Dictionary of Literary Biography

Documentary Series

Yearbooks

Concise Series

Concise Dictionary of American Literary Biography, 6 volumes (1988-1989): *The New Consciousness, 1941-1968; Colonization to the American Renaissance, 1640-1865; Realism, Naturalism, and Local Color, 1865-1917; The Twenties, 1917-1929; The Age of Maturity, 1929-1941; Broadening Views, 1968-1988.*

Concise Dictionary of British Literary Biography, 8 volumes (1991-1992): *Writers of the Middle Ages and Renaissance Before 1660; Writers of the Restoration and Eighteenth Century, 1660-1789; Writers of the Romantic Period, 1789-1832; Victorian Writers, 1832-1890; Late Victorian and Edwardian Writers, 1890-1914; Modern Writers, 1914-1945; Writers After World War II, 1945-1960; Contemporary Writers, 1960 to Present.*

American Travel Writers, 1850–1915

Dictionary of Literary Biography® • Volume One Hundred Eighty-Nine

American Travel Writers, 1850–1915

Edited by
Donald Ross
University of Minnesota
and
James J. Schramer
Youngstown State University

A Bruccoli Clark Layman Book
Gale Research
Detroit, Washington, D.C., London

Printed in the United States of America

The paper used in this publication meets the minimum requirements
of American National Standard for Information Sciences–Permanence
Paper for Printed Library Materials, ANSI Z39.48-1984.∞ ™

Library of Congress Cataloging-in-Publication Data

American travel writers, 1850–1915 / edited by Donald Ross and James J. Schramer.
    p. cm.–(Dictionary of literary biography; v. 189)
"A Bruccoli Clark Layman book."
Includes bibliographical references and index.
ISBN 0-7876-1844-6 (alk. paper)
1. Travelers' writings. American–Bio-bibliography–Dictionaries. 2. American prose
literature–19th century–Bio-bibliography–Dictionaries. 3. American prose literature–
20th century–Bio-bibliography–Dictionaries. 4. Americans–Travel–Foreign countries–
History–Dictionaries. 5. Authors, American–19th century–Biography–Dictionaries.
6. Authors, American–20th century–Biography–Dictionaries.7. Travelers–United
States–Biography–Dictionaries. I. Schramer, James. II. Ross, Donald 1941- . III. Series.
PS366.T73A45 1998
810.9'355–dc21   98-12461
                                                                              CIP

10 9 8 7 6 5 4 3 2 1

To Our Families

Contents

Plan of the Series

. . . Almost the most prodigious asset of a country, and perhaps its most precious possession, is its native literary product — when that product is fine and noble and enduring.

Mark Twain*

The advisory board, the editors, and the publisher of the *Dictionary of Literary Biography* are joined in endorsing Mark Twain's declaration. The literature of a nation provides an inexhaustible resource of permanent worth. We intend to make literature and its creators better understood and more accessible to students and the reading public, while satisfying the standards of teachers and scholars.

To meet these requirements, *literary biography* has been construed in terms of the author's achievement. The most important thing about a writer is his writing. Accordingly, the entries in *DLB* are career biographies, tracing the development of the author's canon and the evolution of his reputation.

The purpose of *DLB* is not only to provide reliable information in a convenient format but also to place the figures in the larger perspective of literary history and to offer appraisals of their accomplishments by qualified scholars.

The publication plan for *DLB* resulted from two years of preparation. The project was proposed to Bruccoli Clark by Frederick C. Ruffner, president of the Gale Research Company, in November 1975. After specimen entries were prepared and typeset, an advisory board was formed to refine the entry format and develop the series rationale. In meetings held during 1976, the publisher, series editors, and advisory board approved the scheme for a comprehensive biographical dictionary of persons who contributed to North American literature. Editorial work on the first volume began in January 1977, and it was published in 1978. In order to make *DLB* more than a reference tool and to compile volumes that individually have claim to status as literary history, it was decided to organize volumes by

*From an unpublished section of Mark Twain's autobiography, copyright by the Mark Twain Company

topic, period, or genre. Each of these freestanding volumes provides a biographical-bibliographical guide and overview for a particular area of literature. We are convinced that this organization—as opposed to a single alphabet method—constitutes a valuable innovation in the presentation of reference material. The volume plan necessarily requires many decisions for the placement and treatment of authors who might properly be included in two or three volumes. In some instances a major figure will be included in separate volumes, but with different entries emphasizing the aspect of his career appropriate to each volume. Ernest Hemingway, for example, is represented in *American Writers in Paris, 1920–1939* by an entry focusing on his expatriate apprenticeship; he is also in *American Novelists, 1910–1945* with an entry surveying his entire career, as well as in *American Short-Story Writers, 1910–1945, Second Series* with an entry concentrating on his short stories. Each volume includes a cumulative index of the subject authors and articles. Comprehensive indexes to the entire series are planned.

The series has been further augmented by the *DLB Yearbooks* (since 1981) which update published entries and add new entries to keep the *DLB* current with contemporary activity. There have also been *DLB Documentary Series* volumes which provide biographical and critical source materials for figures whose work is judged to have particular interest for students. One of these companion volumes is entirely devoted to Tennessee Williams.

We define literature as the *intellectual commerce of a nation:* not merely as belles lettres but as that ample and complex process by which ideas are generated, shaped, and transmitted. *DLB* entries are not limited to "creative writers" but extend to other figures who in their time and in their way influenced the mind of a people. Thus the series encompasses historians, journalists, publishers, book collectors, and screenwriters. By this means readers of *DLB* may be aided to perceive literature not as cult scripture in the keeping of intellectual high priests but firmly positioned at the center of a nation's life.

DLB includes the major writers appropriate to each volume and those standing in the ranks behind them. Scholarly and critical counsel has been sought in deciding which minor figures to include and how full their entries should be. Wherever possible, useful references are made to figures who do not warrant separate entries.

Each *DLB* volume has an expert volume editor responsible for planning the volume, selecting the figures for inclusion, and assigning the entries. Volume editors are also responsible for preparing, where appropriate, appendices surveying the major periodicals and literary and intellectual movements for their volumes, as well as lists of further readings. Work on the series as a whole is coordinated at the Bruccoli Clark Layman editorial center in Columbia, South Carolina, where the editorial staff is responsible for accuracy and utility of the published volumes.

One feature that distinguishes *DLB* is the illustration policy—its concern with the iconography of literature. Just as an author is influenced by his surroundings, so is the reader's understanding of the author enhanced by a knowledge of his environment. Therefore *DLB* volumes include not only drawings, paintings, and photographs of authors, often depicting them at various stages in their careers, but also illustrations of their families and places where they lived. Title pages are regularly reproduced in facsimile along with dust jackets for modern authors. The dust jackets are a special feature of *DLB* because they often document better than anything else the way in which an author's work was perceived in its own time. Specimens of the writers' manuscripts and letters are included when feasible.

Samuel Johnson rightly decreed that "The chief glory of every people arises from its authors." The purpose of the *Dictionary of Literary Biography* is to compile literary history in the surest way available to us—by accurate and comprehensive treatment of the lives and work of those who contributed to it.

The *DLB* Advisory Board

Introduction

The first-class tourist may see the beauties of a country's landscape and scenery from the window of a palace-car, but his vision goes no further—does not penetrate below the surface. To know a country one must fraternize with its people, must live with them, sympathize with them, win their confidence. High life in Europe has been paid sufficient attention by travellers and writers. I was desirous of seeing something of low life; I donned the blouse and hob-nailed shoes of a workman, and spent a year in a "Tramp Trip" from Gibraltar to the Bosphorus. Some of my experiences have been related in letters to the New York *World,* the Philadelphia *Press,* the St. Louis *Republican,* and other American newspapers, and in my official report to the United States Bureau of Labor Statistics, Department of the Interior, Washington, D.C., on the condition of the laboring classes in Europe.

> —Lee Meriwether
> *A Tramp Trip*

Lee Meriwether's introduction to *A Tramp Trip: How to See Europe on Fifty Cents a Day* (1886) represents a declaration of American travel independence. During the infancy of the republic Americans traveled to Britain and the Continent for practical reasons related to diplomatic or commercial ventures. Later, in the two decades prior to the Civil War, Americans began to enjoy themselves more in Europe. The Civil War halted this discovery of the pleasures of European travel. With the end of the war and the emergence of new money, most of it from the industrial North and the developing West, Americans began to travel in increasing numbers to Europe. And while the Continent remained the primary destination for American travelers, there was also growing interest in other parts of the world, including Africa and Asia. "If the social history of the world is ever written," *Putnam's Magazine* declared in 1868, "the era in which we live will be called the nomadic period. With the advent of ocean steam navigation and the railway system, began a travelling mania which has gradually advanced until half of the earth's inhabitants, or least half of its civilized portion, are on the move."

One can get a rough notion of the increases in American travel abroad by the number of passports issued though the statistics understate the number of actual travelers since many traveled without official documents. Before the Civil War about twenty-

THE AUTHOR IN TRAMP ATTIRE.
(From a Photograph taken in St. Petersburg.)

Frontispiece from Lee Meriwether's A Tramp Trip *(1886)*

five hundred passports were being issued per year, this figure doubled to about five thousand through the 1860s, 1870s, and early 1880s. The number rose to ten thousand a year in the mid 1880s, but this increase may be owing in large measure to more widespread passport requirements on the part of foreign countries as well as to the tightening of U.S. laws. Passports had to be reissued for each trip abroad and had to be renewed every two years if one stayed on. By the end of the century the number of issued passports rose to above fifteen thousand. The numbers then increased rapidly, reaching almost one hundred thousand for the year 1919.

Those bold enough to have made their fortunes from the steel mills and oil fields of the East or the forests and mines of the West were not shy about displaying their wealth. They flocked abroad to see and to be seen in the cities and spas of Europe. In *The American* (1877) Henry James fictionalizes and satirizes this exodus and its excesses. With the travail of the journey now removed from travel, the years of the tourist had begun. Like James's Christopher Newman, newly rich Americans were eager to sample all that Europe had to offer.

American travel writing during the latter half of the nineteenth century and the first years of the twentieth century reflects this appetite. In *Anglo-American Landscapes: A Study of Nineteenth-Century Anglo-American Travel Literature* (1983), Christopher Mulvey distinguishes between travel literature that focuses on the "authenticity of statement" and that which is more concerned with the "authenticity of feeling." He finds that "The English travel writer was preoccupied with the first; the American with the second. English travel literature was primarily directed at the intellect and the political imagination. American travel literature was primarily concerned with the sensibility and the cultural memory."

The emphasis on the sensory or the aesthetic experience in American travel literature seems perfectly in consonance with the experience of a people previously so taken up with the arduous and pragmatic concerns of building and then preserving a nation that they scarcely had any time to develop a more reflective sense of taste. As the nineteenth century came to a close, however, and the routine of European travel became more formulaic, Americans such as Meriwether began to abandon the rituals of the Grand Tour in favor of a more intimate level of person-to-person contact, an inquisitive rather than an appetitive approach to travel. This shift in the focus of American travel writing from the subjective, emotive, somewhat unreflective capturing of fleeting sensations to a more reflective, realistic, and other-directed reporting about people and places is one of the themes that emerges from the essays in *Dictionary of Literary Biography 189: American Travel Writers, 1850–1915.*

Literary travel accounts in the late nineteenth century must be seen in the light of decreased travel times and costs, which resulted in the growth of the middle-class tourist industry. Except for crossing into Mexico or Canada by horse or later by train, the only way out of the United States was by ship. In 1838 the *Great Western* (1,300 tons) won a transatlantic race between steam-driven paddle-wheel ships by crossing the ocean in fifteen days. The fare was $145, a princely sum when one considers that a laborer's wage at the time was about one dollar a day. By the late 1850s steamship technology had advanced but fares remained high: $160 for first class

and $80 for cabin passengers. The American-owned Collins line had wooden ships of some 3,000 tons and 300 feet in length that could carry from 160 to 220 passengers. By the 1870s luxury liners, nearly all European, carrying several hundred passengers, made the crossing in a week; the Hamburg-America's *Deutschland* crossed in five days in 1900. Fares in the 1890s were from $100 to $200, an affordable price for the time.

Cutting down on the time and expense of the ocean crossing meant that more middle-class people could get to and from Europe and even Asia for a month or so, rather than having to commit themselves to at least six months for a trip. While many travelers went to business, conduct missionary work, or learn about fine art, many more went just for leisure, for a vacation. And many more could afford to take their families along. The growth of the American middle class and the rising standard of living helped to keep the berths of the ships full.

On the ground in Europe railroad service increased almost exponentially by the end of the century. Railroads not only connected the capital cities but also linked nearly all population centers as well as spas, mountains, and seaside resorts. Trains did much to change travel patterns, as visitors no longer confined themselves to a series of stops along the coast with only short side trips inland; instead, they were able to move freely into the interior of the Continent. Paul Baker in *The Fortunate Pilgrims: Americans in Italy, 1800–1860* (1964) shows how this transition took place in Italy at mid century.

Trains took much of the unpredictability out of travel so that, for example, one could make hotel bookings in advance. As opposed to carriage travel, which encouraged the traveler to tarry at a few spots, trains allowed travelers to move rapidly through a series of stops. This difference made it easier to "cover" the highlights without noticing much of what was between. As early as 1849 John Ruskin laments that the train "transmutes a man from a traveller into a living parcel."

Nostalgia about the good old days of difficult carriage transportation and unscheduled stops at uncomfortable inns was frequently voiced by English travel writers whose experience on the Continent went back to the first half of the century. This regret was not shared by Americans who mostly explored Europe after trains were established. During the bicycle craze of the 1880s and 1890s, the hardy, including Woodrow Wilson and Fanny Bullock Workman, chose to experience a closeness to the bumpy roads of Europe that surpassed even that experienced by the carriage passenger. For the truly adventurous, of course, there were more exotic destinations where the means of travel were still primitive.

In the 1880s Americans enjoyed favorable exchange rates and could budget between $250 to $300 for a comfortable ten weeks in Europe, with good hotels at $2.50 a day. They were anticipated at the Hotel du New York in Florence and the Hotel États Unis and Hotel de l'Oncle Tom in Paris. More and more, though, tourists were facing an increasing number of small fees to visit the important sights. In *The Beaten Track: European Tourism, Literature, and the Ways to Culture, 1800–1860* (1993) James Buzard, after pointing to the charges to see *The Last Supper,* Glastonbury Abbey, and Kenilworth Castle, notes "One could not turn back the turn-stiles through which historic and beautiful places had passed in becoming tourist attractions."

Both at the time and in retrospect, the development of tourism as a concept and as an industry affected ordinary travel, and it became a major theme in travel writing. Dean MacCannell in *Empty Meeting Grounds: The Tourist Papers* (1992) gives an often-cited definition: "[T]ourism is not just an aggregate of merely commercial activities; it is also an ideological framing of history, nature, and tradition; a framing that has the power to reshape culture and nature to its own needs." It is "a primary ground for the production of new cultural forms on a global base." Buzard comments on an 1848 *Blackwoods* article concerning "Modern Tourism" and characterizes the situation this way: "By mid-century the hyperbole so common to criticisms of tourists had set in: the tourists who were 'everywhere' in Europe were pictured as 'all pen in hand, all determined not to let a henroost remain undescribed.'" Tourists were feared to be pouring their writings on the "reading public," without compassion or conscience at the beginning of the "season."

Buzard explains that the traveler was seen to be good while the tourist was bad owing to his or her being a "dupe of fashion, following blindly where authentic travellers have gone with open eyes and free spirits." Citing Paul Fussell, he notes that tourists were a "pure cliché," who went "*en masse,* remaking whole regions in their homogeneous image." The contrast, now familiar, was between "the sensitive traveller" on the one hand and "vulgar tourist" on the other. As Baker explains, the real traveler conducted "truly perceptive studies of the land and the people" rather than making "repetition of the comments and responses of earlier travellers." Mulvey makes a similar point in the context of writing about travel: "Applied to others the term 'tourist' could be nasty, and it was used by most travel writers in the nineteenth century to separate the serious traveller from the frivolous and the serious writer from the superficial." Most readers probably make a similar distinction, for a guidebook is never thought of as literature whereas travel writing might be.

The greater accessibility of travel abroad for Americans had a profound influence on the audience for travel writing. Readers no longer picked up travel books just for vicarious experience but increasingly to help them to make their own travel plans. Some travel writers responded by becoming more informative to serve this need. Others varied their approach to make their writing more interesting. Some abandoned the worked-over field to report on more exotic adventures.

Following the Civil War, many Americans sought what Foster Rhea Dulles in *Americans Abroad: Two Centuries of European Travel* (1964) calls "new cultural ties." Buzard focuses on James as the spokesman for this change: "The great watershed of the Civil War having been passed, James saw both his nation and himself on the brink of new cultural accomplishments, which were to be won by Americans' converting their legacy of cultural impoverishment into an enabling freedom to 'pick and choose' the best among the separate national cultures of Europe." Like James, many believed that high culture had to be imported into the United States. Other Americans, however, did not find Europe so superior to their native land. Another important writer who also reported his visits to Europe, though not with the same reverence for its culture, was Samuel Langhorne Clemens, better known as Mark Twain. Other literary notables who recorded their experiences included Henry Adams, William Dean Howells, William Cullen Bryant, James Russell Lowell, Oliver Wendell Holmes, and Edith Wharton, all of whom are treated in *DLB 189.*

Many of the travel writers included in *DLB 183: American Travel Writers, 1776–1864* had appreciated and tried to capture the "picturesque" experience, the moment when a beautiful natural scene transported the viewer. For later writers the concept changed and became associated more with the idea of culture and society. The new view of the picturesque included concerns about how the peasants or other natives fit in with the landscape.

Travel writing after the Civil War followed the tenets of literary Realism, no longer reflecting the Romantic sensibility of the earlier age. The practical exigencies of tourism, photography, and industrialization caught up with the travel writer and forced him or her to abandon the picturesque and the romantic attitudes that had dominated the earlier nineteenth century. Generally, the focus on the self in an overseas setting became linked to memoir and autobiography, and the focus on place became the centerpiece of travel writing. The changes thus tip the balance a bit on the side of passive capturing of the essence of the place rather than the more dynamic projection of the self.

In *Realism* (1971) Linda Nochlin points out that "The Realists placed a positive value on the depiction of the low, the humble and the commonplace, the socially dispossessed or marginal as well as the more prosperous sectors of contemporary life. . . . Courbet said that the goal of the Realist was to translate the customs, the ideas, the appearances of his own epoch into his art" whether the artist was radical or antidemocratic. Such an emphasis is evident in the travel writing of John William De Forest, for example. Realism in fiction to some degree lent itself to the episodic rather than the crafted, self-conscious, and directed narrative, and those formal preferences lend themselves quite well to the nature of traveling and travel writing.

Realism in travel writing has its appeal in the mimetic and in verisimilitude. But it also joined its cousins in Victorian fiction with an underlying concern with ethical issues—it had a democratic and reformist bias, and many American travel writers looked with disdain on autocratic, nonegalitarian political systems. The basis of the ethical concerns was bourgeois rather than working class so that the social issues most often addressed were ones of courtesy and manners rather than those of social reform or the economic plight of the worker or the peasant. Often travel writing remained pastoral, with an escape to the Campagna the best antidote to an unpleasant encounter with beggars and urban poverty. It seems appropriate to link some of the travel writing of the last decades of the century with the local-color movement in fiction since both shared ideologies, relationships with their metropolitan audience, and a sense of being on the margins from the purely "artistic" novel and short story. Both had a tense relationship with photography and realistic painting.

Travel by Americans to Italy has been especially well researched, and certainly no other European country has received such scholarly attention. The interest in the country was influenced, no doubt, by famous travel writings by James, Twain, and Constance Fenimore Woolson, and increasingly, travel to Italy became a symbol of status among Americans. The country was quite consistently presented by both English and American writers as being a feminized land. James in *Portraits of Places* (1883) writes of "Young Italy, preoccupied with its economical and political future, must be

heartily tired of being admired for its eyelashes and its pose." The concept of "falling in love" with the place is seen often—Buzard points to James's reactions to Florence in 1870 and Venice in 1882, as examples. Americans almost always took on the pose of being the innocents, likely in many ways to be corrupted by a decadent Italy. After Italy became "commonplace" the traveler to that country sought out what Baker calls the "exotic," the medieval, "the oddly picturesque or the bizarre." The traveler could also seek out important or ceremonial events, such as being in Rome during Holy Week or Christmas.

As the nineteenth century progressed American travel writers were hard-pressed to come up with new approaches to render the Old Countries. Something of this frustration may be seen in James's depiction of the sheep in William Shakespeare's Stratford: they "were by no means edible mutton; they were poetic, historic, romantic sheep; they were not there for their weight or their wool, they were there for their presence and their compositional value, and they visibly knew it." The insistence on celebrating England almost exclusively for its past led Americans to hope that the country would not improve itself. In Mulvey's words, "Were England's political system to be updated, her housing modernised, her abuses reformed, and her population given social justice, England would not be worth the tourist's visiting."

Europe was, for some, worn out and predictable. As Mulvey, among others, points out, "The great number of travel accounts of Europe that had already been published [by mid century] were at once an inducement and a deterrent." Other continents attracted travelers with a promise of the exotic—generally associated with the East, a geographical direction defined from a European point of view since Asia is, after all, America's Far West. One result of the work done by travel writers is the proliferation of European and Middle-Eastern place-names in the United States, many based on tourist attractions, especially in midwestern and western states. The Levant was intriguing to American readers because of its biblical resonances. Americans were also interested to read about such faraway lands as Africa, South America, and Australia. American travelers to such distant locales often believed themselves to be true explorers and that their accounts contributed to the West's store of knowledge. Writers such as Elizabeth Cary Agassiz and Frederick Ober saw themselves somewhat in the position of the scientist, the amateur ethnographer. Buzard links James's "sensitive traveler" with Edward Sapir's "sensitive ethnologist," both finding the expanded concept of the picturesque in the places they visited.

Most of the travel writing documented in this volume came before the era of academically defined ethnographers (Frank Boas began his career in the late 1880s). Some strive for completeness, depth, and objectivity, but few are disciplined. For a variety of reasons, travel writers held themselves apart from the cultures they visited so they did not meet the basic criterion of being "participant observers." Similarly, most of the nature writing here is informed by literary rather than scientific standards—it successively follows sublime, picturesque, and, finally, realistic principles. In *The Mind of the Traveller: From Gilgamesh to Global Tourism,* Eric J. Leed writes, "Modern science arose as Europeans were becoming self-conscious travelers inside and outside the boundaries of their culture, experiencing new peoples, plants, animals, and landscapes."

In the nineteenth century some travelers kept their focus on animals and plants—in Barbara Maria Stafford's terms from *Voyage into Substance* (1984), a "landscape freed of culture." They saw their job as gathering facts and rendering them into prose. As part of a moderately successful effort to build his scientific credentials, Paul Belloni Du Chaillu was said by biographer Michel Vaucaire, to have made three copies of his daily journal, "which he intrusted to three different negroes as a safeguard against the carelessness of any one man which might make all the results of the long and difficult undertaking valueless." Scott Slovic in *Seeking Awareness in American Nature Writing* (1992) discusses the "tension between aesthetic celebration and scientific explanation." In the era before high-quality photography, in addition to the prose description, the naturalist was obliged to kill and stuff the specimens and bring the physical evidence—skeletons, heads, skins—back to a museum or scientific society.

The rhetoric of exotic travel writing depends on the writer's relationship to his or her subject. If the subject and author are closely linked and the readers are distant, then the stance is one of the writer's having been there and doing the readers a favor by telling them about the exotic, since they will never be able to follow in the writer's path. If the author links himself closely with the reader, then the position is defined by "our" shared experience: the exotic people and places are not much like our own, but it is interesting, perhaps important, to know about them. The traveler to exotic places almost always winds up back home, with a new appreciation of America.

While the United States officially supported the European colonial powers, especially England, with both rhetoric and attitude, the direct participation overseas of the United States was quite limited in the nineteenth century. With slavery and its aftermath, the long campaign against Native Americans, and an undercurrent of nativism, the country had plenty to do at home. Henry M. Stanley, who had gone to the American West before Africa, writes in *My Early Travels* (1895), "The lessons derived from the near extinction of the Indian are very applicable to Africa. . . . Savages have the minds of children and the passions of brutes, and to place breechloaders in their hands is as cruel an act as to put razors in the hands of infants." To their contacts with people of color, most American travel writers brought a smug pride in their republican institutions as well as a strong belief in the benefits of capitalism and the blessings of Protestant Christianity.

With the notable exception of U.S. administrations in former Spanish colonies such as Puerto Rico, Guam, and the Philippines, Americans were only short-term visitors to Africa, Asia, and the Pacific rather than occupying forces with a stake and some responsibility in the colonial enterprise. Their observations were therefore likely to be superficial, their racism flippant, and their disdain often for both the colonial subjects and their rulers easily expressed. American travel writers joined the other Europeans in judging peoples of color as exotic or primitive and backward, or, in the Near East and part of Eastern Europe, medieval, and worthy of admiration or pity. While American travelers regretted that they could not get close to the ordinary citizens of Europe, on the other continents they rarely thought of closeness as being desirable, and thus did not even miss it. The flora and fauna and the natives all blended into the background for the traveler's transit across the landscape.

For practical purposes Americans were frozen out of both serious scholarly influence and political control over most parts of the world which were being colonized in the nineteenth century. In the Middle East, for example, scholarship and imperialism were dominated by the British and French and the Germans to some degree in scholarship. American travel writers in the area were amateur bit players, and the country did not have the kind of major oriental institutes that would sponsor significant studies or train scholars to conduct such studies. Thus, the United States in general could not take part in what Edward W. Said in *Orientalism* (1979) calls the "long and slow process of appropriation by which Europe, or the European awareness of the Orient, transformed itself from being textual and contemplative into being administrative, economic, and even military."

Travel books do play an important role in the textual phase of this process, and their apparent authority comes to define a place in ways that actual experience does not: "such texts can *create* not only knowledge but also the very reality they appear to describe. In time such knowledge and reality produce a tradition." For the United States, Said's "self-metamorphosis from a scholarly discourse to an imperial institution" shows up in the form of American travel writings about Cuba, Hawaii, and other islands of the South Pacific in the years surrounding the Spanish-American War. As David Spurr argues in *The Rhetoric of Empire* (1993), the colonial gaze "is never innocent or pure, never free of meditation by motives which might be judged noble or otherwise."

The most significant group of American travelers to exotic parts of the world were journalists—people who intentionally or accidentally arrived at "events"—war, revolutions, famine. Such a reporter becomes what David Porter calls a "political witness." Journalism, whether for daily newspapers or monthly magazines, takes on some of the intimacy of letters, although professional journalistic standards put a premium on combining accuracy with telling a good story. As with other retrospective evaluations of nineteenth-century travel writing, critics now recognize the pervasive cultural biases that affect the reporter's ability to see the complexities of "truth," however defined. It is also essential to recall that American newspapers were blatantly partisan, most being explicitly linked to political parties—William Randolph Hearst's role in the Spanish-American War, with Richard Harding Davis as one of the lead reporters, is the most famous symptom of this tendency.

The presence of hundreds of newspapers and magazines in the last third of the century made it possible for one to turn global travel writing into a lifelong career. These men and women, and a few wife-and-husband teams such as Fanny Bullock Workman and William Hunter Workman, managed to hit the correct, popular tone and were able to produce a successful series of books, built on previous publication in the periodicals. Bayard Taylor, for example, was the most famous professional traveler of the century. In 1890 Nellie Bly, on the staff of the *New York World,* went around the world in seventy-two days and wrote her own dispatches and book.

Observations by travel writers have often proved useful to twentieth-century historians and scientists. No matter how clearly postcolonial theories reveal the viciousness of the underlying ideology, ethnographic travel writing transformed the Western world's notions of the past and present. Perhaps more important, travel writing sought and found a mass audience. Aside from government reports and military dispatches, travel writing, whether through the work of amateurs, journalists, or travel professionals, enhanced Americans' awareness of peoples and natural environments in Africa, South America, central Asia, and the Middle East.

Acknowledgments

This book was produced by Bruccoli Clark Layman, Inc. Karen L. Rood is senior editor for the *Dictionary of Literary Biography* series. George P. Anderson was the in-house editor. He was assisted by Tracy S. Bitonti, Karen L. Rood, and Samuel W. Bruce.

Administrative support was provided by Ann M. Cheschi and Brenda A. Gillie.

Bookkeeper is Joyce Fowler.

Copyediting supervisor is Jeff Miller. The copyediting staff includes Phyllis A. Avant, Patricia Coate, Christine Copeland, Thom Harman, and William L. Thomas Jr. Freelance copyeditor is Rebecca Mayo.

Editorial associate is L. Kay Webster.

Layout and graphics staff includes Janet E. Hill and Mark McEwan.

Office manager is Kathy Lawler Merlette.

Photography editors are Margaret Meriwether and Paul Talbot. Photographic copy work was performed by Joseph M. Bruccoli.

Production manager is Samuel W. Bruce.

Systems manager is Marie L. Parker.

Typesetting supervisor is Kathleen M. Flanagan. The typesetting staff includes Pamela D. Norton and Patricia Flanagan Salisbury. Freelance typesetters include Melody W. Clegg and Delores Plastow.

Walter W. Ross, Steven Gross, and Ronald Aikman did library research. They were assisted by the following librarians at the Thomas Cooper Library of the University of South Carolina: Linda Holderfield and the interlibrary-loan staff; reference-department head Virginia Weathers; reference librarians Marilee Birchfield, Stefanie Buck, Stefanie DuBose, Rebecca Feind, Karen Joseph, Donna Lehman, Charlene Loope, Anthony McKissick, Jean Rhyne, and Kwamine Simpson; circulation-department head Caroline Taylor; and acquisitions-searching supervisor David Haggard.

American Travel Writers, 1850–1915

Dictionary of Literary Biography

Henry Adams

(16 February 1838 – 27 March 1918)

Sherrie A. Inness
Miami University

See also the Adams entries in *DLB 12: American Realists and Naturalists* and *DLB 47: American Historians, 1866–1912.*

BOOKS: *Civil-Service Reform* (Boston: Fields, Osgood, 1869);

Chapters of Erie and Other Essays, by Adams and Charles F. Adams Jr. (Boston: Osgood, 1871);

The Life of Albert Gallatin (Philadelphia & London: Lippincott, 1879);

Democracy: An American Novel, anonymous (New York: Holt, 1880; London: Macmillan, 1882);

John Randolph (Boston & New York: Houghton, Mifflin, 1882);

Esther: A Novel, as Frances Snow Compton (New York: Holt, 1884; London: Bentley, 1885);

History of the United States of America during the Second Administration of Thomas Jefferson (1 volume, Cambridge, Mass.: Privately printed, 1885; revised edition, 2 volumes, New York: Scribners, 1890); republished in *History of the United States of America,* 9 volumes (London: Putnam, 1891–1892);

History of the United States of America during the First Administration of James Madison (1 volume, Cambridge, Mass.: Privately printed, 1888; revised edition, 2 volumes, New York: Scribners, 1890); republished in *History of the United States of America;*

History of the United States of America during the First Administration of Thomas Jefferson, 2 volumes (New York: Scribners, 1889); republished in *History of the United States of America;*

History of the United States of America during the Second Administration of James Madison, 3 volumes (New York: Scribners, 1891); republished in *History of the United States of America;*

Historical Essays (New York: Scribners, 1891; London: Unwin, 1891);

Memoirs of Marau Taaroa, Last Queen of Tahiti (N.p.: Privately printed, 1893); revised as *Memoirs of Arii Taimai E Marama of Eimeo Teriirere of Tooarai Teriinui of Tahiti,* as Tauraatua I Amo (Paris: Privately printed, 1901);

Mont-Saint-Michel and Chartres, anonymous (Washington, D.C.: Privately printed, 1904; revised and enlarged, 1912; Boston & New York: Houghton Mifflin, 1913; London: Constable, 1914);

The Education of Henry Adams: An Autobiography (Washington, D.C.: Privately printed, 1907; Boston & New York: Houghton Mifflin, 1918; London: Constable, 1919);

A Letter to American Teachers of History (Washington, D.C.: Privately printed, 1910);

The Life of George Cabot Lodge (Boston & New York: Houghton Mifflin, 1911);

The Degradation of the Democratic Dogma, edited by Brooks Adams (New York & London: Macmillan, 1919);

Sketches for the North American Review by Henry Adams, edited by Edward Chalfant (Hamden: Archon Books, 1986).

OTHER: *Essays in Anglo-Saxon Law,* edited, with an essay, by Adams (Boston: Little, Brown / London: Macmillan, 1876);

Henry Adams, summer 1884 (photograph by Marian Adams)

Documents Relating to New-England Federalism, 1800–1815, edited by Adams (Boston: Little, Brown, 1877);

The Writings of Albert Gallatin, 3 volumes, edited by Adams (Philadelphia: Lippincott, 1879);

Letters of John Hay and Extracts from Diary, 3 volumes, edited by Adams (Washington, D.C.: Privately printed, 1908).

SELECTED PERIODICAL PUBLICATIONS–
UNCOLLECTED: "Captain John Smith," *North American Review,* 104 (1867): 1–30;

"American Finance, 1865–1869," *Edinburgh Review,* 129 (1869): 504–533;

"Civil Service Reform," *North American Review,* 109 (1869): 443–475;

"The Session," *North American Review,* 111 (1870): 29–62;

"The New York Gold Conspiracy," *Westminster Review,* 94 (1870): 411–436;

"The Tendency of History," *Annual Report of the American Historical Association for the Year 1894* (Washington, D.C.: Government Printing Office, 1895);

"The Great Secession Winter of 1860–61," *Proceedings of the Massachusetts Historical Society,* 43 (1910): 656–689.

The works of Henry Adams have received a tremendous amount of critical attention, with the majority of the scrutiny being directed at *Mont-Saint-Michel and Chartres* (1904) and *The Education of Henry Adams: An Autobiography* (1907). These two works, along with *Memoirs of Marau Taaroa, Last Queen of Tahiti* (1893), have established Adams as an important contributor not only to American intellectual history but also to the field of travel writing. The three books all display Adams's concern with using travel writing as a way to re-create lost historical epochs and as a method for reflecting on the course of human development. Adams will be long remembered for using travel experiences to understand human society as well as the soul.

One of the greatest intellectuals and historians the United States has produced, Henry Adams was born in Boston on 16 February 1838 to Charles Francis Adams and Abigail Brooks Adams, members of a wealthy, privileged family that was also one of the most notable political families in the United States. The Adams family lineage produced many famous men, including Henry's father, who served as minister to Great Britain during the Civil War, and two presidents of the United States—Henry's grandfather, John Quincy Adams, and his great-grandfather, John Adams. With such a background Henry Adams seemed destined for great things, a belief that would simultaneously push him onward to his greatest accomplishments and give him a lifelong feeling that his work was paltry and insignificant in comparison to the achievements of other family members.

Adams did not as a matter of course follow eagerly in the footsteps of his famous forefathers. He disliked school and one day announced to the household that he would no longer attend. His grandfather, the former president, overhearing this imperious announcement, marched over to Henry, took him by the hand, and led him all the way to the schoolhouse, not once uttering a word. This taught the young Adams an important lesson: no matter how much one might dislike an assigned task, one must finish it to the best of one's ability out of a sense of duty.

Adams's cynicism about organized education only deepened after he entered Harvard College in 1854, a time when the school's academic program was tradition-bound and less than challenging. Although Adams appreciated the skills of two of his teachers, Louis Agassiz and James Russell Lowell, he later scoffed that his four years of education could have been accomplished in a mere four months. In his later years Adams's disenchantment with formal education led him to search for a means of education outside the walls of academe that would offer the student a greater sense of intellectual and spiritual unity than what was allowed within.

After graduation Adams went to Europe for two years. He planned to study civil law at the University of Berlin but found the German language too difficult. Abandoning his plans for schooling, he went on an informal grand tour that included Belgium, Holland, France, Sicily, Rome, and Germany. These early travels were only the beginning of the extensive traveling that Adams was to do throughout his life. He often found that travel, whether to Europe, the Pacific, the Caribbean, or the Middle East, challenged and changed his perspective on the world. Both travel and travel writing offered him the intellectual opportunity to explore a wide variety of subjects. As Adams wrote to John Hay, "My notion of Travels is a sort of ragbag of everything; scenery, psychology, history, literature, poetry, art; anything in short, that is worth throwing in."

When Adams returned to the United States, he began helping his father¬ then a congressman, with his work in Washington. After a brief stint in the capital Adams traveled abroad with his father, who had been appointed minister to Great Britain by President Abraham Lincoln, serving as his father's secretary from 1860 to 1868. During his long sojourn in England, Adams had enough spare time to become a correspondent for *The New York Times*. He began to develop as a writer but did not blossom as a stylist until he returned to Washington in 1868. He then contributed to national journals such as *The North American Review,* struggling to be heard as an honest voice for reform during the notoriously corrupt administration of President Ulysses Grant.

In 1870 Adams's life changed dramatically when Charles W. Eliot offered him a position as an assistant professor of medieval history at Harvard. Adams, who had no advanced degrees, doubted his abilities to teach the subject and initially declined the job, accepting it only after he was persuaded to do so by his family. He spent seven years at Harvard, during which time he also edited *The North American Review*. He managed to find time in his busy schedule for a summer trip to the Rocky Mountains in 1871, where he met Clarence King, a geologist who became a lifelong friend.

On 27 June 1873 Adams married Marian Hooper, a socially prominent Bostonian. He spent more than a year traveling in Europe and in Egypt with his wife, who shared his interest in history, and the experience reaffirmed for him the importance of travel for intellectual enrichment. During the long wedding trip Adams inevitably played the tourist, a role he adopted self-consciously in his later travel writing. As William W. Stowe points out in his essay "Henry Adams, Traveler," the tourist role allowed him to be "always the ironic observer, the critic rather than the participant." Adams's distance from the subjects he studies is one of the defining characteristics of his travel writing.

When Adams's travels with his new wife came to an end, he returned home to his work. Although his teaching was regarded as outstanding by the students who crowded his classes, Adams in 1877 gave up a life in academe in order to spend more time on his historical writing. Settling in Washington with his wife, he began a productive life as a scholar, edit-

Adams as a student at Harvard University in 1858

ing the papers of Albert Gallatin and writing a biography of John Randolph. These works, however, reveal little of the scope and skill of Adams's nine-volume history of the United States of America during the administrations of Thomas Jefferson and James Madison that he published with Scribners between 1889 and 1891. In these books Adams showed a keen interest in drawing connections between seemingly disparate events, a skill that he was to display repeatedly in his travel narratives as well as his best historical work.

As a break from his multivolume history Adams wrote two novels, *Democracy: An American Novel* (1880) and *Esther* (1884), the first published anonymously and the second pseudonymously, as well as the biographical account *John Randolph* (1882), a work commissioned by John T. Morse Jr., the editor of a series of books on American statesmen. Although Adams did not wish to write about John Randolph, a Virginia politician he found particularly reprehensible, he reluctantly agreed. Adams's account of Randolph's life contains some lively writing and draws a vivid picture of the society in which Randolph was raised, but it does not display the in-

tellectual depth of his best work, perhaps because he found it difficult to become interested in Randolph's life.

Adams never acknowledged that he had written two novels, and few people guessed the truth. *Democracy* is a satire of the American political system that holds up for scrutiny the corruption that Adams thought to be epidemic in Washington. Upon publication it became a best-seller in both the United States and England. Readers were particularly curious about the novel because so many of the characters seemed to have real-life counterparts. Through characters such as Mr. Hartbeest Schneidekoupon, Old Baron Jacobi, the odious Sen. Silas P. Ratcliffe, and the two sisters, Madeleine Lee and Sybil Ross, Adams created a unique analysis of Washington culture and its peculiar foibles.

Adams had *Esther* published with no advertisements because he wanted to see whether the American public would buy a book without a large publicity campaign. The answer seemed clear: only five hundred of the first thousand books published were sold, and Adams was forced to buy up the remaining five hundred. He was always fond of his book despite its poor sales because its heroine, Esther Dudley, was modeled after his wife. The novel addresses the split between science and religion as Esther falls in love with an Episcopalian clergyman but finds it impossible to believe in the doctrines of the church. Much of the book is a long intellectual debate about whether Esther should follow her own ideals or allow her beliefs to be subsumed by those of her husband-to-be.

Adams's life changed suddenly on 6 December 1885 when his wife, depressed by the death of her father, committed suicide by swallowing a fatal dose of potassium cyanide. Her unexpected death haunted Adams for the rest of his life and eventually altered the focus of his work. He attempted to alleviate his grief through traveling and by throwing himself into an exhausting work schedule. More than a means of occupying his mind, travel offered Adams the opportunity to redefine himself, a purpose, one could argue, that was at the heart of his need to travel.

One of the first places where Adams sought a new perspective on the world was Japan, which he visited in summer 1886. He had long been fascinated by the East, discussing it in his letters and in *Esther*. He sought in Japan and other Asian countries the unity that seemed to him so sadly lacking in what he considered to be the confusing "multiplicity" of the West. For Adams the East offered the hope of intellectual and spiritual redemption. The doctrines of Hinduism and Buddhism were particularly interesting to him and influenced his thinking, helping him to take the broad view of religion that was later evident in *Mont-Saint-Michel and Chartres* and *The Education of Henry Adams*. Adams's dreams of unity, however, were not satisfied in Japan or the other countries he visited; he still felt restless, longing for something that Japan did not hold.

Adams returned to live in Washington for three years in order to finish his history of the Jefferson and Madison administrations. In 1890 he and John La Farge sailed to the South Seas, a voyage that was to mark an important turning point in his career. Traveling in Samoa and Tahiti, he was alternately bored and intrigued by the peoples he met. One woman in particular fascinated him: Hinari, a former queen of Tahiti. In long talks with her Adams built up an intricate picture of the Tahitians' genealogy and past history, which he put into writing in *Memoirs of Marau Taaroa, Last Queen of Tahiti,* a chronicle of Tahitian society before and after the arrival of Western forces that shows Adams's interest in women and their power and influence, an interest that would later appear in *Mont-Saint-Michel and Chartres*.

Although Adams's book is bogged down with genealogical details, it does show his moving from the traditionalism of his work on Jefferson and Madison to the more experimental work, combining history and personal reflection, that he was to do in the future. Adams writes about the history of Tahiti not merely to record the past of that island but also to show how the past experiences of Tahiti become a metaphor for the experiences of all humankind. Whether in Tahiti or in France, Adams always sought to discover how the places that he visited represented universal experiences. In *Memoirs of Marau Taaroa,* however, Adams becomes so inundated by historical detail that he is unable to elaborate fully on the connections between Tahiti's inhabitants and those of the rest of the world.

An even more influential trip for Adams was the one he took in the summer of 1895 to France, where he had an opportunity to visit Norman and Gothic cathedrals. The aesthetic beauty of these cathedrals, particularly those at Mont-Saint-Michel and Chartres, offered spiritual uplift and a respite from the mundane reality of his daily life and was a relevation to Adams. He noted Mont-Saint-Michel's almost military quality and could find nothing but praise for Chartres, which he viewed as nearly perfect. From this point on, Adams's interest in Gothic art was a thread throughout much of his writing. To him the eleventh century represented a time of harmony when rich and poor, nobleman and peasant, were connected by their spiritual faith. By writing about his experience Adams hoped to invoke for his

Marian Hooper in 1869, three years before she married Adams

readers, however fleetingly, the spirit of this past age.

Adams often returned to the Gothic cathedrals that inspired him, renting a home in Paris in the summers to visit nearby cathedrals as he worked on *Mont-Saint-Michel and Chartres,* certainly one of the greatest travel narratives ever written. Told as if it were a talk given by an old uncle to his favorite niece as they spend a summer in France visiting cathedrals, this travel account creates an evocative picture of what life must have been like in the Middle Ages. Rather than being a toneless report of an historical period, Adams's work is a poetic, romantic narrative about the cathedrals as the astonishing products of the eleventh, twelfth, and thirteenth centuries. Through his artful use of language Adams attempts to make his readers feel as if they were actually in France themselves. The book is also a philosophical reflection on the Gothic period, which Adams viewed as the time of the greatest spiritual and aesthetic unity that humanity has ever achieved. He was far from alone with this belief since he was writing during a major medieval revival inspired by John Ruskin's belief in the superiority of Gothic architecture. Adams's work stands out as among the best writing produced by this movement.

Adams's book begins with a description of Mont-Saint-Michel, a cathedral that represents the power of the church: "The masculine, military energy of Saint Michael lives still in every stone." But it is the unity that Mont-Saint-Michel represents that lies at the heart of Adams's thoughts. For him the cathedral "expressed the unity of Church and State, God and Man, Peace and War, Life and Death, Good and Bad; it solved the whole problem of the universe." It is exactly this unity that Adams finds so sorely lacking in modern culture and that he seeks to understand by turning his intellectual energies to the medieval period.

Mont-Saint-Michel is the first of three cathedrals that readers visit with Adams. Like tourists, readers follow Adams from Mont-Saint-Michel to Coutances to Chartres, attending as he points out notable features and provides a detailed description of the architectural sensibilities that are reflected in the different cathedrals. The largest part of the tour is spent at Mont-Saint-Michel and Chartres, the two cathedrals that most accurately represent Adams's understanding of the Gothic period, representing as they do the differences between what he calls the Church of Michael the Archangel and the Church of the Virgin Mary. Of these two, Chartres takes up the majority of the book since for Adams it represents humanity's highest accomplishment and deepest emotion: "the struggle of his own littleness to grasp the infinite."

Although Adams includes whole chapters in *Mont-Saint-Michel and Chartres* that focus on Chartres's stained-glass windows and apse, he is even more interested in Chartres as a representation of unity than as a spectacular architectural achievement. At the center of Adams's belief about the unity of the Middle Ages is the Virgin Mary. She fills much of the book as he discusses her influence and power in the Gothic period when she had a central position in Christianity as the Queen of Heaven and stood for "the ideal of feminine grace, charity, and love." Adams believes the Virgin's power in the Middle Ages is impossible to overestimate: "The Virgin filled so enormous a space in the life and thought of the time that one stands now helpless before the mass of testimony to her direct action." One of Adams's most notable accomplishments in this work is his ability to make the Virgin seem not like a distant deity but like a real woman. His humanizing portrayal suggests how people might have perceived her in the Middle Ages as every bit as real as the king or queen.

The Virgin also represented to Adams the importance of the influence of women in the period. While he held that the "superiority of the woman was not fancy, but a fact," he acknowledges that the power and influence the Virgin possessed were doomed to be fleeting. Adams lamented that in the nineteenth century the Virgin looks down "from a deserted heaven, into an empty church, on a dead faith." He believed that the loss of the Virgin and all she represents signaled the loss of unity and the onslaught of multiplicity. All nineteenth-century humanity could do, it seemed, was look back to the golden age of the Gothic period and mourn its passing. In this work Adams provides no hope that such an age can ever return. The travel writer can only strive to make such a period come alive in words.

Adams planned *The Education of Henry Adams* as a companion to *Mont-Saint-Michel and Chartres,* intending it to embody the infinite energy of the twentieth century in contrast to the peacefulness and contemplation that he associated with the twelfth century. Nominally, *The Education of Henry Adams* tracks Adams's education throughout his life, but the book is far more than an autobiography concerning his own experiences. It is an account of what Adams calls a "manikin," a figure that represents Everyman even more than it represents Adams. The book also provides an in-depth look at the changes in society in the 1800s that Adams often associated with the growing movement toward multiplicity. And it is largely through travel that Adams's manikin gains experience in how the world works. As for the young Adams after his graduation from college, travel serves as a far better way to receive an education than formal instruction.

The Education of Henry Adams starts off with Adams's boyhood in Boston and Quincy, each place representing a contrasting ethos to the young boy: "Town was restraint, law, unity. Country, only seven miles away, was liberty, diversity, outlawry, the endless delight of mere sense impressions given by nature for nothing and breathed by boys without knowing it." Although Adams appreciates the lessons he learns in the two distinct households to which he belongs, he condemns the formal education he receives from grade school on into his years at Harvard. Such education always offers Adams little in comparison to what he calls "accidental education," the learning one can pick up through travel. Accidental education is an important part of Adams's years abroad after his college education, far more significant to him than the superficial knowledge he picks up in the classrooms in Germany. The

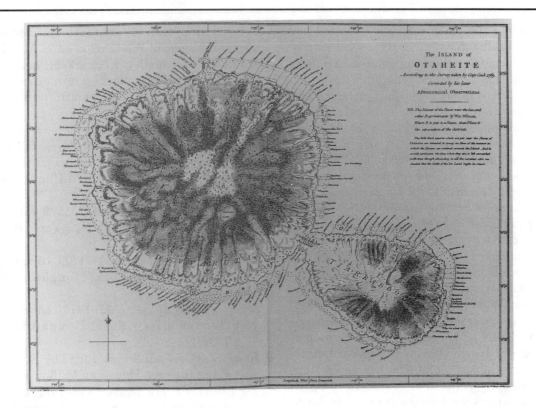

Map from Adams's Memoirs of Arii Taimai E Marama of Eimeo Teriirere of Tooarai Teriinui of
Tahiti *(1901)*

importance of accidental education becomes clear when he is traveling by steamer to Germany and a storm hits: "He learned then a lesson that stood by him better than any university teaching ever did—the meaning of a November gale on the mid-Atlantic—which, for mere physical misery, passed endurance."

Fleeing Germany, the young Adams journeys for eighteen months in Italy, where he continues to pursue his search for education outside of the school. Rome is a revelation to him: "No sand-blast of science had yet skinned off the epidermis of history, thought, and feeling. The pictures were uncleaned, the churches unrestored, the ruins unexcavated." Rome is a place that refuses to "be fitted into an orderly, middle-class, Bostonian, systematic scheme of evolution." Travel enables Adams to recognize the limitations of written history. Visiting a place, he believes, is the only way that an individual can come into contact briefly with a different historical sensibility that eludes textbook description.

When *The Education of Henry Adams* charts Adams's career as secretary to his father during his years in England, what stands out most is his reliance on achieving an education through his own efforts, sometimes simply by observing the people and society around him. Adams, however, still had

little faith in the practical education he had received thus far: "Tossed between the horns of successive dilemmas, he reached his twenty-sixth birthday without the power of earning five dollars in any occupation." Ultimately, Adams considered his years in England, like his years at Harvard, "life wasted." He desired a new start away from England: "If he were ever to amount to anything, he must begin a new education, in a new place, with a new purpose." Traveling to a new place always offered Adams the alluring promise of redesigning his life, of gaining new purpose and meaning.

Adams continues to relate his experiments with life, including his attempts to establish himself as a muckraking newspaper reporter. A particularly important chapter, simply labeled "Failure," explores his years as a professor at Harvard and his overwhelming sense that, except for the companionship of his students, those years offered little to him. After describing his early years teaching at Harvard, Adams skips forward to the year 1892 when he was fifty-three. Scholars have been puzzled by this gap, particularly since the missing years encompass some of Adams's best work. Perhaps Adams wished to avoid the topic of his wife's suicide and the events leading up to it. He makes no mention of Marian in *The Education of Henry Adams* except for a brief discussion of the statue designed by Augustus St. Gaudens for her grave.

In the most famous section of his book Adams renews his attempts to gain an education almost despite himself even though "Nothing attracted him less than the idea of beginning a new education." However, the financial crisis of 1893, which temporarily held Adams "over the gulf of bankruptcy" along with millions of others, served as a "starting-point for a new education." His enthusiasm was also reinvigorated by his visit to the Chicago Exposition of 1893, where he became enraptured by the displays of equipment he saw, seeing in them an energy, a force, that symbolized to him the American mindset as it looked into the twentieth century. The exposition made him think more deeply about the direction of American society and what forces drove it, an interest that he was to have the rest of his days.

Adams's interest in the forces that drive society increased after he visited the Paris Exposition of 1900 and saw a dynamo, which he views as "a symbol of infinity" and a "moral force" as powerful to modern humanity as the Cross was to early Christians. He describes the dynamo as being similar to the Virgin, for both symbolize the channeling of human energies. Adams wonders, however, whether humanity can ever control the power of the dynamo, particularly when that power seems to be escalating every year at a greater rate. Adams elaborates upon his ideas about this force in two of the last three chapters in the book, "A Dynamic Theory of History" and "A Law of Acceleration," the clearest elaboration of his philosophy. He depicts humans walking on a tightrope between using the industrial forces of the world to their benefit or succumbing in the effort to control them. He sees the modern world as the result of a centuries-long "movement from unity into multiplicity" from 1200 until 1900. As a traveler-philosopher, an outsider, Adams is able to recognize the larger pattern of change—doubtless the main reason he considered travel essential to his writing career.

Adams's last book, *The Life of George Cabot Lodge* (1911), in no way achieved the depth and insight of *Mont-Saint-Michel and Chartres* or *The Education of Henry Adams*. A memoir of Sen. Henry Cabot Lodge's son, "Bay," who had died prematurely, it was written at the senator's request and not intended for publication. After suffering a cerebral thrombosis on 24 April 1912, Adams never entirely recovered. Despite his weakened state he traveled to France in 1913 with Aileen Tone, a friend of one of the nieces who served as his companion during his last years. He continued to work but was unable to pursue his intellectual efforts with the zeal and vigor

of his earlier years. He gradually declined until he died at his home in Washington on 27 March 1918. His books, which allow a remarkable look at an intellectual's development, show how essential travel can be for the growth of the human spirit.

Letters:

Letters to a Niece and Prayer to the Virgin of Chartres, edited by Worthington Chauncey Ford (Boston & New York: Houghton Mifflin, 1920; London: Constable, 1921);

A Cycle of Adams Letters, 1861–1865, 2 volumes, edited by Ford (Boston & New York: Houghton Mifflin, 1920);

Letters of Henry Adams (1858–1891), edited by Ford (Boston & New York: Houghton Mifflin, 1930);

Letters of Henry Adams (1892–1918), edited by Ford (Boston & New York: Houghton Mifflin, 1938);

Henry Adams and His Friends, edited by Harold Dean Cater (Boston: Houghton Mifflin, 1947);

The Letters of Henry Adams, 1858–1892, 6 volumes, edited by J. C. Levenson, Ernest Samuels, Charles Vandersee, and Viola Hopkins Winner (Cambridge, Mass.: Belknap Press, 1982–1988).

Bibliography:

Earl N. Harbert, *Henry Adams: A Reference Guide* (Boston: G. K. Hall, 1978).

Biographies:

James Truslow Adams, *Henry Adams* (New York: A. & C. Boni, 1933);

Ernest Samuels, *The Young Henry Adams* (Cambridge, Mass.: Harvard University Press, 1948);

Elizabeth Stevenson, *Henry Adams: A Biography* (New York: Macmillan, 1955);

Samuels, *Henry Adams: The Middle Years* (Cambridge, Mass.: Harvard University Press, 1958);

Samuels, *Henry Adams: The Major Phase* (Cambridge, Mass.: Harvard University Press, 1964);

Earl N. Harbert, *The Force So Much Closer Home: Henry Adams and the Adams Family* (New York: New York University Press, 1977);

R. P. Blackmur, *Henry Adams* (New York: Harcourt Brace Jovanovich, 1980);

Edward Chalfant, *Both Sides of the Ocean: A Biography of Henry Adams, His First Life, 1838–1862* (Hamden, Conn.: Archon Books, 1982);

Patricia O'Toole, *The Five of Hearts: An Intimate Portrait of Henry Adams and His Friends, 1880–1918* (New York: Clarkson Potter, 1990);

Chalfant, *Better in Darkness: A Biography of Henry Adams: His Second Life, 1862–1891* (Hamden, Conn.: Archon Books, 1994).

References:

Ferman Bishop, *Henry Adams* (Boston: Twayne, 1979);

David R. Contosta and Robert Muccigrosso, eds., *Henry Adams and His World* (Philadelphia: American Philosophical Society, 1993);

William Merrill Decker, *The Literary Vocation of Henry Adams* (Chapel Hill: University of North Carolina Press, 1990);

William Dusinberre, *Henry Adams: The Myth of Failure* (Charlottesville: University Press of Virginia, 1980);

Earl N. Harbert, *Critical Essays on Henry Adams* (Boston: G. K. Hall, 1981);

Joanne Jacobson, *Authority and Alliance in the Letters of Henry Adams* (Madison: University of Wisconsin Press, 1992);

Melvin Lyon, *Symbol and Idea in Henry Adams* (Lincoln: University of Nebraska Press, 1970);

William W. Stowe, "Henry Adams, Traveler," *New England Quarterly,* 64 (June 1991): 179–205;

William Wasserstrom, *The Ironies of Progress: Henry Adams and the American Dream* (Carbondale: Southern Illinois University Press, 1984).

Papers:

The primary location of Henry Adams's papers is the Massachusetts Historical Society in Boston. Adams's correspondence and manuscripts are also held by the Houghton Library of Harvard University and by Brown University. The University of Virginia holds a collection of his papers. The Library of Congress has a collection of papers from the Adams family in which Henry Adams is represented.

Elizabeth Cary Agassiz

(5 December 1822 – 27 June 1907)

Linda S. Bergmann
Illinois Institute of Technology

BOOKS: *A First Lesson in Natural History,* as Actaea (Boston: Little, Brown, 1859; revised edition, Boston: Ginn & Heath, 1879);

Seaside Studies in Natural History: Marine Animals of Massachusetts Bay. Radiates, by Agassiz and Alexander Agassiz (Boston: Ticknor & Fields, 1865);

A Journey in Brazil, by Agassiz and Louis Agassiz (Boston: Ticknor & Fields, 1868);

Louis Agassiz: His Life and Correspondence, 2 volumes (Boston: Houghton, Mifflin, 1885).

SELECTED PERIODICAL PUBLICATIONS– UNCOLLECTED: "An Amazonian Picnic," *Atlantic Monthly,* 17 (March 1866): 313–323;

"A Dredging Expedition in the Gulf Stream," *Atlantic Monthly,* 24 (October 1869): 507–517; (November 1869): 571–578;

"The Hassler Glacier in the Straits of Magellan," *Atlantic Monthly,* 30 (October 1872): 472–478;

"In the Straits of Magellan," *Atlantic Monthly,* 31 (January 1873): 89–95;

"A Cruise through the Galapagos," *Atlantic Monthly,* 31 (May 1873): 579–584.

The wife of Louis Agassiz, a famous natural scientist and Harvard professor, and one of the founders and the first president of Radcliffe College, Elizabeth Cary Agassiz was first known as a travel writer for *A Journey in Brazil,* which she wrote with her husband. The book was well reviewed when it came out in 1868 and was widely read by the Cambridge intelligentsia. The Agassizes' discussions of race relations in Brazil were of particular interest to their contemporary readers and reviewers and provide an intriguing window on evolving racial attitudes after the Civil War. *A Journey in Brazil* was translated into French and Portuguese, and new editions in English were brought out until 1909. It was republished in 1969 by Praeger.

Born in Boston on 5 December 1822, Elizabeth Cary was the second of the seven children of Mary Perkins Cary and Thomas Graves Cary, a lawyer. Soon after her birth her family moved to New York City but returned to Boston in 1831. Growing up in enclaves of Cary, Perkins, and Gardiner cousins, she was educated primarily by the family governess, Martha Brewster Lyman. Because of concerns about her health, her only formal schooling consisted of some afternoons at Elizabeth Peabody's Historical School in Boston, which she began attending at age twelve. Influenced by Bronson Alcott, Peabody used the Socratic method of teaching and required her girls to undertake serious reading in history and other subjects. Cary learned Latin and Greek at home, and after her sister Mary's marriage in 1846, she undertook a course of reading with her brother-in-law, Cornelius Conway Felton, a Harvard classics professor (and later president of Harvard from 1860 to 1862). Throughout her life she read widely and seriously, particularly in literature, philosophy, history, and biography.

It was while visiting her sister Mary Louisa (Molly) Cary Felton that Elizabeth came to know the famous Swiss natural scientist Louis Agassiz, who had come to Boston in 1846 to give a series of lectures at the Lowell Institute and was immediately lionized by the Boston and Cambridge elite. They married on 25 April 1850, after the death of his first wife in Switzerland. Childless herself, she helped raise her husband's three children and later took responsibility for the upbringing of the three young sons of her stepson Alexander Agassiz. Despite her heavy family responsibilities, she collaborated with her husband as editor, secretary, and amanuensis.

On 26 September 1855 Elizabeth Agassiz opened a high school for girls in her Cambridge home in order to supplement her husband's $1,500 annual income from Harvard University. Although this was considered a high salary the Agassizes were generally in debt because they lived well and spent large sums on natural history acquisitions. Louis Agassiz, his son Alexander, and other Harvard professors lectured in the school, and his daughter Ida Agassiz (later Higginson) and other local women served as teachers. At this time Elizabeth Agassiz began the practice, which she continued throughout her husband's lifetime, of transcribing his lectures. The school continued for nine years, by which time Louis Agassiz's Museum of Comparative Zoology at Harvard, founded in 1859, was well under way.

Always involved in her husband's work, Elizabeth Agassiz entertained his students and colleagues as he built the museum and established its mission of providing educational and apprenticeship opportunities for future professional scientists. She assisted his efforts to raise funds for the project from private individuals and the state legislature. Happy in her life revolving around home, family, and the intellectual elite of Cambridge, Elizabeth Agassiz began writing about natural science for a popular audience. In *A First Lesson in Natural History,* published in 1859 under the pseudonym Actaea, she writes in the form of letters to the Felton children, her nieces and nephews. She drew her scientific information from her husband's conversations with them about his

specimens and collections during the children's visits to the Agassizes' summer cottage and laboratory at Nahant as well as from her own experiences and observations as she helped her husband collect jelly-fish, anemones, and other shoreline creatures. She later collaborated with her stepson Alexander Agassiz on another book of popular natural science, *Seaside Studies in Natural History: Marine Animals of Massachusetts Bay. Radiates* (1865), published while she was traveling in Brazil.

From April 1865 to July 1866 Louis Agassiz conducted a major expedition to the Amazon River regions of Brazil, financed by the industrialist Nathaniel Thayer, who served as a trustee for the Museum of Comparative Zoology. Elizabeth Agassiz accompanied her husband on the expedition and served as its primary recorder: she kept a diary; wrote an article for the *Atlantic Monthly,* "An Amazonian Picnic," while the expedition was still under way; recorded her husband's lectures; and collected documents relevant to the journey. The Agassizes were accompanied by six Harvard students, among them William James and Van Rensselaer Thayer, and scientific assistants of various specializations from the museum.

From a scientific point of view the immediate results of this expedition were meager, despite Louis Agassiz's claims of its success. He had undertaken the expedition with the avowed intention of disproving Charles Darwin's theory of evolution, of which he had been the foremost American scientific adversary since the publication of *On the Origin of Species* in 1859. Louis Agassiz's observations in Brazil were by most accounts skewed by his desire to see divine design in natural history and were not taken seriously by the scientific community. Moreover, he never had the time to assess the hundreds of barrels of specimens that he had shipped home from Brazil, most of which were not fully examined and classified until 1907, by which time they were used as support for, rather than refutation of, Darwin's theory.

A Journey in Brazil was nevertheless widely read among the New England academic and literary elite. It was applauded for its evocation of the progress of the scientific expedition through the Brazilian landscape and for its smooth melding of travel narrative and scientific observation. The book is constructed from the letters that Elizabeth Agassiz was able to post home at long intervals during the expedition. Early in her correspondence she asked her mother to save her letters for her in the hope of using them later. Her reading the expedition narratives of Alexander von Humboldt, Darwin, and Henry Walter Bates while on the journey suggests

Agassiz in 1852

tributions have become so closely intertwined that we should hardly know how to disconnect them, and our common journal is therefore published, with the exception of a few unimportant changes, almost as it was originally written.

After *A Journey in Brazil* was published, Oliver Wendell Holmes complimented Louis Agassiz in a 5 January 1868 letter: "So exquisitely are your labors blended, that as with the Mermaidens of ancient poets, it is hard to say where the woman leaves off and the fish begins. The delicate observations from the picturesque side relieve the grave scientific observations."

Despite the contentions of Holmes and Louis Agassiz, however, *A Journey in Brazil* is not so untouched by revision, nor are the voices of husband and wife so perfectly melded. The differences between the letters on which the book is based and the book itself are substantial, for Elizabeth Agassiz revised her letters considerably to fit the conventions of the genre. Her original letters to her family are warm and chatty; she allows herself to brag about her experiences and to rejoice in or to complain about the various pleasures and difficulties of the expedition. She offers her family an intimate view of herself experiencing the landscape, and she self-consciously accentuates her anomalous position as a middle-aged Cambridge lady roughing it on a scientific expedition to the Amazon.

In the published book, on the other hand, Elizabeth Agassiz anticipates a wider reading public; she carefully selects letters that focus less on her own experiences and more on the landscape and people themselves, and she subordinates her personal concerns, emphasizing the public events and official discourse of the expedition. She is careful not to offend the imperial family and the Brazilian aristocracy, who had offered help, friendship, and support to the expedition. She reflects on the correspondences between the American and Brazilian cultures and uses the conventions of the picturesque to mediate between the experiences described in the letters—which include her distress at dirty floors, barely dressed slaves, and ladies who spat out of windows—and her desire to represent Brazil as a nation on the brink of modernity.

In *A Journey in Brazil* Elizabeth Agassiz's criticisms of Brazilian conventions, particularly of the subjugation of Brazilian women, become formal and generalized, framed as argument rather than as complaint. The Brazilian ladies, who in the letters are depicted lounging about their houses in dirty muslin wrappers and eating with their fingers, become abstract generalizations, "stifled existences" in need of

that she had publication on her mind from the outset, although she addresses an explicitly familial audience in the original letters.

A Journey in Brazil was published as a joint work since interpolated among excerpts from her letters are her transcriptions of Louis Agassiz's lectures, letters he wrote to various people (including Don Pedro II, the emperor of Brazil, a supporter of the expedition), excerpts from his own expedition notes, occasional footnotes, and an article he had published in *The Atlantic Monthly* concerning the natural history of Brazil. In the preface Louis Agassiz attests to the authenticity of the letters and to the close harmony of the two authorial voices:

> Partly for the entertainment of her friends, partly with the idea that I might make some use of it in knitting together the scientific reports of my journey by a thread of narrative, Mrs. Agassiz began this diary. I soon fell into the habit of giving her daily the more general results of my scientific observations, knowing that she would allow nothing to be lost which was worth preserving. In consequence of this mode of working, our separate con-

the "culture" that contact with America could bring them:

It is, on the contrary, impossible to imagine anything more dreary and monotonous than the life of the Brazilian Senhora in the smaller towns. . . . It is sad to see these stifled existences; without any contact with the world outside, without any charm of domestic life, without books or culture of any kind, the Brazilian Senhora in this part of the country either sinks contentedly into a vapid, empty, aimless life, or frets against her chains, and is as discontented as she is useless.

Her observations of native Brazilians, slaves, and the Portuguese-descended inhabitants of the Amazon basin are similarly formalized.

Despite the perception of Louis Agassiz and Holmes of a close harmony between the two voices in *A Journey in Brazil* and despite her intention to complement her husband's work, what Holmes calls her "delicate observations from the picturesque" do not always accord with what he calls her husband's "grave scientific observations," particularly when she records her observations of the conditions of and interactions between the various races in Brazil. Because Louis Agassiz believed that the different races were different species, his "scientific observations" entail clear differentiation between the races, based on what he perceived as their distinct natures, capacities, and appropriate roles.

Although in her observations of and responses to the peoples of Brazil, Elizabeth Agassiz reflects her husband's hierarchical thinking about race, her distinctions between "civilized" and "savage" are much more fluid than her husband's, and she implicitly contradicts his conviction of essential racial differences. When she observes the easy social and occupational mingling of the racial groups in Brazil she considers the possibility that the Brazilian practice of what seemed to be racial equality might serve as a model for the United States—which was, as she was preparing the manuscript, in the process of Reconstruction:

It seems to me that we may have something to learn here in our own perplexities respecting the position of the black race among us, for the Brazilians are trying gradually and by installments some of the experiments which are forced upon us without previous preparation. The absence of all restraint upon the free blacks, the fact that they are eligible to office, and that all professional careers are open to them, without prejudice on the ground of color, enables one to form some opinion as to their ability and capacity for development. Mr. Sinimbu [a Brazilian senator with whom they traveled] tells us that here the result is on the whole in their favor; he says that the free blacks compare well in intelligence and activity with the Brazilians and Portuguese. But it

must be remembered, in making the comparison with reference to our own country, that here they are brought into contact with a less energetic and powerful race than the Anglo-Saxon.

Although she shares the assumption of Anglo-Saxon superiority with her husband and her culture, Elizabeth Agassiz's descriptions of her encounters with the Brazilian "Indians" indicate that she does not see them only through her husband's dichotomy of "civilized" and "savage" or through his strict racial hierarchy. At times, at least, she conceives of them as individuals of her own kind—not as an undifferentiated mass and not as people of a separate or lower kind. When she describes one set of acquaintances as "people of gentle condition, although of Indian blood," she indicates her awareness of groups and subgroups among the native Brazilians; furthermore, because she identifies them as people of her own kind, she is surprised that they do not share her sense of sexual propriety rather than being shocked by their practices.

Although she uses the condescending term "children of the forest" to describe one group, she displays respect for their knowledge about the natural world in which they live and their skill at living in it. She outlines the reasons or functions underlying native Brazilian practices, rather than dismissing them as "savage"; these too are people from whom Americans might learn something. Comparing them favorably with the New England poor, she sees, for instance, that the twine hammocks in which they sleep and the openness of their houses help keep them free from vermin and odor, as does their habit of frequent bathing. She tells stories about the hospitality of the Indians and admires the suitability of many of their customs to the hot and wet environment in which they live. Indeed, she repeatedly asserts that the lives of the Brazilian Indian women in particular are superior to those of the white women, whom she pictures as victims of indolence and ignorance.

So successful was her first attempt at travel writing that Elizabeth Agassiz kept another journal when she accompanied her husband on a deep-sea dredging expedition aboard the steamship *Hassler*. The *Hassler* departed Boston on 4 December 1871, the party including the Agassizes; a student from the museum; two naturalists, the Count de Pourtales and Franz Steindacher; and Thomas Hill, a former president of Harvard. The voyage took them to the West Indies and Rio de Janeiro and through the Strait of Magellan to the Galápagos Islands before coming to an end in San Francisco in August 1872. Elizabeth Agassiz's work on her Hassler diaries

The Agassiz Gate at Radcliffe College, erected by her descendants in 1916

was interrupted by the death of her husband in December 1873. The only portions published were three articles in *The Atlantic Monthly* in 1872 and 1873 that combine picturesque descriptions of wild and rugged landscapes, some detailed accounts of glacial geology, and amusing stories of picnics, encounters with animals and native peoples, and treks across wild landscapes.

Elizabeth Agassiz reflects on the travails of the early explorers who rounded the tip of South America in uncharted waters and on Darwin's voyage in the *Beagle*—a voyage also on her husband's mind on this expedition, as he reassessed but ultimately maintained his opposition to Darwin's theory of evolution. In these articles her depiction of the "Fuegian Indians" is much less sympathetic than her earlier portrayal of the Brazilians, perhaps because on this trip the expedition members took only short excursions off the ship whereas in Brazil they had extended contact with the local people. Brazil, moreover, offered a lushly exotic landscape as compared with the hostile environment of stormy straits and volcanic islands. She dismisses the Fuegians as noisy and physically repulsive and wonders why people who

build canoes so skillfully do not apply their skills to building better houses and to providing themselves with more and better clothing.

After the death of her husband Elizabeth Agassiz undertook to assemble and write *Louis Agassiz: His Life and Correspondence* (1885), her last book. She fully intended it to be an account of her husband's intellectual development, not a family memoir, and so her authorial presence in this book is much more distant and formal than in her travel narratives. She tells Louis Agassiz's life story to depict him as a great man—or to use one of his favorite terms, a *savant*—as well as an avatar of the newly emerging professional scientist.

This two-volume biography took years to prepare because of the many other demands on Elizabeth Agassiz's time during this period. Immediately after her husband's death she assumed the work of running the household of her stepson Alexander Agassiz, whose wife, Anna Russell Agassiz, died eight days after Louis Agassiz. Alexander took his father's place as head of the Museum of Comparative Zoology, and Elizabeth read and edited many of his publications, as she had done for her husband. Beginning in 1879 she also became involved with a committee working to start a college for women at Harvard, eventually known as Radcliffe College.

Elected president of the Society for the Collegiate Instruction of Women by Harvard Professors, Elizabeth Agassiz was involved in all phases of the process of founding the college. She helped organize the school from the outset, arranged lectures, found housing for the young women, measured windows and hung curtains, raised funds, and negotiated with Harvard president Charles William Eliot and with the Harvard Corporation. When Radcliffe College was finally chartered by the Massachusetts state legislature in 1894, she continued as its first president and served in this capacity until she resigned in 1903 at the age of eighty-one. A serious illness in the summer of 1904 left Elizabeth Agassiz an invalid, but she maintained her love of reading and listening to music as well as her correspondence with family and friends until shortly before she died of a stroke on 27 June 1907.

Elizabeth Agassiz's reputation was inadvertently undermined by her reviewers, eulogizers, and biographers, who downplayed her intelligence and her achievements and stressed her support for her husband, her "helpmate" qualities, and her bearing as a lady. For example, Charles Eliot Norton's eulogy, which was published in Lucy Allen Paton's biography and echoed in its newspaper reviews, dismisses her intelligence while praising her character:

> The whole lesson of her life is a lesson of *character;* she was not a woman of genius or of specially brilliant intellectual gifts; what she did, what she accomplished–and she did and accomplished much more than most women for the good of the society in which she lived,–was not so much due to exceptional powers as to the possession of certain not uncommon qualities in remarkable combination, all perfected by her simplicity of heart.

This is the way she has been depicted–and her strength, intelligence, and wit downplayed–in most accounts of her life.

Biographies:

Lucy Allen Paton, *Elizabeth Cary Agassiz: A Biography* (Boston: Houghton Mifflin, 1919);

Emma Forbes Cary, "A Sketch of Mrs. Louis Agassiz," in *Memories of Fifty Years in the Last Century,* by Caroline Gardiner Curtis (Boston: Privately printed, 1947);

Louise Hall Tharp, *Adventurous Alliance: The Story of the Agassiz Family of Boston* (Boston: Little, Brown, 1959).

References:

Linda Bergmann, "A Troubled Marriage of Discourses: Science Writing and Travel Narrative in Louis and Elizabeth Agassiz's *A Journey in Brazil," Journal of American Culture,* 18 (Summer 1995): 83–88;

Bergmann, "Widows, Hacks, and Biographers: The Voice of Professionalism in Elizabeth Agassiz's *Louis Agassiz: His Life and Correspondence," a/b: Auto/Biography Studies,* 12, no. 1 (1997): 1–21.

Papers:

The Schlesinger Library at Harvard University contains the bulk of Elizabeth Agassiz's letters and diaries, including her original letters from the Thayer Expedition to Brazil. Other important letters are held in the Houghton Library and the Library of the Museum of Comparative Zoology, both also at Harvard University.

Maturin Murray Ballou
(Lieutenant Murray)
(14 April 1820 – 27 March 1895)

Mary K. Edmonds

See also the F. Gleason's Publishing Hall entry in *DLB 49: American Literary Publishing Houses, 1638–1899* and the Ballou entry in *DLB 79: American Magazine Journalists, 1850–1900.*

BOOKS: *Fanny Campbell; or, The Female Pirate Captain,* as Lieutenant Murray (New York: Long, 1844);

Red Rupert, the American Bucanier, as Murray (Boston: Gleason, 1845);

The Protege of the Grand Duke: A Tale of Italy, as Frank Forester (Boston: Gleason, 1845);

The Naval Officer; or, The Pirate's Cave: A Tale of the Last War, as Murray (Boston: Gleason, 1845; London: Pratt, 1849);

Albert Simmons; or, The Midshipman's Revenge: A Tale of Land & Sea, as Forester (Boston: Gleason, 1845);

The Child of the Sea; or, The Smuggler of Colonial Times, And The Love Test (Boston: United States Publishing, 1846);

The Spanish Musketeer: A Tale of Military Life, as Murray (Boston: Gleason, 1847);

Roderick the Rover; or, The Spirit of the Wave, as Murray (Boston: Gleason, 1847);

The Gipsey; or, The Robbers of Naples, as Murray (Boston: Gleason, 1847);

Rosalette; or, The Flower Girl of Paris: A Romance of France, as Murray (New York: French, 1848);

The Duke's Prize: A Story of Art and Heart in Florence, by Murray and others (New York: French, 1848)–also contains "The Prima Donna," by M. V. St. Leon; "The Artist of Florence," by James De Mille; "A Tale of a Crusader," by Charles E. Waite; "The Australian Footman," by De Mille; and "The Corsair of Scio," by De Mille;

The Cabin Boy; or, Life on the Wing: A Story of Fortune's Friends and Fancies, as Murray (Boston: Gleason, 1848);

Maturin Murray Ballou

The Adventurer; or, The Wreck on the Indian Ocean: A Land and Sea Tale, as Murray (Boston: Gleason, 1848);

The Belle of Madrid; or, The Unknown Mask: A Tale of Spain and the Spanish, as Murray (Boston: Gleason, 1849);

The Turkish Slave; or, The Mahometan and His Harem: A Story of the East, as Murray (Boston: Gleason, 1850);

The Magician of Naples; or, Love and Necromancy: A Story of Italy and the East, as Murray (New York: French, 1850)–also contains "The Black Avenger of the Spanish Main," by Edward Z. C. Judson;

The Circassion Slave; or, The Sultan's Favorite: A Story of Constantinople and the East, as Murray (Boston: Gleason, 1851);

The Heart's Secret; or, The Fortunes of a Soldier: A Story of Love and the Low Latitudes, as Murray (Boston: Gleason, 1852);

Life-Story of Hosea Ballou, for the Young (Boston: Tompkins, 1854);

History of Cuba; or, Notes of a Traveller in the Tropics: Being a Political, Historical, and Statistical Account of the Island, from Its First Discovery to the Present Time (Boston: Phillips, Sampson/Derby, 1854);

The Turkish Spies Ali Abubeker Kaled, and Zenobia Marrita Mustapha; or, The Mohammedan Prophet of 1854: A True History of the Russo-Turkish War, as Murray (Baltimore & Philadelphia: Orton, 1855);

The Sea-Witch; or, The African Quadroon: A Story of the Slave Coast, as Murray (New York: French, 1855)—also contains "La Tarantula," by Giddings H. Ballou; "The Goldsmith of Paris," by H. W. Loring; "Miss Henderson's Thanksgiving Day," by Horatio Alger Jr.; and "The Fireman," by M. C. Montaigne;

Miralda; or, The Justice of Tacon: A Drama, in Three Acts (Boston: Spencer, 1858);

The Arkansas Ranger; or, Dingle the Backwoodsman: A Story of East and West, as Murray (Boston: Office of the *Flag of Our Union, Ballou's Pictorial,* and *Ballou's Dollar Monthly,* 1858);

The Pirate Smugglers; or, The Last Cruise of the Viper, as Murray (Boston: Elliott, Thomas & Talbot, 1861);

Captain Lovell; or, The Pirate's Cave: A Tale of the War of 1812, as Murray (New York: Brady, 1870);

The White Brave; or, The Flower of the Lenape Lodge, as Murray (New York: Beadle, 1872; Glasgow & London: Cameron & Ferguson, n.d.);

Due West; or, Round the World in Ten Months (Boston: Houghton, Mifflin, 1884);

Due South; or, Cuba Past and Present (Boston & New York: Houghton, Mifflin, 1885);

Due North; or, Glimpses of Scandinavia and Russia (Boston: Ticknor, 1887);

Genius in Sunshine and Shadow (Boston: Ticknor, 1887);

Under the Southern Cross; or, Travels in Australia, Tasmania, New Zealand, Samoa, and Other Pacific Islands (Boston: Ticknor, 1887; London: Trübner, 1888);

The Outlaw; or, The Female Bandit: A Story of the Robbers of the Apennines, as Murray (Boston: Studley, 1887);

Foot-Prints of Travel; or, Journeyings in Many Lands (Boston: Ginn, 1888);

The Dog Detective and His Young Master, as Murray (New York: Street & Smith, 1888);

Mezzoni the Brigand; or, The King of the Mountains, as Murray (New York: Street & Smith, 1889);

The Masked Lady; or, The Fortunes of a Dragoon, as Murray (New York: Street & Smith, 1889);

The New Eldorado: A Summer Journey to Alaska (Boston & New York: Houghton, Mifflin, 1889);

Aztec Land: Central America, The West Indies and South America (Boston & New York: Houghton, Mifflin, 1890);

Equatorial America: Descriptive of a Visit to St. Thomas, Martinique, Barbadoes, and the Principal Capitals of South America (Boston & New York: Houghton, Mifflin, 1892);

The Story of Malta (Boston & New York: Houghton, Mifflin, 1893);

The Pearl of India (Boston & New York: Houghton, Mifflin, 1894).

OTHER: *Treasury of Thought: Forming an Encyclopedia of Quotations from Ancient and Modern Authors,* compiled by Ballou (Boston: Osgood, 1872);

Pearls of Thought, compiled by Ballou (Boston: Houghton, Mifflin, 1881);

Notable Thoughts about Women: A Literary Mosaic, compiled by Ballou (Boston: Houghton, Mifflin, 1882);

Edge-Tools of Speech, compiled by Ballou (Boston: Ticknor, 1886).

Maturin Murray Ballou spent most of his seventy-five years with a pen in his hand and a notebook on his lap. A prolific journalist and editor who contributed to and published many periodicals, including *Flag of the Union, Gleason's Pictorial Drawing-Room Companion, Ballou's Dollar Monthly,* and the *Boston Globe,* Ballou has also been called "the father of the American dime novel." Indeed, Ballou marketed his first three works of sensational fiction under the inventive heading "shilling novelettes," and they along with other novels solicited from writers such as J. H. Ingraham, Ann Stephens, and Justin Jones (Harry Hazel) became the first such series to be sold so cheaply in America.

Ballou's precedent-setting efforts in fiction and journalism have overshadowed another equally important manifestation of his compulsive writing endeavors: travel books. Like many literary, prosperous, or infirm Americans of the mid-to-late nineteenth century, Ballou traveled frequently abroad. Often in the company of his wife and frequently in search of climates conducive to good health, Ballou journeyed to familiar as well as to exotic regions. His most extensive tours occurred between 1882 and 1895, and he was able to publish ten travel books during the last eleven years of his life. Although these books met with an often negative or indifferent reception during his lifetime as well as after, Ballou wrote much of interest to modern readers of nineteenth-century travel literature.

As a travel writer Ballou views the world through the eyes of a journalist greatly influenced by a spirit of American nationalism, the Protestant work ethic, and a healthy dose of morality. He reports those things that might immediately attract the reader's attention: a country's unique geographical features and climate, the dress and customs—both religious and secular—of its natives, ways of life in urban and rural areas, the quality of hotels and the transportation system, and any historical or contemporary bits of information that might reveal something about the country's development. Moreover, whether he intends to or not, Ballou divulges the prejudices that inform his vision and writing.

Throughout his travel books he displays his impatience with countries that fail to make use of their natural resources and possibilities for trade and commerce. Ballou equates a lack of business acumen with laziness and sloth. He also promotes contemporary cultural stereotypes in his writing: natives turn out to be "savages" or "animals"; the Chinese become the "despised race"; and Jewish people appear as the manipulative "children of Israel." Although Ballou strives, from time to time, to make the case for cultural relativism, his efforts prove infrequent and didactically unconvincing. Finally, Ballou is more of an observer than a mingler. As such, he contents himself with conveying to the reader general observations rather than penetrating insights. The modern reader should not turn to Ballou for sympathetic or probing inquiries into a country's psyche; instead, Ballou's travel writing offers a glimpse into the ways a literate, nineteenth-century American responded to cultures different from his own.

On 14 April 1820 Rev. Hosea and Ruth Ballou welcomed their ninth child, Maturin Murray, into their religious household. The two Bostonians named the child after Maturin Ballou, an ancestral compatriot of Roger Williams who in 1646 owned half of the Providence Plantations. The young Maturin Murray Ballou's ties to religious America were strong: his father was a well-known Universalist minister and author of the popular *Ancient History of Universalism* (1829); two uncles were also Universalist clergymen; and his grandfather was a Baptist minister. The Ballou family's religious heritage went hand in hand with a commitment to education and hard work. Ballou attended public schools in Boston and in 1838 graduated from English High School. Although he took qualifying entrance exams at Harvard and passed, the nineteen-year-old instead decided to pursue a career and opted for a clerkship at the Boston Post Office. In his spare time he contributed material to a local miscellany titled the *Olive Branch,* and he helped his father edit religious journals such as the *Universalist Expositor.* On 15 September 1839 Ballou interrupted both career and writing to marry Mary Anne Roberts, a young woman who, like Ballou, suffered from periodical bouts of ill health. The pair took an extended honeymoon to the West Indies, and it was at this time that Ballou began his practice of keeping journal notes of his travels and writing up these accounts for Boston newspapers.

After the honeymoon the Ballous returned to Boston. In 1840 Mary Ballou bore their only child, Murray Roberts Ballou. To care for this addition to his family Ballou left his post-office job and became a deputy navy agent at the Boston Custom House—a position that provided him with the knowledge of sea, sailors, and boats that would later prove invaluable to his sensational fiction. Shortly thereafter, printer Frederick Gleason approached Ballou in 1844 with the idea of forming two publishing companies—F. Gleason's Publishing Hall and the United States Publishing Company—for the purpose of producing and distributing cheap fiction across America. Ballou soon left the Custom House for a life in publishing he felt confident he could lead.

Ballou's partnership with Gleason was a lucrative one, especially for the printer. Together they created two periodicals: the *Flag of the Union* (1846) and America's first illustrated newspaper, *Gleason's Pictorial Drawing-Room Companion* (1851). Gleason promoted and managed the journals while Ballou served as chief writer and managing editor. He provided stories, poems, aphorisms, and news briefs for the periodicals whenever submissions ran low or were too poor to publish. Throughout his ten-year partnership with Gleason and beyond, Ballou churned out one to three novels a year for serialization or book publication. Masking his identity behind the assumed names Lieutenant Murray and, occasionally, Frank Forester, he penned romance-adventures, beginning with *Fanny Campbell; or, The Female Pirate Captain* (1844), *Red Rupert, the American Bucanier* (1845), and *The Protege of the Grand Duke: A Tale of Italy* (1845). While almost all of his tales take place in exotic locales, the setting proves secondary to the action and romantic intrigue of the stories. Although by modern standards Ballou's style is staid

M. M. BALLOU, {CORNER OF TREMONT AND BROMFIELD STS.}   BOSTON, SATURDAY, JUNE 9, 1855. $3,00 PER ANNUM. 6 CENTS SINGLE. {VOL. VIII., No. 23.—WHOLE No. 205.

GOING TO THE MEADOW.

Mr. Warren has given us here a fine local sketch, truly American in character, and remarkable for its fidelity. The old farmhouse, seen in the distance, has a familiar look. If we have not seen that particular farm-house, we have seen a thousand like it; the homes of strong hands, brave hearts, bright minds. Then look at the sturdy horse in the fills of the hay-rack; he is trotting off as proudly and bravely as if he was aware of his importance, and sensible that he had a mission, as well as his master—his particular mission, or destination, being just now the meadow, where, while his load is being piled up, he will have leisure to amuse himself with the wastage of his fragrant burthen, and to do battle with his deadly enemies, the horse-flies. The children who crowd the rack are full of delight, as they always are when work to be done is associated with the idea of a frolic. It is a pity that all labor cannot be made as agreeable to the toilers of this world, as haying is to children. One of them has lost a hat, and this inci-

dent creates quite as much hubbub and excitement in the juvenile group as a hat overboard does in a bevy of steamboat passengers, or railroad travellers. But there are children of a larger growth in the hay-rack. A few more summers than those which have blessed the little group of boys and girls, have ripened the beauty of that maiden with the straw hat, who is borne along in "maiden meditation, fancy free." Observe with what shy fondness the youth in front glances askant at her, unable to take his eyes from her, and yet modest in his demonstration—a true picture of rustic backwardness. Now, this unconscious maiden may be a farmer's daughter—"sole daughter of the house and heart" of a landed proprietor; and it may be nothing new to her to ride in a hay-rigging to the field, and then assist in the preparation of the dainty food which is to sustain the strong horses and the grateful kine through the long months of the coming winter; and yet, for our part, we strongly suspect her of being an amateur, and going to her voluntary task with the zest that always accompanies new

occupations. We accuse her of being no country damsel, but a city belle metamorphosed for the occasion into an Amaryllis. What dire execution these rusticating belles do on the hearts of such swains as the one in our picture. Everything they lay their delicate hands to, they do with a grace perfectly fascinating. They milk in the style of Maria Antoinette at the Petite Trianon, they make butter or love with equal grace, ride the fastest horses in the most desperate style, break colts and hearts with perfect impunity, and then scamper back to the city, regardless of the damage they have caused. Yet they often are susceptible, and with some of them a manly young farmer has a better prospect of success than a city exquisite. Therefore, in bidding our young swain in the cart adieu, we advise him to "make hay while the sun shines." Many a pleasant life connection has resulted from such merry country scenes and interviews, and some of the pleasantest associations of after-life grow out of the convivial gatherings about the farmer's homestead, and in the fields and meadows,

Front page for one of the three periodicals Ballou edited from 1855 to 1863

and his dialogue stilted, contemporary readers consumed Ballou's shilling novelettes and periodicals with gusto.

After ten years of grueling work Ballou had tired of the burdensome workload that the two journals demanded; he was also tired of failing to receive due recognition for his work. In 1854 he published the first of his travel narratives, the *History of Cuba; or, Notes of a Traveller in the Tropics,* under his real name, hoping that a successful book would serve as an antidote to his increasing ill feeling toward the better-known Gleason. In his preface he wrote of his desire that "this summer book of a summer clime [might] float lightly upon the sea of public favor." A mingling of personal observation, historical anecdote, and information gathered from other sources, the book received favorable notices but did not ease Ballou's resentment of his partner, who he felt did less work and yet could afford to go on more than one European vacation. Ballou wanted the control and the recognition that only sole ownership of the periodicals could bring, and in 1854 the thirty-eight-year-old Gleason sold his share of both weeklies to Ballou.

Ballou remained dissatisfied even in the face of the continuing strong profits from the two journals. In 1855 he created yet another magazine, *Ballou's Dollar Monthly,* with the marketing strategy of selling each issue at only ten cents. Under Ballou's guidance, his *Dollar Monthly* managed to become the second-highest-selling monthly magazine in America. By 1863, however, Ballou had wearied of the incessant writing and managing that juggling three periodicals entailed, so he sold his publications to the Boston publishing house of Elliott, Thomas and Talbot. At the age of forty-three he now had time to recoup his health and to travel with his wife.

After a nine-year hiatus from the publishing industry Ballou collaborated with some fellow Bostonians to establish the *Boston Globe* in 1872. Disagreements over the content of the paper, however, led to initial problems: Ballou preferred to stay away from all political issues while his partners and contributors insisted that politics and hard news stories were what a good newspaper was all about. Ballou resolved the difficulties by resigning his editorship. He then launched a Sunday newspaper titled the *Boston Budget* and the miscellany known as *Ballou's Magazine.* Both publications began circulation in 1879; *Ballou's Magazine* continued until 1893, and the *Boston Budget* lasted until 1895.

While the first part of Ballou's career clearly revolved around fiction writing and periodical publishing, the last half focused on travel and travel writing. With plenty of money in the bank, a grown son, a companionable wife, and a quick interest in other places and cultures, Ballou traveled across the globe, writing about what he saw for an American reading public curious about foreign locales. Ballou truly was a globetrotter, whose itinerary included Hawaii, Japan, Hong Kong, India, Egypt, Spain, Cuba, Scandinavia, Russia, Australia, New Zealand, Alaska, Central America, the West Indies, and South America.

A prototype of Ballou's travel writing, *Due West; or, Round the World in Ten Months* (1884) displays traits that can be found throughout his other works: his dislike of mingling with and getting to know natives; an extraordinary awareness of the physical, whether landscape or the human body; comparisons of people and cultures foreign to him with those of America or other Western countries; a penchant for writing purple prose with a didactic thrust; and his antipathy for Roman Catholicism. Ballou endorses the cultural stereotypes prevalent in America in the nineteenth century, but in comparatively unexplored countries where such stereotypes do not exist he tends to be more tolerant of "otherness." In general he shows himself to be an observer primarily of surfaces.

Ballou tells his readers of two ways of seeing the world—"automatic seeing" and "feeling when seeing"—and recommends the latter. He writes that automatic seeing occurs when the individual looks at his surroundings with a sense of duty rather than of imagination while feeling when seeing happens when the individual finds that "the simplest object in its suggestiveness may be full of beauty." As he further suggests in *Due West,*

> The first business of a traveller upon arriving in a new country is not to look up its history, nor to study its geographic or political economy. He should be at least grounded in these already; he follows his natural instincts, guided by curiosity, shrewdly watching the outdoor life about him, the dress of the people, the architecture of the houses, modes of conveyance, and especially the manners of the women, their status as it regards treatment, occupation, and the respect accorded to them. Nothing is so sure a keynote or test of civilization and progress as this.

The passage illustrates Ballou's belief that the traveler should be occupied with what immediately meets the eye, not what might be hidden from it. Moreover, his use of the typical nineteenth-century Western standard for measuring the refinement of other civilizations—the status of women—leaves little room for appreciating the variety of other cultures.

Ballou begins his journey west by taking a railroad across America and then sailing to Hawaii, Japan, Hong Kong and China, Sumatra, India, Egypt, Malta, Morocco, and Spain. The wide range of cultures available to him for commentary results in an equally broad range of stereotypical and intolerant attitudes representative of the times. Of the Chinese people in Chinatown, San Francisco, he remarks, "They are extremely unpopular with the citizens of all classes, and not without some good reasons, being naturally a filthy race, and in many ways especially offensive." The Chinese fare no better when Ballou visits them in Hong Kong and Canton. In Hong Kong he presents his reader with the prototypical "John Chinaman": "imagine a short, slouching figure, with sloping eyes, a yellow complexion, features characterized by a sort of a loose cloth blouse, half shirt and half jacket, continuations not exactly pants not yet a petticoat, and shoes thick-soled and shearing upwards like a Madras surf-boat, and you have John Chinaman as he appears at home. The portrait is universal. One Chinaman is as like as two peas."

In Canton, Ballou's preference for being an observer rather than a mingler becomes all too apparent as he voices his disgust at the crowded streets:

> We were not disposed to walk any more than was necessary in the public streets, where the foulest odors assailed us at every step, and disgusting sights met the eye in the form of diseased individuals of the most loathsome type. The stranger is jostled by staggering coolies, with buckets of the vilest contents, or importuned for alms by beggars who thrust their deformed limbs into his very face. It is but natural to fear contagion of some sort from contact with such creatures, and yet the crowd is so dense that it is impossible to entirely avoid them.

For Ballou the Chinese equal "contagion," notwithstanding his later admission, "Undoubtedly our type of features is repulsive to the average Chinaman." What the Chinese think of the Westerner matters little as Ballou floats "in palanquins upon the shoulders of the coolies" through the narrow streets where "a most unmistakable surliness" is exhibited "that would have broken into forcible demonstration as we passed through them only for the instinctive cowardice of the Asiatics."

Disgusted by the Indian habit of chewing betel nuts and spitting out the juice in public, Ballou apparently feels compelled to generalize about the bad habits of humanity across the globe: "Wherever we go, among civilized or savage races, upon islands or upon continents, in the chilly North, or the languid, melting South, we find man resorting to some stimulant other than natural food or drink. It seems to be

an instinctive craving exhibited and satisfied as surely in the wilds of Africa, or the South Sea Islands, as by the opium-consuming Chinese, or the brandy-drinking Anglo-Saxons." Carrying his religious background with him, Ballou sniffs out the sins of races and people from the four corners of the globe. In this one respect, at least, he believes that all cultures are equal.

The only positive comments Ballou makes about India come when he either finds similarities between India and the West or views superb gardens and landscapes. He writes with pleasure of a Calcutta promenade, graced with walkers and riders, but seems to find it lovelier still because he can liken it to landmarks such as Hyde Park in London and the Champs Elysées in Paris. He praises Indian gardens, plantations, and mountain ranges in the purple prose typical of a sentimental culture in America that slights the subject for the words. For example, Ballou rhapsodizes about the Himalayas and Mount Everest: "Then the veil of night was slowly removed, as Aurora extinguished the last of those flickering lamps, and the soft amber light touched the brow of each peak, causing it to blush like a beautiful maiden aroused from sleep, at sight of one beloved." He distances the audience from the foreign by indulging in the familiar high rhetoric of nature description.

Ballou's journey westward around the world culminates with brief stops in Morocco, Spain, Belgium, and France. In each of these places Ballou reveals his inclination to criticize that which is different, to laud the American work ethic, and to make bland observations. Ballou dismisses Morocco by finding fault with its coffee: "It was quite the thing to patronize one of the little dingy cafés, and so we patiently endured the punishment of drinking an egg-shell cup of a muddy compound called coffee, but nothing short of compulsion would have induced a repetition of the same."

He finds the Spanish a lazy, unproductive people. In Cordova he declares, "Spain is a country of beggars, but in this ancient town one is actually beset by them." He compares the backward-looking nature of the Spaniards to that of the Chinese:

> the citizens owe it to the energy and skill of foreign engineers that they enjoy the luxury of an ample supply of good water; and foreign engineers are doing or have done the same thing for other Spanish cities, though, in fact, only restoring the ancient supplies first constructed by the quick-witted Moors, and wantonly permitted to crumble into ruin by the Spaniards. They are not sufficiently enterprising or progressive to originate any such scheme for the public good. They even dislike the railroads, though they are compelled to use them; dislike

them because they force them to observe punctuality, the native instinct being of the Chinese school, retrospective and retrograding.

Once arrived in Belgium, Ballou reflects upon his ten-month trip and concludes his journey with some superficial musings on physical differences: "Belgium is a nation of blondes, in strong contrast with its near neighbor, France, where the brunettes reign supreme. It is singular that there should be such a marked difference in communities, differences as definite as geographical boundaries, and seemingly governed by rules quite as arbitrary. Why should a people's hair, eyes, and complexion be dark or light, simply because an imaginary line divides them territorially?" Ballou offers no answers to his own questions; instead, he leaves the reader to ponder them.

Reviews of *Due West* were not kind. The reviewer for the 28 February 1884 issue of *The Nation* ignores the questions Ballou posed and expresses great annoyance not only with Ballou's style but also with his audience. He implies that the work is "effeminate" by observing that Ballou's writing is "known and appreciated on drawing-room tables and in ladies' boudoirs." The reviewer then faults Ballou for his page-long paragraphs and the lack of vitality and color of his prose and condemns him for making "frequent statements of what was fact a decade ago, but is not now." The reviewer concludes his appraisal of *Due West* by hinting that it had been "finished on deck or by rail" and declaring that the only people who might benefit from it are those "who wish to compass the world between two New Year's Days, and have neither the time to do preparatory reading nor the originality to choose their own routes."

Undiscouraged by such hostile reviews, Ballou followed *Due West* with *Due South; or, Cuba Past and Present* (1885). In the preface Ballou states (perhaps in response to criticism of his travel writing) that he intends to give a comprehensive view of the island "past and present"; its "political and moral darkness"; and its inhabitants, vegetation, geography, and commercial potential as a trade partner with the United States. In his book Ballou praises the rich Cuban soil and the fruits, sugar cane, and coffee plantations of the island. But Ballou suggests that the mild climate and luxuriant vegetation encourage sloth in the Cubans: "It would seem that the softness of the unrivaled climate of those skies, beneath which it is luxury only to exist, has unnerved this people." Amid all of the potential for wealth and happiness Ballou sees only Cuban failure to achieve real prosperity. He complains about the nearly bankrupt government as well as the pervasive begging in Santiago, which he finds "synonymous with the Spanish name," and blames "Popery and slavery" for "the low condition of morals." *Due South* demonstrates no coherent or abiding thesis other than its anti-Spanish and anti-Catholic sentiments.

Contemporary reviewers found the three-hundred-page text to be unfocused. The critic for *The Nation* of 29 October 1885 noted, "Original observation, hearsay, gleanings from the author's readings, all mixed pell-mell—one might fancy the leaves of the manuscript scattered by a sudden gust of wind, and hastily gathered up and sent to the printer just as they happened to be put together, so abrupt and sometimes startling are the transitions from topic to topic." The review concludes by praising Ballou's observant eye and bemoaning that the result of his labors was "a very unsatisfactory specimen of bookmaking."

Ballou's next travel volume, *Due North; or, Glimpses of Scandinavia and Russia* (1887)—which takes the reader through Norway, Sweden, Russia, and Russian Poland—met with favorable commentary upon publication. In the May 1887 issue of *The Dial* he was praised for touching upon "every point which an intelligent and observant tourist, seeking for the largest amount of trustworthy knowledge, would find most significant and impressive." The reviewer finds Ballou at his best when explaining the affairs of Poland under the czarist regime and when showing how the Romanoff dynasty, as opposed to popular opinion, was indeed liberal minded. The reviewer correctly notes that the political sections are the more interesting portions of *Due North*—especially when they are compared to his rhapsodies on nature. Ballou's effusions over the natural beauty of the Scandinavian countries—"How Nature enters into our hearts and confides her amorous secrets through winsome flowers!"—correspond to his insistence that one should see with feeling.

Such heartfelt prose, however, pales in interest beside Ballou's political commentary on Russia and Poland and his indifference to extreme government surveillance and rampant anti-Semitism. Ballou rejects the idea that there is any internal revolution growing within Russia; instead, he blames the anti-czar sentiments on foreign, nihilist troublemakers. He concludes that any social ferment is caused by the "scheming, partially educated, idle, disappointed, and useless members of society." Of the socialist, communist, and nihilist movements he asserts: "Socialism is the very embodiment of selfishness; its aim is that of legalized plunder. Communists, Socialists, Nihilists, are one and all disciples of destruction."

Ballou accepts the existence of the Russian police state as a matter of course. When he is in Saint Petersburg, for example, he merely observes that "foreigners are not left alone for a moment" and that "one is forbidden to make even pencil sketches or to take notes in the various palaces." He further remarks, "the author was subjected to constant surveillance in both St. Petersburg and Moscow, which was to say the least of it quite annoying; his correspondence was also withheld from him,—but no serious trouble worth expatiating upon was experienced." While noting this surveillance along with the censorship of the press, Ballou does not speculate about what such tight control might signify about the government or the quality of life in Russia. He is content to make the observation and move on.

As he discusses Poland, then recently deprived of its independent nationhood by Russia, Ballou sees only cheerful and talkative Poles and evil Jews. Just as Ballou exhibits extreme prejudice against the Chinese, so does he condemn the Jewish people living in Poland:

> In every village and settlement, no matter how small, there are always Jews who are ready and eager to administer to this base appetite [Polish love for liquor], and to rob the poor ignorant people of both health and money. It is unpleasant to speak harshly of the Jewish race, especially as we know personally some highly cultured, responsible, and eminently respectable men who form a decided exception to the general rule; but the despised and wandering children of Israel, wherever we have met them, certainly appear to exercise an evil influence upon the people among whom they dwell. We record the fact with some hesitation, but with a strong sense of conviction. Poland appears to be after Palestine a sort of Land of Promise to the Jews; but they are certainly here, if nowhere else, a terrible scourge upon the native race. Their special part of the town—the Jews' Quarter—is a mass of filth, so disgusting, so ill-smelling, that one would think it must surely breed all sorts of contagious diseases; but here they live on in unwholesome dens, amid undrained, narrow streets and lanes, often in almost roofless tenements.

In this extraordinary passage Ballou reveals a deep cultural stereotype pervasive at the time.

It is difficult to reconcile Ballou's inability to move beyond such prejudice with his contention that travel is a learning and illusion-shattering experience. The man who could voice anti-Semitic sentiments in one book could in the same year bring out another volume of travel, *Under the Southern Cross; or, Travels in Australia, Tasmania, New Zealand, Samoa,*

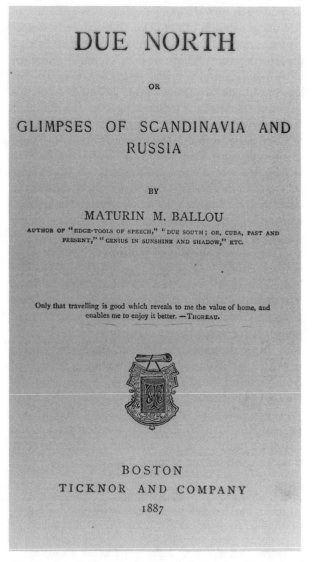

Title page for the 1887 book in which Ballou reveals a strain of anti-Semitism

and Other Pacific Islands (1887), in which he claims in the preface that travel is the "royal road to learning"—a road that can provide enchantment or prove to be "the winding-sheet of many cherished illusions" for the tourist. Despite his assertions for the eye-opening experience of travel Ballou still manages to walk blindly through the lands beneath the Southern Cross.

He retains, for example, his prejudice against the "ubiquitous Chinese" he finds in Hawaii, Australia, and New Zealand: "The pertinacity which enables these Asiatics to get a foothold and maintain themselves in various countries in the face of such universal oppression and unpopularity, is a constant source of surprise to one who has seen them established and prospering in so many foreign lands." His wonder at the continued existence of the Chinese in such unwelcoming societies leads Ballou to add deeper shades of suspicion to his already stereotypical view. At the quartz-mining areas of Tasmania, for instance, Ballou notices "some Chinamen" working with picks, drills, and shovels. Instead of leaving his description at that, Ballou projects his negative feelings by remarking that the Chinese miners were "dark, mysterious figures, who seemed to glare at us from out of the uncertain rays of light as though they were brooding over some fancied wrong, for which they would gladly avenge themselves then and there." Because Ballou cannot understand the Chinese, he characterizes them as inscrutable, shady characters at whose veiled thoughts Westerners could only tremble. When Ballou does guess at what might lie behind the silent Chinese stare, he envisions them brooding over a "fancied wrong," resulting in an antipathy that is no less threatening for being imagined. Far from being a learning experience, then, Ballou's travels seem to reinforce his preexisting prejudices.

In the last sections of *Under the Southern Cross,* in which he discusses the little-known Maoris of New Zealand, Ballou attempts to be open-minded. Having only the preconception that the Maoris are "savages," Ballou praises their physical strength and ancient language. He criticizes their pagan ways and childlike habits but goes beyond surface observations to consider the Maori perspective:

> It is surprising how well these Maoris get along without civilization. It is fully as surprising to see how they wilt and fade away with it. Whether the white man has been upon the whole any advantage to them is certainly an open question. They originally possessed a language composed of a copious vocabulary, and also a complete social system that answered their purpose. Their houses, rude as they were, kept out the heat of the summer sun and retained the necessary warmth in winter,—and this in a degree quite superior to European houses. Their food-supply, eked out by cannibalism, was ample though not varied, while their natural condition involved few necessities. Their wars promoted a condition of robustness as well as a spirit of enterprise and activity. But with civilization came rum, tobacco, and laziness. Far be it from us to argue in favor of the savage life above that of the civilized; but to judge these savage races correctly or fairly, we must look at them from their own standpoint, not from ours.

Why Ballou can respect the differences of Maoris and not those of the Chinese is difficult to explain. Perhaps this gleam of cultural relativism suggests that Ballou, when not influenced and supported by widely accepted cultural stereotypes such as those against the Chinese, was able to recognize to some degree his own prejudices. In any case *Under the*

Southern Cross indicates a significant tension in Ballou's works, for while he generally writes within preexisting cultural stereotypes, he occasionally strives to move beyond them.

Significantly, reviews of the time pay no heed to this tension. Instead, there are comments such as those of the reviewer for *The North American Review:*

> Mr. Ballou's unpretending records of travel are always of interest on account of the bright and comprehensive manner in which he describes strange countries. In his latest volume he takes the reader through some of the islands of the Southern Pacific, describes vividly the objects which would readily attract the attention of the traveler, and imparts, by the way, a wonderful amount of information concerning the natural beauties, wealth and civilization of Australia, Tasmania, New Zealand and lesser islands, which are, for the most part, unfrequented by visitors.

The reviewer's praise for the exclusive focus on external signs such as geography, wealth, and customs suggests the satisfaction of the American audience with the general, almost superficial nature of his works.

Ballou decided to write his next travel book, *Foot-Prints of Travel; or, Journeyings in Many Lands* (1888), for children. In the preface he declares that he wants to "afford pleasing entertainment" and "impart valuable information" to American youth. In particular Ballou wants to ensure that his young readers learn their geography. He advises that "The free use of good maps while reading these *Foot-Prints of Travel,* will be of great advantage, increasing the student's interest and also impressing upon his mind a degree of geographical knowledge which could not in any other way be so easily or pleasantly acquired." Aside from urging his readers to use maps and including black-and-white illustrations for each chapter, Ballou does nothing to appeal to his "students." His descriptive and occasionally didactic writing remains the same as when he writes for adult readers. Moreover, he offers little in the way of adventures to new places. Although Ballou insists that *Foot-Prints* is a mingling of old material and new, it actually recycles old observations.

Ballou returned with fresh experiences in 1889 with the publication of *The New Eldorado: A Summer Journey to Alaska.* In the preface the world traveler urges his readers to "above all . . . first become familiar with the important features of our own beautiful and widespread land before we seek foreign shores, especially as we have on this continent so much of unequaled grandeur and unique phenomena to satisfy and to attract us. It seems to the undersigned that perhaps this volume will have a tendency to lead the reader to such conclusion, and certainly this is its primary object." Throughout his journey Ballou's comments are those of a patriotic American and interested capitalist. Traveling across the American northwest to Alaska, he remarks upon natural phenomena such as geysers, forests, and mountains as well as upon inhabitants such as cowboys, miners, fishermen, and Native Americans.

Ballou's moralistic style and prejudicial attitude remain the same as in his previous books, especially in his comparison of Native Americans to white Americans. Observing Indians outside of Yellowstone, Ballou writes, "No Indians of any tribe are now permitted in the reservation, otherwise, lazy as these aborigines are, they would soon make reckless havoc among the fine collection of wild animals which is gathered here. The Indians are all in the annual receipt of money and ample food supplies from the government; and the killing of extra game and selling the hides would furnish them with only so many more dollars to be expended for whiskey and tobacco. These tribes have no idea of economy, or care for the future. The reliance they place on government supplies promotes a spirit of recklessness and extravagance."

After blaming the Native Americans for their dependence on the United States government, Ballou offers a purely racist portrait of the Indian. He first compares the Indians unfavorably to cowboys in terms of riding skills and then generalizes that the Indians lack the physical and intellectual strength that white Americans possess: "No equestrian feats of the ring equal their [the cowboys'] daily performances, and no Indian of the prairies can compare with them for daring and successful horsemanship. Indeed, an Indian is hardly the equal of a white man in anything, not even in endurance. 'An intelligent white man can beat any Indian, even at his own game,' says Buffalo Bill."

Once Ballou leaves the Indians behind, he is free to focus on America's "new eldorado"–Alaska. This land of gold contains all kinds of wealth as far as Ballou is concerned: plenty of livable, open space; acres of trees; interesting wildlife; fisheries and canneries; and, of course, the much renowned mineral resources. Ballou also notes that much of central Alaska remains unexplored and would be well worth a journey. He concludes his travelogue by addressing the issue of Alaskan statehood–a move he favors for capitalistic reasons.

Ballou's *The New Eldorado: A Summer Journey to Alaska* (1889) was only one of many travel books published on Alaska in the 1880s. The reviewer for the December 1889 *Dial,* who notes that "our national refrigerator" has forged to the front of popu-

lar literary travel topics, deems Ballou's writing that of a "news correspondent" whose moderate observations and "pleasant style" appeal to the general audience. Noting Ballou's keen interest in capitalistic matters, the reviewer emphasizes his enthusiasm over Alaskan timber ("The available timber now standing in the territory might alone meet the ordinary demand of this continent [North America] for half a century") and Alaska's "fur-bearing animals." While *The Dial* does not recommend *The New Eldorado* as a work of art or as a work of exploration, the reviewer does say it has value for those readers generally curious about Alaska.

In his next travel book, *Aztec Land: Central America, The West Indies and South America* (1890), Ballou guides his readers through the rural and urban areas of Mexico. His tour includes a running commentary on false Mexican history, untrustworthy priests, and "roguish," flirtatious Mexican women. Throughout, Ballou spices up his narrative with fervent disquisitions on the right of Texas to secede from Mexico, the benefits of a capitalistic system, and the traveler's need to be tolerant when visiting countries different from his or her own. With a show of embracing the "other," Ballou advises,

The stranger who comes to Mexico with the expectation of enjoying his visit must bring with him a liberal and tolerant spirit. He must be prepared to encounter a marked difference of race, of social and business life, together with the absence of many such domestic comforts as habit has rendered almost necessities. The exercise of a little philosophy will reconcile him to the exigencies of the case, and render endurable here what would be inadmissable at home. A coarse, ill-cooked dinner, untidy service, and an unappeased appetite must be compensated by active interest in grand and peculiar scenery; a hard bed and a sleepless night, by the intelligent enjoyment of famous places clothed with historic interest; foul smells and rank odors, by the charming study of a unique people, extraordinarily interesting in their wretched squalor and nakedness. Though the stranger is brought but little in contact therewith, owing to the briefness of his visit to the country, quite enough is casually seen and experienced to show that there is no lack of culture and refinement, no absence of warmth of heart and gracious hospitality, among the more favored classes of Mexico, both in the northern and southern sections of the country.

Ballou's patronizing attempt at tolerance would be laughable if it were not so clear that he is serious.

Ballou, however, does not try to exercise tolerance when writing about the war Texas fought for independence from Mexico or when describing the false histories of Mexico written by Spanish and Roman Catholic authors. Of the Mexican War, Ballou hotly declares, "It was not this country, but Mexico,

Cover for Ballou's last book, in which he describes the colony of Ceylon, since 1972 the independent nation Sri Lanka

resent anything relative to an idolatrous people save in accordance with the special interests of their own church; or from Spanish historians who had never set foot upon the territory of which they wrote, and who consequently repeated with heightened color the legends, traditions, and exaggerations of others." Ballou then remarks,

One would be glad to get at the other side of the Aztec story, which, we suspect, would place the chivalric invaders in a very different light from that of their own boastful records, and also enable us to form a more just and truthful opinion of the aborigines themselves. That their numbers, religious sacrifices, and barbaric excesses are generally overdrawn is perfectly manifest. Every fair-minded student of history frankly admits this. It was necessary for Cortez and his followers to paint the character of the Aztecs in the darkest hue to palliate and excuse, in a measure, their own wholesale rapine and murder.

Although Ballou does not do much to "form a more just and truthful opinion of the aborigines," he does criticize the Spanish and the clergy at every turn. He condemns the priests for keeping the peasants in poverty by denying them the use of laborsaving technology and by taking any money they might have for church offerings. He calls the Roman Catholic Church "the visible curse of the country."

Ballou's typically chatty style and abuse of Roman Catholics elicited a backlash from book reviewers. In the 9 October 1890 *Nation* the reviewer reports that Ballou seems to have never left his Pullman car when making his observations about Mexico. He faults Ballou not only for having nothing new to say but also for not supporting his argument against Spanish historians. He dismisses *Aztec Land* by saying, "The whole, justice compels us to say, has no excuse for being." While the reviewer for the November 1890 *Catholic World* gives Ballou some praise for his style, it is not surprising that he violently disagrees with Ballou's characterization of the priesthood: "to be just, it must be said that Mr. Ballou's book is readable. He has an easy and correct style, and what he saw for himself in the fields and roadways and market-places he has put with some picturesque force upon his pages. But it must be added, that as what is new in his book is a shade worse than simply untrue, so what is good in it needed no retelling, for the very excellent reason that it had already been better told, and that very recently, and by more than one observer better qualified, less indolent, and more candid than he."

which was the aggressor, and it was her foolhardiness and outrageous insult which brought about the war. There is not a power in Europe which would not have done precisely as this country did when thus attacked. The author knows very well that it is the fashion to berate our government for the punishment it inflicted upon the aggressive Mexicans, but we are not among those who believe that when nations or individuals are smitten upon one cheek they should turn the other for a like treatment. Mexico got what she deserved, that is, a thorough drubbing, and lost one half of her territorial possessions in return for a long series of aggressions."

Ballou goes on to berate the early Spanish and Roman Catholic historians of Mexico, his criticism a part of the larger pattern of anti-Catholic and anti-Spanish remarks that are woven into his story. According to Ballou, "Our information concerning the early inhabitants comes almost solely through the writings of irresponsible monks and priests who could neither see nor rep-

In *Equatorial America: Descriptive of a Visit to St. Thomas, Martinique, Barbadoes, and the Principal Capitals of South America* (1892), Ballou discusses life on a passenger ship and the excitement of "setting foot upon a foreign soil, in mingling with utter strangers, in listening to the voluble utterances and jargon of unfamiliar tongues, while noting the manners, dress, and faces of a new people." He praises the agricultural production of the countries and their use of modern technology such as the telephone, telegraph, and electric lights. Ballou directs his most significant criticism against the Roman Catholic Church and the Peruvian people, whom he regards as indolent.

Ballou's observations lead him to conclude that the Peruvians play only a small role in the commercial life of their country: "Most of the small shops are kept by Italians, and the best hotels by Frenchmen. The banking-houses are usually conducted by Germans, while Americans and Englishmen divide the engineering work, the construction of railways, with such other progressive enterprises as require a large share of brains, energy, and capital." A few pages later he emphasizes the disinterest Peruvians show in work even more:

> One peculiarity is especially noticeable here among the native race: it is that the Peruvians seem to be mere lookers-on as regards the business of life in their country. All of the important trade is, as we have said, in the hands of foreigners. The English control the shipping interests, almost entirely, while the skilled machinists are nearly all Americans, with a few Scotchmen. We repeat this fact as showing the do-nothing nature of the natives, and also as signifying that for true progress, indeed, for the growth of civilization in any desirable direction, emigration from Europe and North America must be depended upon.

According to Ballou the Peruvians and other South Americans are good at raising crops and looking picturesque; however, in terms of real progress, they must rely upon America for the hard work and the brains.

The prefaces of Ballou's final two travel books—*The Story of Malta* (1893) and *The Pearl of India* (1894), which deals with Ceylon—reveal a defensive author, one trying to justify his continued writing about travel. In *The Story of Malta* he states that he received a letter from an "experienced traveler" who claimed "the reading of your [Ballou's] book entitled 'Due North' promptly sent me to view the glories of the 'Midnight Sun,' at the North Cape. I thank you sincerely for the inspira-

tion." Flattered by such a response, Ballou concludes his preface by hoping that "these pen-pictures of the Queen of the Mediterranean may influence others in a similar manner." In his last travel book Ballou again asserts that he writes because his readers ask him to: "That many readers evince a growing satisfaction in contemplating foreign lands through the eyes of experienced travelers, the favor shown to previous books by the author of these pages abundantly testifies. Mutual profit is therefore the outcome of such a work; both the author and reader are gratified."

In each of his final travel books Ballou describes geography, climate, history, agriculture, people, and commerce. He notes with pleasure Malta's temperate climate and large supply of natural fruits; indeed, he likens the island to Elysium. Ballou cannot help but make his habitual comparison of the foreign land to America, but unlike the comparisons made in other such cases it is his own country that he finds lacking:

> It is only as regards its great antiquity that one would contrast Malta with our own country. What we are most deficient in is a background in America,—a background to our national scenery, which in itself is hardly equaled, and nowhere excelled. By the word 'background' we mean the charm of far-reaching history, legend, classic story, and memories of bygone ages. We have no such special inspiration as is presented in the associations of southern Europe and Asiatic localities,—the Bay of Naples and its surroundings, for instance, or the land of Palestine. America is still in the youth of its civilization, while in this isolated Mediterranean group, so circumscribed in space, we have monuments which may nearly equal the Pyramids in age.

Ceylon also delights Ballou with its rich vegetation and historical associations. On one occasion he finds that he has become the object of contemplation: "Loitering beneath the shade of the trees contiguous to their cabins, queer family groups of Singhalese natives watch the passing stranger [Ballou] with curious, questioning eyes." Watching them watch him, Ballou makes a typically condescending observation by noting that the children have "monstrously protruding stomachs, like the little darkies of our Southern States." Ballou draws yet another comparison between Ceylon and America when he determines that Ceylon's climate prohibits its inhabitants from practicing the American work ethic:

> They live from hand to mouth, exercising no forecast, making no provision for the morrow. It is the paradise of birds, butterflies, and flowers, but man

seems to be out of place; he adds nothing to the beauty of the surroundings; he does nothing to improve such wealth of possibilities as Providence spreads broadcast only in equatorial regions. Bishop Heber's lines alluding to Ceylon were certainly both pertinent and true: "Where only man is vile."

Although Ballou thinks little of the capacity of the Ceylonese to work, he does believe that one day they will grow to despise the British who rule them and rise up against them. Ballou was never one to luxuriate in any single place for any length of time. He traveled constantly, wrote constantly, and continued to do so until his death in Egypt on 27 March 1895. Had he not died at that time, the library of travel literature would have contained yet one more volume by the indefatigable Maturin Murray Ballou. Nevertheless, at his death Ballou left behind a body of work that described the most popular countries outside Europe for Americans to travel in the late nineteenth century. Through his books Ballou also bequeathed to modern readers a clear sense of the cultural values and stereotypes Americans held during his time. His travel books provide an enlightening glimpse into the way many Americans traveled and thought about the differences they saw between their ideas about civilization and those of others.

References:

Ralph Admari, "Ballou, the Father of the Dime Novel," *American Book Collector,* 44 (1933): 121–129;

Adin Ballou, *An Elaborate History and Genealogy of the Ballous in America* (Providence, R.I.: E. L. Freeman, 1888), pp. 332–333.

S. G. W. Benjamin

(13 February 1837 – 19 July 1914)

Taimi Olsen
Tusculum College

BOOKS: *Constantinople, the Isle of Pearls, and Other Poems* (Boston: N. J. Bartlett, 1860);

Ode on the Death of Abraham Lincoln (Boston: W. V. Spencer, 1865);

The Turk and the Greek; or, Creeds, Races, Society, and Scenery in Turkey, Greece, and the Isles of Greece (New York: Hurd & Houghton, 1867);

Tom Roper: A Story of Travel and Adventures (Philadelphia: Daughaday & Becker, 1868);

The Choice of Paris; a Romance of the Troad (New York: Hurd & Houghton, 1870);

Contemporary Art in Europe (New York: Harper, 1877);

What Is Art, or, Art Theories and Methods Concisely Stated (Boston: Lockwood, Brooks, 1877);

The Atlantic Islands as Resorts of Health and Pleasure (New York: Harper, 1878);

Our American Artists (Boston: D. Lothrop, 1879);

The Multitudinous Seas (New York: Appleton, 1879);

Art in America; a Critical and Historical Sketch (New York: Harper, 1880);

The World's Paradises: or, Sketches of Life, Scenery, and Climate in Noted Sanitaria (New York: Appleton, 1880);

Troy: Its Legend, History and Literature, with a Sketch of the Topography of the Troad in the Light of Recent Investigation (New York: Scribners, 1880);

Our American Artists, second series (Boston: D. Lothrop, 1881);

A Group of Etchers (New York: Dodd, Mead, 1882);

The Cruise of the Alice May in the Gulf of St. Lawrence and Adjacent Waters (New York: Appleton, 1885);

Persia and the Persians (Boston: Houghton, Mifflin, 1886; London: John Murray, 1887);

Sea Spray; or, Facts and Fancies of a Yachtsman (New York: Benjamin & Bell, 1887);

The Story of Persia (New York & London: Putnam, 1887); republished as *Persia* (New York: Putnam, 1888; London: Unwin, 1888);

The Life and Adventures of a Free Lance, being the Observations of S. G. W. Benjamin (Burlington, Vt.: Free Press, 1914).

S. G. W. Benjamin

SELECTED PERIODICAL PUBLICATIONS–

UNCOLLECTED: "The Bahamas," *Harper's New Monthly Magazine,* 49 (November 1874): 761–772;

"The Channel Islands," *Harper's New Monthly Magazine,* 51 (June 1875): 1–15;

"Wanderings in Brittany," *Harper's New Monthly Magazine,* 51 (July 1875): 205–224;

"Gloucester and Cape Ann," *Harper's New Monthly Magazine,* 51 (September 1875): 465–474;

"Along the South Shore," *Harper's New Monthly Magazine,* 57 (June 1878): 1–14;

"The Sea Islands," *Harper's New Monthly Magazine,* 57 (November 1878): 839–861;

"Rambles in the South of France," *Harper's New Monthly Magazine,* 58 (January 1879): 193–210; (February 1879): 337–354;

"Lake George," *Harper's New Monthly Magazine,* 59 (August 1879): 321–339;

"Portugal's Place in Europe," *Self Culture,* 8 (February 1899): 696–699.

Noted in diplomatic history as the first U.S. minister to Persia (now Iran), Samuel Green Wheeler Benjamin pursued a varied career as journalist, painter, author, diplomat, editor, and amateur sailor. Most of his work was connected in some way to travel overseas; he was a cosmopolitan adventurer who became sickly only when he stayed in one place too long. Contemporaries describe him as a sociable, energetic man of small stature, with a confident pose, intelligent eyes, and an imposing mustache. Critics generally found his books interesting and accurate although not scholarly or well edited. Benjamin prided himself on using firsthand experience in his works, and his enthusiastic recounting of the dangers he met during his many voyages added interest to his writings.

Benjamin was born in Argos, Greece, on 13 February 1837, one of five children of American missionaries, the Reverend Nathan Benjamin and Mary Glading Wheeler Benjamin. The family moved to Athens shortly after his birth, where his father was a Protestant missionary and for several years served as acting consul for the United States. His impressive performance as acting consul led to a permanent offer of the position, but he instead in 1845 chose missionary work in Turkey. The family resided first in Trebizond before moving to Smyrna and finally to Constantinople, cities now known as Trabzon, Izmir, and Istanbul, respectively.

Benjamin's unconventional education was conducted primarily at home by his mother but also at local schools for foreign children. He was allowed time and opportunity for travel, direct inquiry, and self-education. He read from private libraries, listened to the folktales of nannies and the sea yarns of old sailors, built model ships, sketched and painted (he took private instruction in his teens), and toured classical ruins with his father. At seventeen Benjamin published sketches of the Crimean War in the *Illustrated London News.* Exposure to native populations taught him modern Greek as well as some Armenian and Turkish; he also learned French, ancient Greek, and Latin. A facility with languages benefited him as an adult during his travels.

Benjamin enjoyed the rough travel conditions of his youth. During summer trips his family found themselves fighting storms at sea (once on a small Greek *goletta,* or brigantine), sleeping outside in the Greek hills, and on one excursion crossing Greece's "forty-fold river" during a threatening downpour. Of a family journey to Turkey, Benjamin writes in his autobiography *The Life and Adventures of a Free Lance, being the Observations of S. G. W. Benjamin* (1914) that "my sister Frances and I rode in kadjavehs or basket seats slung one on each side of a pack horse." He concludes that he liked the "gamy flavor" of touring. He enjoyed an 1847 voyage to the United States with his family that included sights of "eighty sails" gathering near the Straits of Gibraltar, a reef in the Azores that the ship narrowly avoided, and icebergs appearing out of dense fog in the northern seas. He was put off, however, by the puritanical customs of Williamstown, Massachusetts, which disapproved of his father's mustache while encouraging his family's attendance at lengthy "fire and brimstone" sermons.

Life in Turkey was difficult, as the household had to be wary of hostile strangers, poisonous centipedes, and earthquakes as well as having to protect themselves (as did the natives) from roaming brigands. Owing to unsanitary conditions in the city of Constantinople, his sister Mary became ill and died in 1854. His father died of typhoid fever in 1855, and another sister, Margaret, died the same year. Consequently, his mother moved back to the United States with Benjamin and his remaining brother and sister.

Unimpressed by American culture or its educational system, Benjamin nevertheless enrolled at Williams College in Williamstown to keep a promise to his father and stayed in school out of a sense of duty, earning his bachelor's degree in 1859. His college career, as Benjamin readily admitted, was unremarkable except for poetic and prose contributions to the *Williams Quarterly,* edited by future U.S. president James A. Garfield and future senator John J. Ingalls. During college he also published several poems in the *Independent.* Immediately after college he published his only collection of poetry, *Constantinople, the Isle of Pearls, and Other Poems* (1860), which established his lifelong pattern of publishing short pieces in periodicals and then gathering his material into book form.

In 1861 Benjamin accepted a position as assistant librarian in the New York State Library. He also married Clara Stowell (with whom he later had at least one child, a daughter) and continued to write articles. His three-year tenure at his library position seriously impaired his health, and he fought

DANISH POTTERY.

Illustration of Danish pottery from Benjamin's Contemporary Art in Europe *(1877)*

off a nervous attack that lasted three months before he retired from the job. Thereafter Benjamin maintained his equilibrium by indulging a taste for rigorous travel that often kept him away from his family for half a year or more at a time and by taking short sailing trips along the New England coast with family and friends during the summers he stayed at home. His health was best during ocean voyages, on which he never became seasick. He always had "a voracious appetite at sea . . . never [knew] the qualms of *mal de mer* nor lost a meal on either salt or fresh water." He also claimed that moderate use of alcohol and tobacco benefited his constitution and that owing to his "fondness for tea" he would often let "months elapse without a drop of water passing my lips."

After a yearlong trip to the Mediterranean in 1865, Benjamin published *The Turk and the Greek; or Creeds, Races, Society, and Scenery in Turkey, Greece, and the Isles of Greece* (1867), which sold only five hundred copies. Benjamin faulted his first nonfiction work for being too short—"hastily put together"

from newspaper articles—and realized that, because of his familiarity with the subject, he had sometimes omitted information necessary for the uninformed reader. The book did, however, receive favorable reviews. The critic for the January 1868 issue of *The Nation* laments the shortness of the book but praises Benjamin's "easy, graceful manner."

The style and subject matter of *The Turk and the Greek* ranges from descriptive passages and personal anecdotes to observations of the culture and character of Greeks and Turks to analysis of economic and political conditions. The book is weakest when Benjamin romanticizes topics such as slavery and the purchase of wives and when he generalizes about racial differences. He assumes the inferiority of non-Western culture and remarks that the Turks' "intercourse with superior races seems rather to degrade than to elevate."

The descriptive and anecdotal passages and their detailed information provide the most interesting parts of the book. In the third chapter Benjamin offers the dialect word *Kef* (laziness) as the key to describing the Bosporus, the tiny region of Turkey that separates Europe from Asia. He invites the reader to spend some time there "in a spirit passive to the influence of its charms and devoted to a judicious course of day-dreaming under its pines and plane-trees." After such an experience the reader will understand that Kef connotes restfulness and peace more than idleness. When Benjamin describes Constantinople, he goes to the Galata Bridge, in order to convey the cosmopolitan nature of the city. The pedestrians he sees on the bridge include a Yankee sea captain, a Circassian armed with medieval weapons, a Nubian eunuch, an English lord, a harem of women covered in "green and orange *feredges* and gauze veils," a gypsy girl, a filthy Mohammedan mendicant "friar," a Parisian lady, a Persian man, and a Jesuit missionary. In this passage, as in much of his writing, Benjamin uses generous detail and shows sensitivity to textures and colors.

Following publication of *The Turk and the Greek* Benjamin wrote articles for adolescents on travel and adventure, including the serial featuring Tom Roper, which was published in book form as *Tom Roper: A Story of Travel and Adventures* (1868). Several articles include his own illustrations, the execution of which renewed his interest in pursuing art professionally. In 1869 he studied oil painting with landscape artist S. L. Gerry and marine painter William E. Norton. He then set sail for Newfoundland to gather material for his paintings, believing that "impressions of the majesty of out-at-sea waves can only be obtained . . . from the deck of small sailing ships, rather than from immense steamships."

Benjamin maintained a studio in Boston and then in New York City, in the old University Building on Washington Square whose former occupants included the artists Samuel F. Morse, Edwin White, and Winslow Homer. Benjamin produced most of his paintings during the 1870s and exhibited his work regularly, earning between $60 and $600 per painting; at the end of his autobiography he includes a partial list of the titles he sold. (Interestingly, despite his romanticism, love of the picturesque, and devotion to uncommercialized "true art," Benjamin expresses a great deal of satisfaction when his articles, books, and paintings earn money.) Assessing his own talents as an artist, Benjamin writes that his originality in color, bold composition, and energy "won attention in spite of the occasional crudeness and unpolished technique."

While he pursued his painting career, Benjamin continued to write. He drew on a wide range of classics, including the *Iliad*, the *Odyssey*, the *Aeneid*, the Cyclic poems, and *Agamemnon*, to write *The Choice of Paris; a Romance of the Troad* (1870), a narra-

tive of the siege of Troy. Although the book was not popular, Benjamin thought it was his best prose writing. His publishers, according to Benjamin, considered the title "misleading." His second book on the topic, *Troy: Its Legend, History and Literature, with a Sketch of the Topography of the Troad in the Light of Recent Investigation* (1880)—which he claimed in part to have "dictated while at the same time painting at my easel"—was well received as well as more successful financially. Drawing on much the same material as he used in *The Choice of Paris,* Benjamin narrates the legend of Troy, then discusses in detail the literary sources, particularly Homer's works, and concludes with a consideration of current archaeological research of the plains of Troy. The "topography of the Troad" refers to the regions around ancient Troy, designated as the *Troadic* area (a Latinate term). The reviewer for the March 1881 issue of *The Nation* praised Benjamin for "a very good idea" and having "done the work well."

For *Harper's New Monthly Magazine,* his primary publisher from 1863 to 1881, Benjamin toured Europe and wrote about its art, including an article titled "Modern French Art" and a series called Art Life Abroad. These articles led to books on art history and theory—*Contemporary Art in Europe* (1877) and *What Is Art, or, Art Theories and Methods Concisely Stated* (1877). Benjamin undertook a critical study of American artists with *Art in America* (1880) and two volumes titled *Our American Artists* (1879, 1881), which created conflicts between him and his art colleagues. *A Group of Etchers* (1882) presents the work of what the reviewer for *The Nation* of December 1882 called "the best modern etchers" though the reviewer faulted several of the choices of etchings. During the 1870s Benjamin also served as art editor for *The American Art Review, Literary Table,* and the *Magazine of Art.*

His painting led, naturally, to more travel. His next voyage, to the Azores, was marked by the excitement that seemed to follow Benjamin to sea. While Benjamin's purpose was to study the sea, the ship he sailed on, though ostensibly delivering oranges, was also smuggling young Portuguese men trying to avoid conscription. Both his travel book *The Atlantic Islands as Resorts of Health and Pleasure* (1878) and *The Life and Adventures of a Free Lance* recount his adventures on this ship, the former in more detail but the latter with more exciting descriptions of his personal involvement.

As the ship arrived at the cliffs of Saint George, one of the nine major islands of the Azores, gale winds began to blow. Benjamin describes the danger faced by the refugees and by the ship's skeleton crew that consisted of himself, the first mate, and the captain. In Benjamin's telling of the tale in his autobiography it is his quick action that saves the ship as the Portuguese passengers take to rowboats:

> [They] tumbled aboard, the boats were hastily made fast to the rail with an even chance of being lost, and at the same moment the topsails slapped the masts with a sound of thunder, and the ship shuddered from stem to stern as the shifting squall roared through the rigging. Fortunately I had got a little way on her by watchful steering, enough to bring her into the wind, or she would have gone over. . . . We now had fifteen miles to go to clear the island, and to do it we had to carry a press of sail in a furious sea; it was our only hope, and a slim one at that. If a single spar had gone or a single sheet started, we were doomed.

This near sinking was but one of several dangerous moments in Benjamin's career. In later years he nearly tumbled to his death climbing an island cliff and along with others risked his life for the "zest of danger" posed by taking the last voyage of the leaky U.S. frigate *Constitution,* immortalized as Old Ironsides in the famous 1830 poem by Oliver Wendell Holmes.

Benjamin also spices up his account of his voyage to the Azores with a character sketch of Captain Brown: "He was a weird character . . . [and] had undoubtedly been engaged at one time in the Blackbird or slave trade, and the recollections of it haunted him." His wife left him, and years later, while homeless, "she was murdered in a West Street den. An Algerine called Frenchy was sent for life to State's prison for the crime; but who really committed the murder . . . remains an insoluble problem." Benjamin's quick biography of Brown highlights the sensational details of his life—a selling point of his work.

In addition to the Azores, Benjamin in *The Atlantic Islands* describes the Bahamas, the Channel Islands, Madeira (his favorite), the Bermudas, Tenerife, and others. The book pleased him because of its grounding in factual research—official documents and data, "personal observation," and accounts "from the highest authorities." The reviewer for the August 1878 issue of *The Nation* asserts that the book does not supply enough statistics, maps, or directions to be useful as a guidebook. Referring to Benjamin as a "practical invalid" for mysterious reasons, the reviewer finds that the author "descants upon winds, temperatures, and humidity with a certain personal interest and sympathy."

The narrative of *The Atlantic Islands* moves pleasantly except for dry passages concerning topography and the details of commerce. His specific accounts of localities are usually interesting, as when he describes the town of Funchal, Madeira, with its extraordinarily steep slopes necessitating travel by sled: "the coasting-sledge of Funchal must claim pre-eminence over all known forms of locomotion except sailing. I know of no other place in the world where business men slide down hill to their counting-rooms."

In his next important travel book, *The Cruise of the Alice May in the Gulf of St. Lawrence and Adjacent Waters* (1885), which was first serialized in *Century* magazine, Benjamin recounts further adventures at sea and more personal accounts of various island ports. On arrival at the Magdalen Islands he describes the "extraordinary air of solitude and woebegoneness" of the island coast. At one spot "there are no trees or shrubs, and the wrecks bleaching in the slime or on the beach seem to suggest that this is the grand central spot to which decayed vessels come . . . ." The book was illustrated by M. J. Burns, a specialist in marine drawing who accompanied Benjamin on some of his voyages.

Benjamin's best gathering of his magazine writing is *Sea Spray; or, Facts and Fancies of a Yachtsman* (1887). In researching one of its articles, "A Cruise in a Pilot Boat," Benjamin faced a fierce storm while sailing on the *Caprice,* a schooner whose logbook already recorded several catastrophes:

> [The *Caprice*] had nearly foundered with the weight of ice accumulating on her deck in a northwest gale. The following winter she lost three men in a fearful storm. Two years later she was hove down in a squall and lost a man. The next year she was tipped and filled by a huge wave, and abandoned by crew, who took to the boats and were picked up. Eventually the *Caprice* was unexpectedly found. . . .

Both the *Caprice* and Benjamin were able to weather yet another dangerous situation. The collection also republishes several sea-island stories, the detailed and informative "Evolution of the American Yacht," and an odd piece reminiscent of Mark Twain titled "The Trans-Atlantic Railway," which relates the engineering and cultural history of a hypothetical bridge over the Atlantic. The reviewer in *The Nation* of November 1887 praises only the first entry in the collection, a story titled "We Two on an Island," as a "delightful satire" on the religious and marital conundrums faced by a marooned Scotsman and a Boston lady.

Benjamin's accounts of island cruises, both to the West Indies and to the Magdalen Islands, usually emphasize commercial interests tied to the islands. Capitalists in the late nineteenth century were looking for profits, and the U.S. government

Illustrations of the tomb of Shah Abdûl Azeem (top) and the Royal Palace in Tehran (bottom) from Benjamin's Persia and the Persians *(1886)*

was seeking to secure its naval power in the Atlantic. Benjamin, like many other journalists, sought to meet the increasing interest in the economic and political fortunes of the neighbors of the United States. On the Magdalen Islands, for example, Benjamin records that the seven lobster canneries exported 434,758 lobsters in 1881. "Capitalists," he notes, "have repeatedly offered to purchase the Magdalen Islands of Colonel Coffin, their present owner. There is considerable coloring matter in the soil, which it is thought might be turned to account for pigments."

In 1883 Benjamin was appointed by President Chester A. Arthur to head the U.S. legation and become the first American minister to Persia. Although the United States and Persia had signed a peace treaty in 1856, diplomatic relations were not established until the United States could take advantage of new overseas commercial prospects. An expanding group of American missionaries also required more help than the British Embassy was willing to provide. Benjamin and his family moved to Tehran, the capital, where he served from 1883 to 1885. His first wife had passed away owing to illness, possibly in 1880. He married Fannie Nichols Weed in November 1882; they had one daughter. Although Benjamin rarely mentions his family, he recalls with pride the ability of his second wife and his daughter from his first marriage to travel in primitive conditions. For example, he recounts their horse ride to attend to him, when they heard that he was sick. They traveled along narrow mountain trails, avoiding mule trains driven by rough men; Benjamin remarks that "whatever the circumstances, these ladies never displayed any weakness or timidity."

Upon first reaching Persia, Benjamin was informed that the shah would soon leave the capital and be unable to receive the new minister for more than three months. Benjamin took to horse and galloped eighty to one hundred miles daily, mostly at night, in order to reach the shah in time. Benjamin apparently enjoyed the frantic ride: "The ride by *chappa* [post] is strangely interesting; at long intervals one meets a party going the opposite direction; neither stops, but goes on without a word, as if bound on the unknown errands of Allah." Benjamin reached Tehran, changed into the traditional black suit of an American minister—which he hated, holding the opinion that pomp had its advantages in diplomacy—and greeted the shah on his peacock throne.

During his ministry Benjamin purchased premises and hired staff for the legation. His entire staff, including family members, numbered 112 peo-

ple. He hired a *dragoman* (secretary) and a *moonshee* (translator). Next Benjamin drafted the diplomatic code for the legation and all American citizens in Persia. He then hired workmen to fashion a pole for the American flag. A devoted patriot, Benjamin made sure that the flag would "overtop every other flag at that capital." During all this activity he established relations with government officials and other diplomats. Benjamin's one flaw as minister was his extreme suspicion of Russia and Russian interest in Persia, which led to difficult relations between himself and the Russian diplomat. According to scholar James F. Goode, Benjamin had the prejudices of a "Turkophile" and "attributed difficulties in every area to Russian scheming."

Despite his preoccupation with Russia, Benjamin was evidently an able minister. He fulfilled his first responsibility to help the American missionaries, who were not welcome in Persia, and often, intentionally or unintentionally, crossed the government's restrictive legal limits on Christianity. He once took quick, decisive action to stave off a riot concerning a new missionary church.

Among other difficulties he faced, Benjamin had to contend with dangerous situations involving his family. On one occasion, despite rules of diplomatic immunity, royal guards attacked his carriage for passing the carriages of the shah's wives. Another time a mob gathered at the legation household, and an imminent attack was stopped by Persian officials. Benjamin records that his response to most crises was to use intrigue, schemes, and personal pressure; he could not expect help from the distant U.S. government.

After the attack by the royal guards, Benjamin relates that when he did not receive an immediate apology, he acted quickly and informed the government that he would "haul down his flag" in thirty-six hours and end diplomatic relations. Shocked, the shah immediately sent a cabinet member to his house to apologize. According to other accounts related by Goode, Benjamin, although daring, did not have such complete control over the situation and compromised when officials threatened to demand his recall.

After elections in the United States led to the victory of Grover Cleveland, a Democrat, Benjamin was recalled. He returned to find himself in demand as an expert on Persia and immediately published two volumes, *Persia and the Persians* (1886) and *The Story of Persia* (1887). A hefty book, *Persia and the Persians* was well received by reviewers, who compared Benjamin to Washington Irving, one-time minister to Madrid. In *The North American Review* of February 1887 the reviewer values Benjamin's contribution to an understanding of Persia which will "have permanent value for the sociologist and ethnologist. . . . [By] giving minute delineation of Iran under the present dynasty . . . Mr. Benjamin has produced in a definite and lasting form an important chapter in that exhaustive history of Persia which may ultimately be written." Benjamin describes the peoples of Persia and their customs, religious sects, architecture, geography, arts, commerce, laws, and politics.

Benjamin's fondness and respect for Persia is evident in his knowledge of its cultural history and political power. He tries to draw the Western reader to a deeper appreciation of the country, as when he remarks that the "cultivated imagination kindles at the mention of Persia." Benjamin intuitively relies on the appeal of the exotic and constantly relates details of foreign customs and names. He recalls, for instance, builders laying sun-dried bricks: "They wear long tunics, which are tucked into their girdles when working . . . . The one above sings out in a musical tone, 'Brother, in the name of God, toss me a brick!' The one below, as he throws the brick, sings in reply, 'Oh, my brother! [or, oh, son of my uncle!] in the name of God, behold a brick!'"

Benjamin bolsters his observations and opinions with facts and figures. He explains that nomadic tribes make their living from the sale of butter, cheese, mutton, wool, and textiles and that after taxes—"regular tax is four shahis, or three cents, per month on each sheep and goat"—the tribe retains more than 60 percent of the full value of the animal. Benjamin notes, however, that the tribe's chief and the district governors may get much of the profits. He then points out that the Persian army drafts a large part of its force from the tribes. As with most controversial subjects, Benjamin's political analysis ends quickly, as he concludes that, regardless, the tribes remain "comfortably situated." One of Benjamin's strengths is his ability to explain intricate topics such as the racial origins of various Persian residents, the permutations of language development, and the many religious divisions. Goode concludes that "although the work did not praise all aspects of Iranian culture . . . it showed a depth of understanding uncommon in that period" and a "regard for Iranian culture at a time when most writers despaired of 'primitive' societies."

Benjamin's second book on Persia, *The Story of Persia,* traces important people and events in Persia's history. He begins its founding, continues through the invasion of Alexander, and ends with the rule of the Muslims. Unlike his previous book on Persia, which draws on personal knowledge, *The Story of Persia* uses authoritative sources, though he does not disclose these sources, maintaining they are "well-known." The reviewer for the May 1887 issue of *The North American Review* found the volume "intelligently planned" and praised it for filling gaps left by other popular histories of Persia.

After completing his books on Persia and lecturing for several years on that country, Benjamin retired with his wife to Burlington, Vermont. He continued to publish articles, and his autobiography was published in 1914. Benjamin's contemporaries routinely greeted his writings as interesting, fun, and informative despite poor editing and flaws in style, but the little critical attention his work has received has been mostly limited to his tenure as a diplomat. His travel writings reach their peak with colorful accounts of Greece, Turkey, and Persia. His autobiography may prove worth reexamination simply as the source of information about an adventurous man. Despite hasty organization and occasional dull reminiscences of famous people, Benjamin conveys the excitement of his travels very well. His prose manages to translate events and places with a remarkable sense of immediacy.

Benjamin worked as a journalist to support his need for travel; he remarks in his autobiography that he lacked an ambitious nature and never desired fame. His only regret was that he could not continue his work as a diplomat. After publishing his first book and failing to achieve fame equal to his effort, Benjamin recalls his indifference, writing that he "looked forward to the issue of another work with cynical *sang froid*." Benjamin's best artistic endeavor was life itself. On his varied career he remarks that "if I have failed of achieving the position which can be reached generally only by concentration of effort, on the other hand I have touched life at more points, by this course."

References:

James F. Goode, "A Good Start: The First American Mission to Iran, 1883–1885," *Muslim World,* 74 (April 1984): 100–118;

Abraham Yeselson, *United States-Persian Diplomatic Relations 1883–1921* (New Brunswick, N.J.: Rutgers University Press, 1956).

Nellie Bly
(Elizabeth Cochrane Seaman)

(5 May 1864 – 27 January 1922)

Laurie Delaney
University of Cincinnati

See also the Cochrane entry in *DLB 25: American Newspaper Journalists, 1901–1925.*

BOOKS: *Ten Days in a Mad-House; or Nellie Bly's Experience on Blackwell's Island. Feigning Insanity in order to Reveal Asylum Horrors* . . . (New York: Munro, 1887);
Six Months in Mexico (New York: Munro, 1888);
The Mystery in Central Park (New York: G. W. Dillingham, 1889);
Outline of Bible Theology! Exacted from a Letter by a Lady to the New York World *of 2nd June, 1889* (N.p., 1889);
Nellie Bly's Book: Around the World in Seventy-Two Days (New York: Pictorial Weeklies, 1890).

Nellie Bly was one of the most famous journalists of the late nineteenth and early twentieth centuries. Despite her accomplishments and fascinating life, her work has been largely ignored. With the exception of a few references in early books on women in the press and surges in juvenile biographies in the 1950s, 1970s, and 1980s, little has been published on Bly. Her books are out of print, and no scholarly work was available on her until Brooke Kroeger wrote the first documented biography of Bly aimed at adult readers, *Nellie Bly: Daredevil, Reporter, Feminist* (1994). Authoritatively establishing Bly's important role in American journalism, Kroeger argues that Bly "pioneered the development of 'detective' or 'stunt' journalism, the acknowledged forerunner of full-scale investigative reporting" and helped open the field of journalism to other women. Yet Bly's role in American history and literary studies, especially as it is revealed through her reporting and travel writing and the persona she constructed through that writing, is only beginning to be understood.

Nellie Bly was born Elizabeth Jane Cochran on 5 May 1864 in Cochran's Mills, Pennsylvania. She

Nellie Bly, circa 1895

was the thirteenth child of Judge Michael Cochran, a store owner, gristmill operator, and real estate speculator. Pitts' Mills was renamed Cochran's Mills in 1855, five years after Cochran was elected associate justice of Armstrong County; two years later Catherine, his first wife and the mother of ten of his fifteen children, died. He continued to prosper in his businesses and in real estate after his marriage to his second wife, a widow named Mary Jane Kennedy Cummings, Bly's mother.

In 1869 Judge Cochran sold all his real estate holdings except for those in Cochran's Mills and moved his wife and younger children to Apollo, Pennsylvania, his boyhood home. Cochran died a year later without leaving a will, and his oldest son, Robert Scott Cochran, petitioned to have the judge's estate distributed among his heirs. Mary Jane Cochran was forced to support herself and her young children on a small yearly annuity, including a small allowance from her minor children's inheritance administered by Col. Samuel Jackson, the town banker. She and her children had to move out of the fine house and into a small home.

In 1873 Mary Jane Cochran married again. Her third husband, John Jackson Ford, was verbally and physically abusive. He threatened her life several times, pointing a gun at her more than once. On 14 October 1878 she filed for divorce. Young Elizabeth Jane Cochran testified on her mother's behalf, recounting the brutalities committed by her stepfather. The divorce was granted on 3 June 1879.

Elizabeth Jane Cochran, nicknamed Pink, was educated at the Methodist Episcopal Church in Apollo. In 1879 the fifteen-year-old began the fall semester at the Indiana State Normal School in Indiana, Pennsylvania. She registered as Elizabeth Cochrane, adding a final *e* to her surname, perhaps to separate herself from her father's first family that had left her mother in such poor financial conditions. Her plans to become a teacher fell apart when she had to leave the school after one incomplete semester because of a lack of funds. This marked the end of her formal education.

In 1880 Cochrane and her mother followed her older brothers Albert and Charles to Allegheny City, a community that was later incorporated into Pittsburgh. Little is known about her life during the next few years except that she was certainly angered by her inability to find gainful employment. In 1885 Erasmus Wilson began lamenting about women who were unprepared to fulfill their roles as housewives in his "Quiet Observations" column in the *Pittsburgh Dispatch*. Cochrane sent a letter signed "Lonely Orphan Girl" to the editor of the newspaper, where it caught the attention of managing editor George Madden. Although he did not publish the letter, he responded with a notice in the 17 January 1885 issue that read, "If the writer of the communication signed 'Lonely Orphan Girl' will send her name and address to this office, merely as a guarantee of good faith, she will confer a favor and receive the information she desires." The next day Cochrane appeared in Madden's office and was subsequently hired as a reporter—the first woman to work in that capacity for the newspaper.

The *Dispatch* published Cochrane's first article, "The Girl Puzzle," on 25 January 1885 under the name Orphan Girl. In it she took up the cause of poor workingwomen and implored the wealthy and "believers in women's rights" to "take some girls that have the ability, procure for them situations, start them on their way and by so doing accomplish more than by years of talking." Bly drew on her childhood experiences to write "Mad Marriages," her second article, in which she suggested eliminating divorce by preventing men of bad character from marrying. Madden decided that Cochrane should write under a pen name and borrowed her byline for the article from Stephen Collins Foster's song "Nelly Bly." An important career in American journalism had begun.

Bly did not establish her reputation as a writer through her language skills but through her approach to her subjects. While her limited education almost certainly led to intense editing of her stories for grammar and punctuation, throughout her career she demonstrated the ability to find unique angles for her stories. She provided abundant, explicit detail and was personally involved in every article, passionately defending whatever opinion she had at the time. Her first series, eight articles on the Pittsburgh slums emphasizing the plight of working-class women, aroused public sympathy but also provided titillating details about the lives of the women after work, including descriptions of drunken liaisons with men. Bly never criticized their working conditions, though she sympathized with their lack of a more respectable outlet in which to spend their leisure hours. With the completion of the series Bly was given less controversial assignments.

After a few months of writing typical women's features on fashion and culture, she picked up the theme of workingwomen again in her short-lived weekly column. After criticizing the lack of an organization for women similar to the YMCA, she positioned herself against Bessie Bramble, an established *Dispatch* columnist, who championed the work of the Woman's Christian Association. Bly argued that while that organization certainly helped destitute women, it failed to extend attention to working girls. Despite the popularity of her column, Madden soon put Bly back on the women's beat. In November 1885, less than a year after she began writing for the paper, Bly resigned from her full-time position.

Bly continued to write for the *Dispatch* as a freelance journalist. Accompanied by her mother, she traveled in Mexico, and the pieces describing her journey ran in the newspaper from February through September 1886. They were later repub-

Cochran's Mills in the late 1800s

lished with some minor revisions in her first collection of travel writing, *Six Months in Mexico* (1888). She recounts her various experiences in Mexico City and her various sojourns into other cities and towns in articles such as "A Day's Trip on a Street Car," about an excursion to Jalapa in the state of Vera Cruz.

Bly is seemingly both eclectic and thorough in her depiction of Mexican society. She describes everything from the Mexican army to the way parlors are set up in Mexican homes. No detail is too minute to mention: she notes Mexicans' addiction to cigarettes, often describes their laundry rituals, and frequently documents prices, from the cost of purchasing a newspaper to the cost of constructing and maintaining various buildings. She gives accounts of festivals and even witnesses and depicts the gory details of several bullfights. In addition to portraying the beautiful theaters and poor performances presented in them, she describes Mexican courting rituals in great detail. She mixes her descriptions of tourist spots with local folklore and Mexican history and was especially interested in Benito Juarez, the "Lincoln of Mexico," and Maximilian, of whom she writes, "The worst things the Mexicans ever did for themselves was to shoot Maximilian. They have never had one quarter so good government since."

One recurrent theme in Bly's book is her effort as a journalist to present the truth about Mexico. Against the pleas of Joaquin Miller, who was build-

ing his reputation as a popular poet on romanticized images of Mexico, Bly reveals that the famous floating gardens do not float at all. The pyramid of Cholula is not the grand structure portrayed in illustrations and history books but rather "looks like many of the other queerly shaped hills which one so frequently sees in Mexico." In repeating the various legends and stories she heard, she would often offer a rational explanation, or when that was not possible she would treat them as amusing anecdotes. At the end of the book Bly concludes that "superstition is the ruin of Mexico."

Catholicism played a part in the superstitions of Mexico, and Lenten celebrations held a particular fascination for Bly. She was both unsettled and enchanted by the festivities that she described as "a mixture of religion and amusement . . . to a sightseer it looked as if the two forces were waging a battle to see which would dominate." The fasting forced upon her during Lent further enhanced her homesickness and hatred for Mexican food:

I for one am glad Lent with its eggs, red-pepper, and bad-smelling fishes is gone. What cowards our stomachs make of us all. I really have begun to long for home, or rather home-cooking. I have made out a list which I view every day, and see how much longer I can endure this trash.

The food preparation practices of the Mexicans were especially repulsive to her. She notes the women making tortillas: "They spit on their hands to keep the dough from sticking. . . . Rich and poor buy and eat them, apparently unmindful of the way they are made." She remarks similarly about pulque, an alcoholic beverage made from the sap of various agave plants:

> The pulque is collected in jars that the gatherers carry suspended from their shoulders. It is sucked out of the basin through a hollow bamboo reed, and squirted from the mouth into the jars. A knowledge of this fact does not render the stuff any more palatable to foreigners.

Bly often attributes a town's cleanliness to the low number of pulque shops. Despite her distaste for the cuisine, Bly provides an entire chapter of Mexican recipes.

The volume reflects the shifting moods and opinions of its author. In chapter 7, "A Horseback Ride over Historic Grounds," she notes, "Mexican cemeteries have a certain peculiar beauty, and yet they are ugly." Her description of the cemeteries also reflects her perceptions of the country and the people. She writes, "The Mexicans are certainly misrepresented, most wrongfully so. They are not lazy, but just the opposite. From early dawn until late at night they can be seen filling their different occupations." She later continues along the same lines:

> Those who call the Mexicans "greasers," and think them a dumb, ignorant class should see the paseo on Sunday: tally-ho coaches, elegant dog carts, English gigs, handsome coupes and carriages drawn by the finest studs, are a common sight. Pittsburg, on this line, is nowhere in comparison.

Yet Bly is not so gracious in individual encounters. About being stuck in a train car with an opera troupe, she writes, "Every woman had at least three children, which were cared for by as many nurses. Oh, what a howling, dirty, lazy mob."

Bly cares little for consistency. She condemns the "white-faced stranger" who invaded Montezuma's land and

> outraged his hospitality and trust; stole his gold and jewels and replaced them with glass beads; tore down his gods and replaced them with a new; butchered his people, and not only made him an imbecile but cursed him to die at the hands of his once loving subjects the despised of all people.

Yet she encourages wealthy Americans to buy land in Mexico and take advantage of its natural resources.

Observing the wealthy and poor as they intermingle in the streets and at church, Bly asserts that Mexico is not as class-conscious as America, but throughout the book she emphasizes the differences between the classes in their living conditions and housing. She sympathizes with the poor, especially their children:

> Mexico is the hotbed of children; the land is flooded with them, and a small family is a thing unknown. . . . It is a blessed thing that the natives are able to live in a cane hut and exist on beans and rice, else the lists of death by starvation would be something dreadful.

She portrays the poor and homeless as "worse off by thousands of times than were the slaves of the United States. Their lives are hopeless, and they know it. That they are capable of learning is proven by their work, and by their intelligence in other matters." On the one hand, she finds the poor so clean, hardworking, and honest that she recommends several times that American women consider hiring them as servants. On the other hand, she recounts many instances of Mexicans who try to cheat her by miscalculating hotel receipts and overcharging her for carrying a bag.

Bly is more consistent in projecting her own intelligence and determination as an American and as a woman. She displays her sense of superiority when she feels she becomes aware of a swindle: "I had no intention of allowing a Yankee girl to be cheated by a Mexican." Rather than overpay a *mozo* (youth) to carry her bag, she pays him a fourth of what he asks for and shows the gawking bystanders "that a free American girl can accommodate herself in circumstances without the aid of a man."

Bly is conscious throughout the book about the way women are treated. After crossing into Mexico she quickly sees the deplorable situation of women in the country:

> For the first time I saw women plowing while their lords and masters sat on a fence smoking. I never longed for anything so much as I did to shove those lazy fellows off.
> After we got further south they had no fences. I was glad of it, because they do not look well ornamented with lazy men.

Bly sees that Mexican women have little independence. She notes that the only women who visit Mexican libraries are tourists. After observing the way wives are jealously guarded by their husbands, Bly asserts that "Life to a Mexican lady in an American's view is not worth living." If a woman should separate from her spouse, her life does not improve.

The Nellie Bly game, published in The New York World, *26 February 1890*

Bly describes Manuel Gonzáles's wife, who, unable to get a divorce, "is living in abject poverty, and, like all Mexican women with the door to the way of gaining an honest livelihood barred against her because of her sex."

Although Bly's earlier writing on the plight of workingwomen in the United States suggests that the countries are similar in denying women economic opportunities, Bly usually contrasts the two nations to show the superiority of her native land. She writes of the Mexicans, "One can hardly believe Americanism is separated from them only by a stream. If they were thousands of miles apart they could not be more unlike." She is particularly careful to distinguish between the freedoms allowed in the two countries: "The Constitution of Mexico is said to excel, in the way of freedom and liberty to its subjects, that of the United States; but it is only on paper." She observes that elections and the right to a fair trial are nonexistent in Mexico. When accused criminals were not executed on the spot, they were often sent to overcrowded prisons and kept under horrid conditions. Bly herself was threatened with prison because of an article published while she was still in Mexico that discussed the imprisonment of newspaper editors who opposed the government. The threat of winding up in jail kept her from further exposing Mexico's puppet press and other limitations on freedom until she and her mother returned to the United States on 22 June 1886.

In October 1886 Bly returned to Armstrong County to testify in a lawsuit she filed against Colonel Jackson for mismanaging her inheritance, which had led to her withdrawal from the normal school. She did not see the lawsuit through, however. When she returned to Pittsburgh she resumed her work as a full-time reporter on theater and art.

Again dissatisfied with writing for the women's pages, she left in less than six months and moved to New York City. Though she tried to get a

Bly in traveling attire, 1890

Bly's confidence. She went to see John Cockerill, managing editor for the *World* and one of the editors she had interviewed for her article. He did not hire Bly right away, but he held her on retainer while he considered her story ideas. In late September of 1887 Bly received her first assignment, the one that would make her famous and establish her career in stunt journalism.

To report on the treatment of the insane, Bly devised a plan to have herself committed to the Women's Lunatic Asylum on Blackwell's Island. As Nellie Brown she checked into a shabby lodging house, Matron Irene Stenard's Temporary Home for Women, and proceeded to act like a madwoman until the police were called. She was sent to Bellevue for examination as Nellie Moreno because the judge she appeared before mistook her for Cuban when she responded to questions in broken Spanish. She was then transferred to Blackwell's Island, where she stayed until the *World* obtained her release. In her articles she described in minute detail the poor conditions at the asylum, exposing the violence used to control inmates as well as unsanitary conditions and lack of proper food, clothing, and bedding. She concluded that the cold, filthy environment in which inmates were denied any intellectual stimulation would certainly cause a sane woman to go mad within months and noted that some inmates, particularly women who could not speak adequate English, probably had been sane before they were committed.

Bly's first installment appeared on 9 October 1887. As the series continued, her name moved from byline to headline, where it remained, with few exceptions, for the rest of her career. Before the year was out the series was published in book form as *Ten Days in a Mad-House; or Nellie Bly's Experience on Blackwell's Island. Feigning Insanity in order to Reveal Asylum Horrors . . .* (1887). The book is rounded out with two more examples of her stunts, "Miscellaneous. By Nellie Bly. Trying to Be a Servant" and "Nellie Bly as a White Slave."

All the major papers picked up Bly's madhouse exposé, and her fame brought her enough money to move into a comfortable home with her mother. Her investigative reporting for the *World* continued. Her most famous piece for this period is an investigation of Edward R. Phelps, an Albany lobbyist. Bly bribed him to quash a piece of legislation, and her story caused an investigation that forced Phelps to drop out of politics. Another notable article resulted from her interview of Belva Lockwood, the presidential candidate on the Woman Suffrage ticket.

job at Joseph Pulitzer's *New York World* by volunteering for an assignment chronicling a balloon trip originating in Saint Louis, the home of Pulitzer's *Post-Dispatch,* her offer was rejected, and the paper sent a man to report the event. To support herself Bly continued to write fashion pieces for the *Dispatch* on a freelance basis.

Although she could not get any job offers from the editors of the major New York newspapers, the experience gave her a story idea that furthered her career. On 21 August 1887 the *Pittsburgh Dispatch* published her story on women in journalism in which she used the editors' own words to show the resistance to women entering the profession. The story was picked up by several papers throughout the eastern United States, and apparently it boosted

As her fame as a journalist increased, so did condemnation from her peers. *The Journalist* and *Town Topics,* the two top trade journals, began to ignore or criticize her work. Her one attempt at fiction writing, *The Mystery in Central Park* (1889), was a romantic story about a young man who must prove his love by finding the murderer of a girl found in Central Park before his lover will marry him. The novel was not well received, and Bly returned to investigative journalism, uncovering baby-selling rings, exposing swindlers, interviewing murderers and prizefighters, and reporting on women's achievements. Her report on the religious practices of the Oneida Community impressed community members so much that they had it reprinted as *Outline of Bible Theology! Exacted from a Letter by a Lady to the* New York World *of 2nd June, 1889* (1889).

A few months later, on 14 November 1889, Bly began her most famous stunt: a race around the world. Traveling east, she arrived back in New York on 25 January 1890, beating the eighty days of French novelist Jules Verne's fictional character, Phileas Fogg, with a record of seventy-two days, six hours, eleven minutes, and fourteen seconds. Throughout her trip the *World* reported on her progress and, to keep interest high, sponsored a contest offering a trip to Europe for the person who most closely guessed Bly's time. Upon her return, however, Bly was not pleased with the reception she received at the *World,* and she left reporting once again.

She began a lecture tour, and her recollections of her journey were published in 1890 as *Nellie Bly's Book: Around the World in Seventy-Two Days.* Early in her journey she stopped in Amiens, France, to meet Verne, who showed Bly his library and the map he used to plot Fogg's journey. In her short visit she charmed both Verne and his wife, just as the Vernes charmed her. They both wished her good luck, and Verne toasted her trip even though he had given up drinking for his health. However, because of the necessity of speed, Bly had few opportunities for sight-seeing. She spent most of her time on boats and trains and often recounts her impressions of other passengers. She was particularly fond of criticizing the English. Her trip from Europe through Asia on the *Victoria* provided her with much ammunition, as the passengers as well as the crew were rude: "The impudence and rudeness of the servants in America is a standing joke, but if the servants on the *Victoria* are a sample of English servants, I am thankful to keep those that we have, such as they are." The crew of the *Oceanic* was much more to Bly's liking. They promised to do everything possible to cross the Pacific and return her home in time to beat the record.

Bly's observations are similar to those she made in *Six Months in Mexico.* When she has the opportunity, she gives detailed descriptions of stops, including her stays in Port Said, Egypt; Aden, a port in southern Arabia; Colombo, Ceylon (now Sri Lanka); Singapore; Hong Kong; Canton; and Yokohama, Japan. She tries to rationalize myths and legends in her pursuit of truth, and when she cannot, she dismisses them in an amusing manner. For example, after describing a carved image of a Japanese god who has healing powers, she writes, "I can't say whether it cured them or not, but I know they rubbed away the nose of the god." As in her book on Mexico, she includes many descriptions of food, though in Japan she finds some of what she eats palatable.

She spends much time describing the exotic people she meets and the fashions they wear, especially the beautiful women of Aden and Japan. However, she pays far less attention to the men in this narrative than in her Mexican travelogue. She found the men in Mexico seductive, but the men she encounters on this journey do not seem nearly as attractive to her. She describes her lack of attention to Japanese men: "I know little about the men except that they do not go far as we judge manly beauty, being undersized, dark, and far from presupposing."

She is again interested in cleanliness and is especially repulsed by the requests of Buddhist monks who ask that she remove her shoes before entering their temples. She becomes even more incensed when she is refused admittance to a temple because she is a woman: "'Why?' I demanded, curious to know why my sex in heathen lands should exclude me from a temple, as in America it confines me to the side entrances of hotels."

One of Bly's chief concerns again is to present herself as a strong, independent American woman. In the first chapter of her book she explains that the editors of the *World* wanted to give the assignment to a man because they believed that a woman could not travel alone unprotected and would take too much baggage. But Bly believed she would have the advantage over a male traveler. Although she often took pride in demonstrating her independence, she was never shy in taking advantage of her femininity and knew she could charm men when she needed their help. Just as she waited coyly in Mexico for a chivalrous gentleman to retrieve the hat she lost while horseback riding, she was confident she could depend on men to come to her rescue. "I knew if my conduct was proper I should always find men ready

Postcard advertisement, 1890

Her sympathies, though, often change with her mood. She coaxes an Italian man into accepting some money for his daughter but says the beggars in Port Said

> presented such repulsive forms of misery that in place of appealing to my sympathetic nature, as is generally the case, they had a hardening effect on me. They seemed to thrust their deformities in our faces in order to compel us to give money to buy their absence from our sight.

In her encounters with children she is similarly changeable. She finds Japanese children, like the abundant but well-behaved children of Mexico, beautiful and enchanting, while she finds many of the other children she meets annoying, especially the Chinese.

Many of her sentiments are split along national lines, especially with respect to the Japanese and the Chinese:

> The Japanese are the direct opposite of the Chinese. The Japanese are the cleanliest people on earth, the Chinese are the filthiest; the Japanese are always happy and cheerful, the Chinese are always grumpy and morose; the Japanese are the most graceful people, the Chinese the most awkward; the Japanese have few vices, the Chinese have all the vices in the world; in short, the Japanese are the most delightful of people, the Chinese the most disagreeable.

These attitudes accurately reflect American attitudes of the time. Threatened by the influx of Chinese immigrants in the West, Americans at the same time romanticized Asian culture through images of Japan.

Both Bly and her book are unapologetically pro-American. In Canton she visits the American consulate and reflects on seeing the U.S. flag:

> It is a strange fact that the further one goes from home the more loyal one becomes. I felt I was a long ways off from my own dear land; it was Christmas Day, and I had seen many different flags since I last gazed upon our own. The moment I saw it floating there in the soft, lazy breeze I took off my cap and said: "That is the most beautiful flag in the world, and I am ready to whip anyone who says it isn't."

Perhaps because her awareness of politics developed through her reporting for the *World,* Bly can also be critical of her country despite her loyalty. She asserts that "Japanese patriotism should serve as a model for us careless Americans. No foreigner can go to Japan and monopolize a trade." She even praises the English for loyalty to the queen and regrets that Americans cannot have the same regard

to protect me, let them be Americans, English, French, German or anything else." With this in mind she challenged the *World* editors: "'Start the man and I'll start for some other newspaper the same day and beat him.'" When she received the assignment, she only packed one bag for the journey.

Nellie Bly's Book: Around the World in Seventy-Two Days is often richly detailed. In gruesome detail she describes various forms of Chinese torture and the decaying heads of decapitated prisoners, taking such opportunities to criticize oppression abroad. She is sympathetic to the poor, especially when defending them against the English. She defends the Arab boatmen who demand payment before they reach the shore because otherwise the English would not pay them. Similarly, instead of revealing the trick a juggler in the Bay of Suez used to make a ring disappear, she let him fool his audience: "I wanted to see the juggler get his money, much to the disgust of the Englishman."

for their leaders: "There I was a free-born American girl, the native of the grandest country on earth, forced to be silent because I could not in honesty speak proudly of the rulers of my land, unless I went back to those two kings of manhood, George Washington and Abraham Lincoln."

In 1893 Bly rejoined the staff of the *World*. In the next year she published several important pieces, including an interview with anarchist Emma Goldman, a series on the Pullman strike, and an interview with American railroad union leader Eugene V. Debs. By the time her Debs interview was published, she was no longer working for the *World* full-time. In February 1895 she joined the staff of the *Chicago Times-Herald*. She worked there only five weeks, leaving to marry the seventy-year-old millionaire Robert Livingston Seaman on 5 April 1895.

The marriage got off to a rocky start. When the jealous Seaman had Henry Hansen, the caretaker of his Catskill property, follow Bly, she had Hansen arrested. The couple also fought about friends and family. Seaman's brother and other potential heirs did not like Bly, and she did not care for them. She often left the house and dined alone because she did not like the company her husband kept. Upon her return to the *World* in January 1896, she produced some of her most explicitly radical writing. She used her column to criticize Seaman by discussing what a good husband should be like. She covered the National Woman Suffrage Convention in Washington and published an interview with Susan B. Anthony. By March she was proposing to form an army of women to fight in Cuba during the Spanish-American War and had even designed uniforms. After the Cuba column Bly's work abruptly stopped, and she and her newly attentive husband left for Europe.

Bly did not write about her years in Europe, which she spent taking care of her husband. During this period she convinced him to rewrite his will to leave her, rather than his other potential heirs, the bulk of his inheritance. He began transferring property into her name so she would not have to fight for it in probate. After the Seamans returned to America in 1899, Bly immersed herself in the family business, the Iron Clad Manufacturing Company. With her husband's death on 10 March 1904 a five-year inheritance battle ensued in the courts, but Bly already had most of Seaman's property in her name. She focused on running the business, not on the court proceedings from which she eventually emerged victorious. She treated her employees well and ran the company successfully. Eventually branching out into the making of steel barrels, which she claimed to have designed, Bly founded a new business under the name American Steel Barrel Company.

By 1911 Bly's apparently successful business was in severe financial trouble. Her discovery that her employees had been embezzling for years led to court proceedings that would last for years, during which time Bly would also have to defend herself against creditors. Bly returned to journalism again in 1912, this time for the *New York Evening Journal*. The bankruptcy hearings were settled in January 1914, but Bly still faced an arrest warrant for obstructing justice.

To delay her arrest Bly left for Vienna, arriving just in time for the advent of World War I. She remained in Austria throughout the war and reported from the front for the *Evening Journal*, writing pieces sympathetic to the Austrians that appealed to Americans to send food and supplies for war relief, unaware that she was taking up the side of America's eventual enemy. When she tried to return to America after the war, Bly was debriefed several times by the war department. Although she proudly wore an American flag on her sleeve throughout her Austrian sojourn, American officials had difficulty reconciling her patriotism with her warnings that the Bolsheviks would take over Central Europe and eventually America.

When Bly finally returned home she had to sue her mother and brother Albert for what was left of her company. In the meantime she continued writing for the *Evening Journal*, mainly advice columns, and spent her spare time finding jobs for the destitute and adoptive parents for orphans. She eventually won the lawsuit in February 1920. She died almost two years later on 27 January 1922.

At the time of her death Bly received the respect from her peers for which she had long worked. There were many tributes, including one from a dear friend, the respected journalist Arthur Brisbane. In the 28 January 1922 *Evening Journal* he proclaimed that "Nellie Bly was THE BEST REPORTER IN AMERICA and that is saying a good deal." While most scholars would not agree with Brisbane's assertion, more and more are coming to the conclusion that for her time she was certainly one of the most important reporters in America.

Biographies:

Jason Marks, *The Story of Nellie Bly* (New York: American Flange Manufacturing, 1951);

Nina Brown Baker, *Nellie Bly* (New York: Holt, 1956);

Iris Noble, *Nellie Bly: First Woman Reporter* (Detroit: Messner, 1956);

Mignon Rittenhouse, *The Amazing Nellie Bly* (Freeport, N.Y.: Books for Libraries Press, 1956);

Emily Hahn, *Around the World with Nellie Bly* (Boston: Houghton Mifflin, 1959);

Terry Dunnahoo, *Nellie Bly: A Portrait* (Chicago: Reilly & Lee Books, 1970);

Charles Parlin Graves, *Nellie Bly, Reporter for the World* (Champaign, Ill.: Garrard, 1971);

Ann Donegan Johnson, *The Value of Fairness: The Story of Nellie Bly* (La Jolla, Cal.: Value Communications, 1977);

Tom Lisker, *Nellie Bly: First Woman of the News* (New York: C.P.I., 1978);

Kathy Lynn Emerson, *Making Headlines: A Biography of Nellie Bly* (Minneapolis: Dillion, 1981);

Judy Carlson, *"Nothing Is Impossible," Said Nellie Bly* (Milwaukee: Raintree, 1989);

Elizabeth Ehrlich, *Nellie Bly* (New York: Chelsea House, 1989);

Martha E. Kendall, *Nellie Bly: Reporter for the World* (Brookfield, Conn.: Millbrook Press, 1992);

Marcia Schneider, *First Woman of the News* (New York: CPI Group, 1993);

Brooke Kroeger, *Nellie Bly: Daredevil, Reporter, Feminist* (New York: Times Books, 1994).

References:

Evelyn Burke, "Nellie Bly Started This Globe-Girdling," *Pittsburgh Press,* 31 October 1936;

Sue Davidson, *Getting the Real Story: Nellie Bly and Ida B. Wells* (Seattle: Seal Press, 1992);

Jason Marks, *Around the World in 72 Days: The Race between Pulitzer's Nellie Bly and* Cosmopolitan's *Elizabeth Bisland* (New York: Gemittarius Press, 1993);

Mignon Rittenhouse, "They Called Her the Amazing Nellie Bly," *Good Housekeeping* (February 1955): 48–51;

Ishbel Ross, *Ladies of the Press* (New York: Harper, 1936);

Bennett Wayne, *Women Who Dared to Be Different* (Champaign, Ill.: Garrard, 1973).

William Cullen Bryant

(3 November 1794 – 12 June 1878)

Kristine Harrington
Kent State University, Trumbull Campus

See also the Bryant entries in *DLB 3: Antebellum Writers in New York and the South; DLB 43: American Newspaper Jounalists, 1690–1872;* and *DLB 59: American Literary Critics and Scholars, 1800–1850.*

BOOKS: *The Embargo; or, Sketches of the Times; A Satire; by a Youth of Thirteen,* anonymous (Boston: Printed for the purchasers, 1808); second edition, corrected and enlarged, as Bryant (Boston: Printed for the author by E. G. House, 1809);

An Oration, Delivered at Stockbridge. July 4th, 1820 (Stockbridge, Mass.: Printed by Charles Webster, 1820);

Poems (Cambridge, Mass.: Printed by Hilliard and Metcalf, 1821);

Poems, by William Cullen Bryant, An American (New York: E. Bliss, 1832); edited by Washington Irving (London: J. Andrews, 1832); expanded (Boston: Russell, Odiorne & Metcalf / Philadelphia: Marshall, Clark 1834);

The Fountain and Other Poems (New York & London: Wiley & Putnam, 1842);

An Address to the People of the United States in Behalf of the American Copyright Club, attributed to Bryant, Francis L. Hawks, and Cornelius Mathews (New York: Published by the Club, 1843);

The White-Footed Deer and Other Poems (New York: I. S. Platt, 1844);

A Funeral Oration, Occasioned by the Death of Thomas Cole, Delivered before the National Academy of Design, New-York, May 4, 1848 (New York & Philadelphia: Appleton, 1848);

Letters of a Traveller; or, Notes of Things Seen in Europe and America (New York: Putnam, 1850);

Reminiscences of the Evening Post: Extracted from the Evening Post of November 15, 1851. With Additions and Corrections by the Writer (New York: William C. Bryant, 1851);

Letters of a Traveller. Second Series (New York: Appleton, 1859);

Bryant at age thirty (portrait by Samuel F. B. Morse, National Academy of Design)

A Discourse on the Life, Character and Genius of Washington Irving, Delivered before the New York Historical Society on the 3d of April, 1860 (New York: Putnam, 1860);

Thirty Poems (New York: Appleton, 1864);

Letters from the East (New York: Putnam, 1869);

Some Notices of the Life and Writings of Fitz-Greene Halleck, Read before the New York Historical Society, on the 3d of February, 1869 (New York: Evening Post Steam Presses, 1869);

A Discourse on the Life, Character and Writings of Gulian Crommelin Verplanck, Delivered before the New York Historical Society, May 17th, 1870 (New York: The Society, 1870);

Orations and Addresses by William Cullen Bryant (New York: Putnam, 1873);

Thanatopsis. (A Poem.) (New York: Appleton, 1874);

Among the Trees, by William Cullen Bryant, Illustrated from Designs by Jervis McEntee, Engraved by Harley (New York: Putnam, 1874);

William Cullen Bryant: Representative Selections, with Introduction, Bibliography, and Notes, edited by Tremaine McDowell (New York & Cincinnati: American Book, 1935).

Collections: *Poems,* edited by Bryant, 2 volumes (New York & London: Appleton, 1855);

The Life and Works of William Cullen Bryant, 6 volumes, edited, with a biography, by Park Godwin (New York: Appleton, 1883–1884).

OTHER: *The American Landscape, No. 1,* with contributions by Bryant (New York: E. Bliss, 1830);

Tales of Glauber-Spa, edited, with contributions, by Bryant (New York: E. Bliss, 1832);

The Iliad of Homer. Translated into English Blank Verse, translated by Bryant, 2 volumes (Boston: Fields, Osgood, 1870);

A Library of Poetry and Song: Being Choice Selections from the Best Poets, edited by Bryant (New York: J. B. Ford, 1871);

The Odyssey of Homer, translated by Bryant, 2 volumes (Boston: James R. Osgood, 1871–1872);

Sidney Howard Gay, *A Popular History of the United States, from the First Discovery of the Western Hemisphere by the Northmen, to the End of the First Century of the Union of States,* introduction by Bryant, 4 volumes (New York: Scribner, Armstrong, 1876–1881).

With the publication of *The Embargo; or, Sketches of the Times; A Satire; by a Youth of Thirteen* (1808) William Cullen Bryant began his remarkable career as an important figure in American politics, literature, and journalism. A satire directed at Thomas Jefferson for the 1807 passage of the Embargo Act, the poem drew much attention from critics who doubted it had actually been written by one so young. Bryant's first writing captured the nation's imagination, and American readers continued to view Bryant as a political commentator for the rest of his life. Recognized by his contemporaries most often for his longtime editorship of the *New-York Evening Post* and his poetry, Bryant in his mid fifties added travel writing to his already impressive achievements.

At the urging of his friend Richard Henry Dana Sr., an editor of *The North American Review,* and publisher George Palmer Putnam, Bryant compiled a book of letters about his travels, particularly his trips to Europe. After Putnam's New York firm published *Letters of a Traveller; or, Notes of Things Seen in Europe and America* (1850), Bryant playfully reproved Dana in a letter dated 4 July 1850: "You are the instigator of its publication, and if it be a bad book you must bear your share of the blame." Following on the popularity of travel narratives in American literature in the 1840s, *Letters of a Traveller* was proving to be moderately successful, as Bryant modestly admitted in the same letter: "The periodical press has been civil to it, and the 'Courier' had the magnanimity to set the example of commending the style." Bryant published two more collections of his travel letters: *Letters of a Traveller. Second Series* (1859) and *Letters from the East* (1869).

Bryant was born in Cummington, Massachusetts, on 3 November 1794 to physician Peter Bryant and *Mayflower* descendant Sarah Snell Bryant. By the time he reached eighteen months his mother had successfully taught Cullen, as he was known by his family, the alphabet. He filled the years of his youth reading poetry and preparing for a law career. In 1810 he studied at Williams College, and in 1811 he wrote his first major work of poetry, "Thanatopsis" (some critics speculate he composed the poem in 1813), which was eventually published in the September 1817 issue of *The North American Review.* In "Thanatopsis"—the Greek word translates as "view of death"—Bryant parallels the "tokens of decay" that he saw in nature with the human condition.

Poetry was Bryant's first choice for a career, but he knew that a vocation as a poet would not support him. In 1815 he was admitted to the bar and started his law practice in Plainfield, Massachusetts. He married Frances Fairchild in 1821 and continued to practice law and publish poetry until 1825 when he abandoned his law practice for editorial work in New York. He began as joint editor of the *New-York Review and Athaeneum Magazine,* but the journal was not successful and changed its title to *The New York Literary Review and American Atheneum* and then as *The United States Review and Literary Gazette* before it ceased publication in October 1827. Earlier that year Bryant had begun work as assistant editor at the *New-York Evening Post.* Although he considered newspaper work beneath his poetic sensibilities, he took a practical approach to his career choice. On 16 February 1828 he wrote to Dana: "I do not like politics any better than you do; but they get only my mornings, and you know politics and a bellyful are better than poetry and starvation." In 1829 Bryant succeeded William Coleman as the editor in chief at the *Evening Post,* a position he held for the rest of his life, nearly fifty years.

While newspaper work "got his mornings" and much of his life, Bryant continued to write poetry. In 1832 *Poems, by William Cullen Bryant, An American,* one of his strongest collections, was published in New York and London. He also found the time to pursue other interests, including a love for travel. From 1834 to 1836 he traveled through Europe, often writing home about his observations in letters that were published in the *Evening Post.*

Bryant left the United States on 24 June 1834 during fierce abolition riots, reaching France twenty days later. After passing several weeks in France he made way to Genoa by traveling along the shores of the Mediterranean. He spent eight months in Italy visiting Rome, Florence, Naples, and Pisa. Eventually he journeyed to Heidelberg, where he met with Henry Wadsworth Longfellow. The two poets enjoyed dinner and conversation together on a few occasions before Bryant's abrupt and unexpected departure for America on 25 January 1836, which was precipitated by the request of the dangerously ill William Leggett, assistant editor of the *Evening Post.*

Bryant visited Europe again in 1845 and 1849, and again he chronicled these visits with regular and lengthy correspondence to the *Evening Post.* After Bryant's return to the United States in December 1849, Dana and Putnam soon prevailed upon him to publish *Letters of a Traveller; or, Notes of Things Seen in Europe and America,* a selection of fifty-three unrevised letters spanning fifteen years. Dana was pleased with the result, as he remarked in a letter to Bryant dated 10 May 1859: "The first book I turned to after returning to my room again . . . was yours; and I read on, letter after letter, for it calmed me like a sunlight, gentle and with no glare."

In most of his letters Bryant describes scenery, sites of interest, and the daily life of the people; in some he discusses art and politics. In the first selection in *Letters of a Traveller,* written from Paris on 9 August 1834 and titled "First Impressions of an American in France," Bryant implicitly contrasts the French lifestyle with the American work ethic: "The Parisian has his amusements as regularly as his meals, the theatre, music, the dance, a walk in the Tuilleries, a refection in the cafe, to which ladies resort as commonly as the other sex. Perpetual business, perpetual labor, is a thing of which he seems to have no idea."

Although critics faulted *Letters of a Traveller* for its lack of unity and incoherent narrative structure, readers enjoyed Bryant's descriptions and observations. The letters were unrevised and so lack polish, but they exhibit a natural eloquence and precise use of metaphor. Contemporary critics recognized that the letters broke from Bryant's journalistic style, al-

William Cullen Bryant, circa 1845

lowing him to concentrate on exact description and detail and less on editorial comment.

Two years after the publication of *Letters of a Traveller* Bryant traveled to Europe and the Near East, departing from the United States on 13 November 1852 in the company of Charles M. Leupp, a longtime friend. This trip was the genesis for *Letters from the East,* although the materials were not collected and published until 1869. When Bryant and Leupp arrived in Liverpool, the American books they brought on the journey were confiscated under international copyright laws. Bryant was forced to surrender a book of his own poems that he had brought as a gift for a friend. The experience was the subject of the first letter (London, 29 November 1852) that was later included in *Letters from the East:*

> One of the vexations which a traveller meets on his arrival in this country is the search for contraband books. . . . When a book is found among the baggage of the traveller, which is carefully overhauled for the purpose, the examining officer looks to see if it is printed in America; and if it be, he consults his manuscript list, to see whether it be also published in England. If its title appears on the list, the book is seized.

However distressing the incident, Bryant relayed it in his usual matter-of-fact manner; the rest of the letter was dedicated to a discussion of the floods in England and the large number of English Protestants relocating to Ireland.

After visiting London the men left for Paris, reaching the city on 1 December 1852. From Paris they traveled to Genoa and Naples. They then boarded an English steamer for Alexandria, where Bryant met Mr. Fortune, a botanist traveling to China whose conversations he chronicled in *Letters from the East.* Fortune had visited China twice before to see what kinds of vegetation could be introduced into England and the United States, and he and Bryant shared lengthy conversations on the topic, which Bryant reported in a 12 January 1853 letter from Cairo. After leaving Cairo, the men crossed the Little Desert and eventually reached Jerusalem. During this journey Bryant rode a donkey and a camel, camped in the desert, visited the pyramids and the temple of seraphs, and took a trip up the Nile.

In a typical passage, from a letter written in Jerusalem on 22 February 1853, Bryant describes his impressions of a tomb of a "Mohammedan" saint:

Within the tomb of the saint was a rude sarcophagus of stone, plastered over with mortar and covered with a faded green cloth. Above it was stretched a cord, on which were strung bits of cloth, shells, and little frames of wood and paper stained with various colors, which I afterward learned were suspended there by persons afflicted with diseases, in the belief that there was a virtue in the tomb of a holy man which would work a cure.

In addition to his virtues as a stylist, Bryant here shows a discerning eye for the interests of his readers. He traveled the region for another four months before returning to the United States in June 1853.

In 1857 Bryant again visited Europe. He hoped that a sea journey and rest in southern Europe would help his wife's health. His daughter, Julia Bryant, and her companion, Estelle Ives, accompanied the Bryants, and the four toured many European cities, including Paris, Brussels, Amsterdam, and Madrid. While in Madrid, Bryant viewed his first bullfight, which became the subject of a letter dated 1 November 1857 and later was included in *Letters of a Traveller. Second Series:*

I then perceived, with a sort of horror, that the horse had been blindfolded, in order that he might not get out of the way of the bull. . . . Four other horses were brought forth blindfolded in this manner, and their lives put between the *picador* and the fury of the bull, and each was killed in its turn, amidst the shouts and applauses of the crowd. . . . I had now seen enough, and

left the place. . . . I heard afterwards three more bulls and six horses were killed.

Bryant's understated distaste for the spectacle shows his reluctance to indulge in much editorial comment.

After leaving Spain with plans to sojourn there again later, the Bryant party traveled to Italy and Naples, where in early spring 1858 Sarah Snell Bryant caught rheumatic fever and was confined to her room for four months. Bryant used the time to work on his poetry and wrote five poems, "River by Night," "The Sick Bed," "The Life that Is," "Future Life," and "A Day Dream." When the Reverend Robert Waterston and his family, old acquaintances from Boston and Heidelberg, visited the Bryants, Bryant revealed that he had never been baptized and asked the reverend to perform the ceremony. Waterston baptized Bryant, Julia, and Estelle Ives, and the two families took communion together.

While in Italy, Bryant joined Nathaniel and Sophia Hawthorne in Rome and toured the art centers of the city. In his 21 May 1858 letter to the *Evening Post,* which appeared in *Letters of a Traveller. Second Series,* Bryant remarked on the Grecian artifacts discovered in Rome:

Rome has its rich collections of ancient art in the Vatican, but there is still a richer museum in the earth below. The spade can scarcely be thrust into the ground without turning up some work of art or striking upon some monument of the olden time. Most of the fine statues in the public galleries have, I believe, been discovered in the digging to lay the foundations of buildings; and who can tell what masterpieces of Greek sculpture are yet concealed under that thick layer of rubbish which overlies the ancient level of the city.

After leaving Rome, Bryant visited Robert and Elizabeth Barrett Browning in Florence, where he met with the Hawthornes again.

Bryant's final overseas correspondence to his newspaper came from Eveshame, England, and relayed the tragic news of the death of Helen Waterston, the young daughter of Reverend Waterston. Bryant had met the young woman when her family visited him in Naples and was impressed with her intellect and maturity. Helen became ill while the family was in Naples and suffered for three months before she died. In his 9 August 1858 letter Bryan wrote: "Some of the pleasantest as well as some of the saddest recollections of my present visits to Europe, relate to this charming young person and her premature death. I must say a word of her, and the dangers which, in some cases at least, attend a residence in Naples."

*Bryant posing in a Turkish costume that he bought in Damascus during
the 1852 trip on which he based* Letters from the East *(1869)*

Bryant's memorial to Helen Waterston served as the last entry in *Letters of a Traveller. Second Series.* Published in 1859 by D. Appleton Publishers, the volume contains a total of twenty-five letters dated from 11 June 1857 to 9 August 1858. Again, Bryant chose not to revise, as he notes in the preface:

> These letters, sent home to the United States during recent journeys in several countries of the European continent, are laid before the public just as they were written on the spot, without additions, and with no material corrections. Of their imperfections none can be more sensible than the author; their merit, if they have any, consists in their being a record of observations committed to paper while the impression they made was yet clear and distinct.

After returning to the United States from his European travels, Bryant plunged into American politics. In 1860 he editorially endorsed the nomination of Abraham Lincoln for the presidency but two years later denounced him for timidity in prosecuting the war. Although Bryant did not label himself an abolitionist at the time, he criticized the president for a lack of zeal for the cause of abolition. In 1864

he published *Thirty Poems* and celebrated his seventieth birthday with a dinner at the New York Century Club. The next year brought the assassination of President Lincoln, whom Bryant honored with a memorial tribute.

In 1866 Bryant returned to Cummington, the home of his youth, in an effort to restore the health of his gravely ill wife. On 27 July 1866 she died from what the physician described as "an obstruction of the bile . . . with water on the heart." Bryant finished the summer at Cummington but went back to Roslyn, Long Island, in the fall and wrote the poem "October 1866" as he prepared to travel to Europe again. His goal for the journey was twofold: to relieve some of his own grief and to aid Julia in her recovery from the death of her mother. They left for Europe in October and stayed until the fall of 1867. During the uneventful trip Bryant and Julia visited Paris, Florence, Rome, and parts of Germany, England, and Wales.

At the urging of his publisher Bryant collected letters from his earlier travels for *Letters from the East* while working on other projects, including metrical translations of Homer's *Iliad* (1870) and *Odyssey*

(1871–1872). At this time he was also writing poetry, including "A Brighter Day," "Among the Trees," and "May Evening." Until his death on 12 June 1878, Bryant was regarded as one of the nation's wise men. As a poet, politician, journalist, and grand old man of letters he strove to create an original identity for his maturing nation. His visits to other countries and studies of other cultures only reinforced his desire for an America with its own distinct culture and literature.

Letters:

The Letters of William Cullen Bryant, edited by William Cullen Bryant II and Thomas G. Voss, 6 volumes (New York: Fordham University Press, 1975–1984).

Bibliographies:

Henry C. Sturges, *Chronologies of the Life and Writings of William Cullen Bryant* (New York: Appleton, 1903);

Judith Turner Phair, *A Bibliography of William Cullen Bryant and His Critics, 1808–1972* (Troy, N.Y.: Whitson, 1975).

Biographies:

George W. Curtis, *The Life, Character, and Writings of William Cullen Bryant* (New York: Scribners, 1879);

Parke Godwin, *A Biography of William Cullen Bryant,* 2 volumes (New York: Appleton, 1883);

James Grant Wilson, *Bryant and His Friends: Some Reminiscences of Knickerbocker Writers* (New York: Fords, Howard & Halbert, 1886);

John Bigelow, *William Cullen Bryant* (Boston & New York: Houghton, Mifflin, 1890);

William A. Bradley, *William Cullen Bryant* (New York: Macmillan, 1905);

Allan Nevins, *The Evening Post: A Century of Journalism* (New York: Boni & Liveright, 1922);

Henry Houston Peckham, *Gotham Yankee* (New York: Vantage, 1950);

Curtiss S. Johnson, *Politics and a Belly-Full: The Journalistic Career of William Cullen Bryant* (New York: Vantage, 1962);

Charles H. Brown, *William Cullen Bryant* (New York: Scribners, 1971).

References:

Joan D. Berbich, *Three Voices from Paumanok* (Port Washington, N.Y.: Ira J. Friedman, 1969);

Stanley Brodwin and Michael D'Innocenzo, eds., *William Cullen Bryant and His America: Centennial Conference Proceedings 1878–1978* (New York: AMS Press, 1983);

William Charvat, *The Origins of American Critical Thought, 1810–1835* (Philadelphia: University of Pennsylvania Press, 1936; London: Oxford University Press, 1936);

Bernard Duffey, "Romantic Coherence and Romantic Incoherence in American Poetry," *Centennial Review,* 7 (Spring 1963): 219–236;

William J. Free, "William Cullen Bryant on Nationalism, Imitation, and Originality in Poetry," *Studies in Philology,* 66 (July 1969): 672–687;

Tremain McDowell, Introduction, *William Cullen Bryant: Representative Selections* (New York: American Book, 1935);

Albert F. McLean Jr., *William Cullen Bryant* (New York: Twayne, 1964);

John Paul Pritchard, *Literary Wise Men of Gotham: Criticism in New York, 1815–1860* (Baton Rouge: Louisiana State University Press, 1963);

Floyd Stovall, ed., *The Development of American Literary Criticism,* by Harry H. Clark and others (Chapel Hill: University of North Carolina Press, 1955).

Papers:

The major collections of William Cullen Bryant's papers are the Henry W. and Albert A. Berg Collection, New York Public Library; the Bryant Family Papers, Manuscript Division, New York Public Library; the Bryant Family Association Papers, Bureau County Historical Society, Princeton, Illinois; the Bryant-Godwin Collection, Manuscript Division, New York Public Library; the Bryant Miscellaneous Papers, Manuscript Division, New York Public Library; the Flagg Collection, Manuscript Division, New York Public Library; and the Goddard-Roslyn Collection, including financial records of the *Evening Post,* Manuscript Division, New York Public Library.

George Catlin

(26 July 1796 – 22 December 1872)

Eric Sterling
Auburn University at Montgomery

See also the Catlin entry in *DLB 186: Nineteenth-Century American Western Writers.*

BOOKS: *Catalogue of Catlin's Indian Gallery of Portraits, Landscapes, Manners, Customs, Costumes, &c.* (New York: Piercy & Reed, 1837);

A Descriptive Catalogue of Catlin's Indian Collection, Containing Portraits, Landscapes, Costumes, and Representations of the Manners and Customs of the North American Indians (London: C. Adlard, 1840);

Letters and Notes on the Manners, Customs, and Conditions of the North American Indians, 2 volumes (New York: Wiley & Putnam, 1841; London: Printed for the author by Tosswill & Myers, 1841); republished as *The Manners, Customs and Condition of the North American Indians* (London: Published by the author, 1841); republished as *Illustrations of the Manners, Customs, and Condition of the North American Indians,* 2 volumes (London: H. G. Bohn, 1845); republished as *North American Indians* (London: Chatto & Windus, 187?; Philadelphia: Leary, Stuart, 1913); republished as *Catlin's Indians* (Philadelphia: Hubbard Brothers, 1891);

Catlin's North American Indian Portfolio of Hunting Scenes and Amusements (London: Published by the author, 1844; New York: J. Ackerman, 1845);

Catlin's Notes of Eight Years' Travel and Residence in Europe, with his North American Indian Collection. With Anecdotes and Incidents of the Travels and Adventures of Three Different Parties of American Indians whom he Introduced to the Courts of England, France, and Belgium, 2 volumes (London: Published by the author, 1848; New York: Published by the author, 1848); republished as *Adventures of the Ojibbeway and Ioway Indians in England, France, and Belgium: Being Notes of Eight Years' Travels and Residence in Europe with his North American Indian Collection* (London: Published by the author, 1852);

Souvenir of the North American Indians as They Were in the Middle of the Nineteenth Century, 3 volumes

George Catlin, self-portrait at age twenty-four (Thomas Gilcrease Institute)

(London: Published by the author, 1850; Chicago: C. W. Farrington, 1870);

Life Among the Indians: A Book For Youth (New York: Appleton, 1857; London: Sampson Low, Son, 1861);

Prairie Scenes (New York: Currier & Ives, 1857);

The Breath of Life, or Mal-Respiration. And its Effects upon the Enjoyment & Life of Man (London: Trübner, 1861; New York: J. Wiley, 1861); republished as *Shut Your Mouth* (New York, 1864; London: Trübner, 1869);

An Account of an Annual Religious Ceremony Practised by the Mandan Tribe of North American Indians (London: Printed by Whittingham & Wilkins, 1863–1864);

Last Rambles Among the Indians of the Rocky Mountains and the Andes (New York: Appleton, 1867; London: Gall & Inglis, 1867); republished as *Rambles Among the Indians of the Rocky Mountains and the Andes* (London: Gall & Inglis, 1877);

O-Kee-Pa: A Religious Ceremony (London: Trübner, 1867; Philadelphia: Lippincott, 1967);

The Lifted and Subsided Rocks of America with their Influences on the Oceanic, Atmospheric, and Land Currents and the Distribution of Races (London: Trübner, 1870);

North and South American Indians. Catalogue Descriptive and Instructive of Catlin's Indian Cartoons (New York: Baker & Godwin, 1871).

Collection: *Episodes from* Life Among the Indians *and* Last Rambles, *With 152 Scenes and Portraits by the Artist,* edited by Marvin C. Ross (Norman: University of Oklahoma Press, 1959).

George Catlin, painter and author of books on his travels to Indian tribes throughout North and South America, is an important figure in American history, literature, and art because of the role he played in preserving Native American culture. It was Catlin who first put forward (circa 1832) and promoted the idea of a national park to protect bison, suggesting a location in the northern plains at the confluence of the Yellowstone River with the upper Missouri. He hoped that such a park, which he referred to as the Nation's Park, would sustain the endangered culture of the Plains Indians.

Catlin distinguished himself from contemporaries who wrote journals about their experiences with Indians in that he described the natives as individuals and human beings, refusing to stereotype them. He celebrated and studied sympathetically a culture that most others of his era considered barbaric and worthless. Catlin's admiration for Indian culture caused him to travel to places where few white men had ventured before, a point Peter Matthiessen makes well in his introduction to *North American Indians* (1989):

> If Meriwether Lewis and William Clark were the first white Americans to explore the west half of the continent, from the Mississippi at St. Louis to the northwest Pacific coast, George Catlin traveled at least as many miles on his journeys by canoe and horse from Minnesota and the Montana border south to eastern Texas, as well as forays to the Gulf states and South Carolina, seeking to record the Indians in paintings and journals. Taken together, Catlin's works constitute the first, last, and only "complete" record of the Plains Indians ever made at the height of their splendid culture, so soon destroyed by traders' liquor and disease, rapine and bayonets.

Through Catlin's books and paintings the modern reader or viewer can learn a great deal about the Indian way of life that was overrun by the white man.

George Catlin, the fifth of Putnam and Polly Catlin's fourteen children, was born in Wilkes-Barre, Pennsylvania, on 26 July 1796. When he was an infant, his family built a farm forty miles north of Wilkes-Barre in southern New York. His childhood interest in Indian life may have been sparked by an incident that happened eighteen years before his birth but that bore directly on his life: his mother and grandmother were captured by Indians during the Wyoming Massacre of 4 July 1778, in which British Loyalists and their Indian allies attacked settlers in Wyoming Valley, Pennsylvania. He grew up hearing of the legends and traditions of the Indians from his family as well as others in the community who had tales to tell.

Catlin's choice of avocation may also have been influenced by an incident that occurred when he was nine. While he was hunting in a forest he was startled at the sight of a large buck nearby. An Oneida Indian suddenly appeared, scaring the boy even more, and shot the buck. Fearing for his life, young Catlin was about to fire upon the Indian, but before he could act the Indian departed, carrying the carcass across his back. Shortly thereafter the Oneida, named On-o-gong-way, returned to split the venison with the Catlins and praised the boy for being a good hunter. Catlin was especially glad at this turn of events because no one but his mother had believed him when he claimed to have seen an Indian. As On-o-gong-way explained, white settlers years before had driven his tribe from the area, up the Susquehanna River, to the Oneida and Cayuga Lakes. The story doubtless helped Catlin to understand the precariousness of Indian culture and later fed his desire to paint the portraits of the Plains Indians.

Catlin attended Wilkes-Barre Academy and then attended the Litchfield Law School in Connecticut from 1819 to 1823. Upon passing the bar exam, he practiced in Lucerne County, Pennsylvania, but his father's profession bored him. He carved and drew sketches of criminals and judges on the lawyer's table and the judge's bench. When Catlin abandoned his law practice, he had already established a solid reputation in the area as a portrait painter despite his lack of formal training. In 1823 Catlin ventured to Philadelphia to pursue his new career, relying solely on his natural talent as a portrait specialist and his ability to make friends quickly. His interest in Indians was again engaged in 1824 when he saw an exhibition of live Indians in Philadelphia. Catlin admired the pride and dignity

Plate Nº 3.

A view of the "Red Pipe Stone" Quarry. Côteau des prairies, Source of St. Peters River.

In nearly every part of North Amª the Indians have been found using pipe bowls made of the "Red Pipe Stone" & learning from the various tribes that such pipes all came from the same source, and learning many traditions of that noted place, I made a visit to it in 1837. The Sioux Indians, in whose country it exists, told me I was the first white man who ever visited it, and certainly I was the first to give any account of it. The Indians have many curious traditions relative to this place, amongst which, one of the most important is as follows —— "At an ancient time the Great Spirit, in the form of a large bird, stood upon the wall of rock and called all the tribes around him, and breaking out a piece of the red stone formed it into a pipe and smoked it, the smoke rolling over the whole multitude — he then told his red children that this red stone was their flesh, that they were made from it — that they must all smoke to him through it — that they must use it for nothing but pipes: and as it belonged alike to all the tribes, the ground was sacred, and no weapons must be used or brought upon it. And there is no doubt, as they say, that the various tribes have been in the habit of meeting there as friends, under this injunction, renewing their pipes. The Red Pipe Stone has but one known origin — has been found on analysis to be a new mineral compound, and has been christened "Catlinite". (for a fuller account see Catlin's Notes on the Amⁿ Indians.)

Catlin's handwritten description of how he found and painted the sacred quarry where many North American Indian tribes got the clay for their ceremonial pipes (British Library)

of these people while empathizing with them for the poor treatment they received from white Americans. He sent some of his miniatures to the Philadelphia Academy of Art and was elected to the academy on 18 February 1824. From 1824 to 1829 he lived mainly in Washington, D.C., where his skill was much in demand. His first portrait of an Indian, the Seneca orator Red Jacket, was painted in the capital in 1826.

Catlin would have been quite successful financially had he remained as a portrait painter in the East, yet he enjoyed traveling and wanted to capture Indian culture in his paintings. In 1828 Catlin visited Albany, New York, where he painted portraits of Gov. DeWitt Clinton and many legislators. At one of the governor's parties he met wealthy Clara Bartlett Gregory, whom he married on 10 May 1828. The artist's new wife supported her husband's dream of painting portraits of Indians in the West, as did Catlin's younger brother Julius. The two brothers agreed that they would travel to the West together to paint portraits of Indians. Julius, however, drowned in 1828 in Rochester, New York, while performing an errand for George.

Catlin began painting Indians such as the Senecas, Oneidas, Tuscaroras, Ottawas, and Mohegans

in regional reservations. In 1830 he went to Saint Louis to meet with Gen. William Clark, the famous explorer whose goodwill was important not only because of his knowledge of the West but also because of his political power as superintendent of Indian affairs. The success of travelers and explorers often depended on Clark's willingness to help. Catlin impressed General Clark profoundly and immediately, and the two became friends. Clark especially admired Catlin's artistic talent and his desire to travel to undeveloped areas to paint Indians who had yet to be tainted by white culture. As far as Catlin was concerned, the more primitive the Indian, the more intriguing the subject. Catlin painted Indians who visited Clark to file complaints concerning treaty violations. He was able to sketch rapidly and to picture the subject in his mind so he could finish the portrait accurately at a later time. The Indians usually took a liking to the portrait specialist, which also impressed Clark, for they often did not like the white strangers they encountered.

In 1831 Catlin began visiting tribes, chiefly in the plains. In the fall he took two journeys west of Missouri, painting Indians in Leavenworth (present-day northeast Kansas) and Kansa (on the Kansas River). Catlin claims that during this year he traveled to what is now Wyoming and past the Rocky Mountains to the Great Salt Lake. His account is possible, although some scholars doubt Catlin's story, especially since no documentation or paintings substantiate his claims.

Five years before they were wiped out by a smallpox epidemic, Catlin visited the Mandan Sioux in 1832, becoming the first white man to paint the tribe. The Mandans were unusually friendly and hospitable. (He would later claim in *O-Kee-Pa: A Religious Ceremony* that "no Mandan ever killed a white man.") When Catlin began painting the Mandans they were pleased and considered him a white medicine man because he created human beings in his paintings and could make them laugh and speak. The native women, however, deemed him dangerous because they believed that if he could bring people to life he could also kill them. Catlin consequently was denied the opportunity to complete his paintings until he convinced the men that he was not a medicine man but simply a human being who possessed the ability to paint—a talent they could learn with practice (the Mandans could only draw stick figures). Catlin also played upon the Mandan males' pride, telling them that courageous men never allowed women to dominate them; consequently, the male Mandans overruled the women.

During his three-week stay with the Mandans, Catlin made at least twenty paintings. He was invited by the tribe to watch the O-kee-pa, a four-day religious festival in which tribesmen inflicted cruel punishments upon themselves. At the climax of the ceremony young men were skewered through the pectoral muscles and suspended from lodge poles until they fainted. The ritual that Catlin depicted in four paintings was also witnessed by three other white men, retired fur trader James Kipp, the clerk L. Crawford, and Abraham Bogard. Anticipating the skepticism of others because of the unusual nature of the festival, Catlin convinced the three to write a letter corroborating what they saw, which they immediately did.

In 1835 George and Clara Catlin sailed up the Mississippi River to Fort Snelling, near the Falls of Saint Anthony. There they encountered a significant camp of Ojibways, whom they visited frequently. The Ojibway women greatly admired Clara and the Catlin children and gave the young Catlins maple sugar to eat. Catlin painted the Ojibway babies in their cradles, which were decorated with the umbilicus hanging in front of the babies' faces. Catlin also attended Ojibway dances, such as the Snow-Shoe Dance, in which the dancers thank the Great Spirit for the first snow of the year. The snow allowed the hunters to wear snowshoes, making it easier for them to kill game. These dances fascinated Catlin, and he captured several of them in his paintings.

While Catlin was drawn to the Ojibway, he was disappointed that the Indian tribes he had encountered were not as primitive as the ones he had hoped to see. When an eastern Sioux tribe visited Fort Snelling, Catlin saw firsthand the effects close contact with white men could have on a tribe. The visitors lived far from the beavers and buffalo that other Sioux tribes killed for food and clothing, and they became contaminated by whiskey and smallpox.

From 6 July till the beginning of August 1836 in Buffalo, New York, Catlin held his first important public exhibition. During the following year Catlin sent an extensive collection of paintings and artifacts to Albany, New York, in preparation for Catlin's Indian Gallery, which consisted of 310 portraits of Indians and 200 other paintings of the West as well as items relating to Indian culture, such as ornamental shirts, robes, drums, and headdresses. Although Catlin's gallery received great critical acclaim in the United States and was a financial success for Catlin in New York and Washington, people quickly lost interest. When the gallery proved a financial disappointment in Baltimore and Philadelphia, the U.S. government refused to purchase it and decided against a National Museum of the American Indian that Catlin requested. Facing financial woes, Catlin took his gallery to England in 1839. Harold McCracken notes that Catlin's European patrons included Queen Victoria, the king and queen of Belgium, and the czar of Russia. Catlin also presented many lectures regarding his painting and Indian culture.

Catlin's most famous book, *Letters and Notes on the Manners, Customs, and Conditions of the North American Indians* (1841), contains some of his finest colored plates and engravings as well as many insights regarding the tribes that he visited from 1832 to 1839. Catlin's awareness of the decline of the North American Indian is often manifest. For example, he refers to the Iroquois as "One of the most numerous and powerful tribes that ever existed in the Northern regions of our country, and now one of the most completely annihilated." He attributes their demise to wars with the French, British, and rival Indian tribes as well as to bad living (such as drinking whiskey) and disease.

One of his most affecting descriptions and paintings is of Not-o-way, The Thinker, the chief of the remaining Iroquois. One feels Catlin's respect and admiration for Not-o-way as the painting manifests the chief's feelings of shame for the decline in

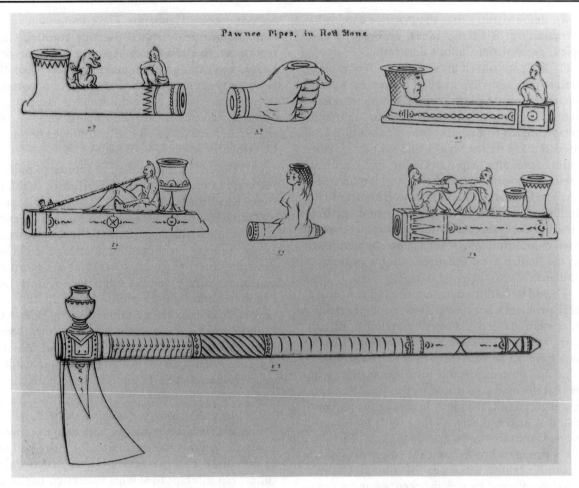

Catlin's pen-and-ink drawings of Indian pipes (The New-York Historical Society)

the fortunes of his tribe. Not-o-way informed Catlin that he was proud to be an Iroquois but that he told others he was a Chippewa because he believed that the Great Spirit sought revenge on the Iroquois for being so bloodthirsty in battle against other Indian tribes. Catlin's matter-of-fact tone deepens the pathos of the story. In the portrait Catlin shows Not-o-way as a somber man. He is dressed in trappings customary for chiefs and holds a tomahawk in his right hand. The many white and dark feathers in his hair indicate both his bravery and his importance in his tribe.

Among the many fascinating and unusual cultures Catlin depicts is the Chinooks, from the lower section of the Columbia River. They were also known as the Flat Heads because of their practice of squeezing and flattening the heads of their infants. A Chinook mother would place her baby on a thick plank, tying the child tightly to the board with thongs and placing moss or rabbit skins behind the head for a supportive pillow. The mother then would

tie another board at an angle on the infant's forehead. This board would be tightened daily with the aid of a cord until it touched the child's nose, thus creating a straight line from the forehead to the tip of the nose. Catlin labeled this procedure cruel yet asserted that its occurrence during infancy rendered it less painful; he also claimed that the procedure changed the shape of the brain while not harming the child's intelligence. As in other cases involving practices of which he disapproved, Catlin respected the custom and did not castigate the Indians for what he could not understand.

Catlin's illustration of a Chinook woman flattening her baby's head shows his tolerance. By illustrating the woman as she holds and supports her child, he demonstrates her love for her baby. Her looking away indicates that she follows the practice whether or not she approves. Catlin's emphasis upon the mother's own flattened head indicates that the procedure continues from generation to generation. The fact that she survived and reared a child of her own demonstrates that the practice cannot be life-threatening. All these ideas, ambiguous and complex, derive from Catlin's illustration.

Catlin jeopardized his reputation for respecting native peoples when in 1843 he became a business partner with Arthur Rankin, a man who mistreated and exploited Indians. Rankin brought nine Ojibway Indians to England for an exhibition and enlisted the aid of the writer and painter. Catlin doubtless agreed to help Rankin for both altruistic and selfish reasons. While he must have believed that he could protect the Ojibways from Rankin's exploitation, he also needed money and realized that the Indians' presence would enhance interest in his own exhibition. Whatever Catlin's motivations were, the British press censured him for exploiting the Indians.

To add to Catlin's dilemma, the Indians caused several problems because of lack of supervision. One, a man named Cadotte, married a British woman, which resulted in a most unhappy union. Rankin gave his permission for the marriage, knowing that his blessing would infuriate Catlin, who knew that the marriage would be doomed. Rankin's plan was to goad Catlin into breaking the partnership so that he could keep all the profits for himself. Marjorie Catlin Roehm, a granddaughter of George Catlin's youngest brother and the editor of Catlin's letters to his family, contends that though Catlin's reputation suffered he was innocent of any wrongdoing. He "was a showman, to be sure, but not a mountebank or huckster!"

In 1845 Catlin moved to Paris to "show" some Iowas, but this venture proved financially unsuccessful. Having lost trust in Catlin because of his relationship with Rankin and the accusations that he had exploited the Ojibways in England, the Indians soon wanted to return to America. As a means of acquiring money to support his children, Catlin subsequently brought some Ojibways to Belgium; the exhibition began in a promising manner, but several of the Indians contracted smallpox and died. Catlin used his profits to pay for their medical expenses and ship them back to America, thus depleting his already meager supply of money.

Catlin's sojourn on the Continent was prolonged by the friendship of important backers. While in Paris he met the renowned scientist Baron Alexander von Humboldt, who proved an ally in the future. Also, King Louis Philippe of France agreed to pay Catlin to create copies of fifteen of his paintings and commissioned twenty-seven more paintings of America and its Indians from the Great Lakes to the Mississippi. The paintings cover the travels of the explorers René-Robert Cavelier La Salle and Louis Hennepin. The commission and the concomitant professional prestige stopped Catlin from leaving Paris for America, a move his wife, Clara, was urging him to make. In December 1845 Catlin was shocked when Clara died of pneumonia, leaving him with four children to support. He blamed himself for his wife's death, thinking that she might have survived had he followed her desires by returning to the United States.

While Catlin remained in France to paint for the king, Louis Philippe was overthrown in the February Revolution of 1848 and the Second Republic was established. Soldiers loyal to the new Republic, recognizing Catlin as a friend of the now powerless Louis Philippe, ransacked his apartment and thrust their bayonets through several of his paintings. Catlin never received the full payment from Louis Philippe, although the paintings he made for the king were later exhibited at the Louvre. Before Catlin was able to leave Paris, his only son, George, died, probably of typhoid. Catlin and his three daughters managed to survive the typhoid epidemic and arrived safely in London with his collection intact.

The publication of *Catlin's Notes of Eight Years' Travel and Residence in Europe, with his North American Indian Collection* (1848), a mixture of satire and biography, did nothing to revive Catlin's financial fortunes. His attempt to sell his collection to the U.S. Congress was rebuffed, thanks in part to the opposition of the ethnologist Henry Rowe Schoolcraft, the "Indian Historiographer to the Congress of the United States." Schoolcraft, who was required to acquire data on all the American Indian tribes and eager to create an extensive encyclopedia financed by the government, had in 1846 approached Catlin, realizing that the inclusion of his paintings would greatly enhance his work. Catlin had refused to allow Schoolcraft to include Catlin's paintings because he wished to reserve his artwork for his own books.

In 1852 Catlin went bankrupt while living in London and was forced by his creditors to sell items from his collection. To the disappointment of Catlin and the chagrin of his creditors, some paintings were sold at an auction for low prices. Catlin then reluctantly mortgaged his paintings to Joseph Harrison Jr. of Philadelphia, one of his creditors. (He was never able to redeem them.) Catlin's in-laws took his three daughters away from him and brought them to the United States. Their uncle, Dudley Gregory, was a multimillionaire and thus could take better care of them than could the painter. Catlin subsequently escaped his creditors by shipping to

Catlin's drawing of torture rites in the Mandan religious ceremony O-kee-pa (New York Public Library)

France a few remaining Indian Gallery paintings he had been copying.

Enticed by legends of lost gold mines in the Crystal Mountains (also called the Tumucamache Mountains) in northern Brazil, Catlin ventured there in search of wealth. He had learned from a friend that Spanish miners in the sixteenth century, after digging out a fortune in gold, perished in an Indian attack. In his search for gold Catlin explored much uncharted territory, traveling to more undeveloped and unknown areas in South America than any white man before him. His account of this journey would appear in the second chapter of *Last Rambles Among the Indians of the Rocky Mountains and the Andes* (1867).

Catlin reports that he traveled from Havana to Caracas, from Venezuela to the Orinoko and Demerara, and finally to the Crystal Mountains in Brazil. Catlin found that these mountains, formed from strata laid down in the paleozoic era, were a formidable barrier. After his mule could venture no farther, Catlin was forced to search for food and shelter, not gold. He received a second chance when he encountered a man, called Senor L in the account, who resided on an island in the Amazon.

Having heard the same legend regarding the gold miners, Senor L agreed to accompany Catlin and pay for the expedition. The party of five—Catlin and his employee, Caesar; Senor L; and two Indian guides—descended the Amazon in a pirogue, a canoe hewn from a tree trunk, along a route that Catlin believed no white man had traversed before. The men followed the Amazon for almost twenty miles, barely able to see the shore because of the massive foliage that extended into the river. The guides led the party to a stream and then on a long, arduous walk in the Amazon forest.

The "road," as the Indian guides called it, was merely a path hacked through the jungle of vines that a man could pass through if he stooped. Catlin could travel no more than twelve miles a day under the difficult conditions, which included an attack by ariguatoes, or howling monkeys. At one point the men encountered an Indian tribe that wanted to view Catlin's portfolio, which Caesar had brought with him on the journey. The Indians were impressed but were afraid to have their portraits painted. For his part Catlin was fascinated by the elaborate dress and appearance of the young Indian girls.

When Catlin finally arrived at the Crystal Mountains, he found them desolate yet beautiful. Having lost their gold washer when a mule stepped on it, they could not pan for gold, so they hoped to dig out gold nuggets. Most of the rocks contained only granite and gneiss, though the prospectors did discover a few nuggets. Informative and compelling, Catlin's riveting account contains minute detail and is both heartbreaking and comical. Catlin blamed himself for his cupidity and seems amused to confess that the entire arduous and life-threatening ordeal allowed him to acquire but two ounces of gold. Catlin concluded, however, that he considered himself a wealthy man because he still had his life, health, intelligence, and his portfolios.

From 1852 to 1855 Catlin spent time exploring Indian villages in South America and painting them. He found the Indians in South America more primitive than those in the United States because they had not been corrupted by white men. While working in the plains in the Midwest, Catlin had used canvas, which he rolled up when he needed to pack for travel, but this technique proved unsuccessful in South America because the canvas dried slowly in the humid climate of the jungles. Catlin began using Bristol board, which proved easier for him to pack and carry and which dried more quickly. This switch permitted Catlin to carry fewer painting materials, and the pictures survived better than they would have had he used canvas. Catlin created his cartoons by delineating the figures on thick cardboard and then painting with oil color.

During these years he produced another collection of works that became known as his Cartoon Collection. He painted most of the works in this collection while living in Brussels, but these were copies of works he originally sketched in South America. Having lost control of his prized collection, he created duplicates by drawing on studies from his notebooks, his sketches, and his excellent memory. He also painted new works of what he witnessed on his trips to South America and the West Coast of North America north of the Rocky Mountains.

In 1861 Catlin published *The Breath of Life, or Mal-Respiration. And its Effects upon the Enjoyment & Life of Man,* which he based on his observations of the sleep of native peoples during his extensive travels throughout North and South America. He described in detail the healthy condition of American Indians, contrasting their excellent physical health with whites who, he claimed, suffered from significantly higher rates of diseases and deformities. Finding it ironic that Indians lived longer than whites when the latter possessed a superior sanitary system, Catlin asserted that the key was the natives' primitive

conditions, which permitted their beauty and teeth to last. He disputed the notions of previous writers who claimed that American Indians had higher rates of early fatalities than civilized nations; he believed that such cases only occurred when Indians were corrupted by members of civilized cultures.

Catlin invited his readers to travel, to visit American Indian tribes throughout the United States and judge for themselves rather than relying upon the prejudiced accounts of other writers who simply copied what they themselves had read. Catlin asserted that the most significant errors that historians and other writers had made regarding American Indian customs were caused by their refusal to investigate native cultures firsthand. Catlin interviewed the Sioux chief Sleepy Eyes, whose tribe resided between the headwaters of the Mississippi and Missouri Rivers; the Mandans in the upper Missouri; Shar-re-tar-rushe, chief of the Pawnee-Picts, at the headwaters of the Arkansas River at the base of the Rocky Mountains; and Ski-se-ro-ka, chief of the Kiowas, who lived by the headwaters of Red River in western Texas. Catlin met with Clermont, chief of the Osages, who asserted that women in his tribe lost children due to firewater brought by white men; Naw-kaw, chief of Winnebagoes in Wisconsin, who said that whiskey had caused early mortality; and Kee-mon-saw, chief of the Kaskaskias, located on the Missouri River, who claimed that whiskey and smallpox were killing off his people. These chiefs and medicine men stated that their people were always healthy until white men brought liquor and disease.

But Catlin did not blame alcohol for premature fatalities. Instead, he believed that the secret to a long, healthy life was quiet, natural sleep. He argued that people in white cultures slept with their mouths open because they were reared and cared for in debilitating extravagance and contrived warmth, which endangered their lives. Whereas infants in civilized nations slept with their mouths open, Catlin noted that Indian babies in primitive societies pressed their lips together when they slept. He cited a North American Indian maxim, "It is sagacious to open one's eyes first, then one's ears, and finally, one's mouth." Catlin remarked, "If I were to endeavor to bequeath to posterity the most important Motto which human language can convey, it should be in *three words—Shut—your—mouth.*"

Catlin's *O-Kee-Pa: A Religious Ceremony* (1867) was written to refute charges made by Schoolcraft in his multivolume encyclopedia, *Historical and Statistical Information Respecting the History, Condition, and Prospects of the Indian Tribes of the United States* (1851–1857). In the third volume of that work, David D. Mitchell, superintendent of Indian Affairs in Saint Louis, refers to Catlin's descriptions of the O-kee-pa ceremony as "almost entirely in the fertile imagination of that gentleman." Schoolcraft, whom Catlin claimed never was within one thousand miles of the Mandans and who indeed never visited them, attacked Catlin for supporting the Madoc theory regarding the Mandans' origin (in *Letters and Notes* Catlin had supported the romantic notion that the tribe was the remnant of the Welsh prince Madoc's legendary medieval colonists) and for claiming that the Mandans were extinct. Because of Schoolcraft's excellent reputation as an ethnologist and because the books were published by the United States government and distributed in important scientific libraries throughout the world, Schoolcraft's accusations had the force of authority. When world traveler Baron Alexander Humboldt received a copy of Schoolcraft's book he suggested that Catlin ask Prince Maximilian of Neuwied, who had also visited the Mandans and witnessed the O-kee-pa ritual, to write a letter supporting his observations. Catlin published the prince's letter opposite his own preface.

In *O-Kee-Pa* Catlin describes in detail the Mandan religious ceremony that he only alluded to in his earlier works. Catlin asserts that the Mandans believed the ceremony brought them buffalo to eat, maintained their very existence, and prevented tragedies from occurring to them. The Mandan ritual was not uncommon in its purpose, for Catlin relates that all of the 120 tribes of North, South, and Central America that he visited had legends of serious tragedies that had befallen them. In such stories only a few survive to rebuild the tribe. Catlin provides several examples, such as the Choctaws, who believed that they were initially crawfish that had lost their ability to live underground.

The Mandan religious ceremony celebrated Mee-ne-ro-ka-ha-sha—the receding of the water after the great water deluge. The ceremony included a "bull dance," which tribesmen believed caused the buffalo to provide them with sustenance, as well as rites of passage for males that involved self-torture. Catlin describes the ceremony vividly, telling about the survivor of the great deluge who returned for the festival and requested a tool at every wigwam to open the Medicine Lodge so the Mandans could perform the required sacrifices to the water, thanking it for receding. Catlin did more than merely recite verbatim what he witnessed: he also questioned and analyzed what he saw. He pondered why the Mandan survivor was represented as white rather than as an Indian. He realized that the Mandans, unlike all other Indian tribes, believed that the first man

Catlin at age seventy-two

was white, partly because Mosaic law had infiltrated the tribe.

O-Kee-Pa sold few copies and proved a financial disappointment; libraries did not wish to purchase a book that contained historical and cultural accounts that a United States government publication deemed fallacious. Catlin tried in vain to recover his reputation by demanding that the United States government purchase copies of his book to send along with Schoolcraft's six-volume set so that readers could decide for themselves. But in a 7 June 1868 letter to his brother Francis, Catlin states that he has given up on his appeal to Congress: "I intended to have been in Washington during this Session, but Mr. Sanford, our Minister here, has constantly told me it would be time & money lost to try anything there during this Session."

In 1871 Catlin exhibited his cartoon collection in New York, but few people expressed interest.

The painter, nonetheless, received permission to exhibit the collection temporarily in Washington, D.C., at the Smithsonian Institution. In later years Catlin's artistic skills suffered, and he also lost his hearing. His large circle of friends gradually declined, and during his last years he became embittered. He died in Jersey City, New Jersey, on 22 December 1872 at the age of seventy-six. In 1879 Harrison's widow sent Catlin's collection to the Smithsonian Institution, where it remains.

Letters:

Marjorie Catlin Roehm, *The Letters of George Catlin and His Family: A Chronicle of the American West* (Berkeley: University of California Press, 1966).

Biographies:

Loyd Haberly, *Pursuit of the Horizon: A Life of George Catlin, Painter & Recorder of the American Indian* (New York: Macmillan, 1948);

Harold McCracken, *George Catlin and the Old Frontier* (New York: Dial, 1959);

Marvin C. Ross, *George Catlin* (Norman: University of Oklahoma Press, 1959);

Robert Plate, *Palette and Tomahawk: The Story of George Catlin, July 27, 1796–December 23, 1872* (New York: McKay, 1962);

Brian W. Dippie, *Catlin and His Contemporaries: The Politics of Patronage* (Lincoln: University of Nebraska Press, 1990).

References:

John C. Ewers, "George Catlin, Painter of Indians and the West," in *Annual Report of the Smithsonian Institution* (Washington, D.C.: Smithsonian Institution Report, 1956), pp. 483–528;

Ewers, *Indian Art in Pipestone: George Catlin's Portfolio in the British Museum* (Washington, D.C.: Smithsonian Institution Report, 1979);

James Gilreath, "George Catlin and Karl Bodmer: Artists Among the American Indians," in *Folklife Annual 1987,* edited by Alan Jabbour and James Hardin (Washington, D.C.: American Folklife Center at the Library of Congress, 1988), pp. 34–45;

Marjorie Halpin, *Catlin's Indian Gallery: The George Catlin Paintings in the United States National Museum* (Washington, D.C.: Smithsonian Institution Press, 1965);

Royal B. Hassrick, *The George Catlin Book of American Indians* (New York: Watson-Guptill Publications, 1977);

James Kipp, "On the Accuracy of Catlin's Account of the Mandan Ceremonies," in *Annual Report of the Smithsonian Institution* (Washington, D.C.: Smithsonian Institution Press, 1873), pp. 436–438;

Peter Matthiessen, Introduction, in *North American Indians* (New York: Penguin, 1989), pp. vii–xix;

George I. Quimby, *Indians of the Western Frontier: Paintings of George Catlin* (Chicago: Natural History Museum, 1954);

William H. Truettner, *The Natural Man Observed: A Study of Catlin's Indian Gallery* (Washington, D.C.: Smithsonian Institution Press, 1979).

Papers:

The major holdings of Catlin's papers include the Bancroft Library, Berkeley, California; the Newberry Library, Evanston, Illinois; the California State Library, Sacramento; the Gilcrease Institute, Tulsa, Oklahoma; and the Amon Carter Museum, Fort Worth, Texas.

Samuel Langhorne Clemens
(Mark Twain)

(30 November 1835 – 21 April 1910)

Jeffrey Alan Melton
Auburn University at Montgomery

See also the Clemens entries in *DLB 11: American Humorists, 1800–1950; DLB 12: American Realists and Naturalists; DLB 23: American Newspaper Journalists, 1873–1900; DLB 64: American Literary Critics and Scholars, 1850–1880; DLB 74: American Short-Story Writers Before 1880;* and *DLB 186: Nineteenth-Century American Western Writers.*

BOOKS: *The Celebrated Jumping Frog of Calaveras County, and Other Sketches* (New York: C. H. Webb, 1867; London: Routledge, 1867);

The Innocents Abroad, or the New Pilgrims' Progress (Hartford, Conn.: American Publishing, 1869); republished in 2 volumes as *The Innocents Abroad* and *The New Pilgrims' Progress* (London: Hotten, 1870);

Mark Twain's (Burlesque) Autobiography and First Romance (New York: Sheldon, 1871; London: Hotten, 1871);

Roughing It (London: Routledge, 1872);

The Innocents at Home (London: Routledge, 1872);

Roughing It, augmented edition (Hartford, Conn.: American Publishing, 1872)–comprises *"Roughing It"* and *The Innocents at Home*;

A Curious Dream; and Other Sketches (London: Routledge, 1872);

The Gilded Age: A Tale of Today, by Twain and Charles Dudley Warner (Hartford, Conn.: American Publishing, 1873; 3 volumes, London: Routledge, 1874);

Mark Twain's Sketches, New and Old (Hartford, Conn.: American Publishing, 1875);

Old Times on the Mississippi, pirated edition (Toronto: Belford, 1876); republished as *The Mississippi Pilot* (London: Ward, Lock & Tyler, 1877);

The Adventures of Tom Sawyer (London: Chatto & Windus, 1876; Hartford, Conn.: American Publishing, 1876);

A True Story, and The Recent Carnival of Crime (Boston: Osgood, 1877);

Samuel Langhorne Clemens

An Idle Excursion (Toronto: Rose-Belford, 1878); expanded as *Punch, Brothers Punch! And Other Sketches* (New York: Slote, Woodman, 1878);

A Tramp Abroad (London: Chatto & Windus / Hartford, Conn.: American Publishing, 1880);

"1601" Conversation, As It Was by the Social Fireside, in the Time of the Tudors (Cleveland, 1880);

The Prince and the Pauper (London: Chatto & Windus, 1881; Boston: Osgood, 1882);

The Stolen White Elephant (London: Chatto & Windus, 1882); republished as *The Stolen White Elephant, Etc.* (Boston: Osgood, 1882);

Life on the Mississippi (London: Chatto & Windus, 1883; Hartford, Conn: Osgood, 1883)—includes *Old Times on the Mississippi*;

The Adventures of Huckleberry Finn (London: Chatto & Windus, 1884); republished as *Adventures of Huckleberry Finn* (New York: Webster, 1885);

A Connecticut Yankee in King Arthur's Court (New York: Webster, 1889); republished as *A Yankee at the Court of King Arthur* (London: Chatto & Windus, 1889);

The American Claimant (New York: Webster, 1892; London: Chatto & Windus, 1892);

Merry Tales (New York: Webster, 1892);

The £1,000,000 Bank-Note and Other New Stories (New York: Webster, 1893; London: Chatto & Windus, 1893);

Tom Sawyer Abroad by Huck Finn (New York: Webster, 1894; London: Chatto & Windus, 1894);

Pudd'nhead Wilson, A Tale (London: Chatto & Windus, 1894); augmented as *The Tragedy of Pudd'nhead Wilson and the Comedy of Those Extraordinary Twins* (Hartford, Conn.: American Publishing, 1894);

Personal Recollections of Joan of Arc by the Sieur Louis de Conte (New York: Harper, 1896; London: Chatto & Windus, 1896);

Tom Sawyer Abroad, Tom Sawyer, Detective, and Other Tales (New York: Harper, 1896);

Tom Sawyer, Detective, as Told by Huck Finn, and Other Stories (London: Chatto & Windus, 1896);

How to Tell a Story and Other Essays (New York: Harper, 1897);

Following the Equator (Hartford, Conn.: American Publishing, 1897); republished as *More Tramps Abroad* (London: Chatto & Windus, 1897);

The Man That Corrupted Hadleyburg and Other Stories and Essays (New York & London: Harper, 1900); enlarged as *The Man That Corrupted Hadleyburg and Other Stories and Sketches* (London: Chatto & Windus, 1900);

A Double Barreled Detective Story (New York & London: Harper, 1902);

My Début as a Literary Person, with Other Essays and Stories, volume 23 of *The Writings of Mark Twain*, Autograph Edition (Hartford: American Publishing, 1903);

A Dog's Tale (New York & London: Harper, 1904);

Extracts from Adam's Diary Translated from the Original MS. (New York & London: Harper, 1904);

King Leopold's Soliloquy: A Defense of His Congo Rule (Boston: P. R. Warren, 1905);

Eve's Diary Translated from the Original MS. (London & New York: Harper, 1906);

What Is Man? (New York: De Vinne Press, 1906); enlarged as *What Is Man? And Other Essays* (New York & London: Harper, 1917);

The $30,000 Bequest and Other Stories (New York & London: Harper, 1906);

Christian Science with Notes Containing Corrections to Date (New York & London: Harper, 1907);

A Horse's Tale (New York & London: Harper, 1907);

Is Shakespeare Dead? (New York & London: Harper, 1909);

Extract from Captain Stormfield's Visit to Heaven (New York & London: Harper, 1909);

Mark Twain's Speeches, compiled by F. A. Nast (New York & London: Harper, 1910);

The Mysterious Stranger, a Romance, edited by Albert Bigelow Paine and Frederick A. Duneka (New York & London: Harper, 1916); enlarged as *The Mysterious Stranger and Other Stories*, edited by Paine (New York & London: Harper, 1922);

The Curious Republic of Gondour and Other Whimsical Sketches (New York: Boni & Liveright, 1919);

Mark Twain's Speeches, edited by Paine (New York & London: Harper, 1923);

Europe and Elsewhere, edited by Paine (New York & London: Harper, 1923);

Mark Twain's Autobiography, 2 volumes, edited by Paine (New York & London: Harper, 1924);

Sketches of the Sixties, by Twain and Bret Harte (San Francisco: Howell, 1926);

The Adventures of Thomas Jefferson Snodgrass, edited by Charles Honce (Chicago: Pascal Covici, 1928);

Mark Twain's Notebook, edited by Paine (New York & London: Harper, 1935);

Letters from the Sandwich Islands Written for the Sacramento Union, edited by G. Ezra Dane (San Francisco: Grabhorn Press, 1937);

The Washoe Giant in San Francisco, edited by Franklin Walker (San Francisco: Fields, 1938);

Mark Twain's Travels with Mr. Brown, edited by Walker and Dane (New York: Knopf, 1940);

Mark Twain in Eruption, edited by Bernard DeVoto (New York & London: Harper, 1940);

Mark Twain at Work, edited by DeVoto (Cambridge, Mass.: Harvard University Press, 1942);

Mark Twain, Business Man, edited by Samuel Charles Webster (Boston: Little, Brown, 1946);

Mark Twain of the ENTERPRISE, edited by Henry Nash Smith (Berkeley: University of California Press, 1957);

Traveling with the Innocents Abroad: Mark Twain's Original Reports from Europe and the Holy Land, edited by Daniel Morley McKeithan (Norman: University of Oklahoma Press, 1958);

Contributions to the Galaxy, 1868–1871, by Mark Twain, edited by Bruce R. McElderry Jr. (Gainesville, Fla.: Scholars' Facsimiles and Reprints, 1961);

Letters from the Earth, edited by DeVoto (New York: Harper & Row, 1962);

Mark Twain's "Which was the Dream" and Other Symbolic Writings of the Later Years, edited by John S. Tuckey (Berkeley: University of California Press, 1966);

Mark Twain's Satires and Burlesques, edited by Franklin R. Rogers (Berkeley: University of California Press, 1967);

Clemens of the "Call": Mark Twain in San Francisco, edited by Edgar M. Branch (Berkeley: University of California Press, 1969);

Mark Twain's "Mysterious Stranger" Manuscripts, edited by William M. Gibson (Berkeley: University of California Press, 1969);

Mark Twain's Hannibal, Huck, & Tom, edited by Walter Blair (Berkeley: University of California Press, 1972);

Mark Twain's Fables of Man, edited by Tuckey (Berkeley: University of California Press, 1972);

Mark Twain's Notebooks & Journals, volume 1, 1855–1873, edited by Frederick Anderson, Michael B. Frank, and Kenneth M. Sanderson; volume 2, 1877–1883, edited by Anderson, Lin Salamo, and Bernard L. Stein; volume 3, 1883–1891, edited by Robert Pack Browning, Frank, and Salamo (Berkeley: University of California Press, 1975, 1979);

Mark Twain Speaking, edited by Paul Fatout (Iowa City: University of Iowa Press, 1976);

Mark Twain Speaks for Himself, edited by Fatout (West Lafayette, Ind.: Purdue University Press, 1978);

The Devil's Race-Track: Mark Twain's "Great Dark" Writings, edited by Tuckey (Berkeley: University of California Press, 1980);

Wapping Alice, Printed for the First Time, edited by Hamlin Hill (Berkeley: Bancroft Library, University of California, 1981);

The Adventures of Tom Sawyer by Mark Twain: A Facsimile of the Author's Holograph Manuscript, 2 volumes (Frederick, Md.: University Publications of America / Washington, D.C.: Georgetown University Library, 1982);

Adventures of Huckleberry Finn (Tom Sawyer's Comrade) by Mark Twain: A Facsimile of the Manuscript, 2 volumes (Detroit: Gale Research, 1983).

Collections: *The Writings of Mark Twain,* Autograph Edition, 25 volumes (Hartford, Conn.: American Publishing, 1899–1907);

The Writings of Mark Twain, Author's National Edition, 25 volumes (New York & London: Harper, 1899–1917);

The Writings of Mark Twain, Definitive Edition, 37 volumes, edited by Albert Bigelow Paine (New York: Wells, 1922–1925);

The Oxford Mark Twain, 29 volumes (New York: Oxford University Press, 1996).

Editions prepared by the University of California Press for the Iowa Center for Textual Studies: *Roughing It,* edited by Franklin R. Rogers and Paul Baender (Berkeley: University of California Press, 1972);

What Is Man? And Other Philosophical Writings, edited by Baender (Berkeley: University of California Press, 1973);

A Connecticut Yankee in King Arthur's Court, edited by Bernard L. Stein (Berkeley: University of California Press, 1979);

The Prince and the Pauper, edited by Victor Fischer and Lin Salamo (Berkeley: University of California Press, 1979);

Early Tales & Sketches, volume 1 (1851–1864), volume 2 (1864–1865), edited by Edgar M. Branch and Robert H. Hirst (Berkeley: University of California Press, 1979, 1981);

The Adventures of Tom Sawyer; Tom Sawyer Abroad; Tom Sawyer, Detective, edited by John C. Gerber, Baender, and Terry Firkins (Berkeley: University of California Press, 1980);

Adventures of Huckleberry Finn, edited by Walter Blair and Victor Fischer (Berkeley: University of California Press, 1988).

For the readers of the late nineteenth century Samuel Clemens was first and foremost a travel writer, not a novelist. He earned his greatest respect and patronage from his contemporaries not for being the author of *The Adventures of Huckleberry Finn* (1884), as most modern readers assume, but for being the endearing narrator of his popular travel books. Excluding collections of short stories and sketches and a short burlesque autobiography, four of Clemens's first seven books published in the United States are travelogues: *The Innocents Abroad, or the New Pilgrims' Progress* (1869), *Roughing It* (1872), *A Tramp Abroad* (1880), and *Life on the Mississippi* (1883). He published his fifth and last travel book, *Following the Equator,* in 1897. These lengthy volumes, along with his many periodical travel pieces that were often incorporated into the books, were instrumental in forming his popular and literary identity. America's most beloved author was, first, its most effective and successful travel writer.

Frontispiece for Clemens's The Innocents Abroad *(1869), which depicts the* Quaker City *in a storm*

It was no coincidence that Clemens made such extensive use of the travel-book format or, moreover, that so many readers admired these works. Clemens recognized the lucrative sales potential of the genre and capitalized on it throughout his varied career. Consistently, his travel books proved to be his best-sellers. His sales figures previous to *The Adventures of Huckleberry Finn* are especially indicative of this success. In its first three years of publication *The Innocents Abroad* sold more than one hundred thousand copies, about seventy thousand of them in the first year. *Roughing It* sold more than seventy-six thousand copies in its first two years, ninety-six thousand by 1879. *A Tramp Abroad* sold sixty-two thousand in its first year. *Life on the Mississippi* was the only one of his early travel books to struggle, yet more than thirty-two thousand copies were sold in its first year.

None of his three fictional works of the same period matched the sales of his travel works. *The Gilded Age* (1873), cowritten with Charles Dudley Warner, took more than six years to sell fifty-six thousand copies. *The Adventures of Tom Sawyer* (1876) sold only twenty-four thousand copies in its first year. And while *The Prince and the Pauper* (1881) sold around eighteen thousand copies in its first few months, according to Clemens's estimate (often optimistic), sales soon dropped off so dramatically that

he was tempted to abandon subscription sales and dump the work on the trade market. For a man who was earning worldwide acclaim with his travel books, the reception of his fiction was feeble at best.

Born on 30 November 1835 to John and Jane Clemens in Florida, Mississippi, Samuel Langhorne Clemens enjoyed a simple childhood in Hannibal, Missouri, where his family moved in 1839. These innocent early years soon gave way to uncertainty and change with the death of his father in 1847. At age twelve Clemens began a lengthy and sometimes tumultuous search for a livelihood, working as an apprentice printer, an apprentice riverboat pilot, a Confederate soldier, a silver prospector, and finally a journalist. His desertion from the Confederate army pushed him west to the territories that fully captured his adventurous and restless spirit. After failing miserably at his prospecting schemes, Clemens became a journalist, a career path that combined with his natural affinity for movement to give him his first real success.

Clemens was always intrigued by travel and its promise of freedom, and although many of his journeys were sometimes physically arduous, he never lost his passion for the symbolic promise of the open road. Likewise, his wanderlust reflects the mood of his times. Americans were on the move as well, and as Clemens notes in *The Innocents Abroad*, he was proud to be "drifting with the tide of a great popular movement." He continues, "Every body was going to Europe–I, too, was going to Europe. Every body was going to the famous Paris Exposition. The steamship lines were carrying Americans out of the various ports of the country at the rate of four or five thousand a week, in the aggregate." The age of mass tourism–fast and furious–had begun, and Clemens became its most thoroughly "American" proponent. But he was not simply "drifting" with the tide; he worked diligently to earn the opportunity to ride it and define the experience for readers back home. For in addition to the thousands of Americans going abroad each year, there were many thousands more who, unable to make their own trips, desired to read about Europe and gain the experience vicariously.

The series of events that enabled Clemens to become the writer for the new mass movement of tourism began on 7 March 1866 as he departed San Francisco on board the steamer *Ajax* bound for Hawaii. Clemens was leaving for his first substantial assignment as a travel writer. He had proposed to the *Sacramento Union* that he become their roving correspondent in the Hawaiian Islands, reporting to the newspaper's readers his experiences in an exotic land. Such an assignment was ideal for Clemens; it allowed him to be on the move and to support himself in the process. His letters from the Sandwich Islands became highly popular sketches of the daily life and history of the islands, punctuated by his humor and contagious energy. These letters would later be incorporated into his second travel book, *Roughing It,* which would be based mainly on his earlier travels and experiences in Nevada and California.

Clemens's temperament and talent adapted well to the conventions and loose narrative structure of travel writing, and his initial trip abroad would always be a favorite for him. Almost twenty years afterward when he wrote to William Dean Howells on 7 October 1884, he claimed that Hawaii for him was "a haven of refuge for a worn and weary spirit." But this trip held more significance for Clemens than the peace its memory allowed: it further revealed his natural affinity for travel writing, a genre that would sustain him when he struggled to succeed as a fiction writer.

Upon his return to San Francisco after four months in Hawaii, Clemens was still eager to keep on the move. Capitalizing on the momentum provided by the *Union* letters, he secured another assignment, this time moving east. Clemens convinced the editors of the *San Francisco Alta California* to pay for him to go to New York in return for a se-

ries of letters chronicling his experiences during the journey and while in the city. His plans were vague, but he intended the New York trip as a segment of a journey that would eventually take him around the globe. On 15 December 1866 he left San Francisco on board the steamer *America.* He then rode on a horse across the isthmus in Central America to board the *San Francisco,* which took him up the Atlantic coast to New York. The journey was a difficult one. The travelers were exposed to cholera while crossing the isthmus, and the disease ravaged the *San Francisco,* claiming at least eight lives. The ship arrived finally on 12 January 1867.

New York City epitomized the bustling energy of the nation, and Clemens was caught up in its mania immediately. He found an abundance of material for his sketches, but the city soon began to overwhelm him. Within a few months he felt alienated by its phenomenal growth and fast pace and claimed to have exhausted New York as a subject. He was eager to move again, and he came across an ideal opportunity, one that would solidify his identity as a travel writer and bring him worldwide attention.

"Isn't it a most attractive scheme?" Clemens wrote to the editors of the *Alta California* on 2 March 1867 regarding the *Quaker City* pleasure excursion to Europe and the Holy Land, the first luxury cruise originating in America. "Five months of utter freedom from care and anxiety of every kind, and in company with a set of people who will go only to enjoy themselves, and will never mention a word about business during the whole voyage." The editors agreed to pay his passage of $2,000 in return for fifty two-thousand-word letters describing the experience. Although supposedly only those with upstanding character had been invited to book passage, Clemens was hardly surprised to find that the passage money helped to solidify his moral standing, especially as other prominent and pious travelers had backed out of the trip and increased the desperation of the promoters. The "wild humorist of the Pacific Slope" was ready to begin a pilgrimage to the Old World in the company of some of the wealthiest and most overtly religious socialites in New York.

The itinerary was ambitious, five months going around the Mediterranean, with scheduled stops in Spain, France, Italy, Greece, Russia, the Holy Land, and Egypt. The excursion would allow for a variety of options with each layover, depending on the tastes and ambitions of each tourist. It promised to be a bonanza that would provide a continual and ever-changing wealth of material to fill his letters home. In addition to his agreement with the *Alta California,* Clemens promised the *New York Tribune*

First page from Clemens's letter to William Dean Howells in which he
suggests changing the title of his "Old Times on the Mississippi"
series in The Atlantic Monthly (Mark Twain Papers,
Bancroft Library, University of California,
Berkeley, and Mark Twain Foundation)

twenty letters and the *New York Herald*–a competitor
of the *Tribune*–several unsigned letters. On 8 June
1867 the *Quaker City* left its Wall Street pier, embark-
ing on the most celebrated tour of the times. Owing
to poor weather, however, the ship remained within
the safe confines of New York harbor for two days
before beginning the voyage proper.

Although more exhausting and certainly less
lively than Clemens had expected, the trip did provide him with ample travel-writing material, though
he was taxed by the constant pressure to produce
written responses to his experiences. His letters
were a sensation, and upon the return of the *Quaker*

City to New York on 19 November 1867, his fame
had been established firmly on both coasts. *The Innocents Abroad,* which he derived from his letters,
would become his best-selling book in his lifetime
and one of the most popular travel books of the
nineteenth century.

As a tourist Clemens was essentially inexhaustible, manic, and hungry for new experiences,
but he also was frequently disinterested, skeptical,
and bitterly disdainful of cultures foreign to his
own. In *The Innocents Abroad* he turned his experiences into a type–the American in the Old
World–and he thus became identified as the spokes-

man for the movement of his countrymen abroad. With his thorough awareness of travel-book convention and the expectations of his readers, Clemens mined the role of tourist for satire as well as self-parody.

Keeping true to convention in the preface, Clemens greets his readers as friends and promises them that he will escort them through the Old World with a consciously "American" perspective. He claims that his purpose is "to suggest to the reader how *he* would be likely to see Europe and the East if he looked at them with his own eyes instead of the eyes of those who traveled in those countries before him. I make small pretense of showing anyone how he *ought* to look at objects of interest beyond the sea...." Clemens went to Europe with the confidence and independence of a man representing a country in its prime, and he encouraged his readers, vicariously, to do the same.

Although modern critics have implied that Clemens in his brashness was setting himself apart from his predecessors and peers, it should be understood that he was not alone in his approach. Many books by Americans in Europe show a similar irreverence for the Old World. Clemens did, however, manage to capture the common sentiment more effectively and consistently than his contemporaries. Quite simply, his innocent swagger engaged readers in a way that no other travel writer could effect. Clemens sought out opportunities to parody not only the assumptions many held concerning European civilization and its supposed cultural superiority but also those pretentious Americans who perpetuated such notions.

One of his favorite targets was art, specifically that of the Old Masters of Italy. As he does so often in *The Innocents Abroad,* he turns a potential weakness—American ignorance of high art and culture—into a virtue. For example, while in Venice, Clemens directly mocks the notion of traveling to learn:

> We have seen pictures of martyrs enough, and saints enough to regenerate the world. I ought not confess it, but still, since one has no opportunity in America to acquire a critical judgment in art, and since I could not hope to become educated in it in Europe in a few short weeks, I may therefore as well acknowledge with such apologies as may be due, that to me it seemed that when I had seen one of those martyrs I had seen them all.

It is important to note that however ironically Clemens confesses his lack of knowledge—his innocence—he aligns himself with the bulk of his readers; moreover, he validates his own opinion by his seemingly humble honesty.

After cataloguing the paintings of martyrs he has seen (thirteen thousand Saint Jeromes; twenty-two thousand Saint Matthews; sixty thousand Saint Sebastians), he extends his apologies to his shipmates who have encouraged him to keep secret his "uncouth sentiments," and he promises to do so. But in the end he must remain true to his honest reactions to the Old Masters. He writes, "It is impossible to travel through Italy without speaking of pictures, and can I see them through others' eyes?" Clemens's apologies are actually celebrations of his and his readers' "uncouth sentiments," and they declare for them a cultural independence from the pretensions of Europe. He thus fulfills the promise made in the preface to view the Old World with fresh, innocent, American eyes—proud and unapologetic.

Such debunking of European civilization permeates *The Innocents Abroad,* and it was a message American readers loved. Clemens well knew the emotional tie the American tourist—perhaps especially the vicarious ones who were his readers—felt for their homeland. Americans were fascinated by Europe, but they were equally interested in themselves and their own identity. Clemens offered his American readers the reassurance that they were living in the best country after all.

The experience of visiting the Old World and writing a best-selling book was crucial for Clemens as a professional writer. The patterns he established and the conventions he followed would thereafter influence his writing and his understanding of his readers and the marketplace. Soon after completing *The Innocents Abroad* he began to explore ideas for a second book, once again capitalizing on the momentum his travel writing had given him. Clemens had found his literary niche.

As his literary star began to ascend, Clemens met and fell in love with Olivia Langdon (Livy), the daughter of wealthy coal merchant Jervis Langdon of Elmira, New York. They were married on 2 February 1870 and settled in Buffalo in a home given to them by Livy's parents. However, Clemens was not happy in Buffalo owing to overcommitments with his work and a series of personal difficulties, including the death of Jervis Langdon on 6 August 1870 and the subsequent collapse of Livy from exhaustion. After a stay in Elmira for Livy's recovery, the family moved in fall 1871 to Hartford, Connecticut, a move enabled by the enormous sales of *The Innocents Abroad* and Clemens's subsequent decision to cut his ties to journalism and devote his energies to his travel books.

In Hartford, Clemens was able to work consistently on *Roughing It*. Although he envisioned the

LIFE ON THE MISSISSIPPI

BY

MARK TWAIN

AUTHOR OF "THE INNOCENTS ABROAD," "ROUGHING IT,"
"THE PRINCE AND THE PAUPER," ETC.

WITH MORE THAN 300 ILLUSTRATIONS

Mississippi Steamboat of Fifty Years Ago.

[SOLD BY SUBSCRIPTION ONLY.]

BOSTON
JAMES R. OSGOOD AND COMPANY
1883

*Title page for Clemens's fourth travel book, which shows his
deep affection for the river*

book as a companion to *The Innocents Abroad,* applying its comic perspective to the American West, its genesis and formation were completely different from its predecessor. *Roughing It* is a record of travel memory. Unlike *The Innocents Abroad,* in which Clemens gives the impression that the text is written contemporaneously with daily experience, in *Roughing It* he adopts the point of view of the older narrator looking back on his youthful journeys. *The Innocents Abroad* ends with a wiser traveler, while *Roughing It* begins with that assumption. Nevertheless, Clemens still records the experiences of an innocent.

Roughing It sold well although Clemens was somewhat disappointed that it was not as successful as *The Innocents Abroad.* In the thick volume—a mishmash of history, anecdote, tall tale, local color, political commentary, and religious treatise—the narrator's fresh perspective on a well-traveled region, just

as in the earlier work, continually surprises the reader. Clemens, though, shifts his sights from the presumptuousness of the Old World to the unbridled optimism of the New. The unifying motif of this often unwieldy narrative is the narrator's continuous struggle to strike it rich, a theme that plays on the common promises of the gold and silver rushes of California and Nevada. The romantic notions of the Wild West were of interest to Clemens's readers, so he carefully presents such a world and then turns it upside down. The narrator's hopes are dashed again and again by bitter reality. Just as in *The Innocents Abroad,* Clemens both meets and mocks the reader's expectations, focusing an ironic, debunking eye on the myths of the West.

The first paragraph of *Roughing It* captures the youthful enthusiasm toward travel and the West: "I never had been away from home, and that word 'travel' had a seductive charm for me." But as he traverses the deserts of the West his excitement begins to wane, and on the edge of another desert Clemens satirizes his innocence: "This was fine—novel—romantic—dramatically adventurous—*this,* indeed, was worth living for, worth traveling for! We would write home all about it." Interestingly, here Clemens also mocks his role as a travel writer "writing home." The romance of the desert is soon shown to be a mirage: "This enthusiasm, this stern thirst for adventure, wilted under the sultry August sun and did not last above one hour. . . . The poetry was all in the anticipation—there is none in the reality." Such disappointments permeate *Roughing It,* but they are ultimately comic in light of the innocent, romantic expectations. In the end Clemens's "record of several years vagabondizing" is a record of misspent dreams and bitter failures—the "rough" lesson the innocent traveler learns in the American West.

Even as he was working to complete *Roughing It* Clemens was contemplating another book, which he planned to base upon a journey to South Africa and its recently discovered diamond deposits. Unwilling to make the trip himself, Clemens hit on what seemed an ideal solution: hire a proxy to make the journey. Upon the proxy's return, Clemens planned to "pump him dry" and write the narrative as his own experience. James Henry Riley, a friend from Clemens's San Francisco days, was excited by Clemens's infectious enthusiasm and volunteered to make the trip. Clemens was manic concerning the prospects of the plan, for he imagined writing a constant stream of travel books that would perpetuate his career as a best-seller indefinitely, all without ever leaving home. As Justin Kaplan notes, Clemens was bent on becoming a "steam-driven, smoke-and-fire-belching" literary machine. Although Riley did go to South Africa and diligently met his part of the bargain, Clemens abandoned the scheme.

Clemens, perhaps, was misguided in his dream of assembly-line literary production, but he was clearly right in his choice of a product. As *The Innocents Abroad* and *Roughing It* had demonstrated, the travel book was his literary diamond mine. After completing *Roughing It,* however, Clemens was desperate to overcome his reputation as a "mere humorist." Wanting to expand his repertoire and to stay as close to home as possible, he abandoned travel writing for other projects, including the collaborative novel with Warner, *The Gilded Age;* a boy's book, *The Adventures of Tom Sawyer;* a collaborative play with Bret Harte, *Ah, Sin* (1876); and a seven-installment reminiscence in *The Atlantic Monthly* titled "Old Times on the Mississippi" (1875), which would later be incorporated into *Life on the Mississippi.* These works illustrated Clemens's ability to write successfully in a variety of contexts, but they also revealed the difficulty in making such work sell on the same level as his travel writing.

In spring of 1878 Clemens decided to return to the genre that had made his career possible and to the continent that had given him his most profitable material. On 11 April the Clemens family boarded the steamer *Holstatia* in New York and headed for Hamburg. Unlike his first trip to Europe eleven years previous, during which Clemens was clearly separated from his touring companions by his limited economic means, his financial stature was now that of those he had parodied in *The Innocents Abroad.* Instead of being a "sinner" among well-to-do "pilgrims," he was now the head of an entourage of family, friends, and servants. Clearly hoping to recapture the literary momentum afforded by his first success, Clemens spent much of the summer of 1878 in Heidelberg and the winter in Munich. During this time Clemens and Reverend Joseph Twichell, who had joined him in August at Clemens's expense, "tramped" across Europe.

Clemens had returned to the notion of a proxy, hoping to gain valuable experience via Twichell as he had earlier hoped to use Riley. In the narrative he often sends Twichell—named Harris—as his agent to perform tasks that Clemens himself preferred not to undertake. In one such instance Clemens has Harris climb the "Ladders" at Gemmi Pass in Switzerland. He writes, "I ordered Harris to make the ascent, so I could put the thrill and horror of it in my book, and he accomplished the feat successfully, through a sub-agent for three francs, which I paid. It makes me shudder yet when I think of what I felt when I was clinging there between heaven and earth in the person of that proxy."

The Clemens family moved to Paris in February 1879; then in July they traveled through Belgium and Holland to London. They boarded the *Gallia* in Liverpool on 23 August to return to the United States, arriving in New York on 3 September. The trip had been pleasant in many ways for Clemens—he thoroughly enjoyed his tramping with Twichell—but it was also a difficult sixteen months because of the constant pressure he felt to produce a salable travel book. He had endured similar pressure during the *Quaker City* excursion, but this time he had much more to lose.

Clemens's low self-confidence made the writing of *A Tramp Abroad* arduous. For this aging innocent wanderer, travel had become a chore. Nevertheless, Clemens did manage to produce a successful narrative by returning to *The Innocents Abroad* in theme and mood, again both using and mocking audience expectations and travel-book conventions. Published in March 1880, *A Tramp Abroad* sold sixty-two thousand copies in its first year, which was only six thousand short of what *The Innocents Abroad* sold in its initial year.

In *A Tramp Abroad* Clemens consciously mimics his previous title—the "innocent" becomes a "tramp"—and features a narrator who is down on his luck from recent disappointments. The book incorporates many of the techniques and themes that worked so well for Clemens in his earlier works. Again he attacks the Old Masters, and despite the intervening years since his first art appraisals in *The Innocents Abroad,* he draws the same conclusions: "the Old Master was a bad painter, the Old Master was not an Old Master at all, but an Old Apprentice." Clemens is still the innocent American art critic, but he no longer has to apologize, however ironically, for his honest eyes.

Perhaps the most interesting cultural observation Clemens makes in *A Tramp Abroad* concerns the growing prevalence among Americans going abroad of "tourists" as opposed to "travelers." The press was full of expressions of distaste by elite travelers for the results of the democratization of foreign travel, made possible by lowering prices, and the consequent growth of package tours. While Clemens had viewed the beginning of widespread middle-class European travel from below in *The Innocents Abroad,* in *A Tramp Abroad* he became America's quintessential man of leisure. Although he ironically calls himself a "tramp" in the double-entendre title, Clemens was unmistakably a tourist, first-class.

To parody his change in status Clemens structures *A Tramp Abroad* around one simple joke: he would let on that he intended to walk

Clemens and his wife, Olivia, circa 1900

(tramp) across Europe—the act of a true traveler—but in actuality would walk very little, opting for whatever leisurely conveyance that was available—the act of a true tourist. He opens the narrative with an explanation of his purpose: "One day it occurred to me that it had been many years since the world had been afforded the spectacle of a man adventurous enough to undertake a journey through Europe on foot. After much thought, I decided that I was a person fitted to furnish mankind this spectacle. So I determined to do it." Thus begins Clemens's adventure, but in the fifth paragraph occurs the first undercutting of his pose: "After a brief rest at Hamburg, we made preparations for a long pedestrian trip southward in the soft spring weather, but

at the last moment we changed the program, for private reasons, and took the express train." Clemens makes such changes in itinerary throughout *A Tramp Abroad,* always extending his self-parody. A bona fide American tourist, he simply will not be inconvenienced no matter what the cost to the aesthetics of traveling.

A Tramp Abroad gave Clemens the financial and literary lift he needed to propel him to his best work. The 1880s would prove to be his most productive decade as an author, and in it he would write his most revered novel, *The Adventures of Huckleberry Finn.* The foundation for his achievement in that novel was laid when he returned to the Mississippi River as a travel writer. In April

Clemens at breakfast in his hotel room in Olympia, Washington, August 1895, during his world lecture tour

1882 the author of books about trips to the American West, the Hawaiian Islands, the countries of Europe, and the Holy Land decided to go home.

The result was his fourth travel book, *Life on the Mississippi* (1883), in which Clemens again manages to mesh traditional travel-book formulas with satire and parody. As he had in his previous travel books, he produced a miscellany of history, autobiography, anecdote, and fiction, all balanced by his most complex narrative perspective. In *Life on the Mississippi* Clemens takes on the persona of the professional travel writer attempting to capture not only the essence of the Mississippi River and its surrounding communities but also his own childhood. *Life on the Mississippi*, like no other of his travel books, reflects a narrative consciousness filled with respect, even awe, and love for his subject.

Clemens left New York on 18 April 1882 headed for Saint Louis to begin his tour of the river. In a little more than a month he traveled down to New Orleans and then back upriver to Saint Paul. His plan was to write a definitive work on the history and life of the Mississippi River, and his reverence for the subject is clear in his opening words: "The Mississippi River is well worth reading about. It is not a commonplace river, but on the contrary is in all ways remarkable." Clemens blends a wide-angled vision, evident in his first two chapters devoted to the history and background of the river, with autobiography and travel experience. Although some critics view *Life on the Mississippi* as an extension of "Old Times on the Mississippi," it is more accurately a wholly new approach to the river.

While the memories evoked in "Old Times on the Mississippi" are an essential part of *Life on the Mississippi*, the core of the book is an exploration into the present, the physical reality of the river basin. Referring to the finished book as an expansion of a purely autobiographical work distorts the complexity of the whole. Clemens's balancing of his past and present allowed him to contrast expectation and reality, but *Life on the Mississippi* has a special quality among his travel writings because the expectations were often personal rather than those of popular culture. During his description of the stay in Hannibal, the struggles between the professional travel writer and the nostalgic middle-aged man are evident:

> During my three days' stay in the town, I woke up every morning with the impression that I was a boy—for in my dreams the faces were all young again, and looked as they had looked in the old times—but I went to bed a hundred years old, every night—for meantime I had been seeing those faces as they are now.

Growing less and less willing to leave his home, he chose not to pursue his travel writing after *Life on the Mississippi*—a book that forced him to face his own mortality—until he was desperate for the economic boost he knew it could provide. The 1880s and 1890s were active ones for Clemens as an author and entrepreneur, an exhausting period that took a heavy toll. By the mid 1890s he simply had no choice but to return to the genre. After declaring bankruptcy on 18 April 1894, Clemens planned to pay off his debts and restore his fortune through a round-the-world lecture tour and a book based on his experiences. The plan worked, and the resulting travel book, *Following the Equator* (1897), was another success, but the yearlong journey was a costly one.

The tour began on 14 July 1895 as Clemens with his wife, Livy, his daughter Clara, and several friends headed for Cleveland, the first stop on the North American leg of the trip. Clemens would visit a hundred cities in all, meeting with enthusiastic and loving fans around the world. The entourage would tour Australia, India, and South Africa and then England, where Clemens planned to write *Following the Equator*. After finishing the tour and setting up home in England, Clemens received the "thunderstroke." On 18 August 1896 he learned that his favorite daughter, Susy, had died from meningitis. She was twenty-four.

It is no surprise that *Following the Equator* is Clemens's most scathing and caustic travel book; the old tourist was exhausted by the trip and the financial woes that necessitated it and devastated by the loss of Susy. In a letter to Laurence Hutton dated 20 February 1898 Clemens commented that the "secret substance" of *Following the Equator* "was all made of bitterness and rebellion." In his last travel book he once again returned to the form of his first, as is suggested by his once considering the title "Another Innocent Abroad."

The conclusion of *Following the Equator* underscores Clemens's disillusion with travel and himself. After noting his personal pride at completing his journey around the world in such a short amount of time, he refers to the recent discovery of "another great body of light" that had appeared in space and which could make the same journey in "*a minute and a half*." The man who had often shared his travels with readers during a span of more than thirty years ended his travel-writing career with a simple observation: "Human pride is not worth while; there is always something lying in wait to take the wind out of it."

The significance of travel writing to Clemens's career has often been overlooked and misunderstood. Critics and readers have preferred to examine these works as merely apprenticeship pieces for his fiction, which has been seen as his more important writing. However, his travel books are not significant simply owing to their historical value or for their connection to other works. The travel books were the financial backbone of Clemens's career and stand as a crucial part of his canon. No other genre encouraged a closer rapport between Clemens and his readers, and no other genre was better suited to his talents and temperament. Examination of his travel writings offers, perhaps more clearly than any other of his works, important insight into both the mastery of Clemens as a literary artist and his keen understanding of American culture in the nineteenth century.

Letters:

Mark Twain's Letters, 2 volumes, edited by Albert Bigelow Paine (New York: Harper, 1917);

Mark Twain's Letters to Will Bowen, edited by Theodore Hornberger (Austin: University of Texas Press, 1941);

The Love Letters of Mark Twain, edited by Dixon Wecter (New York: Harper, 1949);

Mark Twain to Mrs. Fairbanks, edited by Wecter (San Marino, Cal.: Huntington Library, 1949);

Mark Twain-Howells Letters, 2 volumes, edited by Henry Nash Smith and William M. Gibson (Cambridge, Mass.: Harvard University Press, 1960);

Mark Twain's Letters to Mary, edited by Lewis Leary (New York: Columbia University Press, 1961);

The Pattern for Mark Twain's Roughing It: Letters from Nevada by Samuel and Orion Clemens, 1861–1862, edited by Franklin R. Rogers (Berkeley & Los Angeles: University of California Press, 1961);

Mark Twain's Letters from Hawaii, edited by A. Grove Day (New York: Appleton-Century, 1966);

Mark Twain's Letters to His Publishers, edited by Hamlin Hill (Berkeley: University of California Press, 1967);

Mark Twain's Correspondence with Henry Huttleston Rogers, 1893–1909, edited by Leary (Berkeley: University of California Press, 1969);

Mark Twain's Letters, volume 1, 1853–1866, edited by Edgar M. Branch, Michael B. Frank, and Kenneth M. Sanderson; volume 2, 1867–1868, edited by Harriet Elinor Smith and Richard Bucci; volume 3, 1869, edited by Victor Fischer and Michael B. Frank; volume 4, 1870–1871, edited by Fischer, Frank, and Salamo (Berkeley: University of California Press, 1988–1995).

Bibliographies:

Merle Johnson, *A Bibliography of the Works of Mark Twain, Samuel Langhorne Clemens: A List of First Editions in Book Form and of First Printings in Periodicals and Occasional Publications of His Varied Literary Activities,* revised and enlarged edition (New York & London: Harper, 1935);

Thomas A. Tenney, *Mark Twain: A Reference Guide* (Boston: G. K. Hall, 1977);

Alan Gribben, "Removing Mark Twain's Mask: A Decade of Criticism and Scholarship," *ESQ: Journal of the American Renaissance,* 26 (1980): 100–108, 149–171;

William M. McBride, *Mark Twain: A Bibliography of the Collections of the Mark Twain Memorial and the Stowe-Day Foundation* (Hartford, Conn.: McBride, 1984);

Union Catalog of Clemens' Letters, edited by Paul Machlis (Berkeley: University of California Press, 1986);

Union Catalog of Letters to Clemens, edited by Machlis (Berkeley: University of California Press, 1992).

Biographies:

William Dean Howells, *My Mark Twain* (New York & London: Harper, 1910);

Albert Bigelow Paine, *Mark Twain, A Biography,* 3 volumes (New York & London: Harper, 1912);

William R. Gillis, *Goldrush Days with Mark Twain* (New York: Boni, 1930);

Bernard Devoto, *Mark Twain's America* (Boston: Little, Brown, 1932);

Minnie M. Brashear, *Mark Twain, Son of Missouri* (Chapel Hill: University of North Carolina Press, 1934);

Ivan Benson, *Mark Twain's Western Years* (Palo Alto, Cal.: Stanford University Press, 1938);

DeLancey Ferguson, *Mark Twain: Man and Legend* (Indianapolis & New York: Bobbs-Merrill, 1943);

Effie Mona Mack, *Mark Twain in Nevada* (New York: Scribners, 1947);

Kenneth Andrews, *Nook Farm: Mark Twain's Hartford Circle* (Cambridge, Mass.: Harvard University Press, 1950);

Dixon Wecter, *Sam Clemens of Hannibal* (Boston: Houghton Mifflin, 1952);

Paul Fatout, *Mark Twain in Virginia City* (Bloomington: Indiana University Press, 1964);

Margaret Duckett, *Mark Twain and Bret Harte* (Norman: University of Oklahoma Press, 1964);

Justin Kaplan, *Mr. Clemens and Mark Twain* (New York: Simon & Schuster, 1966);

Hamlin Hill, *Mark Twain: God's Fool* (New York: Harper & Row, 1973);

Everett Emerson, *The Authentic Mark Twain: A Literary Biography of Samuel L. Clemens* (Philadelphia: University of Pennsylvania Press, 1984);

Nigey Lennon, *The Sagebrush Bohemian: Mark Twain in California* (New York: Paragon House, 1990);

Margaret Sanborn, *Mark Twain: The Bachelor Years* (New York: Doubleday, 1990).

References:

Leon T. Dickinson, "Mark Twain's *Innocents Abroad:* Its Origins, Composition, and Popularity," dissertation, University of Chicago, 1945;

Dickinson, "Mark Twain's Revisions in Writing *The Innocents Abroad,*" *American Literature,* 19 (1947): 139–157;

Carl Dolmetsch, *"Our Famous Guest": Mark Twain in Vienna* (Athens: University of Georgia Press, 1992);

Dewey Ganzel, *Mark Twain Abroad: The Cruise of the Quaker City* (Chicago & London: University of Chicago Press, 1968);

Ganzel, "Samuel Clemens, Guidebooks, and *The Innocents Abroad,*" *Anglia,* 83 (1965): 78–88;

Ganzel, "Twain, Travel Books, and *Life on the Mississippi,*" *American Literature,* 34 (1962): 40–55;

Alan Gribben, *Mark Twain's Library: A Reconstruction,* 2 volumes (Boston: G. K. Hall, 1980);

Gribben and Nick Karanovich, eds., *Overland with Mark Twain: James B. Pond's Photographs and*

Journal of the North American Lecture Tour of 1895 (Elmira, N.Y.: Center for Mark Twain Studies at Quarry Farm, 1992);

Hamlin Hill, *Mark Twain and Elisha Bliss* (Columbia: University of Missouri Press, 1964);

Robert Stuart Hirst, "The Making of *The Innocents Abroad:* 1867–1872," dissertation, University of California, Berkeley, 1975;

Horst H. Kruse, *Mark Twain and Life on the Mississippi* (Amherst: University of Massachusetts Press, 1982);

Bruce Michelson, "Ever Such a Good Time: The Structure of Mark Twain's *Roughing It*," *Dutch Quarterly Review of Anglo-American Letters,* 17 (1987): 182–199;

Michelson, "Mark Twain the Tourist: The Form of *The Innocents Abroad*," *American Literature,* 49 (1977): 385–398;

Robert M. Rodney, *Mark Twain Overseas: A Biographical Account of His Voyages, Travels, and Reception in Foreign Lands, 1866–1910* (Washington, D.C.: Time/Place Artists and Scholars, 1993);

Miriam Jones Shillingsburg, *At Home Abroad: Mark Twain in Australasia* (Jackson: University Press of Mississippi, 1988);

Jeffrey Steinbrink, "Why the Innocents Went Abroad: Mark Twain and American Tourism in the Late Nineteenth Century," *American Literary Realism,* 16 (1983): 278–286;

Thomas Asa Tenney, "Mark Twain's Early Travels and the Travel Tradition in Literature," dissertation, University of Pennsylvania, 1971;

Dennis Welland, *Mark Twain in England* (Atlantic Highlands, N.J.: Humanities Press, 1978).

Papers:

The major collections of Clemens's papers are at the Bancroft Library, University of California, Berkeley; the Beinecke Library, Yale University; the New York Public Library; the Mark Twain Memorial and Stowe-Day Foundation, Hartford, Connecticut; the Library of Congress; the Houghton Library, Harvard University; the Buffalo and Erie County Public Library; the Harry Ransom Humanities Research Center, University of Texas, Austin; the Mark Twain Museum, Hannibal, Missouri; the Vassar College Library; the Alderman Library, University of Virginia; and the Center for Mark Twain Studies at Quarry Farm, Elmira College, New York.

Richard Harding Davis

(18 April 1864 – 11 April 1916)

James J. Schramer
Youngstown State University

See also the Davis entries in *DLB 12: American Realists and Naturalists; DLB 23: American Newspaper Journalists 1873–1900; DLB 78: American Short-Story Writers, 1880–1910; DLB 79: American Magazine Journalists, 1850–1900;* and *DS 13: The House of Scribner, 1846–1904.*

BOOKS: *The Adventures of My Freshman: Sketches in Pen and Pencil by R. H. Davis, and H. W. Rowley* (Bethlehem, Pa.: Moravian Print, 1883);

Gallegher and Other Stories (New York: Scribners, 1891; London: Osgood, McIlvaine, 1891);

Stories for Boys (New York: Scribners, 1891; London: Osgood, McIlvaine, 1891);

Van Bibber and Others (New York: Harper, 1892; London: Osgood, McIlvaine, 1892);

The West from a Car Window (New York: Harper, 1892);

The Rulers of the Mediterranean (New York: Harper, 1894; London: Gay & Bird, 1894);

Our English Cousins (New York: Harper, 1894; London: Low, Marston, 1894);

The Exiles and Other Stories (New York: Harper, 1894; London: Osgood, McIlvaine, 1894);

The Princess Aline (New York: Harper, 1895; London: Macmillan, 1895);

About Paris (New York: Harper, 1895; London: Gay & Bird, 1896);

Three Gringos in Venezuela and Central America (New York: Harper, 1896; London: Gay & Bird, 1896);

Cinderella and Other Stories (New York: Scribners, 1896);

Dr. Jameson's Raiders vs. The Johannesburg Reformers (New York: Russell, 1897);

Cuba in War Time (New York: Russell, 1897; London: Heinemann, 1897);

Soldiers of Fortune (New York: Scribners, 1897; London: Heinemann, 1897);

A Year from a Reporter's Notebook (New York & London: Harper, 1897); republished as *A Year from*

from a photograph Copyright by Pirie MacDonald

Richard Harding Davis

a Correspondent's Notebook (London & New York: Harper, 1898);

The King's Jackal (New York: Scribners, 1898; London: Heinemann, 1898);

The Cuban and Porto Rican Campaigns (New York: Scribners, 1898; London: Heinemann, 1899);

The Lion and the Unicorn (New York: Scribners, 1899; London: Heinemann, 1899);

With Both Armies in South Africa (New York: Scribners, 1900);

Her First Appearance (New York: Harper, 1901);

In the Fog (New York: Russell, 1901);

Ranson's Folly (New York: Scribners, 1902; London: Heinemann 1903);

Captain Macklin: His Memoirs (New York: Scribners, 1902; London: Heinemann, 1902);

The Bar Sinister (New York: Scribners, 1903);

"Miss Civilization": A Comedy in One Act (New York: Scribners, 1905);

Farces: The Dictator, The Galloper, "Miss Civilization" (New York: Scribners, 1906; London: Bird, 1906);

Real Soldiers of Fortune (New York: Scribners, 1906; London: Heinemann, 1907);

The Scarlet Car (New York: Scribners, 1907);

The Congo and the Coasts of Africa (New York: Scribners, 1907; London: Unwin, 1908);

Vera, The Medium (New York: Scribners, 1908);

The White Mice (New York: Scribners, 1909);

Once Upon a Time (New York: Scribners, 1910; London: Duckworth, 1911);

Notes of a War Correspondent (New York: Scribners, 1910);

The Consul (New York: Scribners, 1911);

The Man Who Could Not Lose (New York: Scribners, 1911; London: Duckworth, 1912);

The Red Cross Girl (New York: Scribners, 1912; London: Duckworth, 1913);

The Lost Road (New York: Scribners, 1913; London: Duckworth, 1914);

Who's Who: A Farce in Three Acts (London: Bickers, 1913);

Peace Manoeuvres: A Play in One Act (New York & London: French, 1914);

The Zone Police: A Play in One Act (New York & London: French, 1914);

The Boy Scout (New York: Scribners, 1914);

With the Allies (New York: Scribners, 1914; London: Duckworth, 1914);

"Somewhere in France" (New York: Scribners, 1915; London: Duckworth, 1916);

The New Sing Sing (New York: National Committee on Prisons and Prison Labor, 1915);

The Lost Road: The Novels and Stories of Richard Harding Davis (New York: Scribners, 1916)—includes "The Man Who Had Everything"; republished as *The Deserter* (New York: Scribners, 1917);

With the French in France and Salonika (New York: Scribners, 1916; London: Duckworth, 1916);

The Boy Scout and Other Stories for Boys (New York: Scribners, 1917).

Collection: *The Novels and Stories of Richard Harding Davis,* Crossroads Edition, 12 volumes (New York: Scribners, 1916); republished as *The*

Novels and Stories of Richard Harding Davis, First Uniform Edition (New York: Scribners, 1920).

PLAY PRODUCTIONS: *The Other Woman,* New York, Theatre of Arts and Letters, 1893;

The Disreputable Mr. Reagan, Philadelphia, Broad Street Theatre, 4 March 1895;

Soldiers of Fortune, New Haven: Hyperion Theatre, 17 February 1902;

The Taming of Helen, Toronto, Princess Theatre, 5 January 1903; New York, Savoy Theatre, 30 March 1903;

Ranson's Folly, Providence, R.I., Providence Opera House, 11 January 1904; New York, Hudson Theatre, 18 January 1904;

The Dictator, New York, Criterion Theatre, 4 April 1904;

The Galloper, Baltimore, Ford's Theatre, 4 April 1904; New York, Garden Theatre, 22 January 1906;

"Miss Civilization," New York, Broadway Theatre, 26 January 1906;

The Yankee Tourist, by Davis, lyrics by Wallace Irwin, and music by Alfred G. Robyn, New York, Astor Theatre, 12 August 1907;

Vera, the Medium, Albany, N.Y., Bleecker Hall, 2 November 1908; revised as *The Seventh Daughter,* Cleveland, Colonial Theatre, 10 November 1910;

Captain Kidd, London, Wyndham's Theatre, 12 January 1910;

Blackmail, New York, Union Square Theatre, 17 March 1913;

Who's Who, New Haven, Hyperion Theatre, 28 August 1913; New York, Criterion Theatre, 11 September 1913;

The Trap, by Davis and Jules Eckert Goodman, Boston, Majestic Theatre, September 1914; New York, Booth Theatre, 19 February 1915;

The Zone Police, Tunkhannock, Pa., Piatts's Opera House, 11 August 1916;

Peace Manoeuvres, Bernardsville, N. J., Somerset Hills Dramatic Association, 13 September 1917;

The Girl from Home, Washington, D.C., 3 May 1920.

OTHER: "Broadway," in *The Great Streets of the World* (New York: Scribners, 1892), pp. 3–35;

Greatest Sports Stories, edited by Tom Meany, contains essays by Davis (New York: Barnes, 1955);

Greatest Stories about Show Business, edited by Jerry D. Lewis, with stories by Davis (New York: Coward-McCann, 1957).

Richard Harding Davis may be better remembered in late-twentieth-century America for being the son of novelist Rebecca Harding Davis than he is for his own literary accomplishments. In late-nineteenth-century America, however, Davis epitomized the American version of Charles Kingsley's ideal of Victorian manhood—the muscular Christian. Perfectly suited by temperament and training to record in his travel writings the flexing of American political and economic muscle in Central and South America and to take up uncritically such causes as the Boers' fight against the British in South Africa, Davis was so closely associated with the values of his age that his writing quickly fell out of favor shortly after his death in 1916.

Today Davis is worthy of study precisely because he so clearly represented mainstream American values in the period from the end of the Civil War to the beginning of World War I. Although his tone and style seem naive and boyish and his politics reflect the racist and imperialist dogmas of his time, Davis's writings mirrored the optimism of late-nineteenth-century America. While modern readers may disagree with his politics and American jingoism, there is much to admire in Davis as a writer and a person. He was passionately devoted to what he saw as struggles for independence. He was capable of profound change in perspective, for during his career he went from viewing war as a crucible in which men were tested to seeing it as the greatest tragedy that can afflict humankind. He genuinely enjoyed travel and insisted on witnessing world events firsthand, bringing splendid observational skills to his task.

Davis wrote six books that specifically focused on his travels: *The West from a Car Window* (1892); *Our English Cousins* (1894); *The Rulers of the Mediterranean* (1894); *About Paris* (1895); *Three Gringos in Venezuela and Central America* (1896); and *The Congo and the Coasts of Africa* (1907). Other travel pieces appear in *A Year from a Reporter's Notebook* (1897) and *Notes of a War Correspondent* (1910). His six books covering the military campaigns he observed—*Cuba in War Time* (1897), *The Cuban and Porto Rican Campaigns* (1898), *With Both Armies in South Africa* (1900), *With the Allies* (1914), *"Somewhere in France"* (1915), and *With the French in France and Salonika* (1916)—also contain passages of travel writing. His travels and his interest in adventurers and soldiers of fortune also shaped the content of his most memorable fiction.

Nature and nurture determined that Richard Harding Davis would be a writer. Born 18 April 1864 to Rebecca Blaine Harding Davis, a noted novelist of the time, and Lemuel Clarke Davis, a lawyer turned newspaper editor, Davis came from a literary family. Davis's parents were his role models and his instructors in his moral and social duties. His parents' causes and interests strongly influenced the development of the young man's literary talent. In their study of Davis, Scott C. Osborn and Robert L. Phillips Jr. remark on the close ties between mother and son. He held his mother's work in high esteem; she, in turn, "encouraged his eye for color and his literary ambition." She was his trusted confidante and critic, to whom he continued to send stories for approval well after he became an established writer. His mother taught him the practical side of the writer's craft. From her he learned to view what he wrote as a marketable commodity, to analyze what magazines wanted, and to hold on to pieces that did not sell for their possible future use. From both his parents Davis learned that "the good Christian had a public duty as an ethical teacher, must hold himself accountable for his talents, and should practice what Clarke Davis called 'the religion of humanity.'"

This humanistic faith, as described by Osborn and Phillips, set aside doctrinal and dogmatic disputes in favor of "simple goodness, humble piety, and love of one's fellow man." Davis was a latitudinarian, finding as much to admire in Islam and Roman Catholicism as in primitive American Protestantism. He preferred primitive simplicity to formalized religion. In 1895 he wrote, "I think I could trace the loss of earnestness in religion from the day they stopped worshipping in the woods and catacombs." Osborn and Phillips contend that Davis's attraction to primitive religiosity explains his "spontaneous partisanship" for the Boers. In *With Both Armies in South Africa* Davis wrote of the "long-bearded, strong-eyed Boers with their drooping cavalier hats": "They rode out to fight for a cause as old as the days of Pharaoh and the children of Israel, against an enemy ten times as mighty as was Washington's in his war for independence." Boer leaders such as the bearded, brooding Paul Kruger impressed Davis as patriarchal, biblical figures engaged in a romantic and hopeless struggle to preserve their independence.

From his mother Davis learned to prize personal and creative independence. In her writings she had criticized the "organization man," and her son, for all of his desire to be an insider in social and political circles, refused to belong to any group that sought to impose its will on its members. Preferring partisanship to passive objectivity, he associated openly with the causes and beliefs of those about whom he wrote. He did not just report on wars as a neutral observer; he took sides. Clarke Davis's belief in the teachings of Charles Kingsley on war as an experience that assayed and purified manly hero-

Davis (standing second from right) and his brother, Charles (standing second from left), with the Lehigh football team

ism also affected his son. Despite his later penchant for taking an occasional poke at John Bull, Davis admired British pluck and resolve. Osborn and Phillips document the influence of British popular culture on Davis: "From Thomas Hughes's Tom Brown books and from Charles Kingsley, young Davis learned lessons in 'good form,' the moral value of sports and war, and 'muscular Christianity.'"

Perhaps the greatest influence on Davis's development as a writer was the theater. He may have acquired his taste for the stage from his father, who was an avid historian of drama. Osborn and Phillips note the theatricality of much of Davis's writing, even his nondramatic work:

> The heroic gestures of tragedy and melodrama appear in his fiction, the brilliant colors of pantomime in his descriptive work, and the flippant witticisms of variety and farce in his dialogue. His stories, usually constructed in playlike, climactic scenes and largely dependent upon dialogue for their development, were often converted with little alteration into plays. His characters frequently seem conscious that they are playing "parts" for the benefit of an audience, and sometimes his stories or chapters of novels end with an obvious "curtain speech."

Davis himself was given to the theatrical gesture and was something of a mimic. Samuel Hopkins Adams, writing in the 20 April 1916 *New York Daily Tribune* shortly after Davis's death, characterized his prose as "speech-English, not pen-English."

Davis's writings reveal conflicts between parental expectations and personal desire. He believed, as his parents had taught him, in doing his Christian duty and acting without regard to social pressures, but he also wanted to be in the inner circle of events and was capable of being as exclusive as those whom he rejected for their exclusivity. He shared his father's keen interest in the stage but not his aesthetic, for the young Davis was interested in acting and had a greater appreciation than his father for theatricality. He willingly took up the cause of the downtrodden in Cuba and South Africa, but in neither instance could he see that the needs and aspirations of nonwhites were being ignored.

Davis made his first venture into writing as a student at Lehigh University in Bethlehem, Pennsylvania, from 1882 to 1885. Osborn and Phillips chronicle this period of his development: "Under the pseudonyms Conway Maur and Theodore Hack, Richard supplied the *Lehigh Burr,* the school magazine, with verse, fiction, editorials, parodies, interviews, dramatic reviews, sports stories, 'grinds,' and jokes." He also gained notice at Lehigh for his resistance to the practice of hazing, which he declaimed was "Silly, undignified, and brutal." Not one to shy away from any contest that he considered dignified and manly, Davis was on the first football squad that Lehigh fielded. Although Davis is credited with scoring the first-ever touchdown for the Lehigh squad, the season proved to be a difficult one as the team lost two of its games by scores of 56–0 and 61–0. In 1883 Davis convinced his mother to publish six of his stories in *The Adventures of My Freshman.* Purely a vanity publication, the collection never sold; Davis's family bought up the first run and stowed it in the family attic.

Davis left Lehigh without a degree in 1885 and sought his father's help in starting a career in journalism. His father put him in touch with Talcott Williams, associate editor of the *Philadelphia Press.* Williams recommended that he enroll at Johns Hopkins for a couple of years to study history and politics before serving his apprenticeship as a newspaperman. Davis spent the 1885–1886 academic year at the school as a special undergraduate. An indifferent student, he registered for six classes but completed only a single course in political economy. Leaving college behind, he used family connections to get a position on the *Philadelphia Press,* where he stayed for almost three years, learning from more-experienced reporters and developing the smile and charm that would be his biggest assets as a reporter.

In June 1889 Davis was sent to cover the Johnstown Flood. The assignment allowed Davis to develop his eye for the "pathetic, the amusing, the ironic" that a tragedy of such magnitude revealed. Commenting on the American desire to help the less fortunate, he wrote that following the flood so many people applied to adopt orphaned children it appeared "no home in America was complete without a Johnstown orphan." As is often the case with disasters, reporters almost outnumbered survivors; Davis observed that the "Thousands of cigars strewn over the mud formed the only dry part of the roadway." His eye for detail and ability to detect the humor in the horrible would become trademarks of Davis's later travel writing.

When he moved to New York in 1889 to take a position with the *New York Evening Sun,* Davis found the social milieu that best suited his talents. From his experiences in New York he created his fictionalized accounts of the affable New York clubman—Courtlandt Van Bibber. Collected in *Van Bibber and Others* (1892), these stories recount the adventures of a man-about-town. A desultory aimlessness characterizes Van Bibber's jaunts around New York. Apparently the heir to unspecified wealth, Van Bibber enjoys a freedom that relieves him of the burden of work and allows him to move in and out of all levels of New York society. Although Davis shared some of Van Bibber's qualities—his good nature, his generosity—he did not identify completely with his aristocratic character.

As Osborn and Phillips observe, "No man attains heroic dimension in Davis's fiction through wealth alone or through business success." Wealthy men like Van Bibber were, however, important; without them there would be no way of rewarding those who have ability but lack wealth. Osborn and Phillips describe how Davis constructed the relationship between the rich and the talented:

> Since art and drama depend upon the upper class for support, the way is open for writers and actors who distinguish themselves by providing entertainment for Van Bibber and his friends. Recognition by the social elite is a reward for the deserving hero who is not born to high estate, and the hero is given no reason to doubt that society and its forms are a proper reward for ambition and accomplishments.

Because of *Van Bibber and Others* Davis's popularity grew both in society and in literary circles. He not only lived in but also helped shape and define the character of the period now called the Gay Nineties.

In *The Confident Years: 1885–1915* (1952) Van Wyck Brooks describes Davis as "a young man who was so dramatic in such a special way that he became the symbol of a 'young man's epoch.'" Brooks cites a remark by Gertrude Atherton's Miss Merrian, a character in *Patience Sparhawk and Her Times* (1895), as the source for the evocative phrase: "A man feels a failure nowadays if he hasn't distinguished himself before thirty." Brooks observes that "Miss Merrian might have been referring to Stephen Crane, Frank Norris, Harold Frederic and Jack London along with Davis." On Davis's importance as a literary figure, Brooks concludes that his greatest influence was "not as a writer but as man, Davis was like the reporter who made himself king, for he was a hero to college boys who gathered from him that the journalist's life was the most picturesque and exciting of all careers."

Davis the man was handsome, dapper, boyish, and healthy. To Brooks "he suggested the well-groomed adventurer who lunched at Delmonico's or Sherry's and was off at three for some new revolution in Hayti or some war in Greece and who returned a few months later leaner and more bronzed than ever to be greeted with nods from all the club windows that he passed." Refer-

Davis (standing to the left of the barrel) and other reporters covering the Johnstown Flood of 1889

ring to the image of the athletic young men and women drawn by Charles Dana Gibson, Brooks observes, "He was the perfect Gibson man who might have married the Gibson girl but preferred a free, untrammeled knight-errant's life watching the shells bespatter the earth while he threw his leg over a saddle and slept in a blanket by a camp fire."

"The Reporter Who Made Himself King," which was published in *Stories for Boys* (1891), reveals the essential components of Davis's adventurer hero. Gordon, the protagonist, leaves Yale without taking a degree and finds a position as a reporter for a New York newspaper. Frustrated in his ambition to be a "great war correspondent" because of a lack of wars, Gordon accepts a position as secretary to the American Consul on Opeki, an island in the Pacific where hostilities are about to break out. When circumstances cause the consul to leave the island, Gordon takes over, negotiates a peace between two warring kings, convinces them to abdicate their thrones, and assumes the unified throne as "King Tellman, the Peacemaker," though he ultimately fails to achieve success.

The story, with its allusion to Rudyard Kipling's "The Man Who Would Be King," shows how Davis transformed Kipling's cockney hero into an American adventurer. Osborn and Phillips observe that "Gordon qualifies as Davis's natural aristocrat because his peers recognize that he is quick-witted, has some common sense, and can assume responsibility." In this and other stories and essays Davis developed his heroic ideal. Grounded on the "Anglo-Saxon idea of chivalry" while being particularly American, Davis's hero shows "respect for manners and decorum, . . . for society and class order, . . . for those interests and traits of character that admit the adventurer to the highest levels, . . . for sportsmanship."

This was the type of hero that Davis personified and that influenced subsequent American writers. Brooks cites the following passage from Sinclair Lewis's *Dodsworth* as an example of that influence:

The vision of himself as a Richard Harding Davis hero had returned wistfully . . . Riding a mountain trail, two thousand sheer feet above a steaming valley; sun-helmet and whipcord breeks; tropical rain on a tin-roofed shack; a shot in the darkness as he sat over a square-face of gin with a ragged tramp of ancestry.

Among the first of his generation to show how small the world had become and how easy it was to get around in it, Davis was the perfect hero for a confident age. It was in his travel writing that Davis advanced this image of himself as a daring man of the world, as familiar with Balkan intrigues and the bazaars of Constantinople as he was with fashionable New York.

Davis's career as a travel writer grew out of his association with *Harper's Weekly,* which began in 1890. After serving for a year as an indifferent managing editor of the magazine, he struck a deal that allowed him to travel half of the year and to write about what he observed. In January 1892 he journeyed west to Texas, Oklahoma, and Colorado. His series of essays on the American West became his first travel book, *The West from a Car Window.* Comparing the westerners he met with the sharply drawn characters of Bret Harte's fiction, Davis found the former uninteresting and dull, "like the negative of a photograph which has been under exposed."

Although he enjoyed himself immensely when he got the chance to ride with cavalry troopers chasing bandits into Mexico, Davis lamented the absence of romance in the West. He thought little of life on the prairie and even less of life in western cities. "I think any man who can afford a hall bedroom and a gas stove in New York City is better off than he would be as the owner of 160 acres on the prairie or in one of those small so-called cities." He observed wryly that "Seven houses in the West make a city." Davis got away with puncturing illusions because he did so with a disarmingly flippant style. Imagining that his readers were much like him and that their views of the West had been shaped by their reading, he played on their expectations. He set them up for the adventures of an Eastern tenderfoot and then wrote about his disillusionment when he learned that real cowboys do not "offer the casual visitor a bucking pony to ride, and then roll around on the prairie with glee" as the visitor tries to ride the bucking horse. *The West from a Car Window* pleased Davis's New York readers but won him few admirers in the so-called cities of the West.

For his next excursion into travel writing Davis changed his style and shifted his direction; in May 1892 he sailed to England with his brother Charles to gather material for the essays that would later be published as *Our English Cousins.* Guided as he often was by his previous reading, Davis was pleased to find that what he saw in England corresponded closely to his expectations. He took great pleasure in attending the "Eights Week" of boat racing and being accepted by the undergraduates at Balliol College as if he were one of them.

Davis was not "an unqualified Anglophile," however, and was quick to point out the differences between "American manners" and those of the English upper classes. Yet, like many Americans of his day, Davis found the English class system comforting. "Each English working man knew his place, dressed for it, and proudly did his job well, whereas in America many working people seemed to think the theory of equality gave them license to be slovenly." While the British lower classes impressed Davis with their dignified acceptance of place, the upper classes impressed him with their willingness to forget their positions. "It is not much better to have royalty at all than to have a democratic royalty that stops to laugh at Punch and Judy shows."

Davis and his brother returned from England in August 1892 and stayed with their parents at Marion on Cape Cod for the rest of the summer. In October he assigned himself to report on the Dedication Exercises for the World's Fair in Chicago. One of the highlights of his Chicago visit was to be "mistaken by a crowd of some thousand people for the P[rinc]e of W[ale]s, and tumultuously cheered. At last I found an inspector of police on horseback, who agreed to get me to the stand if it took a leg. He accordingly charged about 300 women and clubbed eight men—I counted them—and finally got me in." He was back in New York less than four months before the urge to travel and his distaste for editorial work set him on a new course.

In February 1893 he sailed east from New York to Gibraltar, Tangier, Cairo, Athens, and Constantinople. The essays that he wrote about his trip appeared in *Harper's Weekly* from 20 May to 19 August 1893 and were then published in book form as *The Rulers of the Mediterranean.* Commenting on Davis's style and tone as a travel writer, biographer Fairfax Downey observes that "Davis wrote his travel books as if he were a Marco Polo, completely assured that none of his public ever had visited the climes he was discovering." Davis's account of his first sighting of Gibraltar, Spain, and Africa illustrates his belief that the reader is seeing a new world through his eyes:

Spain, lying to the right, all green and amethyst, and flippant and gay with white houses and red roofs, and Gibraltar's grim show of battlements and war, become somehow of little moment. You feel that you have known them always, and that they are as you fancied they would be. But the other land across the water looks as inscrutable, as dark, and as silent as the Sphinx that typifies it, and you feel that its Pillar of Hercules still marks the entrance to the "unknown world."

Once on Gibraltar, Davis was struck by the contrast between the English and Spanish sentries. Considered by himself, the English sentry was unimposing, "a little atom, a molecule," but Davis saw him as part of something larger than himself. "He is one of a great system that obtains from India to Nova Scotia, and from Bermuda to Africa and Australia; and he shows this in the way in which he holds up his chin and kicks out his legs as he tramps back and forward guarding the big rock at his back." On the other side of the Neutral Ground the Spanish sentry sits smoking "and wonders when he will be paid his peseta a day for fighting and bleeding for his country." Commenting on Gibraltar's impregnable defenses, Davis chauvinistically concludes that "It will never be attacked, for the reason that the American people are the only people clever enough to invent a way of taking it, and they are too clever to attempt an impossible thing." In these and other passages in this book, Davis coupled admiration for British military might with chauvinistic devotion to American ingenuity.

When he visited Tangier, Davis overcame the imperialistic jargon of his age and showed that he understood how the local people must feel about the invasion of their country. The Englishman, the Frenchman, the Spaniard, and the American—each "knows that he is not wanted there," that he forces his presence upon the Moors. "But still he comes, and he rides around in his baggy breeches and varnished boots, and he gets up polo games and cricket matches, and gallops about in a pink coat after foxes, and asks for bitter ale, and complains because he cannot get his bath, . . . quite as if he had been begged to come and to stop as long as he liked."

Despite his sympathies for the native peoples of North Africa, Davis wanted them to remain as objectified exotics. He laments that "civilization" had come to Tangier. "On the whole, Tangier impresses one as a fine thing spoiled by civilization. Barbarism with electric lights at night is not attractive. Tangier to every traveller should be chiefly interesting as a stepping-stone towards Tetuan or Fez."

From Gibraltar, Davis traveled to Suez and Cairo, stopping along the way at infamous Port Said. All the sea captains, army officers, and officials that Davis met in the East agreed that Port Said "was the home of the most beautiful women on earth, which is saying a good deal, and that it was the wickedest, wildest, and most vicious place that

man had created and God had forgotten." Davis plays on his readers' expectations of delicious debauchery. "I expected a place blazing with lights, and with gambling-houses and *cafés chantants* open to the air, and sailors fighting with bare knives, and guides who cheated and robbed you, or led you to dives where you could be drugged and robbed by others." The reality of Port Said proved quite different from its reputation. "I bought photographs, a box of cigarettes, and a cup of black coffee at Port Said. That cannot be considered a night of wild dissipation. Port Said may have been a sink of iniquity when Mr. Kipling was last there, but when I visited it it was a coaling station."

Davis found the Suez Canal similarly disappointing. "You have heard so much of the Suez Canal as an engineering feat that you rather expect, in your ignorance, to find the banks upheld by walls of masonry, and to pass through intricate locks from one level to another." Davis described the Canal as if it were an irrigation ditch. As for the great French engineer, "you begin to think that Ferdinand de Lesseps drew his walking-stick through the sand from the Red Sea to the Mediterranean, and twenty thousand Negroes followed him and dug a ditch."

In Cairo he discovered that a city could be picturesque without having stunning buildings, for though both the old and the new architecture was colored dull yellows and grays, the people were of considerable interest: "it is the people who live in it and move about in it, and who are so constantly in the streets that from the Citadel above the city its roar comes to you like the roar of London." Disdainful of the tourists and their predictable costumes—"detective cameras and ready-made ties if they are Americans, and white helmets and pugarees floating over their necks and white umbrellas if they are English"—Davis wrote that the way to see Cairo is to let it wash over you. "So keep away from show-places. Lose yourself in the streets, or sit idly on the terrace of your hotel and watch the show move by, feeling that the best of it . . . lies in the fact that nothing you see is done for show; that it is all natural to the people of the place; . . . that no one is posing except the tourist in his pith helmet."

Despite his love of the noise and liveliness of Cairo, Davis found much to dislike in Egypt. He was particularly upset by the lives of the women, "the enslaved half of Egypt." He asserted that Egyptian women were "as much slaves as were ever the Negroes of our South." Although he sympathized with the Egyptians' desire to be free of foreign domination, Davis argued that freedom begins with granting freedom to one's own people. "If the Egyptians want to be free themselves, they should first

FORDING THE CHAMELICON RIVER

THREE GRINGOS IN VENEZUELA

AND

CENTRAL AMERICA

BY

RICHARD HARDING DAVIS

ILLUSTRATED

NEW YORK
HARPER & BROTHERS PUBLISHERS
1896

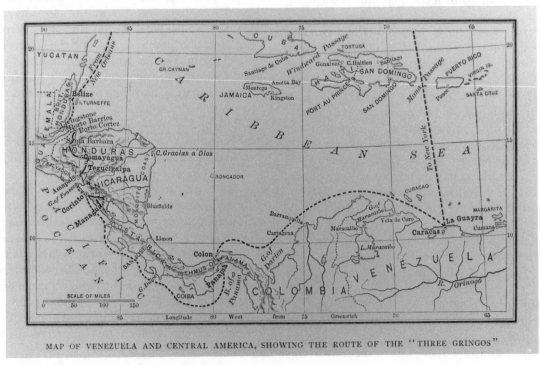

MAP OF VENEZUELA AND CENTRAL AMERICA, SHOWING THE ROUTE OF THE "THREE GRINGOS"

Frontispiece, title page, and map from Davis's fifth book about his travels

free their daughters and mothers." Davis was also critical of the English presence in Egypt. He granted that the English had helped the Egyptians by improving the irrigation system, strengthening the army, and extending the railroad lines: all things for which the English should have been recognized. "But the English to-day not only want credit for having done all this, but they want credit for having done it unselfishly and without hope or thought of reward, and solely for the good of mankind and of Egypt in particular."

The problem with the English was that they wanted the world to ignore the self-interest that had led to their involvement in Egypt. Davis objected to imperialism, but he objected most because the United States had been crowded out of the global real-estate market. "For my own part I find one grows a little tired of getting down and sailing forth and landing again under the shadow of the British flag. If the United States should begin with Hawaii and continue to annex other people's property, we should find that all the best corner lots and post-office sites of the world have been already preempted." Always the journalist, Davis faulted the British press for referring to the eighteen-year-old Khedive of Egypt as a "'sulky boy' who does not know what is best for him." He argued that it would be just as true "to describe him as a plucky boy who wishes to govern his own country and his own people in his own way."

From Cairo, Davis traveled to Athens and Constantinople. He found the "quiet and fresh cleanliness of modern Athens . . . after the dirt and roar of Cairo's narrow lanes and dusky avenues like the touch of damask table linen and silver after the greasy oil-cloth of a Mediterranean coasting steamer." Ever the disappointed tourist, he regretted that the Greek national costume was "not so universally popular as one would suppose from the pictures of Athens in the illustrated papers and by the photographs in the shop windows." Seemingly unaware of the power of American and European marketing, he found it "an inscrutable problem why, with all the national costumes in the world to choose from . . ., the world should have decided on the dress of the Frank, that is, of the foreigner—ourselves." He thought it "a pity" that Athens ". . . should be built of Italian villas, inhabited by people who ape the French, and governed by a King from Denmark."

In Davis's estimation the modern Greeks failed to live up to the standards of their illustrious ancestors:

> I cannot think of any Greek within the last hundred years who has gained world-wide renown, either as a

sculptor, an artist, a soldier, a writer of comedies and satires, a statesman, nor even as an archaeologist; the very historians of Greece and the exponents of its secrets and the most distinguished of its excavators are of other countries.

Although he admitted that the modern Greeks had their own heroes, Davis insisted that none of them were the equal of past ones. He wondered if there would ever come a day when a young Greek would rise in the morning, look up at the Acropolis and say, "To-day I shall do something worthy of that." All that the modern Greek had retained from the past was the Greek language, "which is very creditable to him, as it is a language one learns only after much difficulty, and then forgets it at once." A linguistically impaired American tourist, Davis thought it a "trifle pedantic" that the Greeks go so far "as to put up the names of the streets in Greek."

Seemingly unaware that his own remarks would contribute to the attitude that the modern Greeks were not worthy of the glory they inherited, Davis criticized the British for having stolen Greece's treasures and placed them in an unappealing museum. Napoleon had also stolen the Venus de Milo, but he "placed her in the Louvre, where every one will see her sooner or later; for if he is good he goes to Paris when he dies, and if he is bad he is sure to go there in his lifetime." Davis closed his remarks on Athens with an admonition for the English: "When the people of Great Britain have returned the Elgin marbles to Greece, and the Rock of Gibraltar to Spain, and the Koh-i-noor diamond to India, and Egypt to the Egyptians, they will be a proud and haughty people, and they will be able to hold their heads as high as any one."

Upon arriving in Constantinople, Davis finally found a city that seemed untouched by the civilized elements he had so objected to in Tangier and Port Said. Deprived of his comforts, Davis objected to the city's backward attitude concerning civic improvements. "Of course one does not go to Constantinople to see electric lights and asphalt pavements . . . but it is interesting to find people so nearly in touch with the world in many things, and so far away from it in others. " As had been the case with all the destinations he wrote about in this book, Davis was disappointed by Constantinople. Expecting a "brilliant and flashing city of gilded domes and minarets," Davis felt cheated by a cityscape that was "all white and gray."

In fairness to Constantinople Davis acknowledged that it was a fair-weather city, and as he was visiting it in late winter it was not at its best. "In the winter-time, when the snow and rain sweep over the

The "three gringos": Somers Somerset, Davis, and Lloyd C. Griscom

three hills, and the solitary street of Galata is a foot deep in slush and mud, and the china stoves radiate a candle-like heat in a room built to let in all the air possible, I can imagine no less desirable places than the capital of the Ottoman Empire." In an interview appearing in the 12 April 1896 issue of the *Boston Herald,* Davis recalled the conditions under which he wrote *The Rulers of the Mediterranean:*

> That book, which people have, I'm told, used for a guide book, was written partly, in the winter in Constantinople. My how cold it was! I sat with my legs wrapped around the china stove and wrote on top of it, with my teeth chattering, about "the blue-eyed Bosphorus." There is an instance of getting the facts right down while under the spell of the experience. By the way, how's that for cold realism? I try to make the book interesting for a person who has never been there and does not know anything about the place.

In *The Rulers of the Mediterranean* Davis follows the formula laid down in his first two collections of travel essays. His style is often vividly impressionistic; his tone is sometimes critical. He delights in revealing the mundane reality masked by glittering phrases in guidebooks. He constantly compares the places he visits to his preconceptions of them formed by his earlier reading. While he often finds literature a poor guide to travel, he just as fre-

quently fictionalizes what he sees. Like Lafcadio Hearn, H. Ryder Haggard, and Robert Louis Stevenson, Davis creates a narrative superstructure with an exotic backdrop. On Davis's attitude toward his readers, his brother Charles writes in *The Adventures and Letters of Richard Harding Davis* (1917), "If Richard took it for granted that the reader was totally unacquainted with the peoples of these cities and their ways, it was because he believed that . . . was the best way to write a descriptive article, always had believed it, and believed it so long as he wrote." No matter where he was headed or who had written about the place before him, Davis would say, "It hasn't been done until *I* do it."

Davis's parting advice to readers of *The Rulers of the Mediterranean* who might be interested in the region was for them to travel to Gibraltar, "and from there to Spain and Morocco," which, he assured them, could be seen "in five or six weeks, and at a cost of a very few hundred dollars." He thought this area "the most interesting part" of the Mediterranean coast because it possessed fewer historical sites and therefore had fewer tourists. "A visit to the rest of the Mediterranean," he wrote, was "merely verifying for yourself what you have already learned from others."

Davis left Constantinople in mid April 1893. On 14 April he wrote a letter to his mother from on board the *Orient Express,* "somewhere in Bulgaria," in which he confided that he was happy to be clear of Constantinople, having "shaken [his] fist at the last minaret of that awful city." In a jaunty mood, he enclosed a poem about his travels:

> I'm going back to London, to 'tea' and long frock coats
> I'm done with Cook and seeing sights
> I'm done with table d' hôtes
> So clear the track you signal man
> From Sofia to Pless, I'm going straight for London
> On the Orient Express.

He did not, however, go straight to London; he stopped in Paris, and what he saw there became the material for his next book of travel writing, *About Paris* (1895).

On 11 May 1893 Davis wrote to his mother from Paris that he was still "tentative" about his "opinion of the place." His impressions of the French, however, seem anything but tentative. "They worship the hideous Eiffel Tower and they are a useless, flippant people who never sleep and yet do nothing while awake." Osborn and Phillips note that Davis's tour of Paris "followed the usual course of his travel adventures; he would start out in a burst of enthusiasm, then become depressed as he failed to find what he wanted, and finally salvage from his impressions material to entertain, instruct, or shock the readers at home." Unable to speak French, Davis found Paris much more difficult to navigate socially than London. Frustrated by his unsuccessful attempts to penetrate the upper social orders, Davis lamented that he failed to "see what Harper and Bros. are going to get out of" his trip. Stephen Bonsal cheered him up a bit when he arrived and told Davis that his articles would be different because he hated Paris, "and no one has ever genuinely disliked Paris."

In *About Paris* Davis revealed not only his dislike of but also his inability to understand the French. Although he would later write in his wartime essays about the "spirit of France" being "too alive, too resilient . . . to allow any one thing, even war, to obsess it," Davis's essays from his first trip to France reveal little understanding of or appreciation for that Gallic spirit. He thought French amusements vulgar and boring. After witnessing the friends of a disappointed lover of the actress Marguerite Duclero hissing and spitting at her, he wrote to his mother that "It is a typical incident of the Frenchman and it has made me wrathy." Americans in Paris also came in for their share of his "wrathy" moments. He described the expatriates as a pitiful bunch of frauds who played at being wicked and ris-

qué but were actually models of middle-class American propriety.

Leaving Paris at the end of the spring social season, Davis went on to London, where he stayed for part of the summer before returning to Marion at the end of the season. Except for short visits to see friends in London and Paris, he traveled little for much of 1894. He did leave New York on 9 September 1894 to cover the Sino-Japanese War but stopped the trip at Ottawa and returned to New York.

From January to April 1895 Davis traveled in Latin America; this trip not only gave him the material for three novels, one play, and five short stories but also helped form his attitude toward Latin American peoples and politics during the "Big Stick" era of President Theodore Roosevelt. He had already started working on *Soldiers of Fortune* (1897), which drew on his recollections of a trip to Cuba in 1886, and he thought that a trip to Latin America would freshen the "local color" of this work. Henry Somers Stanley, whom he had met during his stay in Britain, and Lloyd C. Griscom, whose father was involved in a company proposing a Nicaraguan canal and who would himself later become American ambassador to Brazil, accompanied Davis on the trip. Their adventures became the story line for *Three Gringos in Venezuela and Central America.*

After sailing from New Orleans to British Honduras (now Belize) the three men traveled to Guatemala, crossed Honduras by mule, visited the president of Nicaragua, and searched for a nonexistent revolution in Panama. They finished their trip in Caracas, Venezuela, which Davis dubbed the "Paris of South America." In Belize the governor treated them "charmingly," giving them "orderlies, and launches and lunches and advice" and Davis "a fine subject for a short story." The Anglophile Davis admired the Britishness of Belize. "It was not necessary to tell us that Belize would be the last civilized city we would see until we reached the capital of Spanish Honduras. A British colony is always civilized; it is always the same, no matter in what latitude it may be, and it is always distinctly British." It was, however, not always easy to be so properly British. In January 1895 Davis wrote to his family that nothing "has struck me as so sad lately" as the sight of the British governor, Sir Anthony Moloney, "watching us go off laughing and joking in his gilded barge to wherever we pleased and leaving him standing alone on his lawn with some papers to sign and then a dinner tête-à-tête with his Secretary and so on to the end of his life." Davis ended the letter with a curious literary reference, suggesting that the journey from Puerto Cortez, Honduras, to Teguci-

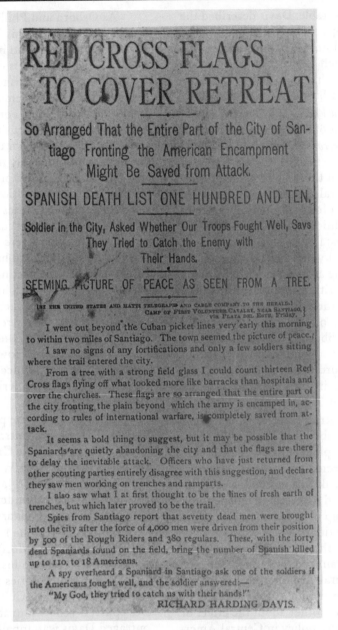

RED CROSS FLAGS TO COVER RETREAT

So Arranged That the Entire Part of the City of Santiago Fronting the American Encampment Might Be Saved from Attack.

SPANISH DEATH LIST ONE HUNDRED AND TEN.

Soldier in the City, Asked Whether Our Troops Fought Well, Says They Tried to Catch the Enemy with Their Hands.

SEEMING PICTURE OF PEACE AS SEEN FROM A TREE.

[BY THE UNITED STATES AND HAYTI TELEGRAPH AND CABLE COMPANY TO THE HERALD.]
CAMP OF FIRST VOLUNTEER CAVALRY, NEAR SANTIAGO,
VIA PLAYA DEL ESTE, Friday.

I went out beyond the Cuban picket lines very early this morning to within two miles of Santiago. The town seemed the picture of peace.

I saw no signs of any fortifications and only a few soldiers sitting where the trail entered the city.

From a tree with a strong field glass I could count thirteen Red Cross flags flying off what looked more like barracks than hospitals and over the churches. These flags are so arranged that the entire part of the city fronting the plain beyond which the army is encamped in, according to rules of international warfare, is completely saved from attack.

It seems a bold thing to suggest, but it may be possible that the Spaniards are quietly abandoning the city and that the flags are there to delay the inevitable attack. Officers who have just returned from other scouting parties entirely disagree with this suggestion, and declare they saw men working on trenches and ramparts.

I also saw what I at first thought to be the lines of fresh earth of trenches, but which later proved to be the trail.

Spies from Santiago report that seventy dead men were brought into the city after the force of 4,000 men were driven from their position by 500 of the Rough Riders and 380 regulars. These, with the forty dead Spaniards found on the field, bring the number of Spanish killed up to 110, to 18 Americans.

A spy overheard a Spaniard in Santiago ask one of the soldiers if the Americans fought well, and the soldier answered:—

"My God, they tried to catch us with their hands!"

RICHARD HARDING DAVIS.

One of Davis's reports on the Spanish-American War (New York Herald, *2 July 1898)*

galpa, the capital city, would be like living a chapter from either *Nostromo* or "Heart of Darkness": "To-day we lie here taking in bananas and tomorrow I will see Conrad, Conrad, Conrad!!"

From Puerto Cortez the trio traveled by rail to San Pedro. Davis's letter from San Pedro explained the setting for an often-reproduced photograph of the "three amigos": "We left the next day on the railroad and the boys finding that two Negroes sat on the cowcatcher to throw sand on the rails in slippery places bribed them for their places and I sat on the sand box." Davis described the countryside as being "very much like Cuba but more luxuriant in

every way." Although he admired the scenery, Davis found little to admire in the people of Honduras. In "The Buried Treasure of Cobre," which he collected in *The Lost Road* (1913), Davis would describe Honduras as a "comic-opera country that was not comic but dead and buried from the world"; its inhabitants were "a savage people, unread, unenlightened, unclean."

Tegucigalpa proved disappointing. The tiny hotel "was a rude shock." The trio had looked forward to beds and clean linens but were offered "a very small room, in which there were three cots, and a layer of dirt all over so thick" that Davis wrote his name in the center of the table. Davis described the inhabitants of Tegucigalpa as "surfeited with leisure and irritable with boredom." A band played in the splendid little plaza each night, but Davis complained that the city had "no color nor ornamentation nor light nor life nor bustle nor laughter."

The Three Gringos in Venezuela and Central America reveals Davis's brand of American imperialism. In *The Rulers of the Mediterranean* Davis had critiqued the British severely for refusing to leave Egypt to the Egyptians. Less than three years later he concluded that "The Central-American citizen is no more fit for a republican form of government than he is for an arctic expedition, and what he needs is to have a protectorate established over him, either by the United States or by another power; it does not matter which, so long as it leaves the Nicaragua Canal in our hands." Writing about a statue in the capital of Costa Rica "in the form of a young woman standing with her foot on the neck of General Walker, the American filibuster," Davis thought "it would have been a very good thing for Costa Rica if Walker, or any man of force, had put his foot on the neck of every republic in Central America and turned it to some account."

Viewing all of Central America as if it were one country, Davis described it as "rich and beautiful, and burdened with plenty." The countryside was fine; what he objected to were the Central Americans. "Its people make it a nuisance and an affront to other nations, and its parcel of independent little states with the pomp of power and none of its dignity, are and will continue to be a constant danger to the peace which should exist between two great powers [Great Britain and the United States]." Davis's views on Central America helped shape American policy on the region. On 31 December 1895 Davis wrote to his brother about the effect of his essays on United States policy in Central America. "The Central American and Venezuelan book comes out on February 1st. Several of the papers here jokingly allude to the fact that my article on the Venezuelan boundary had inspired the President's [Cleveland's] Message. . . . My article was a very lucky thing and is greatly quoted and in social gatherings I am appealed to as an authority." Not everyone was pleased with Davis's views. Annoyed by Davis's tone, one Central American official told a reporter for the *New York Tribune* that it would be "exceedingly unhealthy for Mr. Davis to return to Honduras in the near future." As Osborn and Phillips point out, "The Latin American tour completed Davis's traveling for travel's sake." After 1895, with one exception, Davis's travels were generally related to his assignments as a war correspondent.

As Osborn and Phillips observe, Davis put his travels to good use in his imaginative writing. "The stock of experiences and impressions gathered from 1885 to 1895 became his chief literary capital. With frequent 'refresher' trips to Latin America, and with his vividly retentive memory for sensory images, he easily dubbed in local color in descriptive articles, plays, and fiction." Davis's travels provided the material for his many adventure/romance novels where the hero was predictably moral and justifiably dashing. While the reading public loved his adventure stories with their exotic backgrounds and interchangeable heroes, critics disparaged his lack of literary maturity. They considered his plots hackneyed and his characters insufficiently developed. Taking their criticism to heart, Davis wrote what he thought was the perfect novel, *Captain Macklin: His Memoirs* (1902), in which he traced the psychological development of a character largely based on himself. After it was poorly received, Davis proclaimed his fiction-writing days over and concentrated on his journalistic prose. However, the lure of commercial as well as critical success proved too great, and he returned to fiction writing with *The White Mice* (1909).

During most of the period from 1896 to 1906, however, Davis concentrated his efforts on war reporting. He covered the Greco-Turkish War (1897), the Spanish-American War (1898), the Boer War (1900), and the Russo-Japanese War (1904). His role as a war correspondent allowed Davis to combine his love for the military with his love for travel.

Cuba, to which he had been drawn ever since his first trip in 1885, afforded Davis the opportunity to be an eyewitness to history. By 1896 conflicting (and often untrue) stories raged about what was going on in the Spanish-Cuban war. Journalistic rivalries spurred yellow journalism to a fever pitch. An outraged Davis was appalled by the inaccuracies of war reports that were foisted upon the American public just to sell newspapers. He insisted on traveling to Cuba, where he would uncover the truths about the war.

Davis's essays on Cuba were collected in *Cuba in War Time* (1897), with accompanying illustrations by Frederic Remington. His often-reprinted account of the death of Adolfo Rodriguez, an insurgent executed by the Spanish, illustrates how Davis took the stuff of real life and recast it in dramatic fashion. He carefully described Rodriguez in a manner that was guaranteed to elicit the sympathies of American readers. "He was shockingly young for such a sacrifice, and looked more like a Neapolitan than a Cuban. You could imagine him sitting on the quay at Naples or Genoa, lolling in the sun and showing his

Davis with Col. Theodore Roosevelt in Cuba

white teeth when he laughed." Knowing his readers and their prejudices, Davis emphasized Rodriguez's European features, creating a sympathetic hero.

The handsome young man, calmly smoking a cigarette, was led into an open field and ordered to stand, arms tightly bound to his sides, to await the fatal volley. Davis compared the tightly bound figure to Nathan Hale. What happened during the execution hardly required Davis's dramatic touch. Having steeled himself for the volley, Rodriguez was drawn back into a world he had prepared to leave when the officer in charge of the execution, realizing that the firing squad would hit some of their own men, stepped up to the young man, touched

him on the shoulder, and motioned him to move to another spot. The young man calmly "took up a new position, straightened his back again, and once more held himself erect." The officer raised his sword, dropped his sword arm, and the soldiers fired. The figure slowly sank to the ground; in the place where he had first stood "the cigarette still burned, a tiny living ring of fire." This impressionistic style would remain a characteristic of Davis's war reporting.

Another characteristic of his writing was that he passionately took sides. Prior to going to Cuba Davis had opposed U.S. intervention. However, once on the scene he wrote impassioned accounts of

Davis with an unidentified servant in the Congo, 1907

itzer's *World,* stating it was the *Journal* and not Davis who was to blame for the "deliberate falsehood." Davis never forgave Hearst, "and after the incident never again permitted Hearst to publish anything he wrote."

When Davis traveled to London in March 1897, he was delighted to read that the *London Daily Mail* referred to his dispatches from Cuba as "brilliant." Davis's new status as a celebrity led the London *Times* to offer him a free hand in reporting on the growing war between Greece and Turkey. In April 1897, having ignored the managing editor's suggestion that he report from the Turkish side, Davis joined the Greek troops. On May 4 1897, at the second battle of Velestinos in Thessaly, Davis finally got to see what battle looked like.

He wrote about the battle impressionistically: "the cartridges reminded one of corn-cobs jumping out of a corn-sheller"; the shrapnel did not sound "so much like a shriek as it did like the jarring sound of telegraph wires when someone strikes the pole from which they hang." He even went so far as to turn a Greek artillery officer into an impressionistic artist. "The battle plain below him was his canvas, and his nine mountain guns were his paint brushes. And he painted out Turks and Turkish cannon with the same concentrated serious expression of countenance that you see on the face of the artist." He also began to see that war was a stupid, pointless game of chance. "The dead gave dignity to what other men were doing, and made it noble, and, from another point of view, quite senseless. For their dying proved nothing. Men who could be better spared than they, were still alive in the trenches, and for no reason but through mere dumb chance."

When Davis returned to Cuba to cover the involvement of the United States in the Cuban conflict, his reports were particularly important because of his celebration of Theodore Roosevelt and his Rough Riders. Davis compared the dashing Rough Riders, some of whom were from the elite colleges of the East, to football players. "For the same spirit that once sent these men down a white-washed field against their opponents' rush line was the spirit that sent Church, Channing, Devereux, . . . and a dozen others through the high hot grass at Guasimas, not shouting, as their friends the cowboys did, but each with his mouth tightly shut, with his eyes on the ball, and moving in obedience to the captain's signals." The great heroic moment was Roosevelt at the battle of San Juan Hill, "mounted high on horseback, and charging the rifle-pits at a gallop and quite alone." It was a battle made to order for individual heroics, and Davis wrote about the small, determined groups of men, who pushed forward up the

hunger and disease among the innocent victims of the war. In "The Question of Atrocities" Davis wrote that he "was somewhat skeptical of Spanish atrocities" until he visited Cuba. Among the reasons for his skepticism was the "Cuban war news . . . manufactured on the piazzas" of Key West hotels by "utterly irresponsible newspaper men" who were willing to believe every rumor that drifted across the gulf. After he had been in Cuba for some weeks, Davis found it impossible "to think of the Spanish guerrillas [Davis was referring to the Spanish irregulars] otherwise than as worse than savage animals."

Despite his attempts to report only that which he saw or about which he could be reasonably certain that his sources were accurate, Davis did not escape being misrepresented in American newspapers, a common problem during the war. When one incident that he reported was taken out of context in an effort to increase the readership of William Randolph Hearst's *Journal,* Davis was so outraged that he sent a letter to a rival newspaper, Joseph Pul-

hill. "It was a miracle of self-sacrifice, a triumph of bull-dog courage, which one watched with breathless wonder."

After his reporting from Cuba had made him and Roosevelt famous, Davis married the rich Chicago socialite Cecil Clark on 4 May 1899. Husband and wife were constant companions, and she often accompanied him on his assignments. When Davis went to South Africa to cover the Boer War, Cecil went with him to Cape Town. He dedicated *With Both Armies in South Africa* to his wife. She also went with him on his trip to the Congo and the coasts of Africa in 1907 when reports of Belgian atrocities in the Congo afforded Davis the opportunity for one more travel piece. He also dedicated *The Congo and the Coasts of Africa* to her, "My fellow voyager along the coasts of Africa." The first of their voyages took them to the West Coast of Africa, "One of the places," according to Davis, that civilization "has chosen to ignore."

As usual, Davis paid close attention to his fellow voyagers, particularly the Belgians who had sailed from Antwerp aboard the *Bruxellesville*, which Davis and his wife boarded at Southampton, England. The "Coasters," as they called themselves, were not "Cook's tourists sailing south to avoid a rigorous winter"; they were gamblers engaged in a desperate game. "Nearly everyone of our passengers from Antwerp or Southampton knows that if he keeps his contract, and does not die, it will be three years before he again sees his home. So our departure was not enlivening . . . the exiles prepared us for lonely ports of call, for sickening heat, for swarming multitudes of blacks." Davis believed the odds were against those who chose to spend years in Africa: "The clerk who signs the three-year contract to work on the West Coast enlists against a greater chance of death than the soldier who enlists to fight only bullets."

Davis wondered "How since 1550, when the Portuguese began trading, it has been possible to fill the places of those who have died." A few lines later he answered his own question. "Still, so great are gold, ivory, and rubber, and so many are the men who will take big chances for little pay, that every foot of the West Coast is preempted." From the Spanish colony of Cape Verde in the North on south through French Senegal, British Gambia, French Guinea, British Sierra Leone, the French Ivory Coast, the English Gold Coast, German-held Togo, French Dahomey, English Nigeria, and Spanish Fernando Po and down to the German Cameroons, the coast was a string of "protectorates" broken only by the Republic of Liberia. All along that coast were the sad reminders of the three centuries of slave trading from the West Coast of Africa to the Americas. Citing the estimates of historian George Bancroft, Davis wrote that "in the eighteenth century the English alone imported to the Americas three million slaves, while another 2,500,000 purchased or kidnapped on the West Coast were lost in the surf, or on the voyage thrown into the sea." The slave trade was a great evil in which the sins of the white fathers had fallen upon their children; Davis wrote it is "as though the juju of the African, under the spell of which his enemies sicken and die, has been cast upon the white man," referring to the fevers and malaria that plagued whites.

The residual evil of slavery continued in the Africa Davis visited, for it was the raids of Arab slave traders in the upper Congo basin that had prompted the other European powers to accept Belgium king Leopold's leadership of the International Association to Promote Civilization and Trade in the Congo. In 1885 they appointed him as the "steward" over an area "as large, were Spain and Russia omitted, as Europe." The blacks under Leopold's "protection" suffered more than they ever did at the hands of Arab slavers. Davis reported that Leopold considered the entire Congo as his private property, and he levied taxes that were to be paid in that most precious of commodities—rubber. Davis held Leopold personally responsible for the many atrocities committed in the Congo. Leopold could have stopped the atrocities, but that would have meant stopping the rubber trade, and those "little, roughly rolled red balls, like pellets of coagulated blood, which had cost their weight in blood, which would pay Leopold their weight in gold" were coming into Antwerp in the millions of tons.

While he abhorred Leopold's administration, Davis was less bothered by the presence of the other European colonial powers in Africa. As he did in his other travel pieces, Davis in *The Congo and the Coasts of Africa* lessened the evils of the colonial system by comparing what he saw as good colonialism to the evils of Leopold's Congo Free State. He compared Boma, the capital of the Free State and "the shop window of Leopold's big store," with other European settlements on the West Coast: "To appreciate what Boma lacks one has only to visit the neighboring seaports on the same coast; the English towns of Sierra Leone and Calabar, the French town of Libreville in the French Congo, the German seaport Duala in the Cameroons, but especially Calabar in Southern Nigeria." He considered Southern Nigeria to be a model colony: "Of all the ports at which we touched on the Coast, Calabar was the hottest, the best looking, and the best administered." Davis particularly admired the British insistence on form and

"Somewhere in France"
1905   1915

wishing you all a Happy
New Year RHD

Davis in a trench during World War I

discipline in the face of a hostile climate: "The men of Calabar have learned that when the sun is 110, morals, like material things, disintegrate, and that, though the temptation is to go about in bath-room slippers and pajamas, one is wiser to bolster up his drenched and drooping spirit with a stiff shirt front and a mess jacket."

Davis contrasted what he saw on the French and the Belgian sides of the Congo River, focusing his comparison on the *poste de bois,* the wood posts for the river steamers. "I took photographs of the native villages in all the colonies . . . of the French and Belgian wood posts, the one well stocked and with the boys lying about asleep or playing musical instruments, or alert to trade and barter, and on the Belgian side no wood, and the unhappy white man alone generally shivering with fever." The proof unfortunately did not survive the trip. "Had the photographs only developed properly they would have shown much more convincingly than one can write how utterly miserable is the condition of the Congo Negro." These passages suggest that Davis rarely left the relative comfort and safety of the river steamer; he gathered his evidence for French efficiency and Belgian waste from observations made at the refueling stops. They also show that the horror of Leopold's Congo blinded him to the evils of other, seemingly more benign forms of colonialism.

To put Leopold in the worst possible light Davis was willing to paint an almost pastoral version of French and British colonialism.

When he arrived on the East Coast of Africa, Davis used a method of comparison similar to the one he employed in reporting on the Congo. No European colony in East Africa quite matched the madness and cruelty of the Congo, but the Portuguese, according to Davis, came in a close second. "In the five hundred years in which he has claimed the shore line of East Africa from the south of Lorenço Marquez to north of Mozambique, and many hundreds of miles inland, the Portuguese has been the dog in the manger among nations." The Portuguese (Davis refers to them in the singular as if one stood for all) "has done nothing to help the land or the people whom he pretends to protect."

Davis was convinced that the Portuguese presence in East Africa would not remain much longer because of pressures from the newer British and German colonies. Applying social Darwinism to colonial enterprises, Davis concluded that "It seems inevitable that, between the two great empires, the little kingdom of Portugal will be crowded out, and having failed to benefit either herself or anyone else on the East Coast, she will withdraw from it, in favor of those who are fitter to survive her." Contrasting what he had seen of the Portuguese, German, and English colonies in East Africa, Davis thought that the British colonies were those most suited to survive. "Of these three, the colonies of the Englishmen are, as one expects to find them, the healthiest, the busiest, and the most prosperous." Although he admired what he found in the German colonies such as Dar Es Salaam, Davis argued that "they have still to prove their right to exist."

By 1907 Davis had put aside the anti-British sentiment that characterized his reports from Egypt and South Africa some years earlier. At the end of the nineteenth century America had also become a colonial power after the Spanish-American War ended, and it took charge of Puerto Rico, Guam, and the Philippines. Perhaps Davis admired the English colonies because they reminded him of what he believed was the beneficent American administration of the Philippines, with its official purpose of assuming "the white man's burden."

Always more a marriage of companionship than passion, Davis's marriage to Cecil began to falter, and the couple separated in 1910. On 29 September 1910 the most important woman in Davis's life, his mother, died at the age of seventy-nine. In 1912 Davis secured a divorce from Cecil and married the actress Bessie McCoy (Elizabeth Genevieve McEvoy). His biographers remain unsure how much Davis had told his aging mother about his separation from Cecil or his infatuation with Bessie. One thing is certain—Bessie was the first real love of Davis's life, and she represented a break with the propriety that had long burdened Davis. When she gave birth to his daughter, Hope Davis, on 4 January 1915, Davis, whose articles on the first year of World War I, *With the Allies,* had come out shortly before Hope's birth, was ecstatic.

With the Allies described Davis's trip to Europe at the outbreak of war. It was to be called the Great War, but the excitement of war had worn thin for Davis. As biographer Gerald Langford observes, Davis had changed:

> Richard's compassion for the suffering he saw in Europe was a new experience for him. The war of 1914 was, of course, fought on a larger scale than any of the earlier wars he had covered, but he had seen plenty of suffering and death before now. The difference was more within himself than in outer circumstances. He had come a long way from his insouciance in Cuba and Greece.

As usual, Davis could not refrain from taking sides. In a letter to his wife dated 3 September 1914 Davis wrote about his problems with neutrality:

> Today has been a day of worries. Wheeler cabled me that the paper wanted me to be 'neutral' and not write against the Germans. As I am not interested in the German vote, or in advertising of German breweries (such a hard word to *say*) I thought, considering the *exclusive* stories I had sent them, instead of kicking, they ought to send me a few bouquets. . . . Considering that without credentials I was with French, Belgian, and German armies and saw entry of Germans into Brussels and sacking of Louvain and got arrested as a spy, they were a bit ungrateful. I am now wondering *what* I would have seen *had I had* credentials.

In 1915 Davis donated a copy of *With the Allies* and the passport given to him by the German government at Brussels to the Authors' Club auction for the relief of Belgium. The last travel account Davis wrote was *With the French in France and Salonika.* It was published shortly after his sudden death from a heart attack at Crossroads Farm on 11 April 1916.

Richard Harding Davis seemed destined not to survive World War I, for that conflict destroyed the nineteenth-century attitudes and values that had structured his world. Although he had come to see war as a futile waste and a grim necessity rather than as a test of manhood, he is probably best remembered for describing it as if it were a football game. In his travel writing and his war reporting Davis punctured illusions with his observant eye and sense of justice, but he also displayed all the faults of a confident age. He believed in the survival of the fittest; he questioned but did not deeply examine colonialism; he thought that the world could be a stage for heroic action and that it needed heroes, so he went about creating them. Like Ernest Hemingway and other reporters-novelists who were to follow, Davis was larger than life. His best creation was himself. He lived as an American Quixote, looking for chivalry in a world that was growing distinctly unheroic and unchivalric.

Letters:

The Adventures and Letters of Richard Harding Davis, edited by Charles Belmont Davis (New York: Scribners, 1917).

Bibliographies:

Henry Cole Quinby, *Richard Harding Davis: A Bibliography* (New York: Dutton, 1924);

Fanny Mae Elliot and Lucy Clark, *The Barrett Library: Richard Harding Davis, A Checklist of Printed and Manuscript Works of Richard Harding Davis in the Library of University of Virginia* (Charlottesville: University Press of Virginia, 1963);

John M. Solensten, *Richard Harding Davis (1864-1916)* (Arlington: University of Texas Press, 1970);

Clayton L. Eichelberger and Ann McDonald, *Richard Harding Davis (1864-1916): a Checklist of Secondary Comment* (Arlington: University of Texas Press, 1971).

Biographies:

Fairfax Downey, *Richard Harding Davis: His Day* (New York & London: Scribners, 1933);

Gerald Langford, *The Richard Harding Davis Years: A Biography of Mother and Son* (New York: Holt, Rinehart & Winston, 1961).

References:

J. F. F. Archibald, "Localities and Scenes of Richard Harding Davis's Stories," *Book Buyer,* 25 (1902): 115–121;

Van Wyck Brooks, *The Confident Years, 1885–1915* (New York: Dutton, 1952);

Scott C. Osborn and Robert L. Phillips Jr., *Richard Harding Davis* (Boston: Twayne, 1978);

Harry Thurston Peck, "Richard Harding Davis," *Bookman,* 5 (1897): 462–468;

Joseph M. Rogers, "Richard Harding Davis: A Biographical Sketch," *Book News Monthly,* 29 (1911): 507–510;

John M. Solensten, "The Gibson Boy: A Reassessment," *American Literary Realism,* 4 (1971): 303–312;

Robert Waldron, "Around the World with Swash and Buckle," *American Heritage* (1967): 56–59, 71–74.

Papers:

The three major collections of Davis's papers are the Richard Harding Davis Collection, Clifton Waller Barrett Library, in the Alderman Library at the University of Virginia, Charlottesville; letters on file at Scribners Publishers, New York; and letters in the library of Lehigh University, Bethlehem, Pennsylvania.

John William De Forest

(31 March 1826 – 17 July 1906)

Carole Sims Tabor
Louisiana Tech University

See also the De Forest entry in *DLB 12: American Realists and Naturalists.*

BOOKS: *History of the Indians of Connecticut from the Earliest Known Period to 1850* (Hartford, Conn.: Wm. Jas. Hamersley, 1851);

Oriental Acquaintance: Or, Letters from Syria (New York: Dix, Edwards, 1856);

European Acquaintance: Being Sketches of People in Europe (New York: Harper, 1858);

Seacliff or The Mystery of the Westervelts (Boston: Phillips, Sampson, 1859);

Miss Ravenel's Conversion from Secession to Loyalty (New York: Harper, 1867; revised edition, New York & London: Harper, 1939);

Overland (New York: Sheldon, 1871);

Kate Beaumont (Boston: Osgood, 1872);

The Wetherel Affair (New York: Sheldon, 1873);

Honest John Vane (New Haven: Richmond & Patten, 1875);

Playing the Mischief (New York: Harper, 1875);

Justine's Lovers, anonymous (Boston: Harper, 1878);

Irene the Missionary, anonymous (Boston: Roberts, 1879);

The Bloody Chasm (New York: Appleton, 1881); republished as *The Oddest of Courtships; or, The Bloody Chasm* (New York: Appleton, 1882);

A Lover's Revolt (New York: Longmans, Green, 1898);

The De Forests of Avesnes (and of New Netherland) a Huguenot Thread in American Colonial History, 1494 to the Present Time (New Haven: Tuttle, Morehouse & Taylor, 1900);

The Downing Legends: Stories in Rhyme (New Haven: Tuttle, Morehouse & Taylor, 1901);

Poems: Medley and Palestina (New Haven: Tuttle, Morehouse & Taylor, 1902);

A Volunteer's Adventures: A Union Captain's Record of the Civil War, edited by James H. Croushore (New Haven: Yale University Press / London: Oxford University Press, 1946);

A Union Officer in the Reconstruction, edited by Croushore and David Morris Potter (New Ha-

J W De Forest, 1868

ven: Yale University Press / London: Oxford University Press, 1948);

Witching Times (New Haven: College & University Press, 1967).

Neither a passionate pilgrim, a stalker of the picturesque, nor a satirist of the American fascination with an older world, John William De Forest in *Oriental Acquaintance; Or, Letters from Syria* (1856) and *European Acquaintance; Being Sketches of People in Europe* (1858) presents the details of everyday life he observes in his travels. His eyes were open to the significance of the ordinary and the seemingly trivial, and his ability in these two travel narratives to capture a scene, a moment, or a character foreshadows the strengths he evidenced in his later career as a novelist. Unburdened by the twentieth-century travel writer's awareness that even a "factual" world is to some degree an imaginary construct of the perceiver, De Forest gives us the "real" world of ordinary life as well as the occasional extraordinary adventure of the mid–nineteenth century traveler.

John William De Forest, the fifth and youngest son of John Hancock and Dotha Woodward De Forest, was born in Humphreysville (now Seymour), Connecticut, on 31 March 1826. Of old Huguenot lineage in America, the De Forest family had been permanently settled on American soil since 1636. John Hancock De Forest was at the time of his youngest son's birth a manufacturer of cottons in Humphreysville, a man of social and financial prestige and some importance in the development of cotton manufacturing in America. By 1822 he had built a large, tasteful home for his family. The future writer was reared in a family that was strongly dedicated to its Congregationalist religious faith and that held education in high regard.

Traditionally the De Forests sent their sons to Yale, but because of a chronic bronchial condition—the result of a childhood illness—De Forest was unable to follow two of his older brothers at the college. He lacked the strength for prolonged activity, and he could lift his voice little above a whisper. The ostensible reason for his first trip abroad in 1846 was the possibility of benefit to his health. He would escape the long, damp Connecticut winters for a sojourn in a warmer climate. The twenty-year-old De Forest may also have welcomed the prospect of visiting his brother, Dr. Henry De Forest, a medical missionary in Syria, because he was dissatisfied with his life and needed a change. He was not a productive businessman like others in his family and doubtless felt trapped by a repressive home life with a sickly and sentimentally religious mother (his father had died in 1839). He arrived in Smyrna on 7 February 1846 after a brief stop at Malta; family records do not document the exact date of his return to America, but it was possibly as late as the fall of 1847. *Oriental Acquaintance* was based on the letters De Forest wrote to his family in 1846–1847.

When De Forest left for Syria in 1846 he carried as baggage more than stocks, pantaloons, and flannel undergarments. He carried with him certain intellectual, cultural, and social views common to his upper-middle-class background. He embarked with the respectable middle-class revulsion against the lower orders; firmly fixed in his nature was the New England middle-class distrust of the show of strong emotion and of any tendency toward flattering dissimulation. He was happy to find in his travels others who shared his station in life: Christian gentlemen, both American and British, of culture and mannerly habits.

It would have been nearly impossible for De Forest not to have assumed the superiority (all the more significant because he was unaware of it) that shaped his observation of and his interactions with the "natives" he encountered through his brother's mission. New England also had given De Forest a sense of moral and intellectual confinement that he probably recognized much earlier than his best portrayal of it in the description of New Boston in his finest novel, *Miss Ravenel's Conversion from Secession to Loyalty* (1867). No reader can finish *Oriental Acquaintance* without feeling in it the nature of a young man drawing, perhaps for the first time, a free breath.

The early chapters of *Oriental Acquaintance* (De Forest calls them Letters; there are thirteen in all) are self-consciously fine in style. The "Boston bark" moves "through tediously tempest-beaten" seas, leaving his "western eyes" to feast on "oriental strangeness." The writing is heavily figurative: "A huge, ruinous, glum-visaged castle sat on the lofty hill behind the city, and vainly strove to wrap its brown nakedness in a dilapidated robe of winter." And De Forest's western eyes are ready with their judgments. At Smyrna the "failing timbers of a ruinous wooden quay" symbolized for the young American the "rottenness, of the people and government of the country." Yet there is a comic, self-deprecatory tone at times that enlivens the early letters. After taking an awkward excursion—the tall American rode a donkey while a barefooted Greek boy ran alongside poking the animal with a sharp stick—De Forest records his embarrassment: "I felt like a big ass mounted on a little one."

Parts of the early letters narrate incidents, such as being hemmed into a courtyard by three cur dogs, that must have been exciting and entertaining to the family back in Connecticut, but which do not contain the same charm for a reader unacquainted with the youngest of the De Forest brothers. And too much of the early chapters is predictable: the battle with fleas, comical misadventures with the language, reflections on the multiplicity of nationalities sailing the Aegean and the Mediterranean Seas, a glimpse of a woman's veiled face. From his earliest letters from Smyrna, De Forest is interested in character, not scenery nor atmosphere nor antiquities; however, knowing not a word of the language, he can offer only conjectures about his fellow travelers. The early letters have a young, rather pretentious, essaylike, copybook style, with reflections on the antique greatness of those preceding him on this same journey: "My fancy breathed upon the skeletons of the vast armies of the cross, and restored them to life, glorious with arms, courage, and nobility, ardent with hatred of the unbelievers, inflexible under difficulties and misery, longing only that their mortal eyes might close upon the freed sepulchre of Christ."

There are, however, interesting moments in even the earliest letters as some narratives indicate unfortunate attitudes perhaps not uncommon in America's traveling class. At Rhodes, De Forest and his newly acquired traveling companion, a cheerful American doctor of divinity, encounter a shabby Jewish boy who "seemed to me the most abject creature that ever humanity had occasion to be ashamed of." One had only to look at him, De Forest observes, and he would grovel in the dust at your feet. De Forest has the inclination to kick him but does not wish to dirty his boots. When one of the party does indeed kick the boy several times cruelly hard, the "miserable poltroon responded by a whine, a smile, and a supplicating out-stretched hand." The group decides to take "this disreputable specimen of manhood" into their service as a guide. After they have been guided by the boy around Rhodes, they pay him, and one member of the party gives him a couple of parting kicks.

Once De Forest reaches Beirut and, met by his brother, is introduced to life at the American mission, he begins to observe people and customs with greater knowledge and sympathy. The narrative moves with more vigor, and the young American's genuine interest in the manners and mores of another country sharpens his prose. He is interested in the clothing of the handsome women and the Druze warriors; Syrian agriculture, "about as it was in the suburbs of Eden just after the expulsion of its incautious gardener"; Syrian business practices; a good Arab dinner in which the guest is importuned to eat to exhaustion; and Arab singing, a wild wavering trill that sounds as if the singer were being shaken by something "excessively strong, uneasy, and ill-tempered."

One of De Forest's particular interests is the relation between the sexes. He observes that when a Syrian comes to the missionary doctor, if his son is sick he will say the boy's name, but if it is his wife or daughter who is sick he will say only that "sickness is in the house." In Syria, De Forest is told, it is bad manners to obtrude the existence of one's female relatives on the notice of male friends. In fact, Syrian men use the phrase "may you be elevated above it" in mentioning such things as asses, hogs, Jews, and women.

As De Forest becomes more at ease in the culture, his observations become more intimate. In the home of a Beirut acquaintance he takes his first whiffs through the snakelike coil of the narghile and soon learns to relish greatly the experience. As a native of taciturn New England, De Forest is particularly struck with the elaborate manners of his new Syrian acquaintances: "the conversation shambled and scraped on the legs of compliment, having an appearance of locomotion without really getting on at all." When a Syrian parts from De Forest and his brother with "Please God, we shall yet be Protestants," De Forest inquires: "What do they mean? Will they become Protestants?" His brother replies, "If God wills, to use their own favorite phrase." But, he continues, according to their tenets a man may claim to believe any faith to suit the moment, as long as in his secret heart he keeps the truth; thus "what is on the end of their tongues, is no indication of what is at the bottom of their hearts."

The son of a zealously Christian mother, De Forest especially looked forward to his journey to Jerusalem. A party of four gentlemen, along with mules, donkeys, and five servants, set off on a March day for the Holy City, riding out through crowds of "beggars with sore optics" and "women holding out disgusting babies." De Forest, his health greatly improved, finds the day glorious. Journeying between the Mediterranean Sea and the Galilean Hills—through Sidon, Sarepta, Tyre, Nazareth, and Tiberias—they reach Jerusalem in eight days.

The attractions of Jerusalem have been so widely told (they are shown the exact spot where Christ was buried and the place from where the earth was lifted to make Adam) that De Forest promises to confine his narrative to traveling companions and adventures. He is shocked that a celebration of the burial of Christ degenerates into a bloody battle between followers of the Greek Orthodox and Roman Catholic faiths. An archbishop, several bishops, monks, devotees, and scores of Greeks with cudgels engage themselves in such a tumult that two companies of Turkish soldiers are required to restore order. De Forest, the practical Protestant, scorns the zealotry of what he regards as corrupt medieval religions: "Such scenes will end, I suppose, when the altars are changed into pulpits, the gold and silver lamps are melted into a school-fund, and the church is furnished with pews and lighted with gas."

De Forest recounts another Jerusalem incident during which he became more frightened than he had ever been in his life. In wretched huts in one corner of the city lived a "festered and loathsome" population of lepers. The area horrified him; after

A rhyme in De Forest's hand (John De Forest Collection, Manuscript Department, Alderman Library, University of Virginia)

he learned where the lepers usually wandered, he never went near and was on constant watch in case one of them should catch him unawares. He was so afraid of contagion that he "had a fear of treading upon the very earth which they had touched." One day his party came upon a dozen outside their usual area, holding up their hands to beg. De Forest's whole party was thrown into a panic: "Scared out of my senses lest they should touch me, I drove spurs into my powerful horse and burst away down the hill at full gallop. 'Get Out! That's a pretty set of fingers to stick in a man's face,' roared the doctor [of divinity], as, making his animal rear and plunge, he scattered the lepers like skirmishers before a charge of cavalry."

De Forest was amazed by the faith and gullibility of the people. He was immensely impressed by the annual bathing of the pilgrims in the Jordan River. Calling the ritual "that great spring washing of the dirtiest of possible sheep in the dirtiest of possible rivers," he observes thousands on foot and on donkeys, mules, camels, all "trotting straight to a fool's Paradise" accompanied by a battalion of Turkish infantry to keep the pilgrims from mauling each other. As the pilgrims strip, most covering

themselves with loose bathing garments, and scramble down to the river, De Forest's group sees a man caught by the current and drowned; his body is not even sought for. Back in Jerusalem they witness the "hocus-pocus of the Holy Fire," a fire which, miraculously, would not harm the faithful. One thing, De Forest comments, did have an air of the miraculous, and that was the rapidity with which believers passed their fingers and faces through the flames.

In the heat of the summer the missionary group moved into cooler quarters on Mount Lebanon. In their mountain retreat, with high cedar rafters in which swallows nest, De Forest is able quietly to observe Syrian manners and conversation. He records many visitors to the mission and the tales they tell. An old Maronite priest assures him that swallows acquire every jot of mud for their nests from the tomb of Moses, a site whose whereabouts is known only to the swallows. A Syrian trader in agricultural produce offers De Forest a partnership, which he sometimes fantasizes about accepting. There is also an old Syrian who, when De Forest's brother tells him about the structure and speed of an American locomotive, replies with a grave narration of the performance of a wooden mule that ran between his and the next village. He also finds his fellow travelers fascinating, and he narrates their stories at some length.

By the end of his stay in Syria, De Forest had wandered the northern steppes and the hills of Lebanon, ridden horseback for days in rough terrain, and camped in rugged conditions, surviving occasional dangers. When he chooses to describe ruins and antiquities, it is not the widely famous ones but instead forgotten old temples and cities almost never visited by Europeans. (A modern student of these ruins—for example, the fallen cities of Apamea and Bara—would do well to read De Forest's mid–nineteenth century account.) Although no permanent cure for his bronchial condition had been effected, his health was so much improved that upon his return to America he commenced an extensive scholarly project: research into the history of the Indian tribes of Connecticut.

Keeping steadily at work on the project that required intense mental concentration and strenuous travel to acquire materials, by February 1850 De Forest had completed the manuscript of *History of the Indians of Connecticut from the Earliest Known Period to 1850* (1851). By October, the book having been recommended by the Connecticut Historical Society, De Forest had signed a contract for publication. Having received an inheritance at his mother's death which he invested as a silent partner in his brother Andrew's lumber business, De Forest was free and financially able to set out for Europe in search of health and culture. "Pursued by the fretting enmity of a monotonous invalidism," he left the United States in the late fall of 1850, not to return for nearly five years.

Unlike many Victorian travelers, De Forest was not concerned with mapping or scientifically analyzing a little-known world. He was not intrigued by the extremes of bliss, daring, or danger. He had no profitable business venture in mind. Certainly he was not attempting a guidebook to the monuments of Europe. In contrast to many of his predecessors on the route from London to Paris to Florence to Rome, he does not record his pilgrimages to literary shrines or his emotional reactions to the sublimity of landscape. Nor is moral uplift his purpose in *European Acquaintance*. However, whether he realized it or not, De Forest was finding his way to becoming a realistic novelist, a writer who pays particular heed to the observed world. In *European Acquaintance* the plot is a journey with a goal; the characters are the natives encountered. De Forest was finding a tone—a blend of seriousness and wry humor—and peopling a narrative not with heroes and heroines but with a finely rendered set of people

going about their daily activities in the health spas of Germany and France and the streets of Florence and Rome.

Largely ignoring his time in London and Paris, De Forest begins his narrative at an outdoor table of the Cafe Doney in Florence, where the sculptor Horace Greenough urges him to try hydropathy at Graefenberg, under the direction of homeopath Vincent Priessnitz, the ruling deity of the water cure. Greenough himself could swear by an eighteen-month experience of the place (in Silesia, then a part of Germany near the Czech border). In the company of his Virginian friend George Newton, called Neuville, De Forest in the chilly spring of 1851 passes through Bologna, Ferrara, Pavia, and Venice before arriving at the establishment of Priessnitz. His first impression is of "numbers of people of a cheerfully crazed appearance, wandering confusedly hither and thither, like ants when you scatter their nest"; they are dressed in linen, bareheaded, with clipped hair, and they carry drinking horns across their shoulders.

Just how is Priessnitz's water cure—a treatment for anything and everything—effected? De Forest reports in interesting detail the regime of a hydropathy establishment in the middle of the nineteenth century. A cold, wet sheet is spread; the patient stretches upon it and is quickly wrapped in blankets. At first De Forest is so cold he cannot speak plainly for shivering; then gradually a change comes, a sensation "of absolute physical pleasure." As if purposely to dispel the pleasure, just at that moment the patient is set upright, leaving feet and ankles free, and, steadied by his bathman, is led to a cistern of black water fed by a cold brook. The patient is quickly peeled like an orange and plunged into the icy cistern. When the patient is perfectly iced, he is permitted to step out to be rubbed down with a prickly linen sheet. Next is a cold-air bath before an open window. To aid the air in circulating, the patient flaps his linen sheet as if it were huge wings. Then the patient is sent "nearly as thinly dressed as Adam and Eve" into the misty chill of the woods to wander about and drink at the fountains three or four tumblers of water. This all takes place before breakfast.

The stomach area of the peripatetic seeker of health is then wrapped with broad linen bandages, wet next to the skin. When the bandages are dry, they are rewet. Breakfast consists of sweet and sour milk and rye and barley bread. Before noon the bathman comes to place the patient for fifteen minutes in a tub of cold water; then he is again wrapped in wet sheets. Then comes lunch, the wet sheet again, a half-hour walk, more sour milk, remoistened bandages, and an hour or two of trotting up and down the main hall in the company of other sufferers. At 9:00 P.M. the bandages are wet again, and the patient is put to bed. At 5:00 A.M. he is dragged out of bed by the dreaded bathman, and the process begins anew.

The effect of the water cure on De Forest was "if any thing, more than I had presumed to hope." Having spent years obeying doctors and taking medicines to no avail, he now found a gradual increase in strength, more energy, and a feeling of hope and cheerfulness. Day by day his condition improved. Soon he could walk ten miles over the hills in the early morning and sit down to breakfast so hungry that he felt he could eat "not only the sour milk . . . but the cow that gave it." Yet he decided to leave Graefenberg before his cure was total to find a hydropathic establishment in some more pleasant climate where he could learn French. He had remained a little more than two months, long enough to note a variety of odd spas and cures in the Silesia area, including the Curd Cure, in which curdled milk was applied to the patients both internally and externally, and the Wine Cure, in which patients and doctors were sometimes "all fuddled together." De Forest's ability to observe and present the nature of his fellow patients suggests the future novelist's ability to capture the idiosyncrasies of fictional characters.

In Divonne, a village in southeast France near the Swiss border and about an hour's walk from Lake Leman, De Forest found a highly recommended clinic directed by Dr. Paul Vidart. De Forest was told Vidart's service was at his disposal but that the doctor's language was French. De Forest knew so little French, he writes, that he had used his *dictionnaire de poche* (pocket dictionary) for some months before discovering that Poche was not the author. The pleasant, well-landscaped setting; the courteous sound of the patients' conversation; and the excellent table made De Forest feel that he was again in a civilized country. The clientele, both male and female, was for the most part cultured and well-to-do; some were of minor European nobility. There was music and conversation after dinner, and the gentlemen could if they wished adjourn to billiards and a good cigar. De Forest decided to stay, finish his cure, and become fluent in French. The treatment here was far less "ferocious" so that at first De Forest feared that its "effeminacy" might undo what Priessnitz had accomplished. But Vidart's treatment, which still included a regime of cold baths, proved even more efficacious.

Soon De Forest, having now a tutor in addition to his dictionnaire de poche, plunged into conversation. Many times in *European Acquaintance* he warns that the American traveler cannot expect to learn a language or about a people if he frequents boardinghouses where only English speakers are at the table. He cannot get acquainted with Europeans if he follows the transient path of one or two nights at a hotel. Such a tourist traveler is in danger of returning home carrying the same intellectual baggage with which he started. At Divonne, De Forest was in continual contact with well-educated people from the best classes of European society and heard correct French spoken every hour of the day. For four months he neither heard nor spoke a word of English.

At Divonne some evenings were passed playing games no more sophisticated than "Fox and Goose," a game in which one player chases another around and in and out of a double ring of participants. De Forest one evening taught his fellows what he called "a Negro dance" learned in childhood. A dignified Swiss minister liked the dance so well that, De Forest writes, "I used to hear him double-shuffle or hoe corn and dig potatoes . . . down the passage by way of a reaction after his bath." De Forest's recounting of his evenings in Divonne leave no doubt that he was happy there. The close and continual contact with the same group of people allowed him freely to discuss politics, religion, and social customs. He also was able to note eccentricities of dress and action. De Forest is no naive New Englander by this time in his life, and his patriotic sentiments do not prohibit him from finding the simpler classes of European nobility the "best behaved class of humanity that I ever had the pleasure of observing."

De Forest was so pleased with the establishment at Divonne that, while most of the patients left when winter set in, he decided to stay on for the winter of 1851–1852. After the socializing of the preceding months he was sometimes lonely, being on occasion reduced to making faces at the cat for amusement. Since there were only a handful of people during the winter, De Forest was able to explore the political and religious sentiments of his acquaintances. One of them, Jolivet, was a radical progressive who doubted the old creeds of religion and criticized the existing forms of society. De Forest writes: "As I was orthodox in religion, and believed society in the present shape of the family to be the only society possible, we never talked on these subjects without disputing."

While Jolivet was, "like infidels in general," calm and reasonable, De Forest, "after the fashion of most people who imagine that they have Heaven on their side," was denunciative. When De Forest accused his disputant of being "no more nor less than an atheist," Jolivet shocked him by claiming a belief in God but not in such Christian doctrines as the Fall and Redemption. "It was the second time in my life that I had heard so frank a declaration of infidelity, and I stared in . . . astonishment." De Forest fell back "upon that proof of Christianity which exists in the interior spiritual life of the devout." Then, he writes, he showed his ignorance by claiming that these supernatural emotions are confined entirely to Christians and almost entirely to Protestants. Calmly and courteously Jolivet disagreed, asserting that these spiritual "impressions," as well known to Catholics as to Protestants and also experienced by Buddhists and Moslems, "are nothing but the effects of education acting on a fervent and impressible imagination."

At another time the two talked of theories of society. De Forest advanced America as the freest country and because of that the most stable and equal. Jolivet answered:

> I have no immense admiration for your state of things in America. . . . It is superficial and temporary. It derives from this, that you have ten times more land than you want, and therefore easily raise food enough for everyone. . . . But build cities of a million inhabitants, crowd your country with four hundred souls to the square mile, and you will have as much wretchedness as England or France. . . . You will not reach our discoveries until your masses are as poverty-stricken as ours. We have long ago lived clear through your social existence. . . . A hundred years hence America will be forced to tread in our footsteps.

Conversation was not always serious at Divonne. The guests entertained themselves with ghost stories and accounts of "somnambulism, mesmerism, and their sister mysteries." De Forest's discussion of mesmerism, a subject of widespread interest in the mid nineteenth century, would be particularly fascinating to readers interested in the social history of the period. De Forest stayed eight months in Divonne, having "been raised by the chill potency of pure water to as high a degree of health as is the ordinary award of mortals." No doubt his sheer enjoyment of a gay and tolerant group of people played some part as well in the recovery of his health.

He spent the summer of 1852 after he left Divonne in the Swiss village of Bex and later that year went to Paris, not his favorite city in Europe. Like many other American travelers, De Forest loved Florence, and to there he returned. Little given to enthusiasms, he makes an exception of Florence, feeling "as though my spirit had been born there in

other centuries, and had possessed there long ago a country, a history, love, joy, sorrow, death." He was "drunk with pleasure" at being there again. But after a while he came down to earth again and returned to his acquaintances at the Cafe Doney: Italian gallants, poor artists, a crochety old general, and the lovely flower girl, Enrichetta.

Despite various literary projects—writing verses, translating Nathaniel Hawthorne's work into Italian—De Forest spent his most indolent months in Florence. There were weeks, he writes, when he did nothing more strenuous than pull on his boots or puff on a cigar. He would get out of bed late, spend an hour getting dressed, and reach the café in time to breakfast with his friend Neuville before noon. Then sometimes they would stroll up the Via Tornabuoni and rest for a bit in the cool of the Duomo. Wandering through the Mercato Nuovo, they might buy some strawberries and later lounge around Neuville's rooms in the via Porta Rossa—smoking, talking, reading a little Italian. Around 5:00 P.M. they dressed and headed for dinner at a favorite restaurant, where they would linger with a bottle of Chianti or Montepulciano. They might then drive to the countryside in the cool twilight and back to the city for late-night talk with friends, whose stories of their loves and travels De Forest would record.

De Forest tells several charming tales related to him with simple naiveté by Maria, a pretty seamstress who lodged in the same house as he did: the story of a witch who curses and then cures a young girl; the story of a woman turned into a gigantic, ugly toad and then restored by the benediction of a priest; the story of a man of Siena who inadvertently releases the spirit of a long-dead priest from purgatory; and the story of Martino, a carousing and ungodly youth invited to the palace of Satan and barely escaping to the world of the living. He left Florence in late autumn of 1853 to pass a winter in Rome and Naples. At Rome the deep dissatisfaction with the temporal government of the papacy that De Forest found among the people led him to imagine a change: "Now let the Romans unanimously set teeth into the fat legs of their popes and cardinals instead of kissing their ignominious toes."

De Forest admits that his appreciation for the art of Italy was not strong. No matter how much he tried to study the art around him, he returned always to the beauty of the country, the sunlight on the hills, the starlight on the Arno. He admired the old palaces, but even under their walls he was entranced too much by the beauty of the present day to extol the historical past. James W. Gargano in his admirable essay on De Forest writes that "In con-

De Forest, circa 1900

trast to Henry James's passion for Europe, De Forest's response to the Old World appears to have been dilettantish and lukewarm." In his appreciation of art, this is true. But the Old World is more than art and architecture. De Forest did respond to the Italian culture that he felt to be as alive and contemporary as his own.

De Forest's European sojourn showed that he had the ability to adapt himself easily to surroundings quite different from his accustomed environment. But though he mingled easily with widely divergent types of people, from the pious Protestants of Graefenberg to the dandies of the cafés of Florence, De Forest maintained a quiet detachment. He was enlightened and tempered by his cosmopolitan experiences but not melted down and cast into a new mold. De Forest found what he sought in Europe. He returned to America in early 1855 healthy and hopeful, planning to make a living as a writer.

While De Forest was preparing both *Oriental Acquaintance* and *European Acquaintance* for publica-

tion, he was living in Charleston, South Carolina, although he was occasionally in New Haven. In 1855 De Forest had met his future wife, Harriet Silliman Shepard, whose father, Dr. Charles Upham Shepard, held a joint appointment as professor of chemistry at Amherst and at the Medical College of Charleston. De Forest accompanied the Shepards to Charleston in the fall of 1855 (the marriage took place in New Haven on 5 June 1856) and lived there for most of the next two years. Their only child, Louis Shepard De Forest, was born in Charleston on 23 February 1857.

De Forest edited and expanded the letters from his Smyrna adventure and published them serially in *Putnam's Monthly* from October 1855 to April 1856 before collecting them in *Oriental Acquaintance*. In contrast to *Oriental Acquaintance,* only a portion of *European Acquaintance* was first published in magazine form: a chapter called "Maria and Her Stories" had appeared in *Putnam's Monthly* in October 1856. Both books belong to De Forest's apprenticeship period as a writer.

One of the pleasing aspects of both *Oriental Acquaintance* and *European Acquaintance* is the absence of extended description of scenery and sites of historical and artistic interest. From the street Arabs of Beirut to the cultured Syrians whose homes he visited, from the bathmen of Graefenberg to the minor aristocrats of the spas of Europe, De Forest studied closely the people he encountered. He does not attempt close psychological analysis, but he describes the appearance and actions of people with a fine attention to surface detail. Both works indicate certain tendencies of De Forest the writer that are evident in his better novels: the reliance on humor, his preference for realistic detail rather than the garnishings of the mysterious and exotic, and a natural, matter-of-fact rhetoric far from the enthusiastic eloquence of an overawed American in Europe.

Neither travel book was a best-seller. James H. Croushore reports that when Dix, Edwards and Company, the publisher of *Oriental Acquaintance,* failed in 1857, De Forest purchased the copyright privileges and the plates for thirty dollars. Of *European Acquaintance* he reports that by 1877 about eleven hundred copies had been sold out of an edition of nearly two thousand copies. De Forest must have been pleased, however, by the critical notice his books attracted. In a full-page review in November 1856 the anonymous reviewer in *Putnam's Monthly* praised *Oriental Acquaintance* for its lack of bombast and extravagance, its liveliness, and its use of odd contrasts. The book "reads like the story of a young man, whose heart and mind are so cheerful and well that it makes no difference how the body fares." The book was reviewed as well in *Godey's Lady's Book* and in *The New Englander,* which devoted two pages to quotations and praise for De Forest's exactness of observation and humor. *European Acquaintance* fared even better with the reviewers, being noticed favorably by journals such as *Graham's Magazine, The Knickerbocker Magazine, The North American Review,* and *Harper's Monthly.* In general the reviewers cited De Forest's lack of pretension, his humor, his detailing of the foibles and idiosyncracies of his fellow men, and his eye for detail.

Oriental Acquaintance and *European Acquaintance* are early works of De Forest. Later, in a career spanning more than forty years, he would go on to publish twelve novels and two books of poetry. Two of his finest works, both nonfiction, were published posthumously in book form: the account of his Civil War experiences in *A Volunteer's Adventures: A Union Captain's Record of the Civil War* (1946) and his account of working for the Freedman's Bureau in the Greenville District of South Carolina in *A Union Officer in the Reconstruction* (1948). Jay B. Hubbell calls the section of *A Union Officer* that deals with "chivalrous and semi-chivalrous Southrons" one of the "shrewdest appraisals of the Southern character ever written."

In his best novels De Forest explores the American culture of his time. He treats the Civil War in *Miss Ravenel's Conversion,* the antebellum South in *Kate Beaumont* (1872), and the difficulty of reconciliation after the war in *The Bloody Chasm* (1881). As a political novel, only Henry Adams's *Democracy* (1880) equals De Forest's two novels of political corruption in the Gilded Age: *Honest John Vane* (1875) and *Playing the Mischief* (1875). In other, lesser novels he turns to the American past: the American Revolution in *A Lover's Revolt* (1898) and the Salem witchcraft trials in *Witching Times* (serially published in *Putnam's Monthly* in 1856–1857 but not published in book form until 1967). Without great success he also wrote a novel of manners, *Seacliff or The Mystery of the Westervelts* (1859); a mystery, *The Wetherel Affair* (1873); and a Western, *Overland* (1871).

De Forest died at his son's home in New Haven on 17 July 1906 without finding a publisher for a collected edition. Yet De Forest's novels have not been lacking in critical attention, as a fifty-six page bibliography of critical comment published in *American Literary Realism* (1968) indicates. Edmund Wilson in *Patriotic Gore: Studies in the Literature of the American Civil War* (1962) devotes a lengthy essay to De Forest; Alexander Cowie praises De Forest's work in *The Rise of the American Novel* (1948). Little, however, has been published on De Forest's travel books.

De Forest in his fiction was caught between his desire to depict America objectively and realistically and his desire to reach the large popular audience that would allow him to make a comfortable living as a writer. Often he had difficulty managing tone in his novels, shifting from sharp satire to inexcusable sentimentality. He sometimes moved quickly from finely observed realism to romantic clichés; stiff heroes, nasty villains, and pretty-maids-all-in-a-row are as readily apparent in De Forest's work as in that of any minor writer of his era. With few exceptions, when he depicts women characters, he takes the views of his age: that women must move from being charming and innocent girls to chaste wives and mothers and that women are difficult to school and need the kind but firm hand of a husband or father to guide them.

De Forest's forte was not the imaginative recreation of experience; rational detachment rather than emotional sensitivity served him best. He had the social historian's eye for vivid external detail and for the significance of the commonplace and was less interested in the management of plot than in careful analysis of manners and mores. These are all abilities that served him well in *Oriental Acquaintance, European Acquaintance,* and in his later non-fiction works *A Volunteer's Adventures* and *A Union Officer.*

Fortunately for De Forest the novelist, he lived in interesting times—the Civil War and Reconstruction, the political and economic corruption of the Gilded Age—and his wide personal experience of these times gave him material. But when he had exhausted that personal experience he often seemed to be simply casting his net in what he hoped would be a school of popular topics. Most readers agree that De Forest's reputation rests primarily on *Miss Ravenel's Conversion.* In *My Literary Passions* (1895) William Dean Howells lauds the novel as "of an advanced realism, before realism was known by name" and in an article in the *Atlantic Monthly* of March 1872 insists that De Forest offered "strong proof that we are not so much lacking in an American novelist as in a public to recognize him." Modern critics James F. Light and George F. Whicher consider *Miss Ravenel's Conversion* as perhaps the greatest of Civil War novels. A reading of *Oriental Acquaintance* and *European Acquaintance* shows that in these two apprenticeship works De Forest developed many of the characteristics for which the best of his later works have been praised.

Bibliographies:
E. R. Hagemann, "A Checklist of the Writings of John William De Forest (1826–1906)," *Studies in Bibliography,* 8 (1956): 185–194;

"John William De Forest (1826-1906): A Critical Bibliography of Secondary Comment," *American Literary Realism,* 4 (1968): 1-56.

References:
Alexander Cowie, *The Rise of the American Novel* (New York: American Book, 1948), pp. 505-520;

James H. Croushore, "John William De Forest: A Biographical and Critical Study to the Year 1868," dissertation, Yale University, 1944;

James E. Gargano, ed., *Critical Essays on John William De Forest* (Boston: G. K. Hall, 1981);

William Dean Howells, *My Literary Passions* (New York: Harper, 1895), pp. 223-224;

Jay B. Hubbell, "John William De Forest," in his *The South in American Literature, 1607-1900* (Durham: Duke University Press, 1954), pp. 393-399;

James F. Light, *John William De Forest* (New York: Twayne, 1965);

George F. Whicher, "Literature and Conflict," in *Literary History of the United States,* edited by Robert E. Spiller and others, third edition, revised (New York: Macmillan, 1963), pp. 563-586;

Edmund Wilson, *Patriotic Gore: Studies in the Literature of the American Civil War* (New York: Oxford University Press, 1962), pp. 668-742.

Papers:
The major collection of De Forest materials is the John W. De Forest Collection in the Yale Collection of American Literature, Beinecke Rare Book Library of Yale University. It includes among other materials fifty-seven letters from De Forest to members of his family, ten letters from William Dean Howells to De Forest, and seventeen De Forest manuscripts. The W. D. Howells Collection in the Houghton Library of Harvard University has thirteen letters from De Forest to Howells. The W. C. Church Manuscript Collection of the New York Public Library has seventeen letters from De Forest to the editors of *The Galaxy.* The Columbia University Library has five letters from De Forest to Brander Matthews.

Paul Belloni Du Chaillu

(31 July 1831? – 30 April 1903)

Mary K. Edmonds

BOOKS: *Explorations and Adventures in Equatorial Africa; with Accounts of the Manners and Customs of the People, and of the Chase of the Gorilla, Crocodile, Leopard, Elephant, Hippopotamus, and Other Animals* (New York: Harper, 1861; London: John Murray, 1861; enlarged edition, New York: Harper, 1871);

A Journey To Ashango-Land, and Further Penetration into Equatorial Africa (New York: Appleton, 1867; London: John Murray, 1867);

Stories of the Gorilla Country: Narrated for Young People (New York: Harper, 1867; London: Sampson Low, Son & Marston, 1868);

Wild Life Under the Equator: Narrated for Young People (New York: Harper, 1868; London, 1869);

Lost in the Jungle (New York: Harper, 1869; London: Sampson Low, Son & Marston, 1870);

My Apingi Kingdom; with Life in the Great Sahara, and Sketches of the Chase of the Ostrich, Hyena, &c (New York: Harper, 1870; London: Sampson Low, Son & Marston, 1871);

The Country of the Dwarfs (New York: Harper, 1872 [i.e. 1871]; London: J. C. Hotten, 1872); republished as *The Dark Country. The Country of the Dwarfs: A Work of Stirring Adventure* (London: Blackwood, 1875?);

The Land of the Midnight Sun: Summer and Winter Journeys through Sweden, Norway, Lapland and Northern Finland, 2 volumes (London: John Murray, 1881; New York: Harper, 1881);

The Viking Age: The Early History, Manners, and Customs of the Ancestors of the English-Speaking Nations, 2 volumes (London: John Murray, 1889; New York: Scribners, 1889);

Ivar the Viking: A Romantic History based upon Authentic Facts of the Third and Fourth Centuries (New York: Scribners, 1893; London: John Murray, 1893);

The Land of the Long Night (New York: Scribners, 1899; London: John Murray, 1900);

The World of the Great Forest: How Animals, Birds, Reptiles, Insects Talk, Think, Work, and Live (New York: Scribners, 1900; London: John Murray, 1901);

Paul Belloni Du Chaillu

King Mombo (New York: Scribners, 1902; London: John Murray, 1902);

In African Forest and Jungle (New York: Scribners, 1903; London: John Murray, 1903).

Edition: *Adventures in the Great Forest of Equatorial Africa and the Country of the Dwarfs,* abridged edition (London: John Murray, 1890; New York: Harper, 1890).

SELECTED PERIODICAL PUBLICATIONS–
UNCOLLECTED: "The Great Equatorial Forest of Africa," *Fortnightly Review,* 47 (1 June 1890): 777–790;

"Last Letter from Russia," *Lamp,* 26 (June 1903): 393–394.

He was known as "Chally" or "Spirit" to the tribesmen of the Gabon and interior regions of equatorial Africa and as "Friend Paul" to thousands of juvenile readers. The world knew Paul Belloni Du Chaillu as a charming man with an incessant taste for exploring who was a gifted storyteller. He achieved great fame by becoming the first white man to see and shoot a gorilla and bring specimens of the animal to Europe for scientists to study. Like his contemporaries Heinrich Barth, Richard Francis Burton, John Hanning Speke, David Livingstone, and Henry M. Stanley, Du Chaillu made a career of traveling and writing. He spent the first half of his life defying jungle fevers, wild-animal attacks, and occasional hostile tribes as he rode the imperialist wave into equatorial Africa. After two trips to Africa and seven books on his explorations there, he turned to the chillier Scandinavian countries of Norway, Sweden, Finland, and the Lapland to study their scenery, customs, and history. Had he not died suddenly in Saint Petersburg in 1903, he would have completed a book on czarist Russia to add to his stack of travel narratives.

Du Chaillu's travel books are his chief legacy. He wrote *Explorations and Adventures in Equatorial Africa; with Accounts of the Manners and Customs of the People, and of the Chase of the Gorilla, Crocodile, Leopard, Hippopotamus, and Other Animals* (1861), *A Journey to Ashango-Land, and Further Penetration into Equatorial Africa* (1867), *The Land of the Midnight Sun: Summer and Winter Journeys through Sweden, Norway, Lapland and Northern Finland* (1881), *The Viking Age* (1889), and *The Land of the Long Night* (1899) with the adult reader in mind, while he wrote the other books deriving from his African and Scandinavian travels for children. Both his books for adults and those for children contain vivid descriptions and a lively, dramatic first-person narration that entertained readers but caused some reviewers, especially those of his first book, *Explorations and Adventures in Equatorial Africa,* to doubt his veracity. Despite his critics, Du Chaillu persevered in his work, combining scientific observation of plants, animals, and geography with a humanistic understanding of cultural history and custom to create travel writing that was stimulating, informative, and at times long-winded.

Little is known certainly about Du Chaillu's birth and early years. By some accounts Du Chaillu was born in Paris on 31 July 1835 to French parents. However, according to biographer Michel Vaucaire, the more likely year of birth is 1831–a year Du Chaillu indirectly refers to in the French version of his *Explorations and Adventures in Equatorial Africa.* Vaucaire argues that the 1831 birth year would mean Du Chaillu immigrated to America in 1852 at the age of twenty-one and would make his subsequent activities in Africa (1855–1859) more believable. While those who credit the birth year of 1835 bestow upon Du Chaillu's early explorations an air of precociousness and romanticism, Vaucaire views Du Chaillu more as a bold adult explorer than as a boy hunter heroically journeying into the unknown western interior of Africa.

As with his birth year, there are conflicting accounts of Du Chaillu's childhood and adolescence. Some sources state that Du Chaillu grew up in the West African region of Gabon where his father, Belloni Du Chaillu, served as a successful trade agent for Messrs. Oppenheim of Paris. While his father became one of the earliest and richest traders in the Gabon through negotiating the buying and selling of rubber, dyes, and ivory with the natives, young Paul attended a local mission school. Here he became interested not only in natural history but also in native African languages.

Vaucaire, however, claims that Du Chaillu grew up in France, attended schools there, and went to stay with his father in Africa when he was seventeen. It was only then, Vaucaire believes, that Du Chaillu met the tribesmen and women his father worked with on the west coast of Africa and became well acquainted with their character, customs, and internal trading system. In any case, both versions agree that Du Chaillu did spend time in Africa with his father and that he did meet tribesmen who would become invaluable resources in his later travels.

In 1851 Du Chaillu's father died unexpectedly and left his son the small fortune he had made from his trading. With no ties to the Gabon or to France (his mother had apparently died earlier), Du Chaillu boarded a ship for New York. During the next three years he spent time in New York, Boston, and Philadelphia. He soon discovered that his African experiences interested people he met at social gatherings and that, wherever he went, he was introduced as the young man who had lived in the rich and mysterious trading coast of West Africa. Finding this sort of celebrity attractive, Du Chaillu asked an editor for the *New York Tribune* about writing descriptions of African life for the newspaper. After listening to the young man's proposal for a series of such travel essays, the editor urged Du Chaillu to become an American citizen, seek backing from learned American scientific societies, and return to the Gabon to accumulate more information on the region.

Du Chaillu responded eagerly to these suggestions. After earning his citizenship he then petitioned and received help from the Boston Society of Natural History and the Philadelphia Academy of

Science for his trip back to Africa. In exchange for their support he promised both societies specimens of plant and animal life upon his return. In October 1855 Du Chaillu boarded a ship sailing to the Gabon; he would be away from his new homeland for the next four years.

According to Frank Luther Mott in *Golden Multitudes* (1947), the book Du Chaillu based on his four-year journey, *Explorations and Adventures in Equatorial Africa,* sold nearly three hundred thousand copies in 1861, proving to be one of the best-selling works of the year. In his preface and first chapter Du Chaillu provides an overview of his explorations in the West African interior between January 1856 and May 1859, detailing the hardships he underwent while traveling through the Gabon, Corisco, Camma, Rembo, Ovenga, Biagano, Apingi, and Ogobai countries. His purpose being to understand the nature of the country and its people, he walked "unaccompanied by other white men—about 8,000 miles."

Du Chaillu reports that he "shot, stuffed, and brought home over 2,000 birds, of which more than 60 [were] new species," and "killed upwards of 1000 quadrupeds, of which 200 were stuffed and brought home [to America], with more than 80 skeletons." He estimates that "not less than 20 of these quadrupeds [were] species hitherto unknown to science." While discovering the gorilla and nest-building ape (whom he names *troglodytes calvus*) and exploring the three previously unknown outlets or mouths of the the Ogobai River, Du Chaillu "suffered fifty attacks of the African fever," curing himself with ample doses of quinine, and was exposed to famine, "heavy tropical rains," and "attacks of ferocious ants and venemous flies." It is not surprising that the narration of such exotic experiences appealed to an audience mostly ignorant of Africa.

While the main emphasis throughout *Explorations and Adventures in Equatorial Africa* is on the plant, animal, and tribal life of the Gabon and surrounding regions, Du Chaillu shows himself to be a product of his imperialistic age through his observations on the country's prospects for greater commercialization and "civilization." As with many explorers of Africa in the mid nineteenth century, geography, trade, and Christianity are inextricably bound in Du Chaillu's view of Africa. For example, while he can appreciate the magnificence of the river Rembo Ngouyai, he still

could not help longing heartily for the day to come, when this glorious stream will be alive with the splash of paddlewheels, and its banks lined with trading and missionary posts. Ebony, bar-wood, and India-rubber, palm-oil, bees wax, and ivory, are the natural products of this region, so far as my limited opportunities allowed me to ascertain; and it needs only the cunning hand and brain of the white man to render this whole tract a great producing country.

The Gabon is a region "which is yet virgin ground to the missionary and the trader—those twin pioneers of civilization—and which affords a fertile field for the operations of both." Written in the spirit of his age, Du Chaillu's language clearly appeals to the evangelical and commercial impulses in his readers.

Du Chaillu vividly describes his encounters with fierce animals, the elements, and various tribes. In addition to the gorillas—featured frequently in the winding narrative—he describes many other animals and curiosities, including boas, ants, elephants, crocodiles, leopards, and toucans. He is subject to temperatures ranging from 98 to 106 degrees as he paddles up streams and tramps through tangled underbrush. Du Chaillu also pays careful attention to the people and customs of each tribe he encounters. He notices that each one claims him as *their* white man—almost as if by naming him they own him. According to Du Chaillu a tribe views it as an honor to host a white man bearing beads, cloth, and tobacco as gifts. In a humorous aside he admits that his most frightful encounter is with the Fan tribe, whose intelligence he appreciates but whose cannibalism he cannot.

Du Chaillu examines tribal religions and soon resigns himself to the futility of converting the Africans to Christianity. The African tribesmen stand by their idols and insist that "'white man's God is not our God; *we* are made by a different God.'" And after listening to tribesmen wail their song of mourning at the death of a kinsmen ("'Oh, you will never speak to us any more, / We cannot see your face anymore'"), Du Chaillu writes, "I thanked God that I was not a native African. These poor people lead dreadful and dreary lives. Not only have they to fear their enemies among neighboring tribes, as well as the various accidents to which a savage life is especially liable, such as starvation, the attacks of wild beasts, etc., but their whole lives are saddened and embittered by the fears of evil spirits, witchcraft, and other kindred superstitions under which they labor."

Du Chaillu's treatment of the gorilla—the mysterious animal that was his main reason for returning to the Gabon—was the main draw for his book. He is at his most evocative when he describes his initial sightings of the gorillas he had traveled so far to see:

I could see plainly the ferocious face of the monstrous ape. It was working with rage; his huge teeth were ground against each other so that we could hear the sound; the skin of the forehead was moved rapidly back and forth, and gave a truly devilish expression to the hideous face; once more he gave out a roar which seemed to shake the woods like thunder, and, looking us in the eyes and beating his breast, advanced again.

Several times Du Chaillu says that he feels sick before he shoots a gorilla: "I protest I felt almost like a murderer when I saw the gorilla this first time. As they ran—on their hind legs—they looked fearfully like hairy men; their heads down, their bodies inclined forward, their whole appearance like men running for their lives." He later admits, "I never kill one without having a sickening realization of the horrid human likeness of the beast."

Du Chaillu emphasizes the human quality of these animals even more when one of his companions kills a female *nshiego mbouvé,* an ape who builds nests in the trees, gathering berries for her baby: "Querlaouen, who had the fairest chance, fired, and brought her down. She dropped without a struggle. The poor little one cried Hew! hew! hew! and clung to the dead body, sucking the breasts, burying its head there in its alarm at the report of the gun." The young nshiego resembled a human child so much, as he cried at his loss, that a greatly moved Du Chaillu adopted him, named him Tommy, and proceeded to care for him even though he "behaved very much like a badly-spoiled child."

When Du Chaillu returned to America in 1860, he had already garnered fame for having sent back so many interesting stuffed specimens to the museums of Boston, Philadelphia, New York, and London. Accounts of Du Chaillu's gifts were published in *The Findings of the Academy of Natural Science of Philadelphia* in 1855, 1856, and 1858 and in the *Findings of the Natural History Society of Boston* in 1860. Newspapers and magazines in New York begged him to write articles based on his experiences, and the New York Geographic Society invited him to lecture on his discoveries. All of this publicity ultimately led not only to the writing and publication of *Explorations and Adventures in Equatorial Africa* in 1861 but also to a great deal of controversy over Du Chaillu's honesty in composing and arranging his account.

The greatest attacks on the veracity of *Explorations and Adventures in Equatorial Africa* occurred after Du Chaillu had successfully lectured at the Royal Geographic Society in London and had seen his book published in England by John Murray in 1861. Skepticism first centered on Du Chaillu's itinerary and his claims that he had ventured into areas of in-

terior Africa where no other traveler had gone before. German explorer Heinrich Barth, the world-renowned authority on West Africa and author of the five-volume *Reisen und Entdeckungen in Nord- und Central-Afrika* (*Travels and Discoveries in North and Central Africa,* 1857–1858), faulted Du Chaillu for his unscientific approach to exploration in an article he wrote for *Zeitschrift für allgemeine Erdkunde* in 1861. Barth pointed out that Du Chaillu had not used any scientific instruments to measure the precise mileage he traveled or to determine the exact placement of the villages and geographical sites he described. Barth wrote an article suggesting that Du Chaillu was a fabricator who invented rivers and mountains of a purely imaginary African interior.

Perhaps the most vocal attack came from naturalist and zoologist Dr. John Edward Gray, then chair of the department of natural history of the British Museum. On 14 May 1861 *The Athenaeum* ran an article by Gray in which he questions Du Chaillu's qualifications as a naturalist and argues that none of the specimens that he examined "indicates that the collector had traversed any new region." The impetus for Gray's attack was the warm welcome given Du Chaillu by the Royal Geographic Society and its willingness to give him a room in which to display his stuffed animals. Gray lashes out at what he considers the Royal Geographic Society's naiveté by saying: "From the interest which some of the fellows of the Royal Geographical Society appear to attach to 'Mr., Mrs., and Miss Gorilla,' one would suppose that they thought that the animals were now for the first time brought to Europe, whereas we have been receiving specimens of them for the last fifteen years, both from the missionaries and the traders in those parts, until almost every museum in Europe is provided with specimens. . . ." Gray then concludes, "I am sorry to have to make these observations, but I think the cause of truth and science requires it. We are overburdened with useless synonyma, and Natural History may be converted into a romance rather than a science by travellers' tales, if they are not exposed at the time."

According to the 6 July 1861 issue of *The Examiner,* however, Gray examined only Du Chaillu's specimens of twenty quadrupeds, ignored Du Chaillu's sixty bird specimens, and in this cursory manner determined that Du Chaillu had only described varieties of previously recognized species. Consequently, Gray unfairly took Du Chaillu for a geographical charlatan who had "never travelled into the interior of Africa" and who had, in fact, "bought his specimens."

The Saturday Review also argued that Du Chaillu had been too strongly criticized. *The Satur-*

day Review states that despite the problems with Du Chaillu's book (illustrations done from memory, the occasional giving of new names to old species) Gray's attack stemmed from jealousy. The Royal Geographic Society and members of high society had so lionized Du Chaillu and he had been so brilliant a performer that Gray wanted to see what all the fuss was about. And when he saw Du Chaillu's meager exhibit at the society—his best specimens being in America—Gray was offended that anyone could think Du Chaillu had better materials than his own zoological department at the British Museum. As *The Saturday Review* concludes, "With the feeling that the Geographical Society have been puffing their hero too much, he [Gray] resolves to 'take him down a peg,' and sets to work accordingly."

Adding to this controversy, *The Press* cites a volatile encounter between a Mr. Malone and Du Chaillu at a meeting of the Royal Geographic Society in which Malone disputed Du Chaillu's claim that there existed such a thing as an African tribal harp made from tree-root fibers. According to their report, an inflamed Du Chaillu greeted Malone's skepticism by "touching him on the shoulder," asking him how "he dared to speak of him in the manner he had done, spat in his face," crying out, "there are many persons who dare to vilify an author who are afraid of pistols!"

These harsh personal attacks were followed by more impersonal criticisms in *The North American Review*. The journal found Du Chaillu's writing style "too entertaining,—reminding us too much of the stories of Mayne Reid and Marryatt, and of Robinson Crusoe" to be considered in the same league of scientific works of exploration by Barth, Livingstone (*Travels and Researches*), and Burton. The reviewer notes that the "adventures" in *Explorations and Adventures in Equatorial Africa* are "sufficiently thrilling; happen most dramatically, at the very moment when they ought to happen; hairbreadth escapes abound; and M. du Chaillu is an unquestionable hero, in skill, valor, endurance, and good fortune. Yet, as we read, we have all the time an uneasy suspicion, not merely of exaggeration, but of invention, and we cannot help wishing that another witness might verify these statements of the heroic hunter." *The North American Review* noted that in addition to his lively writing style, "M. du Chaillu has been extremely careless about his dates, and has so confused his several journeys that it is impossible to determine from the volume exactly where he was in his successive months of African travel."

Like *The North American Review*, *The Edinburgh Review* expressed concern over Du Chaillu's difficulties with dates and the apparent confusion with which he constructed his travel narrative from his diary notes. The journal also questioned how Du Chaillu managed to place "his materials into the graphic and attractive form which they have been made to assume" since Du Chaillu the lecturer was noted more for his "many Gallicisms" than for the fluidity of his English. In essence, the review hints that some sort of unattributed "ghostwriting" may have taken place. Despite its questions, *The Edinburgh Review* proved more willing than *The North American Review* to give Du Chaillu the benefit of the doubt and stated that "while the contradictions which at present confuse and disfigure the narrative must . . . detract from the writer's credit, as long as they remain unexplained, we are very reluctant to give up or even call in question M. Du Chaillu's geographical discoveries, and his accounts of the negro tribes with whom his journeys made him familiar." Indeed, the journal praises Du Chaillu's exploration of a region which "more perhaps than any other will open a path into the very heart of Central Africa." Consequently, *The Edinburgh Review* concludes that "until we are in possession of more conclusive and accurate testimony, we shall suspend our judgment, not presuming, at this stage of the inquiry, to pronounce a verdict absolutely condemnatory of M. Du Chaillu's claims to be ranked as a great African discoverer."

Despite the attacks of Malone, Gray, and Barth and the skepticism expressed by leading journals, the Royal Geographic Society, led by its director Sir Roderick Murchison, defended Du Chaillu's work. Moreover, Richard Francis Burton, the famous British explorer and author of *The Lake Regions of Central Africa* (1860), came to Du Chaillu's defense, as did a noted German geographer named Peterman. Peterman published a map of equatorial Africa in 1862 that proved that the regions Du Chaillu visited did indeed exist—though perhaps not as far into the interior as Du Chaillu had estimated. Further support came from the work of French explorers Serval and Griffon du Bellay, who journeyed through some of the areas Du Chaillu had mentioned in his work and confirmed his findings.

After this important validation of Du Chaillu's narrative, the only person left unsatisfied was the explorer himself. The publication of his first book had clearly inspired a divided reception and had raised questions that Du Chaillu felt must be confronted: Had Du Chaillu actually traveled everywhere he claimed and seen every animal he described in his book? Had he in any way embellished his travels? Who really wrote the book? And if Du Chaillu had written the book in English, despite the fact that English was his second language, was his

Illustrations from Du Chaillu's Explorations and Adventures in Equatorial Africa *(1861)*

DEATH OF MY HUNTER.

DEATH OF THE GORILLA.

lecturing style of intermingling Gallicisms with English simply a pose? Indeed, was Du Chaillu himself simply acting a part? To clear his name completely, and to convince any remaining skeptics, Du Chaillu decided upon a second journey to equatorial Africa. And this time he would go armed not only with gifts and guns, but with scientific instruments and cameras.

Du Chaillu introduces his second book, *A Journey to Ashango-Land, and Further Penetration into Equatorial Africa,* by going on the offensive. In the preface he compares his situation to that of an eighteenth-century explorer of Africa, James Bruce, whose published account of his travels in Abyssinia and on the Nile initially met with hoots of disdain and disbelief (Burton and Speke later verified the truthfulness of Bruce's narrative). As an exasperated Du Chaillu complains, "The position of an explorer of unknown countries in England is peculiar, and very difficult. If he returns home with nothing new or striking to relate he is voted a bore, and his book has no chance of being read; if he has some wonders to unfold, connected with Geography, the Natives, or Natural History, the fate of Abyssinian Bruce too often awaits him: his narrative being held up to scorn and ridicule, as a tissue of figments." Clearly, Du Chaillu was not a man to forgive and forget.

Early in his narrative Du Chaillu states that the first object of his two-year return visit to equatorial Africa was "to make known with more accuracy than I had been able to do in my former one, the geographical features of the country" and to represent with even more detail the natives yet "undisturbed by the slave-dealing practices, the proselytism or the trading enterprise of other races." In his preface and again in an appendix Du Chaillu informs his readers that on this second trip to West Africa's interior—a trip which lasted from 1863 to 1865—he brought with him a slew of astronomical and surveying instruments: a sextant, a pair of binoculars, a telescope, compasses, aneroids (barometers), a rain gauge, magnifiers, measuring tape, a protractor, and five watches. He learned how to use these instruments before leaving England in 1863 and attempted to take careful measurements of latitude, longitude, and rainfall as he journeyed from Gabon to Ashango-land. To defend himself even further against charges of unscientific exploration and fabrication Du Chaillu took photography lessons from a M. Claudet and carried a camera with him into the jungle.

As with his first journey into Gabon, this second trip was rife with problems. He landed at Gabon in the midst of a storm, consequently lost several of his key scientific instruments in the bad weather, and found that he needed to stay at this port of call until more instruments could be sent from London. Fortunately, the Commi tribesmen remembered him and bid him welcome. In gratitude Du Chaillu bestowed upon them gifts in the form of beads, cloth, and tobacco. To his favorite, King Quengueza, Du Chaillu gave a coat in the style of a London beadle, a waistcoat, an opera hat, and a staff—the appropriate gifts for a king, for only the kings of the African tribes were allowed to wear such European finery. As Du Chaillu observes of Quengueza: "I felt and still feel the warmest friendship towards this stern, hard-featured old man; and in recalling his many good qualities, cannot bring myself to think of him as an untutored savage."

Despite the warm reception extended him by the tribal chiefs Ranpano, Olenga-Yombi, and Quengueza, Du Chaillu discovered that during his absence in Europe "the assembled chiefs of the Commi clans under the presidency of King Olenga-Yombi . . . had passed a law to the effect that no Mpongwé (the trading tribe of the Gaboon) or white man should be allowed to ascend the river Fernand Vaz or the Ogobai." The reason for this new rule, Du Chaillu discovered, was that these shrewd West Coast tribes wanted to "prevent, if possible, all strangers from penetrating into the interior, even if it be only to the next tribe, through fear that they should lose the exclusive privilege of trading with these tribes." After presenting his case to the tribal chiefs and assuring them that he had no desire to trade, only to explore and collect specimens, the chiefs agreed to let Du Chaillu gain passageway into the African interior. Accompanied by Commi tribesmen as guides and as carriers of his scientific instruments and trunks of gifts, Du Chaillu set off.

This hurdle was not the last Du Chaillu faced on his journey into the interior. He had to keep constant watch over his equipment to ensure that none was mishandled or stolen. He had to venture through villages beset by smallpox. And he had to abandon his camera, along with his film, when an unfriendly African tribe attacked his party near the end of his journey. Despite this bad luck Du Chaillu still managed to approach his sojourn with as much professionalism as possible as he strove to combat the criticism leveled by detractors of his first book.

In response to the criticism of his first book, Du Chaillu makes *A Journey to Ashango-Land* almost into a daily log. He tells the readers the dates on which he traveled, the miles he walked, the latitude and longitude of villages he visited, and the temperature of specific regions. He strives to give scientific names for the animals he sees and tries to discuss them in terms of discoveries by other scientists. For example, he gives a precise description of an *ipi,* an African anteater, shows how it compares to other anteaters described by a Dr. Baikie and Gray, and concludes that his ipi is a new species. He studies the homes and habits of the white ant and termite and collects specimens of them. He further studies the behavior of the gorilla and decides that gorillas are not as aggressive or as solitary as he had previously supposed them to be. In addition to studying Africa's animal and insect life, Du Chaillu collected living plants and sent them back to the scientific director for the Royal Botanic Gardens at Kew.

Further evidence of Du Chaillu's efforts at being scientific occur when he and his men reach the Samba Nagoshi Falls. Here he uses his aneroid barometers to find the altitudes of the falls so that his measurements "will enable geographers to clear up much that was doubtful in the cartography of this part of Africa." As Du Chaillu observes of his scientific endeavors,

> This travelling life is not a lazy one; I am busy from morning till night, and the quiet hours after the people have retired to rest are the only time I have for writing in my journal, projecting my route, and writing out three copies of my astronomical and other observations. In the daytime, besides the time wasted in almost incessant palavering [solving problems of the natives], I am beset by crowds of gaping villagers from sunrise to sundown. At night I have got into the habit of waking frequently and going out to watch for chances of taking observations for longitude and latitude; chances are not of frequent occurrence in this cloudy climate at this time of year.

While Du Chaillu makes it sound as though he did his work in spite of the "gaping villagers," natives were an integral part both of his study and of the success of his journey. Although Du Chaillu does not trade for products such as ivory and palm oil, he is a trader in knowledge. And while his colonialist impulses seem to be undercut by his genuine feeling for individual tribesmen–King Quengueza, for example–the natives do in a sense become part of Du Chaillu's acquisitions as he trades his trinkets for a better understanding of them and the African interior. His trading process is complete when he exchanges this knowledge, which he has turned into a book, for money.

Throughout *A Journey to Ashango-Land* Du Chaillu spends almost as much time describing various tribes, their response to him, and their physiques, clothing, hair styles, crafts, religion, rituals, and habits as he does recording the facts of West African geography and climate. His approach to the natives is also scientific. In the chapter "Ethnology" he lists the various tribes he has encountered, such as the cannibal Fans and the newly discovered Pygmies, and characterizes them by their physical features and habits. He compares his observations of West African tribal politics to what explorers such as Burton, Speke, Grant, and Livingstone had discovered about politics in East Africa. He collected skulls from the graveyards of the Fan, Ashira, and Fernand Vaz tribes so that he might send them to the British Museum to be measured and studied.

Du Chaillu highlights the relative solitude of the interior tribes in regard to encroaching civilization. He reports, for example, the surprise the natives of Niembouai show when he plays a music box for them and then demonstrates how to use a gun:

> The astonishment, the childish wonder and mystification of these primitive people, who had probably never yet seen any article of civilized manufacture, except beads and articles of brass, may easily be imagined. Beer-bottles are to be seen now and then in the interior, and it is astonishing how far inland they have penetrated. They are held in very high estimation by the chiefs, who covet nothing so much as a black bottle to hang by their side, and contain their palm wine; they consider the bottle far superior to the native calabash for this purpose; no doubt, because it comes from a foreign country.

Du Chaillu's observations on this encounter between civilized and uncivilized, between foreign and native, and between beer bottle and calabash lead him to predict the eventual extinction of the African tribes.

Du Chaillu is quick to defend the white man, or civilization, from any role in what he sees as the decline of the native population:

> I have been struck with the steady decrease of the population, even during the short time I have been in Africa, on the coast and in the interior; but before I account for it, let me raise my voice in defence of the white man, who is accused of being the cause of it. Wherever he settles the aborigines are said to disappear. I admit that such is the case; but the decrease of the population had already taken place before the white man came, the white man noticed it but could not stop it.

Du Chaillu goes on to blame the decrease of the African population on the slave trade as continued by Portuguese and Negro agents, polygamy, barren women, high infant mortality rate, plagues, and witchcraft.

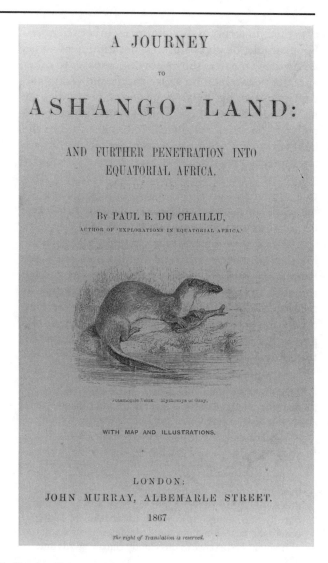

Frontispiece and title page for Du Chaillu's second book

Du Chaillu paternalistically proposes that the civilized peoples help the Africans in their struggle to survive:

> I believe that the negro may become a more useful member of mankind than he is at present, that he may be raised to a higher standard; but that, if left to himself, he will soon fall back into barbarism, for we have no example to the contrary. In his own country the efforts of the missionaries for hundreds of years have had no effect; the missionary goes away and the people relapse into barbarism. Though a people may be taught the arts and sciences known by more gifted nations, unless they have the power of progression in themselves, they must inevitably relapse in the course of time into their former state.

Du Chaillu concludes that since "of all the uncivilized races of men, the negro has been found to be the most tractable and the most docile," that "we ought therefore to be kind to him and try to elevate

him." Such an effort must be made despite the fact that Du Chaillu has "very little doubt" that "[the negro] will disappear in time from his land" and will "follow in the course of time the inferior races who have preceded him." With these somber admonitions Du Chaillu introduces a type of racist Darwinism into his prose and thus draws to a close his observations on life and death in equatorial Africa.

Du Chaillu began writing *A Journey To Ashango-Land* only after his report to the Royal Geographic Society proved successful. Convinced by Du Chaillu's many specimens, the members of the society accepted his new observations of African natural life as well as his modified opinions of the habits of the gorilla. Reassured by this encouraging reception, publisher John Murray urged Du Chaillu to write a book based on his journal, and Du Chaillu's friend,

George Bishop, invited him to stay at his residence in Twickenham for that purpose. H. W. Bates, noted explorer and author of *The Naturalist on the River Amazon* (1863), helped Du Chaillu arrange his notes and organize the book. After enduring two years of life in the wild, Du Chaillu experienced comfort and ease during the year 1866 while he wrote his narrative. When *A Journey To Ashango-Land* appeared in bookstores in 1867, it met with interest, some praise, and criticism.

To judge by the review of *A Journey To Ashango-Land* in the 11 April 1867 issue of *The Nation*, Du Chaillu's book received a lukewarm reception. After giving a plot summary of the text, the reviewer wearily opines, "On the whole, M. Du Chaillu's attempted journey was a great attempt and gallantly prosecuted, but not brought to a successful end. It has added something but not much to what we knew before." The reviewer admits that Du Chaillu's latitudinal and longitudinal measurements have improved the map of equatorial Africa and that he has clarified his previous descriptions of animals such as the ipi, the gorilla, and the chimpanzee. He further acknowledges that Du Chaillu "has done something toward dispelling what little of mystery still lingers over the tribes of Africa." But Du Chaillu's accomplishments—even his discovery and report of a tribe of Pygmies—were apparently not enough to excite the reviewer. Instead he looks forward to other explorers who, inspired by Du Chaillu's "industry and endurance," will travel across the African continent and make their journey "of value to the world."

In late 1867 Du Chaillu, now in his early to mid thirties, sailed from England to New York, where he made his residence at 42 East Thirtieth Street for the next four years. Upon his arrival Harper editors approached him with the idea of translating some of his African adventures into a book for children. Du Chaillu, who must have been disillusioned somewhat by the response to his first two books, agreed. In the second phase of his literary career Du Chaillu would write for a far less demanding audience—adolescent boys. His *Stories of the Gorilla Country: Narrated for Young People* (1867) was the first of nine financially successful books he wrote for children.

Free of the conventions of writing serious, scientific exploration narratives for adults, Du Chaillu in *Stories of the Gorilla Country* adopts a new persona, that of "friend Paul" or "Cousin Paul," who confides that he is here to guide his "dear young folks" through some of his adventures in Africa. As he explains in chapter 1, "In this book I have attempted to relate some of the incidents of life in Africa for the reading of young folks. In doing this I have kept no

chronological order, but have selected incidents and adventures here and there as they seem to be fitted for my purpose." Du Chaillu further appeals to his new audience by saying that he has noticed that "most intelligent boys like to read about the habits of wild animals, and the manners and way of life of savage man; and of such matters this book is composed." The success of Du Chaillu's first children's book was such that he did occasionally read aloud from it to the public. His biographer Michel Vaucaire cites one such reading that Du Chaillu offered on 31 May 1867 at the Board of Foreign Missions of the Presbyterian Church. Du Chaillu introduced himself with such "natural gaiety" and with the friendly announcement that "Cousin Paul is here!" that he won over the hearts of the children in the audience.

The weaknesses that critics noted in his *Explorations and Adventures in Equatorial Africa*—a too lively and dramatic writing style, the presentation of himself as a hero, his disregard for precise dates—become strengths in this narrative for children. Throughout *Stories of the Gorilla Country* Du Chaillu sets up dramatic situations in which he is a key performer and then speaks directly to his audience. This sort of narrative device draws the reader into the narrative and sets up a relationship of camaraderie between Du Chaillu and his young readers. For example, when Du Chaillu eagerly accepts the chance to accompany "savages" on a wildlife hunting expedition, he writes, "If you had been in my place, boys, would you not have felt the same? Would you have left the gorillas alone? I am sure you all shout at once, 'No! No!' Would you have let the elephants go unmolested in the forest? 'Certainly not,' will be your answer."

In addition to these invitations to join in the hunt on an imaginative level, Du Chaillu also invites his readers to experience the emotional and physical sensations of living in the wilds of Africa. While this sort of colorful and evocative writing would never have been acceptable in a scientific tract, it was essential for the sort of writing that would appeal to children. In one instance Du Chaillu reproduces the fears and nightmares that trouble all children when he relates his own experience of going to sleep in a strange place known as a potential home for scorpions:

So when I lay down on my pillow, which was merely a piece of wood, I looked to see if there were any scorpions upon it. I did not see any; but during the night, I awoke suddenly and started up. I thought I felt hundreds of them creeping over me, and that one had just stung me, and caused me to wake up. The sweat covered my body. I looked around and saw nothing but

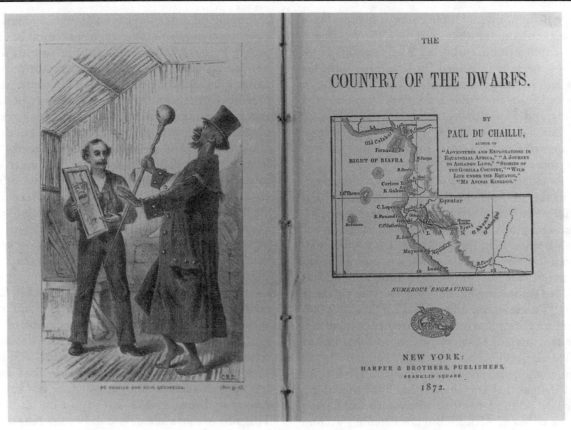

Frontispiece and title page for the first American edition of Du Chaillu's seventh book on Africa

sleeping people. There was no scorpion to be found. I must have been dreaming.

Du Chaillu's initial wariness at his sleeping quarters, followed by the images of "creeping" scorpions and sweat, generates a sympathetic shudder from the reader. Moreover, the short, simple statements that describe his awakening convincingly illustrate the dreamer's disorientation and then relief at discovering a safe reality. The reader is able to relax at the welcome words "I must have been dreaming."

Other dramatic events Du Chaillu relays in *Stories of the Gorilla Country* include killing a snake, shooting a gorilla, meeting a cannibal king, building a village and patriotically naming it Washington, and being offered several native wives as gifts. These exotic stories pale in comparison to his final tale of Tommy the baby gorilla. Du Chaillu spins a delightful yarn about capturing the young gorilla and attempting to domesticate it, only to find that Tommy is a juvenile delinquent who likes to steal food and drink hard liquor. After noting Tommy's escapades and sad death, Du Chaillu bids his readers "farewell till I come

again." And "come again" Du Chaillu did, for he followed *Stories of the Gorilla Country* with four more juvenile books describing his African adventures: *Wild Life Under the Equator* (1868), *Lost in the Jungle* (1869), *My Apingi Kingdom; with Life in the Great Sahara, and Sketches of the Chase of the Ostrich, Hyena, &c.* (1870), and *The Country of the Dwarfs* (1871).

Vaucaire observes that these five children's books were "of great importance in Du Chaillu's life. Their amazing popularity gave him a new reputation; he was no longer just an explorer, but a man of letters, beloved by thousands of readers. He had become that celebrated character, *l'ami Paul!*" Vaucaire is extravagant in his praise, but though Du Chaillu did not win any prizes for being a "man of letters," he certainly did receive financial remuneration and a new direction for his career. In each of the children's books succeeding *Stories of the Gorilla Country*, Du Chaillu became an increasingly assured writer; he also more frequently presented himself as the hero of his own story and showed more of a colonialist attitude toward West Africa, its native population, and its animals.

In *Wild Life Under the Equator* Du Chaillu takes an assertive stance with his "dear young folks," telling them in his first chapter that "I am going to try to make you travel with me in the wild country I have explored." The explorer's young followers will read of all manner of hardships, including hunger and stinging flies. And at the end of the book, Du Chaillu assures them, they will shout, "'What a glorious time we have had with our friend Paul!'"

Wild Life Under the Equator differs little from *Stories of the Gorilla Country* in that Du Chaillu continues to hunt gorillas, leopards, elephants, buffalos, and venomous serpents. He does, however, reveal more about the life of an explorer and his relationship with the natives. Of his work he tells his readers that he will carry home with him "gorillas, hippopotamus, manitee, *nshiego-mbouvé, koola-kamba,* no end of birds (more than two thousand), a great many monkeys, and the skins of several hundreds of animals." He emphasizes that he "had worked hard to kill them, and worked still harder to stuff them, hunting them during the day, and preparing their skins during the night."

Du Chaillu's view of the natives is clearly paternalistic as he observes, "How kind they were to me, how gentle! No children could have been more docile, and yet how fierce, how brave, when the day of battle or of danger came!" Despite this apparent sense of superiority, Du Chaillu is still able to acknowledge King Quengueza as "indeed one of the best friends I ever had anywhere." Ironically, another of Du Chaillu's acquaintances, King Ranpano, appears to exhibit a similar type of paternalistic attitude toward the explorer when he speaks of the feelings he and his tribe have for him: "We are people, we have a heart that feels, we love our white man, for he is the first that ever came to live among us." The native view of Du Chaillu is one of possession just as Du Chaillu's view of them is one of superiority.

Critical reviews of *Wild Life Under the Equator* were somewhat tongue-in-cheek. As the reviewer for the 24 December 1868 issue of *The Nation* remarks, "Nothing could better please adventurous youths than our explorer's narrations." After describing in great detail Du Chaillu's various encounters with wild beasts and wild men in Africa, the reviewer concludes that "All males not yet arrived at the critical or criticizing age will find *Wild Life Under the Equator* a work of fascination." After his encounters with critics for his adult books, such an audience was precisely what Du Chaillu desired.

The popularity of his first two children's books led Du Chaillu to go on the lecture circuit in Boston, Brooklyn, and New York to share his Afri-can experiences with his public. He describes the excitement accompanying these lectures in the first chapter of *Lost in the Jungle:* "Last spring, your friend Paul, not satisfied with writing for young folks, took it into his head to lecture before them." The author is happy to report his success. "Thousands of young folks came to your friend Paul's lectures," and at the lecture in which "friend Paul" actually wore "the old clothes he had worn in Africa" he caused quite a stir. After Du Chaillu volunteered to shake the hand of each and every child present, the "young hearers" rushed to the podium. Their "hearty" handshakes "gladdened the heart" of friend Paul; "he felt so happy as [their] small hands passed in and out of his!"

The positive, energetic contact between author and audience that Du Chaillu thrived on in his lectures is similar to the contact he attempts when he directly addresses the audience in his books. As with his previous two children's books, *Lost in the Jungle* extends a Whitmanesque invitation to the reader to join the author in his expedition. Du Chaillu guarantees that "We will have some very hard times when 'lost in the jungle'; we will be hungry and starving for many a day; we will see how curiously certain tribes live, what they eat and drink, how they build, and what they worship; and, before the end of our wanderings, you will see your friend Paul made KING over a strange people!" To prepare for such fun Du Chaillu offers a final exhortation to his readers, "Let us get ready to start. Let us prepare our rifles, guns, and revolvers, and take with us a large quantity of shoes, quinine, powder, bullets, shot, and lots of beads and other things to make presents to the kings and people we shall meet."

Stalking, hunting, and killing wildlife dominate the story line of *Lost in the Jungle.* As the reviewer for the 16 December 1869 issue of *The Nation* comments, Du Chaillu is "a little sanguinary in his dealings with the brutes which he comes upon in his travels, and kills and skins with a single-eyed ardor for the advancement of science which leads him to recount fearlessly a deal of butchery." The book's "sanguinary" tendencies are evident in its table of contents. For example, the eighth chapter bears the subtitle "See a beautiful Antelope.–Kill it.–," and the subtitle for the ninth chapter announces, "We hear the Cry of a young Gorilla.–Start to capture him.–Fight with 'his Father.'–We kill him.–Kill the Mother.–Capture of the Baby.–Strange Camp Scene." Attended by the three so-called savages, Querlaouen, Malaouen, and Gambo, Du Chaillu kills antelope, *manga* or manatee, and gorilla. Following his habit of naming new species after his

CAPTURE OF THE IPI.

SHOCKING THE ASHANGOS.

Illustrations from Du Chaillu's The Country of the Dwarfs *(1872)*

friends, Du Chaillu names the animal known as manga by the natives "manatus Oweni" after his "most esteemed friend, Professor Owen, of London."

Du Chaillu's spirited dedication to hunting, as manifested in his painting his face and his hands black so that he will appear the same color as his companions, often seems intermingled with an appreciation for animal life, a longing for self-restraint, and suppressed guilt over his actions. After spearing the manga Du Chaillu observes with some wonder, "I could not help thinking what queer animals were found on our globe." Upon seeing an antelope he confesses, "It was the most lovely and beautiful creature of the forest I had ever seen. I stopped. It seemed to me that I had not eyes big enough to admire it. Oh, I thought, it is too beautiful to be fired at and killed. How brilliant was his color!" In the next instant Du Chaillu admits, "I raised my gun almost in sorrow, but I felt that I must kill the beast, in order to bring its skin home; for I knew it was an animal that had never been seen before." And after he kills a baby gorilla's father and mother, he hears the baby howl and interprets the howl as an accusation: "You fellows have killed my mother."

In a rare moment of introspection Du Chaillu actually seems to empathize with the father gorilla and even sees his own resemblance to the creature: "What had he died for? He had died bravely defending his wife and baby from an enemy whom he knew had come to do them harm. He was right. May I and every man of us always have the same motive that big gorilla had!" Later he states, "I could not help feeling sorry. Here lay dead before me a wonderful beast, one of the most strange creatures of the forest God has created. His mate lay dead in another part of the forest, and their offspring was my prisoner." That night Du Chaillu records, "I could not sleep. That big gorilla was always before my eyes." Perhaps the reviewer for *The Nation* was correct in saying, "But we incline to think that his descriptions of his hunting adventures—his account of the shooting of the beautiful gazelle for its hide, and of his capturing the young gorilla which he had orphaned for the sake of the museum—will tend to excite as much pity and sympathy in the young reader as bloodthirstiness."

In *My Apingi Kingdom* Du Chaillu, or "Spirit," as he is called by the natives, is made king by the unanimous decision of the Apingi tribe: "Their king I was, and they respected me, and it was my aim to deserve their respect and love." And because he remembered "the good precepts" his mother had tried to teach him in his boyhood, he becomes a type of great white father to the tribe. Du Chaillu's pater-

nalism dictates the language he uses to describe his benevolent rule: "I cultivated them with truthfulness and kindness of heart. I took care of their sick, I loved their children, I prevented their women from being beaten; I made them feel they could rely upon my word, so that when I promised a thing would be done they knew it would be done. I was firm at the same time. I had to be politic, and there were customs and superstitions which I disliked, but which I knew time and education alone could destroy." His repeated declarative sentences and his constant use of the pronoun *I* indicate Du Chaillu's sense of self-importance and of power in undertaking his new royal role. Moreover, the statements reveal his innate feelings of superiority: Du Chaillu knows best.

Throughout *My Apingi Kingdom* Du Chaillu enacts what Mary Louise Pratt in *Imperial Eyes: Studies in Travel Writing and Transculturation* (1992) has termed "the monarch-of-all-I-survey" role. Under his direction the tribe creates a personal fenced-in hunting ground for Du Chaillu: "wild beasts of all kinds were running to and fro, amad with terror. Hyenas, porcupines, black wild boars, gazelles, antelopes, wild cats, and even snakes were driven helter-skelter within the inclosure." The animals had no chance against Du Chaillu and the Apingi spears: "the slaughter was terrific," and soon "all the game worth killing had been killed, and whatever was too large for a single white man to carry was cut up in small pieces." Thus does King Du Chaillu master his territory.

Du Chaillu does not hesitate to use his guns to impress the tribe. When he wants to get the Apingis' attention, he merely fires his rifles and revolvers in the air until the people sing, "'Oh, Spirit, oh Spirit, thou art our king. . . . Oh Spirit, oh Spirit, do not send disease and death among us.'" On a visit to another village of his Apingi kingdom he tells how he used his ability with firearms to play a godlike role and intervene in a quarrel:

> "Apingi, what do you mean? There must be no war among yourselves. Woe to the man who brings on war in the Apingi country, for I will slay him. I will kill him as sure as I kill that bird." For, luckily, just as I was speaking, a bird flew near the hut where I stood, and gave me the chance to impress the natives with a sense of my skill and power. I shot it flying, and it fell stone-dead just at the feet of chief Andeko. A wild shout of fear was heard through the crowd.

Such a display enforces Du Chaillu's image as dreaded king.

Du Chaillu's imperialistic approach to his tribe is clear in his plans to build a palm-oil factory to increase trade and establish a school for the pro-

FISHERMAN CARRYING A FISH.

THE MONGEFOSS, IN ROMSDALEN.

BERGEN.

Illustrations from Du Chaillu's The Land of the Midnight Sun *(1881)*

motion of civilization were he to remain king. He believes the people must be taught how to read and write so that "in the course of time, from their own free will . . . they might destroy their idols, cast away their superstitions, and believe in God as the great Ruler of the universe." After his lofty rhetoric about civilization and God, Du Chaillu undercuts his vision by humorously imagining that none of the above would occur if he should bring a blonde-haired, blue-eyed wife back from the United States to rule as his queen; he is sure the natives would worship her, like Du Chaillu, as an awe-inspiring spirit.

The final demonstration of colonialism in *My Apingi Kingdom* occurs on New Year's Day 1859 when a weary Du Chaillu makes his way up a hill and ties an American flag to the tallest tree there. He and his Apingi companions watched as the flag "floated in the breeze" and then "gave three cheers for the Star-spangled banner." Although his feet were bleeding and he was in great pain, Du Chaillu says that the sight of the flag gave him "new courage," and he "fired a salute of three guns."

Such a brave salute did not greet Du Chaillu's next children's book, *The Country of the Dwarfs*. In a review in the 21 December 1871 issue of *The Nation* the critic seems bored with the author's approach. He identifies *The Country of the Dwarfs* as "another of M. Du Chaillu's books made over and adapted to the juvenile mind" and remarks that as in the previous books for children "we have M. Paul Du Chaillu again, quite the same Paul that we have previously seen landing on the coast of Equatorial Africa, amid cries of 'Chally, Chally,' from negro tribes and transports of general joy."

While Du Chaillu does recycle material, he varies its presentation by emphasizing different parts of his story. As in *A Journey to Ashango-Land,* Du Chaillu tells of bestowing European clothing and gifts upon the African King Quengueza, but here a garish illustration of the act is also provided, and the description is curtailed. In *The Country of the Dwarfs* Du Chaillu details his adventures taking photographs, an activity he only alludes to in *A Journey to Ashango-Land*. Du Chaillu's attitude toward the natives is also unchanged, though he does vary his approach. Instead of using firearms to awe the tribe as he did in *My Apingi Kingdom,* he amazes the Pygmies with Western inventions such as the music box and the electric battery.

In *The Country of the Dwarfs* Du Chaillu is more self-conscious about his role as a writer than he had previously shown. While sitting before a campfire and reading the works of Herodotus aloud to the Ashango tribe, Du Chaillu tells them that he intends to see the "dwarfish men" that the Greek historian mentions. Amazed at the book and knowing that Du Chaillu writes in a journal every night, the tribesmen cry, "'Oh! oh! It is no wonder that the white man forgets nothing. Chally, will what you write about the strange things we see be remembered in the same manner with what that man Herodotus wrote?'" Du Chaillu seriously replies, "'I do not know. If the white people think that what we saw is worthy of presentation, it will be remembered; if not, it will be forgotten.'" The incident seems contrived in its staginess, but it is hardly surprising that Du Chaillu, always the hero of his own story, should be so concerned with the fate of his work.

Du Chaillu's book is most notable for his vivid descriptions of the Pygmies, or dwarfs. His first encounter with a Pygmy is full of comedy and drama. After approaching a dwarf encampment Du Chaillu tries to coax its inhabitants out with strings of beads. Most of the dwarfs flee, but a few scurry into huts. He recounts his excitement upon finding a Pygmy in one of the darkened huts: "Sweeping my arm from left to right, at first I touched an empty bed, composed of three sticks; then, feeling carefully, I moved my arm gradually toward the right, when—hallo! what do I feel? A leg! which I immediately grabbed above the ankle, and a piercing shriek startled me. It was the leg of a human being, and that human being a Dwarf! I had got hold of a Dwarf!"

Du Chaillu then proceeds to describe the unhappy captured dwarf and her comrades, discovering likenesses to the white man, the Negro, and the chimpanzee:

> They had prominent cheek-bones, and were yellow, their faces being exactly of the same color as the chimpanzee; the palms of their hands were almost as white as those of white people; they seemed well-proportioned, but their eyes had an untamable wildness that struck me at once; they had thick lips and flat noses, like the negroes; their foreheads were low and narrow, and their cheek-bones prominent; and their hair, which grew in little, short tufts, was black, with a reddish tinge.

By likening individual aspects of the dwarf to comparable aspects found in whites, blacks, and chimpanzees, Du Chaillu tries to render the unfamiliar familiar. However, when Du Chaillu blends the three together into one creature and points out the "wildness" of that creatures' eyes, he succeeds in making the dwarf an alien and uncomfortable reflection of humanity. The dwarf becomes one of the "strange things" worthy of being recorded and remembered by book-buying white people.

By spring 1871 Du Chaillu had apparently had quite enough of reliving his African adventures in books for children. In the prime of life, thirty-six or forty years old, he was a wealthy, famous man who had proved himself to be a successful author and lecturer. He might easily have decided to marry and remain settled in New York, but instead Du Chaillu chose to leave his home for seven years to travel throughout Scandinavia. His reason for choosing to explore Scandinavia after Africa is unknown. Perhaps Du Chaillu felt he had nothing else to prove in another exploration of Africa, or perhaps because he suffered from fevers acquired in the hot African climate, he preferred cooler temperatures. Perhaps he simply desired to encounter people, animals, and geography that differed completely from those of equatorial Africa. Vaucaire suggests that he had seen Scandinavian immigrants in America and "had been impressed by their physical perfection and almost epic qualities of appearance and character." Whatever the reason, Du Chaillu's travels in Scandinavia mark the beginning of the second half of his life of exploration and writing. On 1 June 1871 he left behind the heart of darkness for a sojourn in the land of the midnight sun.

Du Chaillu spent the first weeks of June in Sweden wherein he explored Stockholm and met with King Carl XV of Sweden and Norway, who had read *Explorations and Adventures in Equatorial Africa*. Then on 18 June he boarded a steamer that would carry him across the Baltic Sea to Haparanda, a small city that marked the end of the steamer line. Du Chaillu visited the farthermost reaches of Scandinavia—especially areas where no outsider had gone before—to study the people and their ways of living and animal and vegetable life as well as the region's geological and geographical features. Most of all he wanted to see the midnight sun. He toured as much as he could before business required him to sail back to England and then to the United States. By the end of November 1871 he was back in Norway to resume his excursion. He stayed in Scandinavia on and off for the next seven years, save for brief trips to Gotland, an island in the Baltic known for its Viking heritage, and Europe.

Du Chaillu traveled throughout Norway, Sweden, and Lapland by boat, horsecar, reindeer sleigh, skis, and on foot. Usually a native guide would accompany him on his zigzag routes across fjords, lakes, islands, mountains, and glaciers. Because Du Chaillu sought out rural areas, he found resting places at various farmhouses. He enjoyed his stays with these farm families because they gave him the chance to study the people and their culture in a more intimate setting. He found himself accepted by the families, welcomed into their homes as a friend, and included in their work and in their celebrations. Indeed, Du Chaillu felt Scandinavia to be the spiritual home he had not found in France, England, the United States, or Africa.

Du Chaillu left Scandinavia in 1878 and for the next three years shuttled back and forth between residences in New York, Paris, Twickenham, and Denmark. During this time Murray asked him to write a book on his Scandinavian travels, and Du Chaillu agreed. He labored on the book for three years, simultaneously composing the English and French editions, and by the summer of 1881 was checking his proofs and beginning research on a book on the Viking age. *The Land of the Midnight Sun* was published in two volumes in October 1881.

Reviews of *The Land of the Midnight Sun* were, for the most part, favorable. The reviewer for *The Nation* of 8 December 1881 recommended the work for a general audience rather than for scholars: "The work is a thorough, instructive, entertaining and systematic description of the Scandinavian peasants and their physical environment, and as such we most heartily recommend it." While the reviewer notes that no historian or archaeologist would find anything new in the text, he still compliments Du Chaillu on his willingness to learn the Scandinavian languages, meet the people, and describe scenes and scenery well.

While *The Edinburgh Review* was more critical of *The Land of the Midnight Sun,* it tempers its criticism with a good dose of humor and a general endorsement of Du Chaillu's efforts. The reviewer begins by finding fault with Du Chaillu's organization of his material and his apparent inability to include the precise dates and activities of his travel. The reviewer commented on the threads Du Chaillu left dangling, such as when he reports traveling to Haparanda for the sole purpose of seeing the midnight sun at midsummer: "At the end of that month M. du Chaillu reached Haparanda, though, with that innate modesty which refuses to let the vulgar pry into his private devotions, he does not tell us whether he did succeed in worshipping the sun at midnight on midsummer night in 1871. Perhaps he did, perhaps he did not: who can tell?" He then takes Du Chaillu to task for attempting to express his feelings about the midnight sun in poetry:

Chapter I. vol.1. This the reader need not read. It is poetry, and like the American who, in reporting one of the lamented Dean Stanley's lectures, threw down his pencil when he quoted poetry with the remark that poetry was never admitted into the journal which he represented except in obituary notices, we venture to say that, whatever opinion we may have of M. du Chaillu's prose, we think nothing at all of his poetry, and when we come to any of it we throw down the volume in disgust.

The reviewer then proceeds to poke fun at Du Chaillu's personality and experiences by focusing on Du Chaillu's eye for women, his rhapsodies upon nature, and his participation in a Swedish bath. The critic observes that

all through this book, besides the worship of the sun, the worship of another luminary, which may be called the sun of the domestic system, is most apparent. M. du Chaillu has a keen eye for female beauty, and it is wonderful how he discovers pretty girls at every turn. Their light hair, deep blue eyes, rosy complexions, and pearly skins constantly make deep impressions on his heart, and we are convinced, had he devoted himself entirely to society, he would have been a lady- instead of a gorilla-killer.

As for Du Chaillu's appreciation of nature, the reviewer complains, "Nature is good to all of us, but to M. du Chaillu her bounties are excessive. Her manifestations to him are always superlative. If the wind howls to him, no mortal ever heard it howl so loud." And in regard to Du Chaillu's willingness to take a Swedish bath *en famille,* the critic amusedly observes, "when the whole levee had assembled, Du Chaillu followed them in the same scanty costume [nude], which allowed the manly proportions of the great gorilla-hunter to be plainly visible to the undraped eye."

Despite the enjoyment the reviewer takes at Du Chaillu's expense, he does conclude favorably. He acknowledges that Du Chaillu "is a hard traveller and a keen observer, though we do not think travelling in Lapland is so hard as he represents it": "Be that as it may, we now shake hands with Paul, hoping that he will visit many other lands, and leave them as amusing and self-complacent as he has shown himself in the *Land of the Midnight Sun.*"

Between 1881 and 1889 Du Chaillu studied Scandinavian history and traveled with his friend George Taylor to Copenhagen. Du Chaillu then traveled alone to Norway and Iceland to gather material for writing *The Viking Age.* In between these trips Du Chaillu made his home with friends living in New York, Chicago, and Paris. The Chicago journalist John Anderson and his family kept a room in their house designated as "Uncle Paul's

room" for whenever the explorer happened to pay a visit. As Vaucaire notes, "Du Chaillu never attempted to establish a real home"; instead he became the "ideal bachelor" and a "most beloved and amusing guest," charming his friends and acquaintances with stories told in a sly mixture of English and French. His visits, however, were not purely social, for he spent much of his time alone in his designated room writing and correcting proofs of *The Viking Age,* his second book on Scandinavia, the ninth book he had written, and perhaps the most ambitious work of his career.

The massive two-volume works covers all aspects of Viking life: mythology, crafts, rituals, marriage, education, superstitions, laws, weapons, war, trade, and dress. Du Chaillu bases much of his commentary on Viking life and beliefs on the Icelandic sagas and Eddas, bog finds, ground finds, and materials found in various museums. His extraordinary curiosity about the Vikings may have stemmed from his interest in colonization and the transmission of character from one people to another. In the preface Du Chaillu explains that the questions that led to his study of the Vikings include "how is it that over every region of the globe the spread of the English-speaking people and of their language far exceeds that of all the other European nations combined?" and "why is it that, wherever the English-speaking people have settled, or are at this day found, even in small numbers, they are far more energetic, daring, adventurous, and prosperous, and understand the art of self-government and of ruling alien peoples far better than other colonising nations?" The colonialist attitudes he exhibited in his works on Africa rise to the fore again in this study of the Vikings.

Du Chaillu answers these questions at the end of his preface. He asserts that based on its ability to expand, colonize, and rule, England is the premier country. Du Chaillu attributes English success in colonizing and spreading their culture to their "remarkable energy," bravery, and love of conquest—characteristics inherited not from the Romans, who he claims showed no such qualities, but from the Vikings. While Du Chaillu alludes to this argument from time to time in his narrative, he fails to maintain it throughout the course of the two volumes. Occasionally he will attempt to link the two cultures through an observation, as when he asserts that "to this day the love of athletic games is one of the characteristics of their [the Vikings] direct descendants, the English people." Such parallels do little to convince the reader of his argument and become lost amid his descriptions of Viking customs, ships, physical appearance, and lengthy quotations from the sagas.

Reviews of the time praised Du Chaillu for his immense research efforts (much of which he paid for himself) but nevertheless found his overall thesis weak. The reviewer for *The Nation* of 9 January 1890 asserts that Du Chaillu either did not have at his disposal all the facts that might have modified his argument or misinterpreted the facts he did have. According to the reviewer, what is valuable about *The Viking Age* are the translations of Old Norse sagas which shed light on the details of everyday life in ancient Scandinavia.

A friend of Du Chaillu, Rasmus B. Anderson, offered a more enthusiastic endorsement of the work in the December 1889 *Dial*. Rather than focusing on Du Chaillu's stated argument, Anderson examines Du Chaillu's portrayal of the Vikings and insists that his depiction should set to rest any criticism of the Vikings as being a barbaric people. He concludes his review by declaring: "We are indebted to Du Chaillu for placing within reach of the reading public so many facts concerning the hardy Viking. He deserves great credit for the countless quotations from the grand old sagas and eddas, and his publishers are to be congratulated for the elegant appearance of the work. The illustrations alone are well worth the price of the two volumes. Du Chaillu's many old friends and admirers will cheerfully forgive him any shortcomings in his work."

Du Chaillu welcomed in the new year of 1890 by going to Philadelphia to live with publisher George W. Childs and his wife. Here "Prince Paul," as Mrs. Childs called Du Chaillu, completed an abridged version of his first and last books on Africa and published them together as *Adventures in the Great Forest of Equatorial Africa and the Country of the Dwarfs* (1890). He also contributed the article "The Great Equatorial Forest" to the *Fortnightly Review*. Despite many invitations to lecture about his travels, Du Chaillu declined them all and instead satisfied his social nature by attending receptions, balls, dinners, and theaters with friends.

In 1891 Du Chaillu moved from the lively sociability of Philadelphia to a more quiet hospitality in Boston with his close friends Judge and Mrs. Daly. He celebrated the twenty-fifth anniversary of his return from Africa by accepting an honorary silver cup from the American Geographic Society. He left Boston in 1893 for health reasons and journeyed to Hot Springs, Arkansas, to take a cure. Du Chaillu then resumed a busy schedule in Chicago, where he stayed with Anderson and

wrote a few newspaper pieces on the Chicago World's Fair for the *Chicago Herald*. During the time between 1891 and 1893 Du Chaillu also occupied himself with writing yet another children's book, *Ivar the Viking: A Romantic History based upon Authentic Facts of the Third and Fourth Centuries* (1893).

In the introduction to *Ivar the Viking* Du Chaillu asserts that through the life of Ivar he tried to show what it was like to grow up among the Norse in the third and fourth centuries, touching on Norse customs, education, dwellings, worship, athletics, women, marriages, duels, and sports. "In a word," he claims, "the book is a lifelike picture of the period." Du Chaillu also used his introduction to defend his previous work *The Viking Age* from criticism it had received in regard to his assertions that the Vikings, not the Anglo-Saxons, were the true ancestors of the English people. Reviewers of *Ivar the Viking,* however, largely dismissed Du Chaillu's claims about England's Viking heritage and chose to acknowledge the research efforts that went into the book. As the critic for the *Catholic World* of December 1893 observes, "it is only fair to the travelled and erudite author to say that he has produced a work of much value, both from a literary and antiquarian point of view, and has thrown a flood of light, as the result of his patient researches, upon the mode of life, the religious practices, and the social conditions of the early inhabitants of Ultima Thule."

At the publication time of *Ivar the Viking,* Du Chaillu was either fifty-eight or sixty-two years old and felt that he could set aside time for quiet reading and more visits with friends. One such friend, the last great friend of his life, was former chief justice Daly of Sag Harbor, Long Island, New York. When the judge's wife died in 1894, she left a legacy of $40,000 to Du Chaillu on condition that he never leave her husband. Du Chaillu accepted the inheritance gladly; he and the judge were congenial souls, and the judge's library, full of rare and scientific volumes, was one of Du Chaillu's great joys. He spent many hours in Daly's library reading and preparing lectures on geographical subjects for audiences at Hunter's College in New York and the Peabody Institute in Boston. Despite this comfortable domestic arrangement, both men felt the urge to travel. Ten years older than Du Chaillu and in ailing health, Judge Daly still insisted upon sailing to Sweden with him. The two men managed to complete their journey and return safely to New York in November of 1895.

Between 1895 and 1899 Du Chaillu maintained a busy schedule of lecturing at various

"The man had to use all his strength."

"He sat on his haunches and looked at us, uttering a tremendous growl."

Illustrations from Du Chaillu's The Land of the Long Night *(1899)*

Scandinavian societies in Chicago and even campaigning on behalf of presidential candidate William McKinley in 1896. He complained from time to time of severe sinus pain and attacks of bronchitis but refused to let his physical health slow down his mental activity. Always a savvy businessman, he wrote four books for children during this time—books whose publications he purposefully spread out so that his name would continue to be in the press, thus ensuring him of some income in his later years. These books include *The Land of the Long Night* (1899), dedicated to Judge Daly and an adaptation of his adventures in *Land of the Midnight Sun*; *The World of the Great Forest: How Animals, Birds, Reptiles, Insects Talk, Think, Work, and Live* (1900), told from the points of view of African animals; *King Mombo* (1902), an account of Du Chaillu's boyhood adventures in Africa in which he continues to amaze the natives with Western goods; and *In African Forest and Jungle* (1903).

When Judge Daly died on 20 October 1899, Du Chaillu felt the loss keenly. The judge had been not only an intellectual companion but also a father figure to the explorer. Du Chaillu stayed for a while in the house they had shared, but soon the emptiness became too much, and he could not bear to be reminded of his loss and of his own old age and impending death. Consequently, in July 1900 Du Chaillu set off once again for Sweden to revive his spirits. While this trip momentarily satisfied his need for activity and motion, Du Chaillu felt the lack of a greater purpose. After much thought he decided that he needed a new project to work on, choosing Russia as his subject. He planned to learn the Russian language and then wander through the Russian villages, meet with their inhabitants, absorb their customs, and write a final book on the scale of *The Land of the Midnight Sun*.

On 27 June 1901 Du Chaillu set sail from New York on the *Augusta Victoria* bound for Saint Petersburg. He had with him the backing of Scribner's Publishers and his own excitement at beginning a new adventure. He arrived in Russia in the midst of Czar Nicholas II's crackdown on the free press; any protesters against government policy at home and abroad were sent to Siberia. Upon seeing this unrest Du Chaillu hastily changed his travel plans. Instead of going into Russia's more rural areas to meet with the peasants, Du Chaillu decided to visit the big cities of Moscow and Saint Petersburg and meet with citizens of all social classes. During this time he wrote many letters to friends in which he described the people he encountered, the unrest in the cities,

and the prisons. He decided to spend a month and a half in Moscow in November 1902 and midwinter in the province of Archangel. He then traveled north among the Samoyedes in the spring.

Du Chaillu succeeded in making these journeys and continuing his research. On 30 April 1903 he was at the Hôtel de France in Saint Petersburg considering his next stage of writing and research. However, Du Chaillu suffered a stroke and died in the Alexandra Hospital later that evening. While the American ambassador to Russia cabled Du Chaillu's friends in New York for final burial instructions, the Imperial Geographical Society requested the privilege of making all funeral arrangements for Du Chaillu should his body stay in Russia. For a short time Du Chaillu was laid to rest in the Russian cemetery reserved for distinguished men of science and literature. His final resting place was, however, the Woodlawn Cemetery in New York, where he was interred on 25 June 1903.

Obituary notices appeared immediately in such newspapers as the *New York Sun, The New York Times,* and the *New York Tribune* as well as in the journals *Scientific American* and *National Geographic Magazine. The Lamp* of June 1903 even published extracts from Du Chaillu's letters from Russia and included a preface that served as a type of obituary. Here he is remembered as an enthusiastic man whose exuberance was "exhilarating, because it was so genuine, so sound, essentially, and so full of kindliness and fraternal feeling. His unusual good sense formed with even his liveliest enthusiasms an unusual and unusually attractive combination that made him friends everywhere and of all kinds of people."

Other obituaries, no less praiseworthy, focused on Du Chaillu's exploration and scientific achievements. The 9 May 1903 *Scientific American* notes the controversy Du Chaillu excited with his initial reports of the African gorilla and states that he "never overcame the effects of this defamation and vilification, and although he lived to enjoy many honors, he did not reap the full reward due to his achievements." The *National Geographic Magazine* of July 1903 also remembers Du Chaillu's controversial African work by saying that his *Explorations and Adventures in Equatorial Africa* "was greeted with shouts of laughter and derision from one end of the African continent to the other. Mr and Mrs and Miss Gorilla was the common jest, and the name Du Chaillu became a byword for a fanciful storyteller." Nonetheless, the magazine pays tribute to Du Chaillu's exploration efforts and notes that the Geographic Society was the last place Du Chaillu lectured prior to his Russia trip, and it was the first place he was to have visited upon returning from Russia. The 1 May 1903 *New York Daily Tribune* also reports the criticism which the "little but strong limbed man of indomitable energy" received over his gorilla encounters but states that "the truth of his assertions was fully confirmed afterward."

As the obituaries suggest, Paul Belloni Du Chaillu's claim to fame was that of the gorilla discoverer whose vivid prose describing that creature evoked both great interest and doubt from his readers. His strength as a travel writer is not in asserting and maintaining a thesis but rather in conveying a keen sense of people, personality, situation, animals, and place. His African adventures for children, featuring the heroic "friend Paul," make for consistently dramatic, entertaining reading. His work also manifests the imperialist and colonialist impulses of his time.

Biography:
Michel Vaucaire, *Paul Du Chaillu: Gorilla Hunter, Being the Extraordinary Life and Adventures of Paul Du Chaillu, as Recounted for the House of Harper, his Ancient Publishers by his Young Compatriot,* translated by Emily Pepper Watts (New York: Harper, 1930).

Reference:
"Paul du Chaillu," *National Geographic Magazine,* 14 (July 1903): 282–285.

Papers:
The major collection of Du Chaillu's papers is held by the Houghton Library, Harvard University.

Horace Greeley

(3 February 1811 – 29 November 1872)

Martha I. Pallante
Youngstown State University

See also the Greeley entries in *DLB 3: Antebellum Writers in New York and the South* and *DLB 43: American Newspaper Journalists, 1690–1872.*

BOOKS: *An Address before the Literary Societies of Hamilton College, July 23, 1844* (Boston: Andrews Prentiss & Studley, 1844);

Protection and Free Trade: The Question Stated and Considered (New York: Greeley & McElrath, 1844);

The Tariff as It Is, Compared with the Substitute Proposed by Its Adversaries in the Bill Reported to the U.S. House of Representatives by Gen. McKay of N.C. from the Committee of Ways and Means (New York: Greeley & McElrath, 1844);

Association Discussed; or, The Socialism of the Tribune Examined. Being a Controversy between the New York Tribune and the Courier and Enquirer, by Greeley and Henry J. Raymond (New York: Harper, 1847);

Hints Toward Reforms, in Lectures, Addresses and Other Writing (New York: Harper, 1850; enlarged edition, New York & London: Fowlers & Wells, 1853)—includes "Alcoholic Liquors" and "The Crystal Palace and Its Lessons";

Glances at Europe: In a Series of Letters from Great Britain, France, Italy, Switzerland, &c., during the Summer of 1851. Including Notices of the Great Exhibition, or World's Fair (New York: Dewitt & Davenport, 1851);

Why I Am a Whig: Reply to an Inquiring Friend (New York: *Tribune* office, 1852);

What the Sister Arts Teach as to Farming. An Address before the Indiana State Agricultural Society, at Its Annual Fair, Lafayette, October 13th, 1853 (New York: Fowlers & Wells, 1853);

A History of the Struggle for Slavery Extension or Restriction in the United States, from the Declaration of Independence to the Present Day. Mainly Compiled and Condensed from the Journals of Congress and Other Official Records, and Showing the Vote by Yeas and Nays on the Most Important Divisions in Either House (New York: Dix, Edwards, 1856);

Horace Greeley

Aunt Sally, Come Up! or, The Nigger Sale (London: Ward & Lock, 1859);

An Overland Journey from New York to San Francisco in the Summer of 1859 (New York: C. M. Saxton, Barker / San Francisco: H. H. Bancroft, 1860);

The American Conflict: A History of the Great Rebellion in the United States of America, 1860–'65; Its Causes, Incidents, and Results: Intended to Exhibit Especially Its Moral and Political Phases, with the Drift and Progress of American Opinion Respecting Human Slavery from 1776 to the Close of the War for the Union,

2 volumes (Hartford: O. D. Case / Chicago: G. & C. W. Sherwood, 1864–1866);

An Address on Success in Business, Delivered before the Students of Packard's Bryant & Stratton New York Business College, by Hon. Horace Greeley, at the Large Hall of the Cooper Union, November 11, 1867 (New York: S. S. Packard, 1867);

Recollections of a Busy Life: Including Reminiscences of American Politics and Politicians, from the Opening of the Missouri Contest to the Downfall of Slavery; to which are added Miscellanies: "Literature as a Vocation," "Poets and Poetry," "Reforms and Reformers," "A Defense of Protection," etc., etc., Also, A Discussion with Robert Dale Owen of the Law of Divorce (New York: J. B. Ford, 1868);

Essays Designed to Elucidate the Sciences of Political Economy, while Serving to Explain and Defend the Policy of Protection to Home Industry, as a System of National Cooperation for the Elevation of Labor (Philadelphia: Porter & Coates, 1869);

What I Know of Farming: A Series of Brief and Plain Expositions of Practical Agriculture as an Art Based upon Science (New York: C. W. Carleton, 1871);

Mr. Greeley's Letters from Texas and the Lower Mississippi: To Which Are Added His Address to the Farmers of Texas, and His Speech on His Return to New York, June 12, 1871 (New York: *Tribune* office, 1871);

The True Issues of the Presidential Campaign. Speeches of Horace Greeley during His Western Trip and at Portland, Maine. Also, Ex-President Mahan's Letters (New York: Tribune Association, 1872).

OTHER: William Atkinson, *Principles of Political Economy: or, The Laws of the Formation of National wealth, Developed by Means of the Christian Law of Government. Being the Substance of a Case Delivered to the Hand-Loom Weavers' Commission,* introduction by Greeley (New York: Greeley & McElrath / New Orleans: Norman, Steele, 1843);

Epes Sargeant, *The Life and Public Services of Henry Clay, down to 1848,* edited and completed by Greeley (Philadelphia: Porter & Coates, 1852);

S. Margaret Fuller, *Literature and Art,* introduction by Greeley (Philadelphia: Porter & Coates, 1852);

Art and Industry as Represented in the Exhibition at the Crystal Palace, New York–1853–4: Showing the Progress and State of the Various Useful and Esthetic Pursuits. From the New York Tribune, edited by Greeley (New York: Redfield, 1853);

A Political Textbook for 1860: Comprising a Brief View of Presidential Nominations and Elections including All the National Platforms ever yet Adopted; also, A His-

tory of the Struggle respecting Slavery in the Territories, and of the Action of Congress as to the Freedom of the Public Lands, with the Most Notable Speeches and Letters of Messrs. Lincoln, Douglas, Bell, Cass, Seward, Everett, Breckenridge, H. V. Johnson, etc., etc., Touching the Questions of the Day; and Returns of All Presidential Elections Since 1836, compiled by Greeley and John F. Cleveland (New York: Tribune Association, 1860);

The Tribune Almanac for the Years 1838 to 1868, Inclusive, edited by Greeley (New York: *New York Tribune,* 1868);

Charles T. Congdon, ed., *Tribune Essays: Leading Articles Contributed to the New York Tribune, 1857–63,* introduction by Greeley (New York: Redfield, 1869);

"The Tariff, A Protection to Manufacturers," in *The Great Industries of the United States: Being an Historical Summary of the Origin, Growth, and Perfection of the Chief Industrial Arts of this Country,* by Greeley and others (Hartford, Chicago & Cincinnati: J. B. Burr & Hyde, 1873).

Horace Greeley is one of the most discussed and memorable figures of nineteenth-century America. In his career as a journalist and editor for the *New York Tribune* and as a reformer promoting abolition and temperance, he used the power of his pen and his oratorical skills to inform and influence his audiences. As Don C. Seitz asserts in the foreword to his *Horace Greeley: Founder of the New York Tribune* (1926), "No rival American journalist ever created an influence that penetrated so deeply."

Perhaps the deepest impression Greeley made on American culture is his famous exhortation to "Go West, Young Man, go West"–a phrase he borrowed from an article in the *Terre Haute Express.* Greeley's advice concerned the future development of the country–its Manifest Destiny–and had nothing to do with becoming a tourist, for Greeley was more a worker than a traveler. His one book about his travels in the United States, *An Overland Journey from New York to San Francisco in the Summer of 1859* (1860), originated in a trip he took to campaign for a transcontinental railroad.

Greeley's only book about his travels abroad, *Glances at Europe: In a Series of Letters from Great Britain, France, Italy, Switzerland, &c., during the Summer of 1851. Including Notices of the Great Exhibition, or World's Fair* (1851), also was the result of a trip that arose from his position as editor of the *Tribune.* Greeley would not have made such a trip for mere pleasure. Henry Luther Stoddard in *Horace Greeley: Printer, Editor, Crusader* (1946) asserts that Greeley "turned to his greatest adventure reluctantly."

The Tribune *building during Greeley's editorship*

Greeley was born on 3 February 1811 and died on 29 November 1872. During his sixty-one years he lived a life of contrasts and extremes. His rise from poverty to prominence represented the prototype for the late nineteenth-century rags-to-riches stories of Horatio Alger. The son of a failed New England farmer from Amherst, New Hampshire, Zaccheus Greeley, and his wife, Mary Woodburn Greeley, he began his career as a printer's apprentice for the *Northern Spectator* in East Poultney, Vermont, in 1826. The sixteen-year-old Greeley chose to remain behind with the printer when his bankrupt father decided to start fresh in western Pennsylvania. Although he had his parents' consent, Greeley received no encouragement or aid from them.

Greeley labored the next fifteen years to master the newspaper business. He worked as a general employee and ultimately as a printer for several newspapers, including the *Erie Gazette* in Pennsylvania and the *Evening Post,* the *Spirit of the Times,* and the *Morning Post* in New York. His first chance to work as an editor occurred in 1834 for *The New Yorker,* which he and Jonas Winchester founded. He served in similar capacities with the *Jeffersonian* and the *Log Cabin,* which he and his partners ultimately

merged into the *New York Tribune* in 1841. Describing his intention in a 10 April 1841 letter to his partner Thomas McElrath, Greeley said he wanted to produce "a journal removed alike from servile partisanship on one hand, and from gagged and mincing neutrality on the other." Erik Lunde argues that Greeley's work endures the test of time because "his best efforts retain a spark and remain remarkably well balanced and judicious in comment . . . superior in incisive comment, intellectual challenge, diction and effective analysis."

The papers Greeley edited boldly put forward his political views. They supported first Whig and later Republican agendas and candidates. The *Tribune* supported his successful bid for a seat in the House of Representatives as a Whig in 1848 and his unsuccessful campaign as a liberal Republican candidate for the presidency in 1872. The paper promoted Greeley's abolitionist and temperance ideologies in the face of harsh criticism and also expounded the value of western expansion and commercial development as the answer to Americans' collective and personal woes.

Greeley's strong views often led to controversy. He was one of the most vocal advocates of abolition and the war efforts of the Union during the Civil War but stood against the radical Republicans' desire to punish the South in its aftermath. He went so far as to sign the bail bond that allowed for the release of Jefferson Davis from prison. Believing the time to heal had come, Greeley saw his action as consistent with his earlier efforts to maintain the integrity of the republic. The public and his critics saw it otherwise and chastised him for his efforts.

Although Greeley was successful professionally, disappointment often marked his personal life. His marriage to Mary Y. Cheney in 1836 began with hopeful prospects, but those soon faded as his wife suffered from a series of chronic illnesses. Greeley also lived to see the deaths of five of his seven children. Greeley professed to love his family, but he was devoted first to his work and frequently neglected them to fulfill the obligations of his public life. He became a wealthy man, but as Gamaliel Bradford contends in a sketch of Greeley in *As God Made Them: Portraits of Some Nineteenth Century Americans* (1929), "money meant little to him, because he lived sparingly and hardly and had no taste for spending." Bradford describes Greeley as "an instinctive Puritan" who had little patience for either the frivolous or the purely social.

Greeley interspersed his labor as the editor and managing partner of the *Tribune* with the publication of books dealing with a broad range of subjects that were often based on his work for the newspaper. His early writings showed the influence of Charles Fourier and Albert Brisbane, utopian reformers. *Association Discussed; or, The Socialism of the Tribune Examined* (1847) and *Hints Toward Reforms, in Lectures, Addresses and Other Writing* (1850) manifested Greeley's fascination with social utopianism as a cure for the ills of modern urban life. These works also illustrated Greeley's desire for moderation in reform, for he advocated policies that called for cooperative efforts between labor and industry and saw the solution to poverty in mutual associations.

During the 1850s Greeley's life and literary works took several new directions. Besides his continued interest in urban and industrial reform, he showed a growing concern about abolitionist issues. For the 1856 election he outlined the Free Soiler platform in *A History of the Struggle for Slavery Extension or Restriction in the United States, from the Declaration of Independence to the Present Day* (1856). Greeley also wrote three, largely narrative accounts of his travels based on his dispatches to the *Tribune*. In 1851 he traveled to England to act as a judge at the London Exhibition held at the Crystal Palace and used the opportunity to tour and report on selected parts of Europe. His second venture abroad resulted from an invitation to serve in a similar capacity at the Paris Exhibition in 1854. *Glances at Europe* consisted of a series of editorials written during Greeley's sojourn in 1851. In *Recollections of a Busy Life* (1868) he dealt in a narrative fashion with his first trip as well as with his subsequent adventure in 1854.

Greeley stated his purpose in writing *Glances at Europe* in the preface he titled "No Apology": "My aim in writing these letters was to give a clear and vivid daguerreotype of the districts I traversed and the incidents which came under my observation." Greeley worried in his preface that his opinions about Europe and its inhabitants might appear "crude and rash" or that others might be better qualified to comment on these matters, but he asserted his right to voice his concerns: "I see and think, and am not forbidden to speak."

Throughout *Glances at Europe* the reader perceives Greeley's growing disdain for the absurdities of the rigid European social structure and his growing reverence for American egalitarianism. For example, after visiting Queen Victoria's court he commented, "I deeply realize the superiority of Republicanism over Royalty." Greeley continued in this vein in *Recollections on a Busy Life* and asserted that the gaiety and the endless pursuit of amusement that occupied the lives of Europe's elite constituted "a routine that soon tells on one who is inculcated in the habit of making the most of every working-hour."

Revealing his "puritan" tendencies, Greeley also found the moral constitution of most Europeans deficient. Of Paris he stated, "In no other nominally Christian city is the proportion of the unmarried so great as here; nowhere else do families so quickly decay; nowhere else is the proportion of births out of wedlock so appalling." He leveled even harsher criticism at the residents of Rome, stating, "there are very few houses and those are generally poor . . . and the very few inhabitants are so squalid, so abject, so beggarly, that it seems a pity they were not fewer." Greeley wrote the truth as he saw it and rarely if ever masked his opinions with polite words.

Greeley was also impartial in his criticisms and spared not even his fellow countrymen. He suggests that Americans did little to enhance their reputation among Europeans and was extremely critical of the American showing at the London Exposition: "our Manufacturers are in many departments grossly deficient, in others inferior to the best rival productions of Europe." He also suggested that the display of agricultural goods generally acknowledged as superior would do little to improve our standing among Europeans but "serve rather to deepen impressions already too general both at home and abroad, that we are a rude, clumsy people, inhabiting a broad fertile domain." Greeley's bluntness made him well respected but also thoroughly criticized.

Although Greeley denigrated the quality of his European commentaries and suggested in his opening remarks to *Glances at Europe,* "No one can realize more fully than the writer the absence of literary merit in the letters," his critics have not agreed with his estimation. His contemporaries, although often critical of his other work as opinionated and misguided, hailed this series as among his finest works. In *A Memorial of Horace Greeley* (1873), which was published shortly after Greeley's death, the anonymous author proclaimed, "His letters written during his absence to the *Tribune* are among the most interesting productions of his pen."

Lunde focuses on "the majesty of thought and writing style of such a man" and argues that the real value of Greeley's European letters lay in his defense and "renewed appreciation of American culture" and nineteenth-century technological development. Seitz comments that although the modern reader will never know what Europe thought of Greeley, "what he thought of Europe was frankly told in his letters to the *Tribune* such as only Greeley could write." Perhaps Greeley himself best described the enduring quality of his European observations by recognizing their relationship to the human experience. In an early entry in *Glances at*

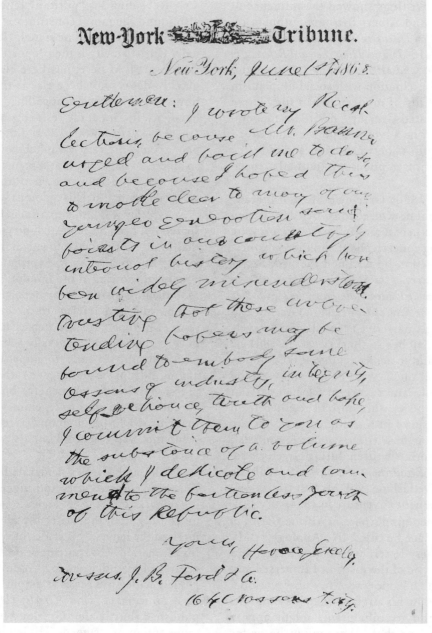

Letter from Greeley to the publisher of his autobiography (from Greeley's Recollections of
a Busy Life, *1868)*

Europe he warned his readers that similar to his
work, "Our human life is either comic or tragic, according to the point of view from which we regard
it." Despite the insightful and colorful character of
Greeley's European observations, his books on the
subject are difficult to find outside of university research libraries.

Greeley continued his frank travel commentaries in *An Overland Journey.* Charles T. Duncan, the
editor of the 1964 edition of this work published by
Knopf, contends that "Greeley had two messages

for readers in his eyewitness reports on the West."
He sought to promote the construction of a transcontinental railroad as well as the promise and opportunities of the American West, but he did not
hesitate to criticize. For example, his account of his
journey through Kansas extolled the territory in its
"natural" state but decried some of the evils imposed on it by its settlers. Squatters, land speculators, and lazy farmers come under fire as he proclaims, "There are too many idle shiftless people in
Kansas . . . To see a man squatted on a quarter-

section in a cabin which would make a fair hog-pen ... is enough to give a cheerful man the horrors."

From 1860 until his death in 1872 Greeley published monographs more deliberately constructed than his earlier works. These latter pieces were the products of analysis and synthesis rather than collections of editorial comments. *The American Conflict: A History of the Great Rebellion in the United States of America, 1860–'65* (1864–1866), *Essays Designed to Elucidate the Sciences of Political Economy* (1869), and *What I Know of Farming* (1871) have a greater organizational unity than his earlier episodic works. In *Recollections on a Busy Life* Greeley authored a deliberate autobiographical account of his life to that point. In the "Apology" that prefaced the work he asserted, "I shall never put so much of *myself,* my experience, notions, convictions, and modes of thought as [in] these *Recollections.*" He went on to describe this literary effort as the "mental history" of his life. Only in *Mr. Greeley's Letters from Texas* (1871) did he return to the episodic structure of his earlier work.

Two decades after Greeley's death in 1872, noted American historian Frederick Jackson Turner, in a famous address to the American Historical Association in 1893 on "the Significance of the American Frontier," described the American character as "Coarseness and strength combined with acuteness and inquisitiveness; that practical, inventive turn of mind, that results in ... buoyancy and exuberance which comes from freedom." Turner did not intentionally describe Greeley, but in his statement he caught the essence of the man. In *A Memorial of Horace Greeley* the author eulogized him as a "self-cultivated man of letters, the philanthropist, the reformer, and unsurpassed journalist, he will be honorably remembered so long as the history of the Republic shall survive."

For the modern reader the importance of Greeley's literary works, particularly his European comments, remains twofold. First, they give us an insightful glimpse of European life during the mid nineteenth century. They supply an American perspective to rival Alexis de Toqueville's or Charles Dickens's commentaries on life in the United States. Second, Greeley's works provide a clear image of a nineteenth-century man hailed by his contemporaries as an ideal. During the last year of his life Greeley published *What I Know of Farming* and in it described the goals of his life and his work. He perceived the driving force to be the "invincible willingness to be made wiser to-day than I was yesterday." These words described not only Greeley's ambitions for himself but also what he hoped to accomplish for his readers and his country.

Letters:

Joel Benton, *Greeley on Lincoln with Mr. Greeley's Letters to Charles A. Dana and a Lady Friend* (New York: Baker & Taylor, 1893).

Bibliography:

Suzanne Schulze, *Horace Greeley: A Bio-Bibliography* (New York: Greenwood Press, 1992).

Biographies:

James Parton, *The Life of Horace Greeley, Editor of the New York Tribune* (New York: Mason, 1855; revised edition, Boston: Fields, Osgood, 1869);

A Memorial of Horace Greeley, anonymous (New York: New York Tribune Association, 1873);

Lurton D. Ingersol, *The Life of Horace Greeley* (Philadelphia: John E. Potter, 1874);

Francis N. Zabriskie, *Horace Greeley, the Editor* (New York: Funk & Wagnalls, 1890);

William Alexander Linn, *Horace Greeley, Founder and Editor of the New York Tribune* (New York: Appleton, 1903);

Don C. Seitz, *Horace Greeley: Founder of the New York Tribune* (Indianapolis: Bobbs-Merrill, 1926);

Henry Luther Stoddard, *Horace Greeley, Printer, Editor, Crusader* (New York: Putnam, 1946);

William Harlan Hale, *Horace Greeley: Voice of the People* (New York: Harper, 1950);

Glyndon G. Van Deusen, *Horace Greeley: Nineteenth Century Crusader* (Philadelphia: University of Pennsylvania Press, 1953).

References:

Gamaliel Bradford, "Horace Greeley," in *As God Made Them: Portraits of Some Nineteenth Century Americans* (Boston: Houghton Mifflin, 1929);

Josiah Bushnell Grinnell, *Men and Events of Forty Years* (Boston: D. Lathrop, 1891);

Erik Lunde, *Horace Greeley* (Boston: Twayne, 1981).

Papers:

Most of Horace Greeley's papers are at the Library of Congress, Chappaqua Historical Society, New York Public Library, and the New York Historical Society. Other important collections include the Rufus W. Griswold Papers in the Boston Public Library, the Margaret Fuller Correspondence in the Harvard Library, the Salmon P. Chase Papers at the Historical Society of Pennsylvania, the Edwin D. Morgan Papers in the Albany State Library, the Mrs. H. C. Ingersoll Papers in the Library of Congress, and the Gerrit Smith Papers in the Syracuse University Library.

John Hay

(8 October 1835 – 1 July 1905)

Barbara Ryan
Michigan Society of Fellows

See also the Hay entries in *DLB 12: American Realists and Naturalists* and *DLB 47: American Historians, 1866–1912.*

BOOKS: *Jim Bludso of the Prairie Belle and Little Breeches* (Boston: Osgood, 1871);
Pike County Ballads and Other Pieces (Boston: Osgood, 1871); republished as *Little Breeches, and other pieces humourous, descriptive, and pathetic* (London: Hotten, 1871);
Castilian Days (Boston: Osgood, 1871; London: John Lane, 1897; revised edition, Boston & New York: Houghton, Mifflin, 1890; abridged edition, Boston & New York: Houghton, Mifflin, 1903; London: Heinemann, 1903);
The Bread-Winners: A Social Study, anonymous (London: Warne, 1883; New York: Harper, 1884);
Dr. Charles Hay: Born February 7, 1801. Died September 18, 1884 (New York: De Vinne, 1884);
Amasa Stone: Born April 27, 1818 Died May 11, 1883 (New York: De Vinne, 1886);
Poems by John Hay (Boston & New York: Houghton, Mifflin, 1890);
Abraham Lincoln: A History, 10 volumes, by Hay and John G. Nicolay (New York: Century, 1890);
Addresses (New York: Century, 1906);
The Complete Poetical Works . . . Including Many Poems Now First Collected (Boston & New York: Houghton Mifflin, 1916);
The Blood Seedling and Other Tales: The Uncollected Fiction of John Hay, edited by George Monteiro (Providence, R.I.: Cut Flower Press, 1972).

OTHER: *Abraham Lincoln, Complete Works: Comprising His Speeches, State Papers, and Miscellaneous Writings,* 2 volumes, edited by Hay and John G. Nicolay (New York: Century, 1894).

Often portrayed as an odd amalgam of talent and lack of ambition, John Hay has confounded many attempts to delve his crowded, productive life. Hay enjoyed presenting himself as one who

John Hay, 1874

shied away from the limelight but was dragged into it by extraordinary gifts. His best friend, Henry Adams, helped to propagate this portrait. Yet the John Hay who appears in *The Education of Henry Adams* (1907), and in the diaries and correspondence that Adams helped to prepare for publication, does not square well with the historical record. As secretary of state under Presidents William McKinley and Theodore Roosevelt (1898–1905), Hay helped to usher in the "American Century," especially by enlarging the U.S. military and economic presence on the international scene. He also co-authored a biography of Abraham Lincoln that reached some one million readers and wrote many essays, poems, speeches, and short stories, as well as a novel and an account of contemporary Spanish manners. He delighted Gilded Age Americans with his dialect poetry and lectured on politics as well as Omar Khayyam; his much-discussed novel, *The Bread-Winners: A Social Study* (1883), was translated into Italian, German, and French. In fact, throughout his adult life in and around the seats of power, Hay was recognized as a brilliant, able, and witty man. In addition to Adams, Lincoln, Jay Gould, and self-made millionaire Amasa Stone, Hay included among his friends Samuel Langhorne Clemens (Mark Twain), Henry James, Walt Whitman, and poet Sarah Helen Whitman, a fiancée of Edgar Allan Poe. Some of these people did see Hay as torn between love of comfort and a sense of duty. Yet none denied his achievements.

Born in Salem, Indiana, on 8 October 1835 to Charles and Helen Leonard Hay, John appreciated the homespun origins of his hero Abraham Lincoln. Yet Hay's forebears were not humble folk. His mother was educated, and his father was a doctor, editor of the local paper, and a lover of the classics. The family moved to Spunky Point (Warsaw), Illinois, in 1841. In 1849 John Hay went to live with his father's brother Milton Hay, a respected lawyer in Pittsfield, Pike County, Illinois, where young Hay attended a private school. After three years in Pittsfield, Hay began his undergraduate career at Illinois State University in Springfield (now Concordia University). He transferred to Brown in Providence, Rhode Island, in 1855. While there Hay investigated spiritualism under the auspices of Sarah Helen Whitman and wrote the class ode, graduating with a master's degree in 1858. By 1859 he was reading law with his uncle, who had moved to Springfield, Illinois, and had an office next door to Abraham Lincoln's. Backing Lincoln's successful 1860 candidacy for the presidency, Hay was rewarded with a White House job. After passing the Illinois bar examination in February 1861, Hay was off to Washington with a Springfield friend, John G. Nicolay.

Although Nicolay was named Lincoln's private secretary and Hay officially worked in the U.S. Pension Office, Hay ended up as an unofficial confidential assistant to the president as well. His January 1864 commission as a major in the Union army indicates the importance of the delicate missions he frequently undertook for the president. (He was promoted to colonel in May 1865.) Hay called Lincoln "the greatest character since Christ." Lincoln,

an exceptionally adept politician, served as Hay's political mentor, and historians give Hay credit for helping to reshape the president's public image when Lincoln's reputation sank to an all-time low during the Civil War. As the war drew to a close Lincoln appointed Hay to the U.S. legation in France. Present at Lincoln's deathbed in April 1865, Hay left soon thereafter for Europe, spending most of President Andrew Johnson's administration in Paris (1865–1866) and Vienna (1867–1868) as secretary of the legation there. After quitting Vienna, Hay was appointed to the American legation in Madrid (1869–1870). He went there, he claimed, to observe a revolution (which did not come to pass while he was there) and to save some money to clear a few pressing debts. The young man kept his eyes open and ended up writing *Castilian Days* (1871), his book about the Spanish way of life.

Returning to the United States in September 1870, Hay took a job writing editorials for the *New York Tribune* and soon became an editor. He also published biographical essays, poetry, and short stories in periodicals. He achieved some notoriety with his dialect poetry, including "Jim Bludso" and "Little Breeches," which were published together as a pamphlet in 1871 before they were collected later that year with Hay's other dialect poems in *Pike County Ballads and Other Pieces*. Many readers were offended by these poems, which excoriated pious hypocrites. Yet at a time when Americans were becoming impatient with sentimental bromides and evangelical Protestantism was losing its influence on their tastes, many other readers relished Hay's rhymed irreverence. His Pike County poems recalled the more high-toned Southwest humorists in their evocations of rough-hewn frontier types who had the right values whatever their lapses in etiquette or grammar. One of the most popular ballads praised Jim Bludso, a bigamous lowlife who died trying to save others by staying at his post faithfully. Another favorite was "Little Breeches," the story of a tobacco-chewing urchin who cares little if angels lurk unseen. Republished in many anthologies, "Little Breeches" was a work that Hay lived to regret as this bit of juvenilia was quoted to him constantly at home and abroad. Even at first Hay downplayed his verses' huge appeal, claiming in a 29 December 1870 letter to William Dean Howells, "I am not to blame for the absurd vogue of my doggerel." Yet a note of pride may be detected in his 19 June 1891 comment to Albert G. Rhoades that *Pike County Ballads* had enjoyed "an appalling run."

Serialized in *The Atlantic Monthly* in 1870 and 1871, *Castilian Days* is written in stylish prose that suggests an intention to distinguish it from Hay's

John Hay, President Abraham Lincoln, and John G. Nicolay at the White House, 1863

popular dialect ballads and demonstrate the sophisticated aspect of his literary repertoire. Witty, often disdainful, and full of badinage, Hay's account of Spanish life flits from one topic to another in an amusing, often dismissive way: "Madrid," he charged, "is a capital with malice aforethought." Most nineteenth-century Americans considered Spain to be the preeminent Catholic monarchy and thus the antithesis of their own progressive, democratic nation-state. Such complacent readers appreciated Hay's frequent, generally implicit contrasts between social practices in Spain, which he depicted as ridden by "the dual tyranny" of king and clergy, and those of an up-to-date republic with separation of church and state. This perspective is apparent in

Hay's observation that Spanish attention to honor and religion is sincere but shallow:

> Nowhere in the world are the forms of religion so rigidly observed, and the precepts of Christian morality less regarded. The most facile beauties in Madrid are severe as Minervas on Holy Thursday. I have seen a dozen fast men at the door of a gambling-house fall on their knees in the dust as the Host passed by in the street. Yet the fair were no less frail and the señoritos were no less profligate for this unfeigned reverence for the outside of the cup and platter.

Such descriptions recall Hay's jibes about pious hypocrites in his *Pike County Ballads*. *Castilian Days* points particularly at the link between Spanish Ca-

*Secretary of State John Hay and Second Assistant Secretary Alvey A. Adee in
Hay's Washington office*

tholicism and a hidebound monarchy. "The Inquisition has been dead half a century," Hay observed, "but you can see how its ghost still haunts the official mind of Spain." Yet Hay expressed confidence in the ability of Spain to establish a republic, asserting in the preface, "There are those who think the Spaniards are not fit for freedom. I believe that no people are fit for anything else." He deleted this claim from the preface to the 1890 edition after a lack of change in Spanish politics. The later excision of several chapters of rather severe commentary from the 1903 edition must be attributed to a statesman's desire to be discreet. Catholics in particular, however, did not forget the scornful criticisms handed out in the first edition.

The press and even Hay's friends took little notice of *Castilian Days*. Yet the book sold well and went through several reprintings. It also paved the way for Hay's translation of the addresses of Spanish Republican leader Emilio Castelar y Ripoll, which were published as "The Republican Movement in Europe" in *Harper's New Monthly Magazine* from June 1872 through October 1875.

On 4 February 1874 Hay married Clara Louise Stone, the daughter of Ohio millionaire Amasa Stone. The happy marriage produced four children. Hay also had harmonious relations with his father-

in-law, with whom he worked as a business associate in 1875–1879, helping to moderate press criticism of Stone's business dealings after a railroad catastrophe. Hay's financial situation and business connections were considerably improved during these years in Cleveland. In November 1879, having been active in Ohio Republican politics, Hay became assistant secretary of state in the administration of President Rutherford B. Hayes. He remained in this post until James Garfield became president in March 1881. Then, refusing an appointment as Garfield's personal secretary, he moved his family from Washington to New York, where he became temporary editor of the *New York Tribune* while his friend Whitelaw Reid was on honeymoon in Europe (April–September 1881). After he returned the editorship to Reid, Hay and his family spent the next year and a half living in England and France. While abroad Hay wrote his only novel, *The Bread-Winners*.

Serialized anonymously in *Century Magazine* from August 1883 through January 1884 and then anonymously published in book form, Hay's antilabor novel provoked intense reactions at a time when labor unrest was widespread. Hay portrayed courageous merchants subduing rebellious, misguided American workers who were unaware of where their own best interests lay. His subject matter was a shocking departure from the usual late nineteenth-century novel, and his insistence on anonymity added mystery, contributing to the popularity of the book. A few liberals liked it in spite of Hay's harsh characterization of the working class. For example, William Dean Howells, who liked and respected Hay, resisted the imputation that *The Bread-Winners* was written to criticize American laborers. Rather, he said, it refused to make heroes of workers and thus sounded a realistic note from which other American fiction writers could learn. *The Bread-Winners* became immensely popular and was acclaimed by the British press. Of course, some people knew, or guessed, who had written the most controversial novel of 1884. Henry Adams's anonymously published novel *Democracy* (1880) was sometimes attributed to Hay as well, a mistake that tickled the devoted circle of friends who called themselves the "Five of Hearts": John and Clara Hay, Henry and Marian "Clover" Adams, and geologist Clarence King.

After the success of *The Bread-Winners* Hay began work with Nicolay on the Lincoln biography they had been researching and tinkering with for years. After it was published serially in *Century* magazine (1886–1890) and as a book in 1890, the two men compiled an edition of Lincoln's works. The biography was a labor of love; yet it was also, and with no contradiction, a deliberate and successful attempt on Hay's part to revive his stalled political career. In fact, Hay's work on *Abraham Lincoln: A History* won him the coveted post of ambassador to Great Britain in 1897. He enjoyed the British capital and was a favorite of Queen Victoria. Yet greater prestige lay ahead for him. In September 1898 President William McKinley recalled Hay to the United States and appointed him secretary of state, a post he held until his death in 1905.

Hay was proud to serve Presidents McKinley and Theodore Roosevelt as secretary of state. He was an able manipulator of the press, an "insider" who knew what editors wanted. At the same time he was unusually gifted at diplomatic negotiation, known for his patience and his long-term view. Yet the highly charged political atmosphere of Washington undoubtedly sapped his waning vitality. Henry Adams thought his old friend was wizened by the job. Foreign policy during the McKinley and Roosevelt administrations was filled with drama. Hay undertook negotiations that made possible the construction of the Panama Canal and won the Samoan island Tutuila, with its strategically important harbor Pago Pago, for the United States. His best-known accomplishment was his articulation of the "Open Door Policy," which permitted all nations to trade freely with China. Throughout this tumultuous period Hay played a key role in global politics; indeed, Adams told him, "You've got literally the world on your shoulders." Hay acknowledged the costs but saw many triumphs too.

Hay and Roosevelt worked well together, even though they sometimes complained about one another in private and to trusted friends. Just how much friction existed between the two men is a subject of some debate, but personal and stylistic differences did not impede the results of their collaboration. During their tenure in office the United States entered a new era in foreign policy, establishing a major role for itself on the world stage. Hay was recognized for his part in this change by the international community: in 1904 France awarded him the Legion of Honor. By this time Hay was exhausted and in poor health. In 1905, after attending Roosevelt's inauguration, Hay and his wife sailed to Europe for a vacation. When he was too ill to accept an invitation from King Leopold of Belgium, the king visited him. Complimented by other royal and diplomatic visits on his travels, Hay returned to the United States in June. While on shipboard Hay dreamed that he reported to the White House and found Lincoln again in charge. Within weeks of his return Hay died at his summer home in New Hampshire.

Whatever his achievements as a diplomat, Hay is probably most fairly classified as an unusually successful dilettante in the field of belles lettres. Talented and much appreciated in his own day, he skipped from one literary form to another without developing his skills in any. While *The Bread-Winners* continues to attract critical attention, it was composed too hastily to survive as a monument of literary art. His dialect poetry, though lively, is ephemeral, and the Lincoln biography is noticeably flat. Hay's letters and diaries gleam with flashing wit, and *Castilian Days* has the same verve but is flawed for late-twentieth-century readers by its self-congratulatory contrast between American republicanism and Spanish monarchy.

Letters:

Letters of John Hay and Extracts from Diary, 3 volumes, edited by Henry Adams and Clara Stone Hay (Washington, D.C., 1908);

A Poet in Exile: Early Letters of John Hay, edited by Caroline Ticknor (Boston & New York: Houghton Mifflin, 1910);

A College Friendship: A Series of Letters of John Hay to Hannah Angell, edited by A. C. Montague (Boston: Privately printed, 1938);

Lincoln and the Civil War in the Diaries and Letters of John Hay, edited by Tyler Dennett (New York: Dodd, Mead, 1939);

Henry James and John Hay: The Record of a Friendship, edited by George Monteiro (Providence, R.I.: Brown University Press, 1965);

John Hay–Howells Letters: The Correspondence of John Milton Hay and William Dean Howells 1861–1905, edited by Monteiro (Boston: Twayne, 1980).

Biographies:

William Roscoe Thayer, *The Life and Letters of John Hay,* 2 volumes (Boston & New York: Houghton Mifflin, 1915);

Tyler Dennett, *John Hay: From Poetry to Politics* (New York: Dodd, Mead, 1933);

Kenton J. Clymer, *John Hay: The Gentleman as Diplomat* (Ann Arbor: University of Michigan Press, 1975).

References:

Robert L. Gale, *John Hay* (Boston: Twayne, 1978);

Howard I. Kushner and Anne Hummel Sherrill, *John Milton Hay: The Union of Poetry and Politics* (Boston: Twayne, 1977);

Patricia O'Toole, *The Five of Hearts: An Intimate Portrait of Henry Adams and His Friends, 1880–1918* (New York: Clarkson Potter, 1990).

Papers:

The two most important collections of Hay manuscripts are at the John Hay Library at Brown University and at the Library of Congress. Letters from Hay may be found in the papers of virtually every American who achieved political or literary prominence between the presidency of Abraham Lincoln and the onset of World War I.

Lafcadio Hearn

(27 June 1850 – 26 September 1904)

Roger Célestin
University of Connecticut

See also the Hearn entries in *DLB 12: American Realists and Naturalists* and *DLB 78: American Short-Story Writers, 1880–1910.*

BOOKS: *Stray Leaves from Strange Literature* (Boston: Osgood, 1884);

Historical Sketch Book and Guide to New Orleans and Environs (New York: Coleman, 1885);

"Gombo Zhèbes": A Little Dictionary of Creole Proverbs Selected from Six Creole Dialects, compiled and translated by Hearn (New York: Coleman, 1885);

La Cuisine Créole (New York: Coleman, 1885);

Some Chinese Ghosts (Boston: Roberts, 1887);

Chita: A Memory of Last Island (New York: Harper, 1889);

Two Years in the French West Indies (New York & London: Harper, 1890);

Youma, The Story of a West Indian Slave (New York: Harper, 1890);

Glimpses of Unfamiliar Japan, 2 volumes (Boston & New York: Houghton, Mifflin, 1894);

Out of the East: Reveries and Studies in New Japan (Boston & New York: Houghton, Mifflin, 1895; London: Osgood, 1895);

Kokoro: Hints and Echoes of Japanese Inner Life (Boston & New York: Houghton, Mifflin, 1896; London: Osgood, 1896);

Gleanings in Buddha-Fields: Studies of Hand and Soul in the Far East (Boston & New York: Houghton, Mifflin, 1897; London: Harper, 1897);

Exotics and Retrospectives (Boston: Little, Brown, 1898);

In Ghostly Japan (Boston: Little, Brown, 1899; London: Sampson, 1899);

Shadowings (Boston: Little, Brown, 1899);

A Japanese Miscellany (Boston: Little, Brown, 1901; London: Sampson, 1901);

Kotto: Being Japanese Curios, with Sundry Cobwebs (New York & London: Macmillan, 1902);

Kwaidan: Stories and Studies of Strange Things (Boston & New York: Houghton, Mifflin, 1904; London: Kegan Paul, 1904);

Japan: An Attempt at Interpretation (New York & London: Macmillan, 1904);

Lafcadio Hearn, circa 1873

The Romance of the Milky Way and Other Studies and Stories (Boston & New York: Houghton, Mifflin, 1905; London: Constable, 1905).

Some Strange English Literary Figures of the Eighteenth and Nineteenth Centuries, edited by Ryoji Tanabé (Tokyo: Hokuseido, 1899);

Leaves from the Diary of an Impressionist (Boston & New York: Houghton Mifflin, 1911);

Fantastics and Other Fancies, edited by Charles Woodward Huston (Boston & New York: Houghton Mifflin, 1914);

Interpretations of Literature, 2 volumes, edited by John Erskine (New York: Dodd, Mead, 1915);

Life and Literature, edited by Erskine (New York: Dodd, Mead, 1917; London: Heinemann, 1920);

Books and Habits, edited by Erskine (New York: Dodd, Mead, 1921);

Essays in European and Oriental Literature, edited by Albert Mordell (New York: Dodd, Mead, 1923; London: Heinemann, 1923);

An American Miscellany, 2 volumes, edited by Mordell (New York: Dodd, Mead, 1923; London: Heinemann, 1923); republished in England as *Miscellanies* (London: Heinemann, 1924);

Creole Sketches, edited by Mordell (Boston & New York: Houghton Mifflin, 1924);

Occidental Gleanings, 2 volumes, edited by Mordell (New York: Dodd, Mead, 1925; London: Heinemann, 1925);

Insects and Greek Poetry (New York: W. E. Rudge, 1926);

Japan and the Japanese, compiled by Teizaburo Ochiai (Tokyo: Hokuseido, 1928);

Lectures on Shakespeare, edited by Iwao Inagaki (Tokyo: Hokuseido, 1928);

Romance and Reason, compiled by Tanabé (Tokyo: Hokuseido, 1928);

Facts and Fancies, edited by Tanabé (Tokyo: Hokuseido, 1929);

Essays on American Literature, edited by Sanki Ichikawa (Tokyo: Hokuseido, 1929);

Victorian Philosophy (Tokyo: Hokuseido, 1930);

Complete Lectures on Poetry, edited by Tanabé, Ochiai, and Nishizaki (Tokyo: Hokuseido, 1934);

American Articles: Literary Essays, Oriental Articles, Buying Christmas Toys and Other Essays. The New Radiance and Other Scientific Sketches, Barbarous Barbers and Other Stories, 5 volumes, edited by Ichiro Nishizaki (Tokyo: Hokuseido, 1939);

Children of the Levee, edited by Orcutt William Frost (Lexington & London: University Press of Kentucky, 1957);

Japan's Religions: Shinto and Buddhism, edited by Kazumitzu Kato (New Hyde Park, N.Y.: University Books, 1966);

The Buddhist Writings of Lafcadio Hearn, edited by Kenneth Rexroth (Santa Barbara, Cal.: Ross-Erikson, 1977).

Collection: The Writings of Lafcadio Hearn, 16 volumes (Boston & New York: Houghton Mifflin, 1922).

TRANSLATIONS: Théophile Gautier, *One of Cleopatra's Nights, and Other Fantastic Romances* (New York: Worthington, 1882);

Anatole France, *The Crime of Sylvestre Bonnard* (New York: Harper, 1890);

Japanese Fairy Tales, 4 volumes (Tokyo: Hasegawa, 1898–1922)–comprises *The Boy Who Drew Cats, The Goblin Spider, The Old Woman Who Lost Her Dumplings,* and *The Story of the Fountain of Youth;*

Gautier, *Tales from Gautier* (New York: Brentano's, 1909);

Gustave Flaubert, *The Temptation of Saint Anthony* (New York & Seattle: Harriman, 1910);

Guy de Maupassant, *Saint Anthony and Other Stories* (New York: Boni, 1924);

Gautier, *Tales from Gautier* (London: Nash & Grayson, 1927);

Maupassant, *The Adventures of Walter Schnaffs and Other Stories* (Tokyo: Hokuseido, 1931);

Pierre Loti, *Stories from Pierre Loti* (Tokyo: Hokuseido, 1933);

Emile Zola, *Stories from Emile Zola* (Tokyo: Hokuseido, 1935; London: Allen, 1935);

Sketches and Tales from the French (Tokyo: Hokuseido, 1935; London: Allen, 1935).

At the turn of the century Lafcadio Hearn was considered one of the finest prose stylists in the United States. His enormous output ranges from early articles written for Cincinnati newspapers to a series of volumes on Japan, the country where he spent the final fifteen years of his life. It is Hearn's work on Japan that has maintained his literary reputation although the locales of his travel writing include New Orleans and the French West Indies as well as Japan. In a relatively short life of fifty-four years Hearn managed to live several different literary lives.

Patrick Lafcadio Tessima Hearn was born on the Ionian island of Santa Maura on 27 June 1850. His father, Charles Bush Hearn, was an Irish surgeon-major stationed in Greece with the British army. His Greek mother, Rosa Tessima, named him Lafcadio after Lefkada, the Greek name for Santa Maura. When Hearn was two years old, his father was posted in the West Indies. Lafcadio, his younger brother, James, and their mother were sent to Ireland to live with her husband's relatives. In 1854 Rosa, unable to adapt to the Irish climate and culture, left her children in the care of her husband's relatives and went back to Greece. Lafcadio, who was raised by his greataunt, Sarah Brenane, never saw his mother or father again.

Hearn's formal education consisted of one year at a Catholic school in France (Guy de Maupassant, who entered the school a year later, became one of Hearn's literary idols) and four years at Saint Cuthbert's in England, where he lost the use of one eye in a playing-field accident. The disfigurement (the blinded eye was whitened; the good eye protruded from overuse) made Hearn a painfully sensitive and shy person for the rest of his life. At seventeen, as a result of financial and personal misfortunes in his great-aunt's family, he was withdrawn from school. A year later his great-uncle gave him passage money to America and advised him to look up a distant relative in Cincinnati.

Hearn arrived in Cincinnati in 1869. When he left eight years later, his journalistic prose reflected the qualities that would characterize his later writings: a responsiveness to the world's outcasts, an obsessive concern with horror, and a tendency to fragment experience into a stream of impressions. Above all, he had learned how to make his narrative personae serve the demands of the story.

First, however, like thousands of Irish immigrants to America, he had to make his way. He wandered the city from day to day in his attempt to survive. He found refuge one night in the hayloft of stables where some English coachmen "fed [him] by stealth from victuals stolen from the house." To his half sister, years later, he catalogued his attempts to find work:

> I endeavored to go as accountant in a business office, but it was soon found that I was incapable of filling the situation, defective in mathematical ability, and even in ordinary calculation power. I was entered into a telegraph office as telegraph messenger boy, but I was nineteen and the other boys were young; I looked ridiculously out of place and was laughed at. I was touchy—went off without asking for my wages. Enraged friends refused to do anything further for me. Boarding-houses warned me out of doors. At last I became a boarding-house servant, lighted fires, shoveled coal, etc., in exchange for food and privilege of sleeping on the floor of the smoking-room. I worked thus for about one and a half years, finding time to read and write stories. The stories were published in cheap weekly papers, long extinct; but I was never paid for them.

No trace of these stories has been found, but Hearn's recollection attests to his early desires to be an author.

In Hearn's earliest experiences in Cincinnati the one fixed center was Henry Watkin, a printer, the first friend he made in the city. Watkin's print shop was Hearn's first resting place. It is probable that Hearn met the older man within a few months of his arrival in the city. He told his version of the meeting to his half sister three decades later:

> I asked him to help me. He took a fancy to me, and said, "you do not know anything; but I will teach you. You can sleep in my office. I cannot pay you, because you are of no use to me, except as a companion, but I can feed you." He made me a paper-bed (paper-shavings from the book-trimming department); it was nice and warm. I did errand boy in the intervals of tidying the papers, sweeping the floor of the shop, and sharing Mr. Watkin's frugal meals.

The paper-shavings bed was only a temporary resting place. The job as errand boy was temporary too. But working around the print shop, Hearn picked up some knowledge of printing that he never lost. He never got far away from activities connected with the printed word.

Hearn's first substantial job in Cincinnati came to him through Watkin's connections: on the printer's recommendation he was taken on by the editor of the trade journal *Trade List* and with some humor given the title of assistant editor. The editor of the journal, Capt. Leonard Barney, sent young Hearn out to solicit advertisements and used him in the office in every kind of job done on a small paper. Hearn found the work dull, but he learned publishing and editorial practices.

His job with *Trade List* did not last. The owner quarreled with him, or more likely he quarreled with the owner. Again Watkin helped him by recommending him to the Robert Clarke Company, book dealers and publishers, as a proofreader. Hearn had now settled into working with words. But the new job was mechanical and tedious. Hearn was aware of another editorial world more favored than this one: the arena of big dailies. The reporters of those papers were virtuosos of the word, men who went out proudly and gaily into the city, looked at all the wickedness it held, and came back to their offices to splash and splatter that wickedness across the pages of their papers. Hearn longed to be one of these privileged men.

In October 1872 he went to the office of the *Cincinnati Enquirer*. The managing editor of that paper, John A. Cockerill, recounted his encounter with Hearn:

> Some twenty years ago I was the editor in charge of the daily newspaper in a western city. One day there came to my office a quaint dark skinned little fellow strongly diffident, wearing glasses of great magnifying power, and bearing with him evidence that Fortune and he were scarce on nodding terms. In a soft shrinking voice he asked if I ever paid for outside contributions. I informed him that I was somewhat restricted in the matter of expenditures, but that I would give consideration to whatever he had to offer. He drew from under his coat

a manuscript, and tremblingly laid it upon my table. Then he stole away like a distorted brownie, leaving behind him an impression that was uncanny and indescribable. Later in the day I looked at the contribution which he had left. I was astonished to find it charmingly written and full of ideas that were bright and forceful.

The article the editor surveyed with some surprise was probably Hearn's review of a lately published part of Alfred Tennyson's *Idyls of the King* (1842). Cockerill did him the favor of printing it—Hearn's first work in print that has been saved—in two issues of the *Enquirer*, on 24 November and 1 December 1872.

When Cockerill accepted the piece, he paid Hearn out of his own pocket. Hearn asked for regular employment, but the editor advised him to hold on to his small, steady job with the Robert Clarke Company. Not willing to lose sight of Hearn, however, Cockerill told him he would consider other contributions, and he let the young man use a desk in his office. Soon Hearn quit his job with the Robert Clarke Company and lived entirely on what the *Enquirer* paid him. By the early part of 1874 he was a regular member of the staff.

Hearn had no style of his own yet, but the fact did not hurt him in the newspaper world. Cockerill, who struggled day after day to get out a readable paper, was interested in approximate results, and he saw that what Hearn wrote was colorful and conscientiously complete. It was Hearn's private problem to work out his own way of writing, to cut down on the crudeness of being colloquial in one paragraph and overly literary in the next, of being objective on one page and subjective on the next.

Even in his first year on the staff Hearn wrote some of the pieces about people at which he later became a specialist. He described a street scene of particular "low life vividness" in "Almost a Riot" on 3 August 1873. On 31 August he investigated "Grave-Digger Baldwin." On 9 November, in "The Golden Balls," he considered the city's pawnshops. On 14 December he ironically admired the "Wonders of Assassination."

Hearn's well-developed sense of the injustice of things was the basis for a series about people working long hours for little money. On 15 February 1874 he wrote about the seamstresses of the city in "Slow Starvation." In a piece that followed in the next month, he wrote about the barbers whose wages were held down by a Barber Ring.

By midsummer of 1874 Hearn's pieces on picturesque poverty were being printed regularly and displayed with headlines, probably devised by Hearn himself, to catch the eye of the daily readers.

A typical story was headlined: "Les Chiffoniers / Rags, Wretchedness and Rascality / The Gnomes of the Dump / How They Live, Work & Have Their Being." Hearn had gained a foothold in the world of journalism, but it was not until the publication of a particularly lurid piece on the murder of a tannery worker named Herman Schilling that Hearn acquired notoriety as a sensational reporter.

The piece is as readable today as when Hearn hastily put it together. It is firm and clear in its presentation of the facts. The order of events is laid out, visualized, and made easy for the reader to grasp. Schilling had been attacked, stabbed with a pitchfork, stuffed into the furnace of the tannery, and cremated. His suspected murderers were quickly found and arrested. There are two parts to Hearn's piece: first, the narration of the events set in motion by the discovery of the body, and second, the imaginative narration of the killing.

The circulation of the *Enquirer* soared with the sale of the story of the Tanyard Case. Writing of Schilling's death, Hearn was confirmed in his role as sensational reporter for the *Enquirer*. It was a role he sought. He was quite canny and cool about the gain. He had good contacts in the coroner's office, and his small, shy figure and one-eyed face did not arouse suspicion among his contacts on the street. Despite Hearn's growing reputation the editor reluctantly fired him after rumors began to circulate that he was living with a woman of mixed race—he had married Mattie Folley, but Ohio law refused to recognize mixed marriages.

Another daily paper, the *Cincinnati Commercial*, hired Hearn immediately. His reporter's work proliferated from 1874 to 1877. He was allowed to contribute brief scholarly essays, local-color stories, and prose poems to the paper as well as the sensational stories that had earned him his reputation. In "Gibbeted" he gave the readers of the *Commercial* the hanging of James Murphy, a hanging so badly mismanaged that it had to be done twice. The rope having broken in the first attempt, the boy, who was only slightly injured, awoke to whisper, "Why I aint dead—I aint dead."

Hearn also wrote several self-consciously literary pieces. He researched curious, morbid, and erudite lore. He tried his hand at prose poems. But his best work was still concerned with the new life of Cincinnati. Paradoxically, there was more art in his "horrible" pieces and his "low-life" sketches than in his consciously artistic and literary essays. His purposely artful pieces were indicative of new interests, but in achievement they were faint, tentative.

Although Hearn achieved a kind of distinction in his daily work, he was constrained to reach out

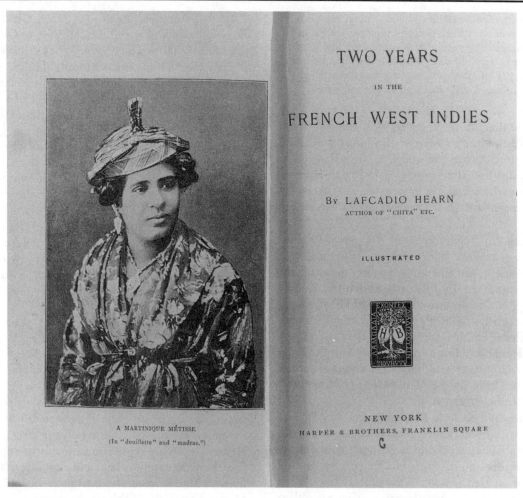

TWO YEARS

IN THE

FRENCH WEST INDIES

BY LAFCADIO HEARN
AUTHOR OF "CHITA" ETC.

ILLUSTRATED

NEW YORK
HARPER & BROTHERS, FRANKLIN SQUARE

A MARTINIQUE MÉTISSE.
(In "douillette" and "madras.")

Frontispiece and title page for Hearn's 1890 book about his travels in Martinique

for something more. He fed his imagination on a different kind of matter in his private time. After fourteen to sixteen hours of newspaper work, he remained in the newspaper building to read, principally in the French romantic-decadent tradition of Gustave Flaubert and Théophile Gautier and, later, in the realist and naturalist tradition of Emile Zola and de Maupassant—all writers whose work he helped introduce to the American public.

The exotic world described by some of these French novelists was diametrically opposed to Hearn's drab, even squalid surroundings. Sneering at Cincinnati, his words echoed those of Gautier's story "One of Cleopatra's Nights": "With our miserable habits we find it difficult to conceive those enormous existences, achieving everything vast, strange, and most monstrously impossible that imagination could devise." In his greatly reduced spare time Hearn translated six stories from Gautier that were later published as his first book: "One of Cleopatra's Nights," "King Candaules," "Arria Mar-

cella," "Clarimonde," "The Mummy's Foot," and "Omphale." These stories were consistently remote in time and opulent in circumstance and consecrated a particular attitude toward physical passion. Passion was exalted, worshiped, but never satisfied.

The stories Hearn translated from Gautier scarcely move; they present historical and supernatural locales in which objects and atmospheres are examined and transformed by an intrusive, ironical narrator. Plot and character exist, yet they too seem more suited for declamation or for the striking of moody attitudes than for active, interested existence. These set pieces may be combinations of blazing eroticism and sighing despair or of antiquarian bric-a-brac and modern sarcasm, but they generally are done with overwhelming care for the elegance of word and of language. What Hearn was finding in translating Gautier and other French writers was affinity, escape, and perhaps most important a means of pursuing his own apprenticeship as a literary writer.

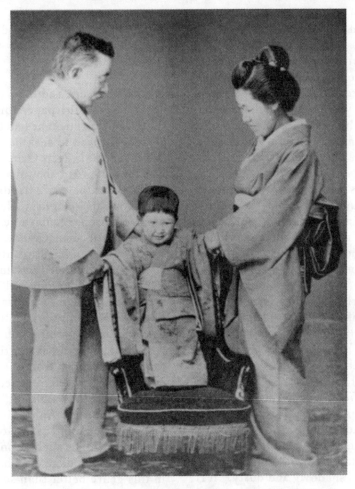

Hearn, his son, Kazuo, and his wife, Setsuo Koizumi, 1895

The pressure and limitations of a Sunday feature column (and perhaps the inevitable artistic temptation) pushed Hearn toward an important breakthrough in his craft as a translator and writer. At first this work was only a step beyond translation—the extract, the high point, the "memorable scene"—but it finally led to the vocation of the years before his death: the folktale renewed, the short story reexperienced. What the handling of fragments from the French did for Hearn was to force him to consider how a narrative had to be reorganized in order to be retold. He had to become aware of what constitutes the attainment of a satisfying end, of how one unwinds the strands making up a long tale and tightens the remaining material for a short one just as intense. More often than not, when he translates from Zola or Pierre Loti, Hearn chooses one of their brilliant portraits of a breathtakingly grim reality or a sunlit, humid island noon and makes the reader fully aware of their poetic value. Often—contrary to the spirit of the French

original, and certainly to its phrasing, punctuation, and paragraphs—Hearn creates a drowsy atmosphere, an increasing quiet, a movement toward an undescribed thoughtfulness, and at last complete vacancy. Through translation a certain type of apprenticeship was over for Hearn, and his exploration of French literature brings him back once again to himself. In the interests of re-creating the hidden world within French art he had ultimately come to discover that translation, to be fully faithful, ended with imitation, not of the word or the spirit but of the artist. Ultimately, sick of Cincinnati and restless with the kind of daily-grind newspaper work he was doing, Hearn quit the *Commercial* in 1877 and left for New Orleans. In an article dated 14 November 1877 he wrote:

> The wealth of a world is here—unworked gold in the ore, one might say; the paradise of the South is here, deserted and half in ruins. I never beheld anything so beautiful and so sad. When I saw it first—sunrise over Louisiana—the tears sprang to my eyes. It was like

young death—a death bride crowned with orange flowers—a dead face that asked for a kiss.

The most noteworthy aspect of Hearn's New Orleans output is its brevity. As a literary man on the staffs of the *New Orleans Item* and *Times-Democrat,* Hearn demonstrates his versatility with the familiar essay, but increasingly his style becomes that of a miniaturist, making humor and fantasy alike take on an aspect of lightness. The average "fantastic" (in the collection *Fantastics and Other Fancies* [1914]) is about a thousand words long; the average "Creole Sketch" about nine hundred words. Frequently Hearn seems to be playing with an idea, winking at the reader as he puts on some grotesquerie or holds a stiffly serious expression as he retells a conversation in all its unconscious absurdity.

The *Creole Sketches* (1924) are intimate bits and fragments of a New Orleans that is seen with the purposely naive eye of a startled outsider. "La Douane," a portrait of the vast, gray Custom House, entertains with a mock-dismal description that ends on a note of betrayal—the narrator laments the statueless niches atop the facade. "Ah, those niches!—Those niches! Why are they accursed with emptiness; why made hideous with vacuity?" The heightened rhetoric and the images of Pharaonic Egypt compare the building to a granite tomb. The structure is a solid nightmare, a sarcophagus, the "ruin of Egypt, vast and shadowy and dusty." It is not called a civic scandal; rather, "rivers of gold have been poured into it; yet it remaineth as before."

The shortest of the *Creole Sketches,* "Why Crabs Are Boiled Alive" (102 words) is perhaps the most brilliant. The sketch is an intricate game: it is written in Creole English, a dialect built almost entirely according to the specification of another language, in this case French. The narrator's only apparent function is that of stenographer, but he is stifling his laughter in the background that the reader has to unravel; the entertainment is inherent, but the fragment is also created with the most careful expressiveness—the brief piece creates someone irate, volatile, naive, and sly, erected out of his own words. Further, the threefold organization of the paragraph sets the stage, seizes the crest of an argument between familiars, and allows the speaker to turn an old joke about crabs into a rebuttal that ends with the perfect insult:

> And for why you not have of crab? Because one must boil dem 'live? It is all dat is of most beast to tell so. How you make for them kill so you not dem boil? You not can cut dem de head off, for dat dey have not of head. You not can break to dem de back, for dat dey

not only be all back. You not can dem bleed until dey die, for dat dey not have blood. You not can stick dem troo de brain, bot dat dey be same like you—dey not have of brain.

With Hearn's addition to the staff more people began to read the paper for its vignettes of local scenes. In Cincinnati he had been the sensational reporter—licensed to seek out fights, riots, suicides, and murders. In New Orleans he began to create a new kind of prose, that of a troubled dreamer who wrote about the city's daydreams and nightmares and about his loneliness. New Orleans colored his dreams with particular hues and supplied certain characteristic images—cracked tombstones and tropical and venomous plants—but the dreams were his own, the troubled daytime musing of an unfulfilled man. In certain self-indulgent moods he seemed unreal himself, a wanderer out of a tale by Edgar Allan Poe, strayed into a strange place where he could find no solid ground or friendship.

He also began at this time to write his fantastics, which ranged from the slight but delicate humor of "The Little Red Kitten," "A Dream of Kites," and "When I Was a Flower" to the relatively elaborate and plotted "Aphrodite and the King's Prisoner," "The Fountain of Gold," "El Vomito," and "A Legend." The slighter ones were usually better, as if something done only half seriously succeeded in this genre better than something done too earnestly. The red kitten, whose wanderings out into the city and whose death Hearn imagined, lived first in observation:

> The kitten would have looked like a small red lion, but that its ears were positively enormous—making the head like one of those little demons sculptured in mediaeval stonework which have wings instead of ears. It ate beefsteak and cockroaches, caterpillars and fish, chicken and butterflies, hash and tumble bugs, beetles and pigfeet, crabs and spiders, moths and poached eggs, oysters and earthworms, ham and mice, rats and rice-pudding—until its belly became a realization of Noah's Ark.

Such fantastics were slight but wise, with the reach of an ingenuous amateur philosophizing. More often the fantastics were vague, soft, and self-indulgent, a morbid dreaming. Scenes of graveyards recurred again and again, such scenery owing its inspiration almost equally to the reality of New Orleans cemeteries and to the pages of Poe.

Hearn found it refreshingly different that New Orleans society accepted the bohemian life of a writer. He was admired and praised as one who was clever with words and appreciative of the local scene. At first, then, the South nurtured the talent that was in Hearn. It set no stumbling blocks in his way. By being its own unself-conscious self, a rich display of a life uniquely different from the American average, New Orleans provided him not only with a climate for writing but also with a fertile kind of material.

From May 1880 until December 1881 Hearn had also been contributing translations to the pages of the *New Orleans Democrat*. Each Sunday there were scenes of splendid frozen horror from Flaubert's *Salammbô* (1862); colorful, amoral descriptions from Loti's Tahitian or African adventures; or a careful lifting of stories from the controversial Zola. When the *Democrat* merged with the *Times,* becoming the largest and perhaps most influential paper in the South, Hearn continued to be a major contributor. Each Sunday literary section carried his translations under the heading "The Foreign Press." Here according to his taste were stories, excerpts from novels, biographical and critical articles, anything at all that he wished to put into English from his daily culling of the French and Spanish papers that cluttered his desk.

Hearn still dreamed of being a literary figure himself. When he was unable to get his stories from Gautier published, he saved $150 from his small salary to pay R. Worthington of New York to publish the book. Thus, in April 1882, when he had been at work for the *Times-Democrat* for five months, Hearn held in his hands the first copy of his first book, his translation of Gautier's *One of Cleopatra's Nights and Other Fantastic Romances*.

On 8 October 1882 Hearn reviewed Herbert Spencer's *Principles of Sociology* and called attention to the author's "synthetic philosophy." This was a modest announcement of a theme that was crucial to Hearn, but it would take the urging of a friend and a rereading to awaken his permanent interest in Spencer. That same year, Hearn also read Edwin Arnold's *The Light of Asia* (1879). This was a decorative retelling of the life of Buddha, pallid if sincere, yet it had a great effect on Hearn. In 1882 he seized every opportunity to write about the East. Although Hearn wrote a good deal, though in a rather superficial manner, about the religion of the East during this period, he had no sense of a destiny turning him particularly toward India or China or Japan. He was at least as interested in Arabic and Jewish folklore and in Finnish mythology. Readers of the *Times-Democrat* could not predict from one day to the next where the errant writer would direct their attention.

Hearn was sparely reviewed, but he enjoyed the small stir of attention even when some reviews and letters reflected a strong mood of disapproval,

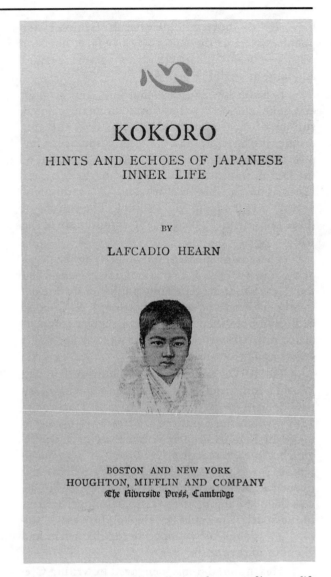

KOKORO

HINTS AND ECHOES OF JAPANESE
INNER LIFE

BY

LAFCADIO HEARN

BOSTON AND NEW YORK
HOUGHTON, MIFFLIN AND COMPANY
The Riverside Press, Cambridge

Title page for Hearn's third collection of essays on Japanese life

even shock. This only further stimulated Hearn, who determined that his next book would go a step beyond his first. This time he would translate the spirit instead of the word. Out of the folktales in his collection he would choose and shape stories, legends, and anecdotes from various traditions of the world. When they were finished, his "stray leaves" would be a varied lot taken from the folk literature of the Egyptian, Eskimo, Polynesian, Hindu, Finnish, Arabic, and Jewish traditions.

In *Stray Leaves from Strange Literature* (1884) Hearn distilled from old tales what he needed for his own aesthetic purpose. He softened his subject matter and indulged himself alternately in eroticism and horror. In "The Corpse Demon," for example, he peopled his dream landscapes with dream-fulfilling women: "He beheld a damsel descending toward him unrobed above the hips, after the fashion of her people. Sweet as the moon was her face; her hair was like a beautiful dark cloud; her eyes were liquid and large as a wild deer's."

Beheadings, suicides, murders, and strange and unimaginable cruelties floated upon the colored surface of these stories. In his best ones the grotesque, the horrible, and the grimly humorous impose their own style, as in "The Lion," a tale out of the Hindu tradition; "The Legend of the Monster Misfortune," a Chinese story; and "A Tradition of Titus," a story from the Talmud. The horror of these tales disturbs the graceful smoothness of the whole.

These tales appeared individually in the pages of the *Times-Democrat*. It was not until spring 1884 that Hearn found a legitimate publisher for the patiently made and polished collection: J. R. Osgood of Boston published the book as a regular commercial venture. Hearn had reached a new stage in his career as a professional writer.

On 16 December 1884 the long-anticipated World's Industrial and Cotton Centennial Exposition opened its gates in New Orleans. During the 1880s, when the Southern leaders were trying to make the South a little more like the North, the region became a romantic place in the Northern imagination. It was a lucky moment for Hearn because it opened a new career to him. After the exposition he was included among the practiced younger writers of the South who could be relied on for essays, stories, and novels all wrapped in the exoticism and glamour of the region.

Hearn found himself engaged in writing Creole pieces again, this time for national publication. The 10 and 17 January 1885 issues of *Harper's Weekly* carried Hearn's "The Creole Patois." In the same magazine on 7 November 1885, with sober words and careful addition of fact to fact, Hearn recreated the life of one of New Orleans's singular persons, Jean Montanet, in "The Last of the Voodoos." Montanet had been a great man among his own people, but in his old age "nothing remained to him but his African shells, his elephant's tusk, and the sewing-machine table that had served him to tell fortunes and to burn wax candles on."

On 3 January 1886 the *New York Tribune* (where Hearn had friends) published his piece "The Creole Doctor." Among curious remedies that the poor people practiced among themselves he listed two he had tried himself: one a cure for fever, the other a cure for inflamed eyes. From his hints one can conjure up a picture of Louise Roche, Hearn's cleaning woman, looking after him in his rooms and

urging him on to recovery from various illnesses as much by her good nature as by her remedies.

Of more importance to Hearn than his revival of his Creole writing was the debut of another of his interests. *Harper's Bazar* published "The Legend of Tchi-Niu," one of his Chinese ghost stories, in October 1885. He was spending his private time on a selection of Chinese tales of which this was only one. There is not much of common life about them. They represent rather the most extreme pitch of verbal perfection he was able to reach. They are extremely polished, and occasionally there is a faint specter of pathos in them. The first story, "The Soul of the Great Bell," and the last, "The Tale of the Porcelain-God," are a double parable about art and the artist. For the perfect bell or the perfect vase, a life must be sacrificed: "'My life for the life of my work!'" cried Pu, the first maker of porcelain, and entered the fire." Working on these Chinese stories—six in all—night after night, during all the weeks and months the exposition lasted, when his day hours were filled with journeyman work, Hearn knew what it was to mix a little of his own life with his works. He accurately estimated the book, *Some Chinese Ghosts* (1887), in a letter to a friend as the "early work of a man who tried to understand the Far East from books—and couldn't; but then, the real purpose of the stories was only artistic. Should I ever reprint the thing, I would change nothing."

In the meantime he rushed into the hasty and makeshift publication of three books he thought the exposition would help to sell. Hearn had only a small share in the one that was best suited for sale at the fair, the *Historical Sketch Book and Guide to New Orleans and Environs* (1885). It was introduced by the publisher as being "edited and compiled by several leading writers of the New Orleans Press." To pad it out to a certain length it included essays as well as factual information on the geography, history, street system, clubs, churches, and charities of New Orleans. It printed and identified a few sketches by Hearn, including his "Scenes of Cable's Romances."

The second book of the small set, *La Cuisine Créole* (1885), issued without any name of author or editor, was Hearn's work entirely, a collection of recipes gathered from the wives of his friends.

The third book, *Gombo Zhèbes: A Little Dictionary of Creole Proverbs* (1885), was a compilation he had completed two years before and that he had put away in his trunk after receiving a rejection. *Gombo Zhèbes* (which is to say "Creole herbs" or "Creole witticisms") belongs to a rare category, the witty personal dictionary. None of the three books did well. When they appeared in April 1885, interest in the exposition was waning. Only the cookbook had a steady sale.

Hearn limited most of his writing about the exposition to a particular interest he had discovered not long after the opening: the Japanese exhibit. He had come upon this small space of quiet and exquisite taste in the middle of the exposition's large bustle and had repeatedly returned to it.

Hearn had read books about the East, but this was touching with his own hands, seeing with his own eyes. Here, in a wash of ink and color upon silk, was the landscape of the East itself: "A flight of gulls sweeping through the gold light of a summer morning; a long line of cranes sailing against a vermilion sky; a swallow twirling its kite shape against the disk of the sun; the heavy eccentric, velvety flight of bats under the moon." So he described what he saw to his readers.

Hearn also returned to tragic tales of the semitropical south. A friend told him of the disaster of 1856 and the horror that had seized New Orleans when news came that Ile Dernière, Last Island, the favorite vacation place of the day, had been swept clean by a storm. Out of a group of summer visitors who had ignored the accelerating storm and recklessly assembled to dance in the hall of a wooden hotel near the beach, only one person survived. The storm had smashed the hotel and washed the dancers out to sea. The survivor, a little girl, was found by a fisherman and brought home to his wife. These two lonely, childless people kept her as their own. It was only years later that a Creole hunter recognized the girl from a trinket she was wearing. She was brought back to her proper place in New Orleans society, but she did not love the civilization that had reclaimed her. She rebelled, returned to the coast, married a fisherman, and, as far as Hearn knew, lived there still.

Hearn resolved to write his own version of the story of the hurricane and the lost child. Now that he had a plot, he could use everything he had observed and experienced at Grande Isle, another island near New Orleans, where he had gone for a short vacation. The book, *Chita: A Memory of Last Island* (1889), became a thing of moods and images. Although weak in structure and characterization, the book is a spontaneous, fervent, emotional prayer to the wildness of sea, sky, sand, and marsh of the first land the writer had loved since he was a boy in Ireland.

With *Some Chinese Ghosts* published and reviewed and *Chita* completed, Hearn felt the desire to travel. He resigned from the *Times-Democrat* at the end of May 1887 and left for the French West Indies by way of New York City. That spring in New

York he stayed at the apartment of a friend from his Cincinnati days, H. E. Krehbiel, now music critic of the *Tribune*. Krehbiel introduced Hearn to Henry Mills Alden, the editor of *Harper's*, who commissioned him to do articles on the West Indies.

After traveling throughout Martinique, Hearn lived for a few months almost entirely in his room, writing, completing sketch after sketch, and then busying himself with a long story about a slave girl who chose to die with the white child entrusted to her care rather than to save herself in a slave rebellion.

He had heard the story, which was based on fact, when he visited the plantation near Grande Anse. *Youma, The Story of a West Indian Slave* (1890) was better than *Chita,* more solid and more human, but it lacked the charm of that frail earlier story. It had too many digressions, curious and interesting though they were. Although when it was first published it was more respectfully reviewed than *Chita* had been, *Youma* never held the continuing audience of the other book. *Youma* had the fault of all Hearn's longer, more elaborate efforts without the particular passion that had filled *Chita;* it had no naturalness of plotting or development. His gift was for short efforts in which the development was all given. What he learned in his best work to do was to convey a single vision, a climax of cause and effect all in one.

Two Years in the French West Indies (1890) comprises two related segments: "A Midsummer Trip to the Tropics" and "Martinique Sketches." Many elements of "Midsummer Trip" reappear in the sketches—not only things from the Martinique landscape but also certain themes, particularly that of the colors and allure of human flesh.

The finest piece of "Midsummer Trip" is chapter 17, in which Hearn's attention is given to the deadly jungle viper, the fer-de-lance. With a loving care for prepared effect, he carries the reader from an evolutionary apocalypse through all the gaudy varieties of the serpent species to increasing delights on the worst possibilities of the poison: "Even when life is saved the danger is not over. Necrosis of the tissues is likely to set in: the flesh corrupts, falls from the bone sometimes in tatters; and the colors of its putrefaction simulate the hues of vegetable decay—the ghastly grays and pinks and yellows of trunks rotting down into the dark soil."

"Martinique Sketches" is also subject to this inner tendency toward breakdown; even the roman-numeral chapter breaks are not enough—other divisions by ellipses and breaks are frequent. Unlike the parts of "Midsummer Trip," however, the Marti-

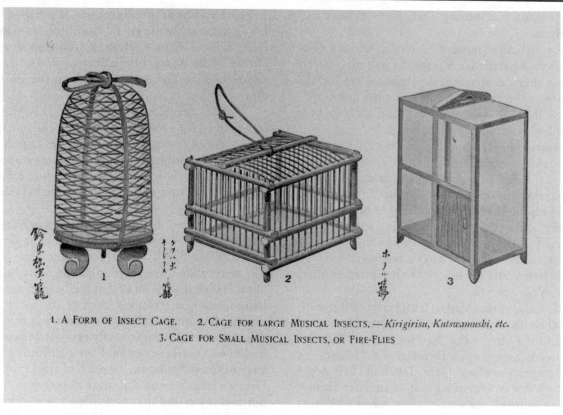

1. A Form of Insect Cage.   2. Cage for large Musical Insects, — *Kirigirisu, Kutswamushi, etc.*
3. Cage for Small Musical Insects, or Fire-Flies

Illustration for "Insect-Musicians," from Hearn's Exotics and Retrospectives *(1898)*

nique pieces usually have such a clear overall purpose that the reader feels uneasy when searching for mere moments of choice impressionism.

"Bête-ni-pié" is designed to inspire disgust. The single-minded sensationalism behind the piece organizes its four sections as an orchestration of effect. Part I uses the device of increasing volume to direct the presentation of a listing of insect and reptile house pests in Saint Pierre. The opening is pleasant—there are no mosquitoes because the town is washed clean by the rivulets in the streets. The next segment is only mildly unpleasant—various inevitable or detestable creatures are brought forward, and a hint is given of the main scent: one should examine one's bed and clothing. Hairy spiders, enormous roaches, and terrifying if silly superstitions about the lizards are mentioned; and finally the *bête-ni-pié,* the huge centipede, appears in more and more distressful attack capabilities: the poison, the length, the choleric endurance, the difficulty of killing, and the strange overtones of the name itself.

In the spring of 1889 Hearn returned to New York, but he only remained in that city for a few weeks. His departure was almost a necessity. He loathed New York and he did not find work there with which to supplement his income from books.

He might have been persuaded to go to the West Indies again or to South America. He had even suggested to Alden that he might go to Greece and make stories from the folk customs of the people of the Greek islands.

The decision to go to the East came as an accident. He was in the process of realizing he could not stay in New York and remain his own man. He would be forced into admitting that the easy part-time job he had talked about was an illusion. He would have to take on a full-time newspaper job. The only answer was flight that could be translated into words which editors would buy. Flight for Hearn was an exercise in integrity, a legitimate movement of his spirit.

A casual suggestion by William Patten, an art editor at Harper's, early in Hearn's stay in New York had ignited the author's imagination. They had been talking of Eastern books, and Patten suggested that Hearn visit Japan. Hearn had just finished reading Percival Lowell's *Soul of the Far East* (1888), and he had earlier read and cherished Arnold's *The Light of Asia.* His earlier longing to go east revived. In addition, Hearn's one chance at a part-time job in New York had failed demonstrably. *The New York Times* had offered him work in reviewing

French books and commenting on French intellectual trends, but nothing was on hand to review when the offer was made, and little turned up.

From the moment Patten spoke to him, Hearn's mind was made up. On 28 November 1889 he wrote an outline of a possible book he might write on Japan. It was detailed, comprehensive, and remarkably prophetic of what he actually did in *Glimpses of Unfamiliar Japan* (1894). In this plan, drawn up to persuade Harper and Brothers that his going was a sensible course, he also stated just what his idea of a travel book was:

> In attempting a book upon a country so well trodden as Japan, I could not hope—nor would I consider it prudent attempting—to discover totally new things, but only to consider things in a totally new way. . . . The studied aim would be to create, in the minds of the readers, a vivid impression of *living* in Japan—not simply as an observer but as one taking part in the daily existence of the common people, and *thinking with their thoughts*.

Hearn thus renewed his explorations of an unfamiliar world, still the American reporter in search of sensation. This time the subject was Japan, but the manner is that of the same traveler who went to the tropics—the impressionist, the sociological amateur, the folktale gatherer, the willing student of a disappearing culture. Hearn's early Japanese years are simply the re-created experiences of an outsider: he is eccentric but is American in his eccentricities. With the utmost devotion to his waiting audience across the Pacific, Hearn's literature does not disturb the expectations created by his handling of New Orleans and Martinique. He was by then well known in America as an impressionistic prose painter of "odd" people and places. For this reputation he was at first celebrated and later deprecated—yet much of his Japanese work is of an entirely different quality and intention. He wrote to his friend Basil Hall Chamberlain in 1893: "After four years studying poetical prose, I am forced now to study simplicity. After attempting my utmost at ornamentation, I am converted by my own mistakes. The great point is to touch with simple words." Perhaps his style shows some tendency to be less obtrusive than it had on other occasions, but that does not mean that it is always more subtly effective. The one noticeable trend in the early collections from *Glimpses of Unfamiliar Japan* to *Gleanings in Buddha-Fields* (1897) is that of objectivity. Hearn makes himself a means, a camera, an interviewing machine, but he rarely finds the locale that balances so much personal effacement.

Hearn had only recently arrived in Japan with C. D. Weldon, an illustrator from *Harper's,* when he broke off relations with the magazine, claiming that he was being exploited. Chamberlain, a professor at Tokyo University, obtained for Hearn a position in a school at Matsue, a small town in which many feudal customs survived. Hearn's stay there provided him with much of the material for *Glimpses of Unfamiliar Japan*. At a fellow teacher's suggestion Hearn married Setsuko Koizumi, the twenty-two-year-old daughter of a samurai, in 1891. He adopted Japanese dress in his home. His wife and students often became his informants for his writing on a people whose language he hardly spoke. In 1895 he became a Japanese citizen and took the name of Koizumi Yakumo.

Glimpses of Unfamiliar Japan, eight hundred pages long, is really twenty-seven pieces joined, as before, by various devices. The subjects include the figure of the children's god Jizō, the loss of Japanese innocence at European hands, Japanese "national soul" or "racial tendency," contrasts and interchanges between Buddhism and Shintō, and, ultimately, the place "never before seen by European eyes." Hearn's approach is deliberately naive: "I do not think this explanation is correct; but it is interesting."

Like the West Indies travel pieces, the Japanese travels are largely ephemeral, lovely successions of trifles, or at worst, information for the uninformed tourist. The "inner life" of Japan, for which the preface lays a claim, scarcely exists in these writings; only "the Japanese Smile" can really be said to strike below the surface. The wise reader of *Glimpses of Unfamiliar Japan* follows, therefore, the warning implicit in the title and waits for those scattered moments of life by which confidence in Hearn's art is restored.

Most fragmentary of all these sketches, "My First Day in the Orient" appears at first to be a hasty collection of notes; instead, it is really an unconscious self-portrait of the impatient, curious, West-hating, impression-seeking, slightly hesitant, intellectual, sentimental new arrival. The only unity lies in the narrator—therefore, he becomes the story. He writes in "My First Day in the Orient":

> There is some charm unutterable in the morning air, cool with the coolness of Japanese spring and wind-waves from the snowy cone of Fuji, a charm perhaps due rather to softest lucidity than to any positive tone,—an atmospheric limpidity extraordinary, with only a suggestion of blue in it, through which the most distant objects appear focused with amazing sharpness. . . . The street-vistas, as seen above the dancing white mushroom-shaped hat of my sandaled runner, have an allurement of which I fancy that I could never weary.

Elfish everything seems; for everything as well as everybody is small, and queer, and mysterious: the little houses under their blue roofs, the little shop-fronts hung with blue, and the smiling little people in their blue costumes. . . .

And perhaps the supremely pleasurable impression of this morning is that produced by the singular gentleness of popular scrutiny. Everybody looks at you curiously; but there is never anything disagreeable, much less hostile in the gaze: most commonly it is accompanied by a smile or half smile.

In "Jizō" there is a sensitive, vivid reconstruction of the town's appearance—coloring, atmosphere, inhabitants, their expressions, gestures—and more, the story of the Hell Scrolls. Using his old technique of recurrence, the narration of an object frozen in time, Hearn uniquely perceives the scroll paintings within the conventions of Asian art. His narrative succession parallels the eye of the instructed beholder:

Floating in glory, Dai-Nichi-Nyorai, Kwannon-Sama, Amida Buddha. Far below them as hell from heaven surges a lake of blood, in which souls float. The shores of this lake are precipices studded with swordblades thickly set as teeth in the jaws of a shark; and demons are driving naked ghosts up the frightful slopes. But out of the crimson lake something crystalline rises, like a beautiful, clear water-spout; the stem of a flower—a miraculous lotus, bearing up a soul to the feet of a priest standing above the verge of the abyss.

Hearn is also the traveler who listens to roadside peddlers, to old inn gardeners, and to the quaint beliefs and tales of the local yokel. His travel stories are decorated profusely with such garnerings; occasionally, though, the reader comes across folk legends that stand on their own in the midst of larger narratives, and the tales usually fall into the categories of zombies and similar returns to Hearn's old American interests.

In "By the Japanese Sea" the weird is put to work to promote the vividness of the tales, which are at once eerie and sentimental: a woman watching her husband and brother drown, and the children whose ghosts haunt the wearers of their quilt. Such tales lead inevitably to the last piece in the collection, "Of Ghosts and Goblins," where only one fragment—a tale of a girl who puts each of her lovers to the task of eating a corpse—produces in the old grisly manner the chills promised by the title. The rest of "Ghosts," being travel or intractably plotted ethnographic material, is merely diverting.

Out of the East (1895) comprises eleven sections of essentially descriptive prose doubled by philosophical considerations and observation of daily life. Hearn is again attempting to penetrate and explain Japanese life. The stories, the folklore researches, the travels, and the descriptions have some of the formal virtues of his previous work, but the choice of subjects used to express his views lacks care. "A Wish Fulfilled," "The Stone Buddha," and "The Red Bridal" are all informative, but their abstract preoccupations only underline their basic, melancholy distraction.

"The Red Bridal" is an attempt to dramatize facts Hearn has reported elsewhere in the volume: love suicide, arranged marriages, and children's thoughts. The story has only one real personage, however, the scheming peasant woman, O'Tama, and her character is almost smothered under moralizing abstractions about her actions and psychology. The children in love remain silly story children, even in their love/death. Even Hearn himself, who steps in at the climax to puncture the effect with a much livelier tale of how a policeman had once detected his foreigner's eye peering through a hole in a shoji screen far above a street, demonstrates both his lack of interest in the tale he is supposedly relating and in the greater liveliness of his own life.

In *Kokoro: Hints and Echoes of Japanese Inner Life,* as the title suggests, Hearn is still striving for the elusive inner Japan, a vain quest that informs about half of the fifteen pieces. The remarkable thing about "At a Railway Station," for example, is how little difference it would make to place the story in Cincinnati or New Orleans: the encounter between a murderer and his victim's child, the crowd scene, and the violence are all reminiscent in both content and style of stories Hearn had written for his Cincinnati and New Orleans newspaper columns. On the whole *Kokoro* is a rather didactic work. Two pieces of war reporting are exceptions to this rule: "After the War" and "A Glimpse of Tendencies." The former has the peculiar advantage of reportage that presents rather than explains, and Hearn himself is sometimes revealed as he confesses his unease at the trumpet sounds of war (the calls of bugles form a motif throughout) because they suggest the sorrows that go with victory. This piece is unusual, too, for its prophetic objectivity about the brutal course of Japanese patriotism (it would be tempting to stress this foresight were Hearn not so blatantly enthusiastic about Japanese chauvinism in other essays).

"A Glimpse of Tendencies" also finds an emotionally divided and less didactic Hearn. Its

Hearn's funeral procession in Okubo, Japan, 1904

theme is the decline and obliteration of foreign options in Japan, but the sketch is particularly vivid in its exploitation of nationalist madness and will. Once again, Hearn is strikingly prescient: he senses war, military dictatorship, and internal disorder.

Gleanings in Buddha-Fields is the last collection of works from Hearn's early Japanese period. Here again is a mix of observations of daily life and more-general, abstract religious and philosophical musings that often threaten to overwhelm intimate, detailed descriptions. The story in the midst of "A Living God," for instance, breaks out of a morass of information and comparative religious experience, but it is the sole memorable fragment. The characters are null, but the moments of panic when the sea runs away from the land—until a character sets fire to the rice stacks—are presented in the most carefully executed rhythm of unease, hint, horror, and desperate search of memory.

"Notes of a Trip to Kyōto" marks at last the merging of Hearn's artistic method with the countryside he has so long desired to capture. The best fragment describes a Western-style restaurant where Westerners have never come. It is out of the way; the client ascends by a ladder, eats with the knives and forks of an abandoned hotel, and listens to a music box and its strangled performance. In this scene, unexplained and unexpected, Hearn demonstrates the validity of his themes: the visit, an unexpected and trivial pleasure, is a small and hidden oddity whose charm lies in its accidental nature. The essay as a whole is performing, however, what it talks about: its fragments are the small, choice, evanescent pleasures that make Japanese life so seductive. The unobtrusiveness of this thematic unity is all the more Japanese; as Hearn comments in the course of the piece, "the greatest applause is silence."

After this early period Hearn's books appeared with almost monotonous regularity. Houghton published *Gleanings in Buddha-Fields* in 1897. Little, Brown published *Exotics and Retrospectives* and Hagesawa of Tokyo published *The Boy Who Drew Cats* in 1898. *In Ghostly Japan* appeared in 1899, *Shadowings* in 1899, and *A Japanese Miscellany* in 1901. The books had a certain sameness, like the slow unrolling of a Japanese scroll painting: there was not much variety, only a difference in settings. It was the ambling journey of a thoughtful, sensuous traveler through a delightful landscape. The little essays, mild disquisitions on such subjects as "Frogs," "Japanese Female Names," "Dragon-Flies," and "Songs of Japanese Children," were now the result of careful research (disguised), not merely of chance observation.

There are listings, compilings, and arrangements of facts designed to give delight and convey knowledge. The naming of things is made to stand for the fundamental qualities of a national life. The stories, into which Hearn poured his most anxious care, are shorter, tighter, and more objective.

After Matsue, whose cold winters had severely affected his health, Hearn had applied for a transfer, and before his first child, a son named Kazuo, was born (1893), he moved to Government College at Kumamoto. Hearn was then in charge of an entire family, his wife's relatives having become part of his household. After teaching at Kumamoto for three years, he resigned and joined the staff of the *Kobe Chronicle* in October 1894; he produced articles for that publication only until December, when he became unable to keep up with the rhythm and pressure of daily newspaper work. It is at this point that Chamberlain found him a position as professor of English at Tokyo Imperial University, a prestigious academic post in the most prestigious school in Japan.

In the last weeks of 1902 Hearn tasted blood in his mouth. During an attack of bronchitis he suffered a dangerous hemorrhage from a burst blood vessel in his throat. He recovered slowly and after days of enforced passivity returned to the classroom. At this time he came up against the gathered forces of those unfriendly to him at the university. His teaching contract, due for a renewal in March 1903, was abruptly announced, but he was informed that henceforth he would be paid as a Japanese citizen; that is, his salary would be sharply reduced. He was also due a sabbatical year, but when he requested it, he was refused.

Hearn made no public statements and only expressed his bitterness in letters to friends in the United States. He resigned from the university and went home, sustained perhaps by the knowledge of another resource. He had received an offer from Cornell University in November 1902 asking him to deliver a series of lectures on the civilization of Japan.

Hearn spent the succeeding months living almost entirely in his work. He completed the book *Japan: An Attempt at Interpretation* (1904), the final form of the Cornell lectures. This study, his last word on Japan, was a somber reversal of many of his first conclusions. He had thought the Japanese spontaneous and free; he described them now as disciplined and determined. The determining factor was the organization of instincts and habits that society had accomplished over hundreds, perhaps thousands, of years. The delicate beauty of manners, dress, and crafts; the subtle adjustments of individual to individual, of person to society; the seemingly unthinking propriety of civil and religious practices—all these good things, he concluded, were the result not of choice but of pressure. Hearn did justice to the deft management, the color, and the subtlety of Japanese living, but he also showed the great price paid for a great good. The book was logical in arrangement and exhilarating in its clarification of a single idea, yet it was not a polemical or argumentative book. Hearn demonstrated what he had found to be true. He left it to the reader to argue the tragic mixture of good and bad in the pattern.

On 26 September 1904 Hearn died of heart failure. He had instructed his eldest son to put his ashes in an ordinary jar and to bury it on a forested hillside. Instead he was given a Buddhist funeral with full ceremony at Zoshigaya, in north Tokyo. Despite Hearn's disappointments in Japan, he had found a measure of contentment there. The lonely youth who had set out from Ireland to find his fortune in America had discovered instead that words were a route to fame, if not to fortune.

Lafcadio Hearn's reputation as a writer and, in particular, as a travel writer, benefited from the initial fascination of the West for the "Mysterious East." Although the present "post-colonial" and "post-modern" context would sometimes make of him the practitioner of a bygone exoticism, the often earnest quality of his work and the sheer quantity of his output—whether set in America, the Caribbean, or Japan—make him a figure to be reckoned with. Today, it is as a pioneer of the literary discovery of the East that Hearn is best remembered.

Letters:

Letters from the Raven, Being the Correspondence of Lafcadio Hearn with Henry Watkin, edited by Milton Bronner (New York: Brentano's, 1907);

The Japanese Letters of Lafcadio Hearn, edited by Elizabeth Bisland (Boston & New York: Houghton Mifflin, 1910);

Some New Letters and Writings of Lafcadio Hearn, edited by Sanki Ichikawa (Tokyo: Kenkyusha, 1925).

Biographies:

Elizabeth Bisland, *The Life and Letters of Lafcadio Hearn,* 2 volumes (Boston & New York: Houghton, Mifflin, 1906);

Edward Larocque Tinker, *Lafcadio Hearn's American Days* (New York: Dodd, Mead, 1924).

References:

Jonathan Cott, *Wandering Ghost: The Odyssey of Lafcadio Hearn* (New York: Knopf, 1991);

Carl Dawson, *Lafcadio Hearn and the Vision of Japan* (Baltimore: Johns Hopkins University Press, 1992);

George M. Gould, *Concerning Lafcadio Hearn* (Philadelphia: G. W. Jacobs, 1908);

Nina H. Kennard, *Lafcadio Hearn* (Port Washington, N.Y.: Kennikat Press, 1967);

Arthur E. Kunst, *Lafcadio Hearn* (New York: Twayne, 1969);

Vera Seeley McWilliams, *Lafcadio Hearn* (Boston: Houghton Mifflin, 1946);

Elizabeth Stevenson, *Lafcadio Hearn* (New York: Macmillan, 1961);

Jean Temple, *Blue Ghost, a Study of Lafcadio Hearn* (New York: J. Cape, H. Smith, 1931);

Edward Larocque Tinker, *Lafcadio Hearn's American Days* (New York: Dodd, Mead, 1924);

Beongcheon Yu, *An Ape of Gods; the Art and Thought of Lafcadio Hearn* (Detroit: Wayne State University Press, 1964).

Papers:

The major collections of Lafcadio Hearn's manuscripts and letters are located in the Houghton Library, Harvard University; the Henry W. and Albert A. Berg Collection of English and American Literature, New York Public Library; and the Humanities Research Center, University of Texas, Austin.

Oliver Wendell Holmes

(29 August 1809 – 7 October 1894)

James E. Canacci
Youngstown State University

See also the Holmes entry in *DLB 1: The American Renaissance in New England.*

BOOKS: *Poems* (Boston: Otis, Broaders, 1836; enlarged edition, London: Rich, 1846; enlarged again, Boston: Ticknor, 1848; enlarged again, Boston: Ticknor, 1849); enlarged again as *The Poetical Works of Oliver Wendell Holmes* (London: Routledge, 1852);

Boylston Prize Dissertations for the Years 1836 and 1837 (Boston: Little & Brown, 1838);

Homœópathy, and Its Kindred Delusions; Two Lectures Delivered before the Boston Society for the Diffusion of Useful Knowledge (Boston: Ticknor, 1842);

The Autocrat of the Breakfast-Table (Boston: Phillips Sampson, 1858; Edinburgh: Strahan / London: Hamilton, Adams, 1859; revised edition, Boston & New York: Houghton, Mifflin, 1883; 2 volumes, Edinburgh: Douglas, 1883);

The Professor at the Breakfast-Table (Boston: Ticknor & Fields, 1860; London: Sampson Low, 1860; revised edition, Boston & New York: Houghton, Mifflin, 1883; 2 volumes, Edinburgh: Douglas, 1883);

Currents and Counter-Currents in Medical Science (Boston: Ticknor & Fields, 1861);

Elsie Venner: A Romance of Destiny, 2 volumes (Boston: Ticknor & Fields, 1861; Cambridge & London: Macmillan, 1861; revised edition, Boston & New York: Houghton, Mifflin, 1883);

Border Lines of Knowledge in Some Provinces of Medical Science (Boston: Ticknor & Fields, 1862);

Songs in Many Keys (Boston: Ticknor & Fields, 1862);

The Poems of Oliver Wendell Holmes (Boston: Ticknor & Fields, 1862);

Soundings from the Atlantic (Boston: Ticknor & Fields, 1864; London: Sampson Low, 1864);

Humorous Poems (Boston: Ticknor & Fields, 1865);

Oliver Wendell Holmes as a young man

The Guardian Angel (Boston: Ticknor & Fields, 1867; 2 volumes, London: Sampson Low, Son & Marston, 1867);

Mechanism in Thought and Morals (Boston: Osgood, 1871; London: Sampson Low, Son & Marston, 1871);

The Poet at the Breakfast-Table (Boston: Osgood, 1872; London: Routledge, 1872; revised edition, Boston & New York: Houghton, Mifflin, 1883; 2 volumes, Edinburgh: Douglas, 1884);

Songs of Many Seasons. 1862–1874 (Boston: Osgood, 1875);

The Poetical Works of Oliver Wendell Holmes, Household Edition (Boston: Osgood, 1877);

The School-Boy (Boston: Privately printed, 1878; Boston: Houghton, Osgood, 1878; London: Routledge, 1879);

John Lothrop Motley (Boston: Houghton, Osgood, 1879 [i.e., 1878]; London: Trübner, 1878);

The Iron Gate, And Other Poems (Boston: Houghton, Mifflin, 1880; London: Sampson Low, Marston, Searle & Rivington, 1880);

The Poetical Works of Oliver Wendell Holmes, Handy Volume Edition, 2 volumes (Boston: Houghton, Mifflin, 1881);

Medical Essays 1842–1882 (Boston & New York: Houghton, Mifflin, 1883);

Pages from an Old Volume of Life: A Collection of Essays 1857–1881 (Boston & New York: Houghton, Mifflin, 1883);

Illustrated Poems of Oliver Wendell Holmes (Boston & New York: Houghton, Mifflin, 1885; London: Macmillan, 1885);

Ralph Waldo Emerson, American Men of Letters (Boston & New York: Houghton, Mifflin, 1885; London: Kegan Paul, 1885);

A Moral Antipathy (Boston & New York: Houghton, Mifflin, 1885; London: Sampson Low, Marston, Searle & Rivington, 1885);

Our Hundred Days in Europe (Boston & New York: Houghton, Mifflin, 1887; London: Sampson Low, Marston, Searle & Rivington, 1887);

Before the Curfew and Other Poems, Chiefly Occasional (Boston & New York: Houghton, Mifflin, 1888; London: Sampson Low, Marston, Searle & Rivington, 1888);

My Hunt after the Captain and Other Papers (Boston & New York: Houghton, Mifflin, 1888);

Over the Teacups (Boston & New York: Houghton, Mifflin, 1891 [i.e., 1890]; London: Sampson Low, Marston, Searle & Rivington, 1890);

The Writings of Oliver Wendell Holmes, Riverside Edition, 13 volumes (Boston & New York: Houghton, Mifflin, 1891; London: Sampson Low, Marston, Searle & Rivington, 1891); volume 14 (Boston & New York: Houghton, Mifflin, 1892);

The Complete Poetical Works of Oliver Wendell Holmes, Cambridge Edition (Boston & New York: Houghton, Mifflin, 1895; London: Sampson Low, Marston, Searle & Rivington, 1895); revised and edited by Eleanor M. Tilton (Boston: Houghton Mifflin, 1975).

The elder Henry James once said to Oliver Wendell Holmes, "You are intellectually the most alive man I ever knew." Holmes replied, "I am, I am! From the crown of my head to the sole of my foot, I'm alive, I'm alive!" Holmes's zest for life provided him with his greatest subject. His works are largely autobiographical in nature, especially *The Autocrat of the Breakfast-Table* (1858), *The Professor at the Breakfast-Table* (1860), and *The Poet at the Breakfast-Table* (1872). In these essays Holmes crystallized a voice in conversation with boarders, family, friends, and fellow Bostonians. A doctor who practiced medicine as a young man and taught anatomy at Harvard for more than thirty-five years, Holmes was also a poet, essayist, and novelist as well as a member of the Saturday Club, a group of the Boston literary elite including Ralph Waldo Emerson, Nathaniel Hawthorne, and Henry Wadsworth Longfellow. He also named and became a leading contributor for *The Atlantic Monthly.* As a travel writer Holmes drew on his keen memories of his first trip to Europe in 1834 and observations in his daughter's personal diary to bring to life his account of his second trip abroad in 1886 in *One Hundred Days in Europe* (1887).

"The year 1809, which introduced me to atmospheric existence, was the birth-year of Gladstone, Tennyson, Lord Houghton, and Darwin," said Holmes in *Our Hundred Days in Europe,* placing himself alongside an English prime minister; a poet laureate; a statesman, poet, and critic; and a natural scientist. He believed, "Men born in the same year . . . especially as the sands of life begin to run low . . . keep an eye on each other." Born in Cambridge, Massachusetts, Holmes was the third child and eldest son of Reverend Abiel and Mary Wendell Holmes. Abiel Holmes, a 1782 graduate of Yale University, not only preached hard religion but also held firm values about his children's education, especially that of his son Oliver. Despite his distress with the intellectual legacy of his Puritan ancestors, living in Cambridge helped to hone young Holmes's intellectual sensibilities. The scholarly spirit of the college village was coupled with the rich historical tradition of its inhabitants—the strategy for the Battle of Bunker Hill had been planned in Holmes's grandmother's attic, where the boy wrote poetry on scraps of paper while standing on one leg. His mother's Dutch ancestors had linked the Wendells through marriage to the old Puritan families of New England; one ancestor was colonial poet Anne Bradstreet. Holmes felt akin to his fellow Bostonians. His passion for the town he dubbed "the hub of the universe" ignited his patriotic disposition. It was that same fervor that drove Holmes to write one of his best-known poems, "Old Ironsides," in 1830.

After attending private day schools in Boston, Holmes entered Phillips Academy in Andover, Mas-

The lodging house where Holmes lived while studying in Paris, 1833–1835

sachusetts, in August 1824. He was a spirited young man with a love for knowledge and aspirations for oratorical and literary greatness. His diligent work earned him a place in Harvard College the following autumn. There Holmes developed lifelong friendships with many of his classmates and professors. The Harvard class of 1829 had as much influence in his life as did the distinguished members of the Saturday Club. He was disappointed with his class rank of seventeenth, but he did well enough to be elected a Phi Beta Kappa scholar and become class poet.

After graduation in 1829 Holmes entered the Dane Law School at Harvard, but he changed his choice of profession at the end of his first year there and took up the study of medicine with a group of Boston doctors connected with a private medical school in Boston (which later merged with the Harvard Medical School).

Soon after moving across the river from Cambridge to Boston, Holmes began preparations for schooling in medicine abroad. This plan, however, required a substantial outlay of capital. He tried to gain financial support on his own, but eventually his parents came up with enough money to send him to the best schools of the day in Europe. Records of his first stay in Europe are scanty, but they offer in-

sights into Holmes's first impressions of Europe, especially France. Holmes's early letters to family and friends at home are filled with descriptions of sites he would revisit more than fifty years later and depict in *Our Hundred Days in Europe*.

On his first sojourn in Europe, Holmes was largely absorbed in his studies, learning everything he could from his mentor, Pierre Charles Alexander Louis, at La Pitié hospital in Paris. At 7:30 each morning Holmes started his day, spending most of the morning attending lectures and observing experiments. He went to breakfast before noon and then continued his study until 5:30 or 6:30, when he ate dinner, usually with fellow Bostonian students or his French tutor. Later in life Holmes said, "I . . . saw little outside hospital and lecture rooms." Yet in a 21 June 1833 letter to his younger brother, John, Holmes wrote, "I feel now as if I had known Paris from my childhood. I am as much at home, day and night, as in the streets in Boston, or almost so."

In the same letter to John, Holmes wrote, "I admire the French so far as I have seen them,—indeed the only very disagreeable people one meets with are generally Englishmen," and he said of the English students he had met in France, "so far as I can learn and observe, they cannot compare with the American." Holmes's arrival in Paris came not too long after the Restoration regime had been replaced by the constitutional Orleanist monarchy of Louis Philippe in the July Revolution of 1830. The French people initially welcomed the new monarch, but he lost favor after his government slid into corruption, and the Revolution of 1848 ultimately ended his reign. In a 14 July 1833 letter to his brother, Holmes observed, "The French are restless people . . . . the papers talk without the slightest ceremony about [Louis Philippe's] defection from the principles of the revolution of July." Holmes admired the patriotic devotion of the young men of France and respected the French for the way in which they faced great adversity. Holmes later said of his compatriots in Paris, "The students from all lands are gathered together, and the great harvest of the year is open to all of us. . . . I enjoy myself as much as I could wish."

Holmes had a wonderful time in Paris, but he was running out of money and dearly missed his family. He said in one of his last letters from France, written on 28 December 1834, "I have the fondest desire to see my parents and my relations and friends—but I keep my heart light in keeping my mind busy and you must also do the same." Before he returned home Holmes described his travels in Switzerland and Italy. He wrote about his adventures in Geneva and Rome and his journey on foot

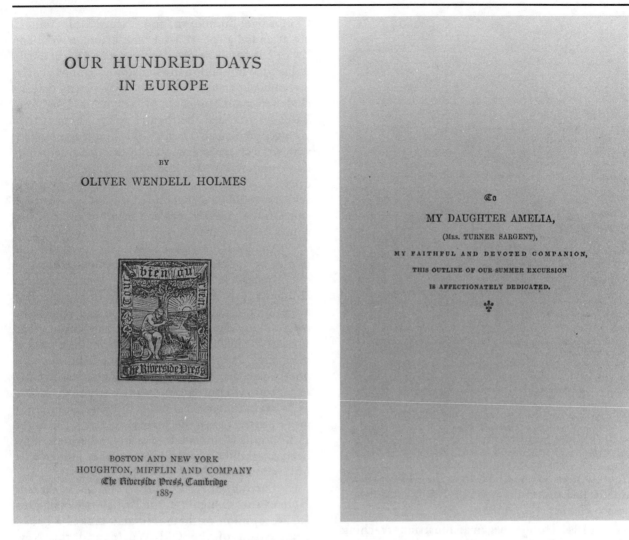

Title page and dedication page for Holmes's account of his 1886 travels in England, Scotland, and France

through a pass in the Alps with the help of mules to carry supplies. Holmes also spoke of his uneasiness in his role as travel writer, saying, "You do not ask from me a description of all I have seen, because I am not a professed traveller, and such only have the time and inclination for this kind of labor, which requires a great deal of elaboration to offer any particular value" (16 August 1835). Leaving Italy, Holmes went to London where he witnessed the Derby of 1834 before he returned to Boston. Later, Holmes wrote in *Our Hundred Days in Europe,* "I think it probable that I had as much enjoyment in forming one of the great mob in 1834 as I had among the grandeurs in 1886."

Holmes returned to America on 14 December 1835, and the following month he submitted "A Dissertation on Acute Pericarditis" to Harvard, which awarded him an M.D. degree in February. Over the next year he published a book of his poems and two

essays on medical topics based on what he had learned in Europe. *Poems* (1836) was well received, and he won Boylston Prizes in 1836 and 1837 for his essays "On the Nature and Treatment of Neuralgia," "Facts and Traditions Respecting the Existence of Indigenous Intermittent Fever in New England," and "On the Utility and Importance of Direct Exploration in Medical Practice," an important accomplishment for a young doctor. The three essays were published as a book in 1838.

Holmes found his new profession tedious and time-consuming. The death of his father soon after Holmes's return from Europe was another setback. In 1839 Holmes took a position as a professor of anatomy at Dartmouth Medical College in Hanover, New Hampshire, remaining there for just one academic year. On 15 June 1840 he married Amelia Lee Jackson. The newlyweds settled in Boston and eventually had three chil-

Holmes in 1892

dren: Oliver Wendell Holmes Jr. (1841–1935), Amelia Jackson Holmes (1843–1889), and Edward Jackson Holmes (1846–1884).

In 1847 Holmes began an illustrious teaching career as the Parkman Professor of Anatomy and Physiology at Harvard Medical School. He was too busy for an active social life, but he loved to meet once a month with his friends in the Saturday Club, which was founded at about the same time as *The Atlantic Monthly,* the highly successful magazine to which he contributed poems, fiction, nonfiction, reviews, and his "Breakfast-Table" essays.

In 1882 Holmes retired from Harvard Medical School, where he was named professor emeritus, and in April–August 1886 he and his daughter, Amelia, traveled in England, Scotland, and France. His opinions of England and France changed dramatically on this second visit.

Obviously worn out by his travels, Holmes repeatedly comments on the tiring nature of travel in *Our Hundred Days in Europe.* His schedule included a string of visits and ceremonies to celebrate his accomplishments not only as a noted physician but also as an esteemed essayist and poet. In June he was awarded honorary degrees at Cambridge, Edinburgh, and Oxford Universities. He attended a speech by Prime Minister William Ewart Gladstone before Parliament and spent much of his time in London in Gladstone's company. He was invited to a meeting of a literary society that included Richard Monckton Milnes, Lord Houghton. Later he attended the theater, where he met two younger gentlemen, Oscar Wilde and Bram Stoker, who were closer in age to Holmes's daughter Amelia. Holmes recorded the event for posterity because, he said, "I know full well that many of my readers would be disappointed if I did not mention some of the grand places and bring in some of the names that lend their lustre to London society."

Amelia Holmes recorded the events of the trip in her personal diary, which her father frequently used as a source of valuable information. Holmes appreciated her fresh view of Europe: her attention to opulent details that he had seemed to overlook by choice and her thoughts about what she saw, which differed so much from his own recollections. Holmes also used lines from his own poetry and that of his friends to help describe his experiences in Europe, speaking of these moments as "a beautiful, poetical series of views, but hardly more poetical than the reality." After a fortnight in London, Holmes felt that he and Amelia had been caught like invited insects in the "golden web of London social life."

Throughout *Our Hundred Days in Europe* Holmes speaks highly of the British, reversing his earlier opinion of them. He also makes a broad comparison of the Old World and the New World, saying, "Everywhere in England a New Englander is constantly meeting the names of families and places which reminds him of the graft from an old tree placed on new stock."

In Stratford-upon-Avon, Holmes spent the best time of his second journey under the branches of a small tree near a small brook. The experience nearly moved Holmes to capture the moment in verse, but he adds that some of his favorite poems were those he never chose to write down, savoring the moment for himself instead of sharing it with others.

If the solitude Holmes found at Stratford was restorative, the isolation he felt in Paris was debilitating. As a young scholar he had treasured the few moments in which he had been able to wander the streets of Paris. Now he felt lonely as he walked those streets alone while his daughter spent most of her time and her father's money in the many shops of the grand city. All his friends and mentors in Paris were deceased or long departed. He felt his time had passed.

In the conclusion to *Our Hundred Days in Europe* Holmes says of traveling in his old age, "I brought home a pair of shoes I had made in London; they do not fit like those I had before I left, and I rarely wear them." His metaphor helps explain not only his fondness of his "second home" in London but also his undying love for his home and family. Like the old shoes he mentions, nothing fit Oliver Wendell Holmes as well as Boston. On 7 October 1894 Holmes died suddenly in his home in Boston while talking to his son and namesake, who had been a Supreme Court justice since 1882.

Bibliographies:

Thomas Franklin Currier, *A Bibliography of Oliver Wendell Holmes,* edited by Eleanor M. Tilton (New York: New York University Press, 1953);

Barry Menikoff, "Oliver Wendell Holmes," in *Fifteen American Authors before 1900,* edited by Robert A. Rees and Earl N. Herbert (Madison: University of Wisconsin Press, 1971), pp. 207–228.

Biographies:

John T. Morse Jr., *Life and Letters of Oliver Wendell Holmes,* 2 volumes (Boston & New York: Houghton, Mifflin, 1896);

M. A. De Wolfe Howe, *Holmes of the Breakfast-Table* (New York: Oxford University Press, 1939);

Eleanor M. Tilton, *Amiable Autocrat: A Biography of Dr. Oliver Wendell Holmes* (New York: Henry Schuman, 1947);

Edwin Palmer Hoyt, *The Improper Bostonian* (New York: Morrow, 1979).

References:

William Lawrence Schroeder, *Oliver Wendell Holmes: An Appreciation* (Philadelphia: R. West, 1977);

Miriam Rossiter Small, *Oliver Wendell Holmes* (New York: Twayne, 1962).

Papers:

The major collection of Holmes's papers is in the Houghton Library at Harvard University. Additional repositories are the Library of Congress, the Francis A. Countway Library of Medicine in Boston, the Harvard University Archives, and the Henry E. Huntington Library in San Marino, California.

Julia Ward Howe

(27 May 1819 – 17 October 1910)

Lisa Logan
Kent State University

See also the Howe entry in *DLB 1: The American Renaissance in New England.*

BOOKS: *Passion-Flowers,* anonymous (Boston: Ticknor & Fields, 1854);

Words for the Hour, anonymous (Boston: Ticknor & Fields, 1857);

The World's Own (Boston: Ticknor & Fields, 1857); another version published as *Leonore; or, The World's Own,* Stuart's Repertory of Original American Plays, no. 1 (New York: Baker & Godwin, 1857);

A Trip to Cuba (Boston: Ticknor & Fields, 1860);

Battle Hymn of the Republic (Boston: Oliver Ditson, 1862);

Later Lyrics (Boston: Tilton, 1866);

From the Oak to the Olive. A Plain Record of a Pleasant Journey (Boston: Lee & Shepard, 1868);

Memoir of Dr. Samuel Gridley Howe . . . With Other Memorial Tributes (Boston: Howe Memorial Committee, 1876);

Modern Society (Boston: Roberts Brothers, 1881);

Margaret Fuller (Marchesa Ossoli) (Boston: Roberts Brothers, 1883);

Is Polite Society Polite? And Other Essays (Boston & New York: Lamson, Wolffe, 1895);

From Sunset Ridge: Poems Old and New (Boston & New York: Houghton, Mifflin, 1898);

Reminiscences 1819–1899 (Boston & New York: Houghton, Mifflin, 1899);

Original Poems and Other Verse Set to Music as Songs (Boston: Boston Music, 1908);

At Sunset, edited by Laura E. Richards (Boston & New York: Houghton Mifflin, 1910);

Julia Ward Howe and the Woman Suffrage Movement: A Selection From Her Speeches and Essays, edited by Florence Howe Hall (Boston: Estes, 1913);

The Walk with God . . . Extracts From Mrs. Howe's Private Journals, edited by Richards (New York: Dutton, 1919).

OTHER: *Northern Lights: An Illustrated Magazine of Tales, Travels, Poems, Sketches, and Essays,* edited by Howe (Boston: Dakin & Metcalf, 1867);

Sex and Education. A Reply to Dr. E. H. Clarke's "Sex in Education," edited by Howe (Boston: Roberts Brothers, 1874).

Julia Ward Howe, reformer, poet, lecturer, and woman's rights advocate, was among the growing number of nineteenth-century American women who published their travel writings. Known among friends and acquaintances for her vibrant, witty, and outspoken personality, Howe perhaps best displayed her energetic and authoritative voice in her books of travel, which take the form of letters, journals, and memoirs.

Born in New York City, the fourth child of Samuel Ward, a successful New York banker, and Julia Cutler Ward, who died four years later, Howe was educated privately. Self-disciplined and intellectually ambitious even as a child, she read widely in the Bible, history, and the classics; mastered German, French, and Italian; and published poetry by age fourteen. In 1843 she married Dr. Samuel Gridley Howe, nicknamed "Chev," a philanthropist, decorated hero in the Greek War of Independence that had begun in 1821, and director of the Perkins Institution and Massachusetts Institute for the Blind. During their often difficult marriage the Howes lived in Boston and had six children.

Howe wrote widely, publishing in a variety of genres, but her work met with limited success. Today she is best remembered for her Civil War poem "The Battle Hymn of the Republic" and for her leadership role in the woman's movement. Concerned with reform and with influencing the public to humane action, whether on behalf of slaves, women, or the citizens of nondemocratic nations, Howe was a gifted lecturer and a brilliant, animated conversationalist.

In the spring of 1859 Howe and her husband accompanied their friend, ailing Unitarian minister Theodore Parker, to Cuba. That year the *Atlantic Monthly* serialized Howe's Cuban travel letters, which she collected soon thereafter as *A Trip to Cuba* (1860). A lighthearted and engaging travelogue describing the people and places, the work begins with caricatures of seasick fellow travelers, including Parker, to whom she refers as "Can Grande," a "heap of shawls" and "moveless mound of woollens" whose "chief food is pickles,—his only desire is rest." Howe's wit extends even to her description of herself:

> A woman, said to be of a literary turn of mind. . . . Her clothes, flung at her by the Stewardess seem to have hit in some places, and missed in others. . . . She is perpetually being lugged about by a stout steward, who knocks her head against both sides of the vessel, folds her up in the gangway, spreads her out on the deck. . . . N.B. This woman . . . rose like a cork, dressed like a Christian . . . and, when ill treated, announced intentions of writing a book.

In this intimate and conversational vein, Howe describes chronologically her various excursions to Havana, San Antonio, Dominica, and Matanzas, highlighting points of interest and devoting considerable energy and wit to obligatory critiques of accommodations, food, prices, and inhabitants. In foreign territory, Howe and her companions pursue the always-elusive cup of tea, and she offers a tongue-in-cheek lament on a "white teapot, with bands of blue" they leave behind. Howe interweaves such whimsical adventures with philosophical, often satiric observations from a feminine perspective about issues facing pre–Civil War Americans.

For both public and personal reasons, Howe's choice of venue and tone represents a savvy feminist strategy. Since childhood, Howe's family (with the exception of brother Sam) saw a conflict between her literary ambitions and a nineteenth-century woman's domestic role. In *Reminiscences 1819–1899* (1899) Howe quotes a comment made by her uncle John Ward: "This is my little girl who knows about books, and writes an article, and has it printed, but I wish that she knew more about housekeeping." Howe's husband was far less indulgent. Believing that a husband has absolute authority over his wife and that only unmarried women should have careers, Chev not only appropriated his wife's yearly income but demanded that she give up her literary aspirations. Her refusal to do so led to his frequent requests for separation, especially following her publication of a book of poems, *Passion-Flowers* (1854), and a play, *The World's Own* (1857), much criticized for its failure to punish the seduced heroine. Unlike poetry, drama, and fiction, however, letter writing was an important component of a wife's social repertoire. In adopting the letter form, Howe not only conformed to the conventions of travel writing and appealed to a wide audience but also managed to move toward what she called her "vision of some important literary work" without compromising wifely propriety. In erudite, amusing, and feminine prose, Howe delivers her outspoken opinions on political issues, suggesting that race, abolition, education, and rights were the appropriate concerns of women.

In 1859 Cuba was a thriving slave port; an estimated thirty thousand African slaves arrived that year on American ships. Samuel Gridley Howe played an active role in abolition: he protested the Kansas-Nebraska bill, which potentially opened unsettled territory to slavery, and as a member of the Secret Six he funded John Brown's antislavery activities. While Howe never addresses the Cuban slave trade or her husband's position, her views, expressed most fully in chapter 18 of *A Trip to Cuba,* complicate her stance as an abolitionist. In a passage that infuriated William Lloyd Garrison, Howe wonders if "compulsory labor be not better than none" for these "tropical" Africans, the "laziest of brutes, chiefly ambitious to be of no use to any in the world." Howe later wrote in *Reminiscences* that she "did not intend it as an argument in favor of slavery.

Samuel Gridley Howe in 1830, in the uniform he wore in the Greek War of Independence (John Hay Library, Brown University)

As an abstract proposition, and without reference to color, I still think it true." This controversial comment and her theory that "[m]uch of the illness among the negroes is owing to their imprudence" undermine her sympathetic descriptions of plantation slave quarters and her chilling account of a black waiter's mistaking Chev's phrenological inspection of his head for a desire to purchase him. Given Howe's lifetime stance as a reformer, her views are disturbing. She believes that slavery will "gradually ameliorate, and slowly die out." While calling for patience, she acknowledges the lessons Cuba offers about slavery, warning "when Death is no longer terrible to the Enslaved, then let the Enslaver look to it." She looks to God for "swift miracles of redemption" for a "wronged people."

Howe's curious vacillation may be traced to several causes. On their trip the Howes had befriended a family, whose Columbia, South Carolina, plantation they visited on their return trip. In addition, as biographer Mary H. Grant suggests, Howe's views on slavery may be an attempt to distance herself from her overbearing husband. But Howe's attitude is perhaps best understood in the context of her consistent aversion to confrontation, which initially turned her away from abolitionists

and which she avoided in her later career as a feminist lecturer.

Howe's less ambivalent critique in *A Trip to Cuba* of women's position is tempered with good-natured wit. Once in Cuba, she too endures the "Oriental imprisonment" of its women. While her male companions visit monasteries, schools, and cockfights, returning with "airs of superior opportunity, and . . . more insufferable than ever," the women are left to "the eternal task of needlework, to which the sex has been condemned ever since Adam's discovery of his want of a wardrobe." Howe attributes women's seclusion in part to the "barbarous manners" of Cubans and "loose administration of Christian principles." Cuban restrictions on women only compounded her frustration with her autocratic husband:

How much easier it is to deal with the article man in his theoretical rather than in his real presence. You may succeed in showing (by every convincement) that you are his master and superior, and that there is every reason on earth why you should command and direct him. "No!–," says the wretch, shaking his fist, and shrugging his shoulders; and whatever your intimate convictions may be, the end is, that you do not.

Howe's feminine perspective becomes a feature of her account. She refers often to Richard Henry Dana Jr., author of *To Cuba and Back* (1859), but asserts her own authority to discuss feminine spheres of shopping, domestic life, and society. Her experienced eye links women's position in Cuba to their silliness: "The ladies are wonderfully got up . . . their children, bedizened like dolls." Their powdered faces tempt her to "rush in amongst them with a feather duster, and lay about one a little." Howe thinly masks her own criticism of Cuban girls' education by reporting a fictitious "jealous-hearted" woman's observation that education should reach beyond woman's mothering role: "'And if she should never be a mother . . . educate her for herself, that she may give good counsel, and discern the noble and the beautiful. For women are good to inspire men, as well as to bear them, and for their own sakes, they have a right to know all that elevates and dignifies life.'"

Howe's convictions emerge not only from a lifetime of study but also from her growing self-confidence, despite her husband's strenuous objections, as an author and public speaker. A March 1860 review in the *Atlantic Monthly,* in which three-quarters of *A Trip to Cuba* had been published previously, recommended the book as "entertainment and instruction," citing Howe's "lively and witty" capacity for description. The reviewer's one reservation was that the book was "a little too personal, and the public is made the confidant of matters in which it has properly no concern."

Howe's growing self-confidence becomes evident in *From the Oak to the Olive. A Plain Record of a Pleasant Journey* (1868). In 1866 Greek leaders asked Samuel Gridley Howe to assist patriots on Crete in their rebellion against Turkish rule, and in March 1867 the Howes, with daughters Julia Romana and Laura, sailed for Europe to distribute aid to Greek refugees. *From the Oak to the Olive,* Howe's record of her third trip to the Continent, reveals a privileged and experienced woman and traveler, a veteran of European attractions, arts, and society. Drawing on her own romantic fascination with Europe from her visits on her honeymoon in 1843 and as a young mother of two in 1850 and conscious of the more than fifty thousand Americans who took the Grand Tour each year and the hundreds of travel books that resulted, Howe positions herself above the average "neophyte," announcing her obligation to "no editor, nor joint stock company." Howe's declaration of leisure announces her privilege to linger over "the three dimensions of time" and indicates her position as a woman of taste and culture, a member of a class of people worth listening to. Howe announces her authority and independence by using the pronoun *I,* describing herself as "an agent one and indivisible," a quintessential American confronting the Old World capably and confidently. Howe chronicles her travels through England, France, Italy, Greece, Germany, Switzerland, and Belgium, avoiding mere description and instead fashioning her daily life as a prominent woman into intellectual reflections on self and culture.

Howe's approach stems at once from her own sense of vocation and from the post–Civil War American literary market. Following the death of her son Sammy in 1863, Howe joined the Unitarian Church, formalizing years of liberal Christian thinking. In 1864, despite the resistance of her husband and eldest daughters, she began giving sermons, lectures, and public poetry readings, acting on a "deep strong impulse." While still in Boston, Howe had written in her diary, "Literary affairs confused, I have no market. Chev takes away my voice and I do not see how or where to print. God keeps me from falling away from my purpose." With the travel book, Howe was assured of a large popular market and a literary vehicle suitable for conveying her reformist values.

Eschewing mere description, Howe instead turns her itinerary into opportunities for musing on the self, religion, politics, art, women's position, and travel and travel writing. Howe is not interested in

Theodore Parker, the Transcendentalist essayist and Unitarian minister who traveled to Cuba with the Howes

describing European tourist sites in detail; for that she consistently refers the reader to Murray's famous guidebooks. "The less we know about a thing," Howe maintains, "the easier it is to write about it." Having thus disposed of the travel writing of amateurs, Howe instead examines what intellectual improvement Americans can derive from the pricey and predictable catalogue of European attractions.

To the older, wiser Howe, Europe seems awash in glittering entrapments and temptations that consistently threaten her with financial ruin. Paris is a "sweating furnace in which humans would turn life everlasting to gold, provided it were a negotiable value." She recalls the fruits of her last trip to Europe, "Roman trash" and "foolish things," which at least one friend "saluted" with a "paroxysm of merriment." Her discussion of Naples summarizes her new attitude:

You have been two days in Naples, the hotel expenses and temptations of the street eating into your little capital. For value received your intellects have nothing to show. Your eyes and ears have been full, your brain

Howe in 1905 (photograph by Underwood)

passive and empty. You rouse yourself, and determine upon an investment. To learn something, you must spend something. These cherished napoleons must decrease, and you must, if possible, increase.

Howe's intellectual "increases" occur as she contextualizes her surroundings in reflections on American political, spiritual, and aesthetic values. Her visit to King Otto's palace in Greece prompts a discourse on democracy, of which America is the standard,

> America, whose shop-girls take music lessons, whose poorest menials attend lectures, concerts, and balls. A democratic people does not acquiesce either in priestly or in diplomatic precedence. Let people perform their uses, earn their bread, enjoy their own, and respect their neighbors; these are the maxims of good life in a democratic country.

Similarly, a cathedral provokes this thought:

> In America we have religious liberty. This does not mean that a man has morally the right to have no religion, but that the very nature of religion requires that he should hold his own conviction above the ordinances of others.

Howe consistently bristles at Catholicism and any national church, satirizing petty church officials and

using visits to cathedrals in Italy and Greece to deliver her own liberal Christian philosophy. Howe's treatment of a Turkish harem, while it extends beyond the typical exoticism of her day, is an occasion to pronounce the American family the root of democracy—its "individuality of centre and equality of obligation" the perfect school for this virtue.

Howe consistently emphasizes American values and reproaches dilettante travelers and travel writers, especially on aesthetic matters:

> Yet, gentle reader, all is not criticism that criticises, all is not enthusiasm that admires. Copious treatises are written on these subjects by people who know as little of them as is possible for a person of average education. Americans have especially to learn that a general tolerable intelligence does not give a man special knowledge in matters of art. Among the herd of trans-Atlantic travellers who yearly throng these galleries, they know most who pretend least to know.

The Great Exposition prompts Howe to suggest that American artists might be improved by bringing European art to them. She argues that success in America is "too cheap and easy. Art-critics are wordy and ignorant, praising from caprise [*sic*] rather than from conscience." Howe thriftily suggests forming an art gallery of twenty of Europe's best pictures to "save a great deal of going abroad, and help to form a sincere and intelligent standard of aesthetic judgment."

Finally, Howe's book is less a record of her journey than a hybrid chronicle, diary, and sketchbook of herself as woman traveler and writer. In her conclusion Howe writes, "I should, perhaps, . . . have occupied acres and acres of attention with superfluous delineation, putting . . . my own portrait in the corner." Yet it is this omnipresent portrait, not, as one contemporary reviewer suggested, the curiosity of a woman's visiting Greece, that distinguishes Howe's voice and book from hundreds of others of its kind, as Mary Suzanne Schriber discusses.

Reminiscences 1819–1899, Howe's autobiographical memoir, includes chapters on her travels abroad, yet the work is most intent on recording her travels in time during a century that "deserve[s] a record among those which have been great landmarks in human history." Given her purpose, "to do justice to the individuals whom I have known, and to the events of which I have had some personal knowledge," Howe focuses her travel recollections around the people she met. Her wedding visit to Europe is presented as a who's who list and includes

Thomas Carlyle, William Wordsworth, Lord Houghton, Maria Edgeworth, and Charles Dickens; and passages from *A Trip to Cuba* and *From the Oak to the Olive* are simply reprinted. Here, even more than in the latter volume, travel is an occasion for reflecting on the self.

Howe's lifelong intellectual and spiritual development are evident in her travel books. She used this popular genre as a vehicle for conveying ideas about social reform—ideas about which, as she grew older, she gained more confidence and spoke more publicly. While Howe's travel volumes are mostly unread today, they were appreciated during her lifetime not only for their liveliness and wit but also for the genius with which she understood and described other places and people. They accurately convey many nineteenth-century Americans' attitudes toward travel in Cuba and Europe. Above all, her travel writing provides an example of one of the vehicles through which nineteenth-century American women spoke.

Biographies:
Laura E. Richards and Maud Howe Elliott, *Julia Ward Howe 1819–1910,* 2 volumes (Boston & New York: Houghton Mifflin, 1916);

Louise Hall Tharp, *Three Saints and a Sinner: Julia Ward Howe, Louisa, Annie and Sam Ward* (Boston: Little, Brown, 1956);

Deborah Pickman Clifford, *Mine Eyes Have Seen the Glory: A Biography of Julia Ward Howe* (Boston: Little, Brown, 1978);

Mary H. Grant, *Private Woman, Public Person: An Account of the Life of Julia Ward Howe from 1819 to 1868* (Brooklyn, N.Y.: Carlson, 1994).

Reference:
Mary Suzanne Schriber, "Julia Ward Howe and the Travel Book," *New England Quarterly,* 62, no. 2 (1989): 264–279.

Papers:
Most of Julia Ward Howe's unpublished papers are in two locations. The largest collection, including letters, diaries, manuscripts, and juvenilia, is at the Houghton Library, Harvard University. Some letters and Howe's own scrapbooks including articles by and about her are at the Schlesinger Library, Radcliffe College. Other papers may be found at Smith College; the John Hay Library, Brown University; the Boston Athenaeum; the Boston Public Library; and in several private collections.

William Dean Howells

(1 March 1837 – 11 May 1920)

Xavier Baron
University of Wisconsin–Milwaukee

See also the Howells entries in *DLB 12: American Realists and Naturalists; DLB 64: American Literary Critics and Scholars, 1850–1880; DLB 74: American Short-Story Writers Before 1880;* and *DLB 79: American Magazine Journalists, 1850–1900.*

BOOKS: *Poems of Two Friends,* by Howells and John J. Piatt (Columbus, Ohio: Follett, Foster, 1860);

Lives and Speeches of Abraham Lincoln and Hannibal Hamlin, life of Lincoln by Howells and life of Hamlin by J. L. Hayes (Columbus, Ohio: Follett, Foster, 1860);

Venetian Life (London: Trübner, 1866; New York: Hurd & Houghton, 1866; expanded, New York: Hurd & Houghton, 1867; London: Trübner, 1867; expanded again, Boston: Osgood, 1872; revised and expanded again, Boston & New York: Houghton, Mifflin, 1907; London: Constable, 1907);

Italian Journeys (New York: Hurd & Houghton, 1867; London: Low, 1868; enlarged, Boston: Osgood, 1872; revised, London: Heinemann, 1901; Boston & New York: Houghton, Mifflin, 1901);

No Love Lost: A Romance of Travel (New York: Putnam, 1869);

Suburban Sketches (New York: Hurd & Houghton, 1871; London: Low, 1871; enlarged, Boston: Osgood, 1872);

Their Wedding Journey (Boston: Osgood, 1872; Edinburgh: Douglas, 1882);

A Chance Acquaintance (Boston: Osgood, 1873; Edinburgh: Douglas, 1882);

Poems (Boston: Osgood, 1873; enlarged, Boston: Ticknor, 1886);

A Foregone Conclusion (Boston: Osgood, 1875 [i.e., 1874]; London: Low, 1874);

Sketch of Life and Character of Rutherford B. Hayes . . . also a Biographical Sketch of William A. Wheeler (New York: Hurd & Houghton / Boston: Houghton, 1876);

The Parlor Car: Farce (Boston: Osgood, 1876);

William Dean Howells in Venice, 1 May 1865

Out of the Question. A Comedy (Boston: Osgood, 1877; Edinburgh: Douglas, 1882);

A Counterfeit Presentment: Comedy (Boston: Osgood, 1877);

The Lady of the Aroostook (Boston: Houghton Osgood, 1879; Edinburgh: Douglas, 1882);

The Undiscovered Country (Boston: Houghton, Mifflin, 1880; London: Low, 1880);

A Fearful Responsibility and Other Stories (Boston: Osgood, 1881); republished as *A Fearful Responsi-*

bility and "Tonelli's Marriage" (Edinburgh: Douglas, 1882);

Dr. Breen's Practice: A Novel (Boston: Osgood, 1881; London: Trübner, 1881);

A Day's Pleasure and Other Sketches (Boston: Houghton, Mifflin, 1881);

A Modern Instance: A Novel (1 volume, Boston: Osgood, 1882; 2 volumes, Edinburgh: Douglas, 1882);

The Sleeping Car: A Farce (Boston: Osgood, 1883);

A Woman's Reason: A Novel (Boston: Osgood, 1883; Edinburgh: Douglas, 1883);

A Little Girl among the Old Masters (Boston: Osgood, 1884);

The Register: Farce (Boston: Osgood, 1884);

Three Villages (Boston: Osgood, 1884);

The Elevator: Farce (Boston: Osgood, 1885);

The Rise of Silas Lapham (1 volume, Boston: Ticknor, 1885; 2 volumes, Edinburgh: Douglas, 1894);

Tuscan Cities (Boston: Ticknor, 1886; Edinburgh: Douglas, 1886);

Poems (Boston: Ticknor, 1886);

The Garroters: Farce (New York: Harper, 1886; Edinburgh: Douglas, 1887);

Indian Summer (Boston: Ticknor, 1886; Edinburgh: Douglas, 1886);

The Minister's Charge; or, The Apprenticeship of Lemuel Barker (Edinburgh: Douglas, 1886; Boston: Ticknor, 1887);

Modern Italian Poets: Essays and Versions (New York: Harper, 1887; Edinburgh: Douglas, 1887);

April Hopes: A Novel (Edinburgh: Douglas, 1887; New York: Harper, 1888);

A Sea-Change; or, Love's Stowaway: A Lyricated Farce in Two Acts and an Epilogue (Boston: Ticknor, 1888; London: Trübner, 1888);

Annie Kilburn: A Novel (Edinburgh: Douglas, 1888; New York: Harper, 1889);

The Mouse-Trap and Other Farces (New York: Harper, 1889; Edinburgh: Douglas, 1897);

A Hazard of New Fortunes (1 volume, New York: Harper, 1890 [i.e., 1889]; 2 volumes, Edinburgh: Douglas, 1889);

The Shadow of a Dream: A Novel (Edinburgh: Douglas, 1890; New York: Harper, 1890);

A Boy's Town Described for "Harper's Young People" (New York: Harper, 1890);

Criticism and Fiction (New York: Harper, 1891; London: Osgood, McIlvaine, 1891);

The Albany Depot: Farce (New York: Harper, 1891; Edinburgh: Douglas, 1897);

An Imperative Duty: A Novel (New York: Harper, 1892 [i.e., 1891]; Edinburgh: Douglas, 1891);

Mercy: A Novel (Edinburgh: Douglas, 1892); republished as *The Quality of Mercy* (New York: Harper, 1892);

A Letter of Introduction: Farce (New York: Harper, 1892; Edinburgh: Douglas, 1897);

A Little Swiss Sojourn (New York: Harper, 1892);

Christmas Every Day and Other Stories Told for Children (New York: Harper, 1893);

The World of Chance: A Novel (Edinburgh: Douglas, 1893; New York: Harper, 1893);

The Unexpected Guests: A Farce (New York: Harper, 1893; Edinburgh: Douglas, 1897);

My Year in a Log Cabin (New York: Harper, 1893);

Evening Dress: Farce (New York: Harper, 1893; Edinburgh: Douglas, 1893);

The Coast of Bohemia: A Novel (New York: Harper, 1893);

A Traveler from Altruria: Romance (New York: Harper, 1894; Edinburgh: Douglas, 1894);

My Literary Passions (New York: Harper, 1895);

Stops of Various Quills (New York: Harper, 1895);

The Day of Their Wedding: A Novel (New York: Harper, 1896); republished in *Idyls in Drab* (Edinburgh: Douglas, 1896);

A Parting and a Meeting: Story (New York: Harper, 1896); republished in *Idyls in Drab*;

Impressions and Experiences (New York: Harper, 1896; Edinburgh: Douglas, 1896);

A Previous Engagement: Comedy (New York: Harper, 1897);

The Landlord at Lion's Head (Edinburgh: Douglas, 1897; New York: Harper, 1897);

An Open-Eyed Conspiracy: An Idyl of Saratoga (New York & London: Harper, 1897; Edinburgh: Douglas, 1897);

Stories of Ohio (New York, Cincinnati & Chicago: American Book, 1897);

The Story of a Play: A Novel (New York & London: Harper, 1898);

Ragged Lady: A Novel (New York & London: Harper, 1899);

Their Silver Wedding Journey, 2 volumes (New York & London: Harper, 1899);

Bride Roses: A Scene (Boston & New York: Houghton, Mifflin, 1900);

Room Forty-Five: A Farce (Boston & New York: Houghton, Mifflin, 1900);

An Indian Giver: A Comedy (Boston & New York: Houghton, Mifflin, 1900);

The Smoking Car: A Farce (Boston & New York: Houghton, Mifflin, 1900);

Literary Friends and Acquaintance: A Personal Retrospect of American Authorship (New York & London: Harper, 1900);

A Pair of Patient Lovers (New York & London: Harper, 1901);

Heroines of Fiction, 2 volumes (New York & London: Harper, 1901);

The Kentons: A Novel (New York & London: Harper, 1902);

The Flight of Pony Baker: A Boy's Town Story (New York & London: Harper, 1902);

Literature and Life (New York & London: Harper, 1902);

Questionable Shapes (New York & London: Harper, 1903);

Letters Home (New York & London: Harper, 1903);

The Son of Royal Langbrith: A Novel (New York & London: Harper, 1904);

Miss Bellard's Inspiration: A Novel (New York & London: Harper, 1905);

London Films (New York & London: Harper, 1905);

Certain Delightful English Towns with Glimpses of the Pleasant Country Between (New York & London: Harper, 1906);

Through the Eye of the Needle: A Romance (New York & London: Harper, 1907);

Between the Dark and the Daylight: Romances (New York: Harper, 1907; London: Harper, 1912);

Fennel and Rue: A Novel (New York & London: Harper, 1908);

Roman Holidays and Others (New York & London: Harper, 1908);

The Mother and the Father: Dramatic Passages (New York & London: Harper, 1909);

Seven English Cities (New York & London: Harper, 1909);

My Mark Twain: Reminiscences and Criticisms (New York & London: Harper, 1910);

Imaginary Interviews (New York & London: Harper, 1910);

Parting Friends: A Farce (New York & London: Harper, 1911);

New Leaf Mills: A Chronicle (New York & London: Harper, 1913);

Familiar Spanish Travels (New York & London: Harper, 1913);

The Seen and Unseen at Stratford-On-Avon: A Fantasy (New York & London: Harper, 1914);

The Daughter of the Storage and Other Things in Prose and Verse (New York & London: Harper, 1916);

The Leatherwood God (New York: Century, 1916; London: Jenkins, 1917);

Years of My Youth (New York & London: Harper, 1916);

The Vacation of the Kelwyns: An Idyl of the Middle Eighteen-Seventies (New York & London: Harper, 1920);

Hither and Thither in Germany (New York & London: Harper, 1920);

Mrs. Farrell: A Novel (New York & London: Harper, 1921);

Prefaces to Contemporaries (1882–1920), edited by George Arms, William M. Gibson, and Frederic C. Marston Jr. (Gainesville, Fla.: Scholars' Facsimiles and Reprints, 1957);

Criticism and Fiction and Other Essays, edited by Clara Marburg Kirk and Rudolf Kirk (New York: New York University Press, 1959);

The Complete Plays of W. D. Howells, edited by Walter J. Meserve (New York: New York University Press, 1960);

W. D. Howells as Critic, edited by Edwin H. Cady (London & Boston: Routledge, 1973);

Editor's Study: A Comprehensive Edition of W. D. Howells' Column, edited by James W. Simpson (Troy, N.Y.: Whitson, 1983);

The Early Prose Writings of William Dean Howells 1853–1861, edited by Thomas Wortham (Athens: Ohio University Press, 1990).

Collection: *A Selected Edition of W. D. Howells,* edited by Edwin H. Cady, Ronald Gottesman, Don L. Cook, and David Nordloh, 20 volumes to date (Bloomington: Indiana University Press / Boston: Twayne, 1968–   ).

OTHER: "The Road to Boston: 1860 Travel Correspondence of William Dean Howells," edited by Robert Price, in *Ohio History,* 80 (1971), pp. 85–154.

William Dean Howells combined a career as an important novelist with that of a journalist. As editor of *The Atlantic Monthly* and later as author of, or contributor to, the "Editor's Study" and "Editor's Easy Chair" columns in *Harper's Monthly,* he was an influential man of letters. Through *The Atlantic Monthly* he introduced a generation of readers to little-known foreign authors and helped young American writers to get started. He wrote forty-three novels as well as short stories, plays, poetry, several volumes of autobiography, two presidential campaign biographies, and a dozen volumes of literary reminiscences, sketches, and essays. In addition Howells wrote ten accomplished travel books, and he used situations and observations from his travels, especially in Italy, in some of his novels and short stories. The encounters of young and often innocent American women with older, more worldly European men figure prominently in his fiction.

Howells was a lifelong traveler. Some of his earliest writings were reports on a river trip to Saint Louis. Most of his travel sketches and travel books

William Dean and Elinor Howells in Venice soon after their marriage in
December 1862

are about the cities of Europe and his journeys to them by boat or train. Following Washington Irving and James Fenimore Cooper, he joined his friends Samuel Langhorne Clemens (Mark Twain) and Henry James in exploring the tensions and contradictions of men and women from the New World confronting the cultural richness and complex historical traditions of the Old World. Influenced by the example of Nathaniel Hawthorne, Howells took an honest approach to art, free from affectation or traditional judgments. He was confident in an intuitive response to traditional art and architecture and was unconcerned about being perceived as anti-intellectual. Often baffled by the historical past—es-

pecially that of Italy—he relied on anecdotal information and conventional observation. Despite his clear belief in the moral superiority of the United States, he was attracted to the cultural charms of Europe and the richness and variety of European customs and rituals.

Keen observation of real places and real experiences is the foundation of literary realism, which Howells defined as "the truthful treatment of material" and which he practiced and preached throughout his career. The travel writer must see and describe the important and convey the immediacy of the actual rather than repeating the formulaic responses of predecessors to frequently visited places.

Howells's innate curiosity and his journalistic veracity contributed to his convictions about the primacy of realism in effective fiction and successful travel writing. For the realist nothing in life was insignificant, nothing unnoteworthy.

Howells also turned to travel writing because it was a variety of the familiar essay that had grown up with the newspaper and journal. The travel essay attracted the curious reader and provided information without seeming idle, and it promised bourgeois readers sophistication and worldliness, even while they stayed settled in their provincial routines. Howells was also temperamentally disposed to travel writing because of his nearly lifelong position as an editor, a position that allowed him to rule on matters of taste, refinement, and culture. This superior tone, attendant on his influential position, sometimes mars his early travel books–*Venetian Life* (1866), *Italian Journeys* (1867), and *Tuscan Cities* (1886)–for he condescended to both the Europeans he wrote about and his American audience. Yet cultural condescension is absent from those he wrote in the twentieth century, particularly *London Films* (1905) and *Roman Holidays and Others* (1908).

William Dean Howells was born in Martin's Ferry, Ohio, on 1 March 1837 to William Cooper Howells and Mary Dean Howells. His father's people were Welsh, and his mother came from German and Irish ancestry in Pennsylvania. His father was a book-loving, cultivated man who delighted in reading aloud. The Howells family, Howells recalled in *My Literary Passions* (1895), owned more books than any other house in town. They had many volumes of poetry, including works by Robert Burns, Thomas Moore, Sir Walter Scott, Alexander Pope, and George Gordon, Lord Byron. When Howells's father became printer and editor of the *Intelligencer* in 1840, he moved the family to Hamilton, Ohio, and by age seven the young Howells was setting type and delivering papers. The family moved again when Howells's father bought the *Dayton Transcript* in 1849. Eighteen months later, when the venture failed, they moved yet again, this time to Eureka Mills, Ohio, where William Cooper Howells attempted to start a commune with his father and brothers. While teaching himself French, Spanish, Portuguese, Latin, and Italian, young William Dean spent hours imitating the styles and techniques of classical authors such as Miguel de Cervantes and William Shakespeare and popular contemporaries including Charles Dickens and William Makepeace Thackeray. His studies were interrupted, however, when the family's need for money forced his parents to send him and his brother Joseph to work in Xenia and later Dayton.

In 1851 Howells's father became a recorder of debates in the Ohio legislature for the *Ohio State Journal* in Columbus, and young William became a compositor for the paper, continuing to contribute his earnings to the family. The following year the elder Howells became editor of the *Ashtabula Sentinel*, which moved six months later to Jefferson, Ohio. William Dean Howells, who had had one poem published in the *Ohio State Journal*, contributed poems and sketches to his father's paper as well as working as a compositor. The elder Howells returned to Columbus in 1856 as a clerk to the state legislature and left the boy in charge of the newspaper. The following year William moved to Columbus, where he and his father produced a daily letter about legislative affairs for the *Cincinnati Gazette*, leaving his brother Joseph in charge of the family paper in Jefferson. Shortly thereafter the *Cincinnati Gazette* offered William Dean Howells a full-time job. He moved to Cincinnati, but after a month the homesick young man was back in Jefferson, and he soon resumed working with his father in Columbus. In May 1858 he took a trip on the Mississippi River to Saint Louis aboard his uncle's steamboat, sending travel letters to the family paper in Jefferson. These pieces are confident without undue smugness, judgmental without undue harshness: "Mississippi scenery for more than an hundred miles below St. Louis, has nothing of the grand or the picturesque, but a great deal of the flat uninteresting" (18 May 1858). "We left St. Louis about noon, yesterday. I confess that I saw, without reluctance, its roofs and spires fading out of sight; and welcomed the pleasant silence and solitude of the river again.–Fairer, in her rudest aspects, than the most pretentious works of man, Nature was unspeakably beautiful to me after five days imprisonment in the dull streets and walls of that city" (26 May 1858).

By November 1858 Howells had become assistant news editor at the *Ohio State Journal*. In addition to publishing poems, sketches, and criticism in this newspaper, Howells contributed to the *Saturday Press* of New York, and *The Atlantic Monthly* accepted five or six poems. His devotion to the poetry of Henry Wadsworth Longfellow and Heinrich Heine inspired him to write verse, resulting in *Poems of Two Friends* (1860), which also includes poems by John J. Piatt. His campaign biography of Abraham Lincoln, published with J. L. Hayes's campaign biography of Hannibal Hamlin (1860), earned him enough money to take a tour through New England to New York, traveling on the Saint Lawrence River to Niagara Falls and Quebec then on to Boston and New York. Arranging to publish travel letters in the *Ohio State Journal* and the *Cincinnati Gazette*, he also

Casa Falier in Venice, where Howells wrote the travel letters that he revised for Venetian Life *(1866)*

planned to gather material for a subscription book about industry in New England and New York, but he quickly lost interest. Howells turned the trip into a literary pilgrimage. In Cambridge, Massachusetts, James Russell Lowell, who had accepted some of Howells's poems for *The Atlantic Monthly,* introduced him to Oliver Wendell Holmes and James T. Fields, who had just replaced Lowell as editor of *The Atlantic* and had accepted Howells's poem "The Pilot's Story" for the magazine. Lowell also gave Howells a letter of introduction to Nathaniel Hawthorne, who sent him to see Ralph Waldo Emerson. While visiting these two writers in Concord, Howells also met Henry David Thoreau, and in New York he met Walt Whitman.

During the Civil War Howells chose not to join the Ohio volunteers. Instead he sought appointment to a diplomatic post, using his Lincoln biography as his political credential. Presidential secretaries John Nicolay and John Hay helped him secure an appointment as U.S. consul in Venice, and he set sail for Italy in November 1861. With his only consular responsibility to report the presence of Confederate ships in Mediterranean waters and occasionally to look after traveling Americans, Howells had a great deal of time for other pursuits. On 24 December 1862, at the American Embassy in Paris, he married Elinor Gertrude Mead of Vermont, whom he had met in 1860 while she was visiting a cousin in Columbus. In his literary work he first wrote mainly unsuccessful verse, but he later turned to travel sketches.

In Venice Howells discovered the Italian dramatist Carlo Goldoni, who became another literary passion, and prepared a study of nineteenth-century Italian literature. His critical essay "Recent Italian Comedy" was accepted by Lowell for the *North American Review,* where it was published in the October 1864 issue. During that same year Lowell praised Howells's travel letters, which had begun appearing in the *Boston Advertiser,* further encouraging Howells to turn from poetry to prose, writing to Howells on 28 July: "I don't forget my good opinion of you . . . I have been charmed with your Venetian letters. . . . They make the most careful and picturesque *study* I have ever seen on any part of Italy. They are the thing itself."

After the letters were published in the *Boston Advertiser* between March 1863 and May 1865, Howells revised them before they were collected as *Venetian Life* (1866). By late 1864 Howells had grown weary of Venice; when the war ended the following spring, he asked to be relieved of his consular duties. He returned to the United States in late summer 1865.

In New York Howells did some freelance writing for *The New York Times* and then worked briefly for *The Nation*. After becoming assistant editor of *The Atlantic Monthly* in March 1866, he settled with his family in Cambridge, Massachusetts, and was soon invited to attend the weekly sessions of the Dante Club, where he listened to Longfellow read from his translation of *The Divine Comedy*. Howells's knowledge of Dante and Italian literature and culture in general helped him to become immediately accepted as a valuable part of this select group. When *Venetian Life* appeared in 1866 it received enthusiastic reviews, with Lowell leading the praise.

Venetian Life became Howells's first literary success. Reprinted several times throughout his life, it has remained the most popular and highly acclaimed of his travel books. Contrasting romanticized descriptions of an imagined and illusory past with ironic or humorous descriptions of a real and factual present, the book sometimes reverses this theme by juxtaposing a dreamy present with a brutal past:

> One longed to fall down on the space of green turf before the church, now bathed in the soft October sunshine, and recant these happy, commonplace centuries of heresy, and have back again the good old believing days of bigotry, and superstition, and roasting, and racking, if only to have once more the men who dreamed those windows out of their faith and piety (if they did, which I doubt), and made them with their patient, reverent hands (if their hands were reverent, which I doubt).

Howells avoided the Venice of romance and Lord Byron and the Venice of art, architecture, and John Ruskin. Instead he observed Venetian everyday life, customs, and people, describing his own life there.

The book begins with a sketch of the present condition of Venice and its background, followed by a description of his arrival by gondola and his general impressions. "Winter in Venice," which includes discussions of stoves and cold, is followed in the fourth chapter by descriptions of the central attractions around the Piazza San Marco. Howells then discusses his domestic life before presenting a cursory examination of Venetian art and architecture. The final two chapters, "Venetian Traits and Characters" and "Society," afford Howells opportunities to report on the minor dramas and players of Venetian street, theatrical, and professional life. In the closing chapter added to the enlarged 1872 edition, "Our Last Year in Venice," Howells indicates that he is not so much interested in rejecting the traditions of writing about Venice as in condemning their excesses and clichés.

Howells's lifelong concern with the faithful presentation of ordinary material is evident throughout *Venetian Life,* but the subject is too weighted down with traditional views of the city for Howells to succeed. He imitates many of the conventions of travel writing despite his attempts to deviate from them by changing tones and shifting points of view. He also gets tripped up in his philistine disdain for the usefulness of critics of art and architecture, such as Ruskin. Without realizing (or at least acknowledging) that he is doing precisely–and not so well–what he criticized Ruskin for doing, Howells often provides suggestions if not the guidance for an aesthetic appreciation and enjoyment of a city that is itself a great and timeless work of art.

Following the success of *Venetian Life,* Howells used his Italian experiences for another book, *Italian Journeys* (1867), based on the travels Howells and his wife made from Venice to Naples and back. Although he presented the book as nonfiction, Howells fashioned a continuous narrative. With their realistic dialogue many episodes read like Howells's fiction. *Italian Journeys* is more fragmented than his Venice book because he covers a larger geographical area and discusses more complicated travel arrangements. He attempted to unify the whole by frequent assertions of the superiority of the present, the destructiveness of time and rejections of "the dead past–the past which, with all its sensuous beauty and grace, and all its intellectual power, I am not sorry to have dead, and, for the most part, buried." Throughout the book Howells never really resolves his tendency toward anti-intellectualism in his derisive attitude toward the past, which he probably meant to please and flatter his American audience. Even if it is less picturesque, he asserted, the present is not so corrupt as the past. The limitations of his argument are suggested in his description of his present-day experience of a room in the Monastero di San Paolo in Parma, which has frescoes by Correggio. Calling it "altogether the loveliest room in the world," Howells acknowledges: "What curious scenes the gayety of this little chamber conjures up, and what a vivid comment on the age and people that produced it!"

Although most of the attention of "The Road to Rome from Venice" in *Italian Journeys* is devoted to Naples, the work concludes with "Roman Pearls," which anticipates Howells's *Roman Holidays*. In *Italian Journeys* Howells explains when a traveler contracts "Roman fever–the longing that burns one who has once been in Rome to go again–that will not be cured by all the cool contemptuous things he

Elinor and William Dean Howells with their children:
Mildred, John Mead, and Winifred, circa 1875

may think or say of the Eternal City; that fills him with fond memories of its fascination, and make it forever desired." Generally he is hostile to Rome, indifferent to its beauties, scornful of the papacy, and intent on showing the vulgarity of the poor. In addition to Naples and Rome Howells describes the trips he and his wife took to Padua, Arquà, Ferrara, Bassano, Passagno, and Como. Vicenza and Verona, which they also visited, get cursory attention. Brief mentions of Torquato Tasso's prison in Ferrara, the marketplace before the Palazzo della Ragione in Padua, Antonio Canova's sculpture in Passagno, and Andrea Palladio's architecture in Vicenza are somewhat balanced by the more extended treatment of "A Pilgrimage to Petrarch's House at Arquà." Homage to the Italian poet is mixed with a tour of the house, delivered with a faint and embarrassed sarcasm. The concluding chapter, "Ducal Mantua," includes a seventy-seven-page summary of the history of the city and its powerful rulers, with passing attention to Virgil.

Howells's two Italian books and his expertise in Italian literature brought him an honorary M.A. from Harvard University in 1867 and in 1869 an invitation from Charles W. Eliot, the new president of the university, to be a special lecturer on contemporary Italian literature. In 1867 *Putnam's Magazine* published Howells's *No Love Lost: A Romance of Travel,* a long poem in unrhymed hexameters that he had written in Venice. Published as a book in 1869, it is characterized by generalized depictions and forgettable verse: "And one finds, to one's infinite comfort, / Venice just as unique as one's fondest visions have made it: / Palaces and mosquitos rise from the water together."

In 1871 Howells was named editor in chief of *The Atlantic Monthly* and collected some of his pieces from that magazine in *Suburban Sketches.* In these sketches Howells describes the daily life of Cambridge in the same manner as he had earlier reported on Venetian life. Encouraged by critics such as Lowell, who compared Howells's style and pow-

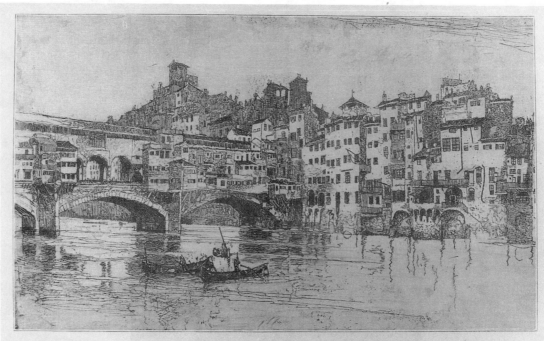

FLORENCE, ON THE ARNO. — PONTE VECCHIO.

A CITY GATE.

FOUNTAIN OUTSIDE OF THE WALL AT SIENA.

Illustrations from Tuscan Cities *(1886)*

ers of observation to Hawthorne's, Howells wrote his first novel, *Their Wedding Journey* (1872), which was serialized in *The Atlantic Monthly*. As in *Italian Journeys*, the plot of the novel is based on a couple's travels, with Mr. and Mrs. Howells becoming Basil and Isabel March, fictional characters Howells used in nine later novels and stories.

During the 1870s *The Atlantic Monthly* flourished, and Howells completed six lengthy works of fiction, tried his hand at playwriting, and wrote short stories, sketches, a volume of poems, and a campaign biography of Rutherford B. Hayes. His novel *A Chance Acquaintance* (1873) also features the framework of the journey, this time in Canada, particularly Quebec, and on the Saint Lawrence and Saguenay Rivers, whose beauties Howells affectionately described. The heroine, Kitty Ellison, from western New York, is traveling with her Milwaukee cousin and his wife from Buffalo to Quebec and eventually back home by way of Boston, a cultural center she holds in awe. Howells uses contrasts in social levels to point up the egalitarian importance of commonplace experience. As Kitty says at one point, "If I were to write a story, I should want to take the slightest sort of plot, and lay the scene in the dullest kind of place, and then bring out all their possibilities. I'll tell you a book after my own heart: 'Details,'–just the history of a week in the life of some young people who happen together in an old New England country-house; nothing extraordinary, little, every-day things told so exquisitely, and all fading naturally away without any particular result, only the full meaning of everything brought out." For all of his and his heroine's attachment to the commonplace, Howells realized the appeal of the exotic and faraway to his American readers and used the setting of French-speaking Quebec for much of the narrative. He continued to use travel and distant places as themes and settings in his next three novels.

His 1874 novel *A Foregone Conclusion* is set in Venice. The work was Howells's first attempt at the international novel and was a considerable success. His next novel was serialized as "Private Theatricals" in *The Atlantic Monthly*, beginning in November 1875. Howells suppressed its publication as a book, and it was published posthumously as *Mrs. Farrell* (1921).

After "Private Theatricals" Howells turned his attention to drama. Most of his efforts went into writing one-act plays, mainly farces and comedies, and he turned out twenty-six of these dramas over the next thirty-five years. His full-length comedy *A Counterfeit Presentment* (1877) was produced with considerable success, and his only other full-length

comedy, *Out of the Question* (1877), was published but never performed professionally.

Howells returned to the international theme with his realistic novel *The Lady of the Aroostook* (1879), about a rural Massachusetts schoolteacher who encounters the sophistication of two young Bostonians on shipboard and the unfamiliar mores of European society in a vividly portrayed Venice. The following year Howells's first big novel, *The Undiscovered Country,* appeared in *The Atlantic Monthly*. When it came out as a book later in 1880, it sold eight thousand copies during the first month.

In 1881 Howells, weary of the routine of editing *The Atlantic Monthly,* now solely owned by Henry Houghton, left his post. Houghton's former partner, James Osgood, who was continuing as a book publisher on his own, offered Howells a weekly salary and royalties to write one novel per year. Howells's frail daughter Winifred was frequently ill, and by the end of the year Howells himself was in a sickbed from overwork. *A Fearful Responsibility,* a novella serialized in *Scribner's* in June and July 1881, is the last work of fiction for which Howells drew on his Venetian experiences. The book is based on a visit to Italy in 1863 by Elinor Howells's sister, Mary Mead, and it again addresses the conflict of an innocent, indiscreet American and a sophisticated and unscrupulous European. A minor work, *Dr. Breen's Practice,* appeared in *The Atlantic Monthly* from August through December 1881. Also in December *A Modern Instance,* an accomplished picture of post–Civil War America, began in *Century.*

In 1882 Howells took his second trip to Italy, having signed a contract with Osgood to publish sketches of thirteen cities. Howells promised to make "each study as attractive as possible with anecdote and adventure. I should seek rather interest than thoroughness, and I believe I should succeed and make some sketches which people would like. It is the ground I know, and I should work con amore." The eventual result was *Tuscan Cities* (1886), which exemplifies Howells's sense of "the travel book as a vehicle for recording reexperienced history."

After a stop in London and literary dinners presided over by Henry James, Howells settled in Switzerland and worked on the novel that is widely considered his worst, *A Woman's Reason* (1883), which he finished in Florence during the winter. He still loved Italy but was more aware of its impoverished aspects than he had been twenty years earlier. He saw shabbiness everywhere, even in Venice, where he once had been "more intensely at home" than anywhere else, "even Boston itself."

Howells in 1899

lisher Roswell Smith estimated that one million people were reading the story as it appeared. Howells's story of the rise and fall of a business entrepreneur also follows the Laphams' failed attempt to gain acceptance in Boston society. This rejection theme is similar to the contrast in Howells's travel books and the related international novels between the young and socially innocent (or inept) and the old, established, and socially sophisticated.

In his preface to *Tuscan Cities* Howells explains that its appearance in "the same size and shape as *Venetian Life* and *Italian Journeys*" was due to "a kind of unity in all three which he hoped might be appreciable to the reader in the uniformity aimed at." If anything, however, Howells had become even more convinced of American superiority and less tolerant of Italian life. His attempts to demonstrate that writing about unimportant places can be as interesting as accounts of visits to the fabled and historical may have been intended to make his American readers feel less intimidated and more at home, but this approach turns out to be condescending and often ridiculous. Insisting that the commonplace is as valuable as the greatest Florentine masterpieces of art and architecture, he claims that he would rather have "the perpetuity of the *cameriere's* smile when he came up with our coffee in the morning than Donatello's San Giorgio, if either were purchasable; and the face of the old chamber-maid, Maria, full of motherly affection, was better than the facade of Santa Maria Novella." More than half the book is a section Howells titles "A Florentine Mosaic," which interweaves the descriptions of the physical scene, people, and sounds of modern Florence with a summary of Florentine history and generalizations about its meaning. About a quarter of the rest of *Tuscan Cities* is made up of "Panforte di Siena," with the remainder of the book evenly divided between "Pitiless Pisa" and cursory descriptions of Lucca, Pistoia, Prato, and Fiesole.

In cities as rich in history as Florence, Siena, and Pisa it seems futile to ignore the past, but Howells did so, sometimes ineffectually, as when he describes a civil wedding or "a session of the police court, which I was willing to compare with the like tribunal at home." At other times this strategy produces some effective writing, principally in those observations of contemporary life such as the drying wash near Dante's house in Florence or the cold, dim death room of Lorenzo de Medici in the Villa Careggi. A description of a young woman of Siena is vibrant and effective: "Her hair was ashen blonde; she was slimly cased in black silk, and as she slowly walked, she pulled forward the skirt a little with one hand, while she drew together with the other a light

After almost a year in Europe, Howells returned home by way of London, where Lowell was American ambassador and where the constant socializing grew tiresome and kept Howells from writing. Once home he finished his novel *Indian Summer* (1886), the most important result of his second visit to Italy. The main character is an American editor who returns to Europe to write a travel book. Disappointed by the sales of this novel, Howells attributed the unenthusiastic reception to American provincialism. He never again placed a story completely in a foreign setting, and he used Venice as a locale only once again, in *Ragged Lady* (1899), a minor work about a New England girl who meets her future husband there.

Back in Boston, Howells wrote his best-known novel, *The Rise of Silas Lapham,* during the spring and summer of 1885. It began appearing in *Century* magazine in November and drew a huge audience. Pub-

shawl, falling from the top of her head, round her throat; her companion followed at a little distance; on the terrace lingered a large white Persian cat, looking after them." So too is his description of the countryside near Pisa, which is compelling despite its generalizations and similarities to versions by other writers.

The metaphors of the mosaic and the "Panforte di Siena," an elaborately decorated Sienese confection that Howells liked because of its "chance and random associations of material and decorative character," are appropriate to the hodgepodge of subjects, styles, and approaches he employed. They suggest more unity than he consistently achieved. Many of the travel pieces are either overwrought or absurd, especially those in which Howells put himself in a dramatic scene, such as his melodramatic re-creation of the attempted assassination of Lorenzo de Medici or the burning of Girolamo Savonarola, or he dramatizes himself and artist Joseph Pennell as old friends reunited with a personified Pisa. Far too often this purported travel book turns into unimpressive philosophical and self-serving ramblings about human nature and its indifference to past and present: "If I had been less modern, less recent, less raw, I should have been by just so much indifferent to the antique charms of the place. In the midst of my reverie of the Pisan past, I dreamily asked the miller about the milling business of the Pisan present. I forget what he said." The haughty voice of the American editor of *The Atlantic* is once again prominent.

A certain weary distrust of his value as a travel writer sometimes shows itself, as when Howells curiously declines to describe the cathedral in Siena and exhorts, "Get photographs, get prints, dear reader, or go see for yourself!" This admonition is surprising not only because *Tuscan Cities* was elaborately illustrated by Pennell but also because Howells, just a few pages earlier, claims that "photographs do well enough in suggestion for such as have not seen the church, but these will never have the full sense of it which only long looking and coming again and again can impart."

With the serialization of *Indian Summer* in *Harper's Monthly* in July 1885 through February 1886, Howells began his association with the publishing firm of Harper and Brothers that lasted until his death. Not only did the firm publish Howells's books, but it also featured Howells's "Editor's Study" (1886–1892) and "Editor's Easy Chair" (1900–1920) columns in *Harper's Monthly*.

In 1886 Howells also published a collection of poems, a farce, and a novel of social concerns, *The Minister's Charge; or, The Apprenticeship of Lemuel Barker*. The following year he produced *Modern Italian Poets,* twenty essays on modern Italian literature and his translations of a hundred years of Italian verse, and *April Hopes,* a novel of manners. In his next novel, *Annie Kilburn* (1888), Howells returned to social concerns, focusing on some of the social and economic problems of late-nineteenth-century New England. *A Hazard of New Fortunes* (1889), Howells's longest novel, is set and was mostly written in New York, where Howells spent the winter of 1888–1889. It gives new emphasis to Howells's growing interest in socialism.

In 1889 Howells and his wife were devastated by the death of their daughter Winifred. After his contract to write "The Editor's Study" for *Harper's Monthly* expired in 1891, Howells and his wife settled in New York. He became editor of *The Cosmopolitan* but resigned after six months. In 1900 he returned to writing a column for *Harper's Monthly*.

In the early 1890s Howells produced two short novels, *The Shadow of a Dream* (1890) and *An Imperative Duty* (1891), and *The Quality of Mercy* (1892), a longer novel in which flight to a foreign country (this time Canada) and exile from the United States are once again prominent in the plot.

The second book for which Howells drew on his 1882 trip to Europe, *A Little Swiss Sojourn,* was published in 1892. Howells's indifference to Switzerland makes the book stale and colorless in comparison with his other travel writings. For most of the book Howells concentrates on explaining how the country, its weather, its food, its customs, and its people are lesser versions of those in the rest of Europe. His attitude toward Switzerland is probably best summed up in his response to getting no examination of baggage from the customs officials: "It was the first but not the last disappointment we suffered in Switzerland." Yet even Howells's disappointments are not deeply registered, contributing to the pervasive superficiality of the work.

Among the novels Howells produced during the remainder of the 1890s were two utopian romances, *A Traveler from Altruria* (1894) and *Through the Eye of the Needle,* which was serialized in part in *The Cosmopolitan* in 1894 but was not published as a book until 1907. At sixty Howells published *The Landlord at Lion's Head* (1897), a study of an amoral New Englander who is rejected by a Boston socialite and his fiancée and escapes to Florence, where he marries a wealthy American.

In the twentieth century Howells completed seven novels. *The Kentons* (1902), which was inspired by Howells's Ohio background, is set there, in New York, and in Holland. *The Son of Royal Langbrith* (1904) and *The Leatherwood God* (1916) are consid-

WESTGATE, SOUTHAMPTON

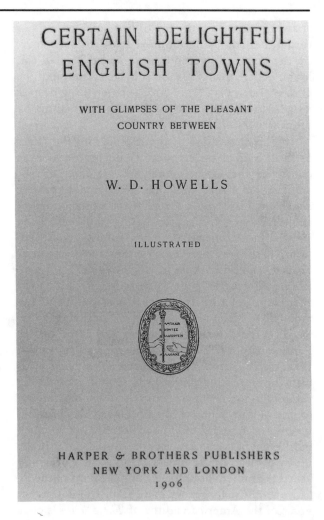

CERTAIN DELIGHTFUL
ENGLISH TOWNS

WITH GLIMPSES OF THE PLEASANT
COUNTRY BETWEEN

W. D. HOWELLS

ILLUSTRATED

HARPER & BROTHERS PUBLISHERS
NEW YORK AND LONDON
1906

Frontispiece and title page for one of the travel books Howells wrote about this 1904 visit to Great Britain

ered major achievements, but the others are minor works. He also produced an important memoir, *My Mark Twain: Reminiscences and Criticisms* (1910).

During the same period Howells also continued to write travel pieces. He began a series of sketches in London in the spring of 1904 and finished them in Italy later that winter. They were first published in *Harper's Monthly* and then collected as *London Films* (1905) and *Certain Delightful English Towns with Glimpses of the Pleasant Country Between* (1906). All Howells's English travel books show the influence of Hawthorne's *Our Old Home* (1863) and Henry James's *English Hours* (1905). Despite an obsession with English weather that commences in a rambling opening chapter, Howells offers astute observations of London, comparing it to other cities, especially New York, "because they are both the effect of an indefinite succession of anarchistic impulses, sometimes correcting and sometimes promoting, or at best sometimes annulling one an-

other." In chapter 3, "Shows and Side-shows of State," he continues the comparisons with telling observations about the interactions of public and private life, about courtesy, and about law and order. Chapter 5, "The Sights and Sounds of the Streets," presents a fascinating account of buses and cabs and "motors, as the English more simply and briefly call automobiles." Because of his interest in politics, it is not surprising that Howells visited the House of Commons but disappointing that he has little to say.

Howells is strongest when avoiding tourist attractions and recounting his observations of London society, most often in parks and on the streets. He touches on the poverty of the East End, comparing it to that of New York and concluding "that the conditions are alike in the Old World and the New, and that the only difference is in the circumstances, which may be better now in New York, and now in London, while the conditions are always bad everywhere for the poor." The vastness of London did not intimidate Howells as it did Henry James, whom Howells echoes when he cautions "that no matter with what devoted passion the American lover of London approaches her he must not hope for an exclusive possession of her heart. If she is insurpassably the most interesting, the most fascinating of all the cities that ever were, let him be sure that he is not the first to find out."

Howells's descriptions of excursions to Hampton Court, to Greenwich, and to watch the Henley Regatta are pedestrian and flat in execution, displaying Howells's probable intention to please and interest his readers with London attractions that do not particularly intrigue him. He is eminently better when he recounts his trek across Tower Bridge to normally unvisited Southwark and makes observations about William Shakespeare's Bankside and John Harvard, then heads back to the city across London Bridge and to Bunhill Fields in pursuit of "American Origins–Mainly Northern" and "American Origins–Mostly Southern." These two chapters are crammed with information and offer a convincing rationale for visiting many of the seventy-four traditional churches of London. The chapters are effective because they impose on the nearly limitless variety of London a requisite tightening of focus that the best of Howells's writing in *London Films* demonstrates.

Although Howells devoted whole books to London, Rome, and Venice and although he lived for much of his adult life in Boston and New York, he never quite identified with city life and maintained the love of the countryside fostered in his rural Ohio boyhood. His preference for smaller towns is part of the charm of *Certain Delightful English Towns with Glimpses of the Pleasant Country Between* (1906), as is his conciliatory tone in responding to the British cultural roots of the United States. For the American visitor, his "English ancestors who really were once there stir within him, and his American forefathers who were nourished on the history and literature of England, and were therefore intellectually English, join forces in creating an English consciousness in him."

Divided into twelve sections, *Certain Delightful English Towns* is the most leisurely of Howells's books but not the most unplanned. Staying mostly in the south of England, he expresses a keen desire to experience its American connections. This framework is effective despite Howells's tendency to treat diverse places as rather uniformly English. Plymouth, where the book commences, is not that much different from Exeter, Bristol, Wells, and the other towns he visits. Some of this uniformity is owing to his visits being afternoon or day trips, but

even a two-week sojourn in Bath yielded only cursory descriptions of sites and views, expanded with historical and literary background and anecdotes. Comparisons to American scenes occur throughout: Bristol to Pittsburgh, Kent to Massachusetts, and Folkestone to Buffalo. In Oxford the "collective tone is that of Old Cambridge, or more strictly, of Harvard." Northampton, last on his itinerary, is of interest because nearby lived the ancestors of George Washington.

Howells's cultural connection to England is readily understandable. The pervasive calmness of his Roman experience after forty years is more difficult to explain. An acceptance of what comes, from a sense of curiosity rather than resignation, is one of the most sensible and useful attributes of a traveler, a reader of travel literature and, indeed, of a wise liver of life. In *Roman Holidays and Others* (1908) Howells enunciates such a readiness: "One of the most agreeable illusions of travel is a sort of expectation that if you will give objects of interest time enough they will present themselves to you, and if they will not actually come to you in your hotel, will happen in your way when you go out." The book began as a series of essays sent to the *New York Sun*. One half of *Roman Holidays* is devoted to Howells's lengthy return visit to the Italian capital, which left him more impressed than he was when he wrote *Italian Journeys* almost forty years earlier. Some of this change of attitude is the result of a more leisurely approach. He traveled first by steamer to Madeira and Gibraltar and then retraced some of his earlier travels to Genoa and Naples before a final preparation for Roman antiquities with a visit to Pompeii. In *Roman Holidays* he is also far less prone to flatter his American audiences: "The pride of Americans in their native scenery is brought down almost to the level of the South Shore of Long Island in arriving home from the Mediterranean voyage to Europe." At the same time he is much more international and able to make knowledgeable generalizations and comparisons. For example, "Berlin is not German as Paris is French, and Rome is not so exclusively Italian. In fact, her greatness, accomplished and destined, lies in just the fact that she is not and never can be exclusively Italian. Human interests too universal and imperative for the control of a single race, even so brilliant and so gifted as the Italian race, which is naturally and necessarily in possession, centre about her through history, religion, art, and make every one at home in the city which is the capital of Christendom."

Howells comments freely on the "New Rome" before his return to the Colosseum and the Forum. His rich sense of the storied beauties of what he ob-

A VIEW OF MONK BAR

[See page 55

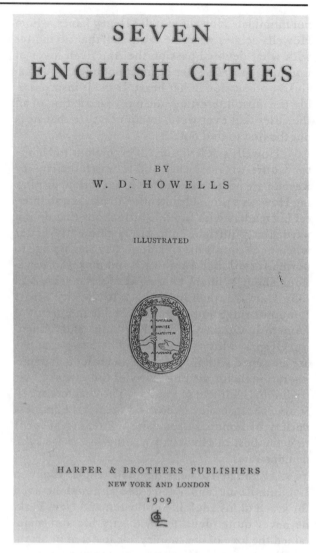

SEVEN
ENGLISH CITIES

BY
W. D. HOWELLS

ILLUSTRATED

HARPER & BROTHERS PUBLISHERS
NEW YORK AND LONDON
1909

Frontispiece and title page for the book that includes Howells's observations on the British people

serves is more sharply defined after an interruption in chapter 5 that takes him to the Anglo-American neighborhood around the Spanish Steps. In the elegant chapter 6, "Personal Relations with the Past," he meditates on the relativity of time and continuity superimposed on and juxtaposed with eternal Rome. He is confident enough in his own curiosity to wander among the many churches, ending at San Paolo fuori le Mura, commenting on its opulence and the timelessness of its rebuilding after a nineteenth-century fire destroyed the fourth-century basilica. His delight in a Rome that his friends believed ruined perplexed Charles Eliot Norton, who could not "believe that the charm of Rome is as great as it was then, and yet my dear old friend Howells who has just returned from a long stay there . . . has fallen under the spell of its charm as completely as if it were the same delightful Rome that we knew so well."

When Howells shifts to contemporary Rome and "Dramatic Incidents," he is effective as a reporter of what he observed with little attempt to contrast it with an illusory past or realistic present. His socialist sentiments are clearly in evidence. Commenting on a two-day strike, he asserts that "it was far the most impressive experience of our Roman winter; in some sort it was the most impressive experience of my life, for I beheld in it a reduced and imperfect image of what labor could do if it chose to do nothing." He moves to "Superficial Observations and Conjectures" and "Casual Impressions" in such a way that the reader accepts the contrast as part of his experience of Rome, presented as it took place. An acceptance of what comes next pervades *Roman Holidays* and introduces the chapter on "Tivoli and Frascati." Howells's final Roman chapter is more American in spirit, opening with a tribute to Hawthorne's Ro-

Decorated binding for Howells's 1913 account of his only visit to Spain

man novel, *The Marble Faun* (1860). After praising his countryman, Howells describes the sculptures at the Capitoline Museum and makes a symbolic visit to the Catacombs of Domatilla and the church of San Gregorio before traveling on to Leghorn (Livorno), Pisa, and Genoa on his way to "Eden After the Fall": Monaco and Monte Carlo. True to the spirit of his most engaging travel book, Howells observes in his concluding words that even in Monte Carlo you are never far from the past, "and closing your eyes to the surrounding glory of alp and sea find yourself again on the Palatine or amid the memorials of the Forum."

For *Seven English Cities* (1909) Howells visited the northern industrial cities of Liverpool, Manchester, and Sheffield; the cathedral cities of York and Durham, and Cambridge; and the "watering-places"

of Aberystwyth and Llandudno in Wales, capitalizing on the successful formula of *Certain Delightful English Towns,* particularly to repeat the many comparisons between Britain and the United States. It is refreshing to find Howells mocking his writing, except that he does so at the expense of the cities he visits, such as Liverpool: "It will be suspected from these reminiscences that I have been studying a page of fine print in Baedecker, and I will not deceive the reader." In the next chapter, he says: "I will suppose the reader not to be going to Oxford, but, in compliance with the scheme of this paper, to Manchester, where there is perhaps no other reason for his going." He is impressed with the grand hotels, but little else. Paraphrased historical and tourist commonplaces continue in "In Smokiest Sheffield." He is more expansive in York because he was there for more than a week and because of all the cathedrals, York Minster is "the grandest and beautifulest in all England." As in the west Midlands, Howells was fascinated with the rich Roman heritage of York. In "Two Yorkish Episodes" he displays that attention to detail and incident that adds human interest to his earlier travel books and contributes to his fiction. In the first episode he describes setting off on a quest for the site of the Battle of Marston Moor. Though he was unsuccessful, he still expresses pleasure with the "recognition of the civility from every one which had so ineffectively abetted my search." The second episode occurred when he took an Ouse river steamer to Bishopsthorpe. He expresses delight with the landscape "all dear and kind and sweet, with a sort of mid-Western look in its softness (as the English landscape often has), and the mud-banks were like those of my native Ohio Valley rivers." He was ferried to and from the shore by a woman who told the story of a murder, which their arrival back at the steamer abruptly interrupted and left without a conclusion. Howells enjoys this little joke.

In the next chapter the Doncaster races get more attention than the greatest of the Norman cathedrals in Durham; the race-day emphasis, however, is less peculiar than his passing over Cambridge to recount a lengthy visit to Boston, England, in "The Mother of the American Athens," which is understandable because of his American audience. Yet the English Boston is comparatively unimportant and rather uninteresting.

The two chapters on Wales represent a decided shift in content and emphasis. Howells's observations are more general: "The country is beautiful in the New England measure, but it is of a softer and smaller beauty; it looks more caressable"; the "air was fresh and sweet"; and "in the town there was no fashion at all, but a general decency and comfort of dress." Perhaps Howells was seeking to validate his own Welsh roots, but he never quite accomplishes that aim. Intimidated by the language, he curiously ignores the annual traditional Welsh music and cultural festival, the Eisteddfod, being held near Llandudno in Rhyl. Even more curious are his observations on the local fascination with "the music of the Pierrots and the Niggers, which those simple-hearted English have borrowed, the one from France and the other from these States. Their passion for our colored minstrelsy is, in fact, something pathetic." He returns to the familiar tourist fare with visits to Conway Castle and the Plas Mawr house.

Seven English Cities concludes with "Glimpses of English Character," in which Howells adds to similar essays on national character by other contemporary visitors to Britain, such as Hippolyte Taine, and writers of previous generations, such as Emerson. Howells acknowledges his "frank superficiality," but he does make some cogent observations. For example, he says the English are a mixture of races; they are not "sort of American." They are loyal to the monarchy and the aristocracy, and accepting of the idea of class. They are socially and linguistically but not politically snobbish. They are great holiday makers.

Howells's anecdotal observations about the rich and the poor are neither profound nor instructive as he realized: "I was always regretting that I got at the people so little, and that only chance hints of what they were thinking and feeling reached me." He is more convincing when he concludes with remarks about the English, who "with all their weight of feudal tradition" managed to invent "the only form of Democratic Christianity the world has yet known," a fact that should not be forgotten. The essay is uneven, but he succeeded in bringing serious and complex issues into a travel book. Few other travel writers even attempt to do so.

Familiar Spanish Travels (1913), Howells's last major travel book, is nostalgic and muted as befits his seventy-four years and his grief over the recent deaths of his wife and good friends Larkin Mead and Mark Twain. His account is structured around the contrasts between boyhood dreams of Spain and his present first experience when he could "grieve for the boy who would have been so disappointed if he had come to the Basque provinces of Spain when he was from ten to fifteen years old, instead of seventy-four." Howells the boy is associated throughout with Don Quixote the dreamer, while the older man is Sancho Panza the realist. After an opening chapter pondering "some sixty years' delay" in finally getting to Spain, twelve chapters traverse the whole of the country from the Bay of Biscay, through Burgos, Valladolid, Madrid, Toledo, Cordova, Seville, Granada, Ronda, and Tarifa. Howells devotes a chapter to each, with one added for the Escorial and another lengthy one for experiences in Seville.

Howells transmits a warmth of tone and a wealth of observation, but *Familiar Spanish Travels* suffers from a wordy style and a sense that he writes out of duty rather than interest or curiosity. His verbosity ruins his enjoyment of the Museo del Prado and Velasquez and contributes to the rambling quality of the entire work. What most fires his prose is an old man's crabbiness about discomfort, so that the high point of his Madrid experience is: "There was not only steam-heating, but the steam was on!"

Howells and his grandsons, William White Howells and John Noyes Mead Howells, 1917

His absorption in the minor annoyances of the traveler reduces the impact of his abhorrence at the degrading and filthy poverty he observes in places such as the gypsy quarter of Seville, into which "every manner of offal had been cast from the beginning of time to reek and fester and juicily ripen and rot in unspeakable corruption." The rambling quality is obvious from beginning to end and finally disintegrates into a distressing feebleness that does an injustice to Spanish vitality.

After *The Leatherwood God* in 1916, Howells never started another novel, but he wrote steadily until the month before he died, including an "Editor's Easy Chair" column once a month for *Harper's Monthly,* insightful introductions to others' works, and his autobiography, *Years of My Youth* (1916). Published the year of his death, *Hither and Thither in Germany* (1920) was compiled from piecing together the descriptions of German cities in *Their Silver Wedding Journey* (1899), with most of the dialogue and any focus other than on the Marches excised. The descriptions of Hamburg, Berlin, and "Frankfort" are left virtually intact as are some provocative comments about German national pride and the "passion for size which is at the bottom of every Ameri-

can heart, and which perhaps above all else marks us the youngest of peoples. We pride ourselves on the bigness of our own things, but we are not ungenerous, and when we go to Europe and find things bigger than ours, we are magnanimously happy in them."

Howells was one of the original seven members elected to the American Academy of Arts and Letters at its founding in 1904, and he served as its president from 1908 until his death. Having caught a cold during the winter of 1919–1920 in Savannah, Howells died at the age of eighty-three on 11 May 1920 in his New York apartment. His funeral was held the next day at the Church of the Ascension in New York, and his ashes were buried near the grave of Henry James in Cambridge Cemetery.

Letters:

Life in Letters of William Dean Howells, 2 volumes, edited by Mildred Howells (Garden City, N.Y.: Doubleday, Doran, 1928; London: Heinemann, 1929);

The Correspondence of Samuel L. Clemens and William D. Howells, 1872–1910, 2 volumes, edited by Henry Nash Smith and William M. Gibson

(Cambridge, Mass.: Harvard University Press, 1960);

Selected Letters, 1852–1872, edited by George Arms and others (Boston: Twayne, 1979);

Selected Letters, 1873–1881, edited by Arms and Christof K. Lohmann (Boston: Twayne, 1979);

Selected Letters, 1882–1891, edited by Robert C. Leitz III (Boston: Twayne, 1980);

John Hay–Howells Letters, edited by George Monteiro and Brenda Murphy (Boston: Twayne, 1980);

Selected Letters, 1892–1901, edited by Thomas Wortham (Boston: Twayne, 1981).

Interview:

Ulrich Halfmann, ed., "Interviews with William Dean Howells," *American Literary Realism,* 6 (1973): 267–416.

Bibliographies:

George Arms and William M. Gibson, *A Bibliography of William Dean Howells* (New York: New York Public Library, 1948);

Edwin H. Cady, "William Dean Howells in Italy: Some Bibliographic Notes," *Symposium,* 7 (1953): 147–153;

John K. Reeves, "The Literary Manuscripts of W. D. Howells: A Descriptive Finding List," *Bulletin of the New York Public Library,* 62 (June 1958): 267–278; (July 1958): 350–363; supplement, 65 (September 1961): 465–476;

James Woodress and Stanley P. Anderson, "A Bibliography of Writing about William Dean Howells," *American Literary Realism,* special number, 2 (1969): 1–139;

Vito J. Brenni, *William Dean Howells: A Bibliography* (Metuchen, N.J.: Scarecrow Press, 1973);

Clayton L. Eichelberger, *Published Comment on William Dean Howells through 1920: A Research Bibliography* (Boston: G. K. Hall, 1976).

David J. Nordloh, "William Dean Howells," in *Fifteen American Authors Before 1900 Bibliographical Essays on Research and Criticism,* edited by Robert A. Rees (Madison: University of Wisconsin Press, 1984), pp. 306–329.

Biographies:

E. H. Cady, *The Road to Realism: The Early Years, 1837–1885, of William Dean Howells* (Syracuse, N.Y.: Syracuse University Press, 1956);

Cady, *The Realist at War: the Mature Years, 1885–1920, of William Dean Howells* (Syracuse, N.Y.: Syracuse University Press, 1958);

Van Wyck Brooks, *Howells: His Life and World* (New York: Dutton, 1959);

Edward S. Wagenknecht, *William Dean Howells: The Friendly Eye* (New York: Oxford University Press, 1969);

Rodney D. Olsen, *Dancing in Chains: The Youth of William Dean Howells* (New York & London: New York University Press, 1991).

References:

William Alexander, *William Dean Howells: The Realist as Humanist* (New York: Burt Franklin, 1981);

Luigi Anicetti, "William Dean Howells, console a Venezia, 1861–1865," *Nuova Rivista Storica,* 41 (1957): 87–106.

George Arms, "Howells' English Travel Books. Problems in Technique," *PMLA,* 82 (1967): 104–116;

Arms, "Howells' Last Travel Book," *The Old Northwest: A Journal of Regional Life and Letters,* 8 (1982): 131–155;

John E. Bassett, *"A Heart of Ideality in My Realism" and Other Essays on Howells and Twain* (West Cornwall, U.K.: Locust Hill Press, 1991);

George N. Bennett, *The Realism of William Dean Howells: 1889–1920* (Nashville, Tenn.: Vanderbilt University Press, 1973);

Bennett, *William Dean Howells: The Development of a Novelist* (Norman: University of Oklahoma Press, 1959);

William W. Betts, "The Relation of William Dean Howells to German Life and Letters," in *Anglo-German and American-German Crosscurrents,* volume 1, edited by Philip A. Shelley and others (Chapel Hill: University of North Carolina Press, 1957), pp. 189–239;

Daniel H. Borus, *Writing Realism: Howells, James, and Norris in the Mass Market* (Chapel Hill: University of North Carolina Press, 1989);

Malcolm Bradbury, *Dangerous Pilgrimages: Transatlantic Mythologies and the Novel* (New York: Viking, 1996);

Van Wyck Brooks, *The Dream of Arcadia American Writers and Artists in Italy 1760–1915* (New York: Dutton, 1958);

Edwin H. Cady, "Howells on the River," *American Literary Realism,* 25, no. 3 (1993): 27–41;

Cady and Norma W. Cady, eds., *Critical Essays on William Dean Howells* (Boston: G. K. Hall, 1983);

Cady and David L. Frazier, eds., *The War of the Critics over William Dean Howells* (Evanston: Row, Peterson, 1962);

George C. Carrington Jr., *The Immense Complex Drama: The World and Art of the Howells Novel* (Columbus: Ohio State University Press, 1966);

Carrington and Ildiko de Papp Carrington, *Plots and Characters in the Fiction of William Dean Howells* (Hamden, Conn.: Shoe String, 1976);

Everett Carter, *Howells and the Age of Realism* (Philadelphia: Lippincott, 1954);

Giuseppe Gadda Conti, *William Dean Howells,* Biblioteca Di Studi Americani 22 (Rome: Edizioni di Storia e Letteratura, 1971);

Delmar G. Cooke, *William Dean Howells: A Critical Study* (New York: Dutton, 1922);

John W. Crowley, *The Black Heart's Truth: The Early Career of W. D. Howells* (Chapel Hill: University of North Carolina, 1985);

Crowley, "Howells in the Seventies: A Review of Criticism," *ESQ,* 25 (1979): 169–189; 235–253;

Crowley, *The Mask of Fiction: Essays on W. D. Howells* (Amherst: University of Massachusetts Press, 1989);

Emily Fourmy Cutrer, "A Pragmatic Mode of Seeing: James, Howells, and the Politics of Vision," in *American Iconology: New Approaches to Nineteenth-Century Art and Literature,* edited by David C. Miller (New Haven: Yale University Press, 1993), pp. 259–275;

James L. Dean, *Howells' Travels Toward Art* (Albuquerque: University of New Mexico Press, 1970);

Joseph A. Dowling, "Howells and the English: A Democrat Looks at English Civilization," *Bulletin of the New York Public Library,* 76 (1972): 251–264;

Dowling, "W. D. Howells' Literary Reputation in England, 1882–1897," *Dalhousie Review,* 45 (1965): 277–288.

Foster Rhea Dulles, *Americans Abroad: Two Centuries of European Travel* (Ann Arbor: University of Michigan Press, 1964);

Ernest Earnest, *Expatriates and Patriots: American Artists, Scholars, and Writers in Europe* (Durham, N.C.: Duke University Press, 1968);

Kenneth Eble, ed., *Howells: A Century of Criticism* (Dallas: Southern Methodist University Press, 1962);

Eble, *William Dean Howells,* revised edition (Boston: Twayne, 1982);

Herbert Edwards, "Howells and the Controversy over Realism in American Fiction," *American Literature,* 3 (November 1931): 237–248;

Clayton L. Eichelberger, "William Dean Howells: Perception and Ambivalence," in *The Chief Glory of Every People,* edited by Matthew J. Bruccoli (Carbondale: Southern Illinois University Press, 1973), pp. 117–140;

Oscar Firkins, *William Dean Howells: A Study* (Cambridge, Mass.: Harvard University Press, 1924);

Olov W. Fryckstedt, "Howells and Conway in Venice," *Studia Neophilologica,* 30 (1958): 165–174;

Fryckstedt, *In Quest of America: A Study of Howells's Early Development as a Novelist* (Cambridge, Mass.: Harvard University Press, 1958);

Joseph Gardner, *Dickens in America: Twain, Howells, James and Norris* (New York: Garland, 1988);

Harry R. Garvin, "Howells, Venice, and the American Novel," *Annali Istituto Universitario Orientale, Napoli, Sezione Germanica,* 5 (1962): 549–561;

William M. Gibson, "Materials and Form in Howells's First Novels," *American Literature,* 19 (1947): 158–166;

Gibson, *William D. Howells* (Minneapolis: University of Minnesota Press, 1967);

Henry Gifford, "W. D. Howells: His Moral Conservatism," *Kenyon Review,* 20 (1958): 124–133;

Alberta Fabris Grube, "Howells e James a Venezia: due scrittori e due mode di interpretare la città," in *Henry James e Venezia,* edited by Sergio Perosa (Florence: Olschki, 1987), pp. 189–202;

Robert L. Hough, *The Quiet Rebel: William Dean Howells as Social Commentator* (Lincoln: University of Nebraska Press, 1959);

Elinor Mead Howells, *If Not Literature: Letters of Elinor Mead Howells,* edited by Ginette de B. Merrill and George Arms (Columbus: Ohio State University Press for Miami University, 1988);

Lois Hughson, *From Biography to History. The Historical Imagination and American Fiction, 1880–1940* (Charlottesville: University Press of Virginia, 1988);

Gary A. Hunt, "'A Reality That Can't Be Quite Definitely Spoken': Sexuality in *Their Wedding Journey,*" *Studies in the Novel,* 9 (1977): 17–32;

Amy Kaplan, *The Social Construction of American Realism* (Chicago: University of Chicago Press, 1988);

Clara M. Kirk, "Reality and Actuality in the March Family Narratives of W. D. Howells," *PMLA,* 74 (1959): 137–152;

Kirk, *W. D. Howells and Art in His Time* (New Brunswick, N.J.: Rutgers University Press, 1965);

Kirk, *W. D. Howells: Traveler from Altruria, 1889–1894* (New Brunswick, N.J.: Rutgers University Press, 1962);

Kirk and Rudolf Kirk, "Howells's Guidebook to Venice," *American Literature,* 33 (1961): 221–224;

Kirk and Kirk, *William Dean Howells* (New York: Twayne, 1962);

Jerome Klinkowitz, "Ethic and Aesthetic: The Basil and Isabel March Stories of William Dean Howells," *Modern Fiction Studies*, 16 (1970): 303–322;

William McMurray, *The Literary Realism of William Dean Howells* (Carbondale: Southern Illinois University Press, 1968);

Edwin S. Morby, "William Dean Howells and Spain," *Hispanic Review*, 14 (1946): 187–212;

Elsa Nettels, *Language, Race, and Social Class in Howells's America* (Lexington: University Press of Kentucky, 1988);

Gail Thain Parker, "William Dean Howells: Realism and Feminism," in *Harvard English Studies*, no. 4, edited by Monroe Engel (Cambridge, Mass.: Harvard University Press, 1973);

Alma J. Payne, "William Dean Howells and the Independent Woman," *Midwest Review*, 5 (1963): 44–52;

Joseph Pennell, "Adventures of an Illustrator: With Howells in Italy," *Century*, 104 (1922): 135–141;

Elizabeth S. Piroleau, *The Circle of Eros: Sexuality in the Work of W. D. Howells* (Durham, N.C.: Duke University Press, 1983);

Piroleau, "William Dean Howells and the Seductress: From *Femme Fatale* to *Femme Vitale*," *Harvard Library Bulletin*, new series 3 (1992): 53–72;

Philip Rahv, ed., *Discovery of Europe: The Story of American Experience in the Old World* (Boston: Houghton Mifflin, 1947);

Daniel Rubey, "Howells' *Venetian Life* as a Vertical Text: Authors/Writers, Text(s), and Copy-Text Theory," *Transactions of the Society for Textual Scholarship*, 5 (1991): 315–338;

Roger B. Salomon, "Realism as Disinheritance: Twain, Howells and James," *American Quarterly*, 16 (1964): 531–544;

Eric Savoy, "The Subverted Gaze: Hawthorne, Howells, James and the Discourse of Travel," *Canadian Review of American Studies*, 21 (1990): 287–300;

Fred G. See, "Howells and the Failure of Desire," in his *Desire and the Sign: Nineteenth-Century American Fiction* (Baton Rouge: Louisiana State University Press, 1987), pp. 95–121;

William W. Stowe, *Going Abroad: European Travel in Nineteenth-century American Culture* (Princeton, N.J.: Princeton University Press, 1994);

Lionel Trilling, "William Dean Howells and the Roots of Modern Taste," *Partisan Review*, 18 (1951): 516–536;

William L. Vance, *America's Rome*, 2 volumes (New Haven: Yale University Press, 1989);

Kermit Vanderbilt, *The Achievement of William Dean Howells: A Reinterpretation* (Princeton, N.J.: Princeton University Press, 1968);

Edward Wagenknecht, *William Dean Howells: The Friendly Eye* (New York: Oxford University Press, 1969);

Robert W. Walts, "Howells's Plans for Two Travel Books," *Papers of the Bibliographical Society of America*, 57 (1963): 453–459;

Morton White and Lucia White, "The Ambivalent Urbanite: William Dean Howells," in *The Intellectual Versus the City* (Cambridge, Mass.: Harvard University Press, 1962), pp. 95–116;

Stanley T. Williams, "William Dean Howells," in *The Spanish Background of American Literature*, volume 2 (New Haven: Yale University Press), pp. 240–267;

James Woodress, "The Dean's Comeback: Four Decades of Howells Scholarship," *Texas Studies in Literature and Language*, 2 (1960): 115–123;

Woodress, *Howells and Italy* (Durham, N.C.: Duke University Press, 1952);

Woodress, "Howells in the Nineties: Social Critic for All Seasons," *American Literary Realism*, 25 (1993): 18–25;

Woodress, "Howells' Venetian Priest," *Modern Language Notes*, 66 (1951): 266–267.

Woodress, "Venetian Life: Background, Composition, Publication, and Reception," *Old Northwest: A Journal of Regional Life and Letters*, 8 (1982): 49–67;

Thomas Wortham, *The Early Prose Writings of William Dean Howells, 1853–1861* (Athens: Ohio University Press, 1990);

Nathalia Wright, "The Enigmatic Past: Howells," in *American Novelists in Italy* (Philadelphia: University of Pennsylvania Press, 1965), pp. 168–197.

Papers:

Harvard University holds the largest collection of Howells manuscripts, containing more than seven thousand letters to and from Howells plus many manuscripts and journals. Significant collections are also housed at the Huntington Library in San Marino, California; the Library of Congress; Yale and Columbia Universities; and the Rutherford B. Hayes Library in Fremont, Ohio.

Helen Hunt Jackson
(14 October 1830 – 12 August 1885)

Elizabeth Hewitt
Grinnell College

See also the Jackson entries in *DLB 42: American Writers for Children Before 1900; DLB 47: American Historians, 1866–1912;* and *DLB 186: Nineteenth-Century American Western Writers.*

BOOKS: *Verses,* as H. H. (Boston: Fields, Osgood, 1870; enlarged, Boston: Roberts, 1874; London: Roberts 1877);

Bits of Travel, as H. H. (Boston: J. R. Osgood, 1872);

Bits of Talk about Home Matters, as H. H. (Boston: Roberts, 1873; London: Low, 1873);

The Story of Boon, as H. H. (Boston: Roberts, 1874);

Saxe Holm's Stories, as Saxe Holm (New York: Scribner, Armstrong, 1874);

Bits of Talk, in Verse and Prose, for Young Folks, as H. H. (Boston: Roberts, 1876);

Mercy Philbrick's Choice, anonymous (Boston: Roberts, 1876; London: Low, 1876);

Hetty's Strange History, anonymous (Boston: Roberts, 1877);

Bits of Travel at Home, as H. H. (Boston: Roberts, 1878);

Nelly's Silver Mine: A Story of Colorado Life, as H. H. (Boston: Roberts, 1878);

Saxe Holm's Stories, second series, as Saxe Holm (New York: Scribners, 1878);

Letters from a Cat: Published by Her Mistress for Her Mistress for the Benefit of all Cats and the Amusement of Little Children, as H. H. (Boston: Roberts, 1879);

A Century of Dishonor: A Sketch of the United States Government's Dealings with Some of the Indian Tribes, as H. H. (New York: Harper, 1881); republished as *A Century of Dishonour: A Sketch of the United States Government's Dealings with Some of the North American Tribes* (London: Chatto & Windus, 1881); enlarged edition (Boston: Roberts, 1885);

Mammy Tittleback and her Family: A True Story of Seventeen Cats, as H. H. (Boston: Roberts, 1881);

The Training of Children, as H. H. (New York: New York & Brooklyn Publishing, 1882);

Helen Hunt Jackson

Report on the Conditions and Needs of the Mission Indians, by Jackson and Abbot Kinney (Washington, D.C.: Government Printing Office, 1883); republished as *Report of Mrs. Helen Hunt Jackson and Abbot Kinney on the Mission Indians in 1883* (Boston: Stanley & Usher, 1887); republished as *Father Junipero and the Mission Indians of California* (Boston: Little, Brown, 1902);

The Hunter Cats of Connorloa, as Helen Jackson (H. H.) (Boston: Roberts, 1884);

Cat Stories (Boston: Roberts, 1884);

Easter Bells: An Original Poem (New York: White, Stokes & Allen, 1884);

Ramona: A Story, as Helen Jackson (H. H.) (Boston: Roberts, 1884; London: Macmillan, 1884);

The Procession of Flowers in Colorado (Colorado
Springs: Gazette, 1885);
Zeph: A Posthumous Story, as Helen Jackson (H. H.)
(Boston: Roberts, 1885; Edinburgh: Douglas,
1886);
A Calendar of Sonnets (Boston: Roberts, 1886);
Glimpses of Three Coasts (Boston: Roberts, 1886);
Poems (Boston: Roberts, 1886–1888);
Sonnets and Lyrics (Boston: Roberts, 1886);
Between Whiles (Boston: Roberts, 1887);
My Legacy (Boston: Carter & Karrick, 1888);
Pansy Billings and Popsy: Two Stories of Girl Life (Boston: Lothrop, 1898);
*Westward to a High Mountain: The Colorado Writings of
Helen Hunt Jackson,* edited by Mark I. West
(Denver: Colorado Historical Society).

TRANSLATION: Jean Pierre Claris de Florian,
Bathmendi: A Persian Tale (Boston: Loring,
1867).

Helen Hunt Jackson, one of the most versatile
and widely admired popular authors of the latter
part of the nineteenth century, did not begin writing
until she was thirty-five years old, shortly after her
second son, Rennie, died of diphtheria. Her first
published poems, "The Key of the Casket" and "It
Is Not All of Life to Live," were sentimental verses
on that death that appeared in *The New York Evening
Post* in 1865. The pseudonym she used, Marah, was
the first of several aliases, including H. H., Rip Van
Winkle, Saxe Holm, and No Name. Such was Jackson's progress as a writer that within three years of
her first publication her literary mentor and editor,
Thomas Wentworth Higginson, considered her sufficiently established to discuss her work in his article "The Female Poets of America." Ralph Waldo
Emerson thought highly enough of her poetry to
comment in the preface to his *Parnassus* (1875): "The
poems of a young lady who contents herself with the
initials 'H.H.' . . . have rare merit of thought and expression and will reward the reader for the careful
attention which they require."

In addition to her poetry Jackson was well
known as a historian and as a writer for children
and is especially remembered for her central role in
the Indian reform movement and for her novel *Ramona* (1884), which popularized the issue of the Indians' plight. Her travel writing was also an important
part of her career. Her first travel book, *Bits of Travel*
(1872), was about her first experiences in Europe
and provided the model for her subsequent efforts.

Born in Amherst, Massachusetts, on 4 October
1830 to Nathan Welby Fiske, a professor of languages at Amherst College, and Deborah Vinal

Fiske, Helen Maria Fiske was educated at a series of
boarding schools. Her life was marked by the early
deaths of people close to her. Fiske's parents died
before she reached her twentieth birthday. After her
marriage on 28 October 1852 to Edward Bissell
Hunt, a mechanical engineer and army officer, the
couple's first son died in infancy. Hunt died in an
accident in 1863 while he was inspecting a submarine weapon he had invented, two years before Rennie's death. Her second husband, Colorado businessman William Sharpless Jackson, whom she married in 1875, survived her.

Although she gained fame through her poetry,
Helen Fiske Hunt early on began to submit essays to
New York magazines. The first essay for which she received remuneration–a gossipy travel letter in which
she recounted her impressions of Bethlehem, New
Hampshire–was published in the *New York Daily Post*.
This nascent interest in travel writing continued when
in 1867 Hunt traveled to Nova Scotia and recorded
her observations in letters, which were published by
both the *Post* and the *New York Independent*. A year later
Hunt set off on her first European tour.

While abroad Hunt continued her habit of sending home "letters," some of which were explicitly intended for publication as essays. The majority of
them, though, were initially intended for a much more
limited audience. Her goal at the beginning was to
send monthly letters that would be passed among
twenty-one friends back in the United States. Because
they were submitted to a group of her acquaintances
and because Hunt wrote many of them during her
stay in Rome, the city of the Pope, she titled these letters "encyclicals." After a time Hunt started writing
two sets of missives: the original round-robin letters
that were sent out and another set addressed to her intimates (many of the same passages and descriptions
can be found in both sets).

The semipublic encyclicals became entirely public, however, when they were published in *The Atlantic
Monthly* in 1871 under the title "Encyclicals of a Traveller" and later in book form as *Bits of Travel*. Yet, even
in the published version of her letters Hunt maintained the conceit that she is writing to individuals
through her impromptu tone. She interrupts her
lengthy descriptions with comments such as "I shall
never get through at this rate. I must lay down the rule
in the outset not to say what I *think*." Moreover, many
are peppered with requests that her correspondents
write back and tell her about the details of their lives:
"If you don't write to me after this, you are the nethermost of millstones; and, once for all, let me say . . . do
write all the most insignificant details."

The originality of Hunt's travel narratives lies in
her attention to the domestic details of life abroad. In-

deed, her first letter from Rome begins, "Dear Souls: Now we are at housekeeping, and this is my house-warming letter."

The remainder of this letter tells of her attempt to find the perfect apartment in Rome and concludes with her discovery of an ideal housemaid, which occasions one of the most rhapsodic moments in her writing:

> I first trod on the stair; they were stone, but clean; the flights were short, and the halls were comparatively light. Such a beauty as opened the door for us! Ah, if you could see her! Just now she came to bring me an egg beaten up in milk, and as she set it on the table, and said, "Signora," the grace and gentleness of her motion, the sweetness of her voice,—ah me, I believe I had tears in my eyes to look at her. I never saw such a human creature before!

The careful depiction of her female caretakers was a consistent theme for Hunt, and the Italian serving girl, Marianina, is a prominent subject in the encyclicals from Rome.

The landlady of the hotel Hunt stayed at in Munich serves as the title subject of "A German Landlady," the essay that became the first chapter of *Bits of Travel*. An engraving of this German landlady, Fräulein Caroline Hahlreiner, serves as the frontispiece to the book. The landlady was important to Hunt not only because she provided such comfortable lodgings but also because she functioned as an intercessor between Hunt and the local population. Hahlreiner forces the Nuremberg jewelers to sell Hunt silver more cheaply than they would have sold it to a tourist and convinces the gatekeeper of a cemetery in Nuremberg to allow Hunt to pick sumac leaves. As her help she receives from the fräulein suggests, two of the subjects that occupy Hunt's attentions while traveling are local flora and fauna and local marketplaces.

In a later essay Hunt asserts, "Markets are always good vantage-grounds for studying the life and people of a place or region. The true traveller never feels completely at home in a town till he has been in the markets." Curiously, her distaste for Paris—of which she says, "I do not care if I never see it again"—seems to come from her apprehension that its shops encourage extravagance among tourists: "What becomes of conscientious convictions on the subject of dress, what becomes of exact calculations as to the proper expenditure of a limited income, in the Paris air, I don't know." More than the luxuriousness of Paris, Hunt seems to disapprove of its marketing itself to tourists. Perhaps she believes such promotion makes a city less interesting for its own sake.

Throughout her travels Hunt is more impressed by the gardens and landscapes she encounters than she is by cities. In her visit to the birthplace of Italian painter Titian, Pieve di Cadore, she is left "speechless" by the meadow of "flowers whose shapes and whose tints were all new to us. . . . We never saw such spot again. It is part of my creed that there is no other such spot in the world." In her essay "May-Day in Albano" Hunt similarly focuses on the abundance of Italian flowers, contrasting it to the paucity of blooms found in New England and giving elaborate descriptions of their many shapes and colors. In "The Valley of Gastein," which Hunt thought one of her best travel essays, she gives an impressionistic rendering of the natural scenery: "Hollyhocks ruled the gardens,—superb stalking creatures, black and claret, and white, and rose-pink and canary-yellow."

Again Hunt is particularly drawn to a picturesque landlady:

> Ah, that Schwarzach landlady! She little dreamed how droll she looked as she stood pompously curtseying in her doorway. . . . Her figure was so square and puffy, it looked as if it had feathers inside, and was made to be sold at a fair, to stick pins in. . . . O, the pride of the pincushion landlady in her feather-beds, her linen, her blankets, her crockery!

Hunt may be poking fun at the landlady's investment in her possessions, but it is also clear that she is scrutinizing these selfsame belongings with great interest: "Most distinctly of all I remember a white wax face stuck on top of an egg-shell painted red."

Although Hunt makes the rounds among the cultural sites one was supposed to visit—the museums, churches, and mansions of Rome, Venice, and Munich—she focuses as much or more attention on food preparation, on beggar children she sees in the street, on the quality of beds and linens, on flower bouquets, and on the women who serve as her domestic servants. Moreover, like many other travel writers, she insists on contrasting her own "tours" to the ones offered in the guidebooks. Indeed, throughout *Bits of Travel* Hunt declares the inadequacy of conventional guidebooks, as in the description of her tour of the Baths of Caracalla:

> Then you sit down on the safest-looking spot you can find, and lean up against a great stone, and think you will never go away. You dare not look over; too dizzy by half. I did wish I knew how high these walls were, but of course *that* wasn't 'put down' in Murray. The few rare bits of knowledge that I do hanker after never *are* in that unpleasant red book.

In one encyclical Hunt vows "never to write about ruins." When in the next letter she does re-

Edward Bissell Hunt, who died in an 1863 accident, and Warren Horsford "Rennie" Hunt, who died in 1865 of diphtheria

port visiting the ruins of the Palace of Cæsars, she spends most of her time describing her surprise that these ruins are "cleaner and more swept and garnished and scrubbed than any old maid's parlor." She expects "to see old women with pail and mops in every corner." Hunt similarly searches for domestic concerns among historical monuments when she visits the Quirinal Palace and sees the Pope's quarters. She describes his "damask footstool" but is more excited to spy a spittoon hidden in his study: "I hope somebody will tell Mr. Dickens; I never saw so many in a hotel in America."

Hunt's description of the spittoon, like much in *Bits of Travel,* is an attempt to vindicate American manners from the calumnies of foreign travelers in the United States. It is this patriotic agenda and her focus on domestic minutiae that occasioned both

criticism and praise from reviewers. A mildly critical reviewer in *The Atlantic Monthly* of August 1872 suggests that her writing suffers because "she does not well observe the bounds that divide gaiety from triviality, and vivacity from flippancy." Yet though the reviewer finds faults that are "characteristic of all lively lady-writers," these same flaws save her from the more serious accusation of a lack of originality.

The reviewer for the April 1872 *Scribner's Monthly* is more positive, claiming that it is Hunt's "sharp apprehension of the ludicrous, odd, and grotesque" that reinfuses interest into those "familiar places, whose charm has been so rubbed away by the iteration of dull innumerable tourists." This same reviewer describes her prose as "a laugh like a child's ripples. . . . Every window of her soul is flung open to sunshine, wind,—the simple joyousness of living." The reviewer explicitly champions Hunt's style in her travel writing over her poetry, in which conversely "the quaint seriousness of a by-gone time moulds her phrase." Hunt's writing about Europe is remarkable because of her New World style: "In her prose the nineteenth-century American treads dizzily on the dangerous edge of slang." Hunt's resistance to the "mouldiness" of the Old World in both style and substance indicates her intention to write for an American audience. With this point the reviewer for *The Atlantic Monthly* reviewer agreed, declaring that the essays in *Bits of Travel* are so "thoroughly American that they may be said to give us a Europe of our own."

Most of the travel essays Hunt submitted for publication were accepted, and at increasingly better magazines. Hunt, for example, thought her travel letters on the Gastein Valley "were far too good for *Hearth and Home* and deserved a place in the *Post*." Accordingly, she sent them to Higginson, who eventually placed them in the even more prestigious *Atlantic Monthly.* When the best of her travel articles were published in *Bits of Travel,* she found that the collection sold well.

Because of the success of her European travel book, Hunt decided she could write to finance an expensive transcontinental tour of the United States by rail in 1872. She was again able to publish articles in leading serials such as the *New York Independent, The Atlantic Monthly,* and *Scribner's Monthly.* Many of the essays were collected and published in *Bits of Travel at Home* (1878), a book she published as H. H. though she had become Helen Hunt Jackson three years earlier after meeting William Jackson in Colorado Springs.

What is most notable about these essays is that while Jackson in her European travel writing had tried to make the foreign familiar, in her American travel writing she takes the opposite approach by stressing the foreignness of the western United States. The collection begins with her praising the "perplexing sense of domesticity" of the Pullman car she boards in Chicago, but once she crosses the Missouri River, the American landscape and its inhabitants become unfamiliar. After she leaves Omaha, she sees her "first Indian." And, whereas the landladies of Europe were described as picturesque managers of their quaint little houses, the Indian woman of Nebraska is described metaphorically as a decrepit house:

We were told it was a woman. It was, apparently, made of old India-rubber, much soaked, seamed, and torn. It was thatched at top with a heavy roof of black hair,

which hung down from a ridge-like line in the middle. It had sails of dingy-brown canvas, furled loosely around it. . . . It was the most abject, loathly living thing I ever saw. I shut my eyes, and turned away.

In 1872 she would look away, but only seven years later Jackson would turn all her attention to the subject of the American Indian.

It is another curious fact of Jackson's career that her interest in Indian reform did not begin until late in her life. In 1879 she attended the Boston lecture of Standing Bear, the Ponca chief who came east to testify to the repeated seizure of his tribe's lands, and almost immediately she became consumed with investigating and reporting on the history of the U.S. government's policy toward its indigenous population. The bulk of her magazine writing from 1879 until her death in October of 1885 reports on the wrongs perpetrated against the Native Americans. The culmination of these labors is found in what Jackson thought to be her most important work, *A Century of Dishonor* (1881), an exhaustive study of America's mistreatment of the Indians.

Jackson made a second European trip in 1880, touring northern England, Scotland, Norway, and Germany. Once again she recorded her journeys in public letters, including another series of "Encyclicals of a Traveller." These letters in large measure resemble her earlier ones in their attention to natural landscapes and native inhabitants, especially women. It comes as no surprise, then, when Jackson declares that the "most picturesque of all the figures to be seen in Edinburgh are the Newhaven fishwives." As in *Bits of Travel* Jackson focuses on the women who serve as both her traveling companions and domestics. The essay "Four Days with Sanna" is titled after a young woman who accompanied Jackson to the Norwegian fjords. Another essay, "The Katrina Saga," concerns Katrina, who travels with her during the remaining stay in Norway. Jackson suggests that it is the presence of these women that marks her travel narrative as different from the standard guidebook: "Murray's Guidebook, that paradoxical union of the false and the true, says . . . 'There is not much interest in the town, and it may be seen in from four to five hours.' The person who made that statement did not have Katrina with him."

Yet despite Jackson's attempt to continue the formula she has used so successfully in *Bits of Travel,* many of the essays from this second tour—for example, her tour of Robert Burns's habitations—seem much like perfunctory guidebook exercises. Jackson admitted in private letters to friends that her attention during her travels abroad was not so much on Europe but rather on her political commitment to the Native Americans at home. Uninspired by her second European tour, Jackson returned to the United States only four months later to oversee the final editing of *A Century of Dishonor*. She distributed a copy of her book to every senator and representative in Congress as part of her continuing efforts to change the governmental policy of forced Indian relocation.

Toward this end she agreed to write a series of articles for *Century* magazine about southern California missions because the project would allow her to continue her research into the history of the American Indian. These articles along with those from her second European visit were collected in the posthumously published *Glimpses of Three Coasts* (1886). Despite her own frustration with her final European travel essays and her disappointment at the end of her life with the reception of *Century of Dishonor,* this final collection of essays was greeted after her death by critical acclaim and interest. The European essays collected in *Glimpses* were cited in the June 1886 issue of *The Critic* as justifying why women should no longer be expected to stay at home: "it is the *pièce justificative* of the emancipated woman."

Biographies:

Jeanne C. Carr, *Helen Hunt Jackson* (N.p.: Woman's Magazine Press, 1885);

Virgina Donaghe McClurg, *The Story of Helen Hunt Jackson's Life* (Colorado Springs: Colorado Springs Gazette, 1924);

Ruth Odell, *Helen Hunt Jackson* (New York: Appleton Century, 1939);

Evelyn I. Banning, *Helen Hunt Jackson* (New York: Vanguard, 1973);

Antoinette May, *Helen Hunt Jackson: A Lonely Voice of Conscience* (San Francisco: Chronicle Books, 1987);

Rosemary Whitaker, *Helen Hunt Jackson* (Boise, Idaho: Boise State University Press, 1987);

Gloria J. Helmuth, *The Life of Helen Hunt Jackson* (Buena Vista, Colo.: Classic Reprographics, 1995).

References:

Susan Coultrap-McQuin, *Doing Literary Business: American Women Writers in the Nineteenth Century* (Chapel Hill: University of North Carolina Press, 1990);

Valerie Shere Mathes, *Helen Hunt Jackson and Her Indian Reform Legacy* (Austin: University of Texas Press, 1990);

Mary Suzanne Schriber, *Telling Travels: Selected Writings by Nineteenth-Century Women Abroad* (De Kalb: Northern Illinois University Press, 1995).

Papers:

The main collections of Jackson's papers are in the Huntington Library, San Marino, California, and in the Charles Leaming Tutt Library, Colorado College, Colorado Springs.

Henry James

(15 April 1843 – 28 February 1916)

Craig White

University of Houston–Clear Lake

See also the James entries in *DLB 12: American Realists and Naturalists; DLB 71: American Literary Critics and Scholars, 1880–1900; DLB 74: American Short-Story Writers Before 1880;* and *DS 13: The House of Scribner, 1846–1904.*

BOOKS: *A Passionate Pilgrim, and Other Tales* (Boston: Osgood, 1875);

Transatlantic Sketches (Boston: Osgood, 1875); revised and abridged as *Foreign Parts* (Leipzig: Tauchnitz, 1883);

Roderick Hudson (Boston: Osgood, 1876 [i.e., 1875]; revised edition, 3 volumes, London: Macmillan, 1879);

The American (Boston: Osgood, 1877; unauthorized edition, London: Ward, Lock, 1877; authorized edition, London: Macmillan, 1879);

French Poets and Novelists (London: Macmillan, 1878);

Watch and Ward (Boston: Houghton, Osgood, 1878);

The Europeans (2 volumes, London: Macmillan, 1878; 1 volume, Boston: Houghton, Osgood, 1879 [i.e., 1878]);

Daisy Miller: A Study (New York: Harper, 1879 [i.e., 1878]);

An International Episode (New York: Harper, 1879);

Daisy Miller: A Study. An International Episode. Four Meetings, 2 volumes (London: Macmillan, 1879);

The Madonna of the Future and Other Tales, 2 volumes (London: Macmillan, 1879);

Confidence (2 volumes, London: Chatto & Windus, 1880 [i.e., 1879]; 1 volume, Boston: Houghton, Osgood, 1880);

Hawthorne (London: Macmillan, 1879; New York: Harper, 1880);

A Bundle of Letters (unauthorized edition, Boston: Loring, 1880);

The Diary of a Man of Fifty and A Bundle of Letters (New York: Harper, 1880);

Washington Square (New York: Harper, 1881 [i.e., 1880]);

Henry James, 1908; portrait by Jacques-Emile Blanche (National Portrait Gallery, Washington, D.C.)

Washington Square, The Pension Beaurepas, A Bundle of Letters, 2 volumes (London: Macmillan, 1881);

The Portrait of a Lady (3 volumes, London: Macmillan, 1881; 1 volume, Boston: Houghton, Mifflin, 1882 [i.e., 1881]);

The Siege of London, The Pension Beaurepas, and The Point of View (Boston: Osgood, 1883);

Daisy Miller: A Comedy (Boston: Osgood, 1883);

Portraits of Places (London: Macmillan, 1883; Boston: Osgood, 1884);

A Little Tour in France (Boston: Osgood, 1885 [i.e., 1884]; revised edition, Boston & New York:

Houghton, Mifflin, 1900; London: Heinemann, 1900);

Tales of Three Cities (Boston: Osgood, 1884; London: Macmillan, 1884);

The Art of Fiction (unauthorized edition, Boston: Cupples, Upham, 1884);

The Author of Beltraffio, Pandora, Georgina's Reasons, The Path of Duty, Four Meetings (Boston: Osgood, 1885);

Stories Revived [*The Author of Beltraffio, Pandora, The Path of Duty, A Day of Days,* and *A Lightman*], 3 volumes (London: Macmillan, 1885);

The Bostonians: A Novel (3 volumes, London: Macmillan, 1886; 1 volume, London & New York: Macmillan, 1886);

The Princess Casamassima (3 volumes, London & New York: Macmillan, 1886; 1 volume, London & New York: Macmillan, 1886);

Partial Portraits (London & New York: Macmillan, 1888);

The Reverberator (2 volumes, London & New York: Macmillan, 1888; London & New York: Macmillan, 1888);

The Aspern Papers, Louisa Pallant, The Modern Warning (2 volumes, London & New York: Macmillan, 1888; 1 volume, London & New York: Macmillan, 1888);

A London Life, The Patagonia, The Liar, Mrs. Temperly (2 volumes, London & New York: Macmillan, 1889; 1 volume, London & New York: Macmillan, 1889);

The Tragic Muse (2 volumes, Boston & New York: Houghton, Mifflin, 1890; 3 volumes, London & New York: Macmillan, 1890);

The Lesson of the Master, The Marriages, The Pupil, Brooksmith, The Solution, Sir Edmund Orme (New York & London: Macmillan, 1892; London & New York: Macmillan, 1892);

The Real Thing and Other Tales (New York & London: Macmillan, 1893; London & New York: Macmillan, 1893);

Picture and Text (New York: Harper, 1893);

The Private Life, The Wheel of Time, Lord Beaupré, The Visits, Collaboration, Owen Wingrave (London: Osgood, McIlvaine, 1893);

Essays in London and Elsewhere (London: Osgood, McIlvaine, 1893; New York: Harper, 1893);

The Private Life, Lord Beaupré, The Visits (New York: Harper, 1893);

The Wheel of Time, Collaboration, Owen Wingrave (New York: Harper, 1893);

Theatricals, Two Comedies: Tenants, Disengaged (London: Osgood, McIlvaine, 1894);

Theatricals, Second Series: The Album, The Reprobate (London: Osgood, McIlvaine, 1895 [i.e., 1894]);

Terminations: The Death of the Lion, The Coxon Fund, The Middle Years, The Altar of the Dead (London: Heinemann, 1895; New York: Harper, 1895);

Embarrassments: The Figure in the Carpet, Glasses, The Next Time, The Way It Came (London: Heinemann, 1896; New York & London: Macmillan, 1896);

The Other House (2 volumes, London: Heinemann, 1896; 1 volume, New York & London: Macmillan, 1896);

The Spoils of Poynton (London: Heinemann, 1897; Boston & New York: Houghton, Mifflin, 1897);

What Maisie Knew (London: Heinemann, 1897; Chicago & New York: Stone, 1897);

In the Cage (London: Duckworth, 1898; Chicago & New York: Stone, 1898);

The Two Magics: The Turn of the Screw, Covering End (London: Heinemann, 1898; New York & London: Macmillan, 1898);

The Awkward Age (London: Heinemann, 1899; New York & London: Harper, 1899);

The Soft Side (London: Methuen, 1900; New York & London: Macmillan, 1900);

The Sacred Fount (New York: Scribners, 1901; London: Methuen, 1901);

The Wings of the Dove (2 volumes, New York: Scribners, 1902; Westminster: Constable, 1902);

The Better Sort (London: Methuen, 1903; New York: Scribners, 1903);

The Ambassadors (London: Methuen, 1903; New York & London: Harper, 1903);

William Wetmore Story and His Friends, 2 volumes (Edinburgh & London: Blackwood, 1903; Boston: Houghton, Mifflin, 1903);

The Golden Bowl (2 volumes, New York: Scribners, 1904; 1 volume, London: Methuen, 1905);

The Question of Our Speech, The Lesson of Balzac: Two Lectures (Boston & New York: Houghton, Mifflin, 1905);

English Hours (London: Heinemann, 1905; Boston & New York: Houghton, Mifflin, 1905);

The American Scene (London: Chapman & Hall, 1907; New York: Harper, 1907);

Views and Reviews, edited by Le Roy Phillips (Boston: Ball, 1908);

Italian Hours (London: Heinemann, 1909; Boston & New York: Houghton, Mifflin, 1909);

The Finer Grain (New York: Scribners, 1910; London: Methuen, 1910);

The Outcry (London: Methuen, 1911; New York: Scribners, 1911);

A Small Boy and Others (New York: Scribners, 1913; London: Macmillan, 1913);

Notes of a Son and Brother (New York: Scribners, 1914; London: Macmillan, 1914);

Notes on Novelists with Some Other Notes (London: Dent, 1914; New York: Scribners, 1914);

The Ivory Tower, edited by Percy Lubbock (London, Glasgow, Melbourne & Auckland: Collins, 1917; New York: Scribners, 1917);

The Sense of the Past, edited by Lubbock (London, Glasgow, Melbourne & Auckland: Collins, 1917; New York: Scribners, 1917);

The Middle Years, edited by Lubbock (London, Glasgow, Melbourne & Auckland: Collins, 1917; New York: Scribners, 1917);

Gabrielle de Bergerac, edited by Albert Mordell (New York: Boni & Liveright, 1918);

Within the Rim and Other Essays, 1914–15 (London, Glasgow, Melbourne & Auckland: Collins, 1919);

Travelling Companions, edited by Mordell (New York: Boni & Liveright, 1919);

A Landcape Painter, edited by Mordell (New York: Scott & Seltzer, 1919 [i.e., 1920]);

Master Eustace (New York: Seltzer, 1920);

Notes and Reviews (Cambridge, Mass.: Dunster House, 1921);

The Notebooks of Henry James, edited by F. O. Matthiessen and Kenneth B. Murdock (New York: Oxford University Press, 1947);

The Scenic Art, Notes on Action & the Drama: 1872–1901, edited by Allan Wade (New Brunswick, N. J.: Rutgers University Press, 1948; London: Hart-Davis, 1949);

The Ghostly Tales of Henry James, edited by Leon Edel (New Brunswick, N.J.: Rutgers University Press, 1948);

The Complete Plays of Henry James, edited by Edel (Philadelphia & New York: Lippincott, 1949; London: Hart-Davis, 1949);

Eight Uncollected Tales, edited by Edna Kenton (New Brunswick, N.J.: Rutgers University Press, 1950);

The American Essays, edited by Edel (New York: Vintage, 1956);

The Future of the Novel: Essays on the Art of Fiction, edited by Edel (New York: Vintage, 1956);

The Painter's Eye: Notes and Essays on the Pictorial Arts, edited by John L. Sweeney (London: Hart-Davis, 1956; Cambridge, Mass.: Harvard University Press, 1956);

Parisian Sketches: Letters to the New York Tribune 1875–1876, edited by Edel and Ilse Dusoir

Lind (New York: New York University Press, 1957; London: Hart-Davis, 1958);

The House of Fiction: Essays on the Novel, edited by Edel (London: Hart-Davis, 1957);

Literary Reviews and Essays, edited by Mordell (New York: Twayne, 1957).

Collections: *The Novels and Tales of Henry James,* 14 volumes (London: Macmillan, 1883);

The Novels and Tales of Henry James, New York Edition, 24 volumes, selected and revised, with prefaces, by James (New York: Scribners, 1907–1909); volumes 25 and 26 (New York: Scribners, 1918);

The Novels and Stories of Henry James, 35 volumes, edited by Lubbock (London: Macmillan, 1921–1923);

The Art of the Novel: Critical Prefaces, edited by Richard P. Blackmur (New York & London: Scribners, 1934; London: Scribners, 1935);

The Complete Tales of Henry James, edited by Edel (Philadelphia & New York: Lippincott, 1949; London: Hart-Davis, 1949);

The Art of Travel: Scenes and Journeys in America, England, France and Italy from the Travel Writings of Henry James, edited by Morton Dauwen Zabel (Garden City, N.Y.: Doubleday, 1958);

The Bodley Head Henry James, 10 volumes, edited by Edel (London: Bodley Head, 1967–1972);

Collected Travel Writings, 2 volumes, edited by Richard Howard (New York: Library of America, 1993).

Traveling often throughout his long and productive life, Henry James wrote fiction and travel literature about Americans in Europe and Europeans in America during the great epoch of transatlantic tourism and exchange in the second half of the nineteenth century. Born to a family of writers in New York City before the Civil War, he died in London during World War I, a distinguished citizen of Great Britain and a major novelist in the "great tradition" of European letters. Though he is best known as a master of the international theme in tales and novels such as *Daisy Miller* (1878), *The Portrait of a Lady* (1881), and *The Ambassadors* (1903), James—like his friends and fellow novelists Edith Wharton, William Dean Howells, and Henry Adams—also wrote letters and sketches that enrich and expand the genre of travel literature while tracing a history of taste, culture, and the writer's art.

James's father, Henry James Sr. (1811–1882), an affluent and well-connected journalist who wrote and lectured on religious subjects, designed a "sensuous education" for his namesake and for Henry's elder brother, William (1842–1910). Like her hus-

Henry James Sr. and Henry James Jr., 1854 (photograph by Mathew Brady)

and Henry spent one academic year at Harvard Law School (1862–1863) and began to publish stories and reviews in American magazines and journals. In 1869 the family financed a grand tour of Europe for him with the intention that, like his brother William (recently returned to Cambridge, Massachusetts), Henry would proceed to Germany to study philosophy and languages. (He was already fluent in French and Italian.)

Committed to a literary life of his own design, however, James, after consorting with the American community and family friends in England, took another path. His voluminous correspondence charts his wandering path through France and Switzerland until at last—as he wrote his only sister, Alice James (1850–1892) on 31 August 1869—he crossed the Simplon Pass on foot into Italy: "the delight of seeing the north melt into the south—of seeing Italy gradually crop up in bits . . . until finally at the little frontier Village of Isella it lay before me warm and living and palpable (*warm,* especially)—all these fine things bestowed upon the journey a delightful flavor of romance." Ecstatically he wrote to William James from Rome on 30 October,

> At last—for the first time—I live! It beats everything: it leaves the Rome of your fancy—your education—nowhere. . . . I went reeling and moaning thro' the streets, in a fever of enjoyment. In the course of four or five hours I traversed almost the whole of Rome and got a glimpse of everything. . . . For the first time I know what the picturesque is.

None of James's family—except for his younger brother Robertson (1846–1910) on a school trip—had visited Italy. To the end of his life it remained a favored destination for Henry James. He used it as a fictional setting and as a topic for travel pieces in which he evoked what Bonney MacDonald has called "a distinctly Jamesian reverence for a grandeur that is larger than himself."

After returning to the United States in spring 1870 James wrote his first novel, *Watch and Ward* (1878), serialized in *The Atlantic Monthly* in August–December 1871, and published his first travel writings, not descriptions of his visit to Europe but sketches of New York and New England resorts, and a description of Quebec, in *The Nation* during 1870 and 1871. According to Ahmed M. Metwalli these pieces already display the "double consciousness" that characterizes James's fiction, the "pull of the past and the push of the present." "Quebec" (*The Nation,* 28 September–5 October 1871), James's first travel piece set outside the United States, suggests the author's passion for sensations beyond the boundaries of the New World as

band, the self-effacing Mary Robertson Walsh James (1810–1882) was descended from Irish immigrants who had prospered in New York State early in the nineteenth century. During the 1840s and 1850s the Jameses relocated from one European or American intellectual and social capital to another, learning foreign languages, reading eclectically, and exploring professional possibilities outside the traditional American world of business. In his first volume of memoirs, *A Small Boy and Others* (1913), Henry James Jr. recalled his "very most infantine sensibility" as beholding a "view, framed by the clear window of the [carriage] as we passed" the Napoleonic column and "monumental square" of the Place Vendôme in Paris. This perception in James's second year of life (confirmed by his parents' recollections) portends the "spirit of place" that the mature James later evoked in his travel writing as well as his fiction.

James's accounts of his juvenile travels in England, France, Switzerland, and Germany appear in his memoirs and letters. During the 1860s the Jameses stayed on the American side of the Atlantic (in Boston, New York, Newport, and Cambridge),

well as his sense that the revolutionary model of American life threatened the Old World. Admiring the "transatlantic wares" of this "picturesque" city, he declared, "not America, but Europe should have the credit of Quebec," which is "belted with its hoary wall and crowned with its granite citadel":

> These walls, to the American vision, are of course the sovereign fact of Quebec. . . . Before you reach the gates, however, you will have been reminded at a dozen points that you have come abroad. What is the essential difference of tone between street-life in an old civilization and in a new? . . . It seems to be the general fact of detail itself—the hint in the air of a slow, accidental accretion, in obedience to needs more timidly considered and more sparingly gratified than the pressing necessities of American progress.

James's perceptions of "tone" and "needs" position him toward the Europhilic end of what Metwalli describes as the "poles of nineteenth-century American temperament"; yet, as Metwalli points out, in nearly forty years of writing travel literature James mediated in complex and varying ways "the conscious need of the public for knowledge, specifically that of its ancestral heritage and of the stable traditions and institutions of old civilizations, and its conscious need for national identity . . . and pride in being American."

However much James admired "old civilizations" or regretted the presence of fellow New-World travelers when he visited the Old World, throughout his career he consciously wrote primarily to an audience of American readers. He did not spurn his "national identity." In "Quebec" he appealed to the highest democratic, capitalistic instincts of his audience to accept the boon of other nations and cultures: "it is of good profit to us Americans to have near us, and of easy access, an ample something which is not our expansive selves." He found, however, that the "expansive selves" that visited the Old World brought New-World profit motives with them: "I suppose no patriotic American can look at all these things, however idly, without reflecting on the ultimate possibility of their becoming absorbed into his own huge state." Thus, as James Doyle has written, "James discovers what appears to be a possible alternative to the raw and often ruthlessly self-centered society of the United States, but the peculiar historical situation of Canada, and the apparent commitment of much of its populace to a quaint, fictive existence, make the continued existence of the country a matter of extreme doubt."

In "Niagara" (*The Nation*, 12–19 October 1871) James revealed tastes that drew him away from his native continent yet gained him no escape from the threat of modern, commercial culture. Approaching the falls "from the edge of the American cliff" as the train is about to cross the bridge to Canada, "You have a lively sense of something happening ahead. . . . And here, in the interest of the picturesque, let me note that this obstructive bridge tends in a way to enhance the first glimpse of the cataract." In line with these views James balanced the "perfect taste" and "matter of line" (which "beats Michael Angelo") of the natural spectacle against the "hideous and infamous . . . hackmen and photographers and vendors of gimcracks," the "horribly vulgar shops and booths and catchpenny artifices which have pushed and elbowed to within the very spray of the Falls." The hyperaestheticism of "this sentimental tourist" thus reaches a shrill pitch, but James's style, here and later, has many tones, including not a little humor, as in the initial climax of "Niagara": "A moment later, as the train proceeds, you plunge into the village, and the cataract, save as a vague ground-tone to this trivial interlude, is, like so many other goals of aesthetic pilgrimage, temporarily postponed to the hotel." In terms of James's developing style, as with many of his tales at this early stage of his career, this passage and others in his travel pieces sound built of old parts. Indeed, in other passages his humor may not even be intentional, as in "Niagara" when he commented on "the unlimited *wateriness* of the whole spectacle" (his emphasis).

In 1872 James crossed the Atlantic again to guide his sister, Alice, on her version of the grand tour in company with their "Aunt Kate," Catherine Walsh (1812–1889). That summer James began composing his first European travel sketches as the three visited American expatriate communities and took in the prescribed sights in England, France, and Switzerland. In a 9 September letter to his parents he called their nights in Venice a "martyrdom" to mosquitoes but he praised the "delightful" days and the "abundant coolness on the water and in the darksome churches." His sketches of these travels appeared in *The Nation* in 1872 and 1873. What James later described as his "church habit" asserted itself as the "pleasure of cathedral-hunting." Four of his pieces were about old British cathedral towns, including "Chester" (4 July 1872), "North Devon" (8 August 1872), and "Wells and Salisbury" (22 August 1872).

Even at this stage of his career James could give voice to "the spirit of place" in the "broken eloquence" of "English ruins" ("Wells and Salisbury"): "in so far as beauty of structure is beauty of line and curve, balance and harmony of masses and dimen-

James in Geneva, 1860

as *The Atlantic Monthly, The Nation, The Galaxy,* and *The Independent,* with some appearing in several installments.

The delicate shadings in James's early sketches associate this part of his career with the literary history of the American travel genre, as when his 1873–1874 series of pieces on Florence and Rome models the role of a "sophisticated" class of tourists who, in Willard Thorp's description, "shun the spots where their meditations might be disturbed by the rushing hordes" and "flee to haunts whose charms had not yet been defiled." "A Roman Holiday" (first published in *The Atlantic Monthly,* July 1873) exposes this conflict in the consciousness of the private traveler whose vocation at least partly lies in reporting his findings, which he treasures for their obscurity yet nonetheless publicizes. James first indulged the pleasure of a cognoscente's knowledge and an artist's pen:

> Even if you are on your way to the Lateran you won't grudge the twenty minutes it will take you, on leaving the Colosseum, to turn away under the Arch of Constantine . . . toward the piazzetta of the church of San Giovanni e Paolo, on the slope of Cælian. No spot in Rome can show a cluster of more charming accidents. The ancient brick apse of the church peeps down into the trees of the little wooded walk before the neighbouring church of San Gregorio . . . ; and a series of heavy brick buttresses, flying across to an opposite wall, overarches the short, steep, paved passage which leads into the small square.

sions, I have seldom relished it as deeply as on the grassy nave of some crumbling church, before lonely columns and empty windows where the wild flowers were a cornice and the sailing clouds a roof." James's conclusion invokes the sublimity and subtlety of his lifelong aesthetic: "These hoary relics of Glastonbury remind me in their broken eloquence of one of the other great ruins of the world—the *Last Supper* of Leonardo. A beautiful shadow, in each case, is all that remains; but that shadow is the soul of the artist."

That October, Alice James and Kate Walsh sailed for home from Liverpool on the transatlantic ship *Algeria,* but the twenty-nine-year-old Henry James stayed abroad to build a professional career as an author, if possible without taxing his family's diminishing resources. James toured and worked steadily, especially in England and Italy, for the next two years, completing several tales and much of his second novel, *Roderick Hudson* (1875), which he finished after his return to the United States in September 1874. He also produced more than a dozen travel sketches for American magazines such

Having further traced the "portico" and "portals" of this square as "the perfection of an out-of-the-way corner," James admitted on second thought that the church of San Gregorio is "a place you would think twice before telling people about, lest you should find them there the next time you were to go."

James's sketches at this stage of his career developed his art of fiction, contributed to the travel-writing genre, and preserved a moment in cultural history. These writings also helped to support him financially and to cultivate an audience for his fiction while at the same time he explored topics and themes that he later used in his novels and tales.

As Carl S. Smith has pointed out, "several dozen" of James's tales and "some ten of his novels . . . derive directly from his travels and travel writings." Alma Louise Lowe judges that his early sketches "bear the same relation to his early fiction as [his] *Notebooks* to his later fiction," and Michael Swan describes them as a "scaffolding" for James's fictional constructions. The indispensable essay on this subject is Morton Dauwen Zabel's introduction to his anthology of James's touring pieces, *The Art of*

James's 8 April 1869 sketch of a scene near Tewkesbury in Gloucestershire (Houghton Library, Harvard University)

Travel (1958), which treats the author's travel and fictional genres in extended parallels. "Travel [for James] is not a marginal matter of romantic atmosphere" or "escapist appeal," Zabel concludes, but "a cognate of the moral and historical drama" and "conflict of culture he saw as basic to his century."

James's travel writings of the 1870s and his great fiction that began to appear later in the decade manifest the "double consciousness" of American travel literature: the desire to penetrate the mysteries of the Old World and a simultaneous respect for the sanctity of such mysteries. Though in his travel pieces James shuns the "swarming democracy" of other tourists and winces at the "English and American families" moving into Italian villas for an "economical winter residence," Christopher Mulvey points out that James, with "curious effects of irony," is "one of the few travel writers who had the self-confidence to identify himself with the sorry being, the tourist," and often "spoke of the 'American tourist' as if both he and the reader might be such a one." James possessed the guilty knowledge that escaping one's kindred masses for obscure corners might not only compromise one's American identity but also might violate the "antiquity, history, [and] repose" the aesthetic traveler came to the Old World to experience.

In subtly negotiating these impulses and precautions James richly complicated the simplicity that Susan Sontag associates with travel literature: "Books about travel to exotic places have always opposed an 'us' to a 'them.' And this is a relation that

yields only a limited number of appraisals." The "us" and "them" of James's early travel writings are not, however, the foreigner and one's alien self but oneself and one's fellow national. Later, less a sentimental tourist and more a working professional, he stood outside this dialectic, mediating between individuals at leisure and a large class of people unemployed against their will. At last, in his late style, he achieved a singularly universal consciousness that risks making any naive reader a "them" to his imperial "us."

James's early travel sketches also document a shift in the history of taste. Throughout the second half of the nineteenth century James's passionate pilgrimage placed his persona in a dialogue with the artifacts of the past, signified by keywords such as *sentimental* and *picturesque*. Responding to changes in fashion, James edited out many relevant references to picturesque aesthetics when he revised his early articles for book publication; his early travel writing fits Willard Thorp's category of a "predominantly sentimental approach" to travel, whose fashion had already begun to fade by the time James wrote in the decades after the Civil War. Partly James's fidelity to the persona of "the sentimental tourist," as he called himself, resulted from the young writer's attachment to his models. In contrast to the overpowering and sometimes finicky self-consciousness that James developed in his later style, his early sketches unabashedly pony on the backs of previous travel writers and cultural critics. He sought support for a description from "Hawthorne, that best of Ameri-

Alice James, circa 1870, two years before she traveled to Europe with her brother Henry

Atlantic, August 1873) when James's narrator finds himself "talking about 'Middlemarch' to a young English lady or listening to Neapolitan songs from a gentleman in a very low-cut shirt."

Ironically, the attraction of picturesque spectacle–multiplied by publication of "the literature of sensibility" and an increasing bourgeois population–threatened the material base of this aesthetic. Gothic rot and decay, F. Hopkinson Smith wrote in *Gondola Days* (1897), are "the guardians of the picturesque." Under the spell of Ruskin in "Litchfield and Warwick" (first published in *The Nation,* 25 July 1872), James discovered "the charm of the spot is so much less that of grandeur than that of melancholy, that it is rather deepened than diminished by this attitude of obvious survival and decay." The only life adhering to an English ruin makes a

sweet accord . . . between all stony surfaces covered with the pale corrosions of time and the deep living green of the strong ivy which seems to feed on their slow decay. Of this effect and a hundred others–from those that belong to low-browed, stone-paved empty rooms where life was warm and atmospheres thick, to those one may note where the dark tower stairway emerges at last, on a level with the highest beech-tops, against the cracked and sun-backed parapet which flaunted the castle standard over the castle woods–of every form of sad desuetude and picturesque decay Haddon Hall contains some delightful example.

cans, who says so somewhere," "fumbled at poor Murray again for, some intenser light on the court," and dug into Walter Pater's *Studies on the History of the Renaissance* (1873) for an appropriate memorial of Sandro Botticelli. "Open Theophile Gautier's *Italia,*" he begs of his reader in "From Venice to Strassburg," "and you will see" (first published in *The Nation,* 6 March 1873).

The most important of James's many models was John Ruskin's *The Stones of Venice* (1851–1853): "Mr. Ruskin . . . beyond any helps us to enjoy" and to seek "the picturesque fact," to observe "a picture, self-informed, and complete" as "the pure picturesque," James wrote in "From Venice to Strassburg." As Bonney MacDonald writes in *Henry James's Italian Hours* (1990), "James's vision in his early Italian sketches is structured by his understanding of the 'picturesque,'" in which impressions "are received by the eye as fully formed, unified, and self-contained." Challenging this power to "see in wholes," however, the objects of James's picturesque searches are often particularly obscure and secretive, as in "Roman Rides" (first published in *The*

The first hints that alien visitors are imperiling James's "picturesque" appear in his description of Wells Cathedral, first published in the 22 August 1873 issue of *The Nation.* Instead of "the melancholy black of your truly romantic Gothic," James's persona finds the structure "too brilliantly lighted for picturesque, as distinguished from strictly architectural, interest." Similar references recur throughout the travel sketches of the 1870s. James's "lively impression of the numbers of people now living, and above all now moving, at extreme ease in the world" gives the ironical clue to a regrettable change: renewed traffic caused by the popularity of visits to such buildings has led to "improvements and embellishments" or "restoration," which "is certainly a great shock. . . . Wherever the hand of the restorer has been laid all semblance of beauty has vanished." Particularly vexing in England was the work of "Gilbert Scott, ruthless renovator." For James the original parts that survived Scott's restorations were a "frowning mockery of the imputed need of tinkering." Later, in *A Little Tour in France* (1884), James asserted:

I prefer in every case the ruined, however ruined, to the reconstructed, however splendid. What is left is more precious than what is added; the one is history, the other is fiction; and I like the former the better of the two—it is so much more romantic.

James admits the subject is "a very delicate question" and does not "undertake a scientific quarrel with these changes; we admit that our complaint is a purely sentimental one."

Yet no judgment is free from changing tastes. "Now it was Ruskin himself I had lost patience with," he later fumed in "Italy Revisited" (first published in *The Atlantic*, April–May 1878), and in "Chester" he evenhandedly remarked that the "actual townsfolk have bravely accepted the situation bequeathed by the past, and the large number of rich and intelligent restorations of the old facades makes an effective jumble of their piety and their policy." His "Florentine Notes" observe, "In the Carthusian Monastery . . . one may still snuff up a strong if stale redolence of old Catholicism and old Italy," but the "ugly" road "outside the Roman Gate" is marked not by the "truly romantic Gothic" of abandoned ruins but is fringed "with tenements suggestive of an Irish-American suburb" (*The Independent*, 23 April–9 July 1874). To James form was obviously superior to function. He approved of the castle of Vincigliata, a ruin rehabilitated by "the millions, the leisure and the eccentricity . . . of an English gentleman," who has "kept throughout such rigid terms with his model that the result is literally uninhabitable to degenerate moderns." Twisting his maxim that the ruin is "history," and the reconstruction is "fiction," James conceded that each apartment at Vincigliata is "as good a 'reconstruction' as a tale of Sir Walter Scott; or, to speak frankly a much better one."

Returning to America in 1874 after spending the better part of two years abroad, the thirty-one-year-old James set about supporting himself as he had in Europe. His second novel, *Roderick Hudson*, concerning an American artist torn between love and vocation in Rome, was serialized in *The Atlantic* (January–December 1875), and he continued to write reviews and tales for magazines. He wrote no travel sketches during stays with his parents in Cambridge or as a bachelor in New York, where he spent the winter of 1874–1875 writing art and theater notes for *The Nation*. He also revised and collected his tales and travel writings for publication as *A Passionate Pilgrim, and Other Tales* (1875) and *Transatlantic Sketches* (1875).

A Passionate Pilgrim, and Other Tales, which he had earlier described to his mother as "a volume . . .

of tales on the theme of American adventurers in Europe" (24 March 1873), appeared first, in late January 1875. *Transatlantic Sketches*, his first collection of travel pieces, was published in April 1875. Both volumes sold respectably for first books, but sales of the travel sketches were nearly triple those of the tales. James, however, had borrowed money from his father to purchase the printer's plates for *Transatlantic Sketches* and thus speed the publication of the book. Consequently, the royalties on this book did not pay off his initial investment until 1906. James never entered such a publishing arrangement again, and the sales figures encouraged him to continue working in this genre.

Writing travel literature extended and developed James's audience, advanced his lifelong campaign to support himself as a man of letters, and directly remunerated him for persevering in the peripatetic life he had known since infancy. Aside from the widely pirated *Daisy Miller*, James's book sales never satisfied his expectations, but he always maintained a firm and well-placed readership. In modern publishing parlance he was a "prestige author" from the start. His publisher was the most distinguished firm in Boston, James R. Osgood and Company (formerly Ticknor and Fields and Fields, Osgood and later Houghton, Mifflin), the house that published the works of Nathaniel Hawthorne, Henry Wadsworth Longfellow, and other American writers of the northeastern literary establishment in the mid nineteenth century.

All twenty-five of the essays in *Transatlantic Sketches* had appeared in magazines in 1872 through 1874. In republishing them James revised them considerably, beginning the process that culminated in the further selection and revision of some of these pieces for *English Hours* (1905) and *Italian Hours* (1909). He changed the titles of some sketches. For instance, he soberly reduced "An Ex-Grand-Ducal Capital" (*The Nation*, 9 October 1873) to "Darmstadt." Among many insertions and revisions, James added seventy-two lines to the opening of "Swiss Notes," first published in the 19 September 1872 issue of *The Nation*. James revised these essays further for *Foreign Parts* (1883), an abridged version of *Transatlantic Sketches* brought out by Tauchnitz, a Leipzig publisher of good-quality, mass-market books. For this volume James omitted four complete essays—"The Parisian Stage," "The After-Season in Rome," "The Autumn in Florence" and "The Splugen"—as well as parts 2, 6, 7, and 8 of "Florentine Notes."

The travel essays in *Transatlantic Sketches* may be his most cosmopolitan. In addition to his earliest published works on England, France, and Italy, the

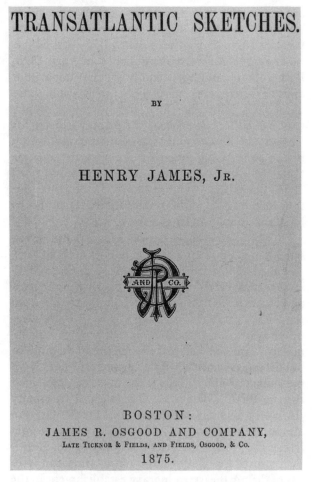

TRANSATLANTIC SKETCHES.

BY

HENRY JAMES, Jr.

BOSTON:
JAMES R. OSGOOD AND COMPANY,
Late Ticknor & Fields, and Fields, Osgood, & Co.
1875.

*Title page for James's first collection of travel writings,
describing visits to England, France, Italy, Germany,
and the Low Countries during 1872–1874*

book includes the author's only travel sketches of Germany and the Low Countries, which were not republished in another collection until the *Collected Travel Writings* appeared 118 years later.

In autumn 1875, just as Osgood was about to publish *Roderick Hudson* in book form, James returned to Europe, having convinced the *New York Tribune* to make him its Paris correspondent on politics and culture "to begin about 25th October, 1875." (He engaged in similar contracts in the 1890s, writing "London Letters" for *Harper's Weekly* and "American Letters" for *Literature*.) An acquaintance, John Hay, recommended James to Whitelaw Reid, the current editor, saying, "He will write better letters than anybody—you know his wonderful style and keen observation of life and character."

Beginning on 11 December 1875 these letters, collected in 1957 as *Parisian Sketches: Letters to the New York Tribune, 1875–1876,* represent James as dangerously out of touch with his genre and audience. As Carl S. Smith writes, "The combination of involve-

ment in and yet disengagement from the world . . . that characterizes travel . . . suited [James's] particular sensibility." In contrast, this intensely social but warily private man found it difficult to write of celebrities and public spectacles. In his fiction he frequently caricatured modern journalists who violate privacy for the sake of a story. Thus, although James became friendly with members of the French literary scene, including the Russian novelist Ivan Turgenev and the circle of Gustave Flaubert, he quailed at taking advantage of his private access to these well-known figures.

In addition James's style presented formal difficulties to a popular readership. His debut letter alone was certainly daunting. How many members of a mass audience would finish a first paragraph of more than five hundred words, including the phrase "mutilate an axiom"? For Leon Edel and Ilse Dusoir Lind, the editors of *Parisian Sketches,* "The letters make rewarding reading if we can surrender ourselves to James's constant need to intellectualize and analyze experience." Instead of indulging such a need the readers of the *New York Tribune* met his chaste descriptions of French politics, exhibitions, and theaters with profound indifference. In July 1876, even though the previous Paris correspondents' letters had begun to appear again in the *Tribune,* James asked Reid for a 50 percent raise. Reid politely denied the request, offering instead the criticism that James's subjects were often "too remote from popular interests" and suggesting his letters were "magazine rather than newspaper work." James sardonically apologized, "If my letters have been 'too good' I am honestly afraid that they are the poorest I can do, especially for the money! I had better . . . suspend them altogether" (30 August 1876). Bemoaning in his notebook his inability "to take the measure of the huge flat foot of the public," James terminated his contract with Reid after twenty letters, the last of which appeared in the 26 August issue.

However frustrating its outcome, James's newspaper work had supported his labor on *The American* (1877), the earliest of his important novels, which was serialized in *The Atlantic* in June 1876–May 1877. It also varied and extended his development of the travel genre. Even in some of his initial letters from Paris, James was not a reporter of current events. Instead he indulged a pictorial mode. In the third, "Versailles As It Is" (8 January 1876), for instance, he shrugged off the "political aspect" of a senatorial election for its "picturesque aspect." Ducking the cliques to assert as a priority that "palaces and gardens should be seen in the chill and leafless season," James wrote about slipping out to "the terraces and avenues of the park," where "long, misty alleys and vistas were covered with a sort of brown and violet bloom which a painter would have loved to reproduce. . . ."

James later revised and republished three of the Paris letters in *Portraits of Places* (1883). Although these three pieces are affected somewhat by his attempt to write for a larger audience, in contrast to the other letters to the *Tribune* they immediately show James in command of one of his native genres and, with it, his maturing voice. In the twelfth letter, "Chartres Portrayed" (29 April 1876), revised as "Chartres," it is April in Paris, and "All the world is in the streets." Yet James denied the journalistic appeal of "the world" and went instead "to the ancient town of Chartres." As populated Paris melts away—"relatively speaking, the church is fairly isolated"—his persona communes with beauty in admittedly inadequate words that may be, however, all his reader, the armchair traveler, will ever have of Chartres and the elevated thoughts it inspires:

> I have seen, I suppose, churches as beautiful as this one, but I do not remember ever to have been so touched and fascinated by architectural beauty. The endless upward reach of the great west front, the clear, silvery tone of its surface, the way a few magnificent features are made to occupy its vast, serene expanse, its simplicity, majesty, and dignity—these things crowd upon one's sense with an eloquence that one must not attempt to translate into words.

James returned again to travel writing for the final two *Tribune* letters, whose perspectives indicate some of the directions his future travel literature took. Perhaps in an attempt to infuse more personality into these journalistic efforts, for instance, "Summer in France" (12 August 1876), revised as "Rouen," anticipates his later travel style with its intimate and expansive first-person narration: "I write these lines at an inn at Havre, before a window which frames the picture of the seaward path of the transatlantic steamers. . . . My head is full of the twenty-four hours I have just passed at Rouen."

In a direct appeal to the travel-writing audience James also began to develop a practical voice that asserted itself later in *A Little Tour in France* (1884), his most successful book of travel writing. He directly addressed his audience in the second person, a tendency that, as Metwalli remarks, invites the reader "to join the traveler in touring."

"Carried to an extreme," Metwalli notes, "this personal approach rendered the travel writer more of a tourist guide . . . and his account can be legitimately described as not written but told." Likewise, Thorp observes that in these decades the "predomi-

The house in Venice where James had "dirty apartments with a lovely view" during an 1881 visit to Italy

nantly sentimental approach begins to yield to the kind of book which offers chiefly information and advice." Correspondingly, "Rouen" concludes, "I have left myself space only to recommend the sail down the Seine from Rouen to the mouth of the stream; but I recommend it in the highest terms," and likewise he signs off his twentieth and last letter, "A French Watering Place" (26 August 1876), revised as "Entretat," by pointing out, "So you may go southward or northward without impediment to Havre or to Dieppe."

In December 1876 James relocated from Paris to London. During the late 1870s he had a phenomenal burst of creative activity that included a resumption of his travel writing for magazines in both the United States and England. Indeed, throughout the 1870s there are few prose genres to which James did not contribute. He continued to produce scores of reviews for *The Nation, The Atlantic,* and *The Galaxy.* Some of these articles and some slightly earlier efforts were collected with minor revisions in *French Poets and Novelists* (1878), published in England by Macmillan, which also published James's critical biography *Hawthorne* (1879) in its English Men of Letters series. Some of his best-known tales also began appearing in magazines, including the international success *Daisy Miller* (*Cornhill Magazine,* June–July

James in 1884

1878), a narrative inspired by an anecdote he overheard in Rome, and *An International Episode* (*Cornhill Magazine,* December 1878–January 1879). By the early 1880s he had also completed four novels—*The Europeans* (1878), *Confidence* (1879), *Washington Square* (1880), and his early masterpiece *The Portrait of a Lady* (1881)—all of which were serialized in magazines before appearing as books in England and the United States.

In this enormously prolific period James also found time to tour extensively and to write nearly twenty travel essays. The late 1870s and early 1880s were his most productive time in this genre. After resigning his job with the *Tribune* in August 1876, James traveled in France to Normandy and the Midi. The record of this tour, "From Normandy to the Pyrenees," appeared in *The Galaxy* the following January. Its first-person discursiveness resembles the narration of his columns for the *New York Tribune;* freed, however, from the need to "gossip" for the mass reader, James sounded new sublimities: sitting "before the first fire of winter," the narrator observes,

> In the crackling flame the last remnant of summer appeared to shrink and vanish. But the flicker of its destruction made a sort of fantastic imagery, and in the midst of the winter fire the summer sunshine seemed to glow. It lit up a series of visible memories.

The first of these visions is "a great cube of white cliff," boding a spatial and intellectual dimensionality the rest of the essay develops. At this early stage James's dialectic of tourist and scene concludes in humorous shock and chagrin. Still writing for an American audience, James directly compared the Old and New Worlds. Regarding the Norman countryside: "This universal absence of barriers gives an air of vastness to the landscape, so that really, in a little French province, you have more of the feeling of being in a big country than on our own huge continent, which bristles so incongruously with defensive palings and dykes."

Relieved of any need to fling himself on the "defensive" barriers with which "our own huge continent" prevents free range to the intellect, James adopted another stratagem: "a comparison between French manners, French habits, French types, and those of my native land." The narrator assures his reader, "These comparisons are not invidious; I do not conclude against one party and in favour of the other." James now saw landscape and human figures less as elements in a completed picture of the past and more as an opening for intellectual and social explorations of an emerging modernity, a shift that signals his change of persona from a "sentimental tourist" to one he later described as "the restless analyst."

In this and other essays of the same year James's style and subject underwent a transformation that paralleled his development from a well-to-do young man to a working writer. Specifically, he questioned the assumptions that formerly motivated him as an "almost professional cherisher of the quaint" and engaged himself in a new world defined by class and commodities. Doubt first arose as he exercised a tourist's nearest approach to labor, walking across a series of swags, or vales: "The first *fond* strikes him as delightfully picturesque.... But ... the fourth is decidedly one too many, and the fifth is sensibly exasperating. The *fonds,* in a word, are very tiresome."

His lesson includes a visit with a shepherd who has been in feudal service for thirty-five years. The fatigued narrator resists reducing the peasant to a pastoral fixture and instead says that this man "professed himself very tired of his life"—a transformation from aesthetic appreciation to cultural compassion that James repeated in "Italy Revisited" (*The Atlantic,* April 1878). A country scene, in which a young man sings as he walks, first appears "generally ... operatic." When he and the young man converse, however, the narrator discovers the human figure in this pastoral spectacle to be a "brooding young radical and communist," "an unhappy, underfed, unemployed young man." James's persona now sees himself as "absurd . . . to have looked at him simply as a graceful ornament to the prospect. . . . Yet but for the accident of my having gossipped with him I should have made him do service, in memory, as an example of sensuous optimism!"

Shaken out of his "sensuous" regard and exposed to the material labor that is wasted on a sentimental traveler, James completed a process that in another context later that year he described as "a sort of Hegelian unfolding" ("Americans Abroad," *The Nation,* 3 October 1878). As this once-sentimental traveler earlier saw tourism transforming its objects of regard by stimulating restoration, now the professional writer and cultural critic perceived another material change in "the old book" and "museum" of Italy: "as we move about nowadays in the Italian cities, there seems to pass before our eyes a vision of the coming years. It represents to our satisfaction an Italy united and prosperous, but altogether scientific and commercial"—an Italy similar, that is, to the industrializing nation from which James and other genteel Americans fled after the Civil War. This inexorable dialectic climaxes when, walking in the Tuscan hills, the narrator pauses at a "wayside shrine, in which, before some pious daub of an old-time Madonna" a votive lamp emits "an incongruous odor":

> I wondered, I gently sniffed, and the question so put me left me no doubt. The odour was that of petroleum; the votive taper was nourished with the essence of Pennsylvania. I confess that I burst out laughing. . . .

In "From Normandy to the Pyrennes" James revealed a similar preference for tradition when he found advantages for French women in arranged marriages: Being a married woman in France "does not mean, as it so often means in America, being socially shelved." In this same sketch, perhaps reflecting on the American masses' rejection of his letters for being "too good," James expressed a humorous scorn of the folk spectacle that sacrifices a "finer" form of manhood. The essay ends with James's only paragraph of travel writing about Spain, whose border he crossed to see a bullfight at San Sebastian:

> Description apart, one has taken a sort of pleasure in the bull-fight, and yet how is one to state gracefully that one has taken pleasure in a disgusting thing? It is a hard case. If you record your pleasure, you seem to calumniate your delicacy; and if you record nothing but your displeasure, you feel as if you were wanting in suppleness. . . . I thought the bull, in any case, a finer fellow than any of his tormentors, and I thought his tormentors finer fellows than the spectators. In truth, we were all, for the time, rather sorry fellows together. A bullfight will, to a certain extent, bear looking at, but it will not bear thinking of.

The self-conscious humor of this passage opens a way to James's later style, which does not follow logical processes (or planned tours) as much as it registers phenomena that await a master's poetic evocation.

In the late 1870s and early 1880s James added George Meredith, James McNeill Whistler, and Alfred, Lord Tennyson, to his list of acquaintances. Despite his astounding productivity and active social life James also toured the British Isles and published fourteen travel sketches or essays on these visits between 1877 and 1883. In these essays, which were published in American magazines, he continued to make explicit comparisons between his host and native countries, tending to favor the conservative institutions of the Old World. Often, however, he abandoned these transatlantic comparisons to face with fresh directness not only the beautiful scenes that reflected the privileged class of society that frequented them but also the overvisited public places that attracted the less-winning elements of the population, a spectacle that portended schisms in the cherished old order.

In "An English Easter" (*Lippincott's Magazine,* July 1877) James wrote with some of the old satisfaction that "for one definite precedent in American life there are fifty in English"; "With us there is infinitely less responsibility; but there is also, I think, less freedom." As on the Continent, however, James found himself little tempted to frame such customs as picturesque; regarding the "universal churchgoing" of England, for instance, he "hardly knows whether to estimate [it] as a great force or a great futility." Further he abandoned an explicit international dialectic for one that places the observer in relation to the object itself: "If one is bent upon observation nothing . . . is trivial."

James's maturing temperament and the "overflow[ing] population" of England were perhaps equally responsible for stimulating this new relationship. Where earlier on the Continent the sight of tourists had sent him "dodging" to find a picturesque focus for his sentiment or an obscure locus for his melancholy, in London and its suburbs he seemed only to glance at any stately frame before he shifted his attention to the human base that once supported it but which threatened now to crack. "London is pictorial in spite of the details," he as-

"La Rochelle: the Hôtel de Ville" and "Dijon," illustrations by Joseph Pennell for the 1900 edition of A Little Tour in France

sured the reader early in "An English Easter," but his sketch relocates the rural, ruined gothic to a site of urban dirt and decay—"from its dark green, misty parks, the way the light comes down leaking and filtering from its cloud-ceiling, and the softness and richness of tone which objects put on in such an atmosphere as soon as they begin to recede." This "pictorial" tone becomes rarer as James's narrator drags himself from place to place only to learn that "there are, selfishly speaking, too many people. Human life is cheap; your fellow mortals are too numerous." Adding to "the hard prose of misery," the "depression of business is extreme and universal." As James wrote in "In Warwickshire" (first published in *The Galaxy,* November 1877):

> with regard to most romantic sites in England, there is a constant cockneyfication with which you must make your account. There are always people on the field before you, and there is generally something being drunk on the premises.

James's exasperation, though repeated at nearly every "romantic site," was short-lived as he reminded himself that when "attempting to gather impressions of a people and to learn to know them, everything is interesting that is characteristic, quite apart from its being beautiful."

It tests the parameters of travel writing to wonder whether these pieces may be properly classified within this genre since they originate from the place where the author had chosen to call home and concern not the classical monuments of nature and civilization but the passing parade of a modern nation's working people. In "An English Easter" James described how he "emerged accidentally into Piccadilly," his own neighborhood, to see a popular spectacle that, however far from "gossip," his *Tribune* audience might have found rewarding: the funeral of George Odger, "an English Radical agitator of humble origin," a shoemaker and a parliamentary hopeful mourned by "the most marked collection of the shabbier English types that I had seen since I came to London." In contrast to his childhood vision of the spectacular Place Vendôme from his parents' well-appointed carriage, James's persona sits in "a hansom cab . . . drawn up beside the pavement" and watches this cortege "as from a box at the play." Not "a tragedy" but "a very serious comedy," the "play" James sees forms "a sort of panoramic view of the under side, the wrong side, of the London world." The "double consciousness" of these English travel sketches thus shifts from James's former oppositions of commercial America versus picturesque Europe, or of a sentimental tourist versus "trooping barbarians," to a rapt but forlorn dialectic between the disintegrating feudal class distinctions of England, where he used to find pleasure, and now discovered that "numerosity . . . swallows up quality." Writings of such gravity will endure in any canon of literature in English. If they are travel writings, however, they make no appeal to "escape," for the class dialectic obsessed James throughout his British travels. Leaving London for the Isle of Wight in "English Vignettes" (first published in *Lippincott's Magazine,* April 1879), he visited a "half-modernized feudal dwelling" belonging to "a rich young man" who "occupied it but for three weeks in the year and for the rest of the time left it a prey" to tourists, including James himself, "the would-be redresser of aesthetic wrongs":

James in Rome, 1899

> It seemed a great aesthetic wrong that so charming a place should not be a conscious, sentient home. In England all this is very common. It takes a great many plain people to keep a "perfect" gentleman going. . . .

People on the platforms at fashionable stops on the railroad give the impression "that the population consists almost exclusively of gentlemen in costumes suggestive of unlimited leisure."

James may have remembered these perfect gentlemen and the "plain people" that keep them going when he wrote "The New Year in England" (first published in *The Nation,* 23 January 1879). In one paragraph he radically shifted from the English "social genius" as illustrated in a "well-appointed, well-administered, well-filled country-house" to the "most ineffaceable impression" of his journey. In a "populous manufacturing region" James's narrator takes a rare dramatic action when he accompanies a lady with a Christmas tree to visit the children in a workhouse to assist in giving them toys. Looking for another Oliver Twist, "I glanced through this lit-

tle herd for an infant figure that should look as if it were cut out for romantic adventures. But they were all very prosaic little mortals." As James's persona looks at the individual wealth of his traveling hostess, "the beautiful Lady Bountiful," he realizes that she stands at the other end of the world from the poverty he sees in "the little multitude of staring and wondering, yet perfectly expressionless, faces."

In December 1883 Macmillan and Company of London published James's first collection of travel sketches to appear in Great Britain. The American printing, from the Macmillan plates, was published in January 1884 by James R. Osgood of Boston with a different introductory note. This collection includes three sketches of France that appeared in *The Galaxy* and *The Atlantic* during 1877 and 1878 as well as three of his 1876 Paris letters to the *New York Tribune;* two chapters on Italy, one that appeared in *Century Magazine* in 1882 and another that appeared in two parts in *The Atlantic* in 1878; eight pieces on England written and published between 1877 and 1879; and the four travel pieces on America and Canada that he wrote for *The Nation* in 1870–1871. Altogether, the range and appeal of *Portraits of Places* bear comparisons with James's collections of tales at this phase of his career.

The introductory notes to the British and American printings of *Portraits and Places* express James's characteristic self-consciousness about his new audience and his old travel sketches, revealing his cultivated style and the changing world it chronicles. His "Note to the English Edition" explains the pieces as resulting from "a stage of observation on the writer's part which belongs to freshness of acquaintance." Pointing out that the sketches were initially "addressed altogether to an American public," the note adds that the writer's "impressions have been modified and enlarged, and he would not today have the temerity to write letters upon England." His note to American readers confesses a different problem: given the rapid modernization of his homeland, his sketches of Saratoga, Newport, Quebec, and Niagara have "only the value of history," for "thirteen years" have brought "many changes." Except for the early sketches, the pieces collected in *Portraits of Places* are more fully essayistic or more finished pictorial "portraits" than those in *Transatlantic Sketches*. The later travel essays mark again the distance James had traveled in a dozen years, from an alienated cultivator of the picturesque to an engaged mediator between the contending poles of his culture.

Yet James's career followed few perfectly linear progressions, and not all the essays in *Portraits of Places* find him absorbed in the cultural analysis he developed in his British explorations. In the opening piece, "Venice," first published in the November 1882 issue of *Century Magazine,* for instance, James is back to reading Ruskin and "dodging" sightseeing troops of "savage Germans." Indeed, despite the sensitivity to class and the material resistance to the picturesque that he found on the Continent after quitting the *New York Tribune,* it appears that, despite his prowess in foreign languages, he reverted to his traditional aesthetics when he toured non-English-speaking countries. This supposition must be weighed with the fact that during the 1880s James developed his skill at the political and cultural critique in novels such as *The Bostonians* (1886) and *The Princess Casamassima* (1886), which sold poorly at their publication but received considerable critical acclaim in the twentieth century.

As with all James's modulations of subject and method, the sacrifice of one developing style is compensated by the delights of another. His next travel volume after *Portraits of Places* is perhaps his most

perfect, climaxing his most active decade in the genre. The chapters of *A Little Tour in France* (1884) appeared first in *The Atlantic Monthly* (July–November 1883 and February, April, and May 1884) as a series of articles titled *En Provence*. In contrast to the sketches of his previous travel books, these articles cover extended touring and so cohere more naturally in book form. Though he worked with no definite commitment, James undertook his autumn 1882 tour for these pieces on the recommendation of an editor at Harper and Brothers. Later, when that firm was not forthcoming with a contract, James sold the manuscript to Osgood. James revised the pieces for book publication and revised them again for the 1900 edition, which had a new preface and "admirable drawings" by Joseph Pennell, making it the first of James's travel books to be illustrated.

A Little Tour in France marks the happy convergence of an author at the height of his powers and a subject ripe for treatment. As he was writing the pieces for *The Atlantic,* he was turning forty, and in November 1883 Macmillan, his London publisher, honored his growing reputation by publishing the first collected edition of James's novels and tales. With its bright, rich prose *A Little Tour in France* may be praised as the *Daisy Miller* of James's travel writings, the text that readers uninitiated to the James canon find most immediately enjoyable and rewarding. James's voluminous writing is often mistaken for ponderousness, and his searches for the picturesque may suggest world-weariness, but in *A Little Tour in France* his joyful speech parallels his traveler's tireless and quick step as he rises from realistic detail to abstract thought: "However late in the evening I may arrive at a place, I never go to bed without my impression."

Much of the thematic content of *A Little Tour in France* is familiar, but James avoided social commentary. In contrast, for instance, to *The American Scene* (1907), with its labored stress on nineteenth-century sexual distinctions, *A Little Tour in France* simply and briskly records James's discovery of "no branch of human activity in which one is not liable, in France, to find woman engaged." Instead of pausing to analyze a "commercial town" such as Bordeaux or Narbonne ("nothing but the market, . . . in complete possession"), James's "insatiate American" simply picks up his pace and pursues his path to Langeais, where he "marks the transition from the architecture of defence to that of elegance."

The charming and disarming tone of *A Little Tour in France* seems, ironically, to owe something to its apparently rapid composition, traces of which remain in the text. More professionally and purpose-

CHESTER CATHEDRAL, WEST FRONT

THE CATHEDRAL CLOSE, CANTERBURY

STRATFORD-ON-AVON CHURCH

CHICHESTER CROSS

Illustrations by Joseph Pennell in English Hours *(1905)*

fully than in his earlier pieces, he employed an avuncular tone to advise the reader on matters both abstract and material. "There is a pleasure sometimes in running the risk of disappointment," and "one always misses something," but—the voice of experience warns the reader—"Breakfast not" in the "terribly dirty" little inn at Azay-le-Rideau. The humor implicit in such quickly scratched details leaps out in little set pieces, as in this description of medieval friezes of the Judgment Day at Bourges:

> The good get out of their tombs with a certain modest gaiety, an alacrity tempered by respect. . . . You may know the wicked, on the other hand, by their extreme shyness; they crawl out slowly and fearfully; they hang back, and seem to say "Oh, dear!"

Yet, however quick and varied its lightness of tone, this book also registers historic events:

> Wherever one goes, in France, one meets . . . the spectre of the great Revolution; and one meets it always in the shape of the destruction of something beautiful and precious. To make us forgive it at all, how much it must also have destroyed that was more hateful than itself!

The "spectre" he traces, like that of Leonardo da Vinci's *Last Supper* or the ruins of the ancient Roman theater at Arles, "makes the present and the past touch each other."

A Little Tour in France is James's most practical and delightful travel book. William H. Pritchard has called it "the closest thing he ever wrote to a guidebook" and has suggested that the book "could be useful still as a guide to southern France." Edel pointed out that the book served "successive generations of tourists in the chateau country and the Midi."

At this point in his career James, only a little more than halfway through his long and productive life, had completed the significant majority of his travel writing about the world outside the United States. In his remaining thirty-two years, as he advanced in the craft of writing fiction, memoirs, and criticism and experimented (disastrously) with playwriting, James wrote only one more original travel book, *The American Scene*. Yet *William Wetmore Story and His Friends* (1903), James's biography of a friend and fellow American expatriate, a sculptor and man of letters who lived in Rome, is also of interest to the history of travel. James took up this biography reluctantly, and ultimately he used the book to evoke and memorialize "the early flowering" of "the old relation, social, personal, aesthetic, of the American world to the European." James also wrote occasional travel articles, especially on Italy, and on a

grander scale he revised and repackaged his previously published sketches of Europe in *English Hours* (1905) and *Italian Hours* (1909), the handsome illustrated editions in which his travel literature has largely come down to later readers. James's new articles and revisions of earlier pieces illustrate a third phase of his style, superseding his personae of sentimental tourist and cultural analyst and duplicating the consciousness he wrought in the novels of his "major phase"—such as *The Wings of the Dove* (1902) and *The Golden Bowl* (1904)—a woven web of sense and memory.

English Hours includes ninety-two illustrations by the distinguished American watercolorist Joseph Pennell, who had begun his collaboration with James by drawing thirteen illustrations for "London" in the December 1888 issue of *Century Magazine* and then did ninety-four illustrations for *A Little Tour in France*. This artist wrote a brief memoir of James, including descriptions of encountering the writer in Rome at the grave of John Keats; or "walking the *calle* of Venice"; or, in a rare evocation of the working writer, at his Kensington flat "standing in a red undershirt, before a high writing-desk in a dark room, which wasn't exactly the usual idea of him"; and at his country house in Rye, where "he showed me the town; but as he always would take his little dog with him, and as motors tore through the streets, he was frightened for the dog. But I was more afraid he would get run over, though I think the dog did in the end." The dusky impressionism of Pennell's illustrations share a harmony of tone with the increasing impressionism of James's mature style.

The title *English Hours* indicates a loose temporal organization extending from James's earliest writings on England in the 1870s to two articles from the turn of the century that had appeared in American magazines but not previously in book form: "Old Suffolk" (*Harper's Weekly,* 25 September 1897) and "Winchelsea, Rye, and 'Denis Duval'" (*Scribner's Magazine,* January 1901). Marius Bewley interprets James's cultural reorientation as a passage from "an admiration . . . for Britain as a power structure—in short, for Victorian imperialism," to an "ironic ambivalence" in which James's late style is "already implicit." James's later travel prose has a self-conscious intensity in which the boundaries dissolve between the speaker and his subject as they do between the interior world of his later fiction and the nonfictional, external world of phenomena.

"Winchelsea, Rye, and 'Denis Duval,'" the last-written piece in *English Hours,* further expands the travel genre by turning it to the purposes of literary criticism and history. Reading William

Caricatures of James published in American newspapers during his 1904–1905 visit to the United States

Makepeace Thackeray's unfinished, posthumously published novel, *Denis Duval* (1864), against its "haunted" setting, James's essay expresses the "impression . . . that the chapters we possess might really have been written without the author's having stood on the spot." Thackeray "conceived" his novel "as a 'picturesque' affair," but that "general *poetic*" is now "left well behind." In fact, "we have never really made out what his subject was to have been." Much the same has been said of many obscure passages in James's later fiction; when this style succeeds, however, it marks his accomplishment of the final stage in his development of an individual yet universal consciousness.

James attempted to effect a similar transformation on his earlier pieces for *English Hours*. A prefatory note concedes, "I have nowhere scrupled to rewrite a sentence of a passage on judging it susceptible of a better turn"—a process Alma Louise Lowe described in part in the introduction to her 1960 edition of *English Hours:* "No longer a sentimental tourist, and aware of the changing taste of the twentieth century, James deleted as often as possible the words 'picturesque' (which sometimes had appeared three or four times on a page), 'sentimental,'

'beautiful,' 'pretty,' and 'delicious.'" As a further indication of the turn James's style was taking, Lowe notes that after seeing *English Hours* through the press James began taking notes for a projected two-volume "romantic-psychological-pictorial 'social'" book of sketches to be titled "London Town," whose "style no doubt would have been as impressionistic, and perhaps as poetic, as *The American Scene* and *Italian Hours*."

From the beginning James conceived of *The American Scene* (1907) as a unified book based on travel notes he had made during a lecture tour in the United States that lasted from late August 1904 until early July 1905. After James's long residence in England, the narrative of *The American Scene* reverses the traditional theme of American writers discovering the Old World. Hoping to write another book about his western travels, James wrote about his impressions of life on the eastern seaboard, evoking his personal past while criticizing Americans' speech patterns, materialism, and tendency to undervalue and thus destroy valuable reminders of the past. Mulvey finds in the book "a strange link with the sense of dispossession experienced by the American landing on the English shore." Critical reception has

Henry and William James, 1905

been mixed: on one side W. H. Auden's preface to a 1946 edition hailed *The American Scene* as "a prose poem of the first order," and Bewley deems it James's "most richly textured and brilliant book of nonfiction." On the other Maxwell Geismar dismisses this "vacant, empty, and chatterbox book" for its "hysterical bursts of verbal virtuosity."

In 1907 James, then in his sixties, toured southern France with his friend and fellow novelist Edith Wharton, who based *A Motor-Flight Through France* (1908) on the trip, and then went on to Italy with Italian explorer and traveler Filippo de Filippi. This visit inspired James to compile *Italian Hours*—as did a need to fill his "flat pocket-book." As he wrote to William Dean Howells, collecting old travel articles into new books had "succeeded a little with 'English Hours,' which have sold quite vulgarly—for wares of mine. . . ."

Published in 1909 with illustrations by Pennell, *Italian Hours* includes two entirely new essays—"A Few Other Roman Neighborhoods" and "Other Tuscan Cities"—and two additions to previously collected essays—part 2 of "Siena Early and Late" and parts 6 and 7 of "The Saint's Afternoon and Others"—as well as two essays previously published in magazines—"Casa Alvisi" (*Cornhill Magazine* and *The Critic*, both February 1902) and "Two Old Houses and Three Young Women" (*The Independent*, 7 September 1899). Fourteen of the twenty-two pieces were originally collected in *Transatlantic Sketches*, making *Italian Hours*, even with James's ex-

tensive revisions, a virtual encyclopedia of his evolving style.

Among James's travel sketches that appeared after *Portraits of Places*, his most splendid European composition is the long essay "The Grand Canal," which first appeared in the November 1892 issue of *Scribner's Magazine* and was collected the following month in an anthology, *The Great Streets of the World*, which also includes contributions by Richard Harding Davis, William Wetmore Story, Andrew Lang, and others. (In both *Scribner's* and this anthology James's essay was illustrated with thirteen drawings by Alexander Zezzos.) James's opening procession down the Grand Canal evokes "a hundred . . . infatuations with which Venice sophisticates the spirit," and the essay ends in his admiration of the "double character" by which things in Venice "share fully in that universal privilege . . . of being both the picture and the point of view." Here and in "Two Old Houses and Three Old Women" James reaches the furthest development of his late style in the travel genre.

The new essays James wrote especially for *Italian Hours* manifest the luminous and hypnotic obscurity of this final manner. In part 1 of "Siena Early and Late," first published as "Siena" in the June 1874 issue of *The Atlantic* and collected in *Transatlantic Sketches*, James precisely savored "the life of sensibility" in "dusky alleys" and the "gossip of an innwaiter"; in his report of the "late" visit added in 1909, however, "the incurable student of loose meanings and stray relics and odd references and

James with Howard Sturgis and Louisa and Edward Boit during James's last visit to Italy, 1907

dim analogies" holds only "a little faded cluster of impressions," an "indestructible mixture of lived things" that "remain bright and assured and sublime—practically, enviably immortal—the other, the still subtler, the all aesthetic good faith." In Carl S. Smith's apt description James now "believed that the most interesting subject for him to see and write about was himself seeing." James absorbed the "double character" or "double consciousness" wholly into himself and projected its essential alienation to the reader, who may find himself excluded or simply beleaguered by James's late style. Like James reading the late Thackeray, "we have never really made out what his subject was to have been," but without doubt the reader has witnessed a fulfillment of the courageous dialectic James tried all his life to advance.

In *Collected Travel Writings* (1993) Richard Howard includes four essays written for various publications during World War I in support of the war effort and on behalf of refugees in Great Britain. These essays serve as a lucid and powerful bookend to the world James began exploring and recording a half-century before. As in his finest travel writing he negotiated again the burdens of self-consciousness and those of the world he meets. In "Refugees in England," first published in *The New York Times* and the *Boston Sunday Tribune* on 17 October 1915, overcoming "an elderly dread of a waste of emotion," he registered the "sobbing and sobbing cry" of a Belgian refugee as "the voice itself of history; it brought home to me more things than I could then quite take the measure of. . . . Months have elapsed . . . ; yet her cry is still in my ears . . . and it plays to my own sense, as a great fitful tragic light over the dark exposure of her people."

In "Within the Rim" (*Fortnightly Review*, August 1917) he compares the effect of war in Europe to the "violence with which the American Civil War broke upon us" and acknowledges "the strangest of savours, an inexpressible romantic thrill, to the harsh taste of the crisis." James ultimately reacted to this crisis in 1915 by resigning his American citizenship and becoming a subject of Great Britain to protest the neutrality of the United States in the conflict. In "Within the Rim" he related his position as a mediator of the Old and New Worlds to the buildings in which "the present and the past touch each other": "I felt as the quiet dweller in a tenement so often feels when the question of 'structural improvements' is thrust upon him."

James died in London in 1916, an internationally recognized master of modern literature. While critics have debated his greatness, an enduring audience of readers has discovered in his life and works a marvelous application of opportunity, integrity, and intellect to subjects that still confront the aesthetic conscience. James's fiction has long been admired for these qualities, but his travel writings also engage those who, like him, want to read about the world in all its truth—pleasure and pain, picturesque past and menacing future.

Letters:

Henry James: Letters, 4 volumes, edited by Leon Edel (Cambridge, Mass.: Harvard University Press, 1974–1984).

Bibliographies:

Kristin Pruitt McColgan, *Henry James, 1917–1959: A Reference Guide* (Boston: G. K. Hall, 1979);

Dorothy McInnis Scura, *Henry James, 1960–1974: A Reference Guide* (Boston: G. K. Hall, 1979);

Linda J. Taylor, *Henry James, 1866–1916: A Reference Guide* (Boston: G. K. Hall, 1982);

Leon Edel and Dan H. Laurence, *A Bibliography of Henry James,* third edition, revised with the assistance of James Rambeau (Oxford: Clarendon Press, 1982);

John Budd, *Henry James: A Bibliography of Criticism, 1975–1981* (Westport, Conn.: Greenwood Press, 1983);

Nicola Bradbury, *An Annotated Critical Bibliography of Henry James* (New York: St. Martin's Press, 1987);

Judith E. Funston, *Henry James: A Reference Guide, 1975–1987* (Boston: G. K. Hall, 1991).

Biographies:

Leon Edel, *Henry James: The Untried Years, 1843–1870* (Philadelphia & New York: Lippincott, 1953); *Henry James: The Conquest of London, 1870–1881* (Philadelphia & New York: Lippin-cott, 1962); *Henry James: The Middle Years, 1882–1895* (Philadelphia & New York: Lippincott, 1962); *Henry James: The Treacherous Years, 1895–1901* (Philadelphia & New York: Lippincott, 1969); *Henry James: The Master, 1901–1916* (Philadelphia & New York: Lippincott, 1972); these 5 volumes revised and abridged as *Henry James: A Life* (New York: Harper & Row, 1985);

R. W. B. Lewis, *The Jameses: A Family Narrative* (New York: Farrar, Straus & Giroux, 1991).

References:

A. Alvarez, "Intelligence on Tour," *Kenyon Review,* 21 (Winter 1959): 23–33;

Michael Anesko, *"Friction with the Market": Henry James and the Profession of Authorship* (New York: Oxford University Press, 1986);

Marius Bewley, "Henry James's *English Hours,*" in his *Masks and Mirrors: Essays in Criticism* (New York: Atheneum, 1970), pp. 119–138;

William F. Buckley Jr., "Mr. James in Motion," *New York Times Book Review,* 12 December 1993, pp. 1, 32–33, 37–38;

James Doyle, *North of America: Images of Canada in the Literature of the United States, 1775–1900* (Toronto: ECW Press, 1983);

Donald Emerson, "Henry James: A Sentimental Tourist and Restless Analyst," *Transactions of the Wisconsin Academy of Sciences, Arts, and Letters,* 53 (1963): 17–25;

Alma Louise Lowe, Introduction to *English Hours,* edited by Lowe (London: Heinemann, 1960);

Bonney MacDonald, "The Force of Revelation: Receptive Vision in Henry James's Early Italian Travel Essays," in *The Sweetest Impression of Life: The James Family and Italy,* edited by James W. Tuttleton and Agostino Lombardo (New York: New York University Press, 1990), pp. 128–148;

MacDonald, *Henry James's* Italian Hours: *Revelatory and Resistant Impressions* (Ann Arbor, Mich.: UMI Research Press, 1990);

Ahmed M. Metwalli, "Americans Abroad: The Popular Art of Travel Writing in the Nineteenth Century," in *America: Exploration and Travel,* edited by Steven E. Kagle (Bowling Green, Ohio: Bowling Green University Popular Press, 1979), pp. 68–82;

Christopher Mulvey, *Anglo-American Landscapes: A Study of Nineteenth-Century Anglo-American Travel Literature* (Cambridge: Cambridge University Press, 1983);

Joseph Pennell, "Adventures of an Illustrator; II—In London with Henry James," *Century Magazine,* 103 (February 1922): 543–548;

William H. Pritchard, "James on Tour," review of *Collected Travel Writings, Hudson Review,* 47 (Summer 1994): 259–268;

Carl S. Smith, "James's Travels, Travel Writings, and the Development of His Art," *Modern Language Quarterly,* 38 (December 1977): 367–380;

Susan Sontag, "Model Destinations," *Times Literary Supplement,* 22 June 1984, pp. 699–700;

Michael Swan, Introduction to *A Little Tour in France* (London: Home & Van Thal, 1949);

Tony Tanner, "Henry James and the Art of Travel Writing," in his *Henry James and the Art of Nonfiction* (Athens: University of Georgia Press, 1995), pp. 1–24;

Willard Thorp, "Pilgrims' Return," in *Literary History of the United States,* revised edition, edited by Robert E. Spiller and others (New York: Macmillan, 1953), pp. 827–842;

James W. Tuttleton and Agostino Lombardo, eds., *The Sweetest Impression of Life: The James Family and Italy* (New York: New York University Press, 1990);

Craig Howard White, Review of *Henry James: Collected Travel Writings,* edited by Richard Howard, in *Henry James Review,* 15 (Winter 1994): 91–95.

Papers:

Most of James's manuscripts are in the Houghton Library at Harvard University. Other significant collections are in the Beinecke Library at Yale University, the Library of Congress, the British Library, the Charles Scribner's Sons archives at Princeton University, the Huntington Library, the Morgan Library, the New York Public Library, the Buffalo Public Library, and the libraries of the University of Leeds, Colby College, the University of Rochester, the University of Chicago, the University of California at Los Angeles, and the Century Association in New York City.

James Jackson Jarves
(20 August 1818 – 28 June 1888)

Jeffrey Alan Melton
Auburn University at Montgomery

BOOKS: *History of the Hawaiian or Sandwich Islands, Embracing Their Antiquities, Mythology, Legends, Discovery by Europeans in the Sixteenth Century, Re-Discovery by Cook, with Their Civil, Religious and Political History, from the Earliest Traditionary Period to the Present Time* (Boston: Tappan & Dennet, 1843; London: Moxon, 1843);

Scenes and Scenery in the Sandwich Islands, and a Trip through Central America: Being Observations from My Note-book During the Years 1837–1842 (Boston: James Munroe, 1843; London: Moxon, 1844);

Parisian Sights and French Principles, Seen Through American Spectacles, anonymous (New York: Harper, 1852; London: Clarke, Beeton, 1853);

Parisian Sights and French Principles, Seen Through American Spectacles, second series (New York: Harper, 1855; London: Clarke, Beeton, 1855);

Art-Hints: Architecture, Sculpture and Painting (New York: Harper, 1855; London: Sampson Low, 1855);

Italian Sights and Papal Principles, Seen Through American Spectacles (New York: Harper, 1856);

Kiana: A Tradition of Hawaii (Boston & Cambridge, Mass.: James Munroe / London: Sampson Low, 1857);

Why and What Am I? The Confessions of an Inquirer. In Three Parts. Part 1. Heart-Experience; or, The Education of the Emotions (Boston: Phillips, Sampson, 1857; London: Sampson Low, 1857);

Art Studies: The "Old Masters" of Italy; Painting (New York: Derby & Jackson, 1861; London: Sampson Low, 1861);

The Art-Idea: Part Second of Confessions of an Inquirer (New York: Hurd & Houghton / Boston: Walker, Wise, 1864); revised as *The Art-Idea: Sculpture, Painting, and Architecture in America* (New York: Hurd & Houghton / Boston: Walker, Wise, 1865);

Art Thoughts: The Experiences and Observations of an American Amateur in Europe (New York: Hurd & Houghton, 1869);

James Jackson Jarves

A Glimpse at the Art of Japan (New York: Hurd & Houghton, 1876);

Italian Rambles: Studies of Life and Manners in New and Old Italy (New York: Putnam, 1883; London: Sampson Low, 1883);

Pepero, the Boy-Artist: A Brief Memoir of James Jackson Jarves, by His Father (Boston: Houghton, Mifflin, 1890).

Although his works rarely gain attention from modern readers and scholars, James Jackson Jarves's contributions both as a travel writer and an art critic were substantial in his lifetime. Jarves was a restless and energetic man who, as his biographer Francis

222

Steegmuller aptly notes, led symbolically two lives, each seemingly distinct and each equally intriguing. In one life he became a charter member of the American Oriental Society and the first historian of the Hawaiian Islands, an effort which remains seminal. In another life Jarves became an honorary member of the Florentine Academy of Fine Arts and builder of the most substantial American collections of Italian Old Masters paintings in the nineteenth century. Within these two lives Jarves also grasped the opportunity to become one of the preeminent American travel writers of his time.

Jarves was born on 20 August 1818 to Deming and Anna Stutson Jarves in Boston. Deming Jarves, an enterprising businessman, founded the Sandwich Manufacturing Company, which later became the Boston and Sandwich Glass Company and eventually made Sandwich Glass world famous. Although Jarves had five brothers and three sisters, his family's economic security was solid and comfortable, especially for him since he seemed to be the favored child as the oldest after the early death of the first-born son. He enjoyed the benefits of private education, entering Chauncey Hall School in Boston at age twelve, and he proved to be quite capable as a student. Unfortunately, when he was fifteen, his eyes weakened, which effectively ended his studies since it prevented reading. In the next few years his eye problems and general physical weakness failed to improve, and doctors encouraged his parents to send him away from the bitter New England climate. He chose Hawaii.

Before leaving Boston he became engaged to Elizabeth Russell Swain of New Bedford, the daughter of Oliver Swain, a merchant. He sailed for Hawaii aboard the brigantine *Peru* in February or March 1837. Arriving in Honolulu on 29 July 1837, Jarves soon, owing to family connections, became affiliated with successful New England merchants and active Presbyterian missionaries. He was hosted initially by Peter Brinsmade, a graduate of Bowdoin College and former student at Andover Theological Seminary and the Yale Divinity School and part owner of a mercantile store, Brinsmade, Ladd, and Hooper, in Honolulu. Brinsmade and his partners were often dubbed the "pious traders," and Jarves was almost immediately included within their social, religious, and business group.

His association with the pious traders allowed him his first opportunity for travel writing. Brinsmade, the editor of the newly created *Hawaiian Spectator,* solicited a travel piece based on Jarves's excursions on the island of Kauai–a trip in which he toured a sugar plantation owned by Brinsmade, Ladd, and Hooper. "Sketches of Kauai" appeared in

January 1838. Not surprising, the article is highly complimentary of the sugar plantation and enthusiastic concerning its prospects, thereby providing its owners with valuable publicity.

Soon afterward Jarves sailed back to Boston to marry his fiancée, departing on 5 December 1837 on the brigantine *Clementine*. The trip proved to be a harrowing ordeal. The ship, after being delayed for days by dead-calm weather, was delayed again in Sonsonate, Guatemala, owing to cholera and civil war. Several of the passengers, including Jarves, decided to make the overland trip through Central America, an exhausting and dangerous journey. Once on the Atlantic side, he went to Belize in British Honduras and remained for more than two months with chills and fever. Finally, after boarding an English brigantine, he arrived in New York in late March 1838. Although he survived the ordeal, he spent the following months resting in Sandwich, Massachusetts, and doing little more than preparing for his wedding.

Jarves and Elizabeth "Libby" Swain married on 2 October 1838 in New Bedford, and they sailed on 20 October for Hawaii on the *Fama*. During another long journey (this time with no overland short cuts) Jarves began another travel piece for the *Hawaiian Spectator,* this one describing his ordeal through Central America. It did not appear until October 1839. The newlyweds arrived in Honolulu with Libby pregnant in April 1839. They first settled in Honolulu but soon moved to Koloa, Kauai, where their first child, Horatio Deming, was born on 10 December 1839. At first he was called James Barnard after a friend in New England, but since the original James Barnard failed to show his appreciation soon enough for the Jarveses' tastes, the child was renamed for a more gracious friend and Jarves's father.

Although he was writing his travel sketch, Jarves was primarily preoccupied with establishing himself as a merchant. He was in Hawaii for more than his health; he intended to make his fortune, and he clearly viewed literary pursuits as simply a diversion. Jarves's business ventures continued to struggle. His primary financial concern was his investment in a silk plantation on Kauai, of which he was a co-owner with Charles Titcomb and Sherman Peck. The plantation, called Mauna Kilika, was destined to fail; by March 1840 Titcomb had abandoned the project to begin his own plantation (which also failed). Drought, aphids, and various other insects destroyed the mulberry trees, and the worms remained unfed. Jarves would later describe the catastrophe at length in *Scenes and Scenery in the Sandwich Islands, and a Trip through Central America*

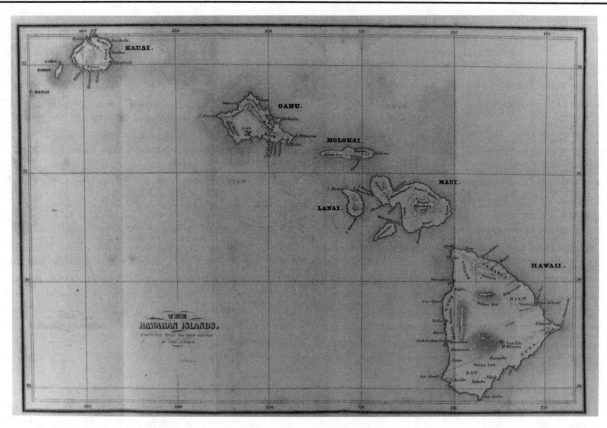

Map from Jarves's first travel book, Scenes and Scenery in the Sandwich Islands, and a Trip through Central America *(1843)*

(1843), adding: "In 1841 the proprietors, unable to bear any further expenses in prosecuting a business against so many obstacles, relinquished the undertaking." The threat to the financial welfare of his new family was formidable if not desperate.

The Jarveses moved back to Honolulu in the spring of 1840 since his presence was no longer necessary on the plantation, and Jarves began in earnest to establish himself more directly as a literary man. On 6 June 1840 Jarves, as editor, published the first issue of a new newspaper, *The Polynesian,* which was intended by the missionaries and pious traders who gave it backing to support their vision of the daily life and future of the Hawaiian Islands. *The Polynesian* appeared every Saturday with four pages; it cost eight dollars for a yearly subscription and five for a half year. With his introductory editorial Jarves described his intentions: "it will endeavor to combine the utility of a commercial paper, with the more solid matter of the periodical, enlivened by the lighter and more amusing topics of a purely literary gazette." After appealing for subscribers he concluded, "with this appeal to the public, doubting not that it will meet with a hearty response, the editor makes his bow, trusting we shall improve upon acquaintance." From its inception *The Polynesian* was

an important source of both historical information and pictures of daily life. The experience of gaining and organizing such disparate material would undoubtedly inform Jarves's future historical and travel writings on the Hawaiian archipelago.

Unfortunately, despite continuous efforts to solicit subscribers *The Polynesian* could never reach any level of solvency. In the 10 October 1840 issue Jarves wrote: "The editors cannot long subsist on gratuitous labor, any more than any other class of the community. Such has been the case with us this far, the subscription list being far from sufficient to cover the printer's bill." Once again Jarves was having to face failure, and during his editorship he was only able to support his family by selling various types of merchandise he imported and by tutoring missionary children. Inevitably, in the 13 November 1841 issue Jarves announced, "*The Polynesian* will be discontinued with No. 26 of the present volume [4 December] completing the half year for which subscriptions have been received." On 14 January 1842 the Jarves family boarded the *Gloucester* and headed home to Boston. Although they, especially Libby, were eager to return to Boston, they were not happy to go home in such financially dire straits. Hawaii had been somewhat beneficial to Jarves's health, but it much more emphatically had proven to be a disaster for the young fortune seeker. As they departed the Honolulu harbor, he seemed to be leaving a failed dream and closing out his first life. But, as it turned out, this life was far from over.

Although he gained no financial security while in the islands, Jarves did not come away empty-handed. He did have a wealth of information—historical, cultural, and even anecdotal—all of which would help him immensely in writing his first two books. His specific intentions were unclear upon his arrival in Boston in the summer of 1842, but apparently he soon began organizing his material, and he received his first honor: being named a member of the American Oriental Society in its organizational meeting on 27 September 1842, a distinction which he would place below his name on the title page of several of his books during his career.

He published his *History of the Hawaiian or Sandwich Islands* (1843) the following winter, thus solidifying his qualifications as a scholar of Hawaiian history and culture. The book earned favorable reviews and remains a staple of historical assessments of the islands. Within a few months Jarves's first travel book appeared: *Scenes and Scenery in the Sandwich Islands, and a Trip through Central America.* As his preface indicates, the volume comprises material from his previously published sketches in the *Hawaiian Spectator* and incidental pieces included within his editorials for *The Polynesian. Scenes and Scenery* demonstrated Jarves to be a capable and often lively travel writer. As nineteenth-century convention demanded, the book is packed with historical and contemporary factual information. Jarves presents such instructive material from a somewhat distant, formal, ostensibly objective narrative stance, despite its often personal nature. The narrative is framed by his first arrival in Honolulu and his first return to Boston.

Scenes and Scenery, especially in conjunction with *History,* provides readers with an exhaustive portrait of Hawaii, one with a comprehensiveness that had not been previously available, and certainly many readers found the South Seas in general fascinating and exotic. Jarves begins in a tone typical of nineteenth-century travel books with the excitement of the arrival to a "new" world: "'LAND, HO!' cried a full, clear voice from the fore topgallant yard of a fast-sailing brigantine, which, but a few years since, had worn out five weary months, on her way from Boston to the Hawaiian Islands." Jarves briefly recounts the arduous voyage and then shows the unparalleled optimism typical of the traveler's first impressions:

> The sun shone out as brightly, and the sky was as blue, as if the ocean had never roughened its surface before a furious blast; the brigantine had donned her fair-weather suit, and royal yard and studding-sail boom were strained by the freshening breeze; while crew and passengers wore smiling faces, the reflection of as many joyous hearts, as if life had ever been to them all sunshine. In the every day concerns of life, there are few sounds that send a more quickened thrill through the frame, than the cry of "land, ho!" to the voyager, who has spent months pent in the narrow confines of a small vessel, and whose heart yearns to greet old friends or new faces ashore, and to exchange the hard deck and his coffin-like bed, for the green fields and ample households of mother-earth.

These opening lines incorporate a metaphor commonly applied to voyages to the South Seas—the rebirth of the traveler from the "coffin-like bed," which implies not only the torturous journey itself but also the life from which the traveler temporarily escapes. The luxuriance of the island landscape and the seeming innocence and simplicity of the native population encourage the initial excitement of the exotic. With this introductory paragraph Jarves effectively brings his readers to the door of paradise.

Jarves had a keen understanding of the value of travel abroad for Americans; despite his relative youth and inexperience at book-length travel writing he soon illustrates his comprehension of the travel impulse. Specifically, he includes in his opening a discussion of travel destinations as reflective of traveler intentions and needs:

> To the young American, the lands of old Europe are fields of storied interest;—of high and noble deeds—of dark and sanguinary passions. In them he sees enshrined the monuments of the proudest genius, records of glory and shame, worth and wickedness, arts and sciences, of the past and the present. In mingling with the living generation, he is everywhere reminded of the vice or virtues of the departed.

According to Jarves, and most nineteenth-century travel writers, the purpose for traveling to Europe was to learn from the accomplishments of the past; he thereby reveals, through word choices such as *enshrined, monuments,* and *departed,* a crucial and basic assumption his contemporaries held: that the essential greatness of Europe dwelt largely in the past.

By implication, American greatness belonged to the present and future. Jarves's assessment of the implicit value of new-world travel points out the other side of the spectrum:

> In perspective, far different are the groups of the South Seas. They seem as the garden-spots of the earth, and distance paints them as redolent with the fragrance and

luxuriance of nature. . . . Imagination, warmed and invigorated by the sunniest and healthiest of all climates, continually presents an undefined yet pleasing image of a perpetual juvenescence; nature retaining a pristine vigor and perennial green.

His descriptions clearly conjure images of Eden, a world promising ever-renewed youthfulness. Such appraisal, starkly contrasted with that of Europe, provides a valuable overview of the hopes, expectations, and dreams of the nineteenth-century travel writer and reader.

Scenes and Scenery includes a wealth of informative, often encyclopedic material balanced by lively sketches of the daily life–political, religious, and economic–of the islanders. Jarves incorporates descriptions of the natural scenery and local customs, dissertations on political history, and observations on the religious future of the islands. Perhaps his most compelling discussions concern the clash of cultures within the growing and varied island communities. Specifically, he examines the effects of the missionaries on the native population. Since Jarves was from the beginning associated with and supported by the missionaries, it is no surprise that on the whole he defends their work.

More interesting are his comments on the racial heritage of the natives in contrast with that of the missionaries themselves and how these differences influence the success of Christianity in Hawaii. In categorizing the natives and their Malaysian ancestry Jarves describes the average islander as

> sensual beyond description; lying and treacherous to friend and foe; a warm, excitable imagination, and docile to instruction; by turns a child or adult in pleasures and passions–weeping the one moment, the other revelling with boisterous mirth; in short, a creature of base sentiments, more like a man who, under the influence of intoxicating gas, acts out that which is uppermost in his nature, than a human being endowed with moral feelings.

Jarves's language is indicative of the common condescension many of his contemporaries held for the native populations of the South Seas. In order to clarify his conclusions about Hawaiian character, as he saw it, he invokes a comparison between Malaysian heritage and that of the Anglo-Saxon:

> Our forefathers [were] offshoots of the noblest race, the Caucasian; cruel heathens but bold, free, and intelligent; sacrificing human victims in obedience to their priests, but, in domestic relations, chaste and affectionate. If their animal passions were strong and conspicuous, their virtues also shone out brightly, and they proved themselves a thinking race.

Jarves defines the Malays as basically savage and childlike while he assures his readers that their own ancestors came from better stock, carefully tempering any potentially negative characteristics such as "heathen" with a superior such as "bold."

Jarves uses these racial stereotypes as an explanation for the less than stellar rate of the natives' conversion to Christianity, and he encourages his readers to consider the differences in temperament when evaluating the successes or failures of the missionaries: "Such are the natural differences between the two, and these must be borne in mind, if a just opinion of the capacity of the Hawaiians for civilization and christianity is to be formed. They should be judged by the standard applicable to their position in the human family, and not by our own." In short, he is reminding readers to keep their expectations relatively low. Interestingly, he follows these observations with an exhaustive accounting of native criminality and licentiousness. In the end, however, he does compliment the work of the missionaries and reasserts his hope that in their earnestness the "remaining dark spots may be washed white."

While in Boston, Jarves had no solid plans, but certainly with the completion and success of his two books on Hawaii he was beginning to reconsider the role the islands might play in his future. He attempted to gain an appointment as United States commissioner to the Hawaiian Islands, but he failed. Although he was disappointed, he nevertheless decided by late 1843 to return to Hawaii, somehow rejuvenated in his hopes of finding his fortune. He was confident that the growing attention given to the islands by the United States government combined with his friendship with G. P. Judd, a recently appointed member of the treasury board for the Hawaiian government, ensured his success. He returned, as he wrote in a 15 September 1843 letter to Judd, to establish a governmental paper. Leaving his child and pregnant wife behind, Jarves sailed for Hawaii in the winter of 1843 and arrived on 8 April 1844 to become once again an editor and publisher.

On 18 May of that year he published the first issue of the new series of *The Polynesian*. The subscription rate was six dollars per year. A few weeks later the newspaper included a subtitle–"Official Journal of the Hawaiian Government"–and included the announcement of Jarves as "Director of Government Printing." As part of his political obligations Jarves had to declare allegiance to the Hawaiian government and Kamehameha III and renounce his U.S. citizenship though the United States did not recognize such declarations, and most people considered them to be simply a necessary formality with little official or emotional import. Jarves

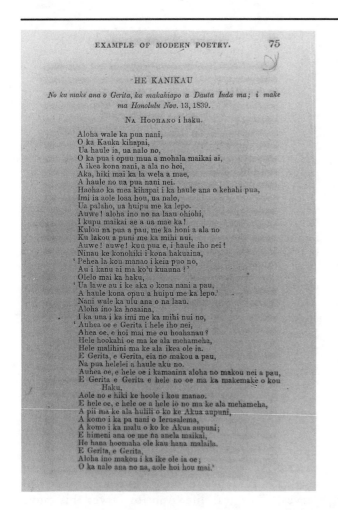

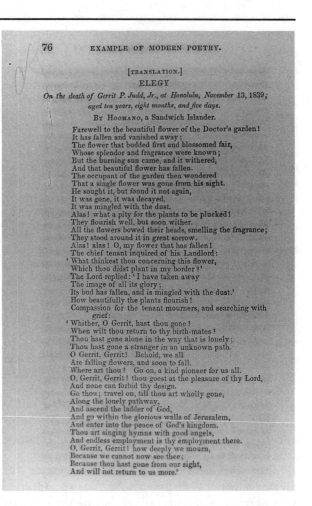

Poem by a Hawaiian and Jarves's translation in Scenes and Scenery in the Sandwich Islands

chose 4 July 1844 for his oath and placed an obscure notice in *The Polynesian:* "Mysterious Disappearance: On the afternoon of the 4th, a young American was seen going down toward the sea-side. The last that was observed of him was near evening; he was near one of the wharves.—Since then he has not been found." Although it is doubtful that Jarves felt in his conscience that he had rejected his United States citizenship, as it turned out he never again lived for more than a few years at a time within its borders. His travels were just beginning.

Jarves edited the new series of *The Polynesian* for close to four years and also continued to dabble as a merchant. Libby and his children, Horatio and Chevalita—born in the spring of 1844—joined him in 1846 somewhat reluctantly. Their marriage had been and continued to be a struggle. The combination of marital strain and the stress of his work began to wear on Jarves, and his health began to deteriorate in much the same way as it had when he was a teenager. On 28 January 1848 he announced in *The Polynesian:* "With this number . . . we take leave

of our readers," and less than two weeks later, on 4 February 1848, Jarves, with only Horatio, departed Honolulu. As in his first departure, he was a financial failure, but this time he was also facing the failure of his marriage. He and Libby had separated, and she and Chevalita remained in Hawaii for the time being. Jarves never returned to the islands.

In Boston, Jarves was once again uncertain of his future. His indecision seemed, temporarily at least, wiped away by President James Polk, who on 5 December 1848 announced the California gold discoveries. Jarves wasted little time in preparing to be part of the gold rush. On 27 March 1849 he boarded the *Obediah Mitchell* and headed for California. But like so many others, Jarves did not make his fortune. However, ostensibly at least, his family was reunited when he met with Libby and Chevalita in San Francisco. They later returned together to Boston to spend the winter of 1849–1850. After another trip to California, this time in an effort to open a store in San Francisco, Jarves returned to Boston and secured letters of introduction from the Reverend Rufus Anderson, secretary of the American Board of Commissioners for Foreign Missions, and statesman Edward Everett. This time Jarves was looking east to the Old World. In the autumn of 1851 the family sailed to Europe and established themselves in Paris, thus beginning Jarves's second life.

Jarves returned to his travel writing almost immediately upon making his family's home in Paris. Late in 1852 his series of travel sketches, most often titled "Life in Paris," began appearing in *Harper's New Monthly Magazine*. The series ran from November 1852 to February 1854, and the house of Harper published Jarves's second travel book, *Parisian Sights and French Principles, Seen Through American Spectacles* (1852). This book, published anonymously, expands the material from the earlier sketches that were appearing in *Harper's* and provides an often provocative assessment of Parisian life. Jarves capitalizes on his American citizenship by explicitly insisting on an American persona in his title and thus taps the readers' tendency to identify with shared and assumed values and perspectives. The *Harper's* pieces and *Parisian Sights* rewarded Jarves by giving his work its most extensive exposure to date, and it earned generally favorable reviews. He remained true to his encyclopedic style of presenting information, so prominent in his earlier work, but he also created a distinct and pointed American perspective that permeates the narrative; despite the obvious prejudices, this persona often provides lively prose.

Such a devoutly American bias was a proven narrative ploy for travel writers throughout the century. As readers enter Jarves's Paris, they begin with a light and lively overview of Parisian daily life in the home, including dining habits and social interaction in Parisian apartment buildings. But Jarves's style soon leads readers into a much more probing and even scientific appraisal of the city and its people. And like so many other nineteenth-century American travel writers in France, he focuses with a deep, abiding interest on the dark, even sordid, aspects of the city of lights. The tendency is not surprising given the desire for many travel writers and readers to reaffirm their complacency in the greatness of American culture by denigrating European cultures.

Jarves simply taps into common assumptions and methodically finds support for them. He devotes much of his attention to the unpleasant and morbid side of Paris. The second chapter, "Sights and Suicides," examines death in Paris and culminates in a trip to the city's morgue—an excursion that attracted many American tourists, including Mark Twain. Jarves writes:

> I entered, and saw three corpses, behind a glass partition, naked, with the exception of waist cloths, and laid out upon inclined slabs, something like a butcher's block. Tiny streams of water were directed over them to keep them fresh.

Jarves's word choices such as *butcher's block* and *fresh* add to the macabre nature of this "sight." Readers cannot help but react with revulsion at such a public display, one they were confident would not occur in America. Jarves continues by describing the moral degradation that such a spectacle encouraged and implies that Parisians who allowed it and took part in it were reflective of a general moral decay. However, Jarves seems unaware of his own part in publicizing this spectacle for his readers. He continues with statistics on death in Paris, including body counts per year (in 1851 the morgue displayed 371 bodies or "parts of corpses"). Despite its preoccupation with death *Parisian Sights* is a highly readable and informative volume. All in all, Jarves's picture of Paris is often compelling, if overly concerned with the sordid and immoral, and consistently comprehensive.

Near the end of a busy and fruitful year in Paris, the family left their apartment, traveled down the Rhone, sailed from Marseilles to Italy, and settled in Florence to begin yet another phase of Jarves's European life. And for Jarves this move would be the most exciting and profound. Except for several cross-Atlantic trips, Jarves remained at home in Florence until his death.

Perhaps the move was owing to Jarves's continual search for a mild climate, but his entrance into Italy became a vital experience not only for his physical health but also for his intellectual and spiritual well-being. For the first time Jarves seems to have become a wholly different person, thoroughly removed from his Hawaiian and even his Boston past. In Italy he began immersing himself in the art world of the Old Masters.

He continued his successful travel pieces for *Harper's* with a series on Italian life, most often appearing under the rubric "Sights and Principles Abroad" and running from March 1854 to November 1855. Moreover, Harper published two more of Jarves's travel books: *Parisian Sights and French Principles, Seen Through American Spectacles,* second series (1855) and *Italian Sights and Papal Principles, Seen Through American Spectacles* (1856). The second series of *Parisian Sights* is a continuation of the first, its contents coming directly from the *Harper's* pieces unused in the first book. Both of the two new books are attempts to capitalize on the suc-

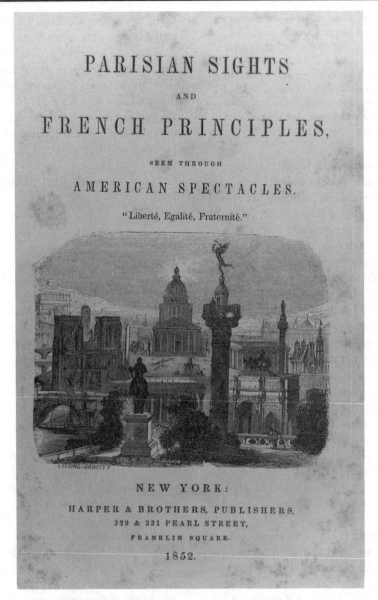

Title page for Jarves's first volume of European sketches

cess of the original *Parisian Sights* and the continuing sketches in *Harper's*.

Italian Sights, using the same title format and American perspective, is another effective travel narrative, comprehensive in its scope and confident in its American posture. Jarves sticks to the format that served him in his earlier travel books: exhaustive studies of history, politics, and religion balanced with lighter, more personal glimpses of daily life. *Italian Sights* does seem to have a more open narrative presence than *Parisian Sights*. Jarves appears more confident not just in his own perceptions but also in his relationship with his readers and his role as a travel writer. One of the most engaging chapters, titled "What

a 'Sight-Seer' Did See One Day," provides a humorous view of a new species of human—the American tourist. In addition to its jaunty tone, the chapter also shows Jarves's desire to differentiate between the "traveler" and the "tourist" (which he also terms "sight-seer" interchangeably).

Jarves enters the dialogue of a growing debate concerning nineteenth-century travel, one that continues today. As more Americans traveled abroad, many began to deplore what they viewed as the loss of the aesthetics of travel. Jarves writes:

> If I were called upon to name the individual of the human species that unites in his or her person the greatest powers of endurance with the utmost impatience, the

most unflagging activity to a body always just ready to drop from fatigue; a mind skeptical from its shallowness, yet ready to ingulf [*sic*] entire kingdoms in its capacious maw, and to bolt miracles and relics by scores—in short, that individual who combines in him or herself the most opposite qualities, whether of body or mind, I should unhesitatingly pronounce that individual to be the modern "sight-seer." Reader mine, has it ever fallen to thy lot to travel with one?

Jarves goes on to relate his unfortunate encounter with one and continues, "Sight-seeing; from its original purpose of information, has been perverted by these traveling pests into a frigid duty. Nothing must be allowed to escape their observation that has attained the dignity of being a 'sight.'" Of course, Jarves's implication is that though a "sight" may have dignity in itself, these "traveling pests" do not, nor can they derive pleasure or knowledge from their efforts because they are motivated by the act of seeing, not comprehending.

Throughout his traveler's view of Italy, Jarves reveals another aspect of his concern for seeing aesthetically: his growing preoccupation with Italian art. This developing passion was nurtured by his living in Florence, a city he called a "vast picture-shop." Unfortunately, as his interest in art grew, his family harmony—already strained—began again to disintegrate. He was a man obsessed by his new life, which had little to do with his family. He devoted himself almost exclusively to the subject of art and to his newfound desire to educate not only himself but also his readers in America about how to appreciate European masterpieces. In turn, he also abandoned travel writing, not to return to it for almost twenty years. During this period, in addition to several articles, he published seven books. Two were reflective of his earlier life: *Kiana: A Tradition of Hawaii* (1857), a short romance published originally in *The Polynesian;* and *Why and What Am I? The Confessions of an Inquirer* (1857), a light, tongue-in-cheek autobiography. His remaining five books of this time were all solely concerned with his new life, art: *Art-Hints: Architecture, Sculpture, and Painting* (1855); *Art Studies: The "Old Masters" of Italy; Painting* (1861); *The Art-Idea: Part Second of Confessions of an Inquirer* (1864); *Art Thoughts: The Experiences and Observations of an American Amateur in Europe* (1869); and *A Glimpse at the Art of Japan* (1876). He also made several trips to Boston and New York to attend to the publication of his books and to attempt to sell his growing collection of Old Masters.

Meanwhile, his family continued to grow. Flora Amy was born in the spring of 1855 while Jarves was in America for the birth of his first art book, *Art-Hints*. The marital difficulties never fully sub-

sided for Jarves and Libby though they remained ostensibly together, if estranged, until her death on 27 August 1861. Libby's death did not slow Jarves's consuming interest in art or keep him from companionship for long. In Boston on 30 April 1862 Jarves married Isabella Kast Hayden of East Cambridge, the twenty-seven-year-old daughter of Ezekial Hayden, a clerk in the Middlesex County Court House. Jarves was forty-three. The couple was trapped in the United States by the Civil War, and Jarves could not take his new bride to Florence until 8 February 1865.

They sailed to Europe to build a home and family, remaining in Paris for the summer of 1865, where Annabel was born. Then they went to Florence, and in the fall of 1867 Italia Hortensia was born—another birth for which Jarves was absent. He had sailed to Boston again to try to secure a home for his Old Masters collection, which had failed for years to gain a suitable and profitable buyer. He finally left the paintings with the Yale University School of Fine Arts with no profit to himself, where they remain today. The Jarveses continued to build what seems to have been a happy and comfortable home in Florence, and in March 1869 Jarves's last child was born—James Jackson Jarves Jr., called Pepero, who displayed artistic interests and abilities.

Although Jarves was never financially well off, he did achieve some level of comfort and peace in the 1860s and 1870s as he established his new family and immersed himself in the world of Italian art. He did return to travel writing once more with *Italian Rambles: Studies of Life and Manners in New and Old Italy* (1883). This book is also a return to the formula of *Italian Sights* and his earlier works, with one clear distinction: the perspective is no longer that of one looking through purely "American Spectacles." Although the volume includes chapters on domestic life, education, and manners, among other topics, *Italian Rambles* is more introspective as a whole; at times the choice of the word *rambles* seems to refer to thoughts rather than physical travels. In describing the Carrara mountain range of the Apennines west of Florence, Jarves writes:

> I had never gazed at these mountains in winter or summer without an involuntary desire to go to them. For they appealed to the inner sense as a resting-place midway between earth and heaven, where body and soul might receive strength for either.

Italian Rambles was the last of Jarves's travel writings. Soon after its publication he faced a series of family tragedies. His two oldest children, Horatio and Chevalita, died in 1883; his youngest and most beloved, Pepero, who had tuberculosis, died at age fifteen in 1884; and his second wife, Isabella, died in 1887. Jarves's last book, *Pepero, the Boy-Artist: A Brief Memoir of James Jackson Jarves, by His Father,* was published in 1890, two years after Jarves's own death. Jarves died of jaundice while he was traveling in Tarasp, Switzerland, with his daughters on 28 June 1888. He is buried in the English cemetery in Rome with Isabella and Pepero.

The tone Jarves had taken in *Italian Rambles* seems especially appropriate not only for his last travel book but for his life as well. He had once asked in the introduction to *Art-Hints,* "To what end travel?" For the specific purpose of that text, he was referring to the seeking of knowledge of other cultures and art. Interestingly, the man who sought his fortune in New England, Hawaii, California, and France finally, perhaps, answered his own question when he found in Florence, Italy, not prosperity but peace of mind.

Biography:

Francis Steegmuller, *The Two Lives of James Jackson Jarves* (New Haven: Yale University Press, 1951).

Reference:

Theodore Sizer, "A Forgotten New Englander," *New England Quarterly,* 6 (June 1933): 328–352.

Papers:

The major collection of Jarves's manuscripts and correspondence is in the Yale University Library.

George Kennan
(16 February 1845 – 10 May 1924)

Kevin J. Hayes
University of Central Oklahoma

BOOKS: *Tent Life in Siberia, and Adventures among the Koraks and Other Tribes in Kamchatka and Northern Asia* (New York: Putnam, 1870; London: Sampson Low, Son, & Marston, 1870); revised and enlarged as *Tent Life in Siberia: A New Account of an Old Undertaking; Adventures among the Koraks and Other Tribes in Kamchatka and Northern Asia* (New York: Putnam, 1910);

Siberia and the Exile System, 2 volumes (New York: Century, 1891; London: J. R. Osgood, McIlvaine, 1891);

Campaigning in Cuba (New York: Century, 1899);

The Tragedy of Pelée: A Narrative of Personal Experience and Observation in Martinique (New York: Outlook, 1902);

A Russian Comedy of Errors, with Other Stories and Sketches of Russian Life (New York: Century, 1915);

The Chicago and Alton Case: A Misunderstood Transaction (Garden City, N.Y.: Country Life Press, 1916);

Misrepresentation in Railroad Affairs (Garden City, N.Y.: Country Life Press, 1916);

E. H. Harriman's Far Eastern Plans (Garden City, N.Y.: Country Life Press, 1917);

The Salton Sea: An Account of Harriman's Fight with the Colorado River (New York: Macmillan, 1917);

E. H. Harriman, A Biography, 2 volumes (Boston & New York: Houghton Mifflin, 1922).

George Kennan, 1865

OTHER: Aleksandr Valentinovich Amfiteatrov and Honoré de Balzac, *Folk-Tales of Napoleon: "Napoleonder" from the Russian; "The Napoleon of the People" from the French of Honoré de Balzac,* translated by Kennan (New York: Outlook, 1902).

George Kennan's travels to Siberia resulted in his two best travel books. *Tent Life in Siberia, and Adventures among the Koraks and Other Tribes in Kamchatka and Northern Asia* (1870) established his reputation as a travel writer and became one of the most popular travel books in nineteenth-century America. *Siberia and the Exile System* (1891), a work that provided the most detailed exposé of the atrocities and injustice of the czarist method for punishing political prisoners, established Kennan as a champion of Russian political exiles and an expert in Russian affairs. *Tent Life in Siberia* has a tender charm while the later book, which Kennan's biographer Frederick F. Travis has called "the *Uncle Tom's Cabin* of Siberian exile," has a forceful though sympathetic authority which leaves the reader absolutely convinced of the injustices perpetrated by czarist Russia.

Kennan in Siberia during the winter of 1885–1886

Born in Norwalk, Ohio, the son of attorney John Kennan and Mary Ann Morse, George Kennan became a telegraph expert during his adolescence. Barred from active service in the Civil War because of physical limitations, Kennan obtained a position as a military telegrapher in Cincinnati. After the war the Western Union Telegraph Company chose Kennan as a member of its Siberian expedition intended to establish an overland telegraph service between America and Europe–an effort which had been made necessary by the failure of the first attempt to lay a cable across the Atlantic Ocean. Western Union planned to build a line from the United States through Canada and Alaska, across the Bering Strait, and overland across Siberia. Kennan left from San Francisco in July 1865, and during the expedition he explored nearly six thousand miles of unbroken wilderness.

Kennan told the story of his experience in *Tent Life in Siberia*. Although other members of the expedition wrote books about their experience–Frederick Whymper's *Travel and Adventure in the Territory of*

Alaska (1868) and William H. Dall's *Alaska and Its Resources* (1870)–Kennan's was the single best book to result from the Russo-American telegraph adventure. He was only twenty at the start of the expedition; his narrative reflects his youth, but that is part of its charm.

Tent Life in Siberia frequently stresses the clash of cultures between members of the American expedition engaged in a state-of-the-art, commercial, technological enterprise and the earthy Russian peasants. Kennan records the difficulty of communicating the idea of telegraph poles to the Siberian locals. Unable to understand the Americans' purpose, they cut poles so stout that they were worthless. Describing the episode, Kennan strikingly conveys the image of the useless, oversized telegraph poles, snow-covered and rotting. Later in the narrative Kennan emphasizes the cultural differences as he describes a Siberian peasant who serendipitously had acquired a copy of *Harper's Magazine* which included an engraved portrait of Maj. Gen. John Adams Dix. Unable to read the magazine text, the peasant appar-

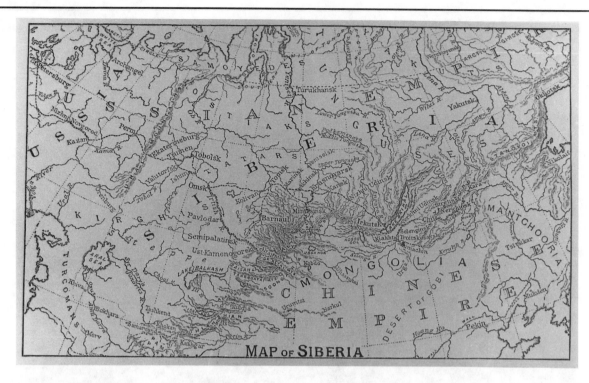

Map from Kennan's Siberia and the Exile System *(1891)*

ently discarded the remainder of the issue, yet saved the engraving, which he and his neighbors worshiped as a Russian saint: "A gilded candle was burning before his smoky features, and every night and morning a dozen natives said their prayers to a major-general in the United States Army!" The episode shows Kennan's characteristic eye for paradox as well as his power of description, a quality which is evident elsewhere in the narrative. *Tent Life in Siberia* comprises the single best description of the northern lights in any American travel narrative.

The final chapter of *Tent Life in Siberia* is touching. Kennan describes going to Gizhiga, a port near the Bering Sea, to await a supply vessel so that he and his men can continue their work. Before their own ship appears, however, another American vessel arrives with the news that the Atlantic cable had been successfully completed and that the Russian-American telegraph enterprise had been abandoned. The telegraph company ship soon arrives with orders for Kennan to end the Siberian expedition and return to America. Kennan writes: "It seemed hard to give up at once the object to which we had devoted three years of our lives, and for whose attainment we had suffered all possible hardships of cold, exile, and starvation; but we had no alternative, and began at once to make preparations for our final departure."

Instead of crossing the Pacific, Kennan took the long way home, going five thousand miles by dogsled across Siberia to Moscow, a journey he did not even describe in his narrative. Undoubtedly, Kennan encountered much more privation and hardship along the way, but apparently he felt the experience inappropriate to include as part of the narrative. His humble ending is a masterpiece of understatement: "On . . . January 3d, after ten weeks of incessant travel, we caught sight of the glittering domes of Moscow, and closed forever the book of our Siberian Experience." Kennan returned to Norwalk in April 1868.

After returning home Kennan lectured on his Russian experiences, and in July 1870 he returned to Russia to study the people of the Caucasus. *Tent Life in Siberia* was published in September 1870 and became a huge success. It went through many editions during the next several years and firmly established Kennan's reputation as traveler, writer, and expert on Russian affairs. Home again in January 1871, he spoke briefly on his experiences in the Caucasus but then took a position with the Union Bank in Medina, New York. In 1876 Kennan moved to New York City, where he lived for two years before moving again to Washington, D.C., to serve as assistant manager of the Washington office of the Associated Press. He married Emiline Rathbone Weld of Medina on 25 September 1879. During the 1870s and 1880s he frequently lectured on Russia.

Much had changed there since Kennan had first visited Siberia. Czar Alexander II had been murdered in 1881, and his son, Alexander III, had assumed leadership. Alexander III actively sought out revolutionary organizations, destroyed them, and sent their leaders to Siberia. Rumors of Siberian atrocities generated support for the Nihilist revolutionaries, and the idea of encountering such figures motivated many American travelers to visit Russia during the 1880s. Several travel narratives resulted from these excursions–J. W. Buel's *Russian Nihilism and Exile Life in Siberia* (1883), John Bell Bouton's *Roundabout to Moscow: An Epicurean Journey* (1887), and William Eleroy Curtis's *The Land of the Nihilist* (1888)–but neither *Tent Life in Siberia* nor any of these accounts prepared the public for what they would read in Kennan's next treatment of Siberia. Though Kennan spent much time in Siberia with the telegraph expedition, he never really encountered exiles. Rather, most of his experiences took place in unpopulated wilderness or among the indigenous people of Siberia. *Tent Life in Siberia* had suggested an overall fondness for the Russians and a generally favorable attitude toward czarist Russia.

In 1885 the Century Company commissioned Kennan, accompanied by the American artist George A. Frost, to revisit Siberia to study the Russian prison system. After a year among the exiled Russian revolutionaries, Kennan's attitudes toward the czarist government completely changed. He became a thoroughgoing partisan of the revolutionary movement and committed himself to exposing the horrors of the exile system in Russia. Kennan's account of the journey appeared serially in *Century* magazine in 1888 and 1889, and it was separately published as a two-volume work, *Siberia and the Exile System* (1891).

Kennan's affection for the Russian exiles is apparent in the preface, in which he briefly mentions their suffering and the intolerance of the czarist government toward opposing political views. Kennan expresses his desire to make the anonymous exiles known to the world, yet he hesitates to mention them by name for fear that he would only make them objects of suspicion and surveillance. Instead, Kennan states, "All that I can do, therefore, to show my appreciation of their trust, their kindness, and their aid, is to use the information which they gave me as I believe they would wish it to be used,–in the interest of humanity, freedom, and good government."

Kennan, as he appeared on the lecture circuit, in the clothing of a Siberian exile (circa 1890)

As Kennan describes his earliest encounters with the political exiles, he takes a rhetorically sophisticated approach to engage the reader's sympathy with the plight of the Russian political exiles. First he describes the initial prejudice he had held before he first met any of them. He had imagined that they were violence-oriented, incomprehensible cranks who possessed little common sense. In short, Kennan explains that he had imagined the political exile as "a long-haired, wild-eyed being who would pour forth an incoherent recital of wrongs and outrages, denounce all governmental restraint as brutal tyranny, and expect me to approve of the assassination of Alexander II." By first expressing his prejudice against the exiles, Kennan creates a camaraderie with his contemporary American readers which makes his change in attitude all the more persuasive. Instead of "incomprehensible cranks," Kennan realized that the exiles were intelligent, rational, well read, cultured, and gentlemanly.

Kennan found the composure of the Siberian exiles especially striking. They often spoke of "intolerable justice and frightful sufferings" with absolute calm. "The men and women who had been sent to the province of Yakútsk for refusing to take the oath of allegiance to Alexander III, and who had suffered in that arctic wilderness all that human beings can suffer from hunger, cold, sickness, and bereavement," Kennan explained,

> did not seem to be conscious that there was anything very extraordinary in their experience. Now and then some man whose wife had committed suicide in exile would flush a little and clinch his hands as he spoke of her; or some broken-hearted woman whose baby had frozen to death in her arms on the road would sob at intervals as she tried to tell me her story; but, as a rule, both men and women referred to injustice and suffering with perfect composure, as if they were nothing more than the ordinary accidents of life.

Still, these stories of injustice, combined with the harsh environment and the mental instability of his traveling companion, Frost, took their toll. Kennan writes that through much of the journey they "were subjected to a nervous and emotional strain that was sometimes harder to bear than cold, hunger, or fatigue." After listening to a particularly heart-wrenching story, Kennan explains, "I could neither sleep nor sit still; and the nervous strain of such experiences, quite as much as to hardship and privation, was attributable to the final breaking down of my health and strength in the Trans-Baikál."

After *Siberia and the Exile System* appeared in 1891, illegal translations circulated in Russia and fueled the revolutionary movement. Kennan's kinsman, George Frost Kennan, who served as U.S. ambassador to the Soviet Union, wrote an introduction to a 1958 University of Chicago Press abridged edition of the book and recalled a longtime member of Stalin's Politburo who referred to the work as "a veritable 'Bible' for the early revolutionists." In the United States the two-volume work, though highly regarded and widely reviewed, did not sell well, but Kennan had another way to bring his message to the American people: the lecture.

Kennan's lecture tours actually reached a much greater segment of the American people than his book. Between 1889 and 1898 Kennan, clad in the costume of the Russian exile (shackles included), delivered more than eight hundred lectures throughout the country. Biographer Travis has estimated that Kennan reached approximately one million people in this way. Almost invariably, reports of Kennan's lectures were positive. One unnamed reviewer commented in the *Jersey Journal:*

> His stories of the cruel, barbarous treatment of the exiles by the Russian Government were extremely thrilling and pathetic. They tended to rouse within his hearers a feeling of revenge against the monarchy that inflicts such horrible treatment on her prisoners. . . . It seems almost incredible that any but the most uncivilized savages could be capable of inflicting on fellow man such awful treatment as the Russian Government does on her exiles to Siberia.

Siberia and the Exile System reinforced Kennan's reputation as a travel writer and firmly established him as the foremost expert in the nation on Russian affairs. As a new century dawned, Kennan continued to travel and serve as a correspondent throughout the world. Shortly after the U.S. Congress demanded that Spain withdraw from Cuba during the spring of 1898, Kennan signed an agreement with *Outlook* to serve as its war correspondent. He visited Cuba during the military engagements that summer and returned in December to stay until February 1899, witnessing the American occupation. His experiences resulted in *Campaigning in Cuba* (1899), a work which describes the activities of the Red Cross, recounting the omnipresence of American journalists and providing a detailed and insightful picture of Santiago. In 1902 Kennan visited Martinique to witness the volcanic activities there. *The Tragedy of Pelée: A Narrative of Personal Experience and Observation in Martinique* (1902) includes much vivid firsthand description of the eruption and its aftermath. In 1904 Kennan traveled to Japan under contract with *Outlook* to serve as war correspondent for the Russo-Japanese War. Kennan reported from the Japanese side, and the experience prompted him to take an interest in Japanese life and culture. Prophetically, he later argued that Americans would need to learn more about Japan.

Besides travel books, Kennan published other works during the early twentieth century. He translated *Folk-Tales of Napoleon: "Napoleonder" from the Russian; "The Napoleon of the People" from the French of Honoré de Balzac* (1902), a work that retells legends about Napoleon's march to Moscow. He also published *A Russian Comedy of Errors, with Other Stories and Sketches of Russian Life* (1915), a moving collection of sketches—some dramatic, some humorous—illustrating Russian politics, government, and social conditions.

Late in life Kennan became fascinated with the railroad executive and capitalist Edward Henry Harriman, and he wrote several pamphlets describing and justifying Harriman's actions. Kennan's interest in Harriman resulted in his most substantial late work, the two-volume *E. H. Harriman, A Biography* (1922). Though Kennan's biography of Harriman was well written and thoroughly researched, it approached hagiography in the treatment of its subject, who had a reputation for ruthless and cold-blooded business acumen. Kennan portrayed Harriman as an exemplar of the American national character, but his reviewers were not fooled, and they criticized Kennan for his blatant partisanship. While Kennan had so effectively used partisan rhetoric to shape *Siberia and the Exile System,* the same type of rhetoric failed in this biography. *E. H. Harriman* was his last book. Kennan died of a paralytic stroke in 1924. He was an important influence on the work of later American political journalists and travel writers such as John Gunther and Lowell Thomas.

Biography:

Frederick F. Travis, *George Kennan and the American-Russian Relationship, 1865–1924* (Athens: Ohio University Press, 1990).

Reference:

George Frost Kennan, Introduction to *Siberia and the Exile System,* by George Kennan (Chicago: University of Chicago Press, 1958).

Papers:

The most important manuscript collection is the George Kennan Papers at the Library of Congress, but the George Kennan collection at the New York Public Library is also significant. Other holdings of Kennan material include the archives of the American Geographical Society in New York and the Western Union Telegraph Expedition Collection, 1865–1867, at the Smithsonian Institution.

Thomas Wallace Knox

(26 June 1835 – 6 January 1896)

James A. Wren
University of Hawaii at Mānoa

BOOKS: *Camp-fire and Cotton-field, Southern Adventure in Time of War: Life with the Union Armies, and Residence on a Louisiana Plantation* (New York: Brelock / Chicago: Kidder, 1865; Philadelphia: Jones, 1865);

Overland through Asia (Hartford, Conn.: American Publishing, 1870); republished as *Overland through Asia: Pictures of Siberian, Chinese, and Tartar Life* (Hartford, Conn.: American Publishing, 1871);

Underground, or Life below the Surface: Incidents and Accidents beyond the Light of Day, Startling Adventures in All Parts of the World, Mines and the Mode of Working Them, Under-currents of Society, Gambling and Its Horrors (Hartford, Conn. & Chicago: J. B. Burr & Hyde, 1873); republished as *The Underground World: A Mirror of Life below the Surface* (Hartford, Conn.: J. B. Burr, 1877);

Backsheesh! or Life and Adventures in the Orient (Hartford, Conn.: A. D. Worthington / Chicago: A. G. Nettleton, 1875); republished as *The Oriental World, or New Travels in Turkey, Russia, Egypt, Asia Minor, and the Holy Land, with Graphic Sketches of Life and Adventures in the Orient* (Hartford, Conn.: A. D. Worthington, 1877);

Journeyings in Russia (Hartford, Conn.: American Publishing, 1877);

The Boy Travellers in the Far East, Part First: Adventures of Two Youths in a Journey to Japan and China (New York: Harper, 1879);

John, or Our Chinese Relations: A Study of Our Emigration and Commercial Intercourse with the Celestial Empire (New York: Harper, 1879);

The Boy Travellers in the Far East, Part Second: Adventures of Two Youths in a Journey to Siam and Java, with Descriptions of Cochin-China, Cambodia, Sumatra and the Malay Archipelago (New York: Harper, 1880);

How to Travel: Hints, Advice, and Suggestions to Travelers by Land and Sea All Over the Globe (New York: C. T. Dillingham, 1880; revised edition, New York: Putnam, 1887);

Very truly Yours
Thos. W. Knox

The Boy Travellers in the Far East, Part Third: Adventures of Two Youths in a Journey to Ceylon and India, with Descriptions of Borneo, the Philippine Islands and Burmah (New York: Harper, 1881);

The Young Nimrods in North America: A Book for Boys (New York: Harper, 1881);

The Pocket Guide for Europe: A Practical Hand-Book for Travelers on the Continent and the British Isles, and through Northern Africa, Egypt and the Holy Land (New York: C. T. Dillingham, 1882; London: American Exchange in Europe, 1882); revised as *The Pocket Guide for Europe: Hand-Book for Travellers on the Continent and the British Isles, and* through Egypt, Palestine, and Northern Africa (New York: Putnam, 1886);

Adventures of Two Youths in a Journey to Egypt and the Holy Land (New York: Harper, 1882); republished as The Boy Travellers in the Far East, Part Fourth: Adventures of Two Youths in a Journey to Egypt and the Holy Land (New York: Harper, 1883);

The Pocket Guide around the World: A Practical Hand-Book for the Globe-Trotter (New York: C. T. Dillingham, 1883);

Adventures of Two Youths in a Journey through Africa (New York: Harper, 1883); republished as The Boy Travellers in the Far East, Part Fifth: Adventures of Two Youths in a Journey through Africa (New York: Harper, 1884);

The Lives of James G. Blaine and John A. Logan: Republican Presidential Candidates of 1884 (Hartford, Conn.: Hartford Publishing, 1884);

Adventures of Two Youths in the Open Polar Sea: The Voyage of the "Vivian" to the North Pole and Beyond (New York: Harper, 1884);

The Boy Travellers in South America: Adventures of Two Youths in a Journey through Ecuador, Peru, Bolivia, Brazil, Paraguay, Argentine Republic, and Chili, with Descriptions of Patagonia and Tierra del Fuego, and Voyages upon the Amazon and La Plata Rivers (New York: Harper, 1885);

A Tour of the American Trosachs, through by Daylight, over River, Mountain and Lake, by Steamer, Stagecoach and Railway (New York: National Press Intelligence, 1886);

The Boy Travellers in the Russian Empire: Adventures of Two Youths in a Journey in European and Asiatic Russia, with Accounts of a Tour across Siberia (New York: Harper, 1886);

The Life of Robert Fulton and a History of Steam Navigation (New York & London: Putnam, 1886);

The Boy Travellers in Australasia: Adventures of Two Youths in a Journey to the Sandwich, Marquesas, Society, Samoan, and Feejee Islands, and through the Colonies of New Zealand, New South Wales, Queensland, Victoria, Tasmania, and South Australia (New York: Harper, 1886);

The Boy Travellers on the Congo: Adventures of Two Youths in a Journey with Henry M. Stanley, "Through the Dark Continent" (New York: Harper, 1887);

Decisive Battles since Waterloo: The Most Important Military Events from 1815 to 1887 (New York: Putnam, 1887);

Life and Work of Henry Ward Beecher: An Authentic, Impartial and Complete History of His Public Career and Private Life from the Cradle to the Grave (Hartford, Conn.: Hartford Publishing, 1887);

The Boy Travellers in Mexico: Adventures of Two Youths in a Journey to Northern and Central Mexico, Campeachey, and Yucatan, with a Description of the Republics of Central America, and of the Nicaragua Canal (New York: Harper, 1889);

The Boy Travellers in Central Europe: Adventures of Two Youths in a Journey through France, Switzerland, and Austria, with Excursions among the Alps of Switzerland and the Tyrol (New York: Harper, 1889);

The Oriental World: A Record of Travel, Adventure and Exploration in Russia, Turkey, Egypt, Asia Minor and the Holy Land; With Descriptions of the Manners, Customs, Habits, Characteristics, etc., of the People, and Sketches of Adventures, Incidents and Experiences among Them (Hartford, Conn.: A. D. Worthington, 1889);

The Boy Travellers in Great Britain and Ireland: Adventures of Two Youths in a Journey through Ireland, Scotland, Wales, and England, with Visits to the Hebrides and the Isle of Man (New York: Harper, 1890);

Horse Stories and Stories of Other Animals: Experience of Two Boys in Managing Horses, with Many Anecdotes of Quadrupedal Intelligence (New York: Cassell, 1890);

Teetotaler Dick: His Adventures, Temptations and Triumphs. A Temperance Story (New York: Ward & Drummond, 1890);

The Boy Travellers in Northern Europe: Adventures of Two Youths in a Journey through Holland, Germany, Denmark, Norway and Sweden, with Visits to Heligoland and the Land of the Rising Sun (New York: Harper, 1891);

A Close Shave, or How Major Flagg Won His Bet (Saint Paul, Minn.: Price-McGill, 1892);

The Republican Party and its Leaders: A History of the Party from its Beginning to the Present Time (New York: P. F. Collier, 1892);

The Boy Travellers in Southern Europe: Adventures of Two Youths in a Journey through Italy, Southern France, and Spain, with Visits to Gibraltar and the Islands of Sicily and Malta (New York: Harper, 1893);

John Boyd's Adventures: Merchant Sailor, Man-of-War's-Man, Privateersman, Pirate, and Algerine Slave (New York: Appleton, 1893);

The Siberian Exiles: A Novel (New York: R. Bonner, 1893);

The Talking Handkerchief and Other Stories (Saint Paul, Minn.: Price-McGill, 1893);

In Wild Africa: Adventures of Two Youths in a Journey through the Sahara Desert (Boston: W. A. Wilde, 1893);

The Lost Army (New York: Werner, 1894);

Boy's Life of General Grant (New York: Merriam, 1895);

The Boy Travellers in the Levant: Adventures of Two Youths in a Journey through Morocco, Algeria, Tunis, Greece, and Turkey, with Visits to the Islands of Rhodes and Cyprus, and the Site of Ancient Troy (New York: Harper, 1895);

Captain John Crane, 1800–1815 (New York: Merriam, 1895);

Dog Stories and Dog Lore: Experiences of Two Boys in Rearing and Training Dogs, with Many Anecdotes of Canine Intelligence (New York: Cassell, 1895);

Hunters Three: Sport and Adventure in South Africa (New York: Dutton, 1895);

The Land of the Kangaroo: Adventures of Two Youths in a Journey through the Great Island Continent (Boston: W. A. Wilde, 1896).

SELECTED PERIODICAL PUBLICATIONS–UNCOLLECTED: "To Pike's Peak and Denver," *Knickerbocker,* 58 (August 1861): 115–128; "The Russo-American Telegraph," *Excelsior Monthly Magazine,* 1 (1869): 241–250.

A self-proclaimed "wandering American," Thomas Wallace Knox was born to Nehemiah Critchett Knox and Jane Wallace Knox in Pembroke, New Hampshire, on 26 June 1835. He was a self-fashioned bohemian spirit with one foot firmly planted in the provincial as well as a jovial companion and sympathetic listener. His early life might be characterized as an attempt to balance the demands of his schooling and the lure of the New Hampshire foothills, though more often than not the latter won out. From his childhood Knox demonstrated skill with the French language (an active interest in languages and linguistic differences would long continue to hold his attention) and exhibited a keen sense of wonder that he would carry with him throughout his life. As an adult this balancing act would manifest itself both in his uncanny ability to ask and to anticipate particular questions of general interest and in his astute powers of observation–he was always looking and continuously jotting down the details of his surroundings. He would find himself pulled between his need to travel (the New Hampshire foothills having been supplanted with grander visions of the world beyond them), an equally compelling need to write (explaining for an audience who might not have his same opportunities), and the world of invention.

Given his own deep-rooted enthusiasm for and ceaseless faith in the value of the educational process, Knox established an academy for students in Kingston, New Hampshire, in 1857 and later became its headmaster. Not content to remain in any one place for too long, in 1860 he moved away from New Hampshire and away from the field of education though his commitment to the process would remain intact. He found himself in Denver, Colorado, where he turned to newspaper reporting. There he fine-tuned his writing skills as the city editor for the *Denver Daily News,* but more important, it is at this point in his early career that he mastered the idiom of popular writing, allowing him to take wholly alien information and make it understandable to a less informed public. He became a journalist in the modern sense of the word: he understood his audience, and he shaped his writing to capture and hold their intellectual curiosity by a characteristic simplification of even the most complicated issues of the day. To this end he asked the five basic questions at the heart of good journalistic reportage–who? what? when? where? and why?–and never more. However mundane or pedestrian Knox's approach, writing with a specific audience in mind led to a large readership for his work.

The financial rewards of such popularity would almost certainly have made themselves felt had the Civil War not broken out only a short six months after Knox arrived in Denver. After much reflection he enlisted as a lieutenant colonel with the California National Guard. Given his keen eye for detail as well as his expertise in encapsulating the issues and making clear the most difficult of problems, it is not surprising that he soon returned to the East to become a war correspondent with the *New York Herald.* In this capacity he was granted free reign for his creative talents, allowing him simultaneously to dabble in the mechanical arts. Consequently, his most significant contribution to the war effort came not from his work as a reporter but as an inventor. Appreciating the necessity of getting battlefield plans from one point to another, Knox set about solving this problem. His method was characteristically practical, based on a realistic assessment of the complicated issues involved. He was eventually granted a patent for transmitting battle plans by telegraph. Ironically, during the process of inventing he became a self-educated expert on the mechanics of the telegraph, having acquired for himself both the theoretical knowledge and the practical skills that would leave him ideally suited for work within the telegraph industry at precisely the time when it was attempting to move its technology across the globe. Accordingly, where the telegraph went, so too went Knox. For a time this relationship would placate his recalcitrant wanderlust.

The Civil War significantly affected Knox for another reason. With his moves from New Hamp-

Map for Knox's 1870 travel book

shire to Colorado to California to New York, Knox had seen firsthand a country experiencing its own growing pains, and he had rejoiced in its vast potential. The war, however, divided the country over moral and economic issues and left the South devastated, and Knox was there to witness it all. His first major work, *Camp-fire and Cotton-field, Southern Adventure in Time of War: Life with the Union Armies, and Residence on a Louisiana Plantation* (1865) is as much a travelogue of the American South as it is Knox's personal testimony to the horrors of the war and a nostalgic lament for a lost era. Sympathetic to the sufferings on both sides of the Mason-Dixon line and astutely aware of the tremendous costs in human lives, Knox could do little more than look on the alienation and the chaos that followed in the wake of the destruction as a grimacing bystander. His immediate impulse seems to have been to move. He longed to travel, to experience the expansiveness of the world, but this impulse betrays a deeper commitment to bringing a wider world into focus for an American readership. Knox believed that

only by educating his readers about the differences that characterize so large a nation while simultaneously stressing the ethical tenets of a universal humanism could similar moments of human folly be averted in the future.

After the war, then, Knox began to travel. He accepted a position with the Russo-American Telegraph Company, and in their employment he embarked upon a journey "undertaken partly as a pleasure trip, partly as a journalistic enterprise, and partly in the interest of the company that attempted . . . to make an electric connection between Europe and the United States by way of Asia and Bering's Straits." His adventures provided the basis for his second travel book, *Overland through Asia* (1870). The immediate success of this work convinced him to pursue as a career what he did best—to travel and to write his impressions.

For Knox the 1870s were characterized in the main by a life on the road or aboard a ship. From European Russia, where his knowledge of French gained him a certain access into high society and rudimentary Russian skills facilitated his ability to move at will, Knox journeyed to the Middle East and Asia Minor. Later he would return to Asia to explore Japan and China. By 1877 he had visited many unfrequented parts of the Orient, amassing a considerable wealth of materials in the form of his journals and notebooks to enable him later to write of his travels.

Whereas Knox spent the 1870s retracing the paths of previous European and American explorers, his travels in the 1880s would be characterized by a pursuit of the exotic. He began with an extended journey through Indochina and Southeast Asia. For his work in introducing these areas to the American reader he was awarded the Order of the White Elephant by the king of Siam. He would later move through Africa, South America, the South Pacific, and finally Mexico and Central America. It appears that what he had written in 1870 held true for all his travels: "It may not be improper to state that the author's official duties were so few, and his pleasures so numerous, as to leave the kindest recollections of the many persons connected with the enterprise."

Knox's writings appealed to the decade's tastes for the spectacle of the exotic, but beyond the wide-eyed adventure and the desire to try something new that characterize all of his travels, his works exhibit a predictability that, no doubt, accounts for their immense popularity during a period of anxiety growing from the expansion of industrial capitalism. Novel and worthy of remark on first notice, they soon become comfortable, even cliché. This is not to dismiss Knox's writings as unimportant but rather to point out that their importance may lie elsewhere than in their originality. A close look at *Overland through Asia* demonstrates that, whatever its shortcomings, the book captures cultural and historical processes at work reshaping the world beyond his narrative. In turning to the Orient, Knox was looking outward and away from the contemplation of internal problems. His recollections, moving increasingly away from the familiarity of regional boundaries, serve to locate the United States squarely within a larger map of the world.

Knox begins the narrative of the journey that would lead him from New York to Moscow and Saint Petersburg by dispensing with the formalities of such a journey. He makes a short visit to a Wall Street banking establishment to obtain a letter of credit. To his question as to whether it will be valid in Irkutsk, Siberia, a banker finally replies, " I am unable to say, if our letter can be used at the place you mention. They are good all over the civilized world, but I don't know anything about Irkutsk. Never heard of the place before."

The episode serves several purposes, illustrating the exotic and the unfamiliar nature of his destination while establishing the picture of the "Ugly American" (obviously not a twentieth-century invention). Yet it does more, for it is in juxtaposition to the banker's provincial attitude that Knox undertakes his journey, implying that he is not such a character. He departs from New York for San Francisco on 21 March 1866 on a voyage that would take twenty-three days, including a port call in Aspinwall, Panama ("a city that could be done in fifteen minutes," he remarks). In San Francisco, a cosmopolitan city with its churches, synagogues, and pagodas standing together (the image of unity is obvious), he affirms that "Californians are among the most genial and hospitable people in America" and that their wines—for Knox the vine is, in general, representative of cultural development—were "already competing with those of France and Germany." Aboard the steamer *G. S. Wright,* Knox departed from San Francisco on 23 June on a journey across the Pacific.

On 6 August members of a delegation representing the Russo-American Telegraph Company departed from Anadyr Bay in Kamchatka, bound for the Amoor River, aboard the *Variag.* They reached the mouth of the Amoor on 11 September and transferred their personal belongings to the *Morje,* a gunboat of the Siberian fleet. On 18 September they changed to the steamer *Ingodah* to ascend the river. Thereafter a considerable part of the narrative is devoted to his travels along the Amoor. After a short journey through Manchuria and into Pekin (Beijing), Knox returned to the Russian frontier, moving to the far reaches of the Russian empire north and south, and eventually made his way to Moscow and Saint Petersburg.

Characteristic of Knox's need to recount all of his observations, the narrative is full of rare and unusual detail (if only from an American perspective), including discussions of the Russian custom of brewing tea in a samovar, the author's childlike fascination with a mirage, and his personal revulsion on witnessing shamanist rituals among the Gilyak natives. There is an inordinate amount of attention paid to Siberian exiles (especially political exiles of aristocratic background) and to foot-binding in China. The plight of the political exiles would certainly have spoken to an American audience still feeling the pains of a country once divided, where fully one-half of its population was still suffering the stigma of having opposed the government. His reports on China, however, leave room for doubt about how closely he adhered to reporting his travel experiences. Whether he actually witnessed footbinding firsthand or whether his reportage is tantamount to hearsay is open to debate, for contradictions in the descriptions abound.

The majority of the narrative, however, records whatever happens to fall within Knox's line of sight in a colloquial, almost chatty manner, often without a coherent thread to bind the whole together. Indeed, although indicative of his mastery of the popular idiom, Knox assumes and thereafter moves with relative ease in and out of several voices as his focus changes and he digresses. Each digression, in turn, becomes the cacophonic site of competing voices inscribed with their own particular interests and desires, always promising something new and exciting along the route of what could potentially become a rather lengthy, drawn-out journey into the mundane. Knox speaks as the seasoned traveler who has long known the hardships of the road and can adapt himself to whatever comes his way. Aboard the *Morje,* where there were no accommodations for passengers, he proposes "to sleep under the table. . . . I knew what I was about, having done the same thing years before on Mississippi steamers. When you must sleep on the floor where people may walk about, always get under the table if possible. You run less risk of receiving boot heels in your mouth and eyes, and whole acres of brogans in your ribs."

It is precisely Knox's practical nature, often flying in the face of conventional wisdom, that separates him from his travel companions, most of whom are (at this stage in his career) more seasoned travelers from the Continent. He speaks with the authority of a sideshow medicine man, caught in the act of peddling his snake oils as a home remedy for seasickness: "The night before going to sea, I take a blue pill (5 to 10 grains) in order to carry the bile from the liver into the stomach. When I rise on the following morning, a dose of citrate of magnesia or some kindred substance finishes my preparation. I take my breakfast and all other meals afterwards as if nothing had happened." For but a moment he becomes the ship's naturalist, knowingly observing that "seven-tenths of the birds of the Amoor are found in Europe, two-tenths in Siberia, and one-tenth in regions further south."

He adopts the superstitions of a sailor's sailor (this from a man who at the outset bemoaned the prospect of traveling aboard a ship in the first place), arguing the virtue of protecting good-luck birds. Anyone who harms a small swallowlike Mother Carey's Chicken, is, he admonishes, "Certain to bring misfortune upon himself and possibly his companions." He positions himself as the avid sportsman, poised to fire upon some hapless whale for sport. "The sport was amusing to all concerned," he would later recall, and then with pangs of conscience, as if having reservations about his participation, adds apologetically, "At any rate the whale didn't seem to mind it, and we were delighted at the fun."

While in China, Knox's comments are those of a seasoned horse trader learning a different way of conducting business: "They have a way of doing trades by drawing their long sleeves over their hands," he notes in surprise, " Making or receiving bids by means of the concealed fingers." Had he ventured a bit farther afield he would almost certainly have noticed the universal applicability of this mode for transacting business (once widespread throughout East Asia, it remains a common practice among fishmongers in contemporary Japan). Upon his arrival in Habarofka, on the mouth of the Oursuree, he notes matter-of-factly that the town is "in a condition of rawness like a western city in its second year." Here again his wide-eyed enthusiasm gains the upper hand as he continues his description. The objective tone he adopts in telling us that somewhere beyond "the principal street we found a store, where we purchased a quantity of canned fruit, meats, and pickles" is as quickly undone by the narrator's enthusiastic musing, "These articles were from Boston, New York, and Baltimore, and had American labels."

It is precisely this subjective eye, given free range, that captivates the reader's attention. If the plurality of voices fails to find a willing listener, Knox's attention to detail almost certainly ensures that the reader will persevere. To this end his text includes both a map and more than two hundred steel engravings. The former keeps the reader informed as to the precise location within larger networks of understanding; the latter were obviously meant as visual accompaniment to be viewed on an equal footing with the text. Knox's descriptions of native costumes are usually followed by illustrative engravings, as when Knox recounts his encounter with a Manjour merchant aboard the steamer *Telegraph.* He describes a man "who possessed an intelligent face, quite in contrast with the sleepy Gilyaks. He wore the Manjour dress, consisting of wide trowsers and a long robe reaching to his heels; his shoes and hat were Chinese, and his robe was held at the waist with a silken cord. His hair was braided in the Chinese fashion, and he sported a long mustache but no beard." These words are accompanied by the seemingly obligatory illustration.

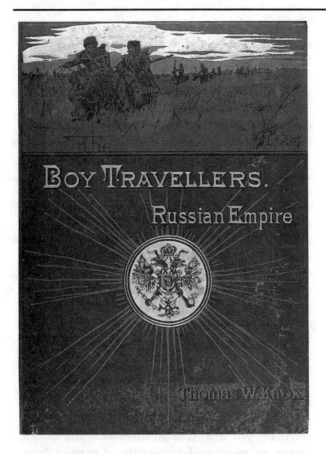

Cover for Knox's 1887 novel featuring American boys in an exotic locale

Taken as a whole, however, the illustrations irritate rather than delight. The London-based artist Frederick Whymper is largely responsible for the pencil sketches that served as the basis of these depictions, which all too often do not match the text or which betray the artist's apparent lack of familiarity with the subject matter. The illustrations seem designed to fit the publisher's desire to append to readers' expectations of an illustrated work rather than truly serving to amplify the written description. The faces of his non-Caucasian subjects, be they African or Asian, are highly conventionalized, stereotypical icons, devoid both of life and any connection to the text. The artistic representation of bound feet clearly contradicts the details of the text and in doing so erects and thereafter perpetuates misinformation among a reading audience who might otherwise never see this phenomenon.

There is also the overt attention to packaging. Reminiscent of the serials appearing in newspapers of his day, Knox utilizes to capacity the cliff-hanger to end each chapter, although he frequently fails to mount much suspense in doing so, and the rhythm of his prose is often interruptive rather than conclusive, almost always less than satisfying. The end of

the twenty-second chapter provides just such an example: "And didn't we enjoy it after riding eight or ten hours over a road that would have shaken skim-milk into butter? You bet we did." In fact, throughout the narrative Knox's concern with framing is evident, fully cognizant as he is that his travelogue will serve some distant readers as a prism of sorts in their understanding of the world that lies outside the United States.

Knox received external impressions during his travels that he later filtered through his memories, in the process altering them. For Knox the mountains of Kamchatka recall "the rocky mountains from Denver or the Sierra Nevadas from the vicinity of Stockton." Midsummer in Siberia is likened to "that of August in Richmond or Baltimore." The odor of drying fish calls forth "the smells in certain quarters of New York in summer, or of Cairo, Illinois, after an unusual flood has subsided." Through Knox's eyes the rapids along the Amoor become like those of the Mississippi in the vicinity of Memphis, Tennessee. This reliance upon inscribing the familiar can be seen as a conscious strategy for underscoring the universality of human nature though simultaneously it has the effect of obfuscating the particularity and the variety of Knox's encounters. Whereas he strives to express the unknown in terms of that which is familiar, the effect of such gross oversimplifications tends to be reductive and thereby diminishes the importance of the moment.

It is, therefore, with a certain irony that this strategy is linked with a conscious attempt at placing the journey within larger issues of history and the historical moment. Certain digressions promise all the excitement of a schoolbook ripe for rote memorization. Underscoring the isolation entailed in sailing around the world, Knox relates how a chance encounter with another ship might lead to an exchange of the news. In this particular incident he hears the words from a distance: "War in progress—France and Austria against Prussia, Italy, and Russia. No particulars." Only later, after a similar encounter with an English steamer, is he informed that "there had been war between Prussia and Austria, but at last accounts all Europe was at peace." His glib conclusion that the War of 1866 "was finished long before I knew of its commencement" diminishes the importance of certain world events. The reader is also instructed with a pedantic air that the purchase of the Alaskan territories from the Russians was, doubtless, a proud expression of our Manifest Destiny:

When the country has been thoroughly examined, it is possible we may find stores of now unknown wealth.

Politically the acquisition is more important. The possession of a large part of the Pacific coast, indented with many bays and harbors, is a matter of moment in view of our national ambition. The American eagle can scream louder since its cage has been enlarged, and if any man attempts to haul down that noble bird, scoop him from the spot.

To focus entirely upon the ex cathedra tone of the peripatetic pedagogue, however, is to miss an additional dimension of Knox's writing skills, namely his ability to situate elements of humor at every opportunity in the manner of Mark Twain's *Innocents Abroad* (1869). At times his wit is light and precarious in its effect: "The Russians have a custom of taking a little lunch," he ventures, "Just before they begin dinner." Longer recollections often digress and serve solely to lighten the moment. Recognizing that the Siberian town of Kamchatka was no more than a glorified trading post for the fur trade, Knox is moved to relate an amusing anecdote about the American frontier:

> There is a story of a traveler who paid his hotel bill in a country town in Minnesota and received a beaver skin in change. The landlord explained that it was legal tender for a dollar. Concealing this novel cash under his coat, the traveler sauntered into a neighboring store.
>
> "Is it true," he asked carelessly, "that a beaver skin is legal tender for a dollar?"
>
> "Yes, sir," said the merchant; "anybody will take it."
>
> "Will you be so kind, then," was the traveler's request, "as to give me change for a dollar bill?"
>
> "Certainly," answered the merchant, taking the beaver skin and returning four muskrat skins, current at twenty-five cents each.

At other times the humorous moment hovers precariously on the edge of the dark, dismissing the lasting outcome of the situation in favor of the momentary joke. In one such instance Knox recalls the unfortunate predicament of a Hong Kong merchant who had invested a considerable sum of money in "a cargo of hams from the Amoor, and when he received it and opened the barrels he found they contained nothing but bones. As the bone market was low at that time he did not repeat his order." These words, however innocent they appear on the surface, in a real sense erase the serious outcome for the merchant by deflecting the attentions of Knox's readers away from—indeed, by erecting a barrier to—the less than savory aspects.

Nevertheless, Knox remains the first to make light of his own predicament: "My apartment had two bunks and no bedding," he complains, "But the deficiency was atoned for by a large number of hungry and industrious fleas." Nor are his foibles immune to such scrutiny. Having summoned an innkeeper, he attempts to put his language skills to use. "*Dai samovar, chi, saher e klehb,*" he begins, fully intending to order the samovar and tea, along with some bread and sugar. To his surprise he is presented with beefsteaks and potatoes. "I spoke the language of the country in a fragmentary way," he argues with himself, noting in his conclusion, "But am certain my Russian was not half as bad as the beefsteak."

It is Knox's reliance upon humor as a mode of communication that leaves him vulnerable to contemporary criticism, for although he attempts covert objectivity, all too often he comes off as offensive (at least from a modern vantage). Again his use of voices reveals as much about Knox as it does of the cultural milieu into which he was born. The reader witnesses the elevation of social mobility and its witless companion, social snobbery, in the frequent references to the "good taste of the owner" in various locations along the journey. Similarly unsettling is the sexist tone that prevails throughout. Notable landmarks along the way are likely to be women: "a couple of pretty girls" or "a pretty grace and figure, more to my fellow traveler's taste than the *pièce de résistance* of our meal." Further, unmistakably racist undertones permeate the narrative. From his musings on "a fair but not undue portion of half breeds" through the frequent references to "John Chinaman" and "shabby Celestials" to instances of anti-Semitism ("in their enterprise and mode of dealing they were very much like the Jews of Europe and America, which may account for their being called Manjours"), racism runs rampant. Knox summarily states that the inhabitants of a particular region are "Russians or half breeds, the former predominating. The half breeds are said to possess all the vices of both races with the virtues of neither." In the face of a variety of ethnic groups Knox's uncontested response reflects his own characteristically hierarchical view of the world (the priorities and privileges of which he never questions): "the Goldees are superior to the Gilyaks in numbers and intelligence," he remarks at one point, "And the Manjours of Igoon and vicinity are in turn superior to the Goldees. The Chinese are more civilized than the Manjours, and call the latter 'dogs.' The Manjours take revenge by applying the epithet to the

Goldees, and these transfer it to the Mangoons and Gilyaks."

These elements, part and parcel of a larger pattern found in his later writings as well, portend that Knox had from the mid 1880s found his niche. From this point in his career he wrote with a clearly limited and limiting eye on the burgeoning middle-class market as his audience of choice. His series of books for boys, for example, were highly formulaic productions focusing on a non-European essence, representing it as something on occasion interesting but always unequal. Overwhelmingly male novels, they place young, resourceful American boys (all of whom are Caucasian) in such exotic locales as Japan and China (*The Boy Travellers to the Far East,* 1879), the Middle East (*Adventures of Two Youths in a Journey to Egypt and the Holy Land,* 1882), the far reaches of the Arctic (*Adventures of Two Youths in the Open Polar Sea: The Voyage of the "Vivian" to the North Pole and Beyond,* 1884), and the Congo (*The Boy Travellers on the Congo: Adventures of Two Youths in a Journey with Henry M. Stanley, "Through the Dark Continent,"* 1887) precisely for the purposes of demonstrating the superior physical stamina, mental acuity, and emotional and spiritual resolve of Anglo-Saxon American youths in coping with problems that the natives could not solve. The nonwhites in these situations readily assent to the young Americans' superiority, accepting as it were Knox's judgment of their own inferiority.

Whether grown weary of the exotic, physically exhausted by being the perpetual outsider, or out of money, Knox turned his hand to hackwork. He churned out several biographies to satisfy the growing demand of a literate if less-than-discerning American readership. Additionally he wrote two animal texts (one on horses, the other on dogs) to sate the same audience. He also made several less-than-successful attempts at fiction.

The decade of the 1890s would witness Knox's encounter with the familiar, having set his sights on exploring those areas most frequented by American travelers of certain social standing. He moved easily through Europe and North Africa. Finishing his adventures in the Sahara, he appeared content that he had seen everything worth seeing.

While he once proclaimed that "there are dozens and hundreds of individuals . . . of all grades and conditions in life, who have placed me under numberless obligations," in the end the reader can hardly characterize Knox or his prodigious writings as either cosmopolitan or international in scope, for to do so would imply an egalitarianism that is much more at home now than it was in post–Civil War American society. Rather he represents in his triumphs as well as his follies what it meant to be a middle-class American in the late nineteenth century: curious and adventuresome, socially mobile and innocent of the pretentions of social climbing, and increasingly urban in outlook, even if fundamentally provincial. It is in this latter light that Knox traveled and wrote, and it is in this light that he died, in New York City on 6 January 1896, a year after having traveled the Sahara. As he once recounted:

> When recalled by the steam whistle we left the village and took a short route down a steep bank to the boat. In descending, my feet passed from under me, and I had the pleasure of sliding about ten yards before stopping. Had it not been for a Cossack who happened my way, I should have entered the Amoor after the manner of an otter, and afforded much amusement to the spectators, though comparatively little to myself. The sliding attracted no special attention as it was supposed to be an American custom, and I did not deem it prudent to make an explanation lest the story might bring discredit to my nationality.

References:

Syed Hussein Alatas, *The Myth of the Lazy Native: A Study of the Image of the Malays, Filipinos, and Javanese from the Sixteenth to the Twentieth Century and Its Function in the Ideology of Colonial Capitalism* (London: Frank Cass, 1977);

Stuart Ewen and Elizabeth Ewen, *Channels of Desire: Mass Images and the Shaping of American Consciousness* (New York: McGraw-Hill, 1979);

Fredric Jameson, *The Political Unconscious: Narrative as a Socially Symbolic Act* (Ithaca: Cornell University Press, 1981);

Walter La Feber, *The New Empire: An Interpretation of American Expansionism* (Ithaca: Cornell University Press, 1963);

Edward W. Said, *Culture and Imperialism* (New York: Knopf, 1993);

Bernard Smith, *European Vision and the South Pacific* (New Haven: Yale University Press, 1985);

Richard W. Van Alstyne, *The Rising American Empire* (New York: Norton, 1974).

James Russell Lowell

(22 February 1819 – 12 August 1891)

Brendan A. Rapple
Boston College

See the entries in *DLB 1: The American Renaissance in New England; DLB 11: American Humorists, 1800-1950; DLB 64: American Literary Critics and Scholars, 1850-1880;* and *DLB 79: American Magazine Journalists, 1850-1900.*

BOOKS: *Class Poem* (Cambridge: Metcalf, Torry & Ballou, 1838);

A Year's Life (Boston: Little, Brown, 1841);

Poems (Cambridge: Owen, 1843; London: Mudie, 1844);

Conversations on Some of the Old Poets (Cambridge: Owen, 1845);

Poems (Cambridge: Nichols / Boston: Mussey, 1848);

A Fable for Critics, or, A Glance at a Few of Our Literary Progenies from the Tub of Diogenes (New York: Putnam, 1848);

Meliboeus-Hipponax: The Biglow Papers (Cambridge: Nichols, 1848; New York: Putnam, 1848);

The Vision of Sir Launfal (Cambridge: Nichols, 1848);

Poems, 2 volumes (Boston: Ticknor, Reed & Fields, 1849);

The Poetical Works of James R. Lowell, 2 volumes (Boston: Ticknor & Fields, 1858);

The Biglow Papers. Second Series (London: Trübner, 1862; Boston: Ticknor & Fields, 1867);

Fireside Travels (Boston: Ticknor & Fields, 1864);

Ode Recited at the Commemoration of the Living and Dead Soldiers of Harvard University, July 21, 1865 (Cambridge: Privately printed, 1865);

Under the Willows, and Other Poems (Boston: Fields, Osgood, 1869);

The Cathedral (Boston: Fields, Osgood, 1870);

Among My Books (Boston: Fields, Osgood, 1870);

My Study Windows (Boston: Osgood, 1871);

Among My Books. Second Series (Boston: Osgood, 1876);

Three Memorial Poems (Boston: Osgood, 1877);

On Democracy: An Address Delivered in the Town Hall, Birmingham, on the 6th of October, 1884 (Birmingham: Cond, 1884);

James Russell Lowell in 1857 (photograph by Mathew Brady)

Democracy, and Other Addresses (Boston & New York: Houghton, Mifflin, 1886);

The Independent in Politics; An Address Delivered Before the Reform Club of New York, April 13, 1888 (New York & London: Putnam, 1888);

Political Essays (Boston & New York: Houghton, Mifflin, 1888);

Heartsease and Rue (Boston & New York: Houghton, Mifflin, 1888);

The English Poets, Lessing, Rousseau: Essays (London: Scott, 1888);

Books and Libraries, and Other Papers (Boston: Houghton, Mifflin, 1889);

Latest Literary Essays and Addresses of James Russell Lowell, edited by Charles Eliot Norton (Boston & New York: Houghton, Mifflin, 1891);

American Ideas for English Readers. Eleven addresses delivered in England from November 6, 1880, to December 23, 1888 (Boston: Cupples, 1892);

The Old English Dramatists, edited by Norton (Boston & New York: Houghton, Mifflin, 1892);

Last Poems of James Russell Lowell, edited by Norton (Boston: Houghton, Mifflin, 1895);

Lowell Leaflets: Poems and Prose Passages from the Works of James Russell Lowell for Reading and Recitation, compiled by Josephine E. Hodgdon (Boston: Houghton, Mifflin, 1896);

The Power of Sound: A Rhymed Lecture, edited by Norton (New York: Privately printed, 1896);

Lectures on English Poets (Cleveland: Rowfant Club, 1897);

Impressions of Spain, compiled by Joseph B. Gilder (Boston & New York: Houghton, Mifflin, 1899);

The Anti-Slavery Papers of James Russell Lowell, 2 volumes (Boston & New York: Houghton, Mifflin, 1902);

Early Prose Writings of James Russell Lowell (London & New York: John Lane, 1902);

The Round Table (Boston: Badger, 1913);

The Function of the Poet and Other Essays, collected and edited by Albert Mordell (Boston & New York: Houghton Mifflin, 1920).

Collections: *The Writings of James Russell Lowell in Ten Volumes* (Boston & New York: Houghton, Mifflin, 1890);

Complete Works, 11 volumes (New York: Sully & Kleinteich, 1892);

The Complete Poetical Works of James Russell Lowell, edited by Horace E. Scudder (Boston & New York: Houghton, Mifflin, 1896);

The Complete Writings of James Russell Lowell, 16 volumes, edited by Charles Eliot Norton (Cambridge: Riverside Press, 1904);

Selected Literary Essays from James Russell Lowell (Boston & New York: Houghton Mifflin, 1914);

James Russell Lowell: Representative Selections, edited by Harry Hayden Clark and Norman Foerster (New York: American Book, 1947);

Essays, Poems and Letters, edited by William Smith Clark (New York: Odyssey, 1948);

Uncollected Poems of James Russell Lowell, edited by Thelma M. Smith (Philadelphia: University of Philadelphia Press, 1950);

Literary Criticism of James Russell Lowell, edited by Herbert F. Smith (Lincoln: University of Nebraska Press, 1969);

The Poetical Works of James Russell Lowell, revised by Marjorie R. Kaufman (Boston: Houghton Mifflin, 1978).

In his later years James Russell Lowell was considered the major man of letters of the age, but posterity has been less kind to him. Today he is little read and is generally regarded as not being in the same league as such fellow New England luminaries as Ralph Waldo Emerson, Henry Wadsworth Longfellow, Edgar Allan Poe, and Nathaniel Hawthorne. This situation is owing in large part to Lowell's failure to compose an acknowledged masterpiece though his two series of *The Biglow Papers* (1848, 1862) were highly regarded and widely read. It is often adduced that Lowell, a man of many talents and interests, spread himself too widely with the resultant sum of the parts being somewhat lacking. Still, he attained high prominence as a poet, literary and social critic, editor, abolitionist, scholar of comparative literature, Harvard professor, and diplomat. Lowell was also a consummate traveler in Europe, where, as an ambassador or as a tourist, he lived many years.

James Russell Lowell was born at Elmwood in Cambridge, Massachussetts, on 22 February 1819, the youngest of the six children of Reverend Charles Lowell and Harriet Traill Spence. In 1834, at the age of fifteen, he entered Harvard, where his subsequent academic career was undistinguished. He was chosen as Class Poet, however, though he was not permitted to read his poem, as he was undergoing temporary rustication for certain dress and academic violations. After graduation he decided to study law, not because of any real calling but rather, as his biographer Horace Elisha Scudder observed, through a process of elimination.

Though he received his bachelor of laws from Harvard in 1840 and was admitted to the bar two years later, by 1843 Lowell had given up the law as a career. An increasing number of magazines were beginning to publish his poems, and his first book of verse, *A Year's Life,* published in January 1841, received favorable reviews. Buoyed by his incipient literary success, Lowell determined to continue exclusively the life of a man of letters.

In 1843 Lowell established the literary journal *The Pioneer* with Robert Carter. Though it only lasted three numbers, the journal published works by Poe, Hawthorne, and Elizabeth Barrett Browning. In the same year Lowell's *Poems* was published, and it was even better received than his first volume of poetry. It had three editions of five hundred copies each. A little more than a year later Lowell published *Conversations on Some of the Old Poets,* a volume of essays on Geoffrey Chaucer, George Chapman, and John Ford.

Toward the end of 1844 Lowell married Maria White. Their first child, Blanche, was born in late 1845 but lived for only fifteen months. A second child, Mabel, the only one of Lowell's four children to reach adulthood, was born in September 1847. During this period Lowell contributed to such journals as the *Pennsylvania Freeman, Graham's Magazine,* the *London Daily News,* the *Liberty Bell,* and the *Boston Courier.* From 1846 to 1852 he was the corresponding editor of the *National Anti-Slavery Standard,* believing strongly that "there are a great many things to be done in this country, but the first is the abolition of slavery." He published almost fifty articles in the *Standard* as well as parts of *The Biglow Papers.*

Lowell's *annus mirabilis,* 1848, was highly productive. In addition to many reviews and articles, he published another volume of *Poems;* the humorous *A Fable for Critics;* a fifteen-page poem, *The Vision of Sir Launfal;* and the satiric and popular first series of *The Biglow Papers.* Lowell's third daughter, Rose, died when she was less than one year old, in March 1850. A son, Walter, was born in December 1850.

In July 1851 Lowell and his family sailed from Boston on their first trip to Europe. After a two-month stay in Florence, "the noisiest town [he] was ever in" but where he particularly enjoyed the walks, Lowell and family traveled to Rome for the winter. Initially he did not like the city. He found the churches nearly all alike and lacking the architectural "spring and soar" of Lombard churches. He was little impressed with the Roman Catholic ceremonies. Moreover, he thought that ostentation was the main characteristic of Rome's modern architecture: he wrote that their churches' "marble incrustations look like a kind of architectural elephantiasis, and the parts are puffy with a dropsical want of proportion."

Still, he gradually began to feel the city's "insensible charm." He appreciated its natural beauty, particularly its mountains, and delighted in the art. He admired its grandeur, glory, and sublimity. He was also convinced that his compatriots, of all people least at home among ruins, were at home there: not only did Americans particularly represent the old Roman power and sentiment, but American talent for politics, law, colonization, aggrandizement, and trade were also "all Roman," according to Lowell. In the early summer of 1852 the Lowells' son died. For the next

Lowell's first wife, Maria White (portrait by Samuel W. Rowse; Harvard University)

few months the family continued their European journey, visiting Venice, the Italian lakes, Switzerland, Germany, and France. On an autumn visit to England, Lowell was particularly pleased by its cathedral towns, especially Ely. At the end of October 1852 the Lowells left Liverpool for America; William Makepeace Thackeray and Arthur Hugh Clough were fellow passengers. During his fifteen-month sojourn in Europe, Lowell had written little apart from letters and journal entries.

After the death of his wife in October 1853 Lowell was deeply despondent and found it difficult to return to literary pursuits. However, in late 1853 he published "A Moosehead Journal," an account of a trip he had taken in Maine that summer with his nephew Charles, in *Putnam's Magazine.* The following year his "Cambridge Thirty Years Ago" and "Leaves from My Journal in Italy and Elsewhere" appeared—the first in *Putnam's,* the latter in *Graham's Magazine.* These three articles were later published as *Fireside Travels* (1864).

Lowell's highly entertaining "Leaves from My Journal in Italy and Elsewhere" presents reflections on and anecdotes about his first trip to Europe. It is also interesting for Lowell's opinion on what constitutes the ideal traveler and model travel writing. Lowell faults modern travelers for seeing "nothing out of sight." They are scientists with doubting and skeptical senses who report "things for other sceptics to doubt still further upon." On the other hand, the journals of older travelers were "prose Odysseys. The geographies of our ancestors were works of fancy and imagination. They read poems where we yawn over items." Though Lowell, despite his many official and unofficial trips abroad, wrote relatively few works concerning his travel experiences, these latter pieces invariably display a poetic imagination that reveals that he himself followed closely in the footsteps of the older travel writers he admired.

During his acclaimed series of lectures titled "The English Poets" at the Lowell Institute in 1855, Lowell received word of his appointment as Longfellow's successor as professor of modern languages and literatures at Harvard. Having obtained permission to spend a year abroad to perfect his knowledge of Spanish and German, Lowell left New York on 4 June 1855. Arriving in France, Lowell spent three "dull" weeks in Paris though he was particularly taken by the Titians at the Louvre. He also made a trip to Chartres Cathedral, a visit that was his inspiration fourteen years later when he composed his poem "The Cathedral." After a month in England, where he met with Thackeray, the Brownings, and Leigh Hunt, he returned to the Continent and settled in Dresden. Grieving over his wife and homesick for New England, Lowell immersed himself in the study of German for the following six months. Paying little attention to society, his "great solace (or distraction)" in Dresden was the theater; Lowell particularly praised the historical accuracy of the costume and scenery. By the end of February 1856 Lowell, feeling a great urge to revisit Italy, traveled through Vienna, Trieste, and Venice and made his way to Rome. His spirits began to revive almost immediately with the beauties of the Italian spring. As he wrote to his father: "My journey in Italy was of much benefit to me." On a mule trip to Sicily with Charles Eliot Norton and two others he greatly admired the island's natural beauty. However, he was saddened by its pervasive poverty, the inhabitants' depressed condition, and at what he considered to be its deplorable political aspect—Sicily, he felt, was "the worst governed country in Europe."

Lowell had planned to spend only one month in Italy; however, this grew to three. Returning to Dresden, Lowell stayed two more months in Europe. By August 1856 he was back in Massachusetts, where he took up his professorship at Harvard.

Lowell married Frances Dunlap in 1857, the same year that he assumed the editorship of *The Atlantic Monthly,* a post he maintained until 1861. His teaching at Harvard and editorial duties claimed most of his energies though he found time over the following years to publish many poems, political and social articles, and literary essays. Lowell also published several books, many of them collections of material that had previously appeared in journals: *The Biglow Papers. Second Series, Fireside Travels, Under the Willows, and Other Poems* (1869), *The Cathedral* (1870), *Among My Books* (1870), and *My Study Windows* (1871).

On 9 July 1872 Lowell, along with his wife, departed for his third trip to Europe, where he remained for two years. After a brief stop in Dublin, which Lowell found "Hogarthian," and a sojourn of several weeks in England the couple settled in Paris, where they remained seven months. Though frequently confessing his homesickness—he declared that he much preferred the walk along Cambridge's Brattle Street to that along the Champs Elysées—Lowell observed that Paris was "certainly the handsomest city in the World." One of his favorite occupations there was scouring the bookshops looking for bargains, above all for works in Old French. He liked the French people, found them more hospitable than the English, and praised the attractiveness of their manners. Still, though the French were "gentle, kindly, patient, and industrious," Lowell complained of their provincialism as manifested in their self-importance: "Every one of them has the flavour of a village great man." In May 1873, during a four-day visit to England, Lowell met Thomas Carlyle, John Ruskin, William Morris, George Henry Lewes, Thomas Hughes, and Leslie Stephen. In June he received an honorary doctor of civil law from Oxford.

Leaving Paris, the Lowells "made a pretty good *giro* in the Low Countries" and then settled in Geneva for two months. In October they were in Italy. Lowell found Venice "incomparable" and after viewing the Tintorettos, the Cimas, the Bellinis, and the Carpaccios declared that he was really happy for the first time since coming abroad. In Florence he wrote one of his best poems, "Agassiz," the ode on the death of Louis Agassiz. Rome saddened him because of past associations. After a spell in Naples, which he found "changed for the worse" and from which he visited the "incomparable Museum" of Pompeii and Herculaneum, he returned to Paris. In

Last photograph of Lowell

July 1874, a month after receiving an honorary doctor of laws from Cambridge University, Lowell was back in America.

In May 1877 Lowell was appointed to the American Ministry in Spain by President Rutherford B. Hayes. In mid August the Lowells were in Madrid. This was Lowell's first trip to Spain, his previous neglect of the country perhaps being because of its chaotic state during the previous decades. He was well aware of the dignity of his new office. After he had been apologized to for a twenty-minute delay in being presented to King Alfonso XII, Lowell replied that the wait meant nothing to him personally, but that it was the United States that had been kept waiting. The work was not too onerous though Lowell frequently found it tedious. He was more concerned with affairs of business, especially customs duties and tariffs, than with major diplomatic issues. He attended many functions of ceremony and court, for example the sumptuous marriage between the twenty-one-year-old King Alfonso to his young cousin Princess Mercedes and the extremely poignant funeral rituals for Mercedes only five months later. He was also active in preparing the official visit of Gen. Ulysses S. Grant to Spain in November 1878.

From the beginning Lowell insisted on conducting official business in Spanish. Though he was a good Spanish scholar, he was more at ease with the Spanish of Pedro Calderón de la Barca and Miguel de Cervantes than with that of his own time. The Spanish and Spain he knew best were those of history. He spent most of his time in Madrid. Having expected something more appropriate to Calderón, this city at first disappointed him by its modern visage. Still, he grew to like it, especially the Prado and the Campiña, which he found grander than the Italian Campagna. He also appreciated the Guadarramas, whose color, he wrote, was at times "so ethereal that they seem visionary rather than real." He visited Barcelona, where he was much taken by its cathedral, and traveled to Seville, Cordova, Granada, and Toledo. He commented on how ruined Toledo was and how indifferent it was to ruin. Still, he felt that there was something oriental in his nature that inclined him to sympathize with the "'let her slide' temper of the *hidalgos.*"

From April to June 1878 Lowell and his wife took leave from Spain and traveled through Tarbes, Toulouse, Carcassonne, Nismes, Avignon, Vaucluse, and Arles. They then continued to Italy, stopping in Genoa, Pisa, and Naples, where they took a steamer to Athens. Though Lowell found Athens somewhat mean and depressing, the Acropolis was "noble in position and sublime even in ruin." After about a week the Lowells proceeded to Constantinople, where Lowell found Santa Sofia to be "very noble, *really* noble" and the Turks "the most dignified-looking race I have ever seen—a noble bearing even in defeat and even in rags." They arrived back in Madrid just in time for the death of young Queen Mercedes.

Lowell turned to his state duties with renewed strength and interest. He attended debates in the Cortes, made acquaintance with important politicians, and read relevant political and intellectual newspapers and journals. At the same time he continued his vigorous study of Spanish language, literature, and history. However, though he deepened his already extensive knowledge of the history of this nation's literature, he almost totally neglected the study of contemporary literary achievements in Spain. Above all, he ignored the great contemporary novelist Benito Pérez Galdós. Still, Lowell's knowledge and interest in Spain were appreciated, and he was elected a corresponding member of the *Academia Española,* whose meetings he diligently attended. He was also appointed an honorary professor in the recently formed *Institución Libre de Enseñanza.*

Lowell, whose preferred acquaintances were intellectuals, scholars, and writers, never gained a deep knowledge of the mass of the Spanish people. However, he liked the Spanish and shared an instinctive sympathy with them for what he felt was their ineptitude for business and lack of interest in money. On the other hand, he described with some distaste the provincialism and pride pervading the Spanish character: "they think they have the best of everything—even of governments, for aught I know. But the everything must be Spain." He noted that Spain, though equipped with constitutional forms, sometimes conveniently ignored constitutional procedures. Still, he believed that it would probably follow France in becoming "a conservative republic." Nevertheless, from his acquaintance with Spanish history and from what he admitted to be his "superficial" knowledge of the national character, he was convinced that change would not come quickly: "The bent of ages is not to be straightened in a day by never so many liberal constitutions." Though the country was making strides promoted by many modern men, Lowell felt that Spain was still back-

ward: "Telegrams are nought, for our distance is really that of time, not space. We are of the last century in so many ways!" To Henry James he wrote that "Spain is as unchangeable as Turkey." Lowell never wrote a book on Spain. His *Impressions of Spain* (1899), published after his death, collects some of his official dispatches to Washington.

In May 1880 Lowell, now a seasoned diplomat, arrived in London and took up his appointment as minister to the Court of St. James. He had had few real diplomatic problems while in Spain. However, as ambassador to England he was much involved in two difficult affairs, the North American fisheries question and the Coercive Law, which suspended habeas corpus in Ireland. Lowell found the latter particularly onerous primarily because some of the Irish imprisoned were American citizens. He disliked the Coercive Law on moral and, as a supporter of Home Rule, political grounds. But because it was an enacted law, he felt that he had to support it. His dealings in this matter were not always well appreciated by the Irish and their American sympathizers, however, and there were demands, even in Congress, for his recall.

Unlike some other of his compatriots who lived for extended periods in England, Lowell always remained distinctly American and was consistently watchful for any slight to his country. English chauvinistic arrogance was particularly galling to him. In 1888 he wrote to Norton: "there is one thing they always take for granted, namely, that an American *must* see the superiority of England. They have as little tact as their *totem* the bull." His caustic views on English prejudice are particularly evident in the section "Mason and Slidell: A Yankee Idyll" in the second series of *The Biglow Papers.* During the Civil War, Lowell had repeatedly castigated England's attitude toward the North. In an April 1866 letter to Leslie Stephen he confessed that he "had an almost invincible repugnance to writing again to England. . . . I cannot forget the insult so readily as I might the injury of the last five years." Even after the war Lowell did not attenuate his criticism of the English sense of superiority, as in his July 1869 article, "On a Certain Condescension in Foreigners."

Nevertheless, Lowell was fond of the English—"I like the people here and always have liked them"—and was a fervent, if by no means uncritical, anglophile. He had particular affection for England's capital. In July 1886 he wrote to his daughter: "I like London better than any place I ever lived in." Though he enjoyed and was very comfortable in fashionable society, Lowell's deepest friendships in England were with men of letters. These included Thomas Hughes, who had introduced the authorized version of *The Biglow Papers* in England in 1859; Leslie Stephen; Robert Browning; and Alfred Tennyson. His own fame as a literary figure was widespread, and he was bestowed with honors as well as invitations to give speeches and addresses. He gave a well-received speech at a commemoration of Henry Fielding in Taunton in September 1883 and spoke at the unveiling of the busts of Longfellow and Samuel Taylor Coleridge in Westminster Abbey in March 1884 and May 1885, respectively. He received an honorary doctor of laws at Edinburgh University in April 1884. In 1883 he was even elected rector of the University of St. Andrews by the students, though he immediately resigned when he became aware of his ineligibility because of his citizenship. On 6 October 1884, as the new president of the Birmingham and Midland Institute, Lowell presented his well-known inaugural address, "Democracy." Earlier that year he was appointed president of the Wordsworth Society. He was also strongly pressured by his friends to allow himself to be nominated for the new chair in English language and literature at Oxford University. However, Lowell, whose wife Frances died in February 1885, preferred to return to New England when his ambassadorial duties were complete. By June he was back home in Massachusetts after eight years outside the United States. During this period he had published little.

His affection for England and the English is manifest in the fact that after his period as ambassador he returned from America on holiday almost each summer until his death. A widower, he looked forward to his summers in England and the social and intellectual contact with his many English friends. As Henry James remarked: "He came back for his friends—he would have done anything for his friends." Often lonely during his winters in Massachusetts, he also greatly enjoyed the social round of lunches, dinners, receptions, speeches, and other engagements in England, where he continued to be very popular. Especially pleasing to him were Saint Ives in Cornwall and Whitby in Yorkshire, which he had visited almost every summer even as minister. In 1889 Lowell spent five months mainly in London and Whitby, the last summer he was to spend in England.

During these years he turned once more to publishing. *Democracy, and Other Addresses,* a collection of speeches he had delivered in England, appeared in 1886. Two years later he published *Political Essays* as well as a volume of poetry, *Heartsease and Rue.* In 1890 a ten-volume edition of his collected works appeared, the preparation of which he oversaw with great care. On 12 August 1891 Lowell

died in Elmwood in the house where he had been born.

Lowell was an extremely prolific writer. However, he produced very little during his lengthy sojourns abroad, apart from letters, the occasional poem, official dispatches, and several addresses. It seems that his creative muse required the stimulus of the New England environment. Though it is difficult to pinpoint how exactly his foreign experiences influenced his writings, it is apparent that they fostered his cosmopolitan intellectual and literary leanings. Lowell was a consummate comparative social, political, and literary critic. Still, despite his many years abroad and his manifest enjoyment, approval, and even love of much that was foreign, Lowell lost not a whit of his Americanism. As he asked rhetorically in 1876: "If I am not an American, who ever was?" Above all, he always remained proud of and deeply rooted in his New England heritage. Consequently, it is perhaps not surprising that his extensive European experiences left this Massachusetts Brahmin "convinced that with all our faults (and nobody is better aware of them or feels them more keenly) we are the happiest and most civilized people on the face of the Earth."

Letters:

Letters of James Russell Lowell, 2 volumes, edited by Charles Eliot Norton (New York & Harper, 1893; London: Osgood, McIlvaine, 1894);

New Letters of James Russell Lowell, edited by M. A. De Wolfe Howe (New York & London: Harper, 1932);

The Scholar-Friends; Letters of Francis James Child and James Russell Lowell, edited by Howe and G. W. Cottrell Jr. (Cambridge, Mass.: Harvard University Press, 1952).

Bibliography:

George Willis Cooke, *A Bibliography of James Russell Lowell* (Boston: Houghton, Mifflin, 1906).

Biographies:

Edward Everett Hale, *James Russell Lowell and His Friends* (Boston: Houghton, Mifflin, 1899);

Horace Elisha Scudder, *James Russell Lowell: A Biography,* 2 volumes (Boston & New York: Houghton, Mifflin, 1901);

Ferris Greenslet, *James Russell Lowell, His Life and Work* (Boston: Houghton, Mifflin, 1905);

Richmond Croom Beatty, *James Russell Lowell* (Nashville: Vanderbilt University Press, 1942);

Leon Howard, *Victorian Knight-Errant: A Study of the Early Literary Career of James Russell Lowell*

(Berkeley: University of California Press, 1952);

Martin B. Duberman, *James Russell Lowell* (Boston: Houghton Mifflin, 1966);

Edward Wagenknecht, *James Russell Lowell: Portrait of a Many-Sided Man* (New York: Oxford University, 1971);

Clemens David Heymann, *American Aristocracy: The Lives and Times of James Russell, Amy, and Robert Lowell* (New York: Dodd, Mead, 1980);

Portrait of a Friendship: Drawn from New Letters of James Russell Lowell to Sybella Lady Lyttelton, 1881–1891, edited by Alethea Hayter (Wilton, U.K.: Michael Russell, 1990).

References:

Henry James, "James Russell Lowell," in *Essays in London and Elsewhere* (London: Osgood, McIlvaine, 1893), pp. 47–85;

Lawrence S. Kaplan, "The Brahmin as Diplomat in Nineteenth Century America: Everett, Bancroft, Motley, Lowell," *Civil War History*, 19 (1973): 5–28;

Lawrence H. Klibbe, *James Russell Lowell's Residence in Spain (1877–1880)* (Newark, N.J.: Washington Irving, 1964);

Robert Charles Le Clair, *Three American Travellers in England: James Russell Lowell, Henry Adams,* *Henry James* (Westport, Conn.: Greenwood Press, 1978);

Claire McGlinchee, *James Russell Lowell* (New York: Twayne, 1967);

E. S. Nadal, "London Recollections of Lowell," *Harper's Magazine*, 132 (1916): 366–372;

Dona Emilia Gayangos de Riaño, "Mr. Lowell and his Spanish Friends," *Century*, 60 (1900): 292–293;

George W. Smalley, "Mr. Lowell in England," *Harper's Magazine*, 92 (1896): 788–801;

William Sommers, "James Russell Lowell as Minister to Spain," *State*, 337 (November 1989): 20–23, 30–31;

Sommers, "James Russell Lowell as U.S. Minister to Great Britain," *State*, 337 (October 1990): 27–30, 67;

Charles Oran Stewart, *Lowell and France* (Nashville, Tenn.: Vanderbilt University Press, 1951).

Papers:

The Houghton Library at Harvard University in Cambridge, Massachusetts, houses the largest collection of Lowell's papers and manuscripts. Other major collections are located at the Berg Collection, New York Public Library; the Hispanic Society, New York City; the Library of Congress; the Massachusetts Historical Society; the National Archives, Washington, D.C.; and the University of Virginia.

Frederick Albion Ober
(13 February 1849 – 31 May 1913)

Alan Spearman
University of North Carolina at Chapel Hill

BOOKS: *Camps in the Caribbees: The Adventures of a Naturalist in the Lesser Antilles* (Boston: Lee & Shepard / New York: C. T. Dillingham, 1880 [i.e. 1879]; Edinburgh: D. Douglas, 1880);

Dungeness, General Greene's Sea-Island Plantation (Philadelphia: Lippincott, 1880);

Young Folks' History of Mexico (Boston: Estes & Lauriat, 1883); republished as *Popular History of Mexico* (Boston: Estes & Lauriat, 1894);

The Silver City: A Story of Adventure in Mexico (Boston: D. Lothrop, 1883); augmented and republished as *John North in Mexico, A Story of the Silver City* (Boston: D. Lothrop, 1892);

Travels in Mexico and Life among the Mexicans (Boston: Estes & Lauriat, 1884 [i.e., 1883]);

Mexican Resources: A Guide to and through Mexico (Boston: Estes & Lauriat, 1884);

The Knockabout Club in the Everglades: The Adventures of the Club in Exploring Lake Okechobee (Boston: Estes & Lauriat, 1887);

Montezuma's Gold Mines (Boston: D. Lothrop, 1888);

The Knockabout Club in the Antilles and Thereabouts (Boston: Estes & Lauriat, 1888), also published as *A Boy's Adventures in the West Indies* (Boston: Estes & Lauriat, 1888);

The Knockabout Club in Spain (Boston: Estes & Lauriat, 1889), also published as *Rambles in Sunny Spain* (Boston: Estes & Lauriat, 1889);

Winter Resorts in Southern Seas, Reached by the New York, Bermuda, and West India Mail Steamship Lines of the Quebec S.S. Co.: A Guide to Bermuda, Porto Rico, and the Windward West India Islands (N.p.: Quebec S.S., 188?);

The Knockabout Club in North Africa (Boston: Estes & Lauriat, 1890);

The Knockabout Club on the Spanish Main (Boston: Estes & Lauriat, 1891), also published as *Adventures on the Spanish Main* (Boston: Estes & Lauriat, 1891);

The Knockabout Club in Search of Treasure (Boston: Estes & Lauriat, 1892);

In the Wake of Columbus: Adventures of the Special Commissioner Sent by the World's Columbian Exposition to the West Indies (Boston: D. Lothrop, 1893);

Josephine, Empress of the French (New York: Merriam / H. M. Caldwell, 1895; London: Unwin, 1901);

My Spanish Sweetheart: An International Romance (New York: F. T. Neely, 1897);

Under the Cuban Flag; or, The Cacique's Treasure (Boston: Estes & Lauriat, 1897; London: D. Nutt, 1898);

Crusoe's Island: A Bird Hunter's Story (New York: Appleton, 1898);

Puerto Rico and Its Resources (New York: Appleton, 1899);

Spain (New York: Appleton, 1899);

The Storied West Indies (New York: Appleton, 1900);

The Last of the Arawaks: A Story of Adventure on the Island of San Domingo (Boston & Chicago: W. A. Wilde, 1901);

Tommy Foster's Adventures among the Southwest Indians (Philadelphia: Henry Altemus, 1901);

For Prey and Spoils; or, The Boy Buccaneer (Philadelphia: Henry Altemus, 1902);

The Navy Boys' Cruise with Columbus: The Adventures of Two Boys Who Sailed with the Great Admiral in his Discovery of America (New York: Burt, 1903); also published as *A Voyage with Columbus: A Story of Two Boys Who Sailed with the Great Admiral in 1492* (New York: Burt, 1903);

"Old Put" the Patriot (New York: Appleton, 1904);

Our West Indian Neighbors: The Islands of the Caribbean Sea, "America's Mediterranean": Their Picturesque Features, Fascinating History, and Attractions for the Traveler, Nature-Lover, Settler and Pleasure-Seeker (New York: J. Pott, 1904);

The War Chiefs: A Story of the Spanish Conquerors in Santo Domingo (New York: Dutton, 1904);

Hernando Cortés, Conqueror of Mexico (New York & London: Harper, 1905);

Pizarro and the Conquest of Peru (New York & London: Harper, 1906);

Columbus the Discoverer (New York & London: Harper, 1906);

Ferdinand De Soto and the Invasion of Florida (New York & London: Harper, 1906);

Vasco Nuñez de Balboa (New York & London: Harper, 1906);

In King Philip's War: A Story of Two Boys Captured by the Great Sachem (New York: Burt, 1907);

Ferdinand Magellan (New York & London: Harper, 1907);

Amerigo Vespucci (New York & London: Harper, 1907);

John and Sebastian Cabot (New York & London: Harper, 1908);

Juan Ponce de Leon (New York & London: Harper, 1908);

A Guide to the West Indies and Bermudas (New York: Dodd, Mead, 1908; London: Unwin, 1908); revised and republished as *A Guide to the West Indies, Bermuda and Panama* (New York: Dodd, Mead, 1913);

With Osceola in Florida: Being the Adventures of Two Boys in the Seminole War in 1835 (New York: Burt, 1908);

Sir Walter Raleigh (New York & London: Harper, 1909).

OTHER: George N. Lawrence, "Catalogue of the Birds of Dominica from Collections Made for the Smithsonian Institution by Frederick A. Ober, Together with His Notes and Observations," includes material by Ober, in *Proceedings of the United States National Museum* (Washington, D.C., 1879), pp. 48–69;

Lawrence, "Catalogue of the Birds of St. Vincent, from Collections Made by Mr. Fred. A. Ober, Under the Directions of the Smithsonian Institution, with His Notes Thereon," includes material by Ober, in *Proceedings of the United States National Museum* (Washington, D.C., 1879), pp. 185–198;

Lawrence, "Catalogue of the Birds of Antigua and Barbuda, from Collections Made for the Smithsonian Institution, by Mr. Fred. A. Ober, with His Observations," includes material by Ober, in *Proceedings of the United States National Museum* (Washington, D.C., 1879), pp. 232–242;

Lawrence, "Catalogue of the Birds of Grenada, from a Collection Made by Mr. Fred. A. Ober for the Smithsonian Institution, Including Others Seen by Him, But Not Obtained," includes material by Ober, in *Proceedings of the United States National Museum* (Washington, D.C., 1879), pp. 265–278;

Lawrence, "Catalogue of the Birds Collected in Martinique by Mr. Fred. A. Ober for the Smithsonian Institution," includes material by Ober, in *Proceedings of the United States National Museum* (Washington, D.C., 1879), pp. 349–360;

Lawrence, "Catalogue of a Collection of Birds Obtained in Guadeloupe for the Smithsonian Institution by Mr. Fred. A. Ober," includes material by Ober, in *Proceedings of the United States National Museum* (Washington, D.C., 1879), pp. 449–462;

Lawrence, "A General Catalogue of the Birds Noted from the Islands of the Lesser Antilles Visited by Mr. Fred. A. Ober; with a Table Showing Their Distribution, and Those Found in the United States," includes material by Ober, in *Proceedings of the United States National Museum* (Washington, D.C., 1879), pp. 486–488;

"Ornithological Exploration of the Caribee Islands," in *Annual Report of the Board of Regents of the Smithsonian Institution for the Year 1878* (Washington, D.C., 1879), pp. 446–451;

"The New Winter Resorts," in *Southern Winter Resorts,* by Ober and F. H. Taylor (New York: Railway & General Printing, 1888);

Brantz Mayer, *Mexico, Central America and West Indies,* edited by Ober (Philadelphia: J. D. Morris, 1907).

SELECTED PERIODICAL PUBLICATIONS–UNCOLLECTED: "Camping among the Seminoles," as Fred Beverly, *Wildlife in Florida* series, *Forest and Stream,* 1 (6 & 13 November 1873);

"A Semi-Tropical Paradise," as Beverly, *Wildlife in Florida* series, *Forest and Stream,* 1 (20 November 1873);

"Shooting at Salt Lake," as Beverly, *Wildlife in Florida* series, *Forest and Stream,* 1 (27 November 1873);

Our Okeechobee Expedition series, as Beverly, *Forest and Stream,* 2 (12 February–7 May 1874);

"Three Months in Florida for a Hundred Dollars," as Beverly, *Forest and Stream,* 3 (8 October 1874);

"In the Wake of Columbus," *National Geographic,* 5 (1894): 187–196;

"Aborigines of the West Indies," in *Proceedings of the American Antiquarian Society,* 9, new series (1895): 270–313.

In *Camps in the Caribbees: The Adventures of a Naturalist in the Lesser Antilles* (1880), lamenting the disorder and lack of cleanliness of the culinary facili-

THE ISLAND OF COCOA PALMS.

Frontispiece for Camps in the Caribbees: The Adventures of a Naturalist in the Lesser Antilles *(1880), Ober's first travel book*

ties in one of his rustic campsites on the island of Dominica, Frederick Albion Ober notes:

> Occasionally the thought obtrudes itself, "They do not have things like this in the States." This often makes me sad, but I raise my eyes, perhaps, and look out over the green slope, down upon the valley bursting with palms, and beyond the hills to the peaceful sea smiling in the sunshine; and I exult in the thought that these enjoyments far outweigh the little annoyances I have described.

His prolific output indicates that travel did indeed provide Ober with abundant recompense for inconveniences and difficulties of all sorts. His voluminous works, in turn, provide readers with an interesting window on a fascinating period of American history. Ober's voice was that of a man never uncertain about the role America and Americans should play as, after a brief phase of isolationism, expansionist impulses were reawakening in the nation and its role as a world power was emerging.

Ober was born in Beverly, Massachusetts, on 13 February 1849. Remaining records concerning his early life are scanty, but it is known that he was seventh in direct line of descent from Richard Ober, who came from England and settled on a royal land grant north of Salem in the vicinity of Mackerel Cove (later Beverly) in 1663. The generations that succeeded this first immigrant remained in northern coastal Massachusetts, where Frederick's father

made his living in the mercantile and manufacturing trades. Young Frederick attended the Beverly public schools, but because of family financial difficulties he was able to do so for only a short time before he had to go out and earn his keep.

Despite this early setback to his formal education, the boy displayed a precocious interest in natural history. In particular he manifested an adolescent fascination with birds that was ultimately to shape his career. On his own he proceeded to become quite knowledgeable about the local avifauna, and he began to acquire and to develop a collection of skins and mounted specimens of birds. Nevertheless, in his early teens Ober seemed condemned to obscurity and lack of opportunity in the learned world. Much of his subsequent effort was employed to lay away this early sense of limitation and of artificially imposed boundaries.

The commencement of the Civil War, however, did little to brighten the prospects of the fledgling ornithologist; circumstances forced the young man to support himself by practical means. In 1862, when he was thirteen, he went into business and worked until 1866 as a shoemaker—certainly an important, though not glamorous, occupation during the war. During these obscure and difficult years, though, he was able to accumulate a small nest egg, and he enrolled himself in the Massachusetts Agricultural College. He attended, however, for only a single term before once again being forced to leave due to lack of funds. From 1867 until the end of the decade he was back in the working world, first as an employee in a drugstore and then once again as a shoemaker.

The beginning of the 1870s did, however, bring several changes that initially must have seemed positive and, in any case, caused reverberations that would last throughout the rest of his life. In 1870 he married Lucy Curtis of Wenham, Massachusetts, but their happiness was short-lived; the new bride died only a few months after the marriage. Despite this loss and the burden of his occupations, Ober did find time to devote to independent study of natural history; by 1872 his collection of stuffed and mounted specimens of Massachusetts birds had attracted the attention of noted scientist Alexander Aggasiz, who arranged for its purchase by the Museum of Natural History at Harvard University. The translation of his collection into more-august confines was Ober's first important intellectual and professional acknowledgment. He was now on his way toward putting his avocation to work and beginning his career as an ornithological explorer and collector.

By late 1872 Ober had accumulated sufficient resources to allow him to gratify his taste for travel (and perhaps to escape from a home that was proving emotionally inhospitable). With the proceeds of the sale of his collections, supplemented by sponsorships from the Smithsonian Institution and *Forest and Stream* magazine, Ober made his way to the wilds of southern Florida. In search of new and unusual birds, he penetrated regions of the state that then were pristine wilderness. Using the pseudonym Fred Beverly, he produced two series of articles on his Florida explorations for *Forest and Stream* in which he detailed his reactions to Lake Okeechobee and the "river of grass" that was the Everglades.

As a result of the success of this enterprise, the Smithsonian commissioned him to collect birds in the southern West Indies. For two years, from 1876 until 1878, Ober pursued a series of highly successful explorations throughout the Lesser Antilles, where he discovered and described twenty-two new species of birds. Two of these species, the *Icterus oberi* (the Montserrat oriole) and the *Myiarchus oberi* (the Lesser Antillean flycatcher), bear his name. He summarized the results of his first Antillean explorations in "Ornithological Exploration of the Caribbee Islands," which appeared in the first *Annual Report of the Board of Regents of the Smithsonian Institution for the Year 1878* (1879). This first publication is also of interest as an early example of his travel writing, for many of the qualities and characteristics of

Ober's later work are observable in the brief compass of the six-page article. Combined with the series of detailed catalogues of West Indian birds compiled by Ober's colleague George N. Lawrence—but which resulted from Ober's work and incorporated his notes and correspondence verbatim—it reveals many of the ideas and themes that would inform Ober's writings for the next forty years.

Although they are ostensibly ornithological and first and foremost scientific, the emphasis in these works is on the difficulties of exploration and mastery of the unfamiliar and dangerous environment. In "Ornithological Exploration of the Caribbee Islands," for instance, Ober interjects accounts of his frustration at being stuck on a reef, of his prostration by fever and contraction of a severe cold, and of a "terrible serpent" peculiar to Dominica and Saint Lucia which caused him "much trouble." In the midst of descriptions of birds he details his methods of proceeding and interacting with the natives, and unsurprisingly he presents himself as in charge of affairs. He often oversees the legwork of others; but it is difficult to sympathize with him as he laments being forced to make a two-day journey on foot while his "mountaineer friends" (three native girls and a man) transport all his baggage—over mountains and across swollen streams—on their heads.

In the first of the seven bird catalogues which appeared in the first volume of the *Proceedings of the United States National Museum* in 1879, Lawrence includes extensive excerpts from Ober's correspondence that describe the landscape and physical features of the island of Dominica. Ober's communication affords the scientific reader glimpses of blue-throated hummingbirds "flitting about in the dark forest, where a gleam of light would penetrate" and where "diminutive insects sport in [a] ray of dusky light." In his accounts of his methods of acquisition he includes a vignette of "little mountain boys" capturing hummingbirds with native birdlime made from the juice of breadfruit trees, and he includes local legends associated with avifauna (such as the "soleil-coucher" bird) and their names. He documents changes occurring in the landscape, such as the abandonment of small farms on many of the islands, as well as practices—such as the market-gunning of plovers on Saint Vincent—which are now things of the past.

The romantic and the sentimental are never far from the surface of Ober's prose; in the Saint Vincent catalogue, for instance, he describes the slope of the central volcano as a "lonely and beautiful spot . . . rendered more enchanting by the singularly melodious notes of a bird [the "invisible souf-

A GROUP OF GAMINS.

CARIB TYPE

MARKET WOMAN.

Illustrations from Camps in the Caribbees

friere bird"], an inhabitant of those upper solitudes." It is not surprising that Ober's accounts lack the objectivity aspired to by the modern ethologist; but his lack of "scrupulosity" was noted by some of his colleagues even in his own day. In almost all his accounts of birds, the scientific is shot through with the subjective and the anthropomorphized. In his description of an endemic blackbird of Grenada, for example, he paints the *Quiscalus luminosus* as "social, gregarious, seeming to delight in company, spending a great part of the day in sportive play." These birds, Ober suggests, "give utterance to a joyous cry, as though giving thanks for the enjoyment" afforded them by a drink of water from a small pool. Less fortunate in Ober's eyes are the island's "poor Anis"; he finds them to be the "same stupid unsuspicious bird everywhere."

Furthermore, some of the prejudices that recur in his later works make their first appearances in these journal entries. As he discusses his attempts to collect an owl known to the natives of Antigua as the "Jumbie bird," he begins lamenting the shortcomings of the darker, "less enlightened" races. The Jumbie bird, Ober writes, has a "hoot [that] strikes terror into the stoutest heart"; "the blacks," he says, "declare that it will not hesitate to tear the eyes out of any individual unfortunate enough to meet it at night. 'Me rudder see de Debbil, any time', is their forcible way of testifying to the powers, supernatural and otherwise, possessed by this . . . Owl." In his account of another owl on Grenada, he writes picturesquely of its lonesome habitations, the "towers of ancient wind-mills, which, in various stages of ruin and dilapidation, are going to decay." These stone towers, he says, are "generally covered with ivy and running vines" and are thus "excellent places of abode for the owl." He adds that "there is rarely a ruin without its occupant to frighten the negroes to the verge of insanity with its nocturnal hootings." Though the owls are (at least aurally) conspicuous, Ober has had little success in collecting a specimen. He laments, "From a superstitious dread of the 'Jumbie bird,' and from the fact that these mills are well hung with the nests of 'Jack Spaniard'—a wasp, it is difficult to get a negro to climb into a tower to dislodge the owl." Ober says all this without the slightest trace of irony.

In the catalogues as a whole, Lawrence preserves much of Ober's anecdotal material, and he hails the explorer as a model of industry and perseverance. Ober, he says in the Dominica catalogue, is to be commended for having his "heart in the enterprise." And the scientific articles read almost like travel accounts with kernels of adventure stories thrown in for good measure. Already Ober was creating a persona, positioning himself at the center of any enterprise as the representative of order and civilization.

As so often happened in the nineteenth century, a travel work resulted from another professional decision: in 1880 *Camps in the Caribbees,* the first of Ober's travel books per se, was published, a by-product of his cataloguing expeditions. In his preface Ober explains its origins, noting that in 1876, "under the auspices of the Smithsonian Institution, I undertook the exploration of these islands with the especial view of bringing to light their ornithological treasures." For two years he visited "mountains, forests, and people" in Dominica, Saint Vincent, Barbuda, Antigua, Guadeloupe, Martinique, Grenada, and the Grenadines "that few if any tourists have reached before." Noting that other travel writers had "never penetrated beyond the line of civilization" and have often reported secondhand information, he prided himself on leaving the beaten path of travel and taking to the woods. He intended, he says, to "tak[e] readers to the forest, where everything reposes in nearly the same primitive simplicity and freshness as when it was discovered by Columbus, nearly four centuries ago."

Camps in the Caribbees is, of course, far more than simply an account of a bird-collecting expedition, although the reader familiar with the articles he produced for the Smithsonian will recognize much of their substance in the book. Ober aimed at creating a work of popular, general interest, and he is decidedly eclectic. He moves from discussion of the various branches of natural history to social history to social criticism with alacrity. This penchant for rambling, which he acknowledges, is also present in his style: "Now and then, in following a thread of history that connects these islands and people with an almost forgotten past, I have availed myself of the language of the historian, but in rare instances." Such circumstances are, of course, not rare in *Camps in the Caribbees*. The discontinuity and elasticity of the genre of travel writing seem to suit Ober perfectly; they allow him to indulge his collector's impulse. Ober rarely, it seems, saw the need to throw away any information in individual works, and over the course of his career he always seemed to be able to reach into his past and find a previously used detail or a story to flesh out a paragraph or a chapter. Each of Ober's works tends to become an accumulation of his thoughts and experiences.

Reception of *Camps in the Caribbees* was generally favorable. The reviewer for the 29 January 1880 issue of *The Nation* noted:

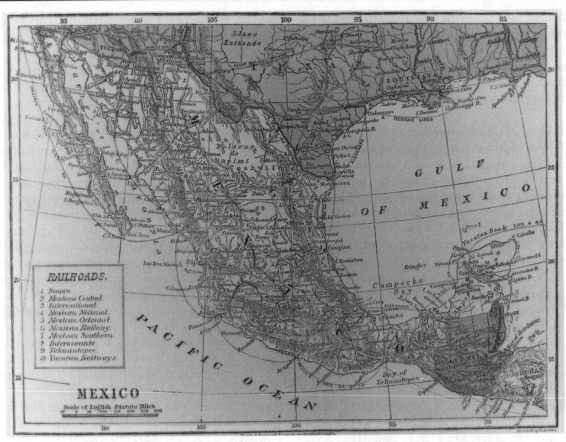

Map of railways in Ober's Travels in Mexico and Life among the Mexicans *(1884)*

Though not at all exhaustive in the topics upon which he touches, he has succeeded in making an interesting work. . . . Mingled with the stories of adventures are descriptions of scenery and comprehensive notes on the plants, the birds, and the Caribs. Some space is devoted to early history and antiquities, and an enjoyable chapter to the home of the Empress Josephine and its surroundings. The primary object of the expedition being a collection of birds, these receive a great deal of well-bestowed attention.

Already, however, early reviews were calling into question the "scientific pretensions" of the work. The same reviewer for *The Nation* detected a "degree of credulity and recklessness in statement not always to be harmonized with the demands of science."

In 1880 Ober returned briefly to the Lesser Antilles on a second collecting expedition. Spurred by an abiding interest in the American past, he also found time to write a thirty-two-page pamphlet on Dungeness, the Cumberland Island plantation of Gen. Nathanael Greene, the ruins of which are one of the most noteworthy historical sites along the Georgia coast. In 1881 Ober journeyed farther

afield to Mexico, where he changed focus somewhat and spent most of his time not in pursuit of ornithological treasures but in visits to sites of archaeological significance. This nine-month sojourn set the stage for most of his activities in the first half of the decade, and he returned to the land south of the border in 1883 and in 1885. His Mexican travels first bore literary fruit in the 1883 publication of the *Young Folks' History of Mexico* and of the novel *The Silver City: A Story of Adventure in Mexico* that same year.

This first foray into the field of adventure fiction concerns the adventures of John North, a thinly veiled reconstruction of Ober himself. John is "a New England boy nineteen years old, coast born and farm bred," who, long ago seduced by the romance of travel books such as those detailing the voyages of Captain Cook, has been commissioned by an unnamed scientific institution to go to Mexico and search for unknown birds. Instead of his native thrushes and swallows, he will now be collecting birds such as the exotic chachalaca and the strange and beautiful ocellated turkey; and he is indeed well fitted for the task. "John," Ober writes, "was a good shot. His long collecting practice in the New England woods had perfected his aim. The neighbors had always said that when John North sighted a bird over a gun barrel, it was as good as dead." This search for birds will be combined with a quest for adventures that will prove his manhood; but most important, it will allow him to search for his father, who disappeared in the jungles of the Yucatan years ago.

Like all of Ober's protagonists and projections of self, John North carries with him a sense of mission and sense of himself, as an American, as privileged and different. At one point in the novel Ober calls attention to the innate and obvious superiority of North and his fellow countrymen to those who held dominion over much of Latin America: "It was one thing to be a Spaniard, quite another to be a North American."

This work, like Ober's ornithological essays, shares many of the features that characterize his travel writing. The narrative of *The Silver City* moves swiftly, but the pace slows from time to time to allow Ober to expatiate on the features of the landscape or on some peculiar natural phenomenon. While it does include material of "scientific pretensions," there are also departures from the truth for the sake of sensation; at one critical moment, for instance, Ober introduces vampire bats as big as pigeons into the story. On a more important level, though, in *The Silver City* Ober underscores several important leitmotivs. At one point early in the work Ober's protagonist looks toward the exotic landscape of the Yucatan, and "with his heart in his eyes" he wonders: "For a moment all was illusion. Could these beautiful white gleaming walls," he asks himself, "be the walls of the Silver City? It was but for a moment. He sat down, smiling at himself for a romantic boy instead of a sensible traveler. Did not the book say the Silver City was far inland?" Aside from suggesting the near-sacred significance of the book as a repository of knowledge, wisdom, and truth, this passage reflects the nearness of the "sensible" and the "romantic" in even the best traveler's psyche. During a long career Ober acknowledged and exploited this proximity.

In 1884 Ober published *Travels in Mexico and Life among the Mexicans,* a weighty tome that purports to be "an impartial view of the present state of Mexico." The work commences, as did his travels, in the Yucatan, moving on to central and southern Mexico and ending with an account of the railway journeys in the border states of both Mexico (Sonora and Chihuahua) and the United States (Texas, New Mexico, and Arizona). He said his intention was to create a wide scope for the book and to include nearly every topic he imagined his audience might find interesting–people, customs, historical references, antiquities, and productions. This goal was an ambitious one, and he attacked it energetically and enthusiastically.

His zeal to fill so many requirements, however, sometimes worked to his disadvantage. The first chapter may be taken as illustrative of some of the shortcomings of Ober's style and approach. He often meanders among scientific facts and economic figures, snippets of history, and firsthand observation of local customs. The impression of disorder is often complicated by the fact that Ober often recycles observations and opinions of previous writers, sometimes with attribution and sometimes without. The effect at times of Ober's attempt at being comprehensive is kaleidoscopic and dizzying, and the work is best when he concentrates upon chronicling those incidental occurrences and happenings along the way. The most interesting parts of *Travels in Mexico* are to be found in details such as his description of an impromptu wild-turkey shoot; in glimpses of dark-eyed senoritas in a festive ballroom; in the story of hearing the news of the assassination of President James Garfield; and in his account from the state of Chihuahua of a "diminutive dog, so small that it leaves nothing to be desired, and so intelligent that it never barks and rarely bites." Sadly, though, the reader must often wade through a lot of murky detail to find these bright places.

In addition to relating the "fascinating story of [Mexico's] history as it is interwoven with scenes visited," Ober also highlights "the wonderful development now taking place through the agency of the millions of American capital invested in railway construction and the exploitation of mines." His agenda of capitalistic expansion is clear. In the preface of *Travels in Mexico* he hails progressive American enterprise; a conviction of the basic laziness and shiftlessness of the darker races underlies his belief in a liberal interpretation of that expansionist doctrine. "As soon as the Border is crossed," he says, "you are impressed with the difference between American energy and Mexican thriftlessness." He castigates Mexicans who mistrust and fear the encroachment of American railroad lines into their traditional farming and grazing lands: "Here, as at Monterey, the 'Greaser' makes his feeble protest against the inevitable advance; he cannot block the wheels of the engine, but he can annoy the engineer." Throughout the text he includes several engravings so "one may trace the extension of our vast system of railways towards its ultimate destination, the continent of South America." Of particular interest along these same lines are his vituperations against those Indian tribes that resisted settlement onto the reservations. He looks forward with satis-

CATHEDRAL AND PLAZA.

THE GREAT KATUNES.

Illustrations of the cathedral of Merida and the katunes, or calendar stones, of Aké, from Travels in Mexico

faction to the extermination of the Chiricahua Apache, a people he deems altogether savage and irreclaimable.

Travels in Mexico was regarded by contemporary reviewers as a sumptuous entry into a field already crowded with other recently published books about Mexico. The reviewer for the 17 April 1884 issue of *The Nation* found Ober's accuracy in comparison with many of these works to be "highly commendable" but was a bit more guarded about the finer points of execution: "The style is not always as clear as one could wish, and sometimes drops into vulgarisms . . . but the whole is smooth and varied." Soon after the lengthy *Travels in Mexico,* Ober published *Mexican Resources: A Guide to and through Mexico* (1884), a commercial complement of its predecessor. Full of railroad maps, train schedules, import instructions, domestic products, and cultural information, it comprises all that the interested North American free-enterprise capitalist might need to establish commercial ties in Mexico and exploit its bountiful resources.

From 1887 to 1892 Ober traveled widely. He had decided to concentrate on documenting the beginnings of the European presence in America, and accordingly in 1888 he went to Spain and North Africa in pursuit of his interest in sites and artifacts dealing with the European conquest. Firsthand acquaintance with the mother country of the Spanish conquistadores and with the homeland of the Moors (whose impression upon Spanish-American civilization intrigued him) was necessary, he felt, for the

conscientious historian. In 1889 he returned from the Old World and traveled in northern South America; and in 1890 he made his way once again to the West Indies. All during this time Ober was making his living from his writings; he had income from the sales of his books and of articles he wrote for popular journals, and he supplemented it with the sale of occasional pieces to newspapers in towns through which he was traveling. His writing was fluent, and his career was approaching its apogee. Misfortune, however, continued to dog his personal life. In the early 1890s Ober married for a second time, but Jean McCloud, the new bride, died shortly after the marriage.

During this tempestuous period Ober poured some of his energy into the writing of six volumes of children's stories, which appeared as the adventures of the "Knockabout Club." Each book took a group of mettlesome young chaps out into a world of high adventure, always along trails Ober himself had blazed (and written about) before. The first of these tales was *The Knockabout Club in the Everglades: The Adventures of the Club in Exploring Lake Okechobee.* It appeared in 1887, and the rest followed apace—*The Knockabout Club in the Antilles and Thereabouts* in 1888, *The Knockabout Club in Spain* in 1889, *The Knockabout Club in North Africa* in 1890, *The Knockabout Club on the Spanish Main* in 1891, and finally *The Knockabout Club in Search of Treasure* in 1892. Also during this time Ober produced a couple of pamphlets—*Winter Resorts in Southern Seas, Reached by the New York, Bermuda, and West India Mail Steamship Lines of the Quebec S.S. Co.: A*

Guide to Bermuda, Porto Rico, and the Windward West Indies Islands (188?) and a section of *Southern Winter Resorts* (1888)—for companies beginning to exploit the developing market for vacation excursions to the Caribbean.

In late 1890 Ober interrupted a series of lectures he was delivering to audiences around the country to accept an appointment as one of the U.S. special commissioners for the approaching World's Columbian Exposition. Officially he was in charge of ornithological exhibits, but the appointment allowed him to do much more than simply go on another collecting expedition; it authorized him to recruit the participation of the islands of the Caribbean in the celebration of the anniversary of Christopher Columbus's discovery and to bring back Carib Indians of pure blood for presentation at the Exposition. From 1892 to 1893 he reexplored routes he had already traveled, visited places associated with Columbus, and built collections not only of ornithological specimens but also of any and every relic of the discovery that he could scavenge. His travels are chronicled in *In the Wake of Columbus: Adventures of the Special Commissioner Sent by the World's Columbian Exposition to the West Indies* (1893). "In this work," he said,

> I aim to present what may be termed the environment of the Admiral; giving scenes with which he was identified, starting with the inception of the enterprise in Spain, carrying the action across the Atlantic to the first landfall, through the Bahamas to Cuba, thence to the scene of the first wreck and the first fort, on the coast of Haiti, the first settlement at Isabella, the initial attempts at discovery in Española, showing where the first gold was found and the first cities started—in fact, following him through all his voyages, writing every description from personal observation, and using the historical events merely as a golden thread upon which to string the beads of this Columbian rosary.

Along the way he investigates such questions as the exact location of Columbus's first landfall and the whereabouts of the explorer's remains, but he does not stick to "hard history"; he allows himself, for instance, an imaginative reconstruction of what the first Christmas celebration in the New World must have been like. *In the Wake of Columbus* is one of Ober's most organized and readable works. He is to some degree limited by someone else's itinerary, and the "golden thread" of the historical events upon which he strings his "literary beads" turns out to be a helpful restraining device.

During his travels he describes with surprise and chagrin any failure to provide aid and cooperation; usually it is the "very intelligent" foreigners (that is, Americans and Britons) who recognize the public benefit and utility of the enterprise and are eager to be of assistance. In this vein he is able to digress for several chapters about a favorite subject—the decline of Haitian civilization. The Haitians, he suggests, are models of laziness, squalor, improvidence, and thriftlessness. Just like the island of Martinique, the republic of Toussaint L'Ouverture is doomed, he thinks, as a result of "black inundation." He does, however, have kind words for the American minister to Haiti, Frederick Douglass. He finds Douglass impressive: "I had good opportunity for comparing this man who had risen to eminence through the force of innate ability and integrity, with those who represented the best products of the Haitian civilization."

Ober recognized early the tug of the romantic. In *In the Wake of Columbus* Ober's stance as a "sensible traveler" is sometimes lost as he indulges in the "romantic nostalgia" of the cultural primitivist. On the island of Saba, for instance, he envies "the primitive simplicity in which man lived and carried on the cultivation of the earth." He thinks the natives "are to be envied, for they are in perpetual possession of the pleasures of childhood—these small gardens being scarcely more than the little spots tilled by children in other lands, and to which man in his memory continually reverts as to a time when he owned the riches of the earth." And Ober is far from being simply a hard-hearted collector of scientific specimens. After alluding to several island stories that point up the vanity of human wishes and the decline of once-noble families, he notes, "I often recur, with a pang of tender solicitude, to my feathered children [on Montserrat], flitting through the depths of the tropical forests . . . and pray that no harm may befall my beautiful *Icterus oberi.*"

After the 1893 Exposition, Ober seems to have taken few distinctly new directions. In 1895 he married Nellie F. McCartney, with whom he had two children; she lived until 1914, a year after his death. During his post-Exposition years Ober continued to revisit places associated with earlier books and travels and continued to recycle and reformat his accumulated knowledge and information. In 1895 he expanded a chapter from *Camps in the Caribbees* on the Martinique home of the future Empress Josephine into a full-length biography. As an historical work *Josephine, Empress of the French* finds little to recommend it; the critic for the January 1896 *American Historical Review* found it "historically worthless; it is a mere rhapsody of admiration . . . and reads more like a volume of devotions in honor of a saint than a sober biography." Attacking Ober's transports of admiration, he finds particularly ridiculous the account of the crayfish who, "bolder than the rest, sallied forth and nipped the future Empress' little toe, thinking—and rightly—that it was a *bonne-bouche* worth some risk to reach." (Ober even reused this incident in connection with another heroine in *The War Chiefs: A Story of the Spanish Conquerors in Santo Domingo,* a 1904 adventure novel.) *Josephine, Empress of the French* may, as the sober critic suggests, be read as interesting testimony to the then-current fascination with all things Napoleonic, but as anything else—history, romance—it is pretty hard going.

More historical romances followed, including *My Spanish Sweetheart: An International Romance* and *Under the Cuban Flag; or, The Cacique's Treasure,* both in 1897. This latter work is particularly interesting, for it once again shows how Ober was able to shuffle materials and genres. Like all his fictional works, *Under the Cuban Flag* is filled with stock characters, rather stilted dialogue, and predictable situations; the development is loosely linked and episodic, with frequent recourse to subplots (some of which are left hanging). It does, of course, make ample use of descriptions of landscapes and physical features that derive directly from his travel observations. In the course of the novel Ober takes his characters from the easternmost point of Cuba to the westernmost, and along the way he describes features of the landscape, such as the anvil-shaped mountain known as the "Yunque," in terms that could have been lifted verbatim from an earlier travel book.

Ober's familiar political and social agenda is much in evidence in *Under the Cuban Flag.* The work is quite clear in its support for the fledgling Nationalists in their struggle for independence from Spain, which is depicted as a power that would stifle the innate and inevitable drive of the Cubans to become productive, hardworking capitalists, just like their northern neighbors. The novel of romantic adventure thus afforded Ober an opportunity for composition much like that given him by the travel work. As he noted in *Camps in the Caribbees,* he was not averse to adding history to landscape where it seemed appropriate; to produce a work of historical fiction, he only had to vary the proportions and add landscape to history.

For Ober the century ended with the production of a cluster of varied works. The first of these, *Crusoe's Island: A Bird Hunter's Story* (1898), was his attempt to assemble textual evidence to prove that the real island upon which Robinson Crusoe was shipwrecked was not Juan Fernandez in the Pacific Ocean, but Tobago in the Caribbean Sea. Not forgetting his adolescent audience, he followed *Crusoe's Island* in 1899 with an history of Spain for young readers. Also in 1899 he produced *Puerto Rico and Its Resources,* a work much like a scaled-down version of his guide to Mexico in con-

ception and execution; it describes the island and its people and suggests ways to exploit the newly acquired territory, a sunny land of apparently limitless potential.

After the turn of the century Ober's career as writer of historical fiction for a juvenile audience continued. In 1901 appeared *The Last of the Arawaks: A Story of Adventure on the Island of San Domingo* and *Tommy Foster's Adventures among the Southwest Indians;* in 1902, *For Prey and Spoils; or, The Boy Buccaneer;* in 1903, *The Navy Boys' Cruise with Columbus: The Adventures of Two Boys who Sailed with the Great Admiral in his Discovery of America;* and in 1904, *"Old Put" the Patriot* and *The War Chiefs.* During this period he also wrote *The Storied West Indies* (1900) and *Our West Indian Neighbors: The Islands of the Caribbean Sea, "America's Mediterranean"* (1904)—both of which present the reader with point of view, detail, and anecdote familiar from earlier works.

By 1905 Ober turned to romantic re-creations of lives of important explorers. He began his Heroes of American History series that year with *Hernando Cortés, Conqueror of Mexico.* This work, like others in the series, is a recycling and popularization of previous scholarship; Ober's retellings added little to their subjects, and the critical reception of the series was often rough. Concerning the biography of Cortés, for instance, the critic for the 16 November 1905 *Dial* noted, "Readable it certainly is, to one who is not fastidious regarding the historical accuracy of the book he is reading." The review in the 14 October *Outlook,* however, was kinder; it recognized the work as a text that might engage the attention and imagination of younger readers: "However the telling is well enough, and the facts seem significant for the purpose in hand. Except for that purpose, the book strikes one as distinctly superfluous." Undeterred by such criticism, Ober followed *Hernando Cortés, Conqueror of Mexico* quickly with *Pizarro and the Conquest of Peru, Columbus the Discoverer, Ferdinand De Soto and the Invasion of Florida,* and *Vasco Nuñez de Balboa* in 1906, and with *Ferdinand Magellan* and *Amerigo Vespucci* in 1907. To top off this flurry of literary activity, Ober published *In King Philip's War: A Story of Two Boys Captured by the Great Sachem* in 1907.

In 1908 Ober entered the real estate business in Hackensack, New Jersey. However, his writing continued with little sign of interruption. For his last major production Ober returned to his roots and completed what remains perhaps his best-known work, *A Guide to the West Indies and Bermudas.* It first appeared in 1908 and was republished in 1913, the year of his death, in revised form as *A Guide to the West Indies, Bermuda and Panama.* By 1920 it had gone through three editions. The work is filled with the timetables and recommendations on drinking water that go into any successful guidebook; but once again the self-reflexive nature of Ober's enterprise is evident. "The West Indies are interesting," he declares, "because here American history, so far as it relates to the white race in these islands and in the Western Hemisphere, had its beginning." He says that the history he relates "is interesting, fascinating, having to do with the beginnings of history in this country, and with the deeds of great men whose lives have become part and parcel of that history, beginning with Columbus, and ending with the heroes of the Spanish-American War." Throughout the guidebook the author seems much more interested in identifying places where George Washington once worshiped or where Alexander Hamilton was born than he is with helping the visitor understand local cultures. Ober's preoccupation with energy and enterprise resurfaces; his emphasis once again rests upon what Americans can and should make out of these places.

The closing years of Ober's life were concerned with production of the final volumes of his Heroes of American History series. *John and Sebastian Cabot* and *Juan Ponce de Leon* came out in 1908; and *Sir Walter Raleigh* rounded out the list in 1909. And Ober's last children's book, *With Osceola in Florida: Being the Adventures of Two Boys in the Seminole War in 1835* (1908), quite fittingly returns its protagonist to the scenes of Ober's first excursions. Ober died on 31 May 1913.

The privations and limitations of Ober's early life, coupled with the losses he experienced in his young adulthood, seem to have conditioned both the form and substance of the books he produced over the more than forty years of his life as an author. In all of his works he presents a consistently articulated persona and a consistently advanced social and political agenda. His work allowed him to create a fictionalized persona as a self-taught, self-made, representative American. Throughout his books he emphasizes the sanctity of one's word of honor, courage in the face of adversity, the virtue and superiority of American enterprise, and a Kiplingesque sense of duty to maintain order and civilization in the face of almost inevitable foreign entropy and chaos. Ober's vision for America and Americans is, of course, clearly imperialistic.

His vision of his calling as an author may be seen to share important elements of this philosophy. Just as he had little tolerance for any barriers that might constrain the expansion of American enterprise abroad, he apparently saw little reason to feel personal constraint with regard to artificial boundaries between types of literature. At the outset of his career the natural commodiousness and elasticity of the travel book allowed Ober to follow what he considered his own genius. He blurred the lines between genres; he incorporated different styles and subjects into a wide variety of types of work. Ober poured a tremendous amount of energy into his enterprise and made the most of his efforts. One trip abroad could thus result in three or four books—a travel book per se, an historical work, an adventure novel, and perhaps a children's book. His ideals and his practice were consistent; for a writer as adamant in his sense of honor, duty, and mission as Ober, this fact would surely seem like high praise indeed.

Raphael Semmes

(27 September 1809 – 30 August 1877)

Anna E. Lomando
Pennsylvania State University, New Kensington

BOOKS: *Service Afloat and Ashore During the Mexican War* (Cincinnati: Moore, 1851); abridged as *The Campaign of General Scott, in the Valley of Mexico* (Cincinnati: Moore & Anderson, 1852);

Memoirs of Service Afloat During the War Between the States (Baltimore: Kelly, Piet, 1869); republished as *My Adventures Afloat: A Personal Memoir of My Cruises and Services on The Sumter and Alabama* (London: Bentley, 1869); republished as *Service Afloat; or, The Remarkable Career of the Confederate Cruisers Sumter and Alabama, During the War Between the States* (New York: P. J. Kenedy, 1869).

Although Raphael Semmes is best known for his success as the captain of a Confederate cruiser during the Civil War, the published records of his journeys on land and sea, during both that war and the Mexican War, have earned him the right to be included within the ranks of travel writers. Raphael Semmes was born on 27 September 1809 to middle-class Roman Catholic parents, Catherine Middleton Semmes and Richard Thompson Semmes, in Charles County, Maryland. Raphael was the elder of two surviving children (another died in infancy) born to this couple. His mother died before her third wedding anniversary, and his father died in 1823. Raphael and his brother Samuel went to live in Georgetown, D.C., with their uncle, also named Raphael Semmes. Although the boys made their home with the elder Raphael, they also visited with another uncle, Benedict Semmes, physician and delegate to the state house.

During his youth Semmes was taught by tutors, and for a time he attended Charlotte Hall Military Academy, located in Saint Mary's County. Like most of his educated contemporaries, Semmes read Latin and the classics, and he was introduced to science, a discipline that continued to fascinate him all his life.

Choosing a career was a challenge for Semmes. Drawn to the sea, he became a midshipman in the United States Navy in 1826. In the days before the establishment of the Naval Academy, young men—often adolescents—went to sea to learn their profession. Although they were taught math and navigation, frequently by a schoolmaster on the ship, the training was informal. Semmes sailed and studied while serving on a succession of ships from 1826 until he returned home in 1831 to study for the midshipman's exam. On 28 April 1832 he not only passed the exam but also ranked second in his class.

Because of the limited opportunities for advancement in the navy, Semmes also studied law. He took his law books to sea and continued his education on shore. He passed the bar in Maryland in

1834, but he did not practice law there. Instead he traveled to Ohio and boarded with Oliver and Electra Spencer. While in Cincinnati he represented and successfully defended two men who were alleged to have damaged a printing press owned by abolitionists. The prosecutor he defeated was Salmon Chase, who would later serve in Abraham Lincoln's cabinet as secretary of the treasury. This trial is emblematic of Semmes's later career in the Confederacy: like burning Yankee commercial vessels, defeating the abolitionists in an individual trial might bring him some personal glory but would do little to change the outcome of the conflict between opposing ideologies.

Semmes's law career was interrupted in March 1835 when the navy called him to serve aboard the *Constellation* on a tour to the Caribbean. On this voyage Semmes had the opportunity to visit Antigua and Jamaica after the 1833 Emancipation Act. He concluded that the effect of the act upon the trade and economy of the islands was negative. In fact Semmes seldom missed an opportunity to point out weaknesses in the social fabric of the countries to which he traveled. His social criticisms usually prompted a comparison with the culture and society of the South, a comparison in which the advantage usually went to the South.

In 1836, during the Second Seminole War, Semmes temporarily commanded the *Lieutenant Izard,* a small steamer, in Florida. He ran her aground, and although no charges were filed, his service in that war ended rather ignominiously. Semmes returned to the *Constellation;* at the end of his tour he was promoted to the rank of lieutenant and began six years of shore duty.

While boarding with the Spencers, Semmes fell in love with their daughter, Anne. Because her family were prominent Protestants, the Catholic Semmes must have been at some disadvantage as a suitor. Yet he and Anne were married in Christ's Church (Episcopal) in Cincinnati in May 1837. Shortly after the wedding Anne converted to Catholicism; she and Semmes went on to raise six children. Few personal details of Semmes's life are available—a fact lamented by biographer John M. Taylor. However, his professional life, especially his naval career, is well documented. Apparently Semmes had not yet made a firm commitment to a career choice, for after his marriage he continued both to practice law and to serve in the navy. Sent first to bases on the Florida coast and the Gulf of Mexico, Semmes was given a post in Pensacola in 1841. He purchased property in Baldwin County, Alabama, and settled in the Deep South.

Semmes received his first major command, the U.S.S. *Poinsett,* in 1843. Assigned to deliver a state department representative to Vera Cruz, he secured permission to accompany the official to Mexico City. Always an acute observer, Semmes spent his time studying the weather, topography, and native plants and animals. Later this knowledge would prove useful to him and his country during the Mexican War.

When that war began, Semmes was first officer on the *Porpoise,* which joined the U.S. naval squadron off Vera Cruz in 1846. Engaged in the blockade of Vera Cruz, Semmes learned much about command and seamanship from his contact with the naval squadron. Although attached to Commodore David Conner's staff, Semmes at first believed that the only opportunity presented by this conflict was for unrelieved tedium. Thus, he was pleased to be placed in command of the *Somers,* a small brig with a shady past—the first mutiny aboard an American ship had taken place on the *Somers* in December 1842—and an even murkier future. The weather proved more dangerous than the enemy, and Semmes's new command sank during a squall. More than half of the crew were lost, and Semmes found himself the subject of a board of inquiry. His conduct was determined to have been appropriate under the circumstances. Following this maritime disaster, Semmes was again assigned to Conner.

But opportunity for active service came again when Semmes became part of an artillery unit, made up of naval personnel, which used the heavy naval guns to aid in the assault on Vera Cruz. Semmes was placed in charge of a thirty-two-pounder. After the surrender Semmes, because of his familiarity with the country and the language, was sent to assist in the negotiations for the release of a midshipman, Clay Rogers, who had been captured during a reconnaissance mission and accused of spying. This assignment sent Semmes on a journey that did not end until he entered Mexico City with Gen. Winfield Scott's army; the trip provided him with the material for his first book of travels, *Service Afloat and Ashore During the Mexican War* (1851).

Semmes's well-written and entertaining book describes not only the war but also the country and its people. He begins with an astute if somewhat biased picture of the society. Obviously a subscriber to the theory of Manifest Destiny, he wastes little time telling his readers that the economic system in Mexico has produced a peasant class living in worse conditions than those of the slaves in the South. Although a devout Catholic, he observes that the church could do more for its people. He admires the clergy who minister to the daily spiritual needs but has little good to say about those who occupy the upper rungs of the hierarchy (whose concern for the sanctity of church prop-

The Alabama *engaged near Pico, one of the Western Islands (illustration from* Memoirs of Service Afloat During the War Between the States, *1869)*

erty blinds them to the needs of their congregation) or to the monks who, behind the walls of their monasteries, "live a life of indolence and ease."

If Semmes's view of Mexican society and culture seems less than objective, he more than compensates for it by his careful scientific descriptions of the landscape and climate of the country:

> the valley of Mexico is situated in the center of the great Cordillera of Anahuac, on a *plateau* of porphyriti and basaltic mountains, extending from N.N.W. to S.S.E. It is of oval shape, and about forty-six miles long, by thirty-two miles broad. . . . the circumference of the valley, reckoning from the crests of the surrounding mountains, is about 180 miles.

Despite the prosaic tone of this passage and the emphasis on detail, frequently Semmes's descriptions are poetic. After explaining that Mexico City appears completely isolated by the mountain range, Semmes continues to describe the valley:

> It thus presents the idea—when seen under favorable circumstances, in all its gorgeous beauty—of a sort of terrestrial paradise, from which the rest of the world has been carefully excluded by ramparts of impassable mountains; some of whose peaks are crowned with snow, and appear to watch over the beautiful valley like jealous sentinels. The city of . . . Mexico . . . sits like a queen upon her throne in the center of this beautiful valley.

Semmes, like other good travel writers, also gives the flavor of the land and its inhabitants. Much of this portion of the work is filled with dry humor, often at the expense of the natives. Semmes recalls

> being highly amused at the distinctions the simple natives drew at the door of the theater, to regulate the price of admission. The population was divided into two parts, the aristocrats and the plebeians; the former included those who wore shoes, and the latter those who went barefoot.

Semmes continued to be amused by the footwear of the natives. In Puebla he notes that "the great majority of the women of *Puebla* go barefoot! Even women well dressed, in other respects . . . may be seen tripping along with their bare feet on the cold flagstones, to mass." Semmes was also fascinated by the freedom of Mexican women to ride astride, smoke cigars, and entertain in dishabille. Yet Semmes admired these women; he describes how one mother and daughter nursed a wounded American officer until his death and then mourned him as though he were a family member. He praises their selfless devotion and the depth of their grief.

The greater portion of the book is devoted to the journey to rescue the midshipman Rogers—although Rogers appears not to have been in any grave danger for long and was freed mainly by his own exertions—and to the battles that Semmes observed while traveling with the army. From Semmes's initial land assignment with the naval battery outside the walls of Vera Cruz to his entrance into Mexico City he proves an able observer. His depictions of battles are relieved by his portrayals of the people and their customs. And his careful descriptions of these battles are augmented by explications of not only the results but also the complex causes for military decisions. For example, Semmes discusses the battle of Molino del Rey from General Scott's order to destroy the fortifications and suspected foundries to General Worth's careful implementation of those orders. Semmes details the costs and consequences of such decisions: "Although this bloody contest failed to effect the object intended by the commander-in-chief it . . . *broke the power of the enemy* more effectively than any other battle of the campaign."

Rewarded for his activity during the conflict by praise from both services, Semmes returned home. In January 1848 he assumed command of the *Electra*. Since the *Electra* was based in Pensacola, Semmes was able to remain close to home when the ship was in port. In spite of Semmes's almost ideal situation, Taylor reports that Semmes was homesick while at sea and complained about missing his son Spencer's tenth birthday. In June he requested shore duty and was given the position of inspector of provisions and clothing for the Pensacola naval yard. The Semmes family later relocated to Mobile to improve the educational opportunities for their children, and Semmes's career continued its plodding pace. In February 1849 he was given command of the *Flirt* and sent to patrol off the coast of Yucatán—an assignment Taylor believes he may have been given because of his fluency in Spanish. It appears that he was successful at gaining military intelligence.

From 1849 to 1851 Semmes was writing *Service Afloat and Ashore During the Mexican War* and attempting to develop a law practice. He made an adequate income from that practice, and his book sold well and earned him some critical attention. Taylor records that the *New York Tribune* and the *Charleston (S.C.) Standard* reviewed the book favorably. However, Semmes's military career was less successful. His requests for active duty were denied until 1855, when he was promoted to the rank of commander. In 1856 he was given the command of the mail steamer *Illinois*.

Semmes was made an inspector of lighthouses along the Gulf Coast in November 1856 and later was appointed secretary of the lighthouse board, discharging his duties with characteristic care and attention to detail. Meanwhile the relationship between the northern and southern states was deteriorating. Although an apologist for slavery, Semmes saw this struggle more in terms of economic, political, and cultural conflict between two societies—the industrial North and the agrarian South—that had shared few common bonds since their combined efforts had freed them from British rule. As he explains in his *Memoirs of Service Afloat During the War Between the States* (1869) Semmes believed that the major philosophical differences of the two sides could be traced to their British origins. He saw the Northerners as direct descendants of Oliver Cromwell's Puritans. For Semmes this meant a people—"Gloomy, saturnine, and fanatical"—who wanted freedom and religious tolerance for themselves, often at the expense of others. Southerners, Semmes claimed, were the heirs of the Cavaliers—a more civilized, tolerant, and cultivated group, imbued with romance and chivalry.

According to Semmes the struggle was precipitated by the Northern economic exploitation of the South. From Semmes's point of view the Constitution did not bind the South to the North irrevocably. Semmes believed in the Southern cause, and when he received a telegram on 14 February 1861 from C. M. Conrad of the Committee on Naval Affairs requesting that he return to Alabama, he resigned from the United States Navy the next day and left for Confederate headquarters in Montgomery on 16 February.

For his first assignment he was sent north to attempt to purchase war materials and hire skilled mechanics to help aid the imminent war effort. At first Semmes's overtures were accepted in the North, but by April 1861 it became evident that the federal government was becoming interested in these activities, and Semmes left for Montgomery. On 4 April 1861 Semmes arrived there; on 13 April, Sumter was fired upon.

Before the hostilities had begun Semmes had suggested that one way for the Confederate navy to injure the North was to commission privateers who would attack Northern commercial ships. His first opportunity to implement his plan came when a small steamer was about to be rejected for service. Semmes claimed the *Havana,* outfitted it, and renamed it the *Sumter* in honor of the recent victory. But the Union blockade proved an obstacle to his plans. Frustrated by both the blockade and the lack of cooperation from the Mississippi River pilots, Semmes waited for a chance to move out into the open sea. On 30 June 1861 the opportunity came.

For most of the war Semmes did not set foot on his native soil, and his record is astounding. He

Semmes aboard the Alabama *in Cape Town (Library of Congress)*

commanded two ships, the *Sumter* and the *Alabama.* Taylor reports that Semmes destroyed sixty vessels, bonded twelve, and had two recaptured and six returned to their owners by Spain. Never long on tact, Semmes was not a diplomat, but his legal background and his determined attitude helped him to secure provisions and limited support from the uneasy authorities at some neutral ports.

Semmes spent the war isolated from family, friends, and even the rest of the Confederate navy as he roamed the oceans. Often his latest news would be old newspapers taken from the ships he destroyed. At other times he would receive news when he refueled at a neutral port.

Semmes's voyages in the *Sumter* and the *Alabama,* as well as his return to a defeated South, are recorded in *Memoirs of Service Afloat During the War Between the States.* This book, unlike his first effort, is concerned mainly with his sea voyages. Written after the war ended, the book also includes his account of the causes of the war and his justification of the position of the South; it reveals Semmes as unreconciled to the fate of the South. Semmes's approach to his material is far more consciously literary in this book. He employs techniques to heighten the dramatic elements. For example, although he usually follows the chronological order of the events he depicts, when Semmes describes

the christening of the *Alabama,* he also foretells her fate:

> From the cradle to the grave there is but a step; and that I may group in a single picture, the christening and the burial of the ship, let the reader imagine, now, some two years to have rolled over—such a two years of carnage and blood, as the world had never before seen—and, strangely enough, another Sunday morning, equally bright and beautiful, to have dawned upon the *Alabama.* This is her funeral morning.

Semmes relates the outline of her final battle on 19 June 1864 and mentions the sad fate that awaited many of her crew. He concludes: "Such were the birth and death of the ship, whose adventures I propose to sketch in the following pages."

Semmes traces the path of the *Alabama* from her commission to her eventual destruction. As Semmes wreaked havoc upon the Northern shipping lines, he became increasingly famous or notorious, depending upon which side was recounting his exploits. He continually reminds his readers of the legality of his actions, but legal or not, his name became anathema to the North, and he was called a pirate, especially by the Northern press. The label rankled; Semmes saw himself as a naval officer following orders, never as operating outside the law.

But he did engage the Union navy. Usually he chose the wiser course and eluded them, but he did

Letter from Semmes to Raphael Semmes Kell that mentions the exploits of the
Alabama *(Michael Masters Collection)*

defeat the *Hatteras* in a brief but exciting episode on 11 January 1863. In reply to charges that the *Alabama* was a larger and more heavily armed ship, Semmes claimed in his book that the *Hatteras* "was a larger ship than the *Alabama* by one hundred tons." He also noted that they each carried eight guns and that their crews were almost equal in strength: "the crew of the *Hatteras* was 108 strong, that of the *Alabama* 110." After describing the positions of the ships during the battle, Semmes reports:

> My men handled their pieces with great spirit and commendable coolness, and the action was short and exciting while it lasted; which, however, was not very long for in *thirteen minutes* after firing the first gun, the enemy hoisted a light, and fired an off-gun, as a signal that he had been beaten.

Following his account of the battle, Semmes reproduces *Hatteras* captain Homer Blake's report and agrees that it is essentially correct. A modest hero, Semmes seems most proud that he was able, at night, to transfer the surviving crew of the *Hatteras* safely to the *Alabama* with no loss of life.

Semmes's emphasis on the code of behavior required of a Southern officer and a gentleman and his perception of the contrast between his conduct and that of the Northern officers is seen in his reference to the difference between his actions in the sinking of the *Hatteras* and those of John Winslow of the *Kearsarge* when the *Alabama* was sinking off Cherbourg. Semmes was convinced that Winslow was tardy in coming to the aid of his crew and was therefore responsible for many of the lives lost when the ship sank.

To the end Semmes was a romantic. Although most of his prisoners, and even Semmes himself, would characterize his crew as a rough lot, Semmes's description of their Sunday morning muster paints an idealized scene:

> We had some dandies on board . . . and . . . these gentlemen would move around the capstan, with the blackest and most carefully polished of pumps, and the whitest and finest of sinnot hats, from which would be streaming yards enough of ribbon, to make the ship a pennant.

Semmes was wounded during the final engagement of the *Alabama*. Rescued by the British yacht *Deerhound,* he was brought to safety in England. To recuperate he took a brief trip to the Continent that he barely mentions: "There reader! I have given you my European tour in a single paragraph; and as I am writing of the sea and of war, and not of the land, and of peace, this is all the space I can appropriate to it." In spite of Semmes's protests that this book was not meant to be a tour guide, he does describe the exotic wildlife of Pulo Condore, an island in the China Seas, and he occasionally is engaged by a scene of pastoral beauty such as this one:

> I was charmed with the appearance of Terceira. . . . The little town of Angra, abreast of which we were anchored, was a perfect picture of a Portuguese-Moorish town, with its red-tiled roofs, sharp gables, and particolored verandas and veranda curtains. And then the quiet and love-in-a-cottage air which hovered over the whole scene, so far removed from the highways of the world's commerce, and the world's alarms, was charming to contemplate.

Perhaps, as Semmes claimed, *Memoirs* is not a traditional travel book. Certainly the work is less focused on a single country and culture than Semmes's first effort was; indeed it covers the oceans of the world and permits the author to vary the tale of his adventures on the privateers *Sumter* and *Alabama* with descriptions of storms at sea, explanations of ocean currents and their effects, and portraits of some of the most exotic ports of the world and their equally exotic inhabitants. Because the focus of this book is primarily the justification of the Confederate efforts to cripple Northern commerce by the use of privateers, it is not surprising that the work did not receive the same critical ac-

claim as that which followed the publication of *Service Afloat and Ashore During the Mexican War.* However, *Memoirs* does what most good travel books do: it gives an understanding of a place that is foreign to the reader—in this case, life aboard a Confederate privateer.

In December 1865 Semmes was arrested on charges of having acted improperly by escaping after the surrender and sinking of the *Alabama,* but he was released by presidential order in April 1866. Initially barred from practicing law, he served briefly as the chair of moral philosophy and English literature at Louisiana State Seminary (now Louisiana State University) and as the editor of the *Memphis Bulletin,* both in 1867. In 1869 he opened a law practice with his son Oliver in Mobile, Alabama, where he lived until food poisoning from bad shrimp ended his life on 30 August 1877. He was buried the following day with high honors.

Biographies:

Gamaliel Bradford, "Raphael Semmes," in his *Confederate Portraits,* Essay Index Reprint Series (Freeport, N.Y.: Books for Libraries Press, 1968), pp. 217–236;

John M. Taylor, *Confederate Raider: Raphael Semmes of the Alabama* (Washington, D.C.: Brassey's, 1994);

Warren F. Spencer, *Raphael Semmes: The Philosophical Mariner* (Tuscaloosa: University of Alabama Press, 1997).

References:

Robert Underwood Johnson and Clarence Clough Buel, eds., *Battles and Leaders of the Civil War,* 4 volumes (New York: Century, 1887–1888);

Warren F. Spencer, *The Confederate Navy in Europe* (University: University of Alabama Press, 1983);

Philip Van Doren Stern, *The Confederate Navy: A Pictorial History* (Garden City, N.Y.: Doubleday, 1962).

Papers:

Repositories of Semmes's material include his papers at the Alabama State Department of Archives and History, Montgomery, Alabama; the Semmes Papers and the C. C. Clay Papers in the Manuscript Department at the William R. Perkins Library, Duke University; and the Manuscript Division at the Library of Congress, which includes his letterbooks.

E. G. Squier

(17 June 1821 – 17 April 1888)

Linda Ledford-Miller
University of Scranton

BOOKS: *Observations on the Aboriginal Monuments of the Mississippi Valley* (New York: Bartlett & Welford, 1847);

Ancient Monuments of the Mississippi Valley: Comprising the Results of Extensive Original Surveys and Explorations, by Squier and E. H. Davis, Smithsonian Contributions to Knowledge, volume 1 (Washington, D.C.: Smithsonian Institution, 1848);

Aboriginal Monuments of the State of New York, Smithsonian Contributions to Knowledge, volume 2 (Washington, D.C.: Smithsonian Institution, 1850); republished as *Antiquities of the State of New York* (Buffalo, N.Y.: G. H. Derby, 1851);

The Volcanoes of Central America, and the Geological and Topographical Features of Nicaragua, as Connected with the Proposed Inter-Oceanic Canal: Being the Substance of the Remarks Made Before the "American Association". . . on the Evening of the 22nd of August, 1850 (New York, 1850);

The Serpent Symbol, and the Worship of the Reciprocal Principles of Nature in America (New York: Putnam, 1851);

Nicaragua: Its People, Scenery, Monuments, and the Proposed Interoceanic Canal, 2 volumes (New York: Appleton, 1851; London: Longman, Brown, Green, and Longmans, 1852); republished as *Travels in Central America, Particularly in Nicaragua: With a Description of its Aboriginal Monuments, Scenery and People, Their Languages, Institutions, Religion, &c.,* 2 volumes (New York: Appleton, 1853); revised in one volume as *Nicaragua: Its People, Scenery, Monuments, Resources, Condition, and Proposed Canal* (New York: Harper, 1860);

Honduras Interoceanic Railway: Preliminary Report (New York: Tubbs, Nesmith & Teall, 1854; enlarged as *Honduras Interoceanic Railway: With Maps of the Line and Ports; and an Appendix, Containing Report of Admiral R. Fitzroy, R.N., the Charter, Illustrative Documents, Treaties, &c.* (London: Trübner, 1857);

E. G. Squier and his wife, Miriam, circa 1864

Notes on Central America; Particularly the States of Honduras and San Salvador: Their Geography, Topography, Climate, Population, Resources, Productions, etc., etc., and the Proposed Honduras Inter-Oceanic Railway (New York: Harper, 1855; London: Sampson Low, 1856); enlarged as *The States of Central America; Their Geography, Topography, Climate, Population, Resources, Productions, Com-*

merce, Political Organization, Aborigines, etc., etc., Comprising Chapters on Honduras, San Salvador, Nicaragua, Costa Rica, Guatemala, Belize, the Bay Islands, the Mosquito Shore, and the Honduras Inter-Oceanic Railway (New York: Harper, 1858); section revised as Honduras: Descriptive, Historical, and Statistical (London: Trübner, 1870; New York: Holt & Williams, 1870);

Waikna; or, Adventures on the Mosquito Shore, as Samuel A. Bard (New York: Harper, 1855; London: Sampson Low, 1855); republished as Adventures on the Mosquito Shore (London: J. Blackwood, 1856; Chicago: Belford, Clarke, 1888);

Information on the Coal Mines of the River Lempa, Republic of San Salvador, Central America (London: Chiswick Press, 1856);

Monograph of Authors Who Have Written on the Languages of Central America, and Collected Vocabularies or Composed Works in the Native Dialects of That Country (New York: C. B. Richardson, 1861; London: Trübner, 1861);

Tropical Fibres; Their Production and Economic Extraction (New York: Scribners, 1861; London: James Madden, 1863);

Peru Illustrated; or, Incidents of Travel and Exploration in the Land of the Incas (New York: Hurst, 1877); also published as Peru: Incidents of Travel and Exploration in the Land of the Incas (New York: Harper, 1877; London: Macmillan, 1877);

Honduras and British Honduras (New York: Scribners, 1880);

Observations on the Archaeology and Ethnology of Nicaragua, edited by Frank E. Comparato (Culver City, Cal.: Labyrinthos, 1990).

OTHER: George T. Lay, The Chinese as They Are; Their Moral and Social Character, Manners, Customs, Language: With Remarks on Their Arts and Sciences, Medical Skill, the Extent of Missionary Enterprise, etc. . . . Containing also, Illustrative and Corroborative Notes . . . , compiled by Squier (Albany, N.Y.: George Jones / New York: Burgess & Stringer, 1843);

William Bartram, "Observations on the Creek and Cherokee Indians," preface by Squier, in Transactions of the American Ethnological Society, 3 (New York: Putnam, 1853), pp. 3–81;

Question Anglo-Américaine: Documents officiels échangés entre les États-Unis et l'Angleterre au sujet de l'Amérique Centrale et du traité Clayton-Bulwer, compiled and translated by Squier (Paris: Stasson et Xavier, 1856);

Collection of Rare and Original Documents and Relations Concerning the Discovery and Conquest of America,

translated by Squier (New York: Norton, 1860);

Frank Leslie's Pictorial History of the American Civil War, edited by Squier, 2 volumes (New York: F. Leslie, 1861–1862);

Arthur Morelet, Travels in Central America, Including Accounts of Some Regions Unexplored Since the Conquest, translated by Miriam Follin Squier, introduction and notes by Squier (New York: Leypoldt, Holt & Williams, 1871).

SELECTED PERIODICAL PUBLICATIONS– UNCOLLECTED: "New Mexico and California: The Ancient Monuments and the Aboriginal, Semi-Civilized Nations . . . with an Abstract of the Early Spanish Explorations and Conquests in Those Regions," American Review, 8, new series 2 (November 1848): 503–528;

"Some New Discoveries Respecting the Dates on the Great Calendar Stone of the Ancient Mexicans, with Observations on the Mexican Cycle of Fifty-two Years," American Journal of Science and Arts, 7, second series (1849): 153–157.

E. G. Squier was a journalist, diplomat, and archaeologist whose extensive travels in Latin America resulted in important and definitive contributions to the study of archaeology in Central America and Peru. An authority on Central America and its antiquities in particular, he published the results of his travels and investigations in several well-received books, many of which were translated into Spanish, French, and German. He was a renowned nineteenth-century Americanist, the first president of the Anthropological Institute of New York, and a member of many learned societies.

Ephraim George Squier was born in Bethlehem, New York on 17 June 1821, the son of Joel Squier, a Methodist minister, and Catharine Külmer Squier. Although he did attend the local school, Squier was raised on a farm, and much of his education came from independent reading fitted around his farm chores. Squier taught school in the winters and studied civil engineering for a time. His involvement with a country paper led him to work at the New York State Mechanic in Albany from 1841 to 1842. From 1843 to 1845 he edited the Evening Journal in Hartford, Connecticut and was actively involved in Whig politics. From Hartford he went to Chillicothe, Ohio, where he edited the Scioto Gazette from 1845 to 1848 and also served as clerk in the Ohio House of Representatives in 1847 and 1848.

While in Ohio, Squier became familiar with the ancient mounds in the Scioto Valley and subsequently initiated a careful investigation of the abo-

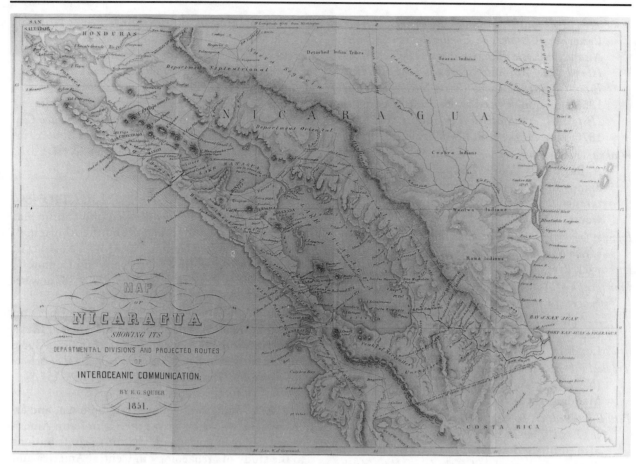

Map from Squier's Nicaragua: Its People, Scenery, Monuments, and the Proposed Interoceanic Canal *(1851)*

riginal monuments of the Mississippi Valley, working with Dr. Edward Hamilton Davis. The results of their investigations were published as *Ancient Monuments of the Mississippi Valley: Comprising the Results of Extensive Original Surveys and Explorations,* which appeared as the first volume of the Smithsonian Contributions to Knowledge series in 1848. This first archaeological experience would change Squier's career. Although he remained active in politics, continued to publish magazine articles, and worked as an editor on occasion, Squier left journalism per se for archaeology, ethnology, and diplomacy.

In 1848, under the auspices of the New York Historical Society, Squier studied the ancient aboriginal ruins of New York State, publishing *Aboriginal Monuments of the State of New York* as the second volume of the Smithsonian Contributions to Knowledge (1850). In 1848 and 1849 Squier also made his first inquiries into the ancient monuments of former Spanish territory, bringing to public attention information gleaned from the report of Lt. J. W. Albert's survey of Mexican lands newly under U.S. jurisdiction following the conclusion of the treaty between Mexico and the United States. He published "New

Mexico and California: The Ancient Monuments and the Aboriginal, Semi-Civilized Nations . . . with an Abstract of the Early Spanish Explorations and Conquests in Those Regions" in *American Review* (1848) and "Some New Discoveries Respecting the Dates on the Great Calendar Stone of the Ancient Mexicans, with Observations on the Mexican Cycle of Fifty-two Years" in *American Journal of Science and Arts* (1849).

Squier's first diplomatic post to Latin America began in 1849 when, through the influence of the historian William Hickling Prescott, he was named chargé d'affaires to all the Central American states. Although his first term in Central America lasted only about a year and a half, he visited each of the republics and negotiated treaties with three of them: Nicaragua, Honduras, and San Salvador. The 1849 treaty that Squier negotiated with Nicaragua, although never ratified, was something of a political embarrassment when presented to the Senate. Squier negotiated a treaty that gave the United States the exclusive right of way for a projected interoceanic canal, along with possession of Tigre Island at the planned western terminus of the canal, in exchange for the U.S. guarantee of a neutral isthmus and protection of Nicaraguan sovereignty. However, British-American negotiations for control of the area were under way at the time. Britain objected to the proposed treaty and in fact seized Tigre Island despite Squier's contention that the island belonged to the United States. U.S. secretary of state John M. Clayton opened discussions with Sir Henry Lytton Bulwer, the British minister to the United States. An accord was finally reached in the Clayton-Bulwer Treaty of 1850, which limited British expansion in Central America but also prevented the United States from proceeding unilaterally on any canal construction. The Clayton-Bulwer agreement remained in effect until 1901, when it was abrogated by the Hay-Pauncefote Treaty.

Squier's next major publication, *The Serpent Symbol, and the Worship of the Reciprocal Principles of Nature in America* (1851), presents a pan-American vision of archaeological study. Dedicated to Chevalier Fomard, president of the Geographical Society of Paris, *The Serpent Symbol* investigates the essential similarity among "the elementary religious conceptions of the primitive nations of the Old and New Worlds," including phallic worship, the "high places" of the United States and Mexico, ancient serpentine earthworks in the United States, and the serpent symbol, particularly as represented in Mexico and Central America. Squier also identifies himself as an Americanist: "I have for some years engaged upon a work of comprehensive design, in which I propose to bring together, under a single view, all such leading and well authenticated facts as may be accessible, relating to the aboriginal monuments of the American continent . . . [and] the ancient and as yet unwritten history of the New World." Further, Squier demonstrates early on his strong advocacy for some developing fields: "no sciences are so eminently inductive as Archaeology and Ethnology, or the sciences of man and Nations; none which require so extensive a range of facts to their elucidation."

In 1853 Squier returned to Central America as secretary of the Honduras Interoceanic Railway Company to examine the proposed route for a railroad that was never built. He used both of his visits to Central America as opportunities for archaeological study and general geographical, ethnological, and commercial investigation. His years in Central America resulted in several influential publications; the first was the two-volume *Nicaragua: Its People, Scenery, Monuments, and the Proposed Interoceanic Canal* (1851). The work is divided into five sections that mix travel narrative with commercial, historical, political, and archaeological observation. Squier himself drew the maps and plans included in the book, while the engravings are "chiefly from the original drawings of Mr. Jas. McDonough, who accompanied [him] to Central America in the capacity of artist."

The first section describes the geography and topography of the country. The second section is a narrative of Squier's journey, mixing historical commentary with personal, ethnographic, and archaeological observations and discoveries such as the idols at Pensacola. With Pacific and Caribbean coasts and contiguous small and large lakes between them (the Lago de Managua and Lago de Nicaragua), Nicaragua was long considered the best location for an interoceanic canal. Section three considers the geography and topography of Nicaragua in light of a projected canal, the history of negotiations with respect to a canal in Nicaragua, and the political and commercial implications of such a canal. The fourth section, "Aborigines of Nicaragua," describes the indigenous nations, their distribution, language, monuments, and customs. Squier closes his text with an "Outline of Political History" that details the history of the Spanish Republics: their revolutions, attempts at republicanism, British interference, and attempts at confederation.

In his preface to the first edition of *Nicaragua* Squier indicates that his purpose is "to give a true picture, not only of the country, but of the character, condition, and relations of the people" of Nicaragua and to "impress the great truth upon this nation, that the United States is the natural head of the great American family." In the revised one-volume edition of 1860 Squier notes that *Nicaragua* remains little changed from his first visit there in 1850 and his subsequent visit in 1854. His belief in Nicaragua as the proper site for an interoceanic canal also remained unchanged: "For, in Nicaragua, and there alone, has nature combined those requisites for a water communication between the seas, which has so long been the dream of enthusiasts, and which is a desideratum of this age, as it will be a necessity of the next."

Squier's visit to Honduras in 1853 called upon his training in civil engineering and resulted in two publications examining the proposed route for a railroad originating at Puerto Caballos on the Bay of Honduras in the Caribbean Sea and running almost due south to the Bay of Fonseca on the Pacific. *Honduras Interoceanic Railway: Preliminary Report* (1854) was enlarged as *Honduras Interoceanic Railway: With Maps of the Line and Ports; and an Appendix, Containing Report of Admiral R. Fitzroy, R.N., the Charter, Illustrative Documents, Treaties, &c,* (1857). Squier worked with Lieutenant William Jeffers, U.S.N., a

Illustration from Nicaragua: Its People, Scenery, Monuments, and the Proposed
Interoceanic Canal

civil engineer whose posting to Brazil immediately after the Honduras expedition delayed the publication of the full report. Like the canal in Nicaragua, the interoceanic railroad in Honduras failed to come to fruition. Nevertheless, the information and experience gained from those investigations helped to educate the people of the United States about their nearest neighbors.

Squier returned to Honduras in *Notes on Central America; Particularly the States of Honduras and San Salvador: Their Geography, Topography, Climate, Population, Resources, Productions, etc., etc., and the Proposed Honduras Inter-Oceanic Railway* (1855). Although *Notes on Central America* gives an overview of the geography, climate, and population of Guatemala, San Salvador, Honduras, Nicaragua, and Costa Rica, the majority of the text focuses on the republic of Honduras, with some attention to the interoceanic railway, and on the republic of San Salvador. Squier concludes the text with "Miscellaneous Notes" on the Bay Islands, the Mosquito Shore (the eastern shore of Nicaragua, named for the indigenous Miskito people), and the Indians of Honduras. Squier refers to his text as a "hurried memoir" that depends almost completely on his own observations, but *Notes on Central America* includes none of the personal narrative found in *Nicaragua*. Rather, it is a scholarly monograph designed to inform public interest in "these hitherto little known yet prospectively important states."

In the same year that *Notes on Central America* appeared Squier also published the novel *Waikna; or, Adventures on the Mosquito Shore* as Samuel A. Bard. Sent by President Zachary Taylor to Central America as chargé d'affaires in an attempt to limit British expansion in the area, Squier would naturally publish pseudonymously a novel based partly on experiences and information garnered while on a diplomatic mission. *Waikna* recounts the adventures of the fictional Samuel A. Bard, an artist who survives a shipwreck on the Mosquito Shore, travels in this new country, meets black Caribs and Indians, and observes the unique local plants and wildlife. Although *Waikna* has been called an "autobiographical novel" presenting the "true adventures" of its fictional protagonist, it seems to bear little relationship to Squier's actual experience. Though Squier drew his own maps, he was not an artist; he hired artists to accompany him on his travels. Nor did Squier ever suffer a shipwreck. The novel appeared in Britain in at least two editions, and scholar Charles L. Stansifer has suggested that Squier's main purpose in writing *Waikna* was to "influence the British public to force abandonment of British holdings in the Central American region." *Waikna* is Squier's only attempt at fiction.

In 1856 Squier was awarded the medal of the Geographical Society of Paris. The next year was even more memorable: Squier announced his engagement to the former actress Miriam Follin on 10 September 1857, describing her in a letter to his parents as "young, not yet 21, highly educated, and very beautiful." They were married on 22 October 1857 in Providence, Rhode Island. Squier was Miriam's third serious relationship and the second of her four marriages. Squier's award of the silver medal of the Royal Society of Arts of Great Britain was announced in the same issue of the *Providence Journal* as his marriage. The couple settled into a quiet domestic and scholarly life: Miriam began the translation of an 1855 play by Alexandre Dumas *fils, Le Demi-Monde,* while Squier worked in the office of the Honduras Railroad Company and prepared *The States of Central America; Their Geography, Topography, Climate, Population, Resources, Productions, Commerce, Political Organization, Aborigines, etc., etc., Comprising Chapters on Honduras, San Salvador, Nicaragua, Costa Rica, Guatemala, Belize, the Bay Islands, the Mosquito Shore, and the Honduras Inter-Oceanic Railway* an 1858 expanded version of *Notes on Central America.*

The States of Central America expands significantly upon the narrow scope of *Notes on Central America,* which focuses principally on Honduras and El Salvador. Like its earlier incarnation, *The States of Central America* is a scholarly monograph. Indeed, Squier's purpose seems, in part, to avoid any flamboyance in his narrative that might discredit it: "What little illustration Central America has received has . . . been at the hands of foreigners; but their works have been, for the most part, rapid narrations of travel and adventure, shallow in observation, and inaccurate in their statements. Few of them have been written by persons competent by education, or accustomed by habit to close and accurate research."

Although Squier bases his text primarily on his own experiences and observations, he demonstrates his education and research by the wide-ranging citation of historians and travelers to the region; he applies the scientist's eye, not the tourist's. His discussion of the unconquered Lacandon Indians of the Petén jungle in Guatemala provides an example:

> As has already been observed, the government of Central America, both in 1831 and 1837, made efforts to bring the Lacandones under its authority, but without success. They still retain their independence, and their country is now no better known than it was in the time of Quiñones and Barrios. They seem . . . to have abandoned their predatory habits. . . . A few occasionally enter the Spanish towns of Chiapa, Tabasco, and Campeachy, bringing down tobacco and a few other articles for sale or exchange. But, according to Waldeck, no sooner have they effected a sale, or procured what they wish, than they suddenly disappear by obscure and unknown paths. This author saw some of the Lacandones near Palenque. They possessed all the savage energy and independence of their fathers.

In May 1858 Squier and his wife sailed for England and visited Paris, Brussels, Cologne, the Rhine, and Switzerland. From Lucerne, Switzerland, Squier wrote to his father that, "no accident intervening, [we] will probably make you a grandfather, before many months." Unfortunately, Miriam's pregnancy terminated early; she and Squier never had children. The Squiers returned to the States, where Miriam used her language skills to help her husband produce the short-lived *Noticioso de Nueva York,* a Spanish-language paper for readers in Cuba and South America.

Sometime in 1859 or 1860 the Squiers met editor and publisher Frank Leslie, who later invited Squier to contribute essays on Central American affairs for the armchair travelers who subscribed to *Frank Leslie's Illustrated Newspaper.* Squier's first contributions, "The Central American Question" and "Honduras," marked the beginning of a long relationship with Leslie, who later moved into the Squier household after leaving his wife. Squier's appointment as editor of *Frank Leslie's Illustrated Newspaper* was announced on 21 September 1861, and under his direction *Frank Leslie's Pictorial History of the American Civil War* (2 volumes, 1861–1862) was produced. Meanwhile, the domestic arrangement of the Squiers and Leslie led to much speculation about the precise nature of their relationship. By February 1863 Miriam Squier had become editor of *Frank Leslie's Lady's Magazine.* Shortly after Miriam undertook the editorship, Squier was offered a post in Peru as commissioner to negotiate claims between Peru and the United States in connection with silver and guano. His physician had recommended a sea voyage and change of scene as the prescription for a period of poor health, so the prospect of a cure for his ills combined with an opportunity to see the aboriginal ruins of Peru made the offer irresistible.

The Squiers arrived in Lima, Peru, in July 1863. By November of the same year Miriam embarked for home, having found the Peruvian climate unpleasant and her marriage increasingly disagreeable. Squier stayed on in Peru for more than a year to pursue archaeological study of ancient Incan ruins. Upon his return to the States, much in debt as a result of his Peruvian expeditions, Squier continued to work for Leslie. Meanwhile, Leslie tried to persuade his wife, Sarah Ann Welham Leslie, to divorce him. In February 1867 Leslie and the Squiers traveled to Europe together. Thanks to a dispatch sent by Leslie, when they disembarked at Liverpool, England, Squier was arrested for nonpayment of £350 borrowed years before in connection with the Honduras Railway and never repaid. Squier was released from Lancaster Castle two weeks later. Leslie and Miriam Squier seem to have spent those two weeks living together in a London hotel. Nonetheless, the trio traveled on together, visiting the Paris Universal Exposition as well as Italy.

In 1868 Squier was appointed consul general to Honduras in New York. He continued working for Leslie, who was still seeking a divorce. In addition to a steady stream of articles for Leslie, Squier

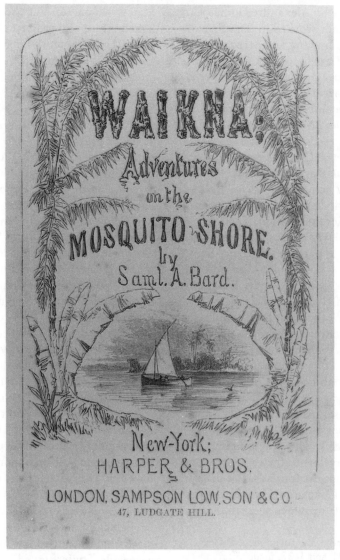

*Decorated title page for Squier's only novel, published under a
pseudonym in 1855*

was working on his notes from his Peruvian journeys. In 1870 the Squiers and Leslie went to London as a trio once again, where Squier attended to diplomatic affairs as consul general. In 1871 Miriam's translation of Arthur Morelet's two-volume *Voyages dans l'Amérique Centrale, l'île de Cuba, et le Yucatan* (1857) was published as *Travels in Central America, Including Accounts of Some Regions Unexplored Since the Conquest* (1871), with Squier providing an introduction and notes. Squier was elected the first president of the Anthropological Institute of New York in the same year. Also in 1871 Miriam Squier was named by Sarah Ann Leslie in her countercharge to her husband's divorce suit. Sarah Ann Leslie claimed that her husband had had carnal knowledge of Miriam Squier since January 1867. Squier immediately responded by accusing Sarah Ann Leslie of trying to

disrupt his friendship and close business relationship with her husband. Frank Leslie was finally free of his wife on 18 July 1872 after persuading her to divorce him on grounds of desertion.

The Squiers' relationship deteriorated rapidly after Leslie's divorce. In April 1873 Miriam asked her brother-in-law, Frank Squier, to remove the pistols from her home, hinting that Squier might rashly harm her or Leslie or himself. Soon after, Squier and Miriam moved to separate addresses. Miriam filed for divorce, claiming that an inebriated Squier had committed adultery in a brothel with a woman known as "Gypsy." Two "friends" testified to Squier's activities, and the divorce was granted in May 1873. There seems to be at least some suggestion that Squier's debauchery was arranged in order to provide grounds for divorce. Perhaps, then, it is no accident that the friends who accompanied him and subsequently testified were artists who literally sketched his predicament. In July 1874 Miriam Squier married Frank Leslie. Less than a month later, Squier was found "a lunatic, not having lucid intervals, so that he was incapable of the government of himself or of the management of his goods and chattels," according to an inquisition at the New York City Courthouse.

Squier was committed at the request of his half brother Frank to the Sanford Hall Asylum in Flushing, Long Island, and forbidden to undertake any further research. Frank Squier became his brother's guardian. Public opinion suggested that Miriam's mistreatment of her husband and her remarriage caused Squier's descent into madness. Yet as early as 1863 Miriam had complained of her husband's "condition" without making clear what that condition was. Squier had also worked feverishly for decades, producing nearly one hundred publications in a career cut short by illness. However, Squier did manage to complete another work, *Peru Illustrated; or, Incidents of Travel and Exploration in the Land of the Incas* (1877), for which he had gathered the materials while serving as commissioner in Peru from 1863 to 1865.

Like his earlier work on Nicaragua, *Peru Illustrated* is a travel narrative as well an archaeological study. Squier traveled with "the compass, the measuring-line, and the photographic camera; knowing well that only accurate plans, sections, elevations, drawings, and views can adequately meet the rigorous demands of modern science, and render clear what mere verbal description would fail to make intelligible." Squier's description of Lima combines the personal observations of the traveler with the quantitative observations of the scientist:

> No other city founded by the Spaniards in America possesses so much interest, historical or otherwise, as does Lima. . . . The Indians can no longer be parcelled out to the favorites of power, and the negro no longer pays the tribute of unwilling labor to the rich proprietors of Lima. But the ancient City of Kings is still rich, still gay, still flourishing, and more luxurious than in her proudest colonial days. . . . Lima is situated in latitude 12° 2' 34" south, and longitude 77° 7' 36" west of Greenwich. Its elevation above the sea is 512 feet.

In his introduction Squier discusses his friendship with Prescott, the eminent historian who inspired him to undertake archaeological investigations. He acknowledges that Prescott's influence had much to do with his diplomatic posting to Central America. Squier's study of the ruins of Central America had fostered a desire to visit the unknown ruins of South America: "To visit the land of the Children of the Sun, and to realize, in some degree at least, his [Prescott's] aspirations, became a leading purpose of my life." But many years had intervened, and then his hopes had seemed dashed by visual problems that threatened blindness:

> at length, owing to undue exposure and protracted over-exertion, the light began to fade away before my eyes, and a dark veil fell between them and the bright and moving world without. The skill of eminent oculists was exerted in vain, and I was told that my only alternative lay between absolute mental rest and total blindness. Rest, and an entire change of scene and occupation, might perhaps restore, at least partially, my failing vision.

The appointment as commissioner to Peru in 1863 had thus provided a timely break from the stress of his life in the United States, and he did not lose his sight until closer to his death.

When Squier's duties as commissioner were concluded, he had begun his last scientific expedition and the basis of this last, and perhaps most influential, major publication. Squier claims to have brought back more than four hundred plans and elevations, and nearly as many drawings and sketches, in addition to many photographs and artifacts. He suggests that his observations point to the existence of pre-Incan civilizations—a commentary that would prove prophetic when archaeologists uncovered the pre-Incan Moche civilizations more than a century later. Squier's drawing of the famous hanging bridge across the Apurimac River, built two centuries before the arrival of the Spaniards, and his description of the gorge traversed by the bridge, intrigued a later scientist. Drawn by Squier's fascinating text and illustrations, the Yale archaeologist Hiram Bingham went to Peru and in 1911 discovered the ruins of Machu Picchu, the ancient sacred city of the Incas.

Squier died in April 1888 in the mental institution where he had been interned for some fourteen years. Although blindness, insanity, or well-meaning relatives and professionals may have prevented Squier from taking on any other projects in the last years of his life, the scope and influence of his achievement was profound. Though a more modern scientist might criticize the accuracy of Squier's measurements and the scale of his drawings, works such as *Nicaragua* and *Peru Illustrated* still entertain and inform the armchair traveler and archaeologist, while his novel, *Waikna*, remains good adventure reading. Along with John Lloyd Stephens, his fellow diplomat-archaeologist-ethnologist, Squier made what are quite probably the most significant contributions to the anthropology and archaeology of the Americas of the nineteenth century. Several of his works remain in print. Perhaps more important, Squier exemplified and promoted inter-Americanism, or pan-Americanism. His was a vision of the Americas as a hemisphere with much similar history and many common causes.

Bibliographies:

Rafael Heliodoro Valle, "E. George Squier, Notas Bio-Bibliográficas," *Hispanic American Historical Review*, 1 (1918): 426–434;

"Squier, Ephraim George (1821–88)," *Huntington Library Bulletin*, 1 (May 1931): 76–77;

Frank Squier, *A Collection of Books by Ephraim George Squier, His Own Copies with Some Recently Acquired Additions and a Few Books by Others* (New York, 1939);

L. Valderrama, "Squier Manuscripts in the Biblioteca Nacional de Perú," *Hispanic American History Review*, 56 (August 1956): 338–341;

Jerry E. Patterson and William R. Stanton, "The Ephraim George Squier Manuscripts in the Library of Congress: A Checklist," *Papers of the Bibliographical Society of America*, 53 (1959): 309–326.

Biographies:

Charles L. Stansifer, "The Central American Career of Ephraim George Squier," dissertation, Tulane University, 1959;

Terry A. Barnhart, "Of Mounds and Men: The Early Anthropological Career of Ephraim George Squier," dissertation, Miami University, 1989.

References:

Daniel E. Alleger, "Introduction," in *Waikna; Adventures on the Mosquito Shore*, by Squier as Samuel A. Bard (Gainesville: University of Florida Press, 1965), pp. ix–xxxvii;

Terry A. Barnhart, "'American Menagerie: The Cabinet of Squier and Davis,'" *Timeline*, 2, (1985–1986): 2–17;

Barnhart, "A Question of Authorship: The Ephraim George Squier-Edwin Hamilton Davis Controversy," *Ohio History*, 92 (1983): 52–71;

D. Lindsey, "Archaeologist, Diplomat, Editor: Ephraim George Squier," *American History Illustrated*, 15 (July 1980): 30–35;

E. Nuñez, "Diplomat on the Trail of the Incas," *Americas*, 13 (April 1961): 3–7;

Michael D. Olien, "E. G. Squier and the Miskito: Anthropological Scholarship and Political Propaganda," *Ethnohistory*, 32, no. 3 (1985): 111–133;

Francis Parkman, *Letters from Francis Parkman to E. G. Squier*, edited by Don C. Seitz (Cedar Rapids, Iowa: Torch Press, 1911);

Alan Reed Sawyer, "Squier's 'Palace of Ollantay' Revisited," *Nawpa Pacha*, 18 (1980): 63–72;

Madeleine B. Stern, *Purple Passage: The Life of Mrs. Frank Leslie* (Norman: University of Oklahoma Press, 1953);

Liliana Irene Weinberg de Magis, "E. G. Squier y la 'causa del progreso' en Nicaragua," *Cuadernos Americanos*, Nueva época 1 (September–October 1987): 74–94;

Ralph Lee Woodward, "Impresiones norteamericanas sobre Centro-América en los siglos XIX–XX," *Anuarios de Estudios Centroamericanos* (Costa Rica), 2 (1976): 375–391.

Papers:

The Library of Congress is the major repository of Squier papers. Holdings include many letters as well as some unpublished manuscripts. Other collections of Squier materials are located at the Huntington Library in San Marino, California; the New York Historical Society; Tulane University; and the Biblioteca Nacional de Perú.

Henry M. Stanley

(28 January 1841 – 10 May 1904)

M. D. Allen
University of Wisconsin Center—Fox Valley

See also the Stanley entry in *DS 13: The House of Scribner, 1846–1904.*

BOOKS: *How I Found Livingstone: Travels, Adventures, and Discoveries in Central Africa: Including an Account of Four Months' Residence with Dr. Livingstone* (London: Sampson Low, Marston, Low & Searle, 1872; New York: Scribner, Armstrong, 1872);

My Kalulu: Prince, King, and Slave: A Story of Central Africa (London: Sampson Low, Marston, Low & Searle, 1873; New York: Scribner, Armstrong, 1874);

Coomassie and Magdala: The Story of Two British Campaigns in Africa (London: Sampson Low, Marston, Low & Searle, 1874; New York: Harper, 1874);

Through the Dark Continent: Or, The Sources of the Nile, Around the Great Lakes of Equatorial Africa, and Down the Livingstone River to the Atlantic Ocean, 2 volumes (London: Sampson Low, Marston, Searle & Rivington, 1878; New York: Harper, 1878);

The Congo and the Founding of Its Free State: A Story of Work and Exploration, 2 volumes (London: Sampson Low, Marston, Searle, & Rivington, 1885; New York: Harper, 1885);

In Darkest Africa: Or the Quest, Rescue, and Retreat of Emin, Governor of Equatoria, 2 volumes (London: Sampson Low, Marston, Searle & Rivington, 1890; New York: Scribners, 1890);

My Dark Companions and Their Strange Stories (London: Sampson Low, Marston, 1893; New York: Scribners, 1893);

Slavery and the Slave Trade in Africa (London: Sampson Low, 1893; New York: Harper, 1893);

My Early Travels and Adventures in America and Asia, 2 volumes (London: Sampson Low, Marston, 1895; New York: Scribners, 1895);

Through South Africa: Being An Account of His Recent Visit to Rhodesia, the Transvaal, Cape Colony, and Natal; Reprinted, With Additions from South Africa

Henry M. Stanley, 1872

(London: Sampson Low, Marston, 1898; New York: Scribners, 1898);

The Autobiography of Sir Henry Morton Stanley, G.C.B., edited by Dorothy Stanley (London: Sampson Low, Marston, 1909; Boston & New York: Houghton Mifflin, 1909);

The Exploration Diaries of H. M. Stanley. Now First Published From the Original Manuscripts, edited by Richard Stanley and Alan Neame (London: Kimber, 1961; New York: Vanguard, 1961);

Stanley's Despatches to the New York Herald 1871–1872, 1874–1877, edited by Norman R. Bennett (Boston: Boston University Press, 1970).

OTHER: "Africa in the Twentieth Century," in *Africa: Its Partition and Its Future,* by Stanley and others, introduction by Harry Thurston Peck (New York: Dodd, Mead, 1898).

Described by Frank McLynn, his most recent and exhaustive biographer, as the "greatest of the African explorers and one of the most fascinating of the late Victorian adventurers," Sir Henry Morton Stanley spent a dozen years of his life undertaking four major expeditions into and across Central Africa. The successful accomplishment of his first journey (1870–1871), from the east coast to Ujiji, on Lake Tanganyika, to find the celebrated explorer Dr. David Livingstone, immediately made him world-famous. His second expedition (1874–1877), made to complete Livingstone's work, crossed the entire continent from east to west and included among its achievements the establishing of the shapes and sizes of Lakes Victoria and Tanganyika and the navigating of the River Lualaba from Nyangwe, deep in the heart of Africa (west of which Livingstone had not traveled), to within fifty miles of the Atlantic Ocean. Stanley also proved the Lualaba to be a tributary of the Congo by discovering the confluence of the two rivers.

The filling in of the blank spaces on the map of Africa had the effect of increasing European interest in hitherto unclaimed regions. Stanley's efforts led to an influx of missionaries and eventual British control in East Africa, while the ambitious King Leopold II of the Belgians quickly recognized the potential of a largely navigable river stretching deep into unappropriated areas. Indeed, Stanley's third stay in Africa (1879–1884) was as an employee of that monarch, and he was thus instrumental in the founding of the infamous Congo Free State. His final major journey (1887–1889) was a controversial second crossing of the continent, this time from west to east, to "rescue" the beleaguered Emin Pasha in Equatoria. His four expeditions together helped change the lives of millions of Africans for both good and ill, encouraging the consolidation of colonial power in the forerunner states of present-day Uganda and the Republic of Congo.

Each of Stanley's explorations was recounted for an Africa-obsessed general public in thick, best-selling volumes that are sometimes cumbersome and wordy but at their best are excellent, quick-moving reportage. These books have had an incalculable impact in creating the idea of Africa in the Western mind, influencing both popular lowbrow authors such as Edgar Rice Burroughs, the creator of Tarzan, and highbrow writers, including Sigmund Freud, Andre Gide, Joseph Conrad, and Michel Leiris. Stanley has also entered popular mythology through his slightly risible inquiry, "Dr. Livingstone, I presume?"

Few who have gone on to considerable achievement and world fame can have had so bleak a beginning as did Stanley. Born on 28 January 1841 in Denbigh, Wales, the man known to history as Stanley was christened John Rowlands for the young, alcoholic farmer who begot him, out of wedlock, upon Elizabeth Parry, a butcher's daughter in her late teens. Parry had more illegitimate children by various fathers and gravely hurt her son, both as boy and man, by her indifference to him. With the exception of his maternal grandfather, who died in June 1846, other relatives given the job of caring for the boy were scarcely more enthusiastic: he was eventually farmed out to a local couple, Richard and Jenny Price. When his blood relatives decided to discontinue their modest weekly payment to the Prices, the latter deceived their charge into entering the Saint Asaph Union Workhouse, not telling him where he was going or why. Stanley never forgot this fresh abandonment and betrayal, writing many years later in *The Autobiography of Sir Henry Morton Stanley, G.C.B.* (1909) of Richard Price "shattering my confidence and planting the first seeds of distrust in a child's heart."

Compensatory fantasy was always a part of Stanley's inner life, complicating the task of the biographer. In *Dark Safari: The Life Behind the Legend of Henry Morton Stanley* (1990) John Bierman authoritatively asserts that Stanley "was a liar and a fantasist on a scale to rival his unquestionably heroic achievements as an explorer." He contends that Stanley invented many of the details of his autobiography, that "he fabricated for himself a suit of armor, which it has taken almost a century to penetrate." It seems likely, for example, that the workhouse was not as brutal a place as he represented it in his *Autobiography*. In particular, Stanley's story of wresting the workhouse schoolmaster's stick from him and applying it to his tormentor seems inspired by a famous scene from Charles Dickens's *Nicholas Nickleby* (1838–1839). Whether or not such an incident was the immediate cause, Stanley left Saint Asaph's in May 1856 at the age of fifteen.

Two and a half years of further petty humiliations followed. He spent some months as a pupil-teacher in a relative's school and then as a laborer on another relative's farm. In August 1858 he sailed to Liverpool in search of a promised clerkship that did not materialize. Obliged to take a job as butcher's boy, Stanley delivered meat to ships anchored on the River Mersey. His Liverpool relatives having proved no more loving or practically helpful than

St. Asaph Union workhouse, which Stanley condemned in his Autobiography *(1909)*

his Welsh kin, he joined the crew of the *Windermere* and set sail for America in December.

The officers of this vessel were in the habit of deliberately treating their deckhands brutally so that they would jump ship, thus forfeiting their wages. After more than seven weeks' sailing the *Windermere* arrived in New Orleans, where the eighteen-year-old still known as John Rowlands, unwilling to face yet more blows but penniless, looked for a job. According to Stanley's account he approached a well-dressed, kindly man and asked, "Do you want a boy, Sir?" The gentleman, Henry Hope Stanley, helped him find employment at Speake and McCreary, Wholesale and Commission Merchants. A week's probation was succeeded by the offer of a permanent position as junior clerk at what must have appeared to Rowlands as the princely salary of twenty-five dollars a month.

The man whom the young Welshman would claim as his foster father in his autobiography and from whom he would take his first and family names (the "Morton" was not to be finally decided on until much later) was a wealthy businessman in cotton and the owner of a plantation near Arcola, Louisiana. According to the *Autobiography* the elder Stanley's personal interest in the young man was first shown by inviting him to his house for Sunday breakfasts and introducing him to his wife. Stanley would allegedly later declare, *"with some emotion, that my future should be his charge!"* The actual nature of the

relationship, however, cannot be determined. Bierman argues that it is likely "that Henry Hope Stanley did, indeed, take an interest in the young Rowlands, but that it was not nearly so intense an interest as the lad had hoped for." While later the older man apparently did find the youth a good position as a store clerk in Cypress Bend, Arkansas, Stanley was to write untruthfully in the *Autobiography* of his protector's wife's death and his putative father's consequent sailing to Cuba as the causes of his removal to Arkansas. When Henry Hope Stanley died in 1878, only a few months after the actual death of his wife, he left no part of his considerable fortune to the youth who claimed to be his adopted son.

Stanley's brief sojourn in Cypress Bend was interrupted by the Civil War. He did not consider himself an American at this stage of his life, or at least not a Southerner, and saw no reason to get involved in the conflict until he received a lady's petticoat in the mail. Stung by the imputation of cowardly unmanliness, he immediately joined the local Confederate regiment. The Dixie Greys completed their basic training in August 1861 and spent nearly four months quietly in Kentucky, but then were thrown into the Battle of Shiloh. Stanley was taken prisoner on 7 April 1862, the second day of the battle. He avoided almost certain death by disease in a prisoner-of-war camp outside Chicago by volunteering to fight for the North, but the Illinois Light Artillery in its turn did not benefit from Stanley's soldierly services for long. Struck with dysentery, he was discharged within a month.

By November 1862 Stanley was back in Liverpool. He made his way to Denbigh, in ill health and obvious poverty, only to be slighted by his mother. Little is known of his life from this time until July 1864, when he extended his familiarity with the armed forces of America by joining the Union navy. He deserted in February of the next year, accompanied by the first in a series of impressionable young male protégés, fifteen-year-old Lewis Noe. Stanley as yet had no means or direction, but he had shown a chameleon-like ability to adapt and survive exploitation by man as well as the buffetings of fate and history.

Stanley made an important step forward by taking up journalism. On the strength of his written descriptions of the Civil War naval battles he had observed from a distance, the editor of the *Missouri Democrat* agreed at least to read any material that Stanley might submit. The would-be journalist went West in search of copy, boating down the Missouri with William Harlow Cook, another freelance journalist, as training in physical hardihood for a projected trip to Asia Minor. Stanley and Cook then traveled to Boston, shipping for Smyrna (now Izmir, on the west coast of Turkey) with Noe along. Stanley's idea seems to have been to find fame and fortune in some way by traveling overland to China.

Soon after their arrival and the commencement of their journey, Stanley and his two companions fought with and were captured by a group of Turks. According to Stanley the trouble began when he struck the leader of the Turks, who was making sexual advances to Noe; however, Noe asserted that the fight was caused by Stanley's miscarried plan to kill and rob one of the Turks. Later, both agree that Noe was sodomized by the Turks. In *Stanley: The Making of an African Explorer* (1898) Frank McLynn contends that "the Turks' [sodomy] brought home forcibly to Stanley the reality of the instincts towards Noe which he was suppressing and which had found their outlet in the bloody beating [Stanley had previously administered to Noe]. The three ruffians were acting out a possibility he could not face."

The Turk chiefly involved, still considering himself wronged, took his three captives to a governor who demanded depositions from both sides. The ensuing court proceedings favored the more articulate Westerner, Stanley, a representative of a powerful country, over the Turkish peasant, although the U.S. minister to Constantinople was puzzled by aspects of Stanley's story. Stanley was com-

pensated financially and traveled to Liverpool before returning to America in January 1867.

Stanley spent 1867 reporting on an expedition against the Plains Indians and later peace conferences. By the end of the year he was sufficiently confident in his increasing reputation to suggest to James Gordon Bennett, owner of the *New York Herald,* that he be sent to Abyssinia to cover a British punitive expedition against the Emperor Theodore, who was holding British subjects hostage. Stanley's eventual brilliant success in Abyssinia was partly the result of his unscrupulousness in bribing the telegraph operator in Suez to send his copy before that of his rivals and partly the result of extraordinary good luck, for after Stanley's first dispatches had been transmitted, the cable broke. Not only was Stanley's report the first news of the triumph of the British army, but for a while it was the only account. In a preview of what would be the British response to his finding of the British hero and saint Livingstone, the "American" Stanley was first accused of lying and then fiercely resented when proved justified.

In winter 1868 Stanley was assigned by Finlay Anderson, the European bureau chief for the *Herald,* to try to interview Livingstone, the celebrated explorer, who after three years unheard from in Africa was rumored to be on his way out of the interior. Livingstone, however, uncooperatively remained incommunicado in the heart of Africa. But the preparations for Stanley's most splendid triumph were not far off. In October 1869 the reporter was called from a mission in Spain to Paris by Bennett, in whose hotel room allegedly took place what is probably the second most famous conversation of Stanley's life:

> After throwing over his shoulders his robe-de-chambre, Mr. Bennett asked, "Where do you think Livingstone is?"
>
> "I really do not know, sir!"
> "Do you think he is alive?"
> "He may be, and he may not be!" I answered.
> "Well, I think he is alive, and that he can be found, and I am going to send you to find him."
> "What!" said I, "do you really think I can find Dr. Livingstone? Do you mean me to go to Central Africa?"
>
> "Yes.... Of course you will act according to your own plans, and do what you think best—BUT FIND LIVINGSTONE."

David Livingstone had gone to Africa in 1840 as a medical missionary. Unsuccessful as such—his one convert later lapsed—he had achieved a reputation as an explorer. He was among the first Europeans to cross the Kalahari Desert, and he discovered for the West both the Zambezi River and Victoria Falls; he was well known as an author, both *Missionary Travels and Researches in South Africa* (1857) and *The Zambezi and Its Tributaries* (1865) being best-sellers. But he had yet more influence as a great British Christian hero, motivated by a steady hatred of the slave trade and a desire to bring Christ to the Africans. In 1866 Livingstone had set off into central Africa hoping to identify the Nile's sources, the greatest mystery of African geography. He planned to explore the uncharted Lualaba River, believing that it emptied into the Nile and constituted its source.

Livingstone's whereabouts had been unknown at the time of the Bennett-Stanley interview for more than three and a half years, and it was not certain that he was still alive. Bennett's plan was for Stanley to make a long journey into Asia, attending first the inauguration of the Suez Canal (17 November 1869), visiting Jerusalem and the Crimean battlefields, moving on to Baghdad and India, and only then returning to find Livingstone, if he were still unaccounted for. Thus, Bennett could profit from Stanley's travel writing if the Livingstone puzzle remained unsolved in the interim, or he could benefit even more from copy about an expedition into Africa if it had not. (Bierman suggests that the East was the main focus of Bennett's interest, and the missionary-explorer a provisional afterthought at best, that, in fact, the celebrated conversation in the Paris hotel room was another of Stanley's fabrications.)

The Asian copy, the product of nine months' travel, was later collected by the then world-famous Stanley to make up the second volume of the potboiler *My Early Travels and Adventures in America and Asia* (1895), the first volume consisting of his dispatches from the American West. Bierman justly writes of the American half of the book, "Recycled journalism rarely reads well, even to a generation still attuned to the literary conventions in which it was composed, and that of *My Early Travels,* with its pomposities, its elephantine attempts at humor, and its long passages lifted verbatim from other writings, is certainly no exception." Nor can one be enthusiastic about the second volume, a collection of five pieces titled "The Suez Canal," "Up the Nile," "Jerusalem," "To the Caspian Sea," and "Through Persia."

Stanley had as yet published nothing between hardcovers, but the expedition he now undertook provided the material for a volume that was to be the best-selling success of 1872, *How I Found Living-*

Stanley at seventeen

stone: Travels, Adventures, and Discoveries in Central Africa: Including An Account of Four Months' Residence with Dr. Livingstone. The achievement is considerable; its recording less so. Not then thirty years old and with no African experience behind him, Stanley set off with his caravan into Central Africa from Bagamoyo on the east coast, opposite Zanzibar, in February 1871. Before leaving the coast he had already learned much about the cloth, beads, and wire he would have to take with him to pay his way; he had also learned something about the men he had to employ to carry them. He would learn more in the coming weeks about William L. Farquhar and John William Shaw, his two white lieutenants, and would also rapidly learn much about East Africa's terrain and people.

The first obstacle to success was fever, the origin of which—the bite of the tsetse fly—was not understood in Stanley's day. Stanley's approach to the onset of sickness among his men, to dispiritedness and fatigue, and to the difficulties of travel generally was to drive and flog his subordinates on: "I was compelled to observe that when mud and wet sapped the physical energy of the lazily-inclined, a dog-whip became their backs, restoring them to a sound—sometimes to an extravagant activity." As whites, Farquhar and Shaw were not flogged. But so tense did matters become that the two men hatched a desperate conspiracy. Shaw attempted to kill Stanley, firing into his tent at night and claiming that he had shot at a thief. Farquhar became so ill that he died five days after the caravan left the village in which he had been abandoned. He was the first of the many white companions who would perish on Stanley's relentless journeys.

Stanley reached Unyanyembe in record time. McLynn reports in *Stanley: The Making of an African Explorer* that he had averaged 6 miles a day for 84 days, thus beating Richard Burton and John Hanning Speke's rate of 3.9 miles a day for 134 days as well as Speke and James Grant's rate of 4.6 miles a day for 115 days. But now he became involved in a war between the Arabs of Unyanyembe and the Africans led by Mirambo. Stanley would make no progress for three months because Mirambo's warriors blocked the route to the next major settlement, Ujiji. Almost killed by fever at this time, Stanley had the additional misfortune of being inveigled into supporting the weaker side. Mirambo ambushed Stanley's Arab allies and wiped them out. When Mirambo withdrew without attacking Stanley's entrenched position, Stanley was able to think again about his main business in Africa and hire new porters to move on.

Unyanyembe did provide one source of solace for the increasingly frustrated and furious explorer. Stanley made a sort of gentleman's gentleman out of Kalulu, a seven-year-old black slave he acquired as a present from an Arab. In one of the dispatches he was sending to the *New York Herald* when opportunity offered, he described Lewis Noe's successor as a "young antelope . . . frisky. I have but to express a wish and it is gratified. He is a perfect Mercury, though a marvelously black one." Stanley's second book would be titled *My Kalulu: Prince, King, and Slave: A Story of Central Africa* (1873). His only attempt at fiction, *My Kalulu* is a boy's book telling of the imagined adventures of an idealized version of Stanley's devoted protégé. At his own adventure's end Stanley had himself photographed with Kalulu; the frontispiece to *How I Found Livingstone* depicts Stanley as the intrepid explorer and the young African in the role of trusty gunbearer.

Because of Mirambo's soldiers Stanley took a detour to the south out of Unyanyembe and then proceded north. He and Shaw were suffering from smallpox, and when Shaw begged to be allowed to retrace his steps, Stanley granted him permission. As McLynn points out, in granting Shaw's request Stanley ensured that he would be the only white to find Livingstone at journey's end. Shaw died soon after. Stanley's position as sole white in the caravan gave him no problems in imposing discipline: a mutiny among the porters ended with him whipping the man he considered its instigator. Crocodiles attacked the caravan as it crossed the River Malagarazi, and Simba, Stanley's favorite donkey, was lost. The expedition lost far more on dry land, however; Stanley was obliged to give up half its goods to tribesmen of the powerful Ha confederation. A second Ha chief demanded more the next day. To avoid further tribute Stanley and his men left the Ha village surreptitiously in the middle of the night, profiting from the offer of a slave who, for a price, took them toward Ujiji by another route.

When Stanley saw Lake Tanganyika, an "immense broad sheet, a burnished bed of silver," he knew he was close to his goal. Upon entering Ujiji, where they were now confident they would find the man they sought, Stanley's men fired volleys and flew the flags of both Zanzibar and the white man (the United States flag). When an expedition member reported that he could see Livingstone, Stanley was hard put to control his feelings. The wish to maintain his dignity as a white man before Arabs and Africans combined with his lifelong sense of social inferiority to produce the greeting that will always be associated with Stanley's name:

> I would have run to him, only I was a coward in the presence of such a mob—would have embraced him, only, he being an Englishman, I did not know how he would receive me; so I did what cowardice and false pride suggested was the best thing—Walked deliberately to him, took off my hat, and said:

> "Dr. Livingstone, I presume?"

In the moment of Stanley's greatest triumph the social and personal insecurities of the workhouse bastard are manifest. Here, when his tenacity, physical and moral courage, endurance, and leadership (even if mixed with and qualified by deeper psychological forces) should have brought their reward of unself-conscious joy and delighted fulfillment, Stanley is wincingly aware of himself, his base origins, and his status as non-English gentleman.

Livingstone was not an English gentleman either, his own origins being Scottish and working-class. Stanley must have realized immediately from the doctor's kindly "Yes" in reply to the greeting that his fears of indifference or rebuff were unfounded. But once news of the conversation had been transmitted to the outside world in the form of a dispatch to the *New York Herald,* it was too late. Stanley was haunted by his phrase for the rest of his life. When he came to write *How I Found Livingstone,*

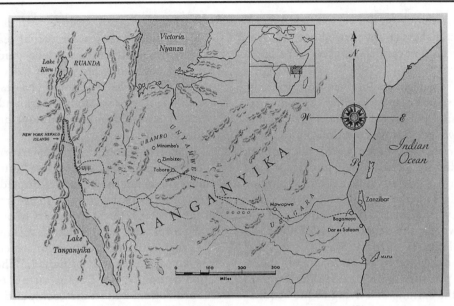

Map of Stanley's route in search of Dr. David Livingstone (from Byron Farwell, The Man Who Presumed, *1957)*

he self-consciously appended a famous paragraph from A. W. Kinglake's *Eothen* about two Englishmen whose paths crossed in the desert: "except that we lifted our hands to our caps, and waved our arms in courtesy, we passed each other as if we had passed in Bond Street."

Stanley delivered the supplies and letters he had brought for Livingstone and presented a white-washed account of why and at whose behest he had come. He could have started the trek back to the coast within twenty-four hours, but he stayed four months as his apparently unlikely friendship with Livingstone developed. The relationship was not as surprising as it may seem at first consideration. Not only did the reputedly saintly British missionary and the wicked American reporter share outsider origins as Celtic plebeians, chronically suspicious of those in the inner circles, but they also shared personality traits. In professional matters both were egocentrics who got on badly with other Europeans in Africa. What each of the two men could offer—and what each needed—were pleasingly complementary. In the American who had survived the Civil War, Livingstone found a new form of his son Robert, who had died of wounds sustained in the conflict. Stanley, in turn, found the father he had never had. "I loved him as a son, and would have done for him anything worthy of the most filial," he wrote to Livingstone's daughter. "He behaved as a son to a father—truly overflowing in kindness," wrote Livingstone to the same person.

In the time they spent together Livingstone and Stanley explored the north of Lake Tangan-

yika. The doctor refused to accompany Stanley back to England, wishing still to establish definitively the Nile's sources, but agreed to wait in Unyanyembe for the supplies that Stanley would send to him there. The final parting occurred on 14 March 1872, with Stanley, at least, "unmanned." "For both," writes McLynn in *Hearts of Darkness: The European Exploration of Africa* (1993), "it meant the end of the only successful human relationship of their lives." Stanley set a new record on the march back to Bagamoyo: 525 miles in fifty-two days, a rate of more than 10 miles a day.

Stanley traveled back to London via France. He was feted in Paris, but in London the response was hostile. His story was doubted, and the Livingstone letters he had brought back with him were said to be forgeries. But after initial English incredulity and snobbish contempt had been overcome, honors followed fast. Stanley was received by the queen, and in October 1872 he was given the Royal Geographical Society's Gold Medal. He was concurrently writing his book.

Livingstone had written to John Murray, the publishers, from Ujiji in favor of the book Stanley was already talking of and had already written to his daughter urging her to cooperate with him. Stanley was eventually to accept a generous offer from Sampson Low: 50 percent of the profits and a £1,000 advance. In the United States Scribners offered another £1,000 for the American rights and in $10,000 advanced royalties. *How I Found Livingstone* rapidly sold seventy thousand copies, making its author a rich man. Florence Nightingale described it as "the very worst book on the very best subject," but Stanley's publishers could crow about "an ovation seldom, perhaps never before, accorded a book of travel."

Most present-day readers would probably agree that in this book Stanley justifies McLynn's estimate of him and Livingstone in *Stanley: The Making of an African Explorer:* "Both were primarily journalists of genius." *How I Found Livingstone* is the product of a fiercely ambitious, penetratingly intelligent man who seeks both worldly advancement and psychological release. It is not the work of a man with a specifically literary interest in the selection and arrangement of words, the development of ideas, or the aesthetic pleasures of form. Stanley's writing was always produced, often at extraordinary speed or under great pressure, with an extraliterary purpose, whether the earning of a living or the acquisition or consolidation of fame. His books were criticized in their time for their sometimes leaden style, but it is possible to read them with pleasure today.

All four of Stanley's major books possess the virtues and vices of *How I Found Livingstone.* The main faults of the first book are those typical of Victorian travel writing of the second rank: occasionally wearisome jocularity; pretentiously Latinate or adjectivally clichéd diction; and a reluctance, or inability, to omit from the travel diary kept en route the banal or extraneous. The striving after humor is illustrated by Stanley's description of the Jesuit mission in Bagamoyo. He notes that the padres and the sisters "all found plenty of occupation in educing from native crania the fire of intelligence." Stanley is also coyly witty about the high quality of the food and wine he is surprisingly served at this outpost: after a reference to the "plats" (dishes) of a "first-class hotel in Paris," he remarks that "I feel assured also that the padres, besides being tasteful in their potages and entrées, do not stultify their ideas for lack of that element which Horace, Hafiz, and Byron have praised so much." Stanley would be taken for a man of the world and wants his reader to understand that he is well read in addition to being well traveled in the highest circles.

Stanley's insecurity as an autodidact fuels both his pedantic Latinisms and his literary response to nature. He remarks that one man suffers from "the infructuosities of the business he has been engaged in, as well as . . . the calor . . . of the climate." A handshake is "an interlacing of digits." When Farquhar and Shaw quarrel, they are "contumacious belligerants." When he feels called upon to praise the beauty of nature, Stanley can write like a well-brought-up young nineteenth-century lady: "as I looked over the grandly undulating plain, lovely with its coat of green verdure, with its boundaries of noble woods, heavy with vernal leafage, and regarded the pretty bosky islets amid its wide expanse, I could not but award it its need of high praise." He is at his worst when he describes African scenery as if it were English parkland, much better when he sees without the dubious help of conventional attitudes.

Stanley seems never satisfactorily to have decided on a narrative stance. His "Introductory" includes the claim that "I have adopted the narrative form of relating the story of the search, on account of the greater interest it appears to possess over the diary form, and I think that in this manner I avoid the great fault of repetition for which some travellers have been severely criticised." The fault of repetition he may avoid, but the virtues of elimination, subordination, and studied composition he does not attain. Despite his disclaimer, he is not above writing, "The following items are extracted in their entirety from my Diary" toward the end of the book, as earlier he had not blushed to claim, implausibly, "I have felt myself compelled to copy out of my Diary the above notes. . . . To me they appear to explain far better than any amount of descriptive writing, even of the most graphic, the nature of the life I led."

The story Stanley tells is also complicated by his own sense of self. He was both a Victorian self-made man of low origins and a link in the chain of increasing Western knowledge of and control over Africa, who hoped that later explorers would find his book more helpful than he had found Burton's *The Lake Regions of Central Africa* (1860). Both voices are evident in Stanley's justification for his inclusiveness: "do not think, if I speak out my mind in this or in any other chapter upon matters seemingly trivial and unimportant, that seeming such they should be left unmentioned. Every tittle related is a fact, and to know facts is to receive knowledge."

The chief merit of *How I Found Livingstone* is Stanley's ability to observe. While his descriptions of natural beauty are often tritely and conventionally expressed, his descriptions of people are usually vivid and hardheaded. The depiction of Hadji Palloo in Bagamoyo reveals Stanley's attention to detail: "His jaws also were in perpetual motion, caused by vile habits he had acquired of chewing betel-nut and lime, and sometimes tobacco and lime. They gave out a sound similar to that of a young shoat, in the act of sucking."

Stanley's account of the chief Mionvu's gorgeous dress is similarly precise: "a crimson robe called Joho, two ends of which were tied in a knot over the left shoulder; a new piece of American

Marker at the place where Stanley met Livingstone in 1871, under a mango tree at Ujiji

sheeting was folded round a turban round his head, and a large carved piece of polished ivory was suspended to his neck." (He apparently chooses the awkward "to his neck" to avoid a third "round" in two lines.) Stanley sculpts Mionvu's features for the reader: "oval in form, high cheek-bones, eyes deeply sunk, a prominent and bold forehead, a fine nose, and a well-cut mouth." McLynn sees "a novelist's perception" in a description of Livingstone in Stanley's journal: "The loose front teeth which play while he talks add to the appearance of age a great deal. He uses humorous Scotticisms frequently . . . he is full of sly jokes. When he begins one of his funny stories, I see how it is going to end by the gleam in his dark hazel eyes, the pucker gathering about his eyes—the uplifted forefinger." Unfortunately the frankness of the journal is diminished in the official portrait of *How I Found Livingstone:* "His eyes, which are hazel, are remarkably bright; he has a sight keen as a hawk's. His teeth indicate the weakness of age; the hard fare of Lunda has made havoc in their lines. . . . the Doctor has a fund of quiet humor, which he exhibits at all times whenever he is among friends." Stanley's journals were scrupulously kept, often in circumstances that were trying indeed. The disciplined will and the alert eye are both admirable.

Stanley's writing often captures the romance and exotic glamor of the strange African world freshly observed: "The lake [Tanganyika] was quite calm; its waters, of a dark-green color, reflected the serene blue sky above. The hippopotami came up to breathe in alarmingly close proximity to our canoe, and then plunged their heads again, as if they were playing hide-and-seek with us." In its narrative sweep, its offer of escape and vicarious excitement, and its flattering juxtaposition of "savage" splendor and gentlemanly Christian virtue, Stanley's book paints what was indeed for many nineteenth-century Westerners "the very best subject" and in a manner that, if flawed, is far from "the very worst." Marianna Torgovnick suggests that Stanley's comment about Livingstone's first book—that no boy should be without it—applies also to his own works. But one may more charitably add that they appeal to boys of all ages.

Stanley's new wealth and fame aroused the jealousy of Bennett, whom Stanley credited with the idea of the Livingstone expedition. To take his employee down a peg Bennett sent him to Spain for his next assignment. However, in November 1873 Stanley was ordered to the Gold Coast in West Africa. It was his second experience of covering a British colonial punitive expedition, this time against the Ashanti, whose stronghold at Coomassie soon fell to the superior weaponry of a technologically advanced army. Stanley's *Coomassie and Magdala: The Story of Two British Campaigns in Africa* (1874) is another collection of recycled journalism. The humid tedium of life in West Africa seems to have affected Stanley's style, which is turgid and lifeless.

His assignment completed, Stanley was back in London in time to be a pallbearer at Livingstone's funeral on 18 April 1874. There is no reason to doubt the sincerity of Stanley's grief at the death of his hero despite its expression in his diary in terms that suggest self-serving Victorian cant with a thin veneer of altruistic Christianity. "Dear Livingstone! another sacrifice to Africa! His mission, however, must not be allowed to cease; others must go forward and close the gap. . . . May I be selected to succeed him in opening up Africa to the shining light of Christianity!"

Resentment and ambition were both part of Stanley's emotional mix. Believing that some still questioned his achievements in Africa in 1870 and 1871, he was determined to silence his critics and to be seen as Livingstone's successor. Stanley received assurance from the *London Daily Telegraph* that it would provide £6,000 for an African expedition if the *New York Herald* would provide a similar sum. Bennett agreed, and Stanley landed in Zanzibar again in September 1874 for the mission that was intended to make undeniable his status as an explorer. When it ended with his arrival in August 1877 at Boma on the west coast, his achievements were indeed overwhelming, but the journalistic dash of his accounts of bloody battles with the tribes who would have barred his way had given his enemies fresh cause to despise him.

Stanley's three-year expedition—the basis for *Through the Dark Continent: Or, The Sources of the Nile, Around the Great Lakes of Equatorial Africa, and Down the Livingstone River to the Atlantic Ocean* (1878)—may conveniently be divided into three parts: his trek to and exploration of Lake Victoria, followed by his dealings with Mutesa, the king of Buganda, which is situated to the immediate northwest of the lake in present-day Uganda; the trek southeast to Lake Tanganyika, which he also circumnavigated, and then northwest into unexplored territory and the River Congo; and the final descent west and south along the Congo to the Atlantic Ocean. He was accompanied by Kalulu and three English companions—Frederick Barker, the clerk at the London hotel where he had been staying and an eager volunteer for the expedition, and Frank and Edward Pocock, two young men from Kent recommended by Stanley's publisher. All four were to die on this trip. Edward Pocock died in January 1875 of typhus, and Barker died of fever while Stanley was exploring Lake Victoria. Kalulu and Frank Pocock perished in the cataracts of the Congo.

The generously underwritten expedition—McLynn in *Hearts of Darkness* asserts that it was "the most lavishly equipped and financed to date" in Africa—began well, reaching the village of Mpwapwa in an impressive twenty-five days. But when Stanley turned northwest toward Lake Victoria, his first major objective, he and his caravan encountered harsh terrain and extremes of climate while being pressed by desertions, extortionate demands for passage money, and "the grievous and bitter pangs of hunger." To feed the company Stanley and Frank Pocock once emptied a "'Torquay dress trunk' of sheet-iron" and concocted a porridge out of a ten-pound bag of oatmeal and four one-pound tins of "revalenta arabica" (lentil flour), fortunately found in the medical stores. But even these difficulties pale into insignificance beside the events of Vinyata, which followed shortly after Edward Pocock's death.

Stanley's frankness about his battles with Africans was to surprise other Africanists, who preferred to maintain a tactful silence about such conflicts. Gen. Charles Gordon asked in a letter, "Why if you had to defend yourself, you said anything about it." Stanley no doubt said something about it out of journalistic training: he knew that battles made good, exciting copy. In the case of Vinyata, however, weakness brought about by sickness and starvation as well as the memory of Livingstone's practice of forbearance made Stanley behave with relative moderation. Stanley narrates how tension increased until they "heard war cries. . . . and presently saw a large body of natives armed with spears, bows and arrows, and shields, appear within a hundred yards . . . outside the camp." At first Stanley avoided a fight by giving cloth to recompense the warriors for an alleged theft. Some, though, wanted action against the expedition anyway. Interpreting Stanley's continued restraint as cowardice, they taunted his band with cries of, "Ye are women, ye are women." The taunts proved too much for Stanley to bear. "It was only then, perceiving that they were too savage to understand the principles of forbearance, that the final word to 'fight' was given. A brisk encounter was maintained for an hour, and then, having driven the savages away, [my men] were recalled to camp." Fighting went on for the next two days but ended in Stanley's victory, at the cost of twenty-four of his men killed and four wounded. He had the local villages burned and looted, thus obtaining grain for six days. The fight at Vinyata was the first of many engagements. A far more damaging one to Stanley's reputation took place at Bumbireh Island in Lake Victoria.

The circumnavigation of the lake, with Stanley

Stanley's inscription to his publisher, J. Blair Scribner, in a copy of Stanley's best-known book (Archives of Charles Scribner's Sons, Manuscript Division, Department of Rare Books and Special Collections, Princeton University Libraries)

taking his usual precise observations, was the first great geographical achievement of the expedition. His party was hospitably received by Mutesa of Buganda, who deceived the explorer into thinking he was ready to embrace Christianity. Stanley's subsequent call for missionaries in a dispatch eventually would lead to an increased British presence in East Africa, but because the call was answered by missionaries of different sects, it also produced sectarian discord. By encouraging missionaries Stanley could style himself as Livingstone's successor as proselytizer as well as explorer.

When Stanley and his men landed on Bumbireh to barter for food, the natives, after simulating friendliness, suddenly dragged Stanley's boat, the *Lady Alice,* ashore. Stanley, both the product and

molder of Western attitudes about the "Dark Continent," portrays the Africans as devils from a Miltonic hell:

> Then ensued a scene that beggars description. Pandemonium—all its devils armed—raged around us. A forest of spears was levelled; thirty or forty bows were drawn taut; as many barbed arrows seemed already on the wing; thick, knotty clubs waved above our heads; two hundred screaming black demons jostled with each other and struggled for room to vent their fury, or for an opportunity to deliver one crushing blow or thrust at us.

In the pages that follow Stanley delivers an exciting, fast-paced narrative. He quietly ordered his men, when he gave the word, to "push [the boat] with the force of a hundred men down the hill and into the water." But this feat having been successfully accomplished, the group was then confronted by other dangers: pursuing natives had to be fought off, as did curious, or hungry, hippopotamuses; the twelve men in the boat had only makeshift paddles, the real ones having been snatched by the men of Bumbireh in an effort to prevent the explorers' escape; and the explorers only had four bananas between them. After seventy-six hours' sailing, the boat beached on an uninhabited island. Stanley shot two ducks, and his men found fruit.

The attack on the *Lady Alice* occurred in late April 1875. Stanley returned to Bumbireh in August with his full expedition and additional warriors supplied by Mutesa. Using modern firearms he inflicted a severe punishment upon the spear-wielders and archers who had insulted him. "The savages, perceiving the disastrous effect of our fire on a compact body, scattered. . . . We then moved to within 50 yards of the shore, to fire at close quarters, and each man was permitted to exercise himself as best he could. . . . a volley was fired into the spearmen, which quite crushed their courage. . . . Our work of chastisement was complete."

Not even Stanley could win every encounter. In December he began the second stage of his journey by traveling northwest as far as Lake George but was obliged to turn back by a hostile chief more powerful than he. He headed south-southwest to Ujiji on Lake Tanganyika, with its memories of Livingstone, and thoroughly explored that lake too. The exploration of Lake Victoria had validated Speke's supposition that the Nile has its source there. Stanley now demolished Burton's belief that the Nile's source flowed north out of Lake Tanganyika.

By August 1876 Stanley was ready to continue northwest to the Lualaba River, which the expedition sighted in mid October. It was Stanley's hope that the river would join with the Congo and lead to the Atlantic, but a conversation with Tippu-Tib, a rich Arab trader who had been operating in Central Africa for some decades, led him to fear it might be "the river that flows North for ever." Certain knowledge of the region had been discouraged by the reported cannibal ferocity of the tribes northwest of Nyangwe. In another memorable piece of bravura journalism Stanley recounts a conversation between himself and Frank Pocock about whether to court danger by heading north or go south to relative safety. Stanley gave Pocock a rupee to toss: "Heads for the north and the Lualaba; tails for the south and Katanga." Six times running tails won; then by drawing short straws Pocock persisted in getting the same unpopular answer. Stanley nevertheless declared to his subordinate, "It is of no use, Frank. We'll face our destiny despite the rupee and straws."

Stanley's decision would lead to Pocock's death and to great suffering for all the expedition, but it yielded unimpeachable glory for its leader. In addition to the hostile tribesmen, Stanley and his men would have to contend with cataracts and again with terrible hunger. Bitter confrontations with natives had already taken place when the expedition encountered the first cataract in the first series. (Stanley would name these cataracts Stanley Falls; they are now Boyoma Falls.) The *Lady Alice* and the canoes had to be pulled along paths slashed through the jungle. Scarcely had the river become navigable again than attacks from tribesmen increased in frequency and intensity. Stanley accepted this opposition philosophically. "In these wild regions our mere presence excited the most furious passions of hate and murder, just as in shallow waters a deep vessel stirs up muddy sediments. It appeared to be a necessity, then why should we regret it?" This comment precedes a description of one of the biggest battles, which occurred at the confluence of the Congo and the Aruwimi.

Falling into the historical present, as is his wont for his most "thrilling" passages, Stanley writes, "Looking up stream, we see a sight that sends the blood tingling through every nerve and fibre of the body, arouses not only our most lively interest, but also our most lively apprehensions—a flotilla of gigantic canoes bearing down on us, which both in size and numbers utterly eclipse anything encountered hitherto!" In the closely observed and enthusiastically described barbaric splendor of the cannibals, one sees the origin of a sterotypical scene in jungle movies:

> A monster canoe leads the way, with two rows of upstanding paddles, forty men on a side, their bodies bending and swaying in unison as with a swelling and barbarous chorus they drive her down towards us. In the bow, standing on what appears to be a platform, are ten prime young warriors, their heads gay with feathers of the parrot crimson and grey: at the stern, eight men, with long paddles, whose tops are decorated with ivory balls, guide the monster vessel; and dancing up and down from stem to stern are ten men, who appear to be chiefs. All the paddles are headed with ivory balls, every head bears a feather crown, every arm shows gleaming white ivory armlets. . . . [We hear the] crashing sound of large drums, a hundred blasts from ivory horns, and a thrilling chant from two thousand human throats.

The ten-to-one numerical superiority of the attackers does little more than the flash of nodding plumes

Stanley and his men at Zanzibar in 1877

or the glint of ivory ornaments against "ripping, crackling musketry." Stanley is unembarrassed in his description of the expedition's enraged blood-lust: "Our blood is up now. It is a murderous world, and we feel for the first time that we hate the filthy, vulturous ghouls who inhabit it." The explorers continued the killing in the streets of the villages where the tribesmen fled and then in the surrounding woods. In the course of the expedition Stanley would record thirty-two such encounters.

Stanley offers his readers scenes other than those of battle and depicts peaceful Africans as well as warriors. As the caravan progressed southwest along the Congo after the seemingly endless northern loop, Stanley heard of more cataracts ahead. Partly to gather information on the terrain and tribes ahead and partly to satisfy hunger, Stanley accepted an invitation from the king of Chumbiri. Some of the 150 engravings that enliven Stanley's *Through the Dark Continent* were produced from his preliminary sketches of the people of Chumbiri. The illustrations in this and his other works of exotic people and places, of native tools and artifacts such as the king's "great pipe," certainly helped make Stanley's books best-sellers. The text is sometimes condescending and shows the unfortunate tendency to jocularity that had marred his first book, but Stanley's eye for the detail that would interest his audience is keen. For example, he "makes a rough calculation" that the king, "a keen and enterprising trader, . . . possesses a portable store of 1396 lbs. of brass," all forged into collars or arm or leg ornaments for his wives and daughters.

After this peaceful interlude followed what Richard Hall in *Stanley: An Adventurer Explored* (1974) calls "a nightmare, an unparalleled disaster that almost destroyed the expedition in the last stage of its 7,000-mile crossing of Africa." He refers to the arduous working of the *Lady Alice* through or around the cataracts of the Lower Congo. The men, increasingly hungry and weak, had to negotiate fierce rapids or manhandle their boats over specially cut trails. They covered only 180 miles in five months. It was here that Kalulu and Frank Pocock drowned. Only at the end of July did Stanley finally decide to leave the river and march the last fifty miles to Boma. His men were now so feeble that he selected four to go on ahead with a letter addressed "To any Gentleman who Speaks English at Embomma" requesting immediate supplies. They arrived a week later, and the 115 men, women, and children who had managed to survive were saved.

Nobody doubted Stanley's word this time, not even the mandarins of the Royal Geographical Society. In the preface to *Through the Dark Continent* Stanley remarks that the king of Italy, the Prince of Wales, and the khedive of Egypt had all offered their congratulations. He then lists sixteen honors its author had been given, and ends "&c." The book became Stanley's second best-seller.

It is a better book, more confident about what it wants to achieve and less hesitant about how to achieve it, than *How I Found Livingstone*. While the coy Latinisms and other flaws are not gone, they are certainly much less in evidence. Less of a hodge-podge than his first book, Stanley's account of his

295

second great journey avoids verbatim transcription from his diary, although it still is closely based on notes made en route. He does not stop the narrative for "Geographical and Ethnographical Remarks," although readers learn more about "Life and Manners in Uganda" than perhaps they wish. Uncomplicated, extroverted, indomitable, *Through the Dark Continent* deserved its popular success.

It does not, however, deserve the extravagant praise heaped upon it by *Harper's New Monthly Magazine* in a contemporary review. The response to Stanley and his work cannot be fully understood without an awareness of his changing nationality and the ways in which reactions to him were often shaped either by anti-Americanism or by Anglophobia. Born a British subject, he was to become an American citizen in 1885 to prevent his books from being pirated in the United States with impunity. In 1892 he reverted to his British nationality in order to satisfy the political ambitions his wife nurtured for him. Queen Victoria had described him after their first meeting as "a determined, ugly, little man—with a strong American twang," and much of the cool wariness of the British establishment, the congratulations of the Prince of Wales notwithstanding, originated in snobbery.

When Stanley was accused of slaughterous indifference to African life, the reviewer for *Harper's* responded as if America had been slandered. The review of *Through the Dark Continent* significantly begins with a comparison of Stanley's exploit with that other great feat of world-changing exploration, the discovery of America: "The work which Stanley set out from Zanzibar to do was perhaps the noblest and most intrepid that had ever fallen to one man since Columbus with a modest fleet of unseaworthy boats sailed forth to discover a world. . . . Columbus began the discovery of America; Stanley finished the discovery of Africa." Playing up the cannibalism of the Africans, the reviewer excused Stanley's actions: "We think the law of self-defense can be put on no higher ground than the dislike to be killed and eaten by your enemy." The American reviewer could even discern a "modest piety" in Stanley and praise his writing as "fine, clear, nervous Saxon English, simple in its strength, with the stamp of truth in its simplicity."

Stanley's life now changed focus without changing direction. He had spent eleven years, from 1867 to 1878, as a journalist, much of it exploring Africa. He now left journalism to become an administrator in the Congo for King Leopold II of Belgium. From 1879 to 1885 Stanley would play a major role in the founding of what would become first the Congo Free State and later the Belgian Congo.

Belgium was a newcomer to colonizing Africa. Portugal, France, and Britain had histories of trading posts and missionary endeavors in the continent that had culminated in the outright possession of thousands of square miles. The newly unified Italy and Germany were also showing an interest in colonization. Belgium, however, lagged far behind, and it seemed that most of Leopold's countrymen did not share the belief of their king that "Il faut à la Belgique une Colonie" (It is necessary for Belgium to have a Colony). Leopold, described by his father as "subtle and sly" and by his interior minister as "artful and deceitful," knew he must proceed with caution to avoid causing anxiety at home or anger abroad. He believed enlisting the services of the greatest African explorer of the age would no doubt help him achieve his goals.

Stanley was approached by the king's messengers at a dinner of the Marseilles Geographical Society. Stanley accepted the proposal because he was convinced of Britain's lack of interest in the Congo and because hard work in the region seemed more attractive to him than what he believed would be a lonely life in London. As Bierman explains, Leopold wished "to supply [Stanley] with 100,000 dollars a year over five years to found a settlement on the Congo and from there to branch out as far as possible around this great river." Stanley would administer the Comité d'Etudes du Haut-Congo—a misleading name, because although the ostensible purpose of the organization was "study" of the Congo basin, Stanley realized that Leopold wished to make the region a Belgian dependency. Stanley arrived at the mouth of the Congo on 14 August 1879. His plans were to build a road along the river (railways were too expensive), transport boats on it to the Stanley Pool, a lakelike stretch of the Congo River, and proceed by water from there. He would also build administrative stations at convenient points.

Stanley was under pressure to move ahead quickly, but four months after his arrival he was still far from the Upper Congo. King Leopold knew of the activities of a French naval officer, Italian-born Pierre Savorgnan de Brazza, who was traveling down from Gabon with the intention of claiming both the north and south shores of Stanley Pool for his adopted country. Unlike Brazza, Stanley in intense heat was road-making and station-building as he went, resisting suggestions from Brussels to increase his pace. "I am not a party in a race for the Stanley Pool, as I have already been in that locality just two and a half years ago and I do not intend to visit it again until I can arrive with my 50 tons of goods, boats and other property, and after finishing the second station." Ultimately, through Brazza's efforts France would acquire French Equatorial Africa, including Gabon and the French Congo, with its capital of Brazzaville on the north side of the pool, while Belgium through Stanley would claim the neighboring Belgian Congo, with its capital of Léopoldville on the southern shore.

While traveling to that second station, Isangila, fifty miles northwest of the first station at Vivi, Stanley met Brazza, who was journeying to Gabon by way of Vivi. Stanley devotes a few pages to Brazza in the dreariest of his four big books, *The Congo and the Founding of Its Free State: A Story of Work and Exploration* (1885): "the French gentleman appears, dressed in helmet, naval blue coat, and feet encased in a brown leather bandage . . . The gentleman is tall in appearance, of very dark complexion, and looks thoroughly fatigued." One gets a more vivid impression of Brazza, as interesting a man as his rival, from the splendid woodcut that illustrates the text than from Stanley's uninspired prose.

But while his Congo years did not produce great writing, they transformed the Congo basin and the lives of those Africans who inhabited it. Stanley's indomitable willpower is as much in evidence as ever. Brazza had looked at the mountain that represented the next obstacle on Stanley's route and observed, "It will take you six months to pass that mountain with those wagons. Your force is too weak altogether for such a work as you are engaged in." Stanley admits the justice of the remark. However, his career hitherto had been built upon overcoming apparently impassible barriers, physical and human. He would pass "the huge mass of Ngoma" in a mere seven weeks. Stanley had earlier related how he acquired the nickname "with which, from the sea to Stanley Falls, all natives of the Congo are now so familiar." A group of chiefs, "wonderingly looking on while I taught my men how to wield a sledge-hammer effectively, bestowed on me the title of Bula Matari–'Breaker of Rocks.'" By February 1881, eighteen months after arriving at the coast, he had established Isangila station and made thirty-eight miles of road. The next station, Manyanga, was to be built ninety miles upriver. The work, arduous as it was, progressed steadily.

It was at Manyanga in early May 1881 that Stanley almost died of malaria. On the eighth day of the fever he took "twenty grains of quinine dissolved in some hydrobromic acid" and then another thirty grains on regaining consciousness. By the fourteenth day he was "so weak that I could scarcely lift my arms, and to sit up in bed was impossible without support." On 20 May, at seven in the morning, he felt that the end had come. Temporarily fortified by sixty grains of quinine, he called for the workers to surround his bed so he could pass on last orders. The effort required was so great that when "the sentence was at last . . . delivered clearly and intelligently . . . I felt so relieved from my distress that I called out, 'I am saved!'" The worst was over, but it was two weeks before he was well enough to walk.

A problem of an entirely different nature next arose. The rate of Stanley's methodical progress up the river had allowed Brazza to claim the north shore of Stanley Pool for France without opposition. Leopold's displeasure was considerable, and Stanley felt himself under yet greater pressure to buy land for Leopold's front organization and to "place under [its] sovereignty, as soon as possible and without losing a minute" the chiefs from the mouth of the Congo all the way upriver to Stanley Falls, almost a thousand miles beyond Stanley Pool.

But securing the southern, unclaimed shore of Stanley Pool, an acquisition that must inevitably precede further movement upriver, proved difficult because of opposition from a tribal chief called Ngalyema. The writing in the two chapters of *The Congo and the Founding of Its Free State* that deal with this colorful rogue is livelier than much of that which surrounds it, as mordant scorn replaced journal-keeping banality or public-man acknowledgments of others' services. Ngalyema, Stanley tells us, "was now about thirty-four years old, of well-built form, proud in his bearing, covetous and grasping in his disposition, and, like all other lawless barbarians, prone to be cruel and sanguinary whenever he might safely vent his evil humour. Superstition had found in him an apt and docile pupil, and fetishism held him as one of its most abject slaves." A former slave who had acquired riches by trading in ivory, Ngalyema commanded a thousand men armed with muskets. Stanley had to win Ngalyema over–not obliterate him–if he was to do his work and survive the judgment of public opinion.

Stanley was fond of Africans. His white subordinates complained that he would always favor the African over the European in any dispute placed before him. But he was of two minds about the relative value of Ngalyema and what he represented on the one hand and Leopold's organization and what Stanley thought it represented on the other. "This was the man," he sardonically notes, "in whose hands the destinies of the Association . . . were held, and upon whose graciousness depended our only hope of being able to effect a peaceful lodgment on the Upper Congo. Had he but known that fact, we should have been obliged to pay a heavier penalty than is conceivable to any reader of these pages." Stanley assures his reader that a "simple narration" will serve to reveal "this African chief in his true col-

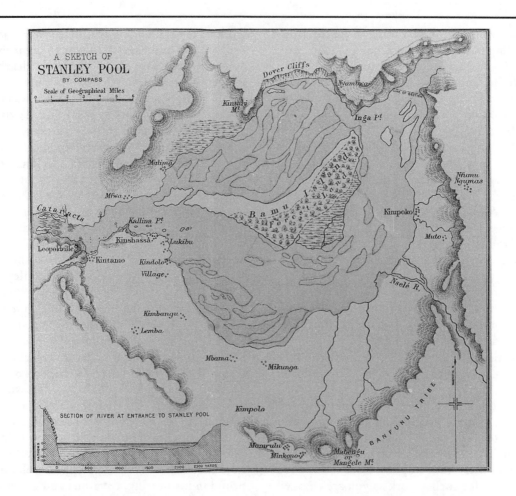

Map and illustration from Stanley's Congo and the Founding of Its Free State *(1885)*

ours." The narration tells how the chief, the extent of whose Western sophistication is symbolized by his warriors' antique muskets, was fooled by a "ruse."

Stanley began by offering presents to the man who was now his blood brother. "My brother being . . . the deepest-voiced and most arrogant rogue among the whole tribe, first demanded . . . two asses, then a large mirror, which was succeeded by a splendid gold-embroidered coat, jewellery, glass clasps, long brass chains, a figured table-cloth, fifteen other pieces of fine cloth, and a japanned tin box with a 'Chubb' lock." Ngalyema gave his staff of office in exchange—then sent back the presents, having been warned by his men not to offer Stanley a grant of land. Among blood brothers this act probably presaged war.

When Ngalyema arrived in the white man's camp accompanied by two hundred soldiers with muskets, Stanley was ready. He had ordered most of his armed men to hide and the rest to feign sleep. Ngalyema entered an apparently defenseless camp, curtly told Stanley to return downriver, and made ready to leave. As he was leaving, he noticed a "large Chinese gong suspended to a cross-bar supported by two forked poles." With seeming reluctance, at Ngalyema's insistent urging, Stanley beat the gong, which he had represented as a "war fetish." It was the signal his men had been waiting for:

> With all my force I struck the gong, the loud bell-like tone sounding in the silence caused by the hushed concentrated attention of all upon the scene, was startling in the extreme, but as the rapid strokes were applied vigorously the continued sound seemed to them like thunder. They had not recovered from the first shock of astonishment when the forms of men were seen bounding over the gunwale of the *En Avant* right over their heads, and war-whooping in their ears. From my tent, and from the gorge behind them, a stream of frantic infuriates emerged as though from the earth. The store-tent was violently agitated, and finally collapsed, and a yelling crowd of demoniac madmen sprang out one after another, every one apparently madder than his neighbour. The listless, sleepy-eyed stragglers burst out into a perfect frenzy of action. From under the mats in the huts there streamed into view such a frantic mob of armed men, that to the panic-struck natives the sky and the earth seemed to be contributing to the continually increasing number of death-dealing warriors.

At the sounding of this war fetish that caused screaming, armed warriors to appear from nowhere, Ngalyema pleaded for protection from Bula Matari. He eventually came to realize that he had been the object of a practical joke, but posed no more serious problems. With the signing of a final agreement Stanley could build his settlement, which he called Léopold-

ville (present-day Kinshasa). It became the capital of the Belgian Congo.

Stanley pushed on, intending to build another station at Mswata, sixty miles upriver. But falling ill, he first returned to Vivi and then, on 15 July 1882, sailed for Europe. He thought he had finished his work in the Congo and assumed that the three-year contract he had signed with one of Leopold's front organizations superseded and canceled a previously signed five-year contract with another. He was surprised and dismayed when asked to go back as soon as his health permitted. But go back he did, leaving Brussels in November and arriving once more at the Congo's mouth in the middle of the next month. His work was now to establish stations on the Upper Congo and to make treaties with the chief there.

It was often dispiriting work. The most haunting pages in *The Congo and the Founding of Its Free State* describe the ravaged villages around Stanley Falls and the fate of their inhabitants, victims of Arab slavers. After Stanley's descent of the Congo the slavers realized that their earlier fears of the river tribes had been excessive, and fresh areas to plunder lay before them. Stanley passed through deserted and burned villages and crops in what had once been populous areas. Desolated survivors spoke of a night attack. Further along the river, one of his men turned over with a boat hook "some object, of a slaty colour, floating downstream." It turned out to be the bodies of two women, bound together with cord. A few hours later, Stanley's party caught up with the "banditti." Just as he could not bring Ngalyema to heel by force, as the employee of a nonviolent organization, Stanley now felt unable "to avenge these devastations and massacres of sleeping people."

But perhaps he did a little to bring an end to such scenes of wretchedness by imagining and relating them so clearly:

> Little perhaps as my face betrayed my feelings, other pictures would crowd upon the imagination; and after realising the extent and depth of misery presented to me, I walked about as in a kind of dream, wherein I saw through the darkness of the night the stealthy forms of the murderers creeping towards the doomed town, its inmates all asleep, and no sounds issuing from the gloom but the drowsy hum of chirping cicadas or distant frogs—when suddenly flash the light of brandished torches; the sleeping town is involved in flames, while volleys of musketry lay low the frightened and astonished people, sending many through a short minute of agony to that soundless sleep from which there will be no waking.

By the time he sailed back to Europe on 8 June 1884, Stanley had directed the construction of what amounted to the infrastructure of a new nation. He had established twenty-two stations on the Congo and its tributaries, built roads, and gained sovereignty of the land from more than four hundred chiefs.

The Congo and the Founding of Its Free State appeared in July 1885, Leopold having previously read the proofs to make sure there was no harm in it from his perspective. The product of a world-famous man about a fascinating subject, it sold well but surely must have disappointed many of its purchasers. Too often it reads like a bland company report: "On the 13th of October the *Belgique* began running up; then the Englishmen, Mr. John Kirkbright of Birmingham, and Mr. A. B. Swinburne of London, were ordered up to the scene. . . . The *Belgique* towing the large steel lighter commenced transporting the wooden house and iron stores so well constructed by Francis Morton & Co. of London." Biographer Richard Hall considers that "The most lively part of the whole production is the cover design, showing steamboats, naked cherubs, cacti, pineapples, and scenes of the Stanley Pool."

Leopold now considered Stanley a tool of dubious value. Irreplaceable as the manager of the project, he was a potential embarrassment when diplomacy was needed. Leopold's tortuous diplomatic maneuverings culminated in brilliant success at the end of the Berlin Conference of 1884–1885, called to adjudicate disagreements between the great powers in regard to the African colonies. The powers recognized nine hundred thousand square miles of the Congo basin as Leopold's personal possession. The "stone breaker" was kept idle in London on an extended contract and given the Order of Leopold as a sop.

Stanley began looking for a wife, asking Livingstone's son-in-law for moral support in the search. His relations with women had been consistently unfortunate. He still had not recovered from being jilted by Alice Pike, the daughter of an American millionaire after whom the *Lady Alice*—the boat of his second great expedition—had been named. Alice had accepted his proposal before he left for Zanzibar in 1874 and promised to wait. When, full of love and anxiety, he arrived in London and read through his accumulated mail in 1877, he discovered that she had married someone else. In 1886, after agonizing doubts and hesitations, he proposed marriage to Dorothy Tennant, a thirty-four-year-old society hostess and artist. She turned him down.

Stanley took refuge in preparing for what he must have known would be his final adventure in Africa. Although followers of the Mahdi Mohammed Ahmed had killed British general Gordon in Khartoum in 1885, one of Gordon's subordinates was still pluckily in place. Dr. Emin, or Emin Pasha, a German-born medical doctor and a convert to Islam, was an unlikely figure to arouse British public sympathy but nevertheless became a rallying point for the nation's pride. Emin still held power in the province of Equatoria in southern Sudan, but it was unclear for how much longer he could hold it against the Mahdi's rebels. Although the British government was reluctant to commit forces to Emin's relief, popular and missionary calls for intervention coincided with a growing interest in east Africa as a possible British prize in the scramble for new colonies. The Emin Pasha Relief Committee and the Imperial British East Africa Company were founded within two months of each other in 1886–1887. Plainly, Stanley was the man to go into Central Africa and do the job.

Portrayed at the time by Stanley and others as a great triumph, the mission to aid Emin was a dubious achievement at best. In his subsequent book on the adventure, *In Darkest Africa: Or the Quest, Rescue, and Retreat of Emin, Governor of Equatoria* (1890), Stanley attempts to dignify the expedition as a quest. Despite his exalted subtitle, the expedition was marred by as many blunders as his Turkish trip of 1866. But the errors of 1886–1889 were committed on a much larger stage and led both to loss of life and considerable lasting bitterness directed against Stanley.

The newly energized Stanley, once more operating in a world he understood, ordered fifty Winchester repeating rifles from America, later to be supplemented by over five hundred Remingtons and a Maxim machine gun, and selected his assistants. Maj. Edmund Barttelot, who would be the expedition's second-in-command, came from a privileged background—an important fact, as social resentments and snobberies would play a role in the disintegration of the mission. The young adventurers Herbert Ward, Capt. Robert Nelson, Lt. William Stairs, Lt. John Rose Troup, and William Bonny, a former sergeant in the army medical service, were also accepted, as were two more civilians, James Jameson and Arthur Mounteney Jephson, after they had contributed £1,000 each to the fund for the expedition. Jameson was a big-game hunter and amateur naturalist. He would bring notoriety to the expedition by allegedly buying a young African girl and watching as she was killed and eaten by cannibals. Jephson was a product of the Anglo-Irish gentry who would survive both the expedition and its leader. Stanley had reconciled himself to doing without a doctor when the man chosen backed out, but he later accepted the volunteer Thomas Parke. All

Stanley (second from right) with his wife, Dorothy, on tour in the United States

of Stanley's assistants, apart from the Canadian Stairs, were British.

The first indication that Emin's well-being was not the only concern of those organizing his relief was the route Stanley took to Equatoria. He led his small army of 620 Zanzibaris, 60 Sudanese, 12 Somalis, and 10 whites (counting his young servant William Hoffmann) with their weapons and supplies south from Zanzibar and around the Cape to the Congo River, which he ascended. He then marched five hundred miles through the Ituri rainforest. Stanley had chosen this route to serve the interests of his backers. Leopold wanted Stanley to open up a route across the unknown territory between the Free State and Equatoria, with a view to absorbing the latter within the former. Stanley's British backers, on the other hand, wanted him to sell Emin on the idea of a British East Africa.

The mission's contradictory aims were not the only complicating factor. Barttelot, the racist scion

of an aristocratic background, and Stanley, the defensive former workhouse brat who could at least command the respect and obedience of his African troops, soon began to get along badly. Their relationship was not helped by Stanley's decision to split the expedition into two parties at Yambuya, a thousand miles up the Congo. He proposed to dash ahead with an advance-column party to give Emin the ammunition he needed; Barttelot would stay behind in charge of the rearguard. He would thus not be present at the climax of the mission, the meeting with Emin. Stanley announced that he would be back within four months and set out to trek through the unexplored Ituri forest.

It was a grimmer—and more time-consuming—journey than he anticipated. It took Stanley 160 days to hack through the dank, overgrown forest: "Nothing but miles and miles, endless miles of forest, in various stages of growth and various degrees of altitude, according to the ages of the trees, with varying thickness of undergrowth according to the character of the trees which afforded thicker or lighter shade." It was "a region of horrors," the cannibal and Pygmy inhabitants of which were terrified by strangers and therefore terrifying in their responsive violence. The advance column largely subsisted on fungus, roots, berries, lizards, snakes, and ants. Each of Stanley's white companions came near death, from disease, hunger, mutiny, or poisoned arrow.

When Stanley successfully reached Emin Pasha, who was in so much better repair than his "rescuers" that it was a moot question who was to aid whom, he was then obliged to return for the rear column. He had expected to rejoin them in December 1887; he did not do so until August 1888, by which time a Conradian tale of madness and disintegration had unfolded. As the months passed and he still heard nothing from Stanley and as food became scarcer, Barttelot, trapped in an alien world for which his training and code had not prepared him, rigidly imposed harsh sentences of flogging for those caught stealing food or attempting to desert. Having been given ambiguous orders by Stanley—to stay at Yambuya or to follow on as seemed best—in June 1888 he decided to follow Stanley. One morning he got involved in an altercation with a native woman whose loud drumming to celebrate a "festival of the moon" annoyed him. Her husband shot him dead. Of his white subordinates, Stanley found only Bonny, the former sergeant, alive. He turned around again and for the third time slashed and hacked through the terrible Ituri forest to unite his expedition.

There had been no mockable greeting at the first encounter with the man Stanley had come so far to meet and for whose sake he had suffered and caused others to suffer so much: "At eight o'clock, amid great rejoicing, and after repeated salutes from rifles, Emin Pasha himself walked into our camp, accompanied by Captain Casati and Mr. Jephson, and one of the Pasha's officers. I shook hands with all, and asked which was Emin Pasha?" Nor would there follow any lifelong friendship between Stanley and Emin, nor even much mutual regard. Emin struck Stanley as an indecisive figure who at first would not choose between King Leopold and Queen Victoria; later, when a rebellion had made clear to all how precarious his position was, he could not decide between staying where he was and moving to the coast. Eventually, Stanley presented him with an ultimatum: in April 1889 he would begin his march to Bagamoyo. Emin and those of his men who were still loyal, together with their women and children, set out in the company of Stanley and

his much-reduced expedition. They reached Bagamoyo in early December. A final note of absurdity was added to the undertaking when Emin, the man whose safety had been the expedition's raison d'être, fell over a balcony and cracked his head open at a celebratory banquet. He recovered, accepted employment with his fellow Germans in East Africa, and was murdered by an Arab slaver in 1892.

A Catholic missionary, Father Schynse, had accompanied Stanley and Emin on the last leg of their journey from Lake Victoria. According to Hall in *Stanley: An Adventurer Explored,* the missionary soon noticed the American's habit of disappearing into his tent to write up his notes and surmised the result: "When he returns to Europe, the impatient world won't have long to wait for some interesting reading." Stanley had signed a contract to write a book about the mission with his publishers Sampson Low before setting out and was already working to fulfill his obligation. Upon his return to civilization Stanley accepted congratulations—from the queen, Kaiser Wilhelm, King Leopold, the president of the United States, and the khedive of Egypt—and duly attended a state banquet given by the khedive, but he was soon back at work on his book.

A fascinating insight into Stanley's attitude toward writing and his way of working is provided in an article in the August 1890 issue of *Scribner's Magazine* titled "How Stanley Wrote His Book," by Edward Marsden, a member of his publishing firm. It was worked up into a little book that was published that same year by Stanley's British publishers, *How Stanley Wrote* In Darkest Africa: *A Trip to Cairo and Back.* Marsden begins by noting that "Everything relating to Mr. Stanley seems to possess a special and peculiar interest for a very large portion of the public of many nationalities. . . . [and] probably no book has ever been more eagerly looked for in every part of the civilised world, and in many languages than [*In Darkest Africa*]." This is more than publisher's puffery: Stanley had to seclude himself strictly in Egypt in order to get the book written.

Noting that it is rare for a publisher to be summoned to give practical help in the preparation of the manuscript, Marsden makes the telling admission that "The truth . . . was that a great book had to be written within a certain period of time, and if not completed by that time, there was every chance that it would never be completed at all." Marsden goes on to write that Stanley

as a rule . . . shut himself up in his bedroom, and there he wrote from early morning till late at night, and woe betide anyone who ventured unasked into this sanctum. He very rarely went out, even for a stroll round the garden. His whole heart and soul were centred on his work. He had set himself a certain task, and he had determined to complete it to the exclusion of every other object in life. He said of himself, 'I have so many pages to write. I know that if I do not complete this work by a certain time, when other and imperative duties are imposed upon me, I shall never complete it at all.'

Marsden also describes the notebooks kept so assiduously by his author:

> His constant habit was to carry a small note-book 6 x 3 inches in his side pocket: in this he pencilled notes constantly and at every resting-place. Of these note-books he has shown me six of about one hundred pages each, closely packed with pencil memoranda. These notes, at times of longer leisure, were expanded into six larger volumes of about two hundred pages each of very minute and clear writing in ink. . . . In addition to these field note-books and diaries, there are two large quarto volumes, filled from cover to cover with calculations of astronomical observations, etc.

The chairman of Sampson Low estimated that in the fifty days he spent writing the book, Stanley converted the notes into prose at the rate of eight thousand words a day. (In fact, he did not work so uniformly: his rate ranged between a hundred words a day and nine pages an hour.)

Although great books may have been written in this way, *In Darkest Africa* is not one of them. Like *Through the Dark Continent,* which it resembles in more than title, it is a piece of serviceable journalism, occasionally clogged by excessive detail. Oscar Wilde said on publication of the book, "The difference between journalism and literature is, that journalism is unreadable and literature is unread." But Stanley's éclat was such that his book did extraordinarily well, his publisher estimating that the paper used in its production, "if it had been laid out in single sheets, would have formed a white carpet for Mr. Stanley to have walked upon from the Congo to Zanzibar, or if laid sheet upon sheet it would have formed a tower something like the Tour Eiffel." It was translated into twelve languages, including Russian and Arabic.

The Times of London claimed *In Darkest Africa* was "as moving and enthralling a tale as ever was told by man." *The Daily News* called it "a great performance, alike in what it relates, and in the manner of its relation." *The Standard* revealingly asserted, "Mr. Stanley's animated pages . . . will continue to be read as long as there remains amongst Englishmen any taste for adventure, and any honour for manliness." An indication of the degree to which Victorians venerated "manliness" are the endpapers in *How Stanley Wrote* In Darkest Africa, which adver-

tise the productions of William Clowes & Sons, with titles such as *The Waterloo Roll Call, Exercises for Light Dumb-Bells,* and *A Key to Infantry Drill: 1889.* The front papers advertize *London Street Arabs,* "by Mrs. H. M. Stanley (Dorothy Tennant)," for Stanley had proposed again and been accepted. They were married on 12 July 1890.

Stanley would live for another fourteen years but added little more to the splendid list of his accomplishments. In the autumn of 1890 he began a highly successful lecture tour of the United States. In 1891 he made another in Britain. Stanley's wife was the daughter of a former member of Parliament, and she encouraged her husband to go into politics. After an unsuccessful attempt in 1892 he was elected in 1895. Stanley hated being an M.P. and disliked the House of Commons. He declined to seek reelection in 1900.

The workhouse bastard was now rich and honored. *In Darkest Africa* continued to do well, and with the proceeds Stanley in 1899 bought Furze Hill, a mock-Tudor house near Pirbright in Surrey. In this same year the queen conferred upon him the Grand Cross of the Bath. John Rowlands was now Sir Henry Morton Stanley, G.C.B. Stanley's last years were saddened by continuing reports of atrocities in the Congo Free State. He had returned ill from his third stay in Africa and exhausted from his fourth. His health declined during his years as an M.P. In April 1903, he had a stroke that paralyzed his left side. Suffering from gastritis, fever, and heart trouble, Stanley died on 10 May 1904. His last words, uttered as he heard Big Ben strike the hour, were, "How strange! So that is Time!" Lady Stanley had a granite monolith removed from Dartmoor to her husband's Pirbright grave. On it she had a cross cut, and beneath the cross, "HENRY MORTON STANLEY, BULA MATARI 1841–1904, AFRICA."

Letters:

Lettres de H.-M. Stanley recontant ses voyages, ses aventures et ses découvertes à travers l'Afrique équatoriale, de 1874 à 1877, edited by H. Bellinger (Paris: Maurice Drefous, 1878);

The Story of Emin's Rescue as Told in Stanley's Letters, edited by J. Scott Keltie (London: Sampson Low, 1890; New York: Harper, 1890);

Stanley: Lettres inédites, edited by Albert Maurice (Brussels: Office de Publicité, 1955; translated and republished as *H. M. Stanley: Unpublished Letters,* edited by Albert Maurice (London: W. & R. Chambers, 1957; New York: Philosophical Library, 1957).

Bibliographies:

Théodore Heyse, "Centenary Bibliography of Publications Concerning Henry Morton Stanley," *Journal of the Royal African Society,* 42 (1943): 91–98;

Théodore Heyse, *Bibliographie de H. M. Stanley, 1841–1904,* Bibliographie Belgica, no. 85 (Brussels: Commission belge de Bibliographie, 1961);

Max Liniger-Goumaz and Gerben Hellinga, *Henry Morton Stanley: Bibliographie* (Geneva: Les Editions du Temps, 1972);

James A. Casada, *Dr. David Livingstone and Sir Henry Morton Stanley: An Annotated Bibliography,* Garland Reference Library of Social Science, volume 21 (New York & London: Garland, 1976).

Biographies:

Cadwalader Rowlands, *Henry M. Stanley: The Story of His Life from His Birth in 1841 to His Discovery of Livingstone, 1871* (London: John Camden Hotten, 1872);

Frank Hird, *H. M. Stanley: The Authorized Life* (London: Stanley Paul, 1935);

Ian Anstruther, *I Presume: Stanley's Triumph and Disaster* (London: Geoffrey Bles, 1956; New York, Dutton, 1956);

Bryon Farwell, *The Man Who Presumed: A Biography of Henry M. Stanley* (London: Longmans, Green, 1957; New York: Holt, 1957);

Richard Hall, *Stanley: An Adventurer Explored* (London: Collins, 1974; Boston: Houghton Mifflin, 1975);

Frank McLynn, *Stanley: The Making of an African Explorer* (London: Constable, 1898; Chelsea, Mich. & Chicago: Scarborough House, 1990);

John Bierman, *Dark Safari: The Life Behind the Legend of Henry Morton Stanley* (New York: Knopf, 1990; London: Hodder & Stoughton, 1991);

Frank McLynn, *Stanley: Sorcerer's Apprentice* (London: Constable, 1991).

References:

Patrick Brantlinger, "Victorians and Africans: The Genealogy of the Myth of the Dark Continent," *Critical Inquiry,* 12, no. 1 (1985): 166–203;

James A. Casada, "Henry Morton Stanley: The Explorer as Journalist," *Southern Quarterly,* 15 (1977): 357–369;

Felix Driver, "Henry Morton Stanley and His Critics: Geography, Exploration and Empire," *Past & Present,* 133 (November 1991): 134–166;

Dorothy Hammond and Alta Jablow, *The Africa That Never Was: Four Centuries of British Writing about Africa* (New York: Twayne, 1970);

Edward Marston, *How Stanley Wrote* In Darkest Africa*: A Trip to Cairo and Back* (London: Sampson Low, Marston, Searle, & Rivington, 1890);

Frank McLynn, *Hearts of Darkness: The European Exploration of Africa* (New York: Carroll & Graf, 1993);

Beau Riffenburgh, *The Myth of the Explorer: The Press, Sensationalism, and Geographical Discovery* (London: Belhaven, 1993), pp. 57–69;

Marianna Torgovnick, *Gone Primitive: Savage Intellects, Modern Lives* (Chicago: University of Chicago Press, 1990), pp. 26–34;

Tim Youngs, *Travellers in Africa: British Travelogues, 1850–1990* (Manchester & New York: Manchester University Press, 1994), pp. 113–207.

Papers:

The Stanley Family Archives are held by the Musée royal africaine, Tervuren, Belgium. Copies of most of these papers, excluding the diaries of Lady Stanley and her husband, are to be found in the British Library, London. The Royal Geographical Society, London, holds many letters from and about Stanley, and the Archives du Palais royal, Brussels, contain correspondence between him and King Leopold. Other collections of Stanley's letters are held by the School of Oriental and African Studies, London (Mackinnon Papers); the National Library of Scotland, Edinburgh; the Wellcome Medical Library, London; the Sanford Memorial Library, Sanford, Florida; and the privately owned Quentin Keynes Collection, London.

Harriet Beecher Stowe

(14 June 1811 – 1 July 1896)

Sarah Bird Wright
College of William and Mary

See also the Stowe entries in *DLB 1: The American Renaissance in New England; DLB 12: American Realists and Naturalists; DLB 42: American Writers for Children Before 1900;* and *DLB 74: American Short-Story Writers Before 1880.*

BOOKS: *Primary Geography for Children, on an Improved Plan with Eleven Maps and Numerous Engravings,* by Stowe and Catharine Beecher (Cincinnati: Corey & Fairbank, 1833);

Prize Tale: A New England Sketch (Lowell, Mass.: Gilman, 1834);

The Mayflower; or, Sketches of Scenes and Characters among the Descendants of the Pilgrims (New York: Harper, 1843); enlarged as *The Mayflower and Miscellaneous Writings* (Boston: Phillips, Sampson, 1855); republished as *Tales and Sketches of New England Life* (London: Sampson Low, Son, 1855);

Uncle Tom's Cabin: or, Life Among the Lowly, 2 volumes (Boston: Jewett / Cleveland: Jewett, Proctor & Worthington, 1852; London: Clarke, 1852);

A Key to Uncle Tom's Cabin; Presenting the Original Facts and Documents upon Which the Story is Founded. Together with Corroborative Statements Verifying the Truth of the Work (London: Sampson Low, Son, 1853; Boston: Jewett / Cleveland: Jewett, Proctor & Worthington / London: Low, 1853);

Uncle Sam's Emancipation; Earthly Care, A Heavenly Discipline; and Other Sketches (Philadelphia: Hazard, 1853);

Sunny Memories of Foreign Lands, 2 volumes (London: Sampson Low, Son, 1854; Boston: Phillips, Sampson / New York: Derby, 1854);

First Geography for Children, edited by Catharine Beecher (Boston: Phillips, Sampson / New York: Derby, 1855); revised by "an English Lady" as *A New Geography for Children* (London: Sampson Low, Son, 1855);

The Christian Slave. A Drama Founded on a Portion of Uncle Tom's Cabin (Boston: Phillips, Sampson, 1855; London: Sampson Low, Son, 1856);

Harriet Beecher Stowe (The Schlesinger Library, Radcliffe College)

Dred: A Tale of the Great Dismal Swamp, 2 volumes (London: Sampson Low, Son, 1856; Boston: Phillips, Sampson, 1856); republished as *Nina Gordon: A Tale of the Great Dismal Swamp* (Boston: Ticknor & Fields, 1866);

Our Charley and What To Do With Him (Boston: Phillips, Sampson, 1858; London: Routledge, 1859);

The Minister's Wooing (London: Sampson Low, Son, 1859; New York: Derby & Jackson, 1859);

The Pearl of Orr's Island: A Story of the Coast of Maine (2 parts, London: Sampson Low, Son, 1861, 1862; 1 volume, Boston: Ticknor & Fields, 1862);

Agnes of Sorrento (London: Smith, Elder, 1862; Boston: Ticknor & Fields, 1862);

A Reply to "The Affectionate and Christian Address of Many Thousands of Women of Great Britain and Ireland, to Their Sisters, The Women of the United States of America" (London: Sampson Low, Son, 1863);

House and Home Papers, as Christopher Crowfield (Boston: Ticknor & Fields, 1865; London: Sampson Low, Son, 1865);

Stories About Our Dogs (Edinburgh: Nimmo, 1865);

Little Foxes, as Christopher Crowfield (London: Bell & Daldy, 1866; Boston: Ticknor & Fields, 1866);

Religious Poems (Boston: Ticknor & Fields, 1867); republished as *Light After Darkness: Religious Poems* (London: Sampson Low, Son & Marston/Bell & Daldy, 1867);

The Daisy's First Winter, and Other Stories (Edinburgh: Nimmo, 1867);

Queer Little People (Boston: Ticknor & Fields, 1867; enlarged edition, New York: Fords, Howard & Hulbert, 1881);

The Chimney-Corner (London: Sampson Low, Son & Marston/Bell & Daldy, 1868); as Christopher Crowfield (Boston: Ticknor & Fields, 1868);

Men of Our Times; or, Leading Patriots of the Day (Hartford, Conn.: Hartford Publishing Company / New York: Denison / Chicago: Stoddard, 1868; London: Sampson Low, Son & Marston, 1868); enlarged as *The Lives and Deeds of Our Self-Made Men* (Hartford, Conn.: Worthington, Dustin / Cincinnati: Queen City Publishing / Chicago: Parker, 1872);

Oldtown Folks (3 volumes, London: Sampson Low, Son & Marston, 1869; 1 volume, Boston: Fields, Osgood, 1869);

The American Woman's Home, by Stowe and Catharine Beecher (New York: Ford / Boston: Brown, 1869);

Lady Byron Vindicated: A History of the Byron Controversy, from Its Beginnings in 1816 to the Present Time (Boston: Fields, Osgood, 1870; London: Sampson Low, Son & Marston, 1870);

Little Pussy Willow (Boston: Fields, Osgood, 1870; London: Sampson Low, Son & Marston, 1870);

Pink and White Tyranny (London: Sampson Low, Son & Marston, 1871; Boston: Roberts, 1871);

My Wife and I; or, Harry Henderson's History (New York: Ford, 1871; London: Sampson Low, Marston, Low & Searle, 1871);

Oldtown Fireside Stories (London: Sampson Low, Marston, Low & Searle, 1871; Boston: Osgood, 1872); enlarged as *Sam Lawson's Oldtown Fireside Stories* (Boston: Osgood, 1872; enlarged again, Boston: Houghton, Mifflin, 1881);

Six of One by Half a Dozen of the Other: An Everyday Novel, by Stowe, Adeline D. T. Whitney, Lucretia P. Hale, Frederic E. Loring, Frederic B. Perkins, and Edward E. Hale (Boston: Roberts, 1872; London: Sampson Low, Marston, Low & Searle, 1872);

Palmetto-Leaves (Boston: Osgood, 1873; London: Sampson Low, Marston, Low & Searle, 1873);

Woman in Sacred History (London: Sampson Low, Marston, Low & Searle / New York: Ford, 1874); republished as *Bible Heroines* (New York: Ford, Howard & Hulbert, 1878);

We and Our Neighbors; or, The Records of an Unfashionable Street (London: Sampson Low, Marston, Low & Searle, 1875; New York: Ford, 1875);

Betty's Bright Idea. Also, Deacon Pitkin's Farm, and The First Christmas of New England (New York: Ford, 1876 [i.e., 1875]; London: Sampson Low, Marston, Low & Searle, 1876);

Footsteps of the Master (New York: Ford, 1877; London: Sampson Low, Marston, Low & Searle, 1877);

Poganuc People: Their Loves and Lives (New York: Fords, Howard & Hulbert, 1878; London: Sampson Low, Marston, Low & Searle, 1878);

A Dog's Mission; or, The Story of the Old Avery House, and Other Stories (New York: Fords, Howard & Hulbert, 1880; London: Nelson, 1886).

Collections: *The Writings of Harriet Beecher Stowe,* 16 volumes (Boston & New York: Houghton, Mifflin, 1896);

Regional Sketches: New England and Florida, edited by John R. Adams (New Haven, Conn.: College & University Press, 1972).

SELECTED PERIODICAL PUBLICATIONS–UNCOLLECTED: "Immediate Emancipation: A Sketch," *New-York Evangelist,* 16 (2 January 1845): 1;

"An Appeal to the Women of the Free States of America, On the Present Crisis in Our Country," *Liberator,* 24 (3 March 1854): 57;

"Letters from Europe: No. 1," *Independent,* 9 (22 January 1857): 1;

"Letters from Europe: II," *Independent,* 9 (29 January 1857): 1;

"Letters from Mrs. Stowe in Europe: III," *Independent,* 9 (5 February 1857): 1;

"Letters from Mrs. Stowe in Europe: III [*sic*]: The First Day in Rome," *Independent,* 9 (23 April 1857): 1;

"A Letter from Mrs. Stowe," *Independent,* 11 (1 December 1859): 1;

"A Letter from Mrs. Stowe," *Independent,* 11 (15 December 1859): 1;

"A Letter from Mrs. Stowe," *Independent,* 11 (22 December 1859): 1;

"The Freedom of Florence: A Letter from Mrs. H. B. Stowe," *Independent,* 11 (22 December 1859): 1;

"A Letter from Mrs. Stowe," *Independent,* 11 (29 December 1859): 1;

"Letter from Mrs. Stowe: Milan Cathedral," *Independent,* 12 (5 January 1860): 1;

"Letter from Mrs. Stowe: Church of St. Ambrose, Milan," *Independent,* 12 (12 January 1860): 1;

"Letter from Mrs. Stowe: Florence," *Independent,* 12 (12 January 1860): 1;

"Letter from Mrs. Stowe," *Independent,* 12 (16 February 1860): 1;

"The Carnival at Rome," *Independent,* 12 (5 April 1860): 1;

"A Day at Tivoli," *Independent,* 12 (12 April 1860): 1;

"An Eventful Week in Rome," *Independent,* 12 (19 April 1860): 1;

"Pencilings from Rome," *Independent,* 12 (3 May 1860): 1;

"How People Like the Pope," *Independent,* 12 (10 May 1860): 1;

"A Panoramic Picture: Cream-Colored Oxen on the Campagne [sic]–Sea Sickness on the Mediterranean–Sights from a Hotel Window in Naples–Herculaneum and Pompeii–Out-of-Door Life," *Independent,* 12 (21 June 1860): 1;

"Sketches of Rome: Vatican Gardens–Mass Prayer-Meeting at St. Peter's," *Independent,* 12 (28 June 1860): 1;

"A Picture of Rome," *Independent,* 12 (5 July 1860): 1;

"Housekeeping in Rome," *Independent,* 12 (12 July 1860): 1;

"The Ascent of St. Peter's," *Independent,* 12 (19 July 1860): 1;

"The Sistine Chapel," *Independent,* 12 (26 July 1860): 1;

"Sunday in Rome," *Independent,* 12 (23 August 1860): 1;

"Letter to Lord Shaftesbury," *Independent,* 13 (1 August 1861): 1;

"A Winter in Italy," *New York Ledger,* 21 (12 August–28 October 1865);

"Palmetto Leaves from Florida," *Christian Union,* 5 (7 February–19 June 1872).

Harriet Beecher Stowe, who has been described as "a 'genius' in a family of eccentrics," is best known for her 1852 antislavery novel *Uncle Tom's Cabin: or, Life Among the Lowly.* Few American books have as spectacular a publishing history. The novel launched tumultuous discussion that, according to Ralph Waldo Emerson, "encircled the globe." Three thousand of the initial printing of five thousand copies were sold the first day, and within a year of publication there had been 120 editions and sales of more than 350,000. The succeeding year George L. Aiken's dramatic version of the book was produced in New York. The play was exceptionally successful. Later in the decade as many as sixteen companies were presenting the play throughout the United States, and it was popular well into the twentieth century.

When Stowe visited the White House in 1862, President Abraham Lincoln is said to have greeted her with the remark, "So you're the little woman who wrote the book that started this great war!" Translated into dozens of languages–including Swedish, Japanese, Hindustani, Gujarati, Welsh, and Russian–the book was praised by many celebrated writers of the day, including Henry Wadsworth Longfellow, Charles Dickens, and George Sand.

The success of *Uncle Tom's Cabin* has obscured to some extent Stowe's other literary achievements. She was a prolific writer throughout her life, producing nine other novels as well as short fiction, poetry, and nonfiction, including travel sketches. *Sunny Memories of Foreign Lands* (1854), about Stowe's 1853 travels in Great Britain and on the continent of Europe, placed her in the burgeoning ranks of female travelers abroad and added her recollections to a growing body of nineteenth-century travel books by American women. Before the Civil War there were nearly 30 such accounts by women, and by the turn of the century there were nearly 170. Many of these books were informal, chatty memoirs, compilations of letters written to family members and often published first in local newspapers. The majority of American women authors valued their status as ladies, and thus, like Stowe, traveled under the protection of male relatives: husbands, fathers, sons, and brothers. Stowe, already famous as the author of *Uncle Tom's Cabin,* was in an unusual position. She hoped, as Mary Suzanne Schriber has put it, to seek "knowledge of the Old World and fresh insights into reform and education to take back to the New World."

Stowe was born Harriet Beecher on 14 June 1811 at Litchfield, Connecticut, where her father, noted minister Lyman Beecher, was pastor of the Congregational Church. A fiery evangelist, he treated his children with a harsh benevolence. They appear to have preferred their mother, Roxana Foote Beecher, who died in 1816, leaving eight children

Harriet and Calvin Stowe in 1853 (The Schlesinger Library, Radcliffe College)

who idealized her memory. Among them were the distinguished educator Catharine Beecher and the well-known clergyman Henry Ward Beecher, pastor of Plymouth Church in Brooklyn, New York. At her mother's death Harriet Beecher was taken to live for about a year with an aunt in Guilford, Connecticut, where she was trained in the catechism, needlework, the Episcopal prayer book, and hymns and poems. After Lyman Beecher married Harriet Porter in 1817, Harriet returned to Litchfield, where her father and his new wife eventually had four children. (Seven Beecher sons became clergymen.)

For the next few years Harriet Beecher attended Miss Sarah Pierce's school in Litchfield, where she read widely and began writing compositions. She had the run of her father's library and became familiar with theology, literature, and history. At the age of thirteen Stowe was sent to study at the Hartford Female Seminary under the stern supervision of her sister Catharine Beecher, eleven years

her senior, who had founded the school with their sister Mary and bullied her younger sister Harriet even as she exerted a strong intellectual influence over her. Harriet Beecher spent eight years at the school learning Latin, French, and Italian as well as teaching herself and studying history and moral theology. She became a teacher at the Hartford Female Seminary in November 1827, and by the time she was twenty-two her education had made her, in the eyes of her father and brothers, something of a "bluestocking," more likely to be a teacher than to marry.

In 1832 Lyman Beecher accepted the presidency of Lane Theological Seminary in Cincinnati, and Catharine and Harriet Beecher accompanied him there to start another school for young women. The following year Harriet published her first book, *Primary Geography for Children* (1833), largely written by her and edited by Catharine Beecher. In Cincinnati the sisters met many of the local literati by joining the Semi-Colon Club, a literary organization that met on alternate weeks, often at the mansion of their uncle Samuel Foote, who had moved to Cincinnati a few years before them. Harriet also began writing essays and stories, and in Cincinnati she first became aware of the issue of slavery.

She soon met Eliza Tyler Stowe and her husband, Calvin Stowe, who was a professor of theology at Lane Theological Seminary. In 1834, after her friend Eliza Stowe died, Harriet Beecher's empathy for the widower developed into an enduring attachment, and they were married on 6 January 1836. She described her husband as a man "rich in Greek and Hebrew, Latin and Arabic, and, alas! rich in nothing else." Their first children were twins, Eliza Tyler and Harriet Beecher Stowe, born on 29 September 1836; Calvin Stowe insisted that his daughters bear the names of both of his wives. By 1850 Stowe had given birth to five other children; one of her sons died of cholera when he was a year old. Her youngest son, Charles Edward, the only one to survive her, became her biographer.

During these years in Cincinnati, Stowe supplemented her husband's income by writing stories for magazines, including *Godey's Lady's Book.* Fifteen of her stories and sketches were collected in *The Mayflower; or, Sketches of Scenes and Characters among the Descendants of the Pilgrims* (1843). She also became sympathetic to the antislavery movement. In 1850 the Stowes moved to Brunswick, Maine, where Calvin Stowe became a professor at Bowdoin College, and Harriet Stowe, spurred by the passage of the Fugitive Slave Law and reports of the resulting re-enslavements of African Americans, began writing *Uncle Tom's Cabin,* which was serialized in the abolitionist weekly *National Era* from 5 June 1851 through 1 April 1852. Stowe not only became one of the best-known American women authors, but she was also much praised abroad, especially in England.

In speaking out publicly against slavery and endorsing the cause of the slave, Harriet Beecher Stowe was taking a risk and, as Joan D. Hedrick puts it, placing her "own womanhood on the line." *The Times* (London) said Stowe's novel could only appeal to readers with "strong hearts and weak intellects." It was denounced as poorly written and unfeminine, the product of malice and greed. William J. Grayson, a South Carolina poet, denounced Stowe as "a moral scavenger" who "sniffs up pollution with a pious air . . . and trades for gold the garbage of her toils." Charleston novelist William Gilmore Simms regarded *Uncle Tom's Cabin* as a moral battle cry and later blamed Stowe for the slaughter of many Confederate soldiers. Such attacks im-

Charles Beecher, who accompanied his sister and other family members to Europe in 1853 and kept a journal that Stowe used in her 1854 book, Sunny Memories of Foreign Lands *(The Stowe-Day Foundation, Hartford, Connecticut)*

pelled Stowe to justify her claims by producing the evidence behind *Uncle Tom's Cabin.* In 1853 she published *A Key to Uncle Tom's Cabin,* a polemical defense of the novel buttressed by thirty-five chapters of southern newspaper advertisements for sales of slaves and rewards for returned escapees.

Criticism was somewhat mitigated by her position as the wife of a minister and the mother of seven children and by her widespread public support. In 1853 more than half a million women in England, Scotland, and Ireland signed a petition on behalf of the slave, "An Affectionate and Christian Address of Many Thousands of Women of Great Britain and Ireland to Their Sisters, the Women of the United States of America," and Stowe was invited by the Glasgow Ladies' Anti-Slavery Society and the Glasgow Female New Association for the Abolition of Slavery to tour Scotland and England. Partly to escape the furor succeeding publication of *Uncle Tom's Cabin,* she accepted the invitation and planned to add a tour of northern Europe.

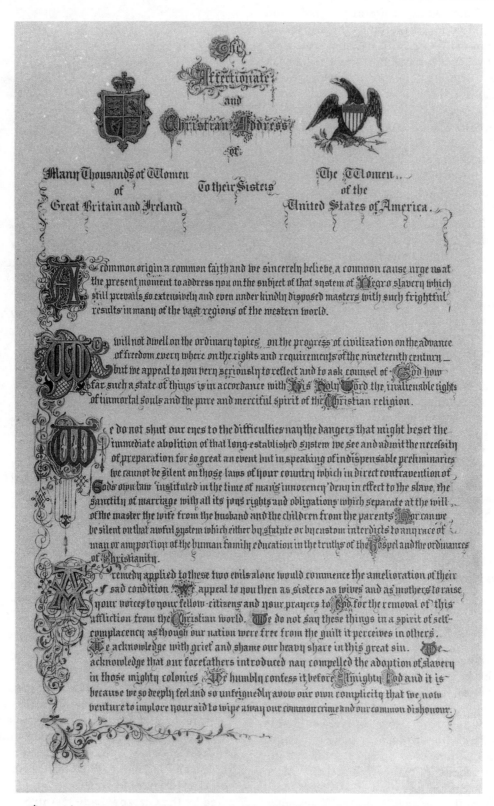

The antislavery petition signed by more than half a million English, Scottish, and Irish women and presented to Stowe in 1853 (The Stowe-Day Foundation, Hartford, Connecticut)

On 30 March 1853 the Stowe party sailed for Liverpool. The group consisted of Harriet and Calvin Stowe; her brother Reverend Charles Beecher, who came as her secretary; her wealthy Rochester sister-in-law Sarah Buckingham Beecher (widow of George Beecher, who had accidentally shot himself in 1843); Sarah's brother, Rochester businessman William Buckingham; and Sarah's son, George Beecher Jr., who hoped to become a painter. Of this group only Calvin Stowe had previously been abroad.

While Stowe's fame secured introductions to well-known figures in the British Isles, including clergymen, writers, and members of the nobility, it may also have narrowed her opportunities to get an unbiased perspective on British attitudes toward America and the question of slavery. Throughout her tour, at breakfast parties and tea parties, she was introduced to members of the working and middle classes as well as the aristocracy, who also invited her to dine in their homes.

From the time her ship docked at Liverpool and it became known that Stowe was aboard, a large crowd began gathering at the wharf. To her astonishment the men removed their hats and bowed to her. The party was taken in hand by the Croppers, a family of wealthy merchants and philanthropists, who were delighted to have the privilege of introducing Stowe to the city and entertained them at a large breakfast the next morning. In a letter to her father Stowe described the elaborate meal, which was followed by an official welcome delivered by Reverend Dr. Hugh McNeile, whom Stowe described as one of the leading Church of England clergymen in Liverpool. Calvin Stowe responded to McNeile's greeting, as it would have been considered unlady-like for Stowe herself to speak publicly.

Those invited to meet Stowe had read and in general endorsed the views expressed in *Uncle Tom's Cabin*. For months the book had been widely sold in railway stations and bookstores and had been dramatized in theaters. An inexpensive Sunday-school edition introduced thousands of children to Stowe's depiction of the South and the Underground Railway. Readership of *Uncle Tom's Cabin* cut across all classes and, to some extent, revised British concepts of American literature. Calvin Stowe's introduction to the American edition of *Sunny Memories of Foreign Lands,* his wife's book about her travels, includes an account of her appearance in Dundee, Scotland, where a Mr. Gilfillan admitted that American works previously had been viewed with "contempt or patronizing wonder," although Washington Irving's *The Sketch Book of Geoffrey Crayon* (1819, 1820) was considered "a very good book to be an

American's." Nevertheless, he continued, "the most popular book of the century has appeared on the west side of the Atlantic." This book, "and by a woman, too!," had invalidated any idea of "the poverty of American brains, or the barrenness of American literature." During the Stowes' travels by train in England and Scotland, crowds often gathered all through the night thronging the railway stations of small towns to watch her train pass by.

The ardor of British readers to see Stowe was matched and even exceeded by Stowe's lifelong wish to make a literary pilgrimage to England and Scotland. She had written Eliza Lee Cabot Follen, a Boston aristocrat and abolitionist who was living in London, in February 1853: "If I live till spring I shall hope to see Shakespeare's grave, and Milton's mulberry-tree, and the good land of my fathers,—old, old England! May that day come!" As they sailed up the Mersey River before landing at Liverpool, she reflected that "an American, particularly a New Englander, can never approach the old country without a kind of thrill and pulsation of kindred. Its literature, laws, and language are our literature, laws, and language. . . . Our very life-blood is English life-blood."

Written in the epistolary tradition of travel writing prevalent throughout the nineteenth century, *Sunny Memories of Foreign Lands* is described in the preface and introduction as a collection of letters written to family members and friends and edited by Calvin Stowe. Yet some scholars believe that Stowe may have adopted the epistolary form later and not sent the "letters" to the people to whom they are addressed. Although the second volume includes sections written by Charles Beecher, only Harriet Beecher Stowe's name is on the title page. The book was published in two volumes, both of which include illustrations by Hammatt Billings. The first, about England and Scotland, comprises eighteen letters with descriptions of people, public appearances, ecclesiastical and domestic architecture, landscape, horticulture, meals, and details about carriages and railway cars. The second volume comprises letters 19 through 49, interspersed with twelve excerpts from Charles Beecher's travel journal. The first twelve letters in this volume, about the Stowe party's continued stay in and near London, are followed by eighteen others about their Continental travels. It concludes with Charles Beecher's account of crossing the Channel to England and Stowe's description of their visit to York and embarkation at Liverpool for New York.

Volume one includes several accounts of public meetings held in Scotland and England at which Calvin Stowe spoke on his wife's behalf against the

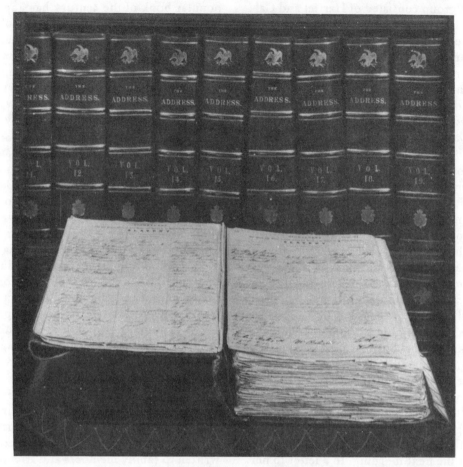

Some of the twenty-six bound volumes of signatures to "An Affectionate and Christian Address of Many Thousands of Women of Great Britain and Ireland to Their Sisters, the Women of the United States of America," presented to Stowe in 1853 (The Stowe-Day Foundation, Hartford, Connecticut)

practice of slavery, which he called "a canker, a poison, in the very heart of our republic." Throughout her tour Stowe met crowds of people who sympathized with her position. Among them were many members of the Scottish and English working class, which she praised as producing "orators and writers." Toward the end of the volume she wrote, "all my way through Scotland, and through England, I was associating, from day to day, with people of every religious denomination, and every rank of life." She was entertained by members of the nobility, especially in London, where her party dined with the progressive George William Frederick Howard, seventh Earl of Carlisle, and his family. Later they dined at Stafford House, home of George Granville Leveson-Gower, third Duke of Sutherland, and his wife, Harriet Elizabeth Georgiana, the earl of Carlisle's sister and an influential friend of Queen Victoria. The purpose of the reception was the reading to Stowe of "An Affectionate and Christian Address of Many Thousands of Women of

Great Britain and Ireland to Their Sisters, the Women of the United States of America."

Stowe was often asked to explain the paradox of Americans who were active churchgoers yet accepted and even condoned slavery. Such questions began in Liverpool, where Dr. McNeile asked her to make the situation "plausible." Stowe presented the "most plausible view": that many Christians regarded the institution of slavery as "a sort of wardship or guardian relation, by which an inferior race were brought under the watch and care of a superior race to be instructed in Christianity."

After eight weeks of traveling and being entertained, Calvin Stowe, who had helped to absorb attacks on his wife, decided to cut his trip short. He returned to America at the end of May, urging Stowe to continue on to the Continent as soon as possible. She and others in the party remained in London for another week to meet various commitments. Stowe was often exhausted by her duties as guest of honor at official functions and by her attempts to talk with

Inkstand presented to Stowe by the ladies of Surrey Chapel, London, in June 1853 (The Stowe-Day Foundation, Hartford, Connecticut). The figures on the top represent Stowe giving a Bible to a slave while another person removes the slave's fetters.

as many individuals as possible among her crowds of admirers. The Lord Mayor of London gave a dinner for Stowe's party and Charles Dickens; they were both toasted "as having employed fiction as a means of awakening the attention of the respective countries to the condition of the oppressed and suffering classes." Stowe found herself too tired to accept an invitation to dine with Dickens. She also met William Ewart Gladstone and Thomas Babington Macaulay.

Throughout *Sunny Memories of Foreign Lands* Stowe also revealed her interest in social problems in Britain. In Scotland she and her party attended a "*soirée* got up by the working classes." She concluded that their condition was "world-wide different from that of the slave." In London, after Anthony Ashley Cooper, seventh Earl of Shaftesbury, took her to visit model tenements that had replaced filthy lodging houses, she stated that this reform could be improved by reforms in temperance legislation. She also visited a charitable borough-school for boys in London and was stunned when they could respond to questions on Christian doctrine by citing chapter and verse. She devoted a chapter to improvements Lord Shaftesbury had instituted in the working conditions of milliners and dressmak-

ers, including good ventilation, fewer hours, better pay, and free medical care.

Raised on the poetry and fiction of Sir Walter Scott, Stowe was a zealous pilgrim to sites associated with his work. While touring the ruins of Bothwell Castle on the banks of the Clyde, she felt "every nerve shiver" as she recalled the "dim melodies of the Lady of the Lake." In describing Scott's home at Abbotsford, then inhabited by his only surviving daughter, she referred to Washington Irving's account of the house as it was being built, with Scott himself "humorously descanting on various fragments of sculpture, which lay scattered about" to be incorporated in the building. She gives an English translation of the Latin epitaph on the grave of Scott's dog, quotes his poem on the Eve of Saint John at Dryburgh, and recalls, by the River Tweed, his *The Lay of the Last Minstrel* (1805). In the second volume of *Sunny Memories of Foreign Lands* she recommends William Shakespeare, John Bunyan, and Daniel Defoe as authors to be studied by anyone aspiring to the most effective use of the English language.

British novelist George Eliot pronounced *Sunny Memories of Foreign Lands* "feeble" compared with Stowe's fiction, and at times *Sunny Memories of Foreign*

Lands is overly sentimental, but Stowe also incorporated an element of almost fictional invention in her travel writing. While visiting Shakespeare's birthplace at Stratford-upon-Avon she fancied him as a "bright-eyed, curly-headed boy" creeping up the stairs. She ascribed the character of Desdemona to the "impression on the child's soul of a mother's purity." She declared that John Milton's epics were marred by his knowledge of Latin and Greek and prevented from being "wrought" into "the energy of new productions." The book often seems to address an untraveled, naive American audience unaccustomed to the splendor of Europe and perhaps too democratic to countenance the possessions of the aristocracy. Warwick Castle, for example, has a "bewildering display of magnificent apartments, pictures, gems, vases, arms and armor, antiques, all, in short, that the wealth of a princely and powerful family had for centuries been accumulating." Despite its flaws the book compares favorably with many other travel books of the time, written by men as well as women. *Sunny Memories of Foreign Lands* reveals Stowe as both informed and literate and much aware of her British lineage. She was observant and discriminating about architecture, particularly Gothic, and had sketches drawn of gargoyles she liked. She was also interested in horticulture and exacting in her descriptions of various plants and the ways in which they differ from their American counterparts. Throughout the text she attempted to obey the mandate issued by Shakespeare's Valentine of Verona to his friend Proteus in *Two Gentlemen of Verona,* which serves as the epigraph to volume two: "When thou haply seest / Some rare note-worthy object in thy travels, / Make me partaker of thy happiness."

On the Continent Stowe became less a polemicist and more a tourist. In Paris they stayed with Mrs. Maria Weston Chapman, a wealthy Bostonian who had espoused the cause of abolition. Accompanied by her sister and three daughters, whom she wished to introduce to France, she was living on the ground floor of a townhouse on the Rue de Verneuil in the elite Faubourg Saint-Germain. Sarah Beecher, William Buckingham, and George Beecher left the group temporarily in Paris to embark on a tour of Italy. Stowe and her brother Charles, who spoke French, explored Paris in the company of Maria Chapman and her sister—shopping, sightseeing, and visiting museums. Stowe was particularly enthralled by the Louvre, having had a lifelong ambition to see its treasures and resolve her "imaginings of what art might be." She admired the works of "great, joyous, full-souled, all-powerful" Peter Paul Rubens and, most of all, the Venus de Milo. Experts had ascribed

it to the time of Phidias, and Stowe declared, "as this is a pleasant idea to me, I go a little further and ascribe her to Phidias himself."

She met Louise Swanton Belloc, the French translator of *Uncle Tom's Cabin,* and her husband, Jean-Hilaire Belloc, later the grandparents of the British writer Hilaire Belloc. Jean-Hilaire Belloc had refused to read *Uncle Tom's Cabin* until French poet, novelist, and dramatist Alfred de Musset exclaimed to him, "say nothing about this book! There is nothing like it. This leaves us all behind—all, all, miles behind!" Charles Beecher's journal describes the opportunities they had in Paris to attend salons and meet the distinguished French people—including professors, members of the nobility, Napoleonic soldiers, and Russian exiles. "Nothing can surpass the ease, facility, and genial freedom of these *soirées,*" Beecher wrote.

When the entire party was reunited, they made a kind of grand tour of northern Europe, setting out for Luxembourg, Switzerland, Germany, and Belgium. Stowe's letters from Switzerland are in the vein of the picturesque as she attempted to describe glaciers, mountains, mountain streams, and meadows. In the valley of Chamouni, gazing at a vertical glacier on the side of one of the Alps, Stowe writes, "I thought to myself, 'Now, would it be possible to give to one that had not seen it an idea of how this looks?' Let me try if words can paint it." She admits, however, that "every prospect loses by being made definite," and, once they were close to the mountain and glacier, she was unable to absorb or describe it. Throughout the book she addresses her reader directly, earnestly endeavoring to make him or her see Europe in terms of America, particularly New England. The party continued to various sites in Switzerland and several German states, back to Paris, and then on to London.

If the weeks in Britain had been structured about the memory of Sir Walter Scott, the journey to the Continent was devoted to Martin Luther. Protestant to the core, they had attended a Roman Catholic service at the Church of the Madeleine in Paris, replete with incense and altar hangings. In a journal entry Charles Beecher described his "kind of Puritan tremor of conscience at witnessing such a theatrical pageant on the Sabbath." In Basle, Stowe visited the museum, where she saw several of Luther's original letters. Putting her hand on one, she "thought his hand also had passed over the paper; which he has made living with his thoughts." At Wittenberg they visited the church where Luther had nailed his theses to the door (the actual door had been destroyed by the French), the bronze monument to him in the marketplace, the church

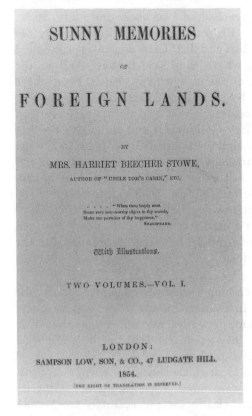

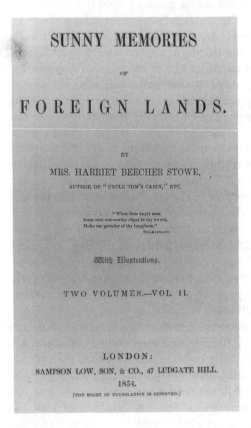

Frontispieces and title pages for Stowe's book about her first trip to Europe, a popular guidebook for American travelers throughout the second half of the nineteenth century

where he preached, and his house and study. Stowe found this "Protestant Mecca" unfortunately obscured by dust and dirt. Their pilgrimage continued to Erfurt, where they saw Luther's cell in the Augustine convent, and to Eisenach. From there they went by carriage to Wartburg Castle, where Luther's bedstead, books, and clothes press were on display. Their Continental tour ended at Antwerp, where Longfellow had instructed them to see the Rubens paintings. Stowe had told him she did not expect to like them. "You will, though," he replied. Seeing *The Descent from the Cross,* Stowe conceded that Longfellow was right: "Art has satisfied me at last." After a brief stay in Paris, the party returned to England, and from there they sailed for the United States.

Sunny Memories of Foreign Lands was well received, becoming a widely used guidebook. By the end of her first visit to Europe, Stowe was no longer the innocent, provincial person who, as she wrote her father, "had never seen any ruin more imposing than that of a cow house" and was "ravenous for old towers." As Hedrick explains, Stowe was aware that a culture of consumption was emerging in America as the middle class became increasingly prosperous, and that there was a growing appetite for foreign travel and the social prestige associated with it. According to Hedrick, Stowe saw her audience as "a nation in the throes of a vast cultural transformation" and considered her role one of "reassuring them, pointing out new roads, criticizing the past so as to help ease them into the future." Anticipating the coming era of mass travel as an activity increasingly open to middle-class Americans, Stowe tried to come to terms with the secular culture of Europe by tying it to tradition and, ultimately, to the polarization between democracy and monarchy. In pondering the problem of the lax Continental Sunday, for example, she concluded that the Protestant Sabbath could be correlated with a "popular" form of government. "Protestant Switzerland, England, Scotland, and America cover the whole ground of popular freedom," she declared, because "the very element of a popular government must be self-control in the individual."

Stowe presumed that her American audience was highly literate and resolutely Protestant. On their behalf she rejected the Baroque treatment of religious subjects that later fascinated Edith Wharton, Henry James, and other American writers. On seeing Correggio's *Notte* (or Nativity of Jesus) in Dresden, she remarks "that I should prefer a seraph's head to his heels; and that a group of archangels, kicking from the canvas with such alarming vigor . . . does not illustrate either glory to God in

the highest, or peace on earth and good will to men." *Sunny Memories of Foreign Lands* exhibits the same paradoxical mixture of Europhilia and chauvinism about the national self-image that Samuel Langhorne Clemens (Mark Twain) expressed fifteen years later in his European travel book *The Innocents Abroad.*

Stowe made two other trips to Europe, in 1856 and 1859. During both she sent travel letters to *The Independent* that have not been collected in book form. In 1856 in London she was introduced to John Ruskin, who escorted her to Camberwell, where they saw his collection of paintings by J. M. W. Turner. In Florence, she met Annie Fields, the wife of James Fields, junior partner in Ticknor and Fields of Boston, who became Stowe's publishers. Later to become Stowe's closest woman friend, Annie Fields was twenty-six and already known in Boston for her brilliance, but she was overwhelmed at meeting Stowe. She spoke for many young American women when she said, "We . . . saw her wrapped about, as it were, with a kind of sacred awe." Stowe's letters to *The Independent* during her third trip to Europe, in late 1859, describe Italian sites that she visited.

In the late 1860s, the Stowes were drawn to Florida because of the warm climate. Stowe; Charles Beecher; her nephew Spencer Foote; his wife, Hannah; and their baby first visited the state in 1867, going by sea from New York. When she saw the mouth of the Saint John's River, she wrote her family, "In all my foreign experience & travels I never saw such a scene. . . . The fog was just up as we came in—the river broad as the Connecticut in its broadest parts. . . . The shores white and dazzling like driven snow & out of this dazzling white rise groves of palmetto pine." Stowe convinced her husband that they should purchase a house at Mandarin, Florida. Calvin Stowe joked to James Fields that she had found "the Paradise described in the last chapters of Revelation, banning the alligators."

The Stowes spent winters in Mandarin from 1869 to 1884. The house was on a bluff overlooking the Saint John's River, with live oaks, an orange grove, date palms, and a view of passing steamboats. She regarded herself as chatelaine of her outpost in "this queer country, this sort of strange, sandy, half-tropical dreamland," and tried to tempt her northern friends to join them. "Here is where we read books. . . . Up North nobody does,—they don't have time."

In 1870 Stowe's brother Henry Ward Beecher bought out the *Church Union* and established the *Christian Union,* a rival to *The Independent.* Stowe and her husband began contributing three columns a week, Calvin basing his on his New Testament stud-

Calvin and Harriet Stowe at their house in Mandarin, Florida, circa 1880 (The Stowe-Day Foundation, Hartford, Connecticut)

ies and Harriet writing about her travels, her views on current events, and her scriptural meditations. Other family members were also regular contributors, including Catharine Beecher, Edward Beecher, Thomas Beecher, and Eunice Beecher. Between February and June 1872 Harriet Stowe contributed several articles about Florida, which were later collected in *Palmetto-Leaves* (1873).

Stowe's biographer Forest Wilson calls these articles "probably the first promotion-writing for Florida ever done." Stowe urged other writers to visit Florida; they would find it a mecca, she declared: "Hawthorne ought to have lived in an orange grove in Florida.... You have no idea how small you all look, you folks in the world, from this distance. All your fusses and your fumings, your red-hot hurrying newspapers, your clamor of rival magazines,—why, we see it as we see steamboats fifteen miles off, a mere speck and smoke."

Many of the essays are somewhat sentimental, but some of the vignettes of people are convincing and fresh, such as that of the former slave "Commodore Rose," "no mean example of female energy and

vigor." The de facto commander (actually "stewardess") aboard the river steamer *Darlington,* she saved the life of the captain (her former owner) in a steamboat disaster. According to Stowe, "It is asserted that the whole charge of provisioning and running the boat, and all its internal arrangements, vests in Madame Rose; and that nobody can get ahead of her in a bargain, or resist her will in an arrangement."

Stowe, like Edward King in *The Great South* (1875), gives thoughtful attention to the situation of blacks in the post-Reconstruction South. From a sociological point of view *Palmetto-Leaves* is optimistic in its profiles of various black figures whose lives have been improved during Reconstruction. Stowe is less judgmental than King, finding the problems of freed African Americans a matter of poignant concern. She wrote about Cudjo, who had raised cotton on the land he had been deeded and then nearly had it taken away by a foreign intruder before sympathetic white neighbors gave him legal redress.

Stowe's most typical attitude toward blacks is one of condescension. She conceives of them as

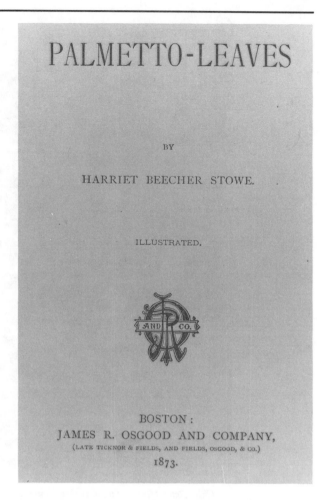

PALMETTO-LEAVES

BY

HARRIET BEECHER STOWE.

ILLUSTRATED.

BOSTON :
JAMES R. OSGOOD AND COMPANY,
(LATE TICKNOR & FIELDS, AND FIELDS, OSGOOD, & CO.)
1873.

Frontispiece and title page for the collection of articles about Florida that Stowe wrote for the Christian Union *in 1872*

happy, energetic workers, their vitality blossoming under the hot sun; for her they were emblematic of the New South in their adjustment to freedom. Blacks, she says, are more suitable for physical labor than Chinese, Swedes, or Germans. She insists that black laborers toil under the hot sun "more actively, more cheerfully, than during the cooler months. The sun awakes all their vigor and all their boundless jollity."

Stowe is even more a naturalist in *Palmetto-Leaves* than she was in *Sunny Memories of Foreign Lands*. In Europe she had time to note different species of plants and animals, but not to observe their life cycles. Florida seemed a natural habitat, at least for part of each year, for the essential Stowe. David Miller observes that to Stowe the swamp was almost genteel, a bright and vivid place, with flamboyant vegetation. In February parties go out into the pinewoods and pick yellow jessamine to mail north. The letters describe organized walks to see an "oak-hammock," or grove of live-oak trees, and they recommend watching a sunset through "a grove drap-

eried with gray moss. The swaying, filmy bands turn golden and rose-colored; and the long, swaying avenues are like a scene in fairyland." Stowe continually cautioned her *Christian Union* readers, many of whom had written asking her to mail them flowers from Mandarin, that the task was impossible. Florida could not be exported. It was like a piece of embroidery with two sides, one side "all tag-rag and thrums, without order or position; and the other side showing flowers and arabesques and brilliant coloring."

Palmetto-Leaves was directed to a northern audience that was coming to Florida in increasing numbers. Stowe wrote Annie Fields in 1872 that fourteen thousand northern tourists had been to Florida that year. Stowe's intimate glimpse of the leisurely domestic life in Mandarin was appealing to readers, and it is likely that many tourists came to Florida in response to Stowe's articles in the *Christian Union*. The Stowes welcomed neighbors, seemingly unaware of the implications of her vision of the future: "we look forward to the time when there shall be many more; when, all along the shore of the St. John's, cottages and villas shall look out from the green trees." Stowe's letters depict Florida both as an unspoiled tropical paradise, which it would remain until the advent of the railroad and the automobile, and as a suffocating wilderness. Nature in Florida is an "easy, demoralized, indulgent old grandmother, who has no particular time for any thing, and does every thing when she happens to feel like it."

In *Sunny Memories of Foreign Lands* Stowe's persona is a feminine equivalent of Henry James's Chad Newsome, "made over" by Europe. She does not soften her Puritan stance, but by the end of her tour she is far more cosmopolitan, at ease in the presence of nobility as well as Quakers and working people, and different in many ways from the timid person besieged by admirers when she arrived at Liverpool. Twenty years later Stowe was less eager traveler than self-sufficient homesteader. Her persona in *Palmetto-Leaves* is that of a cicerone to the rewards and perils of owning a plantation in Florida. The political sphere has subsided in favor of a private and domestic one. In Florida, Stowe was distanced from her public by the fact that the mail boat bringing letters from readers came only twice a week. She was still a highly professional and productive writer, her column indeed a "pulpit." Her social concerns are evident in her dissections of local culture and mores, and she acted as something of a missionary to black children and illiterate adults.

Stowe wrote little during the 1880s and 1890s. Calvin Stowe died in 1886, and by 1889 Stowe herself was suffering from senile dementia and forgetfulness. She continued to receive public acclaim and was honored at the World's Columbian Exposition in Chicago in 1893 with a display of her books in the Woman's Building. She died on 1 July 1896 at the age of eighty-five. In 1902 the writer Henry Adams compared Stowe and Queen Victoria as two women who had left an indelible stamp on their age and who had been "morally determined to recreate civilization in their own image and likeness." Nevertheless, twentieth-century scholars have not considered *Uncle Tom's Cabin* a classic of American literature, perhaps because of its emotionality and its accessibility to ordinary readers as well as its lack of structural complexity. Jane Tompkins has observed that "the most powerful book ever written by an American has been excluded from our literary canon precisely *because* of its power."

In her travel writings Stowe helped Americans see themselves and a wider world. Her positive reception in the British Isles, especially the praise and tumultuous welcome extended by ordinary citizens, confirmed widespread support abroad for her attack on slavery. Her travel letters from the Continent enabled her readers to partake of a Europe they might never see. They could identify with Stowe as a genteel American lady traveler, escorted and protected, even as they admired her capacity for observant and eloquent commentary. *Palmetto-Leaves* taught Stowe's readers of natural splendors in their own country that were equal to those of Europe. Stowe's travel writings from abroad gave her American readers many insights into the customs and sights of the British Isles and the Continent. It may be argued, however, that their most enduring impact was in their portrayal of Stowe as an increasingly informed and literate American, holding her own in an enigmatic Old World. *Palmetto-Leaves* complemented this image as Stowe fashioned a life of cultured industry against the background of a society as alien to her native New England as Europe.

Letters:

Life of Harriet Beecher Stowe Compiled from Her Letters and Journals, edited by Charles Edward Stowe (Boston & New York: Houghton, Mifflin, 1889);

Life and Letters of Harriet Beecher Stowe, edited by Annie A. Fields (Boston & New York: Houghton, Mifflin, 1897).

Bibliographies:

Margaret Holbrook Hildreth, *Harriet Beecher Stowe: A Bibliography* (Hamden, Conn.: Archon, 1976);

Jean Ashton, *Harriet Beecher Stowe: A Reference Guide* (Boston: G. K. Hall, 1977).

Biographies:

Charles Edward Stowe and L. B. Stowe, *Harriet Beecher Stowe, The Story of Her Life* (Boston: Houghton Mifflin, 1911);

Forest Wilson, *Crusader in Crinoline: The Life of Harriet Beecher Stowe* (Philadelphia: Lippincott, 1941);

Noel B. Gerson, *Harriet Beecher Stowe: A Biography* (New York: Praeger, 1976);

Joan D. Hedrick, *Harriet Beecher Stowe: A Life* (New York & Oxford: Oxford University Press, 1994).

References:

John R. Adams, *Harriet Beecher Stowe,* revised edition (Boston: Twayne, 1989);

Elizabeth Ammons, ed., *Critical Essays on Harriet Beecher Stowe* (Boston: G. K. Hall, 1980);

Charles Beecher, *Harriet Beecher Stowe in Europe: The Journal of Charles Beecher,* edited by Joseph S. Van Why and Earl French (Hartford, Conn.: Stowe-Day Foundation, 1986);

Sculley Bradley, "Pilgrim's Return," in *Literary History of the United States,* third edition, edited by Robert Spiller (New York: Macmillan, 1963);

Charles Foster, *The Rungless Ladder: Harriet Beecher Stowe and New England Puritanism* (Durham, N.C.: Duke University Press, 1954);

David Miller, *Dark Eden: The Swamp in Nineteenth-Century American Culture* (Cambridge & New York: Cambridge University Press, 1989);

Mary Suzanne Schriber, ed., *Telling Travels: Selected Writings by Nineteenth-Century American Women Abroad* (DeKalb: Northern Illinois University Press, 1995);

Jane Tompkins, "Harriet Beecher Stowe," in *The Heath Anthology of American Literature,* volume 1, edited by Paul Lauter (Lexington, Mass.: D. C. Heath, 1990);

Edward Charles Wagenknecht, *Harriet Beecher Stowe: The Known and the Unknown* (New York: Oxford University Press, 1965).

Papers:
Harriet Beecher Stowe's papers are in the Beecher-Stowe Collection at Schlesinger Library, Radcliffe College, Harvard University, and at the Stowe-Day Foundation in Hartford, Connecticut.

Bayard Taylor

(11 January 1825 – 19 December 1878)

James L. Gray
Indiana University of Pennsylvania

See also the Taylor entry in *DLB 3: Antebellum Writers in New York and the South.*

BOOKS: *Ximena; or, The Battle of the Sierra Morena, and Other Poems* (Philadelphia: Herman Hooker, 1844);

Views A-Foot; or, Europe Seen with Knapsack and Staff (New York: Wiley & Putnam, 1846); augmented as *Pedestrian Tour in Europe. Views A-Foot; or, Europe Seen with Knapsack and Staff* (New York: Putnam, 1848); revised (New York: Putnam / London: Sampson Low, Son, 1855);

Rhymes of Travel, Ballads and Poems (New York: Putnam, 1849);

Eldorado; or, Adventures in the Path of Empire: Comprising a Voyage to California, via Panama; Life in San Francisco and Monterey; Pictures of the Gold Region, and Experiences of Mexican Travel, 2 volumes (New York: Putnam, 1850; London: Richard Bentley, 1850);

The American Legend: A Poem Before the Phi Beta Kappa Society of Harvard University, July 18, 1850 (Cambridge, Mass.: Bartlett, 1850);

A Book of Romances, Lyrics, and Songs (Boston: Ticknor, Reed & Fields, 1852);

A Journey to Central Africa; or, Life and Landscapes from Egypt to the Negro Kingdoms of the White Nile (New York: Putnam, 1854); republished as *Life and Landscapes from Egypt to the Negro Kingdoms of the White Nile: Being A Journey to Central Africa* (London: Sampson Low, Son, 1854);

Poems of the Orient (Boston: Ticknor & Fields, 1855 [i.e., 1854]);

The Lands of the Saracen; or, Pictures of Palestine, Asia Minor, Sicily, and Spain (New York: Putnam, 1855 [i.e., 1854]); republished as *Pictures of Palestine, Asia Minor, Sicily, and Spain; or, The Lands of the Saracen* (London: Sampson Low, 1855 [i.e., 1854]);

A Visit to India, China, and Japan, in the Year 1853 (New York: Putnam / London: Sampson Low, Son, 1855);

Poems of Home and Travel (Boston: Ticknor & Fields, 1855);

Northern Travel: Summer and Winter Pictures of Sweden, Lapland, and Norway (London: Sampson Low, Son, 1858 [i.e., 1857]); republished as *Northern Travel: Summer and Winter Pictures of Sweden, Denmark, and Lapland* (New York: Putnam, 1858 [i.e., 1857]);

Travels in Greece and Russia, with an Excursion to Crete (New York: Putnam, 1859; London: Sampson Low, Son, 1859);

321

At Home and Abroad: A Sketch-Book of Life, Scenery, and Men (New York: Putnam, 1860 [i.e. 1859]; London: Sampson Low, Son, 1860 [i.e., 1859]);

At Home and Abroad: A Sketch-Book of Life, Scenery, and Men, . . . Second Series (New York: Putnam, 1862; London: Sampson Low, Son, 1862);

The Poet's Journal (Boston: Ticknor & Fields, 1863 [i.e., 1862]; London: Sampson Low, 1863 [i.e., 1862]);

Hannah Thurston: A Story of American Life (New York: Putnam, 1863; 3 volumes, London: Sampson Low, Son, 1863);

John Godfrey's Fortunes; Related by Himself. A Story of American Life (New York: Putnam/Hurd & Houghton, 1864; 3 volumes, London: Sampson Low, Son & Marston, 1864);

The Poems of Bayard Taylor (Boston: Ticknor & Fields, 1865 [i.e., 1864]);

The Story of Kennett (New York: Putnam/Hurd & Houghton, 1866; 2 volumes, London: Sampson Low, Son, 1866);

The Picture of St. John (Boston: Ticknor & Fields, 1866);

Colorado: A Summer Trip (New York: Putnam, 1867);

By-Ways of Europe (New York: Putnam, 1869); also published as *Byeways of Europe,* 2 volumes (London: Sampson Low, Son, & Marston, 1869);

The Ballad of Abraham Lincoln (Boston: Fields, Osgood, 1870);

Joseph and His Friend: A Story of Pennsylvania (New York: Putnam / London: Sampson Low, Son & Marston, 1870);

Beauty and the Beast: And Tales of Home (New York: Putnam, 1872; London: Sampson Low, Marston, Low & Searle, 1872);

The Masque of the Gods (Boston: James R. Osgood, 1872);

Diversions of the Echo Club: A Companion to the "Autocrat of the Breakfast-Table," anonymous (London: Hotten, 1872); augmented and republished as *The Echo Club, and Other Literary Diversions* (Boston: James R. Osgood, 1876);

Lars: a Pastoral of Norway (Boston: James R. Osgood, 1873; London: Strahan, 1873);

The Prophet: A Tragedy (Boston: James R. Osgood, 1874);

Egypt and Iceland in the Year 1874 (New York: Putnam, 1874; London: Sampson Low, Marston, Low & Searle, 1875);

A School History of Germany: From the Earliest Period to the Establishment of the German Empire in 1871 (New York: Appleton, 1874); republished with an additional chapter by Marie Hansen-Taylor as *A History of Germany From the Earliest Times to the Present Day* (New York: Appleton, 1894);

Home Pastorals, Ballads and Lyrics (Boston: James R. Osgood, 1875);

Boys of Other Countries: Stories for American Boys (New York: Putnam, 1876; augmented, New York & London: Putnam, 1901);

The National Ode: July 4, 1876, facsimile of manuscript (Boston: James R. Osgood, 1876); republished as *The National Ode: The Memorial Freedom Poem* (Boston: W. F. Gill, 1877);

Prince Deukalion: A Lyrical Drama (Boston: Houghton, Osgood / Cambridge, Mass.: Riverside, 1878; London: Trübner, 1878);

Studies in German Literature, edited by Marie Hansen-Taylor (New York: Putnam, 1879; London: Sampson Low, Marston, Searle, 1879);

Critical Essays and Literary Notes, edited by Hansen-Taylor (New York: Putnam, 1880; London: Sampson Low, Marston, Searle, 1880).

Collections: *The Poetical Works of Bayard Taylor* (Boston: Houghton, Osgood / Cambridge, Mass.: Riverside, 1880);

The Dramatic Works of Bayard Taylor, edited by Marie Hansen-Taylor (Boston: Houghton, Mifflin / Cambridge, Mass: Riverside, 1880).

OTHER: *Hand-book of Literature and Fine Arts,* edited by Taylor and George Ripley (New York: Putnam, 1852);

Cyclopaedia of Modern Travel: A Record of Adventure, Exploration and Discovery, for the Past Fifty Years: Comprising Narratives of the Most Distinguished Travelers Since the Beginning of This Century, edited by Taylor (Cincinnati: Moore, Wilstach, Keys, 1856); revised and enlarged as *Cyclopaedia of Modern Travel: A Record of Adventure, Exploration and Discovery, for the Past Sixty Years . . . ,* 2 volumes (Cincinnati: Moore, Wilstach, Keys, 1860);

"The Golden Wedding: A Masque," in *The Golden Wedding: Joseph Taylor, Rebecca W. Taylor, October 15, 1868,* by Taylor, Richard Henry Stoddard, and George Henry Boker (Privately printed, Philadelphia: Lippincott, 1868);

Faust: A Tragedy by Johann Wolfgang von Goethe; the First Part, Translated, in the Original Metres, by Bayard Taylor (Boston: Fields, Osgood, 1871 [i.e., 1870]);

Faust: A Tragedy by Johann Wolfgang von Goethe; the Second Part, Translated, in the Original Metres, by Bayard Taylor (Boston: James R. Osgood, 1871);

Japan in Our Day, edited by Taylor (New York: Scribners, 1872);

Travels in Arabia, edited by Taylor (New York: Scribner, Armstrong, 1872);

Travels in South Africa, edited by Taylor (New York: Scribner, Armstrong, 1872);

The Lake Regions of Central Africa, edited by Taylor (New York: Scribner, Armstrong, 1873);

Central Asia: Travels in Cashmere, Little Tibet and Central Asia, edited by Taylor (New York: Scribner, Armstrong, 1874);

Picturesque Europe: A Delineation by Pen and Pencil of the Natural Features and the Picturesque and Historical Places of Great Britain and the Continent, edited by Taylor, 60 parts, also published in 3 volumes (New York: Appleton, 1875–1879).

Baynard Taylor was one of the most popular travel writers of his time, producing eleven volumes of his own accounts and lecturing throughout the United States to large audiences. From the time his first travel book appeared in 1846 virtually until his death, he never really quit traveling or writing about it. Always adventurous, he went to places and attempted feats not usual for travelers, thereby making accessible largely unknown regions of the world to a popular audience and making himself a romantic figure. Describing people and places vividly, he enthusiastically participated in several of the cultures he visited, often attempting to assume the characteristics of those persons whom he was observing; by this means he engaged his readers more fully than most other travel writers of his time.

Bayard Taylor (occasionally listed, incorrectly, as James Bayard Taylor) was born of English and German ancestry in Kennett Square, Chester County, Pennsylvania, and raised as a Quaker. Never happy on the farm, he enjoyed school, and early on he showed a flair for poetry. He relished spending almost three years in West Chester (1837–1839) while his father was sheriff, and in 1842 he returned to West Chester apprenticed to a local printer. He had by then published some poetry; encouraged by Rufus Griswold, in 1844 he produced a small volume of verse, *Ximena; or, The Battle of the Sierra Morena, and Other Poems,* hoping to raise money to travel to Europe. Even this early Taylor revealed his high enthusiasm for poetry and his desire to cultivate established figures, sending inscribed copies to Henry Wadsworth Longfellow and James Russell Lowell. With some money from the volume, the help of Nathaniel Parker Willis, and the agreement of two newspapers to publish his letters, he obtained his release from the apprenticeship and sailed to Europe, arriving on 26 July 1844.

Taylor, the penniless, striving, awestruck youth, walked across Europe for nearly two years,

seeking out every tourist and cultural site he could find, gathering material for the book that would make his reputation and remain his best-known work. *Views A-Foot; or, Europe Seen with Knapsack and Staff* (1846) can be understood best as a struggle for culture. Taylor strives to get to Europe; he scrapes for money while he is there; he walks in the rain if necessary. Against all odds he will acquire a culture and a history by positioning himself in those of Europe. He almost never lets an opportunity pass: given a free hour, he looks for a church or a ruin, and places which have neither bore him. He even criticizes those English travelers who do not see everything; conscious that they are part of the culture, they do not feel the need to see all of its artifacts to participate in it. Taylor will not fail to see anything, and his youthful and romantic enthusiasm for all of it could not fail to find a response in his readers.

Taylor is sometimes disconcerting in his desire to be certain the reader observes and learns as much as he does: on his first day in Ireland he describes several landmarks, including the Giant's Causeway, the Giant's Well, the Giant's Loom, the Ladies' Chair, the Giant's Organ, and the Chimneys; then he adds a narrative of a Spanish ship that was wrecked off the Chimneys. Later he describes a Robert Burns festival and a visit to Abbotsford in similar detail. In London he visits all the conventional tourist sites and describes them in appropriately reverential terms. About Westminster Abbey, for example, he asserts: "A place so sacred to all who inherit the English tongue is worthy of a special pilgrimage across the deep. To those who are unable to visit it, a description may be interesting; but so far does it fall short of the scene itself."

From London, Taylor traveled through Belgium to Heidelberg. In Ghent, having an hour before his train to Heidelberg, he "went to see the cathedral of St. Bavon." From Heidelberg he walked to Frankfurt, where he spent several weeks meeting with students and visiting composer Felix Mendelssohn. Then he went on to Leipzig and Dresden, from there into Austria and Bohemia and Moravia, back to Vienna, through the valley of the Danube, then to the Austrian Alps—almost always walking. He frequently refers to his need for money and to how little he is spending. He is impressed by the size of libraries and by picture galleries, but his concept of art emphasizes regularity, order, and elaborateness. Of Stuttgart he says: "Stuttgard has neither galleries, ruins nor splendid buildings to interest the traveller, but it has Thorwaldsen's statue of Schiller, calling up at the same time, its shame and its glory." From Stuttgart he hiked through the Black Forest and Switzerland into Italy. In Milan he finds only

Frontispiece for the 1848 edition of Taylor's best-known travel book, Views A-Foot; or, Europe Seen with Knapsack and Staff *(1846)*

four things worth seeing: "the Duomo, the triumphal arch over the Simplon, La Scala and the picture gallery." Soon he had "already finished seeing Milan" and was on his way.

Florence has the *Venus de Medici* sculpture, which he twice calls "faultless." In that city he reaffirms his adulation for what he considered art and culture:

> But we are pilgrims to the shrines of Art and Genius; the dwelling-places of great minds are our sanctuaries. The mean dwelling in which a poet has battled down poverty with the ecstasy of his mighty conceptions and the dungeon in which a persecuted philosopher has languished are to us sacred.

A few pages later he produces a paean to Italy, where "there is a silent, intense poetry that stirs the soul through all its impassioned depths. With warm, blissful tears filling the eyes and a heart overflowing with its own bright fancies, I wander in the solitude and calm of such a time, and love thee as if I were a

child of thy soil." He also demonstrates what became a consistent habit when he visited the sites of ancient culture. His appreciation is for the ancient Italy, and he rather dislikes contemporary Italians: "The Italians, as a race, are indolent and effeminate. Of the moral dignity of man they have little conception."

Taylor's idea of culture did not include the gross. Of one group of lifelike wax figures he writes: "There are enough forms of beauty and delight in the world on which to employ the eye, without making it familiar with scenes which can only be remembered with a shudder." Of Michelangelo's *Drunken Bacchus* he says, "It may be doubted whether the artist's talents might not have been employed better than in ennobling intoxication." Taylor remained in Florence longer than he wished because he lacked money; he had to give up plans to visit Greece for the same reason. In his brief time in Rome he was the typical tourist, seeing the sights and praising the art. From Rome he returned through France to London, where he worked briefly in a clerical capacity for publisher George Putnam while he awaited the money that would pay his passage home.

Certain characteristics stand out in Taylor's account of his tour. For one thing, Taylor is always in a hurry, impatient to be moving on to see new things and to absorb traditional European culture as quickly as possible. His tour is not a Continental one in the usual sense of the time; he is acquiring cultural credentials. Thinking himself a culturally deprived young man, he seeks out virtually every artifact he can find, often admiring the objects only as representative of the culture; for instance, several times he reports how many volumes a library possessed. His desire for credentials means Taylor ordinarily limits himself to the conventionally cultural in what he sees and in how he responds to it. Business and economy mean nothing to him, and his view of art emphasizes the regular and the correct. He never expresses a surprising or an outrageous idea.

Taylor also frequently refers to the United States but usually only in traditional terms as representative of freedom, individual rights, and self-reliance. He emphasizes that Europeans of all classes admire the United States and want to talk with him about it. He never misses an opportunity to note positive European response to American writers and artists, even expressing the belief that the United States is potentially a future aesthetic center: "What country possesses more advantages to foster the growth of such an art than ours? Why should not the composer gain mighty conceptions from the grandeur of our mountain-scenery, from the howling of the storm through our giant forests, from the eternal thunder of Niagara."

Finally, he made as much as possible of the sentimental and romantic possibilities of a young man so eager to acquire culture that he would travel to Europe almost without money and would walk from country to country, often going without food, in order to achieve his goal. From the beginning Taylor understood the commercial value of the persona he was creating for himself.

Although *Views A-Foot* was an immediate success when it was published in 1846 after his return to the United States, Taylor needed to find a way to support himself and earn enough money to marry Mary Agnew, his childhood sweetheart. First he attempted to set himself up as a newspaper editor and publisher, buying a local Pennsylvania paper, the *Phoenixville Pioneer,* and running it for about a year. Then he moved to New York City, seeking employment that included schoolteaching. There he moved in intellectual circles and made several friends including two, Richard Henry Stoddard and George Henry Boker, with whom he became close. He was soon working for Horace Greeley and editing Caroline M. Kirkland's *Union Magazine* for a few months while she was in Europe. Although the success of *Views A-Foot* was his entry into New York literary circles, Taylor's ability to cultivate literary friends helped him to establish himself once he was there.

Greeley gave Taylor the major assignment that led to his next book, sending him in 1849 to San Francisco and the gold camps of California to chronicle both the gold rush and the formation of a government. Taylor went by way of the Isthmus of Panama and spent five months in California, returning alone by horseback through Mexico in a bit of bravado that was to become typical of him. Thus, Taylor's second travel book, *Eldorado; or, Adventures in the Path of Empire: Comprising a Voyage to California, via Panama; Life in San Francisco and Monterey; Pictures of the Gold Region, and Experiences of Mexican Travel* (1850), took him in a different direction in space and in time than his European travels had in *Views A-Foot.* He saw western North America rather than western Europe, and he focused on a new and developing culture rather than on a traditional one.

Eldorado also demonstrates stylistic and attitudinal changes. Taylor first published a series of letters about his travels in the *New York Tribune* and then the two volumes in book form, including an account of his solitary journey across Mexico. Although he had published letters from his European journey, this latest series concentrated as much on the process of travel as on the sights and scenes of his destination. Writing them required a shift in stylistic focus; the book reflected the impressionistic nature of letter writing. Taylor recorded events, impressions of persons, and sights as he experienced them, producing the book so rapidly that he had little time to revise and provide more thoughtful analysis. The requirements of letter writing tended to make him a tourist.

Two other stylistic features surface as early as his description of Chagres, on the Isthmus of Panama. First, he demonstrates his knack for putting the reader in his position, making the reader feel as if he or she were witnessing the scene with Taylor. Second, his description of the Spanish fortification reveals his cultural bias. He contends that a more assertive people would make more of it: "Strong as it is by nature, and would be in the hands of an enterprising people, it now looks harmless enough with a few old cannon lying lazily on its ramparts." Perhaps under the influence of Greeley, but certainly affected by the general optimism and assertiveness of the times, Taylor believed that aggressive Anglo-Saxons could improve virtually any place. Anglo-Saxons not only brought civilization but also were more able and worked harder. He was capable of some self-awareness, however; a few pages later he describes "the American habit of going at full speed" coming into contact with the deliberate residents of the Isthmus of Panama.

Taylor had sought cultural stability in Europe. Now, in San Francisco, he enthusiastically reports cultural transition. Taylor's first impression of California was of overturned values; he experienced "a complete sense of bewilderment," not only about business and money but also about all other values: "Never have I had so much difficulty in establishing, satisfactorily to my own sense, the reality of what I saw and heard." This new place changed the way one understands. Leaving San Francisco for the gold camps separates one even more from civilized values, but here the separation is conventionally positive: "cut off, for the time, from every irksome requirement of civilization, and cast loose, like a stray, unshackled spirit, on the bosom of a new earth, I seemed to take a fresh and more perfect lease of existence." In the gold camps themselves, Taylor describes a circumstance in which people banded together to develop rules appropriate to the conditions, noting, "The capacity of a people for self-government was never so triumphantly illustrated."

That capacity was matched by the agricultural and financial possibilities of the area—possibilities he thought were further illustrated by the constitutional convention that he witnessed and reported. He approved the Declaration of Rights in the constitution of the California Territory because it prohibited slavery, gave married women the right to property, and established "a liberal system of education." He notes that Californians (apparently those of total Spanish ancestry) are superior to Mexicans, and he comments with disappointment that suffrage was denied to African Americans and, except under special circumstances, to Native Americans. Nevertheless he believed that the constitution reflected "harmony evolved out of so wonderful, so dangerous, so magnificent a chaos" and was the product of the same spirit that permitted the mining camps to establish order. Paradoxically, perhaps, the disruption of order had made possible the establishment of an even more effective order, a quality he sees resulting from the American capacity for self-government: chaos here leads to "the highest form of civil order—the broadest extent of liberty and security."

For Taylor, California became a model for American democracy and, in most respects, also a model for peaceful and productive relationships among groups. California even produced a new kind of person: "A man, on coming to California, could no more expect to retain his old nature unchanged, than he could retain in his lungs the air he had inhaled on the Atlantic shore." Such men demonstrated "an increase of activity, and proportionately, of reckless and daring spirit." Those who risked most gained most. Had they been less assertive, they (and California) would have been less successful. Although Taylor particularly wanted to praise this energy, he also noted that the same expense of that energy caused traditional signs of civilization to diminish in importance. Whatever their background, men did not read books in California, and even Taylor was unable to become interested in Jane Porter's *Scottish Chiefs* (1810), a book he had enjoyed when a child.

Taylor could not leave California without one romantic and heroic act. Thus, he returned home by sailing down the coast for some time and then riding alone some twelve hundred miles across most of Mexico to Vera Cruz, describing the Mexicans he meets and giving significant space to being robbed, a circumstance which did not really frighten him. He found many of the Mexicans to be docile and kindly, but contented and not especially progressive, often expecting, he thought, to be ruled by Americans some day. On the other hand, he found the mosquitoes, fleas, sand flies, and "venomous bugs" a real problem. Taylor was not particularly interested in Mexican politics or antiquities, preferring Mexican War

battlefields for his sightseeing. By the time he arrived in New York on 10 March 1850, he had been gone for eight months and eight days.

Scholar Paul C. Wermuth believes that *Eldorado,* which sold well enough, made travel so profitable to Taylor that he could not quit. Certainly *Eldorado* is a better book than *Views A-Foot;* Taylor remains essentially a tourist, but he no longer feels obliged to see everything and to admire it. He acquires more of the characteristics of the observer, reporting (however optimistically) what he thinks necessary and important. Further, Taylor reports a culture as new and fascinating to his readers as to himself. As an early explication of the importance and meaning of California (and thereby the West Coast), *Eldorado* is an important book. In that sense, and in Taylor's treatment of Mexico generally, *Eldorado* also served to justify the Mexican War. The confident young man presenting a vision of the future in *Eldorado* was as attractive as the impoverished young man walking across Europe in a continuing search for his cultural roots. Whether or not he recognized it at the time, Taylor had demonstrated that he could report travel in relatively unknown and exotic areas as effectively as he could describe travel in Europe; in so doing he had prepared himself for further travel which would take him to areas that Americans knew well and to those that they hardly knew at all.

Taylor had long been engaged to Mary Agnew, but the two had been waiting until he could better afford to marry her. Now, both knowing that she was dying of tuberculosis, they married on 24 October 1850. She died less than two months later on 21 December. Taylor seems to have been devastated by her death and left as soon as possible for Egypt on what became a long recuperative trip—much of it into areas where few, if any, Europeans or Americans had traveled. This trip and the three volumes he subsequently produced mark the zenith of his career as traveler and travel writer.

A Journey to Central Africa; or, Life and Landscapes from Egypt to the Negro Kingdoms of the White Nile (1854) reveals both his growing interest in and appreciation of Middle Eastern life and his desire to see and describe sights few westerners had experienced. Clearly seeking the exotic and the unknown, and describing it well because he so enjoys it, Taylor is now a much more confident writer. Although his desires to see everything important and to travel rapidly remain, his judgments are surer. He is less eager to worship at the feet of culture except when that culture is clearly part of his own western European background. Taylor also discovers a new approach to travel: he declares himself "attracted less by historical and geographical interest of those regions than by the desire to participate in their free, vigorous, semi-barbaric life." His unstated goal is to help his reader share in that participation.

His attitude on the way along the Nile from Alexandria to Cairo reveals his desire to adopt a new attitude toward life: "My conscience made me no reproach for such a lazy life. In America we live too fast and work too hard, I thought: shall I not know what Rest is, once before I die?" He is already fitting himself into what he understands as an Arabian view of life. In Cairo he immediately tries the Narghileh, or Persian water pipe, and begins to wear Egyptian clothing, although he plans to learn more of the language before adopting the costume completely.

Soon he is heading toward Khartoum on a riverboat, stopping briefly at the Pyramids, adopting the costume fully, and lauding the pleasure of a relaxed life: "I do not reproach myself for this passive and sensuous existence. I give myself up to it unreservedly, and if some angular-souled utilitarian should come along and recommend me to shake off my laziness, and learn the conjugations of Coptic verbs or the hieroglyphs of Kneph and Thoth, I should not take the pipe from my mouth to answer him." In Luxor he describes in some detail (but without much sensuousness) the performance of dancing girls, defending his decision to see them on the grounds that he is traveling for instruction.

Another result of Taylor's confidence in his opinions is some easy racism: he claims to recognize distinct Persian, Jewish, and Ethiopian racial characteristics in a three-thousand-year-old drawing on a tomb. To him this suggested the accuracy of the idea of the separate origin of different races. He comments that Nubian children have cunning, but not intelligent, faces and eyes with "an astonishingly precocious expression of sensuality." Later he asserts that Egyptians had no "negro features" and that "there is no evidence in all the valley of the Nile that the Negro Race ever attained a higher degree of civilization than is at present exhibited in Congo and Ashantee." He finds Ethiopia beautiful but thinks that it "might become, in other hands, the richest and most productive part of Africa." Taylor is comforted by "the knowledge that the highest Civilization, in every age of the world, has been developed by the race to which we belong." Taylor is often discomfited by, and comments on, what he considers the lack of attractiveness and intelligence of the Africans whom he sees. On the other hand he believes that "that superior intelligence which renders the brute creation unable to bear the gaze of a human eye, is the defence of the civilized man against the barbarian."

Taylor's greatest pleasure came from going beyond Khartoum into what he considered uncharted territory, and in his language he makes the most of it: "I felt for the first time that I was alone, far in the savage heart of Africa." He finds "Central Africa as I had dreamed it—a grand though savage picture, full of life and heat, and with a barbaric splendor even in the forms of Nature." He describes the wildlife at some length, both in numbers and size, providing the reader with a sense of that "barbaric splendor." Taylor's goal had been to reach the Shilluks in the interior of what is now Sudan, and he succeeds, describing the meeting with obvious pleasure and characterizing the Shilluks as large and muscular but not graceful or attractive. That point marked the extent of his journey to the interior, and he wrote a set-piece final paragraph to the section, concluding: "though I was leaving the gorgeous heart of Africa, I was going back to Civilization and Home."

After his return to Khartoum, Taylor, in a decision reminiscent of his riding alone across Mexico to Veracruz, chose to ride through the desert, apparently wishing to experience the extreme heat and report its effect to his readers. At first Taylor finds that the heat had "a bracing effect," inspiring "a sensation of fierce, savage vigor." After an attack of sunstroke ("desert intoxication") he finds the heat less exhilarating and wants out of it. Soon he begins to find conditions almost unbearable, especially during a sandstorm. Still, he can appreciate what he calls "that strange feeling of happiness which the contemplation of waste and desolate landscapes always inspires" and can write romantically of the Nile struggling through the area on its way to Egypt: "There was, to me, something exceedingly touching in watching his course through that fragment of pre-Adamite chaos—in seeing the type of Beauty and Life stealing quietly through the heart of a region of Desolation and Death." Later he provides a similar romantic and pictorial description of the Nile forcing its way through the mountains of Batn El-Hadjar: "It is a wonderful picture of strife between two material forces, but so intricate and labyrinthine in its features, that the eye can scarcely succeed in separating them, or in viewing it other than as a whole."

A significant part of Taylor's travels on and near the Nile took him to places seldom visited by westerners and through adventures (including crossing the desert) seldom experienced by them. Although Taylor never thought of himself as an explorer, it was clearly important to him to recount to a popular audience travel and conditions well beyond what most tourists encountered. He was, in a sense, taking the tourist impulse beyond its logical extremes in going to Khartoum, in traveling farther to visit the Shilluks, and in

Illustration of Robert Burns's home in the 1884 edition of Views A-Foot

crossing the desert. The second book of this trilogy, *The Lands of the Saracen; or, Pictures of Palestine, Asia Minor, Sicily, and Spain* (1855), describes more familiar territory, the Holy Land, but Taylor carefully points out in the preface that part of it was generally new and rarely visited by tourists.

Three attitudes toward the subject matter characterize *The Lands of the Saracen:* first, Taylor the tourist is appropriately moved by the Holy Land and by Grecian antiquities; second, his appreciation for things Arabic increases; third, he seeks new experiences and new places to describe to the reader. Since these attitudes are not always compatible, Taylor occasionally appears ambivalent, even contradictory.

All of these attitudes appear early. Quarantined at Beirut, at the beginning of his journey, Taylor cultivates the friendship of a Muslim holy man and decides that Muslims demonstrate less bigotry than Christians. Further, Taylor adopts Arab dress as more comfortable, and in the Holy Land he enjoys being taken as an Arab, even possibly a thief. On the other hand Taylor describes the Holy Land in conventionally Christian terms, suggesting that just touching the earth would consecrate him and going almost into raptures as he approaches Jerusalem. He often lauds the pastoral quality of the area in the first few pages and suggests that it needs only "Christian hands" once more to "flow with milk and honey," a remark he will make frequently throughout this book. He twice compares Palestine to the beauty and fertility of the California he had described in *Eldorado.* Unwilling to

avoid any interesting experience, Taylor swims in the Dead Sea and bathes in the Jordan River.

In the chapter on Jerusalem, Taylor finds the city characterized by "filth, ruin, poverty, and degradation" and Christians sufficiently contentious that any neutral person would choose to be Muslim. Although Taylor appeared somewhat anti-Semitic in his earlier works and seemed especially so in later ones, here he finds Jews to be attractive, retaining "a noble beauty" that persuaded him they were descended "from the ancient princely houses of Israel." In fact, he sees one man who reminds him of Christ as drawn by Raphael. After a monk, not recognizing that Taylor's rosary is Islamic, sprinkles rose-water on it, Taylor suggests that Jerusalem reminds him of Christ the man and briefly pursues the idea of a "divinely-inspired man," recognizing that this attitude might offend some readers but clearly presenting it in the context of the divided religious sympathies of a city considered holy by Jews, Christians, and Turks.

Taylor is ecstatic about Damascus for what he sees as its oriental qualities, finding it "Beauty carried to the Sublime" when viewed from a distance. In Damascus he experiments with two forms of oriental pleasure and reports fully on both—hashish and the oriental bath. That each experiment leads to the breaking of taboos does not deter him. He introduces taking hashish (which he had tried in smaller quantities in Cairo) by referring to the "insatiable curiosity which leads me to prefer the acquisition of all lawful knowledge through the channels of my own personal experience." Inadvertently taking six times the normal amount, he experiences "deeps of rapture and of suffering" not otherwise possible. Taylor contends that he has described the experience so fully to convey a lesson to others, but his effort to dissuade seems no more than halfhearted.

In the next chapter Taylor makes the bath an oriental luxury, describing in detail a physical sensuousness that could "bestow a superior purification and impart a more profound enjoyment." He moves from that description to assert that Arab bodies have become soft, but the women are especially beautiful. Then he argues the beauty of the nude body: "The necessary disguise of dress hides from us much of the beauty and dignity of Humanity. I have seen men who appeared heroic in the freedom of nakedness, shrink almost into absolute vulgarity when clothed." He clearly objects to "our dress, our costumes, and our modes of speech [which] either ignore the existence of our bodies, or treat them with little of that reverence which is their due." The physical sensuousness of the bath thus leads to a discussion of art and of the body that stands in clear opposition to the usual standards of mid Victorianism.

From Damascus, Taylor traveled to Baalbek, Lebanon, Antioch, and Aleppo, pausing on the way to express his pleasure in two more oriental delights—tobacco (especially the water pipe) and coffee. For the rest of the journey he mentions enjoying both at virtually every stop. Taylor is, in fact, moving through quite a bit of Asia Minor, with little more than short descriptions, until he enters Greece, where he once more falls into conventional superlatives—finding a "sublime wilderness" and "such primeval magnitude of growth, such wild luxuriance." This movement from Asia Minor into Europe signals an interesting change:

> The camp-fire is extinguished; the tent is furled. We are no longer happy nomads, masquerading in Moslem garb. We shall soon become prosaic Christians, and meekly hold out our wrists for the handcuffs of Civilization. Ah, prate as we will of the progress of the race, we are but forging additional fetters, unless we preserve that healthy physical development, those pure pleasures of mere animal existence, which are now only to be found among our semi-barbaric brethren. Our progress is nervous, when it should be muscular.

At Constantinople, Taylor describes the end of the sacred month of Ramadan with care but says he will not describe Constantinople itself because so many others have described it so well. A discussion of mosques gets him into religious and aesthetic confusion again, however. One mosque is described as "a product of the rich fancy of the East, splendidly or-

nate" but with a symmetry of ornament rather than the Grecian symmetry of form: "It requires a certain degree of enthusiasm—nay, a slight inebriation of the imaginative faculties—in order to feel the sentiment of this Oriental Architecture. If I rightly express all that it says to me, I touch the verge of rhapsody. The East, in almost all its aspects, is so essentially poetic, that a true picture of it must be poetic in spirit, if not in form."

Taylor seems caught between his appreciation for Islam and his belief that he must remain Christian, and between his appreciation of the aesthetic qualities of the mosque and his belief that true art comes from Grecian models. He had similarly been caught between his appreciation of Arab life and his commitment to European and Christian models: "While I look forward, not without pleasure, to the luxuries and conveniences of Europe, I relinquish with a sigh the refreshing indolence of Asia." Taylor's appeal lay in his ability to model a response to the Muslim world, allowing his readers to revel in his descriptions of its sensuousness and luxurious indolence without having to give up their European and Christian values.

The third book of the trilogy, *A Visit to India, China, and Japan, in the Year 1853* (1855), is less satisfying than the first two. Taylor, in his most obvious tourist mode, visits and describes three nations in a single volume; not even his stated purpose of joining Commodore Matthew Perry on his famous trip to open Japan to the West can overcome the sprawl. In addition, Taylor's strong aversion to the Chinese and his general sense of the cultural superiority of the European world become problematic.

Taylor's course was from Gibraltar, where the previous volume ended, through the Mediterranean and across Suez, and finally to Bombay. On the voyage he mixes derogatory comments about Africans ("hideous, monkey-faced Negroes from Mozambique," "mongrel natives of the African coast," "wild Africans") with an explicit statement that the British fortress at Aden demonstrates

> the power of that civilization which follows the Anglo-Saxon race in all its conquests, and takes root in whatever corner of the earth that race sets its foot. Here, on the farthest Arabian shore, facing the most savage and inhospitable regions of Africa, were Law, Order, Security, Freedom of Conscience and of Speech, and all the material advantages which are inseparable from these. Herein consists the true power and grandeur of the race, and the assurance of its final supremacy.

Taylor's assertions in the previous volume that European Christians could have made more of a particular spot become a direct statement of the meaning and order Anglo-Saxons bring to a "savage sterility."

"The Valley of Unna in Loo-Choo," frontispiece for the 1878 edition of Taylor's A Visit to India,
China, and Japan, in the Year 1853 *(1855)*

In India a visit to the cave temples of Elephanta leads to the assertion that those who fail to recognize the positive qualities in every religion can neither "understand nor appreciate the Art" that comes from them; the Christian should respect religious shrines and the faint truth that inspired them. He does reassure the reader that his respect does not mean that he believes such religious forms.

Though Taylor was due in China in two months, his usual eagerness to see and experience as much as possible (however fleetingly) and his desire to evaluate British rule in India led to a hurried journey primarily by mail cart from Bombay to Calcutta. On the route he finds some Englishmen a little short-tempered or obnoxious while others are kind to him. He finds the Indian native much like the Egyptian fellah—"the same natural quickness of intellect, the same capacity for deception, the same curious mixture of impudence and abject servility, and the same disregard of clothing." He finds them particularly subservient but thinks "it is natural to them." Taylor is steadily offended by what he regards as the stupidity and lack of effort exhibited by mail-cart drivers. Later he says of native workmen that they can imitate but can never learn "more than is taught them, never using their knowledge as a lamp to explore the unknown fields of science or art."

By the time Taylor is two-thirds of the way through the section on India he is asserting,

I can, however, feel neither the same interest in, nor respect for, the natives of India, as for the Arab races of Africa and Syria. The lower castes are too servile, too vilely the slaves of a degrading superstition, and too much given to cheating and lying. One cannot use familiarity towards them, without encouraging them to impertinence.

Religious leaders appear dirty and opportunistic, even disgusting and corrupt. Efforts to convert the natives to Christianity seem not worth the effort expended; Taylor suspects that many converted for practical gain and that many others saw Christianity as only another form of mythology. On the other hand he accepts polyandry as a natural outcome of the conditions under which those who practiced it lived, and he is hardly concerned by what he sees as phallic implications in some forms of worship: "There is a profound philosophical truth hidden under the singular forms of this worship, if men would divest themselves for a moment of a prudery with regard to such subjects, which seems to be the affectation of the present age." The Sikhs gain almost unqualified approval.

In Akbarabad he finds Saracenic architecture that greatly impresses him, as does the Taj Majal, which he considers the high point of Saracenic art and of which he says, "If there were nothing else in India, this alone would repay the journey." He adds, "Nothing can better illustrate the feeling for proportion which prevailed in those days—and proportion is Art."

By the end of his journey he has decided that despite its flaws, the East India Company has on the whole been good for India: "Despotic as the Company's government certainly is, it is a well-regulated despotism, and its quiet and steady sway is far preferable to the capricious tyranny of the native rulers." But he never learns to like the social attitudes toward natives.

The reader cannot forget, however, that Taylor was in India for only two months. Clearly most of his impressions were quite hasty; equally clear from what he says is that much of what he passed on as direct observation was really a collection of stories related to him or opinions expressed by the Englishmen with whom he spoke. Perhaps more than in any of his previous books, the originality of Taylor's impressions of India is suspect.

If Taylor at least felt sorry for the natives of India, he never learned to like the Chinese. From Calcutta, Taylor made his way to Singapore and then to Hong Kong. His first impression of the Chinese is of "dull faces" and "half-naked unsymmetrical bodies" that produce an "unconquerable aversion." Shanghai led him to comment on "the disgusting annoyances of a Chinese city." Taylor focuses on the stench, which he says stayed with him outside the city, and on what he considers the lack of artistic qualities: "I have seen no article of Chinese workmanship which could positively be called beautiful, unless it was fashioned after a European model." He asserts that "There is no sense of what we understand by Art—Grace, Harmony, Proportion—in the Chinese nature, and therefore we look in vain for any physical expression of it." Taylor seems here to be caught in his culture's conception of what art is, although he had no such limitations when dealing with Arab architecture.

Taylor also seems amazed that most Chinese have no interest in the revolution that soon will be threatening them; he finds a Chinese military review ludicrous, "without order or organization," "a Chinese travesty of Don Quixote." He is offended by all parts of Chinese life, particularly by their use of manure for fertilizer. For him the major problem is a lack of that harmony "which throbbed like a musical rhythm through the life of the Greeks." For Taylor it is even a matter of character. Declaring the Chinese "morally the most debased people on the face of the earth," Taylor urges that they never be allowed to come to the United States. He thinks that the one missionary he meets is simply wasting his time.

At Shanghai, Taylor signed on as an officer in Commodore Perry's expedition to open up Japan. The expedition sailed to Loo-Choo (the present Ryukyu Islands) and explored several islands before visiting Japan. Taylor's focus on Perry's mission is essentially nationalistic, emphasizing the "firmness, dignity and fearlessness" of Americans as opposed to the "artful and dissimulating policy" of the Japanese. The contrast extended to physical appearance as well: "There certainly was a marked contrast between the regular, compact files of our men, and their vigorous, muscular figures, and the straggling ranks of the mild, effeminate-featured Japanese." For Taylor the meeting was a victory of the "simple, straightforward, resolute course adopted by Commodore Perry" over the "cun-

ning and duplicity" of the Japanese. Later, in describing Perry's desire to set up a naval station in Loo-Choo, Taylor asserts that "there is no course so effective as plain common sense, backed up by a good reserve of physical force." Taylor evidently anticipated Theodore Roosevelt's "Speak softly and carry a big stick" by several decades.

During the return to Hong Kong, Taylor devotes a chapter to his opinions on such matters as naval promotions (they should not be based on seniority) and the abolition of corporal punishment ("one of those mistaken acts of philanthropy which are founded on abstract ideas of humanity rather than a practical knowledge of human nature"). In Hong Kong he comments on British society; from there he sails to Macao, and back to New York with a stop at Saint Helena, arriving in New York on 20 December 1853.

Taylor, always energetic, immediately set to work to profit from his travels, beginning a lecture tour and publishing the first two volumes of his account as quickly as possible. According to Albert Smyth he lectured ninety times between January and May 1854, and another 130 times in the fall. He wished to make enough money to build Cedarcroft, a family home in Kennett Square. He also put together the well-received volume *Poems of the Orient* (1855), writing in the genre he thought most congenial. By now travel, travel writing, and lecturing about travel had become a means to other ends—writing poetry and building and furnishing Cedarcroft. In 1856 he was back in Europe with two sisters and a younger brother. His plan was to give them a taste of European travel and to visit August Bufleb, with whom he had become friends in Egypt. Bufleb had given Taylor a home in Germany, near his own. In December 1856 Taylor and a companion went to Stockholm and set out on the trip he recounted in *Northern Travel: Summer and Winter Pictures of Sweden, Denmark, and Lapland* (1858).

Northern Travel seems almost a sport among Taylor's travel narratives. Taylor wanted to be able to say that he had seen both a day in which the sun did not rise above the horizon and a day in which the sun did not set. To achieve that goal he made two trips into the far north, one during the winter and one during the summer. Taylor used the trips to exhibit his hardiness and ability to withstand extreme cold, and he managed to spend a significant amount of time evaluating the cultures he saw—although, as on other journeys, he frequently relied on the opinions of others. Despite noticeable exceptions, Taylor frequently criticized the people he saw, especially the Norwegians and the Laplanders. The reasons are unclear: perhaps he too much preferred warm environments to cold;

perhaps he had lost some of his capacity simply to enjoy the people whom he met; perhaps he was becoming more persuaded of Anglo-Saxon superiority (at least so far as the Laplanders were concerned). At times the reader's pleasure in learning about new areas is lost in the querulous tone of Taylor's writing.

From Stockholm, Taylor started northward in sleds. The journey begins with brilliant winter scenery and strong, healthy persons not given to false modesty. The inhabitants of the Norrland region of Sweden are "noble specimens of the physical man," married to women "who, I venture to say, do not even suspect the existence of a nervous system," a combination that leads to morality, honesty, happiness, contentment. Taylor asks, "Where shall we find such among our restless communities at home?" A Swedish serving girl earns his respect for the calm way she works in his and his companion's presence in their bedroom.

Taylor's description of Arctic twilight is especially effective, notably the change of color as the sun rose only briefly: "Nothing in Italy, nothing in the Tropics, equals the magnificence of the Polar skies." However, by Muoniovara, in Lapland, the scene has become entirely desolate, and of Lippajarvi he says, "I have rarely seen anything quite so bleak and God-forsaken as this village. A few low black huts, in a desert of snow—that was all."

By this time he is traveling in sleds pulled by reindeer, and he decides that "the filth, the poverty, and the discomfort" in which the Lapps lived make him unwilling to repeat this experience. He asserts that the Lapps were interesting as pagans but are no longer. Now "pious and commonplace," they have retained "nearly all that is repulsive in their habits of life" and lost the qualities that might make them interesting to the traveler.

In his analysis of the Finns, Taylor seems to find no irony in relying heavily on a man he met there who knew the people well because he had lived among them for three years. He reports that they are honest, honorable, and morally chaste but not prudes. They are also slow, indolent, and improvident; Taylor believes their geographic position makes them fatalistic: "The polar zone was never designed for the abode of man." But Taylor then seems to reject the conventions of the period one more time when he says, "You who spend your lives at home can never know how much good there is in the world. In rude refined races, evil naturally rises to the surface, and one can discern the character of the stream beneath its scum. It is only in the highest civilization where the outside is goodly to the eye, too often concealing an interior foul to the core."

The following summer Taylor returned to the Arctic Circle, this time through Norway, finding the people "awkward," "uncouth," animal-like, and immoral. He believes that the early Viking seafarer (to judge by his descendants) was "a stupid, hardheaded, lustful, and dirty giant, whom we should rather not have had for a companion." The scenery is even less attractive. Such terms as *grey, naked, barren,* and *sterility* dominate his description. Probably the perceived lack of order and regularity causes Taylor's attitude: "One is bewildered in the attempt to describe such scenery. There is no central figure, no prevailing character, no sharp contrasts, which may serve as a guide whereby to reach the imagination of the reader. All is confused, disorder, chaotic."

Shortly after his return from Norway, Taylor married Marie Hansen, niece of Bufleb's wife, and by the end of the year he was with her in Greece gathering material for *Travels in Greece and Russia, with an Excursion to Crete* (1859). In this volume, the first section of which describes his long-anticipated travels in the country he considered the source of Western culture, Taylor continues his disparagement of cultures he considered inferior and his praise for Anglo-Saxons. In his preface he discusses what he considers to be the debased condition of modern Greece: "I can only record my complete conviction of the truth of the views entertained by Fallmereyer, that the modern Greeks are a mongrel race, in which the slavic element is predominant, and that the pure Hellenic blood is to be found only in a few localities." Early in the volume he finds Corfu another example of the importance of the English, who provide what Greece most needs—"civil order and good roads." Although Taylor is eager to see all the revered sites, this is clearly for him a journey through history, seeking culture, not a visit to a now-vibrant land. It confirms his conception of the superiority of Anglo-Saxon culture.

Early in the book Taylor writes that it may be good that "the mist of antiquity enlarges, glorifies, and transfigures everything." He emphasizes his veneration for the Parthenon by contrasting it with modern Athens. As the work progresses his distaste for modern Greece grows; one chapter emphasizes that neither the present king nor the queen is helpful to Greece, while another introduces the idea that the plethora of saints' holidays means that little work is done. Saints are "honored by a general loafing-spell"; Taylor sees these holy days as "sanctifying indolence." The music of the church is "chaotic discord," so depressing that Taylor even attempts one of the rare puns in his travel writing: "To return to the Te Deum, the tedium of which I endured for half an hour." He even suggests that Crete needs "an enlightened despotism."

 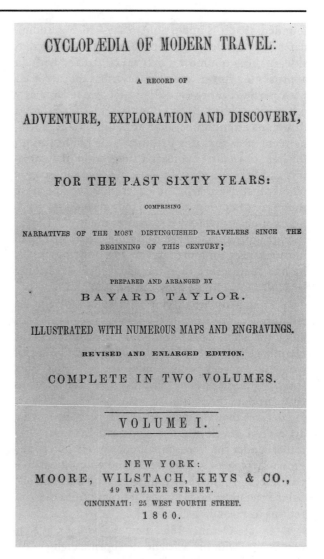

Frontispiece and title page for the revised edition of a book edited by Taylor

The region of Arcadia also needs a sufficiently despotic governor, in Taylor's view. The ruins are impressive only for their historical associations; otherwise the region disappoints. Arcadia suggests an "ideal loveliness, skies of perpetual Spring, and a pure and happy race of men," but in reality it is a "bleak region, surrounded by cold, naked mountains, with its rough barbaric Slavonian population, and its filthy den of a capital." Only in the mountain district of Maina does he find the real descendants of the ancient Greeks, including a woman he describes as Ariadne, who exhibited beauty and grace that could not be found on Broadway. She makes "ancient art a reality." Of course, physical beauty was the result of retaining "the purity of the ancient blood."

In an approach unusual for him Taylor concludes the section on Greece with an evaluation not only of the people and the government but also of the economic potential of the country, topics about which he has made occasional comments earlier. He sees little positive, suggesting for example that the bad conditions of the roads make economic development unlikely.

Taylor's route took him through Constantinople, then Kraków and Warsaw into Russia, traveling now quite openly with the aid of Murray's guidebook. His anti-Semitism becomes more evident. In Warsaw he says of Jews: "a more vile and filthy race (except the Chinese) cannot disgust the traveller." In central Russia he finds the Jews "disgusting to behold," greasy and shabby, even with a "peculiar bodily odor. . . . You can scent them quite as far as you can see them."

Moscow impresses Taylor as a cosmopolitan city where "Europe and Asia, the Past and Present, the Old World and the New are so blended and confounded, that it is impossible to say which predominates." He carefully describes the city from the outside, making it almost a natural landscape with an approaching storm, and then describes the city itself with perhaps more care than he has used for any other city. Saint Basil's Church in the Kremlin draws his attention because although it lacks form, he recognizes that it is striking: "It is not beautiful, for Beauty requires at least a suggestion of symmetry, and here the idea of proportion or adaptation is wholly lost. Neither is the effect offensive, because the maze of colors, in which red, green, and gold, predominate, attracts, and cajoles the eye." Taylor spends more than a page describing the church, an unusual space for him to devote to a building, just as he had spent more than the usual lines describing how Moscow looked from outside the city.

From Moscow, Taylor takes a train to Saint Petersburg (commenting on the importance of railroads along the way), where he enjoys the paintings in the Hermitage but reveals his usual haste when he says it would take a week really to know the collection. Saint Isaac's Church does not impress him, except for its cost, nor does the equestrian statue of Peter the Great. He decides that although art is supported in Russia, art cannot develop in the academies because "they rather hinder the free, spontaneous development and growth which all Art demands, and without which it will never produce anything great and permanent." Saint Petersburg ends his real journey; from there he returns to Poland.

In late October 1858 Taylor was back at Kennett Square with his wife and newborn daughter. For the next nine years he lectured, worked on travel books and fiction, began his 1871 translation of *Faust,* wrote poetry, and traveled frequently between Germany and the United States, even going back to Saint Petersburg when he inaccurately thought that he would be appointed minister to Russia. Smyth reports that between 1858 and 1867 he published nine volumes and gave six hundred lectures. He especially enjoyed playing the gracious host at Cedarcroft after it was completed in early 1860, but the expenses of maintaining it and the bad will that had developed between him and his neighbors made Cedarcroft a less comfortable place. Despite his constant writing and lecturing, Taylor was never financially secure during this period.

One lecturing trip led to another significant travel book. *Colorado: A Summer Trip* (1867) differs from most of Taylor's travel narratives for two reasons. First, though he wrote letters to the *New York Tribune* describing the trip, his primary purpose was to lecture. Second, the American setting meant he was describing an area relatively accessible to his readers.

But all the standard attitudes remain. He wants to see scenery and announces that there are only "three points which are at all picturesque" between Saint Louis and Jefferson City. The "ugliest of all rivers," the Missouri, is "deserted, monotonous, hideous, treacherous," "seeming to repel settlement, even as it repels poetry and art." The "Great American Desert," however, is a myth, no more than forty or fifty miles wide. He thinks that much of it will disappear with farming, because cultivation of the land will change the climate. Taylor is as optimistic about the possibilities of Colorado as he had been about California.

Interestingly, he describes the Rocky Mountains in terms of the Swiss Alps, regarding the Alps as the known landscape to which the new landscape should be compared. He does find the Rocky Mountains beautiful, and a horseback trip through a section of them was a highlight of his two months there; nevertheless, he remains convinced that the Alps are aesthetically superior.

In Colorado itself, however, law and order has not arrived. Taylor points to an example of "rude and violent justice" in which a Mexican was hanged for attempting to assault two ladies, and thinks that "affairs of this kind make an unpleasant impression." Taylor does not seem to doubt that the man deserved hanging; he seems only to have preferred a trial before the execution. Taylor somewhat conventionally finds the population of the mining areas, having escaped from Eastern restraint, to be "more natural, and hence more interesting. . . . The staid New Englander. . . . has simply cast off his assumed shell and is himself; and I must confess I like him all the better." He seems unconcerned that the hanging he has just mentioned is part of that casting off of convention.

Mining fever and mining language fascinate Taylor. In one of the few efforts in his travel writing to be humorous, he quotes the language extensively, making his own language the obvious contrast, thereby distancing himself from those who use the lingo:

> The Colorado dialect, in other respects, is peculiar. A dwelling-house is invariably styled "shebang;" and the word, in many cases, is very appropriate. The Spanish *corral* (always mispronounced *correll*) has become completely naturalized, and is used as a verb, meaning to catch or collect. A supply of any kind is an "outfit"; a man does not shout, but "lets a yell out of him"; and one who makes a blunder "cuts open a dog." I cannot recall, at this moment, half the peculiarities of the dialect, but I am learning them as fast as possible, in order to conform to the ways of the country.

Taylor observes the mining camps rather than becoming part of them. Twice he mentions a new kind of face he saw in his lecture audiences in Colorado—first describing it as representing the point at which the rowdy became the gentleman, then suggesting that perhaps it was the result of some combination of climate, "the circumstances of life," and racial background: "The Celtic and Saxon elements seem to supply each other's deficiencies, and to improve the American breed of men more than any other mixture. The handsome Colorado type may be partly derived from this source." He thinks this new face foretells a great future for the American West.

After 1867 Taylor committed most of his energies to the translation of *Faust* and to other German studies, as well as to literary biography. As his health grew increasingly bad and lecturing was neither congenial nor profitable, he could no longer afford Cedarcroft; in 1871 he offered it for sale, moving to Germany in 1872. During these years and earlier, he published other, generally less interesting volumes of travel, most often collections of shorter pieces, and edited several more volumes, primarily to make money to support his other activities. In 1878 he was appointed minister to Germany, dying in Berlin not long after he assumed the duties.

For much of his career Taylor was the best known and most prolific travel writer in America, enjoying a high critical reputation. In his early search for culture, his later desire to visit almost every area in the world for the excitement and the adventure of it, and his steady confidence in the superiority of Anglo-Saxon culture and the future of the United States, he reflected American attitudes at their best and their worst, sometimes at their most maudlin.

Taylor has never received much critical consideration. Marie Hansen-Taylor and Horace E. Scudder's *Life and Letters of Bayard Taylor* (1884) offers more letters than biography. Albert Smyth's *Bayard Taylor* (1896) in the American Men of Letters series emphasizes long quotations from Taylor's literary works. Richmond Croom Beatty's *Bayard Taylor: Laureate of the Gilded Age* (1936) seems intended more to defend Beatty's views on slavery and his support for segregation of the races than to analyze Taylor; moreover, Beatty is relatively uninterested in the travel works. John Tomsich's *A Genteel Endeavor: American Culture and Politics in the Gilded Age* (1971) is not much concerned with Taylor's travel but discusses his relationship to his time sympathetically. Richard Cary's quite short *The Genteel Circle: Bayard Taylor and His New York Friends* (1952) focuses on Taylor's letters deposited at Cornell University. Paul C. Wermuth's *Bayard Taylor* (1973) in the Twayne series provides the best analysis of the travel writing. Most often Taylor is now ig-

nored, or nearly so. Terry Caesar's *Forgiving the Boundaries: Home as Abroad in American Travel Writing* (1995) gives him two sentences, separated by forty pages. Perhaps the extent to which he spoke for a large segment of his era cost him popularity in the twentieth century.

Letters:
Marie Hansen-Taylor and Horace E. Scudder, eds., *The Life and Letters of Bayard Taylor,* 2 volumes (Boston: Houghton, Mifflin, 1884);
John R. Shultz, ed., *Unpublished Letters of Bayard Taylor in the Huntington Library* (San Marino, Cal.: Huntington Library, 1937);
Charles Duffy, ed., *The Correspondence of Bayard Taylor and Paul Hamilton Hayne* (Baton Rouge: Louisiana State University Press, 1945);
Richard Cary, *The Genteel Circle: Bayard Taylor and His New York Friends* (Ithaca, N.Y.: Cornell University Press, 1952).

Biographies:
R. H. Conwell, *The Life, Travels, and Literary Career of Bayard Taylor* (Boston: B. B. Russell / New York: C. Drew, 1879);
Edmund Charles Stedman, *Poets of America* (Boston: Houghton, Mifflin, 1885), pp. 396–434;
Albert Smyth, *Bayard Taylor* (Boston: Houghton, Mifflin, 1896);
Richmond Croom Beatty, *Bayard Taylor: Laureate of the Gilded Age* (Norman: University of Oklahoma Press, 1936).

References:
Terry Caesar, *Forgiving the Boundaries: Home as Abroad in American Travel Writing* (Athens: University of Georgia Press, 1995), pp. 22, 62;
John T. Krumplemann, *Bayard Taylor and German Letters* (Hamburg: Cram, De Gruyter, 1959);
Richard Henry Stoddard, *Recollections, Personal and Literary* (New York: A. S. Barnes, 1903);
Marie Hansen Taylor, *On Two Continents: Memories of Half a Century* (New York: Doubleday, Page, 1905);
John Tomsich, *A Genteel Endeavor: American Culture and Politics in the Gilded Age* (Stanford, Cal.: Stanford University Press, 1971);
Paul C. Wermuth, *Bayard Taylor* (New York: Twayne, 1973).

Papers:
The principal collections of Taylor's letters are in the Cornell University Library, Ithaca, New York, and the Huntington Library, San Marino, California.

Edith Wharton

(24 January 1862 – 11 August 1937)

Sarah Bird Wright
College of William and Mary

See also the Wharton entries in *DLB 4: American Writers in Paris, 1920–1939; DLB 9: American Novelists, 1910–1945; DLB 12: American Realists and Naturalists; DLB 78: American Short-Story Writers, 1880–1910;* and *DS 13: The House of Scribner, 1846–1904.*

BOOKS: *Verses,* anonymous (Newport, R.I.: C. E. Hammett, 1878);

The Decoration of Houses, by Wharton and Ogden Codman Jr. (New York: Scribners, 1897; London: Batsford, 1898);

The Greater Inclination (New York: Scribners, 1899; London: John Lane, 1899);

The Touchstone (New York: Scribners, 1900); republished as *A Gift from the Grave* (London: John Murray, 1900);

Crucial Instances (New York: Scribners, 1901; London: John Murray, 1901);

The Valley of Decision (2 volumes, New York: Scribners, 1902; 1 volume, London: John Murray, 1902);

Sanctuary (New York: Scribners, 1903; London: Macmillan, 1903);

Italian Villas and Their Gardens (New York: Century, 1904; London: John Lane, 1904);

The Descent of Man and Other Stories (New York: Scribners, 1904; enlarged edition, London & New York: Macmillan, 1904);

Italian Backgrounds (New York: Scribners, 1905; London: Macmillan, 1905);

The House of Mirth (New York: Scribners, 1905; London & New York: Macmillan, 1905);

Madame de Treymes (New York: Scribners, 1907; London: Macmillan, 1907);

The Fruit of the Tree (New York: Scribners, 1907; London: Macmillan, 1907);

The Hermit and the Wild Woman, and Other Stories (New York: Scribners, 1908; London: Macmillan, 1908);

A Motor-Flight Through France (New York: Scribners, 1908; London: Macmillan, 1908);

Edith Wharton, 1897

Artemis to Actæon and Other Verse (New York: Scribners, 1909; London: Macmillan, 1909);

Tales of Men and Ghosts (New York: Scribners, 1910; London: Macmillan, 1910);

Ethan Frome (New York: Scribners, 1911; London: Macmillan, 1911);

The Reef (New York: Appleton, 1912; London: Macmillan, 1912);

The Custom of the Country (New York: Scribners, 1913; London: Macmillan, 1913);

Fighting France, from Dunkerque to Belfort (New York: Scribners, 1915; London: Macmillan, 1915);

Xingu and Other Stories (New York: Scribners, 1916; London: Macmillan, 1916);

Summer (New York: Appleton, 1917; London: Macmillan, 1917);

The Marne (New York: Appleton, 1918; London: Macmillan, 1918);

French Ways and Their Meaning (New York & London: Appleton, 1919; London: Macmillan, 1919);

The Age of Innocence (New York & London: Appleton, 1920);

In Morocco (New York: Scribners, 1920; London: Macmillan, 1920);

The Glimpses of the Moon (New York & London: Appleton, 1922; London: Macmillan, 1923);

A Son at the Front (New York: Scribners, 1923; London: Macmillan, 1923);

Old New York, 4 volumes (New York & London: Appleton, 1924);

The Mother's Recompense (New York & London: Appleton, 1925);

The Writing of Fiction (New York & London: Scribners, 1925);

Here and Beyond (New York & London: Appleton, 1926);

Twelve Poems (London: Medici Society, 1926);

Twilight Sleep (New York & London: Appleton, 1927);

The Children (New York & London: Appleton, 1928);

Hudson River Bracketed (New York & London: Appleton, 1929);

Certain People (New York & London: Appleton, 1930);

The Gods Arrive (New York & London: Appleton, 1932);

Human Nature (New York & London: Appleton, 1933);

A Backward Glance (New York & London: Appleton-Century, 1934);

The World Over (New York & London: Appleton-Century, 1936);

Ghosts (New York & London: Appleton-Century, 1937);

The Buccaneers (New York & London: Appleton-Century, 1938);

The Collected Short Stories of Edith Wharton, 2 volumes, edited by R. W. B. Lewis (New York: Scribners, 1968);

Fast and Loose: A Novelette, as David Olivieri, edited by Viola Hopkins Winner (Charlottesville: University Press of Virginia, 1977);

The Cruise of the Vanadis, edited by Claudine Lesage (Amiens: Sterne Presses de L'Ufr Clerc Université Picardie, 1991);

Edith Wharton Abroad: Selected Travel Writings 1888-1920, edited by Sarah Bird Wright (New York: St. Martin's Press, 1995);

The Uncollected Critical Writings, edited by Frederick Wegener (Princeton: Princeton University Press, 1996).

OTHER: Hermann Sudermann, *The Joy of Living (Es lebe das leben),* translated by Wharton (New York: Scribners, 1902);

"My Work among the Women Workers of Paris," *New York Times Magazine* (28 November 1915): 1-2;

The Book of the Homeless (Le Livre de Sans-Foyer), edited by Wharton (Paris, 1915; New York: Scribners / London: Macmillan, 1916);

"Life and I," in her *Novellas and Other Writings,* edited by Cynthia Griffin Wolff, The Library of America, volume 47 (New York: Viking, 1990), pp. 1069–1096.

Henry James observed in an August 1902 letter to Edith Wharton's sister-in-law, Mrs. Cadwalader Jones, that Wharton "must be tethered in native pastures, even if it reduces her to a back-yard in New York." At almost the same time, he wrote Wharton, begging her to permit him to "admonish" her "in favour of the American subject" while she was "young, free, expert." He hoped she would "profit, be warned by my awful example of exile and ignorance." Biographer R. W. B. Lewis terms James's plea "the wisest literary advice Edith Wharton ever received." Clearly, however, James did not foresee publication of the travel books that constitute a vital and enduring segment of her work. They provide a framework within which she could introduce her intellectual abilities and interests without the constrictions of plot and character imposed by fiction. Moreover, her travel writing validates her role as connoisseur and cicerone of the first magnitude, well able to enlighten her countrymen about the subtleties of taste and aesthetic achievements of the Old World.

Edith Newbold Jones was born on 24 January 1862, the third child and first daughter of George Frederic and Lucretia Rhinelander Jones, members of the social hierarchy of aristocratic old New York. Her father was a gentleman of leisure and her mother a society matron. Although they did not live ostentatiously, they enjoyed considerable affluence, with servants, a governess for Edith, carriages, a summer home in Newport, a townhouse in New York, and frequent dinner parties. However, the Civil War caused a decline in New York real estate values and a corresponding decrease in their in-

The steam yacht Vanadis, *on which the Whartons and James Van Alen took an Aegean cruise in 1888 (courtesy of Mystic Seaport Museum, Mystic, Connecticut)*

come. In 1866, taking along their younger son Harry, then sixteen, and Edith, four, the Joneses went to Europe, where they might live more economically, for six years.

During their residence abroad Edith absorbed the landscape, art, and architecture of France, Italy, Germany, and other European countries. The experience permanently shaped her outlook and gave her, for the rest of her life, a "background of beauty and old-established order," as she later put it in her 1934 memoir, *A Backward Glance*. As an adult she recalled "the lost Rome" of her "infancy," the "warm scent of the box hedges on the Pincian, and the texture of weather-worn sun-gilt stone." From an arduous trip to Spain during the second year of their European residence she "brought back an incurable passion for the road." Few writers of travel have been better equipped for such a task. "Perhaps, after all, it is not a bad thing to begin one's travels at four," Wharton reflected at the age of seventy-one.

Even before she learned to read, Wharton became ardently devoted to what she called "making up." Washington Irving's *The Alhambra* (1832) was the "Pierian fount" of her inspiration. Learning to read converted her delight in "making up" into a "frenzy," even though it was not an activity her parents encouraged. In general, she later recalled, authorship was considered "something between a black art and a form of manual labor" with her parents' circle of friends.

When the Jones family returned to New York, Edith was only ten, but as she recalled in the undated autobiographical fragment, "Life and I," she had been "fed on beauty since my babyhood"; her first thought upon seeing the city again was " '*How ugly it is!*'" She insisted she had "never since thought or felt otherwise than as an exile in America" and had often dreamed her family was returning to Europe. She would wake "in a state of exhilaration which the reality turned to deep depression." Six decades after her early disillusionment she could still recall her abhorrence of the New York cityscape, "cursed with its universal chocolate-coloured coating of the most hideous stone ever quarried, cramped horizontal gridiron of a town without towers, porticoes, fountains or perspectives, hidebound in its deadly uniformity of mean ugliness." The houses lacked "external dignity" and were "crammed with smug and suffocating upholstery." Not only was the vernacular architecture of America poorly proportioned and inharmonious, but, as she wrote to her friend Sara Norton in May 1904, the American landscape had no "accumulated beauties."

Wharton's principal compensation in returning to New York was her entry into the "kingdom" of her father's library. She continued to internalize her European experience, reading widely in literature, history, and philosophy. John Ruskin, John Milton, Alexander Pope, Lamartine, Plutarch, Dante, Percy Bysshe Shelley, John Keats, and the art historian Franz Kugler were only a few of the authors she recalled reading. In her memoir she reflected about her inner life as a young girl: "though living authors were so remote, the dead were my most living companions." As a result of her wide reading, her works of travel are marked by erudition. Mary Suzanne Schriber observes in a 1987 article for *American Literature* that in her travel books Wharton "displays a formidable knowledge of political, literary, and art history. She understands Correggio in relation to Zucchero and the town of La Châtre in the light of the novels of George Sand." She was fluent in French, German, and Italian as well as English and conversant with literature in all four languages.

In 1880, when Edith was eighteen, the Joneses returned to Europe for two years because of her father's bad health; he died at Cannes in 1882. The second visit confirmed Edith's attachment to Europe; she "felt the stir of old associations," especially when she and her father followed "step by step Ruskin's arbitrary itineraries" in Florence and Venice.

Wharton's upbringing, her wide reading, and her extensive early travels endowed her with a substantial capital of what Pierre Bourdieu calls "the competence of the 'connoisseur.'" This quality derives from long contact with cultured persons and places, and it is what distinguishes Wharton's travel books from many contemporary accounts. They manifest not only a thorough knowledge of art and architecture but also an ability to juxtapose them against a complex background of theology, classical mythology, history, and literature. Wharton's cultural competence, or taste, allows her to integrate the scholarly and imaginative approaches to travel, the quality most desired by her audience. This audience consisted not only of affluent Americans who went regularly to Europe, as their parents and grandparents had done, but also of literate middle-class travelers who were able, before World War I, to travel to Europe on a more modest level—or who, at least, could travel vicariously by purchasing her books.

Wharton's love of travel was lifelong and shared by her husband, Edward "Teddy" Wharton, whom she married in 1885. They spent four months of each year abroad, principally in Italy. Her biographer Lewis has said that for Wharton, Italy was a "recurring act of discovery." The Whartons' travels continued each year for nearly two decades, not only in Italy but also in France, England, and other countries. In 1888 they took an Aegean cruise on a chartered steam yacht, the *Vanadis*.

In 1897 Wharton published her first book-length prose work, *The Decoration of Houses,* written with the architect Ogden Codman. Although not a travel book in the usual sense, it comprised an elaborate codification of European principles of harmony and design that could be imported on a domestic scale by wealthy Americans in their house planning. Many of its principles, such as "proportion is the good breeding of architecture," were formulated during Wharton's early years in Europe,

and in some ways the work constitutes an archive on which she drew in much of her travel writing. The European settings she describes and the principles of design she lays out are the foundation of her later observations about Italian, French, and Moroccan garden and house architecture.

By 1902 the Whartons had sold their house at Newport and built The Mount in Lenox, Massachusetts, where they spent part of each year and entertained such friends as Henry James, Gaillard Lapsley, Howard Sturgis, and others. It was in Lenox that Edith wrote the novels *The Valley of Decision* (1902) and *The House of Mirth* (1905) and the nonfiction *Italian Villas and Their Gardens* (1904) and *Italian Backgrounds* (1905). In 1904 the Whartons gave up their annual pilgrimage to Italy in favor of explorations in France, a significant shift in preference heralding Wharton's later expatriation. Her residence in France began in 1907, when she and her husband, who had spent the summer and autumn at The Mount, went to Paris and sublet the apartment of the George Vanderbilts in a "stately Louis XIV *hôtel*" (or town house) in the Rue de Varenne in the elite quarter of the Faubourg St. Germain.

Teddy became increasingly unstable and volatile. Their stays in Paris emphasized his ineptitude at speaking French and conversing on a literary level with her friends. He was more at home at The Mount, where he could indulge in hunting and other outdoor pursuits. He used part of Wharton's inheritance to establish a mistress on Beacon Hill in Boston; he later repaid the debt, but Wharton then refused to let him administer her property and financial holdings. In January 1910 the Whartons moved into another apartment at 53 Rue de Varenne. She lived there until 1919, when she acquired the Pavillon Colombe just outside Paris in St.-Brice-sous-Forêt. The same year she leased a second home at Hyères on the Côte d'Azur, a convent built within the ruins of the Château Sainte-Claire which she renovated and later purchased. For the rest of her life she divided her time between the two homes, living at the Pavillon Colombe from June to mid December and at the Château Sainte-Claire from mid December through May.

In 1911 Wharton left The Mount for the last time, having decided to separate from Teddy and sell the property. She had hesitated about seeking a separation because of Teddy's unstable state of mind, his attachment to their home, and his pride in overseeing it. Lewis observes that she also "foresaw in the sale of The Mount the abandonment of her last American home and the loss of a central element in her own identity." After The Mount was sold, she proceeded with her divorce, which was granted in

An island garden in Lake Maggiore, illustration by Maxfield Parrish in Wharton's Italian Villas
and Their Gardens *(1904)*

Paris on 16 April 1913. By this time Europe had become "home." Wharton only returned to America twice more: in 1913 for the wedding of her niece Beatrice Jones to Max Farrand, and in 1923 to accept an honorary degree from Yale University, the first bestowed on a woman by a major university. Her bicontinental habitation for more than two decades had led almost inexorably to her decision to settle permanently in France, although in some respects it was an enigmatic choice, made just at the peak of her achievement in two literary genres: fiction and travel writing.

In the years preceding and following her divorce, Wharton made many trips with such close friends as Mary and Bernard Berenson, Walter Berry, James, Sturgis, Lapsley, Minnie and Paul Bourget, and others. She often stayed with the Berensons at the Villa I Tatti outside Florence and with the Bourgets at their villa at Costebelle, near Hyères. In England she stayed at Lamb House in Rye, James's home; and at Queen's Acre ("Qu'Acre") in Windsor, Sturgis's home. Her zest for travel was frequently alarming, especially to James. As Lewis observes, James was "disturbed by the rush and movement" of her life and characterized her visits to him: "General eagle-pounces and eagle-flights of her deranging and desolating, ravaging, burning and destroying energy. . . . the Angel of Devastation was the mildest name we knew her by." She never gave up her American citizenship and was disappointed when James did so in 1915 because of his feeling that America should have entered World War I.

The quarter century in which Wharton's trav-el texts were published—from her first travel article in *Scribner's Magazine* in 1895 during the Gilded Age to her final book of travel in 1920—was one of tumultuous change. The years saw the legacy of the "genteel" literary era eroded by the materialistic Gilded Age, the explosion of middle-class and mass travel, the turmoil of World War I, and the beginning of the affluent decade of the 1920s. During this period the network of learned literary periodicals and their readers sustained and to some extent transformed the earlier belletristic tradition of travel writing practiced by Irving, Nathaniel Hawthorne, and others into the more modern connoisseurship embodied by Wharton. To Wharton the depictions of Europe given by such writers as Irving and Hawthorne were too much in the vein of the picturesque to be entirely credible. They hoped, in Daniel Borus's words, to bring "civilization to an unformed nation," and their work was rooted in European models. Wharton discounted their evaluations of art and architecture, which, to her, were naive and uninformed. She despaired of the taste of her parents and their contemporaries, who believed that "Hawthorne's 'Marble Faun', Bulwer's 'Last Days of Pompeii' and Washington Irving's 'Alhambra' were still the last word on Spain and Italy." She dismissed the writers favored by these "artless travellers" who preferred "scenery, ruins and historic sites; places about which some sentimental legend hung, and to which Scott, Byron, Hans Andersen, Bulwer, Washington Irving or Hawthorne gently led the timid sight-seer. [To them]. . . . snow-mountains, lakes and water-falls—especially water-falls—were endlessly enjoyable." Her own works of travel, with their focus on obscure byways and informed aestheticism, were a corrective to the mania for the picturesque and the sentimental that had prevailed during much of the nineteenth century.

The Cruise of the Vanadis (written in 1888 but not published until 1991) is Wharton's earliest known piece of travel writing. Until 1991 it had been supposed that Wharton traveled principally for enjoyment and general cultural development during the many European journeys of her early married life. Although she was occupied with her house and garden, she recalled in her memoir that she had deplored the "watering-place amenities" of Newport and welcomed the months of travel each year. Writing in 1975, Lewis suggested that "no intention had yet formed in her mind of converting her European experiences into literature. She was simply expanding on the knowledge and cultivating the taste acquired in her childhood and her premarital years." He believed, however, that she was also gathering materials, especially in Italy, for fiction. Wharton's first novel, The Valley of Decision, was set in northern Italy in the late eighteenth century just before Napoleon's Italian campaign.

It is now known that Wharton's travel writing, at least in private, had almost as early a genesis as her fiction and poetry. Moreover, she might also have been pondering the later use of her initial efforts. In 1991 a French scholar, Claudine Lesage of the University of Amiens, discovered a detailed diary Wharton had kept of the Mediterranean cruise she and her husband, along with James Van Alen, took aboard the chartered steam yacht Vanadis when Wharton was twenty-six. Lesage states in her introductory note that the reasons Wharton did not publish the diary are unknown. She observes that the diary counters the widely held notion that Wharton's "beginnings as a writer were a mere accident, an occupation for an idle rich woman." Instead, she argues, it is clear that "just as a violinist diligently practises her scales before appearing in front of an audience she had been writing extensively though privately." Lesage calls the diary Wharton's "maiden Odyssey into literature."

It is unlikely that Wharton ever intended the diary to be published, since in later years she denied or failed to recall having written it at all. She declares in A Backward Glance, "until 1918 I never kept even the briefest of diaries." It is conceivable that she thought of it less as a conventional diary than as a sequence of notes that she might later use in constructing a travel account. While the journal is still firmly within the "private domestic sphere" described by Amy Kaplan, in both concept and phrase-

ology it comprises the nucleus of her later travel writing.

Wharton's profound craving for travel is suggested by her choice of the epigraph to The Cruise of the Vanadis: lines 1122–1125 of Part I of Johann Wolfgang von Goethe's Faust (1808, 1832; translated, 1823, 1838). Faust, who harbors the conflicting "souls" of repose and exertion in his breast, tells the pedantic, sedentary Wagner he wishes for a magic cloak so that he might soar into fremde Länder, or foreign lands; he would not trade such a garment for a Königsmantel, or king's crown and robe. Faust appeals to the spirits of the air to enable him to escape a life of peace and quiet and convey him to a new, many-hued existence in other realms. The Vanadis diary and its epigraph suggest that travel not only met a deeply felt inner need on the part of Wharton but also offered a means of escape from what had turned out to be a disappointing marriage. Clearly, the reenacting of travel through writing about it was vitally important to Wharton. The epigraph imparts a motive of impetuous and romantic escapism, of freedom from earthbound concerns, which agrees with her later characterization in A Backward Glance of the cruise as having been undertaken improvidently and enthusiastically. She is a voracious, intellectual wanderer, open to all experiences and often interpreting the sights she sees in the light of the extensive historical and classical reading she had undertaken in her youth.

As an examination of the Vanadis diary shows, Wharton was not, in her mid twenties, a novice at writing. In the diary she depicts vivid physical scenes and enriches her observations with wide-ranging literary and historical references. Moreover, she already evinces a bias against restoration; here she follows Ruskin in preferring structures that are enduring testaments to the ages in which they were constructed. She comments ironically on the fortress of Euryalus at Syracuse in Sicily: "Luckily it has escaped the distinction of being restored." She is an interpreter of sights, not simply a reporter. Her ability to correlate style and period shows that she is alert to the larger religious and aesthetic context of the sights she visits. At Amorgos, for example, she is privileged to see rich vestments, illuminated manuscripts on "velum," altar-cloths, "eikons," and "other wonders that would have rejoiced the hearts of Curzon and Tozer."

So far as is known, the chapter "Mount Athos," describing the closed peninsula in Greece with more than twenty Byzantine monasteries, is the first account of that place written by an American. Since Mount Athos is closed to women, Wharton was not permitted to land there; she based her account on her observations from offshore and the sights her companions reported. Even so, the chapter has historical significance.

Wharton's experiences on the Mediterranean cruise went far toward extending the cosmopolitan outlook first formed by her early travels and providing a visual context for the classical sites she already knew thoroughly from her reading. Over the next few years further reading and travels led to the consolidation of her aesthetic principles and further cultivation of her taste, both of which were apparent in her next work of travel, *Italian Villas and Their Gardens.*

Italian Villas is a compilation of several articles Wharton was commissioned to write for *Century Magazine* to accompany the watercolors of Maxfield Parrish. When Richard Watson Gilder, the *Century* editor, decided to offer his readers a series of illustrated articles, it was entirely in keeping with the ideals of the genteel era. He was prepared to splurge on color watercolors. For the text he turned to Wharton, who had already been praised for articles on Italy that had appeared in a competing periodical, *Scribner's Magazine,* and who was both pleased and honored to receive the commission. As she recalled in her memoir, "I was only beginning to be known as a novelist, but on Italian seventeenth and eighteenth century architecture, about which so little had been written, I was thought to be fairly competent."

The book turned out to be the most frustrating and least satisfying experience in her travel writing, although its impeccable scholarship is still valued today and it is considered a classic of its kind. It is primarily a learned survey of garden architecture and ornamentation rather than a study of the villas. She visited the gardens in 1903 with a scholar's eye, detecting, beneath the palimpsest of eighteenth-century horticulturists bent on transforming every garden into an English park, the original garden outlines and plantings. She sketches the history of the villas, most of which were built during the Renaissance and Baroque periods. She sometimes brings their inhabitants to life; for example, in describing the fortified villa of Caprarola, near Rome, built by Cardinal Alexander Farnese and designed by the renowned sixteenth-century architect Vignola, she invents scenes that could have occurred in her historical novel about Italy, *The Valley of Decision.* She imagines the cardinal's soldiers guarding the fortress from the platform above the village, while within the walls "one has a vision of noble ladies and their cavaliers sitting under rose-arbours or strolling between espaliered lemon-trees, discussing a Greek manuscript or a Roman bronze, or listening to the

last sonnet of the cardinal's court poet." Such fictional interpolations are rare, however. Wharton's essential mission is to evoke for the reader the tripartite relationship between villa, garden, and surrounding landscape and to deduce the original features of the gardens from what remains.

The project was marked by disputes with her editors over the illustrations and the text. She assumed that garden plans would supplement the illustrations by Parrish, and as she stated in a 20 December 1902 letter to Gilder, she believed readers wanted practical details more than "pretty pictures." Gilder refused to allow more than one garden plan and asked her to provide "sentimental and anecdotic commentaries" to make the text more compatible with the spirit of the illustrations. She refused to modify the scholarly nature of the text and tried to prevent publication of the articles, but they ran anyway in *Century* in 1903 and 1904. When the book was published, she still did not feel the essays were in keeping with the Parrish pictures, which should have been used to illustrate "some fanciful tale of Lamotte Fouqué, or Andersen's 'Improvisatore,'" as she commented in *A Backward Glance.* Exact garden plans indicating the overall design, with placement of walkways, plantings, and statuary, which she very much wanted to include, would have been a far more useful supplement to the scholarly exactitude of her text.

Italian Villas includes descriptions of more than seventy-five villas and their gardens. The volume has a bibliography of reference works in four languages, capsule biographies of fifty-five architects and landscape gardeners of the fifteenth through the eighteenth centuries, and a detailed index. The work is a tour de force explaining and illustrating the aesthetic principles lying behind Italian gardens. Wharton cautions affluent Americans against trying to fashion their own Italian gardens by importing bits of statuary and laying out English-style lawns without understanding the principles behind Italian "garden-magic." She is careful to point out that *villa,* in Italian, connotes both house and pleasure-grounds rather than the house alone; throughout the book her emphasis is on the gardens.

In *Italian Backgrounds* Wharton is both scholar and connoisseur of paintings, sculpture, and architecture. The volume includes essays about towns, landscapes, and cities mixed with analyses of paintings, sculpture, frescoes, courtyards, and architecture. The two books reflect, in a sense, mirror images of her travels in Italy spanning two decades. Whereas *Italian Villas* comprises an analysis of the exterior grounds and gardens of many historic villas, focusing on vernacular architecture, *Italian Back-*

Illustration of Parma by Ernest Peixotto, in Wharton's Italian
Backgrounds *(1905)*

grounds is largely concerned with museums, churches, monasteries, palaces, and civic buildings and only tangentially with domestic architecture. She discusses her travels in Parma, Milan, the northern Italian lakes, Venice, Syracuse, Vallambrosa, and several other places.

At the opening of *Italian Backgrounds* Wharton and her party are summering in one of the upper Grison villages of Switzerland below the Splügen Pass. They find, however, that they seem to be "living in the landscape of a sanatorium prospectus"; the healthy walks and climbs are insufficient. Then they discover the problem: "Splügen was charming, but it was too near Italy. One can forgive a place

three thousand miles from Italy for not being Italian; but that a village on the very border should remain stolidly, immovably Swiss was a constant source of exasperation." Italy, in contrast, is a "sophisticated landscape where the face of nature seems moulded by the passions and imaginings of man." Each evening the stagecoaches from Thusis (Switzerland) and Chiavenna (Italy) arrive in the town square and return the next morning to their respective towns. Would it be better, she pondered, "to be cool and look at a water-fall, or to be hot and look at Saint Mark's? Was it better to walk on gentians or on mosaic, to smell fir-needles or incense?"

They board the Chiavenna coach, seeking the

"parentheses of travel" and specifically hoping to tour the Bergamasque Alps. These mountains have connotations of the commedia dell'arte, the improvisatory sixteenth-century theater with such characters as Harlequin and Columbine that exerted a strong influence for several centuries on European comedy and provided a recurrent trope in Wharton's travel writing. She imagines Lake Iseo as a backdrop for a performance of such a comedy "in the Bergamasque dialect, with Harlequin in striped cloak, and Brighella in conical hat and wide green and white trousers strutting up and down before the shuttered house in which Dr. Graziano hides his pretty ward. . . . if ever the boundaries between fact and fancy waver, it may well be under the spell of the Italian midsummer madness." In the dusty ducal theater at Parma, Wharton can "hear" the commedia players "build on the scaffolding of some familiar intrigue the airy superstructure of their wit."

Italian Backgrounds has few details about lodging or meals; instead there are observations about little-known byways and undiscovered treasures of art. She often sees the landscape in terms of art, imagining, for example, that as they travel they are moving through a gallery hung with the paintings of Claude Lorrain, about to come upon "one of Bonifazio's sumptuous picnics." Wharton's first success in the field of art history had come with the reattribution in 1893 of the groups of terra-cotta statues on the Via Crucis at the monastery of San Vivaldo, Italy. They had long been attributed to Giovanni Gonnelli, a seventeenth-century artist, but she was convinced they were much earlier, and Florentine authorities later agreed and reattributed them to Giovanni della Robbia. She published an account of her discovery, "A Tuscan Shrine," in the January 1895 *Scribner's Magazine;* the chapter is included in *Italian Backgrounds.*

The book as a whole confirms Wharton's distrust of architectural restoration and her defense of ruins. She describes the monastery of Chiaravalle, near Milan, with its "noble colonnaded cupula," as one of the "conspicuous objects" in the landscape near Milan. Its appeal, however, lies in the fact that the interior is "falling to ruin . . . one feels the melancholy charm of a beautiful building which has been allowed to decay as naturally as a tree. The disintegrating touch of nature is less cruel than the restoring touch of man." She also has an antipathy to guidebooks, which describe the "catalogued riches" of a place and leave no room for serendipity, for the traveler to discover his or her own treasured byways.

The "abroad" that Wharton evokes in her first two published works of travel largely predates the automotive era and partakes far more of the nineteenth century than the twentieth. She and her party traverse little-known Italian routes at a leisurely pace by horse-drawn carriage and stagecoach, lingering in the aura of the commedia dell' arte, Goethe, Hester Piozzi, Lady Mary Montague, and Stendhal. Between *Italian Backgrounds* and *A Motor-Flight Through France* (1908) she crosses a Rubicon; henceforth, leisurely exploration gives way to rapid visitation, and Italy succumbs to France. Her travel writing becomes less a compilation of heuristic essays than a chronicle of sites and routes. Wharton's first book of motor travel and her first about France, *A Motor-Flight Through France,* is in many ways in dialogue with her last work of travel, *In Morocco* (1920). It is particularly consonant with that volume in its brisk pace; for the first time, constraints of time configure the itinerary. *A Motor-Flight Through France* appears to be uncharacteristically concerned with routes and speed and villages sighted but ruled out for lack of time. Wharton was accommodating herself to the new realities of transport: the motorcar that had been a stunning innovation in 1903, when she visited many of the villas that were to figure in *Italian Villas and Their Gardens,* is now a staple of transport.

A Motor-Flight Through France, based on three automobile journeys taken in 1906 and 1907, points up the perfections of France during the Belle Epoque. In May 1906 the Whartons, accompanied by Edith's brother, Harry Jones, made what she described as a "giro" around portions of France. Picking up their car at Boulogne, they went via Arras to Amiens, on to Beauvais and Rouen, down the Seine to Les Andelys, Versailles, Fontainebleau, and into Auvergne, visiting George Sand's home at Nohant.

In March 1907 Edith and Teddy Wharton made a second motor tour, accompanied by Henry James, who had greatly envied Wharton her visit to Nohant. Teddy had closed in the Panhard-Levassor automobile and added an electric light along with "every known accessorie and comfort" as he wrote Sara Norton. He took pleasure in catering to his wife's "nice, to me, worldly side" even though he was admittedly "no good on Puss's high plain of thought." Shari Benstock observes that "Teddy proved a resilient and good-humored companion" whose "spirits seemed to soar at the prospect of motor-flights." Their second "flight" took them on an itinerary of more than two thousand miles, from Paris to Poitiers, the Pyrenees, and Provence. The final "flight" was a tour of the northeast section of France, including Rheims, Saint-Quentin, Senlis, Chantilly, along the Oise, and back to Paris. Ironically, some of the towns described, such as Meaux,

Wharton, Henry James, the chauffeur, and Edward Wharton in her Panhard automobile, 1907

would later figure in *Fighting France, from Dunkerque to Belfort* (1915) as examples of the devastation caused by World War I.

Wharton begins the book by extolling the way in which "the motor-car has restored the romance of travel." Her journeys are more rapid and free of the "bondage to fixed hours and the beaten track" that have characterized railway travel. The many towns visited and described suggests that the motorcar could, and did, cover far more territory than the carriages and diligences of her Italian journeys. She cautions the traveler, however, that rapid travel entails the sacrifice of many charming byways and little-known places that are well worth seeing. Although she sees the motorcar as an improvement over the uncertainties of travel once experienced by her "posting grandparents," the slow tours and pilgrimages of Irving, Hawthorne, James Fenimore Cooper, and Ralph Waldo Emerson had their value in thorough observation and assimilation of sights. Mobility has eroded leisure by opening more and more possibilities; her habituated responses are adapting to the changes in travel. The freedom of the motorcar almost undergoes a metamorphosis into tyranny. The unexplored towns of France fly by as the motorcar rushes through the various provinces; it is impossible to see every town in the time allotted. The new mode of transport suggests that

Wharton is abandoning the scholarly stance that had been the hallmark of *Italian Backgrounds;* her arguments are directed less at refuting art critics and more at guiding her fellow travelers.

The book is marked by what Wharton terms the *"bon mouvement"* of the imagination when she embellishes her descriptions with flights of fancy; whimsy often supplants aesthetic discourse. Even as she reenacts her geographical passage, she records her intellectual passage. At times her historic sense yields completely to the imperative of fiction; for example, she describes the frenetic stonecutters of the doomed cathedral of Beauvais, whom she envisions as crying, "We simply can't keep it up!" The imaginary cry is a paradigm for the speed of their tour.

From Vichy they embark on a "long run" to Orleans, "having to take as a mere parenthesis the charmingly complete little town of La Palisse on the Bèbre" and the "fine old town" of Moulins on the Allier. The itinerary becomes "spokes of the wheel" as they travel toward the Spanish border, passing by tempting gorges, vales, and passes in the "comet-flight of the motor."

Wharton's French travels also served to justify her expatriation. Schriber notes in her introduction to a new edition of *A Motor-Flight Through France* that America is actually a strong component of the book; she argues that Wharton's French motor trips "offer us a journey back into early twentieth-century America. The hum and buzz of American culture, the issues of the era, the insecurity of America in the face of the cultural superiority of Europe are the intertexts of Wharton's text." This observation may suggest that Wharton was attempting to reinforce her decision to live in France permanently. In a rather oblique way she also indicts Newport and the American cash nexus when she praises the resort of Vichy, a town that is "to the American observer . . . most instructive just because it is not the millionaire's wand which has worked the spell; because the town owes its gaiety and its elegance, not to the private villa, the rich man's 'showplace,' but to wise public expenditure of the money which the bathers annually pour into its exchequer." Here she discloses her objections to the insular American culture, so evident at Newport, whose shortcomings in values and taste presaged her expatriation.

A Motor-Flight Through France is the first of Wharton's travel books to provide itineraries that might be reenacted by travelers today. Wharton was conscious of time constraints, and as a result she often mentions the terrain covered and the town in which the party spent the night, giving a precise description of the route they followed. *Italian Backgrounds,* on the other hand, represents a conflation of the Whartons' many perambulations taking place over several years. Although she devotes single chapters to major cities such as Milan and Parma, the exact roads and railways are seldom designated. Occasionally day excursions away from a major center are mentioned and may be replicated today, such as the Brenta Riviera outside Venice, where the aristocracy spend the *villeggiatura,* or vacation season (mid June/July and October/mid November), in country manor houses. When the Whartons visited the villas described in *Italian Villas and Their Gardens,* they did not follow a systematic itinerary; they often stayed in a central city, such as Florence, Genoa, or Rome, and made special journeys out to villas. Wharton was not always certain of securing admission; many were privately owned and only opened as a special favor. Although some villas are presently open to the public, such as the Villa d'Este at Cernobbio on Lake Como, now a luxury hotel, the majority are private residences or are closed for other reasons.

The onset of World War I brought an end to Wharton's travels and her life in the Faubourg, which had been well balanced with social interaction, travel, and disciplined writing. The war also caused a profound transformation in her outlook. She used her position as a well-respected public figure to become an impassioned humanitarian, launching major war-relief efforts and seeking material assistance from her countrymen. Throughout the war she stayed in Paris, ministering as best she could to a France "paralyzed with horror."

The war had a powerful effect on Wharton's writing, making the social satire of her preceding novels irrelevant and acting as a catalyst to reshape her creative direction and ally it with her relief work. She wrote two books based on her experiences during the war: *Fighting France, from Dunkerque to Belfort,* a compilation of articles about her journeys to the front; and *French Ways and Their Meaning* (1919), a study of French mores and character as shaped not only by long-standing traditions but also by the war. She also edited *The Book of the Homeless (Le Livre de Sans-Foyer),* published in Paris in 1915, soliciting contributions from well-known writers and artists to aid victims of war.

In early 1915 Wharton was asked by the French Red Cross to visit military hospitals at the front and report on their needs, a journey that led to several other visits. These expeditions resulted in six magazine articles for *Scribner's,* calculated to alert her "rich and generous compatriots" to the desperate needs of hospitals and to bring home to her American readers "some of the dreadful realities of war." She went to the rear of the fighting lines; hence the title of the book in which the articles were collected, *Fighting France, from Dunkerque to Belfort.*

Wharton keenly felt the unendurable human cost of the war. *Fighting France* is eloquent testimony to her stance as a recorder and interpreter of the national cultural heritage. In the conclusion she valorizes the French spirit: "The war has been a calamity unheard of; but France has never been afraid of the unheard of. No race has ever yet so audaciously dispensed with old precedents; as none has ever so revered their relics." At the outbreak of war France evinced a "white glow of dedication," but whether the sacrifices necessary for prolonged resistance could be mustered was uncertain. However, she remarks, "baser sentiments were silenced: greed, self-interest, pusillanimity seemed to have been purged from the race."

Wharton describes attending vespers in a small country church in the village of Blercourt in the Argonne that housed four rows of cots with gravely ill soldiers. The congregation consisted only of women and a few soldiers posted in the village; all the other men were fighting. After the Latin cadences were finished, the curé began chanting the Canticle of the Sacred Heart, composed during the Franco-Prussian War of 1870; it was taken up by the "trembling voices" of the women and able-bodied soldiers:

> *Sauvez, sauvez la France,*
> *Ne l'abandonnez pas!*

The church "looked like a quiet grave-yard in a battlefield." The deep-seated hatred of Germany that had smoldered in French hearts since the war of 1870 impressed Wharton deeply; she returns to it again in her postwar novel *A Son at the Front* (1923), depicting an elderly veteran of that war attempting to join the army. Making clear the indomitable spirit of the French people, she emphasizes the tragic loss of artistic and domestic treasures: the "torn traceries" of the ruined church of Clermont-en-Argonne and the many "murdered houses" in whose "exposed interiors the poor little household gods shiver and blink like owls surprised in a hollow tree. . . . whiskered photographs fade on morning-glory wallpapers, [and] plaster saints pine under glass bells."

Her descriptions of the havoc of war, based on several visits to the front lines, are more vivid than those of many seasoned journalists. The primary thrust of *Fighting France* may be to indoctrinate her countrymen about the realities of the war; but it is also cathartic for Wharton and a continuing vehicle for expression of the connoisseurship that had long been the hallmark of her travel writing.

Despite her complete engagement in support for the French cause, Wharton did not conceive of herself as anything but American—alienated from pacifist opinion in America, but still firmly a citizen. She did not hesitate to use her position as a highly visible writer to enlist American opinion in support of France. In November 1915 she wrote an article for *The New York Times Magazine* about her *ouvroir* (workshop), American hostels, and the Children of Flanders Rescue Committee. She explained that she was not attempting a survey of all Paris war charities but simply giving an account of the "particular patch of misery" she had tried to relieve.

The war years were an enduring agency of Wharton's assimilation to France, no small part of which was the wrenching but supremely rational adjustment of the country itself to the calamity. The "triumph" of France, she says in *Fighting France,* is that its "myriad fiery currents flow from so many hearts made insensible by suffering, so many dead hands feed its undying lamp." It can almost be said that she loved the country in its wounded and vulnerable, but heroic, state more than she did its majestic, sometimes impervious, countenance as presented in the Belle Epoque. Her final book about France is a celebration of that heroic spirit.

French Ways and Their Meaning was written in part to interpret France to America, especially to young American servicemen who fought in France and were stationed there after the war ended. In one way the volume responds to the superficial misunderstandings her compatriots had experienced in the trenches and villages of France. It was ordered to be placed in all ships' libraries by the U.S. Department of the Navy. She insisted that a primary purpose in writing it was to impart the full splendor of the French faculty for the "whole business of living" to servicemen who might otherwise have judged the country only by its "brave appearance of 'business as usual'" after four difficult years of war. Seeing France only in a "topsy-turvy state," they would inevitably make erroneous generalizations. It would be similar, she remarked, to impressions of America formed by foreigners if Germany had held the Atlantic seaboard for four years with a "fighting-line stretching to Pittsburg and Buffalo."

She discusses four salient qualities of the Gallic spirit: reverence, taste, continuity, and intellectual honesty. The French, she observes, have a reverence for their long history and political life that counteracts their desire for the "new" thing. In their attachment to the "republic" of precedence (the rigid laws of rank at the dinner table), for example, they are not being snobbish but obeying the rules of *les bienséances,* or "always-have-beens." An appreciation of arts and graces is a first step in the formation of taste. Wharton asserts that French people have taste "as naturally as they breathe: it is not regarded as an accomplishment, like playing the flute." The two other traits round out her depiction of the country as the supreme reservoir of the best culture, "homogeneous and uninterrupted, the world has ever known." The honesty of the French is exceeded only by their intellectual curiosity. She praises the crowds of ordinary people who not only patronize music halls but also attend the Odéon or the Théâtre Français and enjoy, for instance, the plays of Jean Racine or Victor Hugo. The French embrace the culture Americans disdain, being "persuaded that the enjoyment of beauty and the exercise of the critical intelligence are two of the things best worth living for."

Throughout *French Ways,* Wharton contrasts the intellectual and aesthetic attitudes of France and America, always to the disadvantage of America. Although her announced intention in writing it was to educate American servicemen about the essential France, it is possible that the unfavorable comparison also served to justify her own expatriation. Although her decision to live permanently in France had much to do with its cultural history, it may be

Postcard Wharton sent to her friend Sara Norton in 1907, after one of her Atlantic crossings (Beinecke Rare Book and Manuscript Library, Yale University)

argued that her reception there as a woman writer was even more significant in bringing about her final decision.

Constrictions of gender are expressed in detail in *French Ways,* which in many ways reinforces the concept of the proper role of American women she espoused in *A Backward Glance.* There she deplored the "'monstrous regiment' of the emancipated young women taught by their elders to despise the kitchen and the linen room, and to substitute the acquiring of University degrees for the more complex art of civilized living." Gender is not an altogether clear-cut matter with Wharton, but she never wavers in her belief that French women are better-rounded and more competent wives than American ones. The latter are not being "grown up" as French women are. Even though they may dress well and even cook, they are still in "kindergarten," in a "Montessori-method baby-school." American women, although they may have more legal rights, actually enjoy only a "semblance of freedom." The middle-class Frenchwoman is always her husband's business partner, for no one else can have such a vested interest in the success of the business. She "rules French life . . . under a triple crown, as a business woman, as a mother, and, above all as an artist." The American woman in her prime, who has advanced from the freedom of girlhood to the responsibilities of marriage, motherhood, and her household, is suddenly "withdrawn from circulation." Her "liberation" and "progress" are a mirage because her economic security and social standing depend on marriage. The French woman, on the other hand, is a free spirit, and her position improves after marriage. Young girls are protected and sheltered, for the woman "does not count till she is married," when she then enjoys "extraordinary social freedom."

Intellect is more important to French women than wealth; keeping up with books and letters is essential for full participation in social life. As Wharton states in her memoir, "In Paris no one could live without literature." She argues that both men and women, when truly cultivated with varied interests, thrive on the "stimulus of different points of view, the refreshment of new ideas as well as of new faces." In her own practice, for the remaining twenty years of her life, Wharton clearly enacted the role of her version of a Frenchwoman far more than that of an American. She led a life of intense engagement on several fronts: the social and the domestic, the business, and the aesthetic. She was an "artist" in a dual sense: not only did she write every morning, but she also practiced the special skills of French women in steering conversation and participating in it and in deftly arranging guests with an ideal mix of interests and achievements. She frequently entertained houseguests, participated in social life in Paris and at Hyères, organized local sightseeing excursions and distant journeys, and often, in the evenings with close friends, enjoyed their reading aloud.

What may have begun as a polemical treatise gives way to astute analysis by an outsider who tries to be thoroughly assimilated to the country by sensitive perception, deep attachment, and tireless service. As an expatriate Wharton still remains apart from French genteel culture, yet she is replicating it by using her own good breeding and connoisseurship. America is increasingly classless, but France, with its anachronistic institutions and traditions and respect for literary attainment, bolsters her social posture and validates her intellectual status. But she also means to defend her decision to make her home permanently in France by bisecting "patria"—the country of her birth has many shortcomings but, being young, may change and cannot be wholly relinquished; the country of her maturity so nurtures her, despite its foibles, that it secures her full canonical allegiance—but not to the point of surrendering her native citizenship.

Wharton's last travel book, *In Morocco,* is based on her visit to that country in 1917. This journey was the result of an invitation from a French friend, Gen. Hubert Lyautey, resident general of French Morocco. He invited her to tour one of the annual industrial exhibitions that he had been organizing in the French colony since 1914 in order to impress on French subjects that World War I had not affected the normal activities of the country. Lyautey had been encouraged to invite guests from allied and neutral countries. Few foreign travelers had visited Morocco at that time, and Lyautey sent Wharton, accompanied by Walter Berry, on a three-week motor tour of the colony. Upon her return to France her war effort demanded all her energy, and she did not write about the trip until 1920.

In Morocco is imbued with Wharton's appreciation of French contributions to that country. Her journey confirms the value of French expertise, brought benevolently to bear in promoting the traditional crafts and in conserving the aesthetic treasures of the country. It is evident from the acknowledgments that she spoke and read French throughout the journey and relied on more French than English sources to round out and substantiate her facts. Throughout the book Wharton never forgets that her status in Morocco is that of guest of the resident general of France and not that of a professional writer. In the acknowledgments she insists that she is not addressing those who wish "authoritative utterances," which are principally available in French, but the "happy wanderers" who may be planning to visit Morocco. She supplies what she terms a "slight sketch of the history and art of the country" but asserts that its chief merit is "absence of originality"; she makes a point of thanking various "cultivated and cordial French officials," such as the director of the French School of Fine Arts in Morocco and the historian of the Portuguese Mazagan.

Such disclaimers cannot mask the achievement

of *In Morocco,* which is one of the most finely wrought of her travel books. She records the sounds and sights (many of them forbidden to women before that time) of a little-known *"country without a guide-book."* Even visiting such a country, she declares, is "a sensation to rouse the hunger of the repletest sight-seer." In the preface to the first edition she acknowledges that some readers might have expected her to remedy this deficiency and supply a complete guide. She has been unable to do so, however, because the approach of the rainy season limited her time, and the conditions under which she traveled were "not suited to leisurely study of the places visited." With this admission Wharton might seem to have done an about-face with respect to guidebooks. A country without one should be ripe for her own imprint; she could plausibly be an authoritative guide, initiating readers to the unknown Morocco. What she actually does, however, suggests that she had never taken the idea of writing a guidebook seriously. She presents a book that includes few dates and facts and little systematic description, yet which captures the essence of the country in a timeless way. She remains a connoisseur, freeing herself from all necessity for historical particulars and focusing on imaginative description and interpretation. This approach allows her to state, for example, that the "fallen columns and architraves" of the ruins at Volubilis "strew the path of Rome across the world" yet imposes no obligation to depict the ruins in a realistic way or give the precise history of the settlement.

The preface points the reader toward useful works about Morocco in French, and a separate chapter summarizes Moroccan history as a whole. Wharton's chapters on Fez, Marrakech, and other cities, however, oppose the conventional guidebook, just as her essays on Parma, Milan, and the Pennine Alps did in *Italian Backgrounds.* Her interpretation of sites takes its start from this opposition, her generalizations conferring an authenticity that enumerations of individual places would not have had. In Fez, for example, she visits palaces old and new, inhabited and abandoned, "and over all lay the same fine dust of oblivion, like the silvery mould on an overripe fruit."

One of the most interesting chapters of *In Morocco* is "Harems and Ceremonies," describing her visits to several harems during a time when Western women were rarely admitted to the country and even more rarely to harems. Throughout the text Wharton is critical of the deleterious effects on women of lives spent within harems and the "shadowy evils of the social system that hangs like a millstone about the neck of Islam." In the harem at Mar-

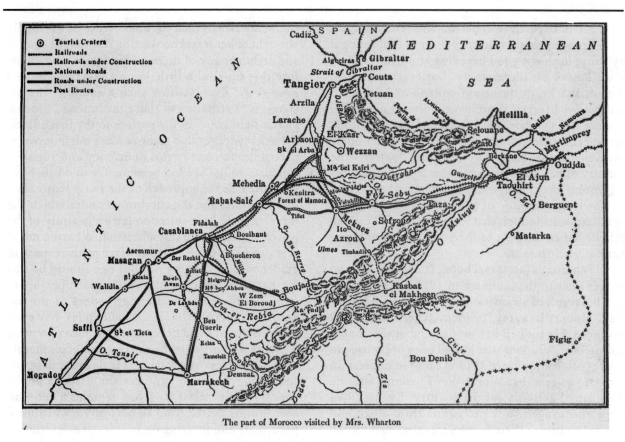

The part of Morocco visited by Mrs. Wharton

Map from In Morocco *(1920), Wharton's last travel book*

rakech she finds a stifling atmosphere in which the young female inhabitants are idle and without curiosity. Elizabeth Ammons states that in Morocco Wharton sees for herself "patriarchal sex pushed to its logical, primitive—and very depressing—extreme" and concludes that "the free expression of female sexuality represents a profound threat to patriarchal power." Seated in the harem before tea, trying to make conversation with the other women, Wharton concedes that the "languid women on their muslin cushions toil not, neither do they spin. The Moroccan lady knows little of cooking, needlework or any household arts." She concludes that in Morocco both sexes "live till old age in an atmosphere of sensuality without seduction." This statement puts a strict limit on the sensuality she celebrates in France, where she argues for its Rabelaisian outlook and condones *"le plaisir"* as standing for the "frankly permitted, the freely taken, delight of the senses, the direct enjoyment of the fruit of the tree called golden."

Wharton's visit to Morocco points up the necessity of finding a balance between conservation and restoration. The French administration had insisted on saving examples of native art and historic buildings. Wharton approves, for instance, of the ef-

forts by General Lyautey and the Moroccan Director of Fine Arts to repair the tombs of the Saadian Sultans at Marrakech. The alternative in Morocco would be, presumably, total obliteration because Moroccan building materials have no endurance and acquire no "bloom of *vétusté*," the phrase she uses in *A Motor-Flight Through France* to describe "venerable architectural relics" that have escaped renovation. She observes that, were it not for French intervention, the "charming colonnades and cedar chambers" of the college of the Oudayas in Rabat would be "a heap of undistinguished rubbish—for plaster and rubble do not 'die in beauty' like the firm stones of Rome."

Morocco is a "land of perpetual contradictions," projecting a mixture of "democratic familiarity and abject servility." She describes plump, slippered merchants riding abroad behind footmen, dignitaries of the sultan's government traveling with their servants, water-carriers, beggars, sorcerers, Jews, university students, Islamic beggars, and veiled women; she describes visits to bazaars along with famous traditional ceremonies such as the Sacrifice of the Sheep. At the latter event the contrast between the serene, plump sultan, a "hieratic" figure on a grey horse, and the "wild factious precipitate hordes" typifies "the strange soul of Islam, with its impetuosity forever culminating in impassiveness." It is as though Morocco, unlike France, is not "grown-up" but is dominated by talented adolescents who have an attitude of carpe diem.

In Morocco was Wharton's final travel book. It is unclear why she did not return to this genre, except that financially the returns from writing fiction were far greater than from nonfiction. She apparently considered at one time writing a book about Spain as a companion volume to A Motor-Flight Through France, because there is an unpublished and undated fragment dealing with travel in Spain in the Edith Wharton Collection in the Beinecke Library at Yale. It consists of an untitled page and a half laying out a journey following "the way of the Pilgrims across the Pyrenees" and mentioning the authors whose books had whetted her appetite for the undertaking. This segment is followed by four pages, numbered consecutively, titled "A Motor-Flight Through Spain." Even in this brief fragment her descriptive powers are at their height. She describes the old churches of Jaca as "the oases of those waterless lands," with their "palm-trunk shafts, their branching vaults, their water at the threshold, their shadows and rustlings and hidden places full of soothing."

As her writing career progressed, Wharton's increasing attachment to the Continent reflected her classicist stance, strengthened her dissociation from what she saw as the banality and ugliness of Victorian life in America, and led to her residence in France for the majority of her later life. Relying in part on her stored impressions of artists and writers, she inscribed a new iconography of place for her readers to consume. Her travel writings integrate her touristic experience and her aesthetic precepts. They are the embodiment of her connoisseurship, a reflection of her visual sensibility, retentive memory, and imaginative powers.

"We were all travelers before we were novelers," wrote William Dean Howells in an essay about his relationship with the house of Harper. Wharton, too, was first a traveler, and her journeys enabled her to develop in her travel writing the persona of the connoisseur and to establish the cultural voice which is embodied most powerfully in her fiction. Her travel writings are not only a product of her own biography but also a culmination of the identity she most valued. If Wharton had not been a "traveler" before becoming a "noveler," her works of fiction might have been much impoverished, and conceivably quite different. As Wharton became more preoccupied with the writing of fiction and the care of her two French homes, she ceased to write works of travel. Those she did write, however, have a timeless quality that justifies Blake Nevius's assessment of them as "brilliantly written and permanently interesting."

Letters:

The Letters of Edith Wharton, edited by R. W. B. Lewis and Nancy Lewis (New York: Scribners, 1988);

Henry James and Edith Wharton: Letters: 1900–1915, edited by Lyall H. Powers (New York: Scribners, 1990).

Bibliographies:

Vito J. Brenni, Edith Wharton: A Bibliography (Morgantown: West Virginia University Library, 1966);

James W. Tuttleton, "Edith Wharton: An Essay in Bibliography," Resources for American Literary Study, 3 (Fall 1973): 163–202;

Marlene Springer, Edith Wharton and Kate Chopin: A Reference Guide (Boston: G. K. Hall, 1976);

Stephen Garrison, Edith Wharton: A Descriptive Bibliography (Pittsburgh: University of Pittsburgh Press, 1990);

Kristin O. Lauer, Edith Wharton: An Annotated Bibliography (New York: Garland, 1990).

Biographies:

R. W. B. Lewis, Edith Wharton: A Biography (New York, Evanston, San Francisco & London: Harper & Row, 1975);

Shari Benstock, No Gifts from Chance: A Biography of Edith Wharton (New York: Scribners, 1994);

Eleanor Dwight, Edith Wharton: An Extraordinary Life (New York: Abrams, 1994).

References:

Elizabeth Ammons, Edith Wharton's Argument with America (Athens: University of Georgia Press, 1980);

Louis Auchincloss, Edith Wharton (Minneapolis: University of Minnesota Press, 1961);

Auchincloss, Edith Wharton: A Woman in Her Time (New York: Viking, 1971);

Millicent Bell, ed., The Cambridge Companion to Edith Wharton (Cambridge, Mass. & New York: Cambridge University Press, 1995);

Daniel Borus, Writing Realism: Howells, James, and Norris in the Mass Market (Chapel Hill: University of North Carolina Press, 1989);

Pierre Bourdieu, Distinction: A Social Critique of the Judgement of Taste, translated by Richard Nice (Cambridge, Mass.: Harvard University Press, 1984);

Janet Goodwyn, *Edith Wharton: Traveller in the Land of Letters* (London: Macmillan, 1990);

Irving Howe, ed., *Edith Wharton: A Collection of Critical Essays* (Englewood Cliffs, N.J.: Prentice-Hall, 1962);

Henry James, *The Letters of Henry James,* edited by Leon Edel (Boston: Harvard University Press, 1984);

Katherine Joslin, *Edith Wharton* (New York: St. Martin's Press, 1991);

Joslin and Alan Price, eds., *Wretched Exotic: Essays on Edith Wharton in Europe* (New York: Peter Lang, 1993);

Amy Kaplan, *The Social Construction of American Realism* (Chicago: University of Chicago Press, 1988);

Percy Lubbock, *Portrait of Edith Wharton* (New York: Appleton-Century-Crofts, 1947);

Blake Nevius, *Edith Wharton: A Study of Her Fiction* (Berkeley: University of California Press, 1953);

Alan Price, *The End of the Age of Innocence: Edith Wharton and the First World War* (New York: St. Martin's Press, 1995);

Mary Suzanne Schriber, "Edith Wharton and Travel Writing as Self-Discovery," *American Literature,* 59 (May 1987): 257–267;

Schriber, *Gender and the Writer's Imagination: From Cooper to Wharton* (Lexington: University Press of Kentucky, 1987);

Schriber, "Introduction," in *A Motor-Flight Through France,* by Edith Wharton, edited by Schriber (DeKalb: Northern Illinois University Press, 1991), pp. xvii–l;

James Tuttleton, Kristin O. Lauer, and Margaret P. Murray, eds., *Edith Wharton: The Contemporary Reviews* (New York: Cambridge University Press, 1992);

Cynthia Griffin Wolff, *A Feast of Words: The Triumph of Edith Wharton* (New York: Oxford University Press, 1977);

Sarah Bird Wright, *Edith Wharton's Travel Writing: The Making of a Connoisseur* (New York: St. Martin's Press, 1997).

Papers:

The most important collection of Wharton's papers is in the Beinecke Library at Yale University. The Houghton Library at Harvard University, the Firestone Library at Princeton University, and the Lilly Library at the University of Indiana, Bloomington, also have large collections of papers and photographs.

Constance Fenimore Woolson

(5 March 1840 – 24 January 1894)

Sarah Wadsworth
University of Minnesota, Twin Cities

See also the Woolson entries in *DLB 12: American Realists and Naturalists* and *DLB 74: American Short-Story Writers Before 1880.*

BOOKS: *The Old Stone House,* as Anne March (Boston: Lothrop / Dover, N.H.: Day, 1873);

Castle Nowhere: Lake-Country Sketches (Boston: Osgood, 1875; London: Trübner, 1875);

Two Women: 1862 (New York: Appleton, 1877);

Rodman the Keeper: Southern Sketches (New York: Appleton, 1880);

Anne: A Novel (New York: Harper, 1882; London: Sampson Low, 1883);

For the Major: A Novelette (New York: Harper, 1883; London: Sampson Low, 1883);

East Angels: A Novel (New York: Harper, 1886; London: Sampson Low, 1886);

Jupiter Lights: A Novel (New York: Harper, 1889; London: Sampson Low, 1889);

Horace Chase: A Novel (New York: Harper, 1894; London: Osgood, McIlvaine, 1894);

The Front Yard and Other Italian Stories (New York: Harper, 1895);

Mentone, Cairo, and Corfu (New York: Harper, 1896);

Dorothy and Other Italian Stories (New York: Harper, 1896);

Constance Fenimore Woolson, volume 2 of *Five Generations (1785–1923), Being Scattered Chapters from the History of the Cooper, Pomeroy, Woolson and Benedict Families, with Extracts from Their Letters and Journals, as well as Articles and Poems by Constance Fenimore Woolson,* edited by Clare Benedict (London: Ellis, 1930; revised and enlarged, 1932).

A New Englander raised in the Western Reserve of Ohio, a northerner who resided for many years in the South, and an American who lived in Europe for the last fourteen years of her life but never considered herself an expatriate, Constance Fenimore Woolson earned her reputation as well as her living by writing four novels, a novella, short

Constance Fenimore Woolson

stories, poems, travel sketches, reviews, and other short nonfiction pieces that mixed realism, regionalism, and romanticism. With her keen powers of observation and her talent for evoking unfamiliar, exotic locales, she began her career as a writer of expository travel articles. She never entirely abandoned this genre, but her career reveals an increasing interest in characterization, particularly the psychological and material effect of setting on the individual. This concern forms the basis of Woolson's most successful writings–the short fiction inspired by her residency in the Great Lakes region, the southern states, and Europe. One of the first northerners to write with sensitivity about the defeated South after the Civil War and one of the first New England–born authors to write appreciatively about

Woolson, circa 1840

Seminary, where she began to develop her talent for composition.

During her school years Woolson frequently traveled with her family around the Great Lakes. She often accompanied her father on summer trips to Wisconsin and the Zoarite community of the Tuscarawas Valley in Ohio. In 1855 she took the first of several summer trips to Mackinac Island, in the straits between Lakes Huron and Michigan. These excursions provided her with abundant material on which she later drew for her sketches and early fiction. She described the Zoar community in her first magazine article, "The Happy Valley" (*Harper's New Monthly Magazine,* July 1870), as well as in the short stories "Solomon" (*The Atlantic Monthly,* October 1873) and "Wilhelmina" (*The Atlantic Monthly,* January 1875). Mackinac was the subject of her second article, "Fairy Island" (*Putnam's Magazine,* July 1870) and several short stories. It was also the primary setting for her first novel, *Anne* (1882).

Woolson completed her formal education at Madame Chegaray's finishing school in New York City. After graduating at the top of her class in 1858, she accompanied her family on a pleasure trip to various places where her parents had lived during the early years of their marriage. Woolson experienced firsthand the gaiety of the fashionable resorts near Boston, which she later depicted in *Anne,* and the more staid New England of her paternal ancestors. Woolson was in her early twenties and living once more with her family in Cleveland when the Civil War erupted. Dedicated to the Union cause, she was deeply affected by the war, a factor that heightened her interest in the South and inspired her Southern sketches.

Following the death of her father in August 1869 Woolson left Cleveland and accompanied her mother, sister, and niece to New York City, where she wrote descriptive sketches that were published in the *Daily Cleveland Herald* during late 1870 and early 1871. Her earliest travel sketches had appeared in print six months earlier, and with this initiation into the literary world Woolson turned her hand to fiction. In 1873 she published her first book, *The Old Stone House,* a semi-autobiographical juvenile novel that appeared under the pseudonym Anne March.

From 1870 to 1879 Woolson divided her time among New York, Ohio, and the southeastern states as she attended to her mother, whose failing health required winters in a temperate climate. She made her first trip to the South in the fall of 1873, and for the next six years she lived principally in Florida and the Carolinas. She frequently visited Charleston, South Carolina, which she described in "Up the

the Florida peninsula, Woolson has been most consistently admired for her "Southern sketches"; her novella, *For the Major* (1883), set in the mountains of North Carolina; and her novel *East Angels* (1886), set in Saint Augustine, Florida. Nevertheless, her vivid portrayals of the Great Lakes and rural Ohio place her securely in the company of such local colorists as Bret Harte (whose stories she admired) and Sarah Orne Jewett while her perceptive treatments of Americans in contact and conflict with the Old World are noteworthy contributions to the international fiction most frequently associated with her longtime friend Henry James.

Born in Claremont, New Hampshire, on 5 March 1840, Woolson was the sixth child of Charles Jarvis Woolson, a businessman and native of Vermont, and Hannah Cooper Pomeroy Woolson, of Cooperstown, New York, a niece of James Fenimore Cooper. When Woolson was only a few weeks old, three of her five sisters died of scarlet fever, a tragedy that prompted the family's removal to Cleveland, Ohio, a few months later. The Woolsons settled there, and eventually two more daughters and a son were added to the family. Woolson attended Miss Hayden's School in the 1840s, and during the 1850s she was enrolled in the Cleveland Female

Ashley and Cooper" (*Harper's Monthly*, December 1875). When the Florida heat became too intense, she sought refreshment in the mountains of North Carolina, Tennessee, and Virginia. Woolson became fond of this unspoiled country and made it the setting for her short story "Up in the Blue Ridge" (*Appleton's Journal*, August 1878); her novella, *For the Major;* her last novel, *Horace Chase* (1894); and her travel sketch "The French Broad" (*Harper's Monthly*, April 1875). Her true home in the South, however, was Saint Augustine, Florida, the subject of "The Ancient City" (*Harper's Monthly*, December 1874 and January 1875) and the principal setting of *East Angels.*

During her sojourn in the South, Woolson was a careful observer of her natural surroundings, from the Florida swamps and pine barrens to the peaks and valleys of the Great Smoky Mountains. She was aided by a profound love of nature and long-standing interest in botany. She was also a close observer of the society she encountered: the fallen aristocracy of the South, the newly freed blacks, the Minorcan fishermen of the Florida coast, and the wealthy northerners who brought to Saint Augustine what Woolson once described as "that tiresome atmosphere of gold dust and ancestors." It was Woolson's practice to store up these impressions and images and allow them to germinate, often over a period of several years, before she used them in her writing. Thus, she wrote much of her Southern fiction after she had permanently left the South. During the first years of her residency in Florida and the Carolinas she wrote of the Lake Country settings she had known as a girl.

Woolson wrote nearly two dozen stories set in the Great Lakes and Ohio. Nine of them, the best of the group, appear in *Castle Nowhere: Lake-Country Sketches* (1875). Steeped in regional culture and natural history, these stories are largely concerned with disappointed love, misplaced loyalty, and self-renunciation. The characters are often outcasts, recluses, or exiles, such as the wrecker Fog of the title sketch and the visionary of "St. Clair Flats" who resides with his wife in the swampy straits between Lake Huron and Lake Michigan. Sometimes the outsider is a displaced easterner or European who is ultimately rejected by the frontier people, as the protagonist of "Jeannette" is spurned by the French-Indian girl with whom he falls in love. The most enduringly popular of the stories is "The Lady of Little Fishing." In this tale the rowdy inhabitants of a frontier settlement are won over by a saintly missionary who succeeds in reforming them until she is discovered to be in love with the one man who is indifferent to her. In a review for *The Atlantic Monthly*

(June 1875) William Dean Howells favorably compared this sketch to Bret Harte's "The Luck of Roaring Camp" (1868), noting that Woolson's story "has that intended harmony which is the only allegiance to probability we can exact from romance, and it has a high truth to human nature never once weakened by any vagueness of the moral idea in the author–as happens with Mr. Harte's sketches, the only sketches with which we should care to compare it. . . ."

Later in her residency in the South, Woolson began writing fiction with Southern settings and themes. The best of her short fiction from this period appears in *Rodman the Keeper: Southern Sketches* (1880). These ten stories range from a narrative of the devastation wrought on a Carolina family by the Union army ("In the Cotton Country") to tales of northerners confronting the aftermath of the Civil War ("Rodman the Keeper," "Old Gardiston," "King David"), and romances replete with the local color of Florida and North Carolina ("Miss Elisabetha," "The South Devil," "Up in the Blue Ridge"). These sketches earned Woolson many admirers, including James, who wrote, "As the fruit of a remarkable minuteness of observation and tenderness of feeling on the part of one who evidently did not glance and pass, but lingered and analyzed, they have a high value, especially when regarded in the light of the *voicelessness* of the conquered and reconstructed South." Although neither *Castle Nowhere* nor *Rodman the Keeper* has had an audience in the twentieth century commensurate with this contemporary enthusiasm, both collections have begun to benefit from the attention of feminist critics who have provided valuable new insights into the texts and sought to expand their readership.

During this period Woolson also wrote travel sketches about the South in which she often followed a practice she had established with her Lake Country articles, populating their pages with fictionalized travelers. According to Hamilton Holt, "Her method in her descriptive articles never varied. Always an excursion, and always an old soldier in the party to explain battlefields and battles, always an erudite scholar who lectures on antiquities, a scientist to name the flowers and trees, and a poet to point out the inherent beauty in earth and river and sky."

Woolson left the South in November 1879, following her mother's death the previous February. Traveling with her sister and niece, she spent several weeks sightseeing in London before journeying to the Riviera. She lived for nearly three months in the French village of Mentone, whose attractions she later described in "At Mentone" (*Harper's Monthly*, January and February 1884). The trio then spent

Palazzo Semitecolo, the house in Venice where Woolson was staying at the time of her death

several months in Florence, where Woolson became acquainted with James, who often accompanied her on gallery visits and sightseeing excursions. Despite (or perhaps because of) a lack of surviving documentation, the nature of the friendship between Woolson and James has proved to be a point of lively, although largely speculative, debate among twentieth-century biographers and critics.

In the spring of 1880 Woolson traveled north to Venice, Milan, Como, and Lugano. She spent the summer in Switzerland, staying in Beckenried, on the shore of Lake Lucerne, and visiting Interlaken, Berne, and Geneva. Spending winters in Italy—mainly Florence, Venice, and Rome—and summers in Switzerland, Germany, or England became a pattern with Woolson over the next three years. In the fall of 1883 she moved to England and lived chiefly in

London and Leamington, Warwickshire. She returned to Florence in the spring of 1886, and for the next two and one-half years she lived at Bellosguardo in Florence, overlooking the Tuscan countryside.

During her years in Europe, Woolson devoted a great deal of time to her novels—*Anne, East Angels, Jupiter Lights* (1889), and *Horace Chase*—and her novella, *For the Major*. Amid the shifting scenes, lively conversations, and subtle humor of these longer works, Woolson further developed the themes of self-sacrifice and the conflicting demands of love and duty. In *East Angels,* often considered her best novel, the conflict centers around Margaret Harold, who denies her love for Evert Winthrop in order to fulfill her duty to a faithless husband. Although *East Angels* has been faulted for its diffuseness of plot and minuteness of style, many have praised Woolson's adept characterizations and psychological analyses. Of merit too is Woolson's rendering of Gracias á Dios, a fictional town based on Saint Augustine. Just as in the early chapters of *Anne* Woolson painted a charmingly convincing portrait of Mackinac Island and its inhabitants, so in *East Angels* she deftly brought to life the Florida backdrop. As an anonymous reviewer for *The New York Times* (6 June 1886) remarked, "You go to Florida when you read 'East Angels,' and pass your day in lazy bliss."

During her years abroad Woolson also wrote short stories with European settings and themes. Most of these are set in Italy. (Writing to a friend, Samuel Livingston Mather, on 23 February 1886, Woolson called Italy "the country I love best of all European ones" and added, "It comes next in my heart after Florida.") *The Front Yard and Other Italian Stories* (1895) comprises six sketches. Several are notable for their striking depictions of Italian scenes: Paestum, with its Greek ruins, in the melodramatic "Neptune's Shore"; Sorrento in the romance "A Pink Villa"; and the Grand Canal in "A Christmas Party" and "In Venice." The title sketch, which was well reviewed at the time, remains one of Woolson's most admired pieces. It tells of Prudence Wilkin, a provincial New Hampshire woman, no longer young, who marries an Italian waiter in Assisi. Antonio Guadagni misleads Prudence into believing he is "all alone in the world," so she is surprised to discover that he is in fact responsible for "innumerable children" from a previous marriage, an orphaned nephew, "a bedridden grandam," and "a disreputable old uncle." When Antonio dies a year later, after exhausting most of his bride's savings, the care of the family falls to Prudence. Over the ensuing years her dream of replacing an eyesore of a shed that stands in front of the Guadagni house with a decorative New England–style garden is repeatedly sacrificed to the unremitting demands of her selfish in-laws and stepchildren. When finally her dream is realized through the beneficence of an American tourist, Prudence is near death, her vitality sapped by a life of arduous labor and deprivation.

"The Street of the Hyacinth," although not generally singled out in contemporary reviews, has received attention in the late twentieth century for its suggestions about Woolson's relationship with James and for its analysis of a female artist struggling under the tutelage and criticism of a male mentor. This artist-heroine theme, as Cheryl B. Torsney has classified it, also appears in the uncollected story "In Sloane Street" (*Harper's Bazar,* June 1892), the only tale Woolson set in England, and in "Miss

Grief " (*Lippincott's Magazine,* May 1880), a story now judged one of Woolson's strongest.

Five more European stories—"Dorothy," "A Transplanted Boy," "A Florentine Experiment," "A Waitress," and "At the Chateau of Corinne"—appear in *Dorothy and Other Italian Stories* (1896). All are set in Italy except for the last, which takes place on Lake Geneva near Coppet, where Madame Germaine de Staël lived in exile. Like other Woolson stories with an artist-heroine motif, "At the Chateau of Corinne" was often dismissed as mere romance and has only recently come into its own through reappraisal by feminist critics. Previous generations were appreciative of "A Transplanted Boy," the story of a semiorphaned American lad who must fend for himself one summer in Rome. Having lived most of his life abroad Maso is accepted neither as an American nor an Italian. When he is unexpectedly left on his own the boy endures a lonely, pathetic existence until his mother, returning from a vacation, discovers his destitute condition and arranges his belated return to the United States.

Late in 1889 Woolson traveled to Greece and Egypt. Leaving from Brindisi, she journeyed by steamer to Corfu and then sailed to the islands of Paxo, Santa Maura, Zante, and Missolonghi before continuing to Athens and Cairo. At the conclusion of her journey to "the Orient" Woolson wrote of the need to "exorcise the ghosts of Cairo and Corfu," confiding in a letter to Katharine Livingston Mather, "The notes and manuscripts I wrote in Cairo would make a large book instead of two magazine articles" (13 June 1890). Woolson succeeded in condensing her impressions into two fairly lengthy sketches, "Cairo in 1890" (*Harper's Monthly,* October and November 1891) and "Corfu and the Ionian Sea" (*Harper's Monthly,* August 1892), which were later republished in *Mentone, Cairo, and Corfu* (1896) along with "At Mentone" (first published in *Harper's Monthly,* January and February 1884).

Woolson's only travel essays to be published in book form, the sketches in *Mentone, Cairo, and Corfu,* vary in format and style. In "At Mentone," the longest of the three, Woolson adopts the persona of "Jane Jefferson," a fifty-year-old American woman. Along with her twenty-eight-year-old niece Margaret Severin, Jane has "accumulated" several other American travelers, including Mrs. Trescott and her comely daughter Janet, a pair of youths who vie for Janet's attention, and Professor Mackenzie, whose selective information Mrs. Trescott describes as "quite Cyclopean." Joined by two English artists who entertain themselves by sketching Janet in picturesque settings, the party explores the village of

Woolson's grave in Rome

Mentone on the French Riviera along with neighboring sites in Italy and Monaco. From the palms of Bordighera to the village of Sant Agnese, from the monastery of L'Annunziata to the casino of Monte Carlo, the members of the group are alternately improved by the commentary of their erudite companions and amused by the more frivolous of the travelers. The narration is at times witty (Jane observes, for example, that the customhouse at Ventimiglia is "modelled patriotically upon the circles of Dante's 'Inferno'") and at times ironic or wistful, but it is always attentive to details of the landscape, flora, architecture, and the beauty of the Mediterranean Sea.

In "Cairo in 1890" and "Corfu and the Ionian Sea," Woolson dispenses with the device of the group of travelers, as well as the thinly fictionalized narrator, in favor of a more direct expository style. While "At Mentone" is loosely structured according to the itinerary of the fictional travelers, "Cairo in 1890" is subdivided topically, with brief sections treating subjects such as "The Climate," "Mosques," "The Bazaars," "Domestic Architecture," "The Pyramids," and "The Reigning Dynasty." As she related her impressions and descriptions, supplementing them with abundant information on Egyptian history, culture, and politics, Woolson simultaneously expressed awe at the antiquity of ancient

Egypt ("the imagination will not rise; it is crushed into stupidity by such a vista of years") and misgivings about how rapidly modern Egypt was propelling itself toward the twentieth century. The Suez Canal brought 180,594 travelers to Egypt in 1889, and to Woolson evidence of European and American interlopers seemed nearly ubiquitous. Of the pyramids of Gizeh, she observed, "modernity is already there. There is a hotel at the foot of Cheops and one hardly knows whether to laugh or to cry when one sees lawn-tennis going on there daily." In a more philosophical vein Woolson wrote of the Nile:

> It comes from the last remaining unknown territory of our star, and this very year has seen that space grow smaller. Round about it stand today five or six of the civilized nations, who have formed a battue, and are driving in the game. The old river had a secret, one of the three secrets of the world; but though the North and South Poles still remain unmapped, the annual rise of its waters will be strange no longer when Lado is a second Birmingham. How will it seem when we can telephone to Sennaar (perhaps to that ambassador beloved by readers of the Easy Chair), or when there is early closing in Darfur?

In contrast to Cairo, Woolson found Corfu "not . . . in the least modern." A stroll down the Corfiote esplanade provided her with an opportunity to discourse on the foreign influences evidenced in its various monuments, institutions, and architectural styles, but despite the incursions of outsiders, for Woolson the genuine Corfu remained intact. Like the other sketches in the collection, "Corfu and the Ionian Sea" asserts a distinctly American point of view that is sometimes self-mocking. For example, writing of the American reverence for things antique, Woolson described herself at the Etruscan track near Bellosguardo "making furtive archaeological pokes with my parasol." At other times, however, her viewpoint is full of national pride, as in the remark that the struggles of Greece are of profound interest to Americans "because the country, in spite of its form of government, is a democracy." Woolson devoted the greater portion of the essay to Corfu itself, with brief comments on Paxo, Parga, Santa Maura, Zante, Missolonghi, and Patras. Throughout the article she interjected her observations on topics of literary and cultural interest.

After returning to England, Woolson lived in Cheltenham and Oxford from the spring of 1890 until the summer of 1893, when she took up residence on the Grand Canal in Venice. She had always adored the "Water City," but, sadly, she was afflicted during her few months there by depression, poor health, and hearing loss, which had begun to affect her some years earlier. She became ill with influenza in January 1894–the second occurrence in recent months–and it is possible that she also contracted typhoid fever. Suffering from a combination of fever, depression, and perhaps delirium, Woolson died on 24 January 1894 after plummeting from her bedroom window to the pavement two floors below.

Over the course of her brief career Constance Fenimore Woolson enjoyed the critical acclaim of the most respected literary minds of her time, including Edmund Clarence Stedman, Howells, and James, as well as the enthusiastic endorsement of the most prestigious publishers. Although largely neglected by the twentieth-century reading public, her best work, particularly her short fiction, has had several distinguished admirers and continues to be held in high critical regard. Increasing attention from feminist scholars, who have been instrumental in the republication of Woolson's writings, promises to expand her rather limited audience. As Joan Myers Weimer has remarked, Woolson's "work deserves to be better known for its complexity, ambiguity, irony, and wit; for its close observation of people and their environments; for its keen analysis of unacknowledged motives; and for the range of voices and tones its style accommodates."

Letters:

Constance Fenimore Woolson, volume 2 of *Five Generations (1785–1923), Being Scattered Chapters from the History of the Cooper, Pomeroy, Woolson and Benedict Families, with Extracts from Their Letters and Journals, as well as Articles and Poems by Constance Fenimore Woolson,* edited by Clare Benedict (London: Ellis, 1930; revised and enlarged, 1932);

Jay B. Hubbell, "Some New Letters of Constance Fenimore Woolson," *New England Quarterly,* 14 (December 1941): 715–735;

Leon Edel, ed., *Henry James: Letters,* volume 3 (Cambridge, Mass.: Harvard University Press, 1980), pp. 523–562;

Alice Hall Petry, "'Always, Your Attached Friend': The Unpublished Letters of Constance Fenimore Woolson to John Hay," *Books at Brown,* 29–30 (1982–1983): 11–108.

Biography:

John Dwight Kern, *Constance Fenimore Woolson: Literary Pioneer* (Philadelphia: University of Pennsylvania Press, 1934).

References:

Sharon L. Dean, *Constance Fenimore Woolson: Homeward Bound* (Knoxville: University of Tennessee Press, 1995);

Leon Edel, *Henry James: The Conquest of London, 1870–1881* (New York: Lippincott, 1962);

Edel, *Henry James: The Middle Years, 1882–1885* (New York: Lippincott, 1962);

Henry James, "Miss Constance Fenimore Woolson," *Harper's Weekly,* 31 (12 February 1887): 114–115; republished in his *Partial Portraits* (London & New York: Macmillan, 1888);

Rayburn S. Moore, *Constance Fenimore Woolson* (New York: Twayne, 1963);

Cheryl B. Torsney, *Constance Fenimore Woolson: The Grief of Artistry* (Athens: University of Georgia Press, 1989);

Torsney, ed., *Critical Essays on Constance Fenimore Woolson* (New York: G. K. Hall, 1992);

Joan Myers Weimer, Introduction to *Women Artists, Women Exiles: "Miss Grief" and Other Stories* (New Brunswick, N.J.: Rutgers University Press, 1988).

Papers:

A significant collection of Woolson's manuscripts, letters, and memorabilia is housed at Rollins College in Winter Park, Florida. Woolson's letters to Katherine and Samuel Mather are in the Mather Family Papers at the Western Reserve Historical Society in Cleveland. Letters to Edmund Clarence Stedman are in the Edmund Clarence Stedman Papers in the Rare Book and Manuscript Library at the Butler Library, Columbia University. Letters to Henry James are in the Houghton Library at Harvard University. Other collections are in the Beinecke Library at Yale University; the Pierpont Morgan Library; the William R. Perkins Library at Duke University; the John Hay Library at Brown University; and the Alderman Library at the University of Virginia.

Fanny Bullock Workman

(8 January 1859 – 22 January 1925)

Stephanie A. Tingley
Youngstown State University

BOOKS–by Fanny Bullock Workman and William Hunter Workman: *Algerian Memories: A Bicycle Tour over the Atlas to the Sahara* (London: Unwin, 1895; New York: A.D.F. Randolph, 1895);

Sketches Awheel in Fin de Siècle Iberia (London: Unwin, 1897); also published as *Sketches Awheel in Modern Iberia* (New York: Putnam, 1897);

In the Ice World of Himalaya: Among the Peaks and Passes of Ladakh, Nubra, Suru, and Baltistan (London: Unwin, 1900; New York: Cassell, 1900);

Through Town and Jungle: Fourteen Thousand Miles A-Wheel Among the Temples and People of the Indian Plain (London: Unwin, 1904);

Ice-Bound Heights of the Mustagh: An Account of Two Seasons of Pioneer Exploration and High Climbing in the Baltistan Himalaya (London: Constable, 1908; New York: Scribners, 1908);

Peaks and Glaciers of Nun Kun . . . A Record of Pioneer Exploration and Mountaineering in the Punjab Himalaya (London: Constable, 1909; New York: Scribners, 1909);

The Call of the Snowy Hispar: A Narrative of Exploration and Mountaineering in the Punjab Himalaya (London: Constable, 1910);

Two Summers in the Ice-Wilds of Eastern Karakoram: The Exploration of Nineteen Hundred Square Miles of Mountain and Glacier (London: Unwin, 1917; New York: Dutton, 1917).

OTHER: "Among the Great Himalayan Glaciers," *National Geographic Magazine,* 3 (November 1920): 405–406.

Fanny Bullock Workman was an aggressive, determined, and uncompromising turn-of-the-century American woman traveler. Together with her husband, William Hunter Workman, she explored and reported on the flora, fauna, people, and sights of Europe, Africa, and Asia; she was one of the first women to work as a professional mountaineer and surveyor and to write about the expeditions she and her husband took to the most remote reaches of the Himalayas. She was an outspoken advocate of woman suffrage and made it clear that she considered herself to be a role model for other women travelers and mountaineers.

Born in Worcester, Massachusetts, on 8 January 1859, Fanny Bullock was the daughter of Alexander Hamilton Bullock, who served as governor of Massachusetts, and Elvira Hazard Bullock. She received a good education both in the United States and abroad, first at Miss Graham's Finishing School in New York City and then at schools in Paris and Dresden. Bullock returned to her hometown in 1879, and on 16 June 1881 she married William Hunter Workman, a local doctor. The Workmans had one daughter, Rachel, who later became a geologist and the wife of Sir Alexander Mar-Robert of Aberdeenshire, Scotland. The Workmans began traveling and writing about their adventures in 1889 when ill health forced William to retire from the practice of medicine. Just before World War I, after their long years of traveling and exploration had ended, the Workmans retired to the south of France. Fanny died at Cannes on 22 January 1925. Her body was cremated at Marsailles, and her ashes were brought back to the Rural Cemetery at Worcester.

Fanny Bullock Workman wrote all eight of her travel books in collaboration with her husband. Their collaborative careers as travel writers fall into two parts: their first travels were to Europe and Asia, while their later years as adventurers focused on their mountaineering expeditions in the Himalayas. They also kept photographic records of their journeys that they used as illustrations for their volumes. The couple's travel books were popular with their contemporaries, as excerpts from two reviews of their 1908 volume, *Ice-Bound Heights of the Mustagh: An Account of Two Seasons of Pioneer Exploration and High Climbing in the Baltistan Himalaya,* found on the endpapers of their book *Peaks and Glaciers of Nun Kun . . . A Record of Pioneer Exploration and Mountaineering in the Punjab Himalaya* (1909), make clear. Writing in the newspaper *The Standard,* one critic remarks:

We have no hesitation in saying that Dr. and Mrs. Workman have written one of the most remarkable books of travel of recent years. . . . The book before us is full of thrilling stories of adventure in places remote from civilisation, where at almost every step the travellers carried their lives in their hands, and where the least miscalculation would have landed the whole expedition in disaster. Mrs. Workman has had the world at her feet in a sense that no other woman past or present can claim, for she has climbed to an altitude of 23,300 ft., a height which no one of her sex, and very few men, have ever attained.

The sentiments of *The Standard* are echoed by the book critic of the *Glasgow Herald,* who writes that

a volume of travel or mountaineering by Dr. and Mrs. Workman is a treat which the reading public have learned to appreciate and enjoy. This wonderful record of pioneer exploration and climbing in the Baltistan Himalayas will enhance the authors' reputation, not only as topographers and mountaineers, but as literary and photographic artists.

Later scientists and mountaineers have criticized the Workmans for not being as meticulous with their measurements and their topographical details as they might have been, however.

Between 1889 and 1905 the Workmans traveled to India, Ceylon, Java, Sumatra, southern Europe, Africa, Egypt, and Greece. They were considered pioneers in part because they logged most of the thousands of miles using bicycles, which were just becoming popular in the 1890s. In the preface to their second volume of travel writing, *Sketches Awheel in Fin de Siècle Iberia* (1897), which recounts the tour of Spain they took in the spring and summer of 1895, they comment on their reasons for touring on bicycles and the advantages of this mode of transportation, explaining that

the tour was made on bicycles, not to satisfy the spirit of adventure commonly ascribed to Americans, though something of adventure must be expected in a country like Spain, nor because there was anything novel to us in this mode of travel–the novelty had long since worn off–but as being the means of conveyance best adapted to our purpose, enabling us in entire independence of the usual hindrances of the traveller to pass through the country at leisure, stopping where and when we pleased.

Later they describe the sensation they created by riding into isolated communities on these newfangled contraptions, reporting that "the men and boys could not keep their hands off our bicycles, ringing the bells, feeling the tyres, and pressing the saddles as if these vehicles were on exhibition for their particular entertainment and instruction." The overreaction of the villagers is placed in sharp contrast to the description of the camels' response:

It is a pity that roads cease in the land where the camel reigns, for he takes the presence of bicyclists, and especially of women bicyclists, much more calmly than either European animals or people. He neither accosts a woman with the trite remark, "Das is nicht schön," as the German often does, nor does he run up a sand-hill to escape from her presence. But he bears the unusual sight with composure, and, with only a gentle look of surprise in his large soft eyes, he pursues his line of march, not varying an inch because two bicyclists happen to invade his domain.

Here and elsewhere the Workmans seem particularly amused at the stir caused by the sight of a woman riding a bicycle, reporting with tongues firmly in cheeks in their first book, *Algerian Memories: A Bicycle Tour over the Atlas to the Sahara* (1895), that "it has been our experience that horses, oxen and mules are much more liable to be frightened by a woman on a bicycle than by a man. Dogs also bark at the former more frequently. It may be that dogs, which seem to regard themselves as a sort of special police, consider women out of place on a wheel, and in need of correction."

The books that recount these travels through Europe and Asia focus on describing the people, art, and architecture of each place or region. In these volumes, then, the Workmans contribute their own insights and observations to a well-established tradition of travel writing in which tourists report their impressions of famous or well-known sights. In one passage in *Sketches Awheel in Fin de Siècle Iberia,* for example, they acknowledge the difficulty of saying something new about places and experiences that have been seen and written about often and indicate that they have read the work of earlier travel writers: "If in 1820 Irving could say the Alhambra had been so often described that little remained to be said, how much more applicable is this remark today?" In the preface to *Algerian Memories,* too, they include a self-conscious disclaimer that explains how hard it is to select what details and experiences would most interest their readers, adding:

A book composed entirely of personal experiences and adventures may become nauseous; one dealing extensively with history is open to the charge of being unoriginal or guidebookish, even though the facts may have been gathered from sources far removed from guidebooks, while one devoted largely to architectural description is considered dry. All these subjects as well as the natural scenery, antiquities, and customs of the people have a bearing on the interest of a Spanish tour, and a writer must cull from all if he would present an intelligible picture of a portion of what may be seen in Spain to-day. . . . This book makes no pretention to being an exhaustive treatise on the subjects touched upon.

The volumes that focus on their southern European and Asian travels often follow what feminist critic Sara Mills, in her 1991 study *Discourses of Difference: An Analysis of Women's Travel Writing and Colonialism,* has identified as the western European and American colonial and postcolonial travelers' habit of describing the local inhabitants and their behavior at best as exotic or unusual, at worst as primitive or even subhuman. In other words, Fanny and William Workman look at the sights through the lenses afforded by their own cultural biases.

To cite one brief example from *Through Town and Jungle* (1904), in which the racist bias is obvious, they describe the Indian natives this way: "It is astonishing what a small space an Indian will occupy when sitting. He will roost on a chair, the head of a cask, or the top of a rounded stone, on his haunches with his feet drawn up closely against them in exactly the position of a monkey, taking up only a third of the room required by a European." Similarly, the natives who serve as coolies for their mountaineering excursions are often described as lazy, unreliable, self-serving, and inferior in every way to European guides. Still, there are just as many passages in which the Workmans seem aware of their biases and work to transcend them. Their most direct comment on the subject of cultural relativism occurs, ironically enough, less than a hundred pages after their unflattering description of the Indian. They write:

> It is with a curious sensation, that one, accustomed by education to the feeling of superiority and pity perhaps not unmingled with mild contempt usually entertained in Christian lands toward the unfortunate class of humanity known as heathen, finds himself regarded, at least by one sect of these very heathen, in a similar light. The discovery is not flattering to his *amour propre* and shows him that the sentiment in question is not a monopoly of the Christian.

Their collaborative prose is most often written in the first-person plural or third-person singular, a practice that usually makes it impossible to determine which words or ideas might have originated with William and which with Fanny. Despite what often seems to be the objectivity and uniformity of this unified voice, however, there are many passages in which it is possible to detect what might be called a female sensibility or sensitivity that may well mark Fanny Bullock Workman's contribution.

In any case the Workmans regularly interrupt their descriptions of people and places to focus on the experiences of Fanny as a pioneering female traveler, as in this anecdote from *Sketches Awheel in Fin de Siècle Iberia,* which describes, with humorous descriptive detail, Fanny's fall from a mule:

> The monotony of the journey was broken for the first time an hour after the march had been resumed by the carelessness of the driver who led the mule ridden by the lady of the party. Having become somnolent from the smoking of hashish at luncheon, he stumbled into a slough and drew the mule in after him. While he was floundering knee deep in the filth, the mule in its efforts to get out threw the rider, whose foot caught in the stirrup from which it was impossible to extricate it. After she had been dragged sufficiently far to become covered with mud to her waist, badly shaken up and frightened, Salem rescued her. She sat on a stone recovering herself and reflecting upon the prospect of riding five hours longer with mud and water dripping from her skirts and oozing from her boots.

Despite the comical, undignified fall, Fanny Workman makes it clear that she is unfazed by the event, for she resumes the journey without complaint.

There are also anecdotes in each of the travel volumes that highlight native women's experiences and often offer an implicit feminist criticism of women's hardships and inferior social status in many societies, as in the description in *Through Town and Jungle* of Fanny's taking tea with two English-speaking Indian women who were confined to their homes because of the custom of purdah:

> Mohammedan ladies, in purdah, never accompanied their husbands into society. One of us, whose sex permitted, was invited to tea with two of these ladies. . . . Tea was served in the English manner. As the visitor was leaving, the hostess remarked with a sigh, "I am very glad to have seen you, you have told me so much that is new to me, and I should like to see the world as you see it. But that can never be. It is not our custom you know." And her eyes grew sad as she spoke.

Beginning in 1907 when they undertook the adventures described in *Ice-Bound Heights of the Mustagh,* the Workmans began a series of mountaineering expeditions that allowed them to test their expertise as scientists—geographers, surveyors, and geologists—as well as satisfy their thirst for the unusual travel experience. Fanny's list of scientific, scholarly credentials, listed with William's on the title pages of their later volumes, includes membership in both the Royal Geographical and the Royal Scottish Geographical Societies. Fanny was also the recipient of the highest medals of honor from ten European geographic societies and was an *officier de l'instruction pub-*

lique of France as well as the first American woman to lecture at the Sorbonne in Paris.

The travel volumes that describe the Workmans' mountaineering trips highlight the perils they encountered on a daily basis. In the introduction to *In the Ice World of Himalaya: Among the Peaks and Passes of Ladakh, Nubra, Suru, and Baltistan* (1900), for example, they begin by making sure their readers understand the dangers, both natural and human, that they faced:

> Mountaineering in the Himalayas is quite a different thing to mountaineering in Switzerland and the Tyrol. In the Himalayas, there are no villages and hotels within a few hours' distance of the summits, no shelter huts, where the climber may break the journey and spend a fairly comfortable night, no corps of guides, who in case of need are ready to render assistance.

> In the Himalayas, the mountaineer must go, fully provided with mountain and camp outfit, many days' march beyond even semi-civilised villages, into the savage and trackless wastes, that surround the giants he would conquer. He must brave fatigue, wet, cold, wind and snow, and the effects of altitude, for the bases of many peaks rest upon buttresses, that are higher than the summit of Mont Blanc. Worst of all, he must wrestle with the peccidilloes of the half barbarous coolies, on whom he must rely for transport, who care nothing for him or his object, and who are likely to refuse to go with him, as soon as any especial difficulty is encountered.

> It has been asserted, that, aside from their altitude, the Himalayas are very easy mountains to ascend. Let no one cherish this delusion.

In contrast to the earlier focus on people, places, and their cultures, the trips described in the Workmans' last four travel books were to largely uninhabited and rarely explored places—the peaks and glaciers of the high Himalaya Mountain range. Their sense of audience seems to differ, too, for they sought in these later books to write for a popular as well as a scientific audience—to write interestingly for the general reader yet establish and maintain their credibility in the scientific community as serious and accomplished mountaineers and geologists. In *In the Ice World of Himalaya* they describe the beauties of the sunset at elevations above twenty thousand feet: "As the sun flung its last flames of fire on the towering ice pinnacles, and the purple fangs of what might be called the Himalayan aurora shot upward from the dull horizon to the blue zenith, as the twilight silence of the Arctic regions fell over the snow land, one felt, not only the overwhelming beauty, but also the intangibility of a scene, that seemed in no way of this world." Lyrical descrip-

tions such as this alternate with detailed lists of the site's geographical features, such as the height of the peaks, the conditions of the climb, and the depth and texture of the glacial ice. Most amazing to them was the "absolute silence" they encountered at the highest elevations, a condition in which "one has the feeling of having completely lost touch with the material world, and the imagination, uncontrolled by the suggestions of ordinary sounds, runs riot among fancies and possibilities neither wholly pleasing nor reassuring."

Fanny was particularly eager to highlight her contributions to these expeditions since she was a pioneer among women who combined the sport of mountain climbing, which she had first practiced as a girl in New England, with the science of mountaineering and surveying. She set many records for women climbers, including her altitude record—which stood for twenty-eight years—for her climb of Pinnacle Peak (22,737 feet). William broke the world's record for men by climbing to a height of 23,394 feet up the same mountain. An ardent and outspoken feminist and advocate of votes for women, Fanny was concerned that her readers appreciate how her contributions to the field of mountaineering reflected women's potential for achievement in the world of work. Indeed, there is a photograph of Fanny on the top of a mountain, ice ax in hand, holding a placard aloft with the words "Votes for Women" written on it in large letters. Ironically, her most direct and extended feminist defense of her career occurs in a footnote at the end of their last travel book, *Two Summers in the Ice-Wilds of Eastern Karakoram: The Exploration of Nineteen Hundred Square Miles of Mountain and Glacier* (1917):

> Lest book-critics, sometimes prone to "take one up," should dispute the expression "one woman," . . . I would add that several women have ascended Himalayan passes of 18,000 and 19,000 feet, and particularly missionaries in Tibet have faced long, hard journeys in pursuit of their calling, while two or more women have, I think, successfully crossed the Pamirs, but no other has carried out the exploration and climbing of great glaciers and high peaks in Asia.

> That they will now begin to compete with men in this field, as in all others, is greatly to be hoped, and to those who may contemplate so doing I would here express my sincere good wishes for the success of their undertakings. They will have to toil and overcome, but by persistent effort they will achieve, not all they desire, but much knowledge, and, on the trail to still untrodden heights and lands, enjoy to the full the most glorious and freest of lives, in comparison with which all ordinary so-called civilized existence is of the deadliest commonplace. I have had what no man or woman can take

from me, what is above all price, the satisfaction of my work, which I have made as good as circumstances would admit of, and which, I trust, will receive a favourable verdict from those who come after me.

Fanny delights in presenting herself as questioning or violating the norms of Victorian female propriety, a trait that her writing shares, Mills notes, with other female-authored travel texts. Mills explains that "the characters subvert the notion that the woman's place is in the home and that women are too frail to go outside the home and to physically exert themselves." Fanny Bullock Workman regularly does this in her discussions of how easily she endures the physical demands of bicycling long distances in hot humid places or the rigors of mountaineering in high altitudes and cold temperatures.

In two instances late in their writing careers the Workmans broke with their practice of writing in a unified, professional, and often dry reportorial or scientific voice that characterizes most of their travel prose. A chapter from *In the Ice World of Himalaya* devoted to exploring the effects of altitude on climbers is divided between them. Fanny writes section 1 in her own voice, as she tells readers, "for the benefit of women, who may not yet have ascended to altitudes above 16,000 feet but are thinking of attempting to do so, I will here give my experiences for what they are worth." She goes on to explain how she had exercised on strenuous bike trips in tropical Java but had not done invigorating exercise since except a little walking, confessing that, "in starting out, I was in no especial training for mountain work. . . . I am not a light weight and am a slow climber. Still my powers of endurance on long days of climbing, and in weeks of continued cycle touring, have, for a number of years, been good." She adds, "As good a bodily condition as possible is, of course, desirable to enable one to combat successfully the facture *majeure* in high climbing, diminished oxygen, as well as to endure fatigue and the extreme cold often met with at high altitudes."

William's section of the chapter follows a disclaimer about his unease with writing in the first person: "Although averse, as a rule, to the mention of subjective phenomena, as savouring too much of autobiography, since the effects of high altitude can only be determined by the collation of individual experiences, I give mine here." He goes on to describe how high altitude may cause disturbances such as insomnia, headache, nausea, and indigestion, as well as difficulties with circulation and respiration. He seems even more interested in the effects of altitude on the mind, reporting that

the simplest actions assume formidable proportions, and even photography and the taking of readings, which one recognizes as of great importance and which at ordinary altitudes are not difficult processes, become bugbears; while the ascent of a peak, a really arduous undertaking at high altitudes, looms up as an almost impossible proposition. One has, therefore, often to call the will into play to its utmost power to force oneself to carry out what has been proposed. Those who are destined to raise the mountaineering altitude-record much higher than it now stands will undoubtedly be persons of strong will and self-control.

This division of the writing into pieces attributable to a single author is expanded in the couple's last book, *Two Summers in the Ice-Wilds of Eastern Karakoram*. As William explains in the preface, they wanted to find a way to write freshly after three previous books about Himalayan mountaineering, and he adds:

Endeavouring to steer a safe course among these shoals and currents, in Part I of this volume I will attempt to portray such features of the expedition of Mrs. Bullock Workman and myself to the Eastern Karakoram in 1911 as seem to me worthy of record leaving to her the task of recording the story of our exploration of the great Siachen and Kaberi glaciers in the latter portion of our 1911 and on our 1912 expedition, with an addition by myself of an account of some of the physiographical features of those glaciers and their basins.

In her section Fanny makes it clear that she was in complete charge of the second expedition, telling her readers that "Dr. Hunter Workman accompanied me, this time, in charge with me of commissariat and as photographer and glacialist, but I was the responsible leader of this expedition, and on my efforts, in a large measure, must depend the success or failure of it." The voice of the scientist, which explains that "As the nomenclature of this glacier and of the pass at its head is of no small importance to the geography of this region in the future, I must expand somewhat on this subject," dominates in Fanny's section of the book, but the most engaging part of the text is the extended narrative that vividly describes the fall of Chenoz, a porter, into an ice crevasse and the man's subsequent death from his injuries and prolonged exposure to the elements. What impresses Fanny and her readers most is how lucky she was to escape a similar fate since she was following right behind the unfortunate Chenoz. She concludes her story with a meditation on fate and luck, writing:

My own escape from sharing his dire fate was quite miraculous. Those who share the Oriental belief in "Kismet" might say his passing here was fore-ordained, while others, believing in the "survival of the fittest," have said that I, having the work to carry on, was, by not taking the one step more, and by chance not being roped, saved to accomplish it.

Here and elsewhere, Fanny seems much more comfortable than her husband with writing in the first person. When she is left to write in her own voice, her work is more narrative, intimate, personal, and humorous than the constraints of the collaborative, collective Workman voice.

Although later mountaineers and surveyors have questioned some of Fanny and William Workman's methods, measurements, and conclusions, there is no disputing their collaborative place in the record books as travelers, adventurers, and writers. Fanny Bullock Workman deserves a place in her own right both in mountaineering history and women's history for her pioneering climbing adventures. Her actions, as well as her feminist statements, invigorated and illuminated the turn-of-the-century debate over woman's rights and highlight her place as a strong woman who was exceptional for her time and place.

References:

Sara Mills, *Discourses of Difference: An Analysis of Women's Travel Writing and Colonialism* (New York: Routledge, 1991);

Jane Robinson, *Wayward Women: A Guide to Women Travellers* (New York: Oxford University Press, 1990), pp. 30–31;

Arthur Winslow Tarbell, "Mrs. Fanny Bullock Workmen [*sic*]. Explorer and Alpinist," *New England Magazine,* 33 (December 1905): 487–490.

American Travel Writing, 1850–1915

This checklist of selected primary sources is designed to provide some idea of the vast range of American travel writing during the period from 1850 to 1915, with particular attention to writings by women travelers. It is intended as a supplement to the essays in this volume and as guide to further research.

Ackerman, Jessie A. *Australia from a Woman's Point of View.* London: Cassell, 1913.

Adams, Emma Hildreth. *Jottings from the Pacific. Life and Incidents in the Fijian and Samoan Islands.* Oakland, Cal.: Pacific, 1890.

Adams. *Jottings from the Pacific, No. 2. The Tonga Islands and Other Groups.* Oakland, San Francisco, New York & London: Pacific, 1890.

Adams. *To and Fro, Up and Down in Southern California, Oregon, and Washington Territory, with Sketches in Arizona, New Mexico and British Columbia.* Cincinnati & Chicago: Cranston & Stowe, 1888.

Banks, Elizabeth L. *Campaigns of Curiosity: Journalistic Adventures of an American Girl in London.* Chicago & New York: F. Tennyson Neely, 1894.

Barlosius, Mrs. C. F. *Recollections of a Visit to England, France and Germany, Made in 1862, and to Germany in 1885.* Fredericksburg, Va.: Free Land, 1887.

Baum, Maud Gage. *In Other Lands than Ours.* Chicago: M.G. Baum, 1907.

Bixby, Olive Jenny. *My Child-Life in Burmah; or, Recollections and Incidents.* Boston: Corthell, 1880.

Blake, Mary Elizabeth (McGrath). *Mexico: Picturesque, Political, Progressive.* Boston: Lee & Shepard, 1888.

Blake. *A Summer Holiday in Europe.* Boston: Lee & Shepard, 1890.

Bonsal, Stephen. *The Fight for Santiago: the Story of the Soldier in the Cuban Campaign from Tampa to the Surrender.* New York: Doubleday & McClure, 1899.

Bonsal. *Morocco as It Is, with an Account of Sir Charles Evan Smith's Recent Mission to Fez.* London: Allen, 1894.

Bonsal. *The Real Condition of Cuba Today.* New York: Harper, 1897.

Bottome, Margaret (McDonald). *A Sunshine Trip: Glimpses of the Orient. Extracts from Letters Written by Margaret Bottome.* New York & London: Edward Arnold, 1897.

Bouligny, Mary E. (Parker). *Bubbles and Ballast. Being a Description of Life in Paris During the Brilliant Days of Empire; a Tour through Belgium and Holland, and a Sojourn in London. By a Lady.* Baltimore: Kelly, Piet, 1871.

Brooks, Abbie M., as Silvia Sunshine. *Petals Plucked from Sunny Climes.* Nashville, Tenn.: Southern Methodist Publishing, 1880.

Brown, Alice. *By Oak and Thorn: a Record of English Days.* Boston: Houghton, Mifflin, 1896.

Buckout, Mrs. B. M. *Aftermath: from City and Country, Berg and Thal. Gathered and Garnished.* New York: W. B. Smith, 1882.

Burnham, Sarah Maria. *Pleasant Memories of Foreign Travel*. Boston: Bradlee Whidden, 1896.

Carleton, George Washington. *Our Artist in Cuba. Fifty Drawings on Wood. Leaves from the Sketch-Book of a Traveller, during the Winter of 1864–5*. New York: Carleton, 1865.

Carleton. *Our Artist in Cuba, Spain, Peru, and Algiers. Leaves from the Sketch-Book of a Traveller. 1864–1868*. New York: Carleton, 1865.

Carleton. *Our Artist in Peru. Leaves from the Sketch-Book of a Traveller, during the Winter of 1865–6*. New York: Carleton, 1866.

Carpenter, Mary Thorn. *A Girl's Winter in India*. New York: Randolph, 1892.

Carpenter. *In Cairo and Jerusalem: an Eastern Notebook*. New York: Randolph, 1894.

Carrothers, Julia D. *The Sunrise Kingdom; or, Life and Scenes in Japan, and Woman's Work for Woman There*. Philadelphia: Presbyterian Board of Publications, 1879.

Child, Theodore. *The Praise of Paris*. New York: Harper, 1893.

Child. *The Spanish-American Republics*. New York: Harper, 1891.

Child. *Summer Holidays; Travelling Notes in Europe*. New York: Harper, 1889.

Claflin, Agnes Elizabeth. *From Shore to Shore. A Journey of Nineteen Years*. Cambridge, Mass.: Riverside, 1873.

Clark, Francis Edward. *Fellow Travellers: a Personally Conducted Journey in Three Continents, with Impressions of Men, Things, and Events*. New York & Chicago: Fleming H. Revell, 1898.

Clark. *Our Journey around the World; an Illustrated Record of a Year's Travel of Forty Thousand Miles*. Hartford, Conn.: Worthington, 1894.

Clark. *Our Vacations: Where to Go, How to Go, and How to Enjoy Them*. Boston: Estes & Lauriat, 1874.

Clemens, Eliza Jane McCartney. *La Plata Countries of South America*. Philadelphia: Lippincott, 1886.

Codman, John. *An American Transport in the Crimean War*. New York: Bonnell, Silver, 1897.

Codman. *The Round Trip by way of Panama, through California, Oregon, Nevada, Utah, Idaho and Colorado; with Notes on Railroads, Commerce, Agriculture, Mining, Scenery and People*. New York: Putnam, 1879.

Codman. *Ten Months in Brazil; with Incidents of Voyages and Travels, Descriptions of Scenery and Character, Notices of Commerce and Productions, Etc.* Boston: Lee & Shepard, 1867.

Collins, Laura G. (Case). *Bygone Tourist Days: Letters of Travel*. Cincinnati: Robert Clarke, 1899.

Collis, Septima Maria (Levy). *A Woman's Trip to Alaska; Being an Account of a Voyage through the Inland Seas of the Sitkan Archipelago in 1890*. New York: Cassell, 1890.

Cort, Mary Lovina. *Siam; or, the Heart of Farther India*. New York: Randolph, 1886.

Coston, Martha Jay (Scott). *A Signal Success; the Work and Travels of Mrs. Martha J. Coston: an Autobiography*. Philadelphia: Lippincott, 1886.

Cox, Samuel Sullivan. *Arctic Sunbeams; or, from Broadway to the Bosphorus by way of the North Cape*. New York: Putnam, 1882.

Cox. *A Buckeye Abroad; or, Wanderings in Europe, and in the Orient*. New York: Putnam, 1882.

Cox. *Diversions of a Diplomat in Turkey*. New York: Webster, 1887.

Cox. *The Isles of the Princes; or, the Pleasures of Prinkipo*. New York: Putnam, 1887.

Cox. *Orient Sunbeams; or, from the Porte to the Pyramids by way of Palestine*. New York: Putnam, 1882.

Cox. *Search for Winter Sunbeams in the Riviera, Corsica, Algiers and Spain*. New York: Appleton, 1870.

Crawford, Cora Hayward. *The Land of the Montezumas*. New York: Alden, 1889.

Culler, Lucy Yeend. *Europe, through a Woman's Eye*. Philadelphia: Lutheran Publication Society, 1883.

Curtis, William Elroy. *The Capitals of Spanish America*. New York: Harper, 1888.

Curtis. *The Land of the Nihilist. Russia: Its People, Its Palaces, Its Politics. A Narrative of Travel in the Czar's Dominions*. Chicago: Belford, Clarke, 1888.

Curtis. *The Yankees of the East: Sketches of Modern Japan*, 2 volumes. New York: Stone & Kimball, 1896.

Curtis. *Venezuela: a Land Where It's Always Summer*. New York: Harper, 1896.

Dahlgren, Madeleine (Vinton). *South Sea Sketches: A Narrative*. Boston: Osgood, 1881.

Davenport, Homer. *My Search for the Arabian Horse*. New York: B. W. Dodge, 1909.

Davis, Sarah Matilda Henry. *Norway Nights and Russian Days*. New York: Fords, Howard & Hulbert, 1887.

Day, Susan DeForest. *The Cruise of the Scythian in the West Indies*. London & New York: F. T. Neely, 1899.

Deane, Margery, as Marie J. Pitman. *European Breezes*. Boston: Lee & Shepard, 1882.

Deering, Mabel Clare (Craft). *Hawaii Nei*. New York: Wieners, 1899.

Dickins, Marguerite. *Along Shore with Man-Of-War*. Boston: Arean, 1893.

Dodd, Anna Bowman (Blake). *Cathedral Days: a Tour through Southern England*. Boston: Roberts, 1887.

Dodd. *In and Out of Three Normandy Inns*. New York: Lovell, Coryell, 1892.

Dodd. *On the Broads*. New York: Macmillan, 1896.

Dorr, Julia Caroline (Ripley). *Bermuda. An Idyl of the Summer Islands*. New York: Scribners, 1884.

Dorr. *A Cathedral Pilgrimage*. New York: Macmillan, 1896.

Dorr. *"The Flower of England's Face": Sketches of English Travel*. New York: Macmillan, 1895.

Dudley, Lucy Bronson. *Letters to Ruth*. New York & Boston: Gilson, 1896.

Dyer, Catherine Cornelia (Joy). *Sunny Days Abroad; or, the Old World Seen with Young Eyes*. New York: Whittaker, 1873.

Eddy, Daniel Clarke. *Eddy's Travels in Asia and Africa*. Boston: Brown, 1893.

Eddy. *Eddy's Travels in Europe*. Boston: Brown, 1893.

Eddy. *Europe; or, Scenes and Society in England, France, Italy, and Switzerland*. Boston: Bradley, Dayton, 1859.

Eddy. *Rip Van Winkle's Travels in Foreign Lands*. New York: Crowell, 1881.

Evans, Mary L. *Glimpses by Sea and Land, during a Six Months' Trip to Europe*. Philadelphia: Jacob Smedley, 1885.

Fay, Amy. *Music-Study in Germany. From the Home Correspondence of Amy Fay*. Edited by Fay Pierce. Chicago: Jansen, McClurg, 1881.

Field, Henry Martyn. *Among the Holy Hills*. New York: Scribners, 1884.

Field, H. M. *The Barbary Coast*. New York: Scribners, 1893.

Field, H. M. *From Egypt to Japan*. New York: Scribners, Armstrong, 1877.

Field, H. M. *From the Lakes of Killarney to the Golden Horn*. New York: Scribners, 1876.

Field, H. M. *Gibraltar*. New York: Scribners, 1888.

Field, H. M. *The Greek Islands, and Turkey after the War*. New York: Scribners, 1885.

Field, H. M. *Old Spain and New Spain*. New York: Scribners, 1896.

Field, H. M. *On the Desert; with a Brief Review of Recent Events in Egypt*. New York: Scribners, 1883.

Field, H. M. *Our Western Archipelago*. New York: Scribners, 1895.

Field, H. M. *Summer Pictures: from Copenhagen to Venice*. New York: Sheldon, 1859.

Field, Kate. *Hap-Hazard*. Boston: Osgood, 1873.

Field, K. *Ten Days in Spain*. Boston: Osgood, 1875.

Fielde, Adele Marion. *A Corner of Cathay: Studies from Life among the Chinese*. New York & London: Macmillan, 1894.

Fielde. *Pagoda Shadows: Studies from Life in China*. Boston: Corthell, 1884.

Finck, Henry Theophilus. *Lotos-Time in Japan*. New York: Scribners, 1895.

Finck. *The Pacific Coast Scenic Tour: from Southern California to Alaska, the Canadian Pacific Railway, Yellowstone Park and the Grand Canyon*. New York: Scribners, 1890.

Finck. *Spain & Morocco: Studies in Local Color*. New York: Scribners, 1891.

Fisher, Harriet. *A Woman's World Tour in a Motor Car*. Philadelphia: Lippincott, 1911.

Fogg, William Perry. *Arabistan; or, the Land of "The Arabian Nights."* Hartford, Conn.: Dustin, Gilman, 1875.

Fogg. *"The Land of 'The Arabian Nights,"* Being Travels through Egypt, Arabia and Persia to Bagdad. New York: Scribners, 1882.

Fogg. *"Round the World": Letters from Japan, China, India, and Egypt.* Cleveland: Cleveland *Leader,* 1872.

Francis, Harriet Elizabeth (Tucker). *Across the Meridians, and Fragmentary Letters.* New York: DeVinne, 1887.

Francis. *By Land and Sea: Incidents of Travel, with Chats about History and Legends.* Troy, N.Y.: Nims & Knight, 1891.

Franck, Harry A. *A Vagabond Journey Around the World: A Narrative of Personal Experience.* New York: Century, 1910.

Gage, William Leonard. *The Isles of Shoals in Summer Time.* Hartford, Conn.: Case, Lockwood & Brainard, 1875.

Gage. *The Land of Sacred Mystery, or the Bible Read in the Light of Its Own Scenery.* Hartford, Conn.: Worthington, Dustin, 1871.

Gage. *A Leisurely Journey.* Boston: Lothrop, 1886.

Gage. *Palestine, Historical and Descriptive; or, the Home of God's People.* Boston: Estes & Lauriat, 1883.

Galpin, Barbara N. *In Foreign Lands.* Boston: New England Publishing, 1892.

Gibbons, Phebe H. (Earle). *French and Belgians.* Philadelphia: Lippincott, 1879.

Gillis, Charles J. *Another Summer; the Yellowstone Park and Alaska.* New York: Privately printed, 1893.

Gillis. *Around the World in Seven Months.* New York: Privately printed, 1891.

Gillis. *A Summer Vacation in Iceland, Norway, Sweden and Russia.* New York: J. J. Little, 1898.

Griffin, Mary (Sands). *Impressions of Germany, by an American Lady.* Dresden: Privately printed, 1866.

Griffin. *Old Facts and Modern Incidents, Supplementary to Impressions of Germany.* Dresden: C. Heinrich, 1868.

Griffin. *Vagaries from the Old Note Book of an American Lady.* Dresden: C. Heinrich, 1867.

Guild, Curtis. *Abroad Again; or, Fresh Forays in Foreign Fields.* Boston: Lee & Shepard, 1888.

Guild. *Britons and Muscovites, or Traits of Two Empires.* Boston: Lee & Shepard, 1878.

Guild. *Over the Ocean; or, Sights and Scenes in Foreign Lands.* Boston: Lee & Shepard, 1871.

Hale, Susan. *A Family Flight through Spain.* Boston: Lothrop, 1883.

Hale. *Young Americans in Spain.* Boston: Lothrop, 1899.

Hall, Adelaide Susan. *Two Travelers in Europe.* Chicago: Stanton, 1898.

Hall. *Two Women Abroad: What They Saw and How They Lived While Traveling among the Semi-Civilized People of Morocco, the Peasants of Italy and France, as well as the Educated Classes of Spain, Greece, and Other Countries.* Chicago & Philadelphia: Monarch, 1897.

Hamm, Margherita Arlina. *Manila and the Philippines*. London & New York: F. T. Neely, 1898.

Hamm. *Porto Rico and the West Indies*. London & New York: F. T. Neely, 1899.

Hapgood, Isabel Florence. *Russian Rambles*. Boston & New York: Houghton, Mifflin, 1895.

Harrington, Adelaide L. *The Afterglow of European Travel*. Boston: Lothrop, 1882.

Harris, Lucy Hamilton. *Each Day's Doings; or, a Trip to Europe in the Summer of 1875. Journal of Lucy Hamilton Harris. (Printed for Friends)*. Albany, N.Y.: Weed, Parsons, 1875.

Harris, Miriam (Coles), as Mrs. S. S. Harris. *A Corner of Spain*. Boston & New York: Houghton, Mifflin, 1898.

Hauser, Mrs. I. L. *The Orient and Its People*. Milwaukee: I. L. Hauser, 1876.

Hayes, Isaac Israel. *An Arctic Boat Journey, in the Autumn of 1854. By Isaac I. Hayes, Surgeon of the Second Grinnell Expedition*. Boston: Brown, Taggard & Chase, 1860.

Hayes. *The Land of Desolation: Being a Personal Narrative of Observation and Adventure in Greenland*. New York: Harper, 1872.

Hayes. *The Open Polar Sea: a Narrative of a Voyage of Discovery Towards the North Pole, in the Schooner "United States."* New York: Hurd & Houghton, 1867.

Hayes. *Pictures of Arctic Travel. Greenland*. New York: J. J. Little, 1881.

Henderson, Alice Palmer. *The Rainbow's End: Alaska*. Chicago & New York: H. S. Stone, 1898.

Henson, Matthew A. *A Negro Explorer at the North Pole*. New York: Frederick Stokes, 1912.

Hitchcock, Mary E. *Two Women in the Klondike: the Story of a Journey to the Gold Fields of Alaska*. New York: Putnam, 1899.

Holyoke, Maria Ballard. *Golden Memories of Old World Lands; or, What I Saw in Europe, Egypt, Palestine, and Greece*. New York: Charles H. Herr, 1893.

Hoppin, James Mason. *Greek Art on Greek Soil*. Boston & New York: Houghton, Mifflin, 1897.

Hoppin. *Notes of a Theological Student*. New York & London: Appleton, 1854.

Hoppin. *Old England: Its Scenery, Art, and People*. New York: Hurd & Houghton, 1867.

Hunnewell, James Frothingham. *The Historical Monuments of France*. Boston: Osgood, 1884.

Hunnewell. *The Imperial Island; England's Chronicle in Stone*. Boston: Ticknor, 1886.

Hunnewell. *The Lands of Scott*. Boston: Osgood, 1871.

Hurlbert, William Henry. *France and the Republic; a Record of Things Seen and Learned in the French Provinces During the 'Centennial' Year 1889*. New York: Longmans, Green, 1890.

Hurlbert. *Gan-Eden: or Pictures of Cuba*. Boston: Jewett, 1854.

Hurlbert. *Ireland under Coercion: the Diary of an American*. Boston & New York: Houghton, Mifflin, 1888.

Hurlbert. *Pictures of Cuba*. London: Longmans, Brown, Green & Longmans, 1855.

Hutton, Laurence. *Literary Landmarks of Edinburgh*. New York: Harper, 1891.

Hutton. *Literary Landmarks of Florence*. New York: Harper, 1897.

Hutton. *Literary Landmarks of Jerusalem*. New York: Harper, 1895.

Hutton. *Literary Landmarks of Rome*. New York: Harper, 1897.

Hutton. *Literary Landmarks of Venice*. New York: Harper, 1896.

Iglehart, Fanny (Chambers) Gooch. *Face to Face with the Mexicans: the Domestic Life, Educational, Social, and Business Ways, Statesmanship and Literature, Legendary, and General History of the Mexican People, as Seen and Studied by an American Woman During Seven Years of Intercourse with Them*. New York: Fords, Houbard & Hulbert, 1887.

Jackson, Julia Newell. *A Winter Holiday in Summer Lands*. Chicago: McClurg, 1890.

Judd, Laura Fish. *Honolulu: Sketches of Life, Social, Political and Religious, in the Hawaiian Islands from 1828–1861*. New York: Randolph, 1880.

King, Edward Smith. *Descriptive Portraiture of Europe in Storm and Calm, Twenty Years' Experiences of an American Journalist*. Springfield, Mass.: Nichols, 1885.

King. *Echoes from the Orient, with Miscellaneous Poems*. London: C. K. Paul, 1880.

King. *My Paris: French Character Sketches*. Boston: Loring, 1868.

Kirchner, Adelaide Rosalind. *A Flag for Cuba: Pen Sketches of a Recent Trip across the Gulf of Mexico to the Island of Cuba*. New York: Mershon, 1897.

Knapp, Frances. *The Thlinkets of Southeastern Alaska*. Chicago: Stone & Kimball, 1896.

Knox, Adeline (Trafton). *An American Girl Abroad*. Boston: Lee & Shepard, 1872.

Krout, Mary Hannah. *Hawaii and a Revolution: The Personal Experiences of a Correspondent in the Sandwich Islands during the Crisis of 1893 and Subsequently*. New York: Dodd, Mead, 1898.

Krout. *A Looker On in London*. New York: Dodd, Mead, 1899.

Lee, Mrs. S. M. *Glimpses of Mexico and California*. Boston: Ellis, 1887.

Leighton, Caroline C. *Life at Puget Sound; with Sketches of Travel in Washington Territory, British Columbia, Oregon, and California, 1865–1881*. Boston: Lee & Shepard, 1884.

Leitch, Mary. *Seven Years in Ceylon: Stories of Mission Life*. New York: American Tract Society, 1890.

Leland, Lilian. *Travelling Alone. A Woman's Journey around the World*. New York: American News, 1890.

Lent, William Bemet. *Across the Country of the Little King. A Trip through Spain*. New York: Bonnell, Silver, 1897.

Lent. *Gypsying beyond the Sea; from English Fields to Salerno Shores*. New York: Randolph, 1893.

Lent. *Halcyon Days in Norway, France, and the Dolomites*. New York: Bonnell, Silver, 1898.

Lent. *Holy Land from Landau, Saddle, and Palanquin.* New York: Bonnell, Silver, 1899.

LePlongeon, Alice (Dixon). *Here and There in Yucatan. Miscellanies.* New York: Bouton, 1886.

LePlongeon. *The Monuments of Mayach and Their Historical Teachings.* Albany, N.Y., 1897.

Locke, David Ross. *Nasby in Exile; or, Six Months of Travel in England, Ireland, Scotland, France, Germany, Switzerland, and Belgium, with Many Things Not of Travel.* Toledo & Boston: Locke Publishing, 1882.

Lowell, Percival. *Chosen, the Land of the Morning Calm; a Sketch of Korea.* Boston: Ticknor, 1885.

Lowell. *Note: An Unexplored Corner of Japan.* Boston & New York: Houghton, Mifflin, 1891.

Lowell. *Occult Japan; or, the Way of the Gods; an Esoteric Study of Japanese Personality and Possession.* Boston & New York: Houghton, Mifflin, 1895.

Mackin, Sarah Maria Aloisa (Britton) Spottiswood. *A Society Woman on Two Continents.* New York & London: Transatlantic, 1896.

Mason, Clara (Stevens) Arthur. *Etchings from Two Lands.* Boston: Lothrop, 1886.

Mather, Helen. *One Summer in Hawaii.* New York: Cassell, 1891.

McAllister, Agnes. *A Lone Woman in Africa: Six Years on the Kroo Coast.* New York: Hunt & Eaton, 1896.

McCollester, Sullivan Holman. *Afterthoughts of Foreign Travel in Historic Lands and Capital Cities.* Boston: Lothrop, 1883.

McCollester. *Babylon and Nineveh through American Eyes.* Boston: Universalist Publishing, 1892.

McCollester. *Mexico Old and New: a Wonderland.* Boston: Universalist Publishing, 1899.

McCollester. *Round the Globe in Old and New Paths.* Boston: Universalist Publishing, 1890.

McGahan, Januarius Aloysius. *Campaigning on the Oxus, and the Fall of Khiva.* New York: Harper, 1874.

McGahan. *The Turkish Atrocities in Bulgaria. Letters of the Special Commissioner of the "Daily News," J. A. McGahan, Esq.* London: Bradbury, Agnew, 1876.

McGahan. *Under the Northern Lights.* London: S. Low, Marston, Searle, & Rivington, 1876.

Miller, Mrs. D. L. *Letters to the Young from the Old World: Notes of Travel, by Mrs. D. L. Miller.* Mount Morris, Ill.: Brethren's Publishing, 1894.

Miln, Mrs. Louis (Jordan). *Quaint Korea.* New York: Scribners, 1895.

Mitchell, Mrs. Murray. *In Southern India: Mission Stations in Madras.* London: Religious Tract Society, 1885.

Moulton, Louise (Chandler). *Lazy Tours in Spain and Elsewhere.* Boston: Roberts, 1896.

Moulton. *Random Rambles.* Boston: Roberts, 1881.

Muir, John. *Travels in Alaska.* Boston: Houghton Mifflin, 1915.

Nevius, Helen Sanford (Coan). *Our Life in China.* New York: Carter, 1869.

Newman, John Phillip. *Aurora Borealis amid the Icebergs of Greenland's Mountains.* New York: Hunt & Eaton, 1896.

Newman. *From "Dan to Beersheba": or, the Land of Promise As It Now Appears. Including a Description of the Boundaries, Topography, Agriculture, Antiquities, Cities, and Present Inhabitants of That Wonderful Land.* New York: Harper, 1864.

Newman. *The Thrones and Palaces of Babylon and Nineveh, from Sea to Sea: a Thousand Miles on Horseback.* New York: Harper, 1876.

Newman, Mrs. John Philip. *The Flowery Orient: Temples and Shrines in Heathen Lands.* New York: Nelson & Phillips. 1878.

Nichols, Francis H. *Through the Hidden Shensi.* New York: Scribners, 1902.

Nieriker, Abigail May (Alcott). *Studying Art Abroad, and How to Do It Cheaply.* Boston: Roberts, 1879.

Ninde, Mary Louise. *We Two Alone in Europe.* Chicago: Jansen, McClurg. 1886.

Norton, Minerva (Brace). *In and around Berlin.* Chicago: McClurg, 1889.

Palmer, Frederick. *George Dewey, Admiral; Impressions of Dewey and the Olympia on Their Homeward Progress from Manila.* New York: Doubleday & McClure, 1899.

Palmer, F. *Going to War in Greece.* New York: Russell, 1897.

Palmer, F. *In the Klondyke; Including an Account of a Winter's Journey to Dawson.* New York: Scribners, 1899.

Palmer, Lucia A. (Chapman) "Mrs. H. R. Palmer." *Grecian Days.* New York & Chicago: Revell, 1896.

Palmer, L. A. *Oriental Days.* New York: Baker & Taylor, 1897.

Parker, Mrs. William. *Wandering Thoughts and Wandering Steps. By a Philadelphia Lady.* Philadelphia: Lippincott, 1880.

Parry, Emma Louise. *Life among the Germans.* New York: Lothrop, 1887.

Peake, Elizabeth. *Pen Pictures of Europe. When and How We Went, and What We Saw during a Seventeen Months' Tour.* Philadelphia: Lippincott, 1874.

Peary, Josephine (Diebitsch). *My Arctic Journal: A Year among the Ice-Fields and Eskimos; with an Account of the Great White Journey across Greenland, by Robert E. Peary.* New York & Philadelphia: Contemporary, 1893.

Pennell, Elizabeth (Robins). *Over the Alps on a Bicycle.* New York: Century, 1898.

Pennell, Joseph. *A Canterbury Pilgrimage: Ridden, Written and Illustrated by Joseph and Elizabeth Robins Pennell.* New York: Scribners, 1885.

Pennell. *Our Journey to the Hebrides.* New York: Harper, 1889.

Pennell. *Our Sentimental Journey through France and Italy.* New York: Longmans, Green, 1888.

Pennell. *Play in Provence, Being a Series of Sketches Written and Drawn by Joseph Pennell and Elizabeth Robins Pennell.* New York: Century, 1892.

Pennell. *The Stream of Pleasure: a Narrative of a Journey on the Thames from Oxford to London.* New York: Macmillan, 1891.

Pennell. *Two Pilgrims' Progress: from Fair Florence to the Eternal City of Rome.* Boston: Roberts, 1887.

Pfirshing, Mena C. *Memories of Italian Shores.* Chicago: Dial, 1895.

Post, Loretta J. *Scenes in Europe; or, Observations by an Amateur Artist.* Cincinnati: Hitchcock & Walden, 1874.

Preston, Margaret (Junkin). *A Handful of Monographs, Continental and English.* New York: Randolph, 1886.

Prime, Samuel Irenaeus. *The Alhambra and the Kremlin. The South and the North of Europe.* New York: Randolph, 1873.

Prime. *The Bible in the Levant; or, the Life and Letters of the Rev. C. N. Righter, Agent of the American Bible Society in the Levant.* New York: Sheldon, 1859.

Prime. *Letters from Switzerland.* New York: Sheldon, 1860.

Prime. *Travels in Europe and the East: a Year in England, Scotland, Ireland, Wales, France, Belgium, Holland, Germany, Austria, Italy, Greece, Turkey, Syria, Palestine, and Egypt.* 2 volumes. New York: Harper, 1855.

Proctor, Edna Dean. *A Russian Journey, from the Narrows to the Golden Gate.* Boston: Osgood, 1872.

Rankin, Melinda. *Twenty Years among the Mexicans, a Narrative of Missionary Labor.* Saint Louis & Cincinnati: Central Book Concern, 1875.

Rees, Miss L. L. *We Four. Where We Went and What We Saw in Europe.* Philadelphia: Lippincott, 1880.

Rideing, William Henry. *At Hawarden with Mr. Gladstone, and Other Transatlantic Experiences.* New York & Boston: Crowell, 1896.

Rideing. *In the Land of Lorna Doone and Other Pleasurable Excursions in England.* New York & Boston: Crowell, 1895.

Rideing. *Thackeray's London: His Haunts and the Scenes of His Novels.* Boston: Cupples, Upham, 1885.

Ripley, Eliza Moore (Chinn) McHatton. *From Flag to Flag: a Woman's Adventures and Experiences in the South during the War, in Mexico, and in Cuba.* New York: Appleton, 1889.

Robinson, Louise B. *A Bundle of Letters from Over the Sea.* Boston: Cupples, 1890.

Rollins, Alice (Wellington). *From Palm to Glacier; with an Interlude: Brazil, Bermuda and Alaska.* New York & London: Putnam, 1892.

Roosevelt, Theodore. *The Rough Riders.* New York: Scribners, 1899.

Roulet, Mary F. (Nixon). *With a Pessimist in Spain, by Mary F. Nixon.* Chicago: McClurg, 1897.

Salm-Salm, Agnes (Joy). *Ten Years of My Life.* New York: Worthington, 1877.

Sanborn, Helen Josephine. *A Winter in Central America and Mexico.* Boston: Lee & Shepard, 1886.

Schneider, Eliza Cheney (Abbot). *Letters from Broosa, Asia Minor, by Mrs. E. C. Schneider, with an Essay on the Prospects of the Heathen and Our Duties to Them.* Chambersburg, Pa.: German Reformed Church, 1846.

Schwatka, Frederic. *Along Alaska's Great River. A Popular Account of the Travels of the Alaska Exploring Expedition of 1883, along the Great Yukon River from Its Source to Its Mouth, in the British North-West Territory, and in the Territory of Alaska.* New York: Cassell, 1885.

Schwatka. *In the Land of Cave and Cliff Dwellers.* New York: Cassell, 1893.

Schwatka. *Nimrod in the North; or, Hunting and Fishing Adventures in the Arctic Regions.* New York: Cassell, 1885.

Schwatka. *A Summer in Alaska. A popular Account of the Travels of an Alaska Exploring Expedition along the Great Yukon River, from Its Source to Its Mouth, in the British Northwest Territory, and in the Territory of Alaska.* Philadelphia: Huber, 1891.

Scidmore, Eliza Ruhamah. *Alaska; Its Southern Coast and the Sitkan Archipelago.* Boston: Lothrop, 1885.

Scidmore. *Appleton's Guidebook to Alaska and the Northwest Coast, Including the Shores of Washington, British Columbia, Southeastern Alaska, the Aleutian and Seal Islands, the Bering and Arctic Coasts.* New York: Appleton, 1893.

Scidmore. *Java, the Garden of the East.* New York: Century, 1897.

Scidmore. *Junrikisha Days in Japan.* New York: Harper, 1891.

Scidmore. *Westward to the Far East, a Guide to the Principal Cities of China and Japan with a Note on Korea,* fourth edition. Montreal: Canadian Pacific Railway, 1893.

Scott, Anna (Kay), as Mrs. Mildred Marston. *Korno Siga, the Mountain Chief; or, Life in Assam.* Philadelphia & New York: American Sunday School Union, 1889.

Sessions, Francis Charles. *From the Land of the Midnight Sun to the Volga.* New York: Welch, Fracker, 1890.

Sessions. *From Yellowstone Park to Alaska.* New York: Welch, Fracker, 1890.

Sessions. *In Western Levant.* New York: Welch, Fracker, 1890.

Sessions. *On the Wing through Europe. By a Business Man.* Columbus: Derby, 1880.

Sheldon, Louise Vescelius. *Yankee Girls in Zulu Land, by Louise Vescelius-Sheldon.* New York: Worthington, 1888.

Sheldon, Mary (French). *Adventures in East Africa; or, Sultan to Sultan: the Narrative of a Woman's Adventures among the Masai and Other Tribes of East Africa.* Boston: Dana Estes, 1892.

Shepard, Isabel Sharpe, as Mrs. L. G. Shepard. *The Cruise of the U.S. Steamer "Rush" in the Behring Sea: Summer of 1889.* San Francisco: Bancroft, 1889.

Sherwood, Mary Elizabeth (Wilson). *Here and There and Everywhere; Reminiscences.* Chicago & New York: Stone, 1898.

Shoemaker, Michael Myers. *Eastward to the Land of Morning.* Cincinnati: Clarke, 1893.

Shoemaker. *Islands of the Southern Seas; Hawaii, Samoa, New Zealand, Tasmania, Australia, and Java.* New York & London: Putnam, 1898.

Shoemaker. *The Kingdom of the "White Woman." A Sketch.* Cincinnati: Clarke, 1894.

Shoemaker. *Quaint Corner of Ancient Empires; Southern India, Burma, and Manila.* New York & London: Putnam, 1899.

Shoemaker. *Trans-Caspia: the Sealed Provinces of the Czar.* Cincinnati: Clarke, 1895.

Smith Ann Eliza (Brainerd), as Mrs. J. Gregory Smith. *Notes of Travel in Mexico and California.* Saint Albans, Vt.: Messenger & Advertiser, 1886.

Smith, Francis Hopkinson. *Gondola Days; with Illustrations by the Author.* Boston & New York: Houghton, Mifflin, 1897.

Smith. *Venice of Today.* New York: Thomas, 1896.

Smith. *Well-Worn Roads of Spain, Holland and Italy. Travelled by a Painter in Search of the Picturesque.* Boston & New York: Houghton, Mifflin, 1887.

Smith. *A White Umbrella in Mexico.* Boston & New York: Houghton Mifflin, 1889.

Steele, James William. *Cuban Sketches.* New York: Putnam, 1881.

Steele. *The Klondike; the New Gold Fields of Alaska and the Far North-West.* Chicago: Britton, 1897.

Steele. *To Mexico by Palace Car. Intended as a Guide to Her Principal Cities and Capital, and Generally as a Tourist's Introduction to Her Life and People.* Chicago: Jansen, McClurg, 1884.

Stetson, Evelyn R. *Rapid Transit Abroad.* New York: Miller, 1879.

Stevens, Thomas. *Africa as Seen by Thomas Stevens and the Hawkeye.* Boston: Blair Camera, 1890.

Stevens. *Around the World on a Bicycle.* 2 volumes. New York: Scribners, 1887–1888.

Stevens. *Scouting for Stanley in East Africa.* New York: Cassell, 1890.

Stevens. *Through Russia on a Mustang.* New York: Cassell, 1891.

Stevenson, Sara (Yorke). *Maximillian in Mexico; a Woman's Reminiscences of the French Intervention, 1862–1867.* New York: Century, 1899.

Stoddard, Charles Augustus. *Across Russia from the Baltic to the Danube.* New York: Scribners, 1891.

Stoddard, C. A. *Cruising among the Caribbees, Summer Days in Months.* New York: Scribners, 1895.

Stoddard, C. A. *Spanish Cities; with Glimpses of Gibraltar and Tangier.* New York: Scribners, 1892.

Stoddard, Charles Warren. *A Cruise under the Crescent; from Suez to San Marco.* Chicago & New York: Rand, McNally, 1898.

Stoddard, C. W. *Hawaiian Life: Being Lazy Letters from Low Latitudes.* Chicago & New York: Neely, 1894.

Stoddard, C. W. *The Lepers of Molokai.* Notre Dame, Ind.: Ave Maria Press, 1885.

Stoddard, C. W. *Mashallah! A Flight into Egypt.* New York: Appleton, 1881.

Stoddard, C. W. *Over the Rocky Mountains to Alaska.* Saint Louis: Herder, 1899.

Stoddard, C. W. *Summer Cruising in the South Seas*. London: Chatto & Windus, 1874.

Stoddard, C. W. *A Trip to Hawaii*. San Francisco: Passenger Department of the Oceanic Steamship Company, 1885.

Stoddard, John Lawson. *Athens-Venice*. Chicago: Belford, Middlebrook, 1897.

Stoddard, J. L. *China*. Chicago: Belford, Middlebrook, 1897.

Stoddard, J. L. *Egypt*. Chicago: Belford, Middlebrook, 1897.

Stoddard, J. L. *India*. Chicago: Belford, Middlebrook, 1897.

Stoddard, J. L. *Japan*. Chicago: Belford, Middlebrook, 1897.

Stoddard, J. L. *Jerusalem*. Chicago: Belford, Middlebrook, 1897.

Stoddard, J. L. *Norway*. Chicago: Belford, Middlebrook, 1897.

Stoddard, J. L. *Red Letter Days Abroad*. Boston: Osgood, 1884.

Stoddard, J. L. *Switzerland*. Chicago: Belford, Middlebrook, 1897.

Stone, James Samuel. *From Frankfort to Munich*. Philadelphia: Porter & Coates, 1893.

Stone. *The Heart of Merrie England*. Philadelphia: Porter & Coates, 1887.

Stone. *Over the Hills to Broadway*. Philadelphia: Porter & Coates, 1893.

Stone. *Woods and Dales of Derbyshire*. Philadelphia: Jacobs, 1894.

Stone, Mary Amelia (Boomer). *A Summer in Scandinavia*. New York: Randolph, 1885.

Straiton, Mrs. M. *Two Lady Tramps Abroad, a Compilation of Letters Descriptive of Nearly a Year's Travel in India, Asia Minor, Egypt, the Holy Land, Turkey, Greece, Italy, Austria, Switzerland, France, England, Ireland, and Scotland. By Two American Ladies*. Flushing, N. Y.: Evening Journal Press, 1881.

Sweetser, Delight. *One Way around the World*. Indianapolis: Bowen-Merrill, 1899.

Tadlock, Clara Moyse. *Bohemian Days: a Narrative of a Journey around the World*. New York: Alden, 1889.

Taylor, William. *Christian Adventures in South Africa*. New York: Phillips & Hunt, 1881.

Taylor. *Four Years' Campaign in India*. New York: Nelson & Phillips, 1876.

Taylor. *Story of My Life; an Account of What I Have Thought and Said and Done in My Ministry of More Than Fifty-Three Years in Christian Lands and among the Heathen*. New York: Hunt & Eaton, 1895.

Terhune, Mary Virginia (Hawes), as Marion Harland. *Home of the Bible: What I Saw and Heard in Palestine . . . To Which Has Been Added the Story of Martyred Armenia*. Chicago: National Book Concern, 1895.

Terhune. *Loiterings in Pleasant Paths*. New York: Scribners, 1880.

Teuffel, Blanche Willis (Howard) von. *One Year Abroad*. Boston: Osgood, 1877.

Thaxter, Celia (Laighton). *Among the Isles of Shoals*. Boston: Osgood, 1873.

Thompson, Ella Williams. *Beaten Paths; or, a Woman's Vacation*. Boston: Lee & Shepard, 1874.

Todd, Mabel (Loomis). *Corona and Coronet: Being a Narrative of the Amherst Eclipse Expedition to Japan in Mr. James' Schooner-Yacht Coronet, to Observe the Sun's Total Obscuration, 9th August, 1896*. Boston & New York: Houghton, Mifflin, 1898.

Trail, Florence. *My Journal in Foreign Lands*. Baltimore: Stork, 1884.

Tyler, Fannie A. *Home Letters from Over the Sea*. Boston: Williams, 1883.

Tyler, Josephine. *Waymarks; or, Sola in Europe*. New York & Chicago: Brentano, 1885.

Tyler, Katherine E. *The Story of a Scandinavian Summer*. New York: Putnam, 1881.

Vincent, Frank. *Actual Africa; or, the Coming Continent: A Tour of Exploration*. New York: Appleton, 1895.

Vincent. *Around and about South America. Twenty Months of Quest and Query*. New York: Appleton, 1890.

Vincent. *In and out of Central America, and Other Sketches and Studies of Travel*. New York: Appleton, 1890.

Vincent. *The Land of the White Elephant: Sights and Scenes in Southeastern Asia. A Personal Narrative of Travel and Adventure in Farther India, Embracing the Countries of Burma, Siam, Cambodia, and Cochin-China (1871–72)*. New York: Harper, 1874.

Vincent. *Norsk, Lapp, and Finn; or, Travel Tracings from the Far North of Europe*. New York: Putnam, 1881.

Vincent. *Through and Through the Tropics, Thirty Thousand Miles of Travel in Oceania, Australia, and India*. New York: Harper, 1876.

Wallace, Mrs. E. D. *A Woman's Experiences in Europe. Including England, France, Germany and Italy*. New York: Appleton, 1872.

Wallace, Susan Arnold (Elston), as Mrs. Lew Wallace. *Along the Bosphorus, and Other Sketches*. New York & Chicago: Rand, McNally, 1898.

Wallace, S. A. *The Repose in Egypt; a Medley*. New York: Alden, 1888.

Wallace, S.A. *The Storied Sea*. Boston: Osgood, 1883.

Walworth, Ellen Hardin. *An Old World, As Seen through Young Eyes; or, Travels around the World*. New York: Appleton, 1877.

Warner, Charles Dudley. *In the Levant*. Boston: Osgood, 1876.

Warner. *Mummies and Moslems*. Hartford, Conn.: American Publishing, 1876.

Warner. *My Winter on the Nile, among the Mummies and Moslems*. Hartford, Conn.: American Publishing, 1876.

Warner. *On Horseback; a Tour in Virginia, North Carolina and Tennessee. With Notes of Travel in Mexico and California*. Boston & New York: Houghton, Mifflin, 1888.

Warner. *A Roundabout Journey*. Boston & New York: Houghton, Mifflin, 1884.

Warner. *A Roundabout Journey*. Boston & New York: Houghton, Mifflin, 1884.

Warner. *Saunterings*. Boston: Osgood, 1872.

Warner. *Studies in the South and West, with Comments on Canada*. New York, Harper, 1889.

Warren, Mary Bowers. *Little Journeys Abroad*. Boston: Knight, 1895.

Wetmore, Elizabeth (Bisland). *A Flying Trip around the World*. New York: Harper, 1891.

Wheeler, Susan Anna (Brookings). *Missions in Eden: Glimpses of Life in the Valley of the Euphrates*. New York & Chicago: Revell, 1899.

White, Caroline (Earle). *A Holiday in Spain and Norway*. Philadelphia: Lippincott, 1895.

Whitney, Caspar. *Hawaiian America: Something of Its History, Resources, and Prospects*. New York & London: Harper, 1899.

Whitney. *On Snow-Shoes to the Barren Grounds: Twenty-Eight Hundred Miles after Musk-Oxen and Wood-Bison*. New York: Harper, 1896.

Whitney. *A Sporting Pilgrimage: Riding to Hounds, Golf, Rowing, Football, Club and University Athletics. Studies in English Sport, Past and Present*. New York: Harper, 1895.

Wieting, Mary Elizabeth. *Prominent Incidents in the Life of Dr. John M. Wieting, Including His Travels with His Wife around the World*. New York & London: Putnam, 1889.

Williams, Lucy Langdon, and Emma V. McLoughlin. *A Too Short Vacation . . . with Forty-Eight Illustrations from Their Own Kodak*. Philadelphia: Lippincott, 1892.

Wills, Mary H. *A Summer in Europe*. Philadelphia: Lippincott, 1876.

Wilson, Alpheus Waters. *Letters from the Orient to Her Daughters at Home*. Nashville, Tenn.: M. E. Church, South, 1890.

Winter, William. *Brown Heath and Blue Bells; Being Sketches of Scotland, with Other Papers*. New York & London: Macmillan, 1895.

Winter. *English Rambles: and Other Fugitive Pieces, in Prose and Verse*. Boston: Osgood, 1883.

Winter. *Gray Days and Gold, in England and Scotland*. New York: Macmillan, 1891.

Winter. *Old Shrines and Ivy*. New York & London: Macmillan, 1892.

Winter. *Shakespeare's England*. Boston: Ticknor, 1886.

Winter. *The Trip to England*. New York: Lee & Shepard, 1879.

Wolf, Annie S., as Emily. *Pictures and Portraits of Foreign Travel*. Philadelphia: Claxton, 1881.

Woodman, Abby (Johnson). *Picturesque Alaska: a Journal of a Tour among the Mountains, Seas, and Islands of the Northwest, from San Francisco to Sitka*. Boston & New York: Houghton, Mifflin, 1889.

Woodruff, Julia Louisa Matilda (Curtiss), as W. M. L. Jay. *My Winter in Cuba*. New York: Dutton, 1871.

Wright, Margaret Barker (Upham). *Hired Furnished. Being Certain Economical Housekeeping Adventures in England.* Boston: Roberts, 1897.

Wright, Marie (Robinson). *Picturesque Mexico.* Philadelphia: Lippincott, 1897.

Checklist of Further Readings

Adams, Percy G. *Travel Literature and the Evolution of the Novel.* Lexington: University Press of Kentucky, 1983.

Adler, Judith, "Origins of Sightseeing." *Annals of Tourism Research,* 16 (1989): 7–29.

Andrews, Malcolm. *The Search for the Picturesque: Landscape Aesthetics and Tourism in Britain, 1760–1800.* Stanford, Cal.: Stanford University Press, 1989.

Baker, Paul R. *The Fortunate Pilgrims: Americans in Italy, 1800–1860.* Cambridge, Mass.: Harvard University Press, 1964.

Behdad, Ali. *Belated Travelers: Orientalism in the Age of Colonial Dissolution.* Durham, N.C. & London: Duke University Press, 1994.

Bendixen, Alfred. "Americans in Europe before 1865: A Study of the Travel Book." University of North Carolina dissertation, 1980.

Bowen, Frank C. *A Century of Atlantic Travel: 1830–1930.* Boston: Little, Brown, 1930.

Brooks, Van Wyck. *The Dream of Arcadia: American Writers and Artists in Italy, 1760–1915.* New York: Dutton, 1958.

Buzard, James. *The Beaten Track: European Tourism, Literature and the Ways to "Culture" 1800–1918.* Oxford: Clarendon Press/Oxford University Press, 1993.

Caesar, Terry. "'Counting the Cats in Zanzibar': American Travel Abroad in American Travel Writing to 1914." *Prospects,* 13 (1989): 95–134.

Clifford, James. "Notes on Theory and Travel." *Inscriptions,* 5 (1989): 177–188.

Cole, Garold L. "The Travel Account as a Social Document: A Survey of Recent Journal Articles." *Exploration: Journal of the MLA Special Session on the Literature of Exploration and Travel,* 7 (1979): 42–55.

Culler, Jonathan. "Semiotics of Tourism." *American Journal of Semiotics,* 1, nos. 1–2 (1981): 127–140.

Dulles, Foster Rhea. *Americans Abroad: Two Centuries of European Travel.* Ann Arbor: University of Michigan Press, 1964.

Dulles. *Yankees and Samurai: America's Role in the Emergence of Modern Japan.* New York: Harper & Row, 1965.

Dunlop, M. H. *Sixty Miles from Contentment: Traveling the Nineteenth-Century American Interior.* New York: Basic Books, 1995.

Earnest, Ernest. *Expatriates and Patriots: American Artists, Scholars, and Writers in Europe.* Durham, N.C.: Duke University Press, 1968.

Leed, Eric J. *The Mind of the Traveler: From Gilgamesh to Global Tourism.* New York: Basic Books, 1991.

Lochsberg, Winifred. *History of Travel.* Leipzig: Edition Leipzig, 1979.

Lockwood, Allison. *The Passionate Pilgrims: The American Traveler in Great Britain, 1800–1914.* New York: Cornwall Books, 1981.

Long, Orie William. *Literary Pioneers: Early American Explorers of European Culture.* Cambridge, Mass.: Harvard University Press, 1935.

MacCannell, Earle Dean. *Empty Meeting Grounds: The Tourist Papers.* London: Routledge, 1992.

MacCannell. *The Tourist: A New Theory of the Leisure Class.* London: Macmillan, 1976.

Memmi, Albert. *The Coloniser and the Colonised.* New York: Orion Press, 1965.

Meriwether, Lee. *A Tramp Trip: How to See Europe on Fifty Cents a Day.* New York: Harper, 1886.

Metualli, A. M. "Americans Abroad: The Popular Art of Travel Writing in the Nineteenth Century." *Exploration: Journal of the MLA Special Session on the Literature of Exploration and Travel,* 4 (1976): 115–124.

Mills, Sara. *Discourses of Difference: An Analysis of Women's Travel Writing and Colonialism.* New York & London: Routledge, 1991.

Mulvey, Christopher. *Anglo-American Landscapes: A Study of Nineteenth-Century Anglo-American Travel Writing.* Cambridge: Cambridge University Press, 1983.

Mulvey. *Transatlantic Manners: Social Patterns in Nineteenth-Century Anglo-American Travel Literature.* London: Cambridge University Press, 1990.

Ong, Walter J. *Orality and Literacy: The Technologizing of the Word.* London: Metheun, 1982.

Passport Office, U.S. Department of State. *The United States Passport: Past, Present, Future.* Washington, D.C.: U.S. Department of State, 1976.

Porter, Dennis. *Haunted Journeys: Desire and Transgression in European Travel Writing.* Princeton: Princeton University Press, 1991.

Pratt, Mary Louise. *Imperial Eyes: Travel Writing and Transculturation.* New York & London: Routledge, 1992.

Pratt. "Scratches on the Face of the Country; or, What Mr. Barrow Saw in the Face of the Bushman," in *Race, Writing, and Difference,* edited by Henry Louis Gates Jr. Chicago: University of Chicago Press, 1986, pp. 138–162.

Rahv, Philip. *Discovery of Europe: The Story of the American Experience in the Old World.* Boston: Houghton Mifflin, 1947.

Rice, Warner G., ed. *Literature as a Mode of Travel.* New York: New York Public Library, 1963.

Said, Edward. *Orientalism.* New York: Vintage, 1979.

Said. *Culture and Imperialism.* New York: Knopf, 1993.

Salamone, A. William. "The Nineteenth-Century Discovery of Italy: an Essay in American Cultural History. Prolegomena to a Historiographical Problem." *American Historical Review,* 73 (1968): 1359–1391.

Schivelsbusch, Wolfgang. *The Railway Journey: The Industrialization of Time and Space in the Nineteenth Century.* Berkeley: University of California Press, 1986.

Scholes, Robert, and Robert Kellogg. *The Nature of Narrative*. London: Oxford University Press, 1966.

Schriber, Mary-Suzanne, ed. *Telling Travels: Selected Writings by Nineteenth-Century American Women Abroad*. De Kalb: Northern Illinois University Press, 1994.

Sears, John. *Sacred Places: American Tourist Attractions in the Nineteenth Century*. New York: Oxford University Press, 1989.

Slovic, Scott. *Seeking Awareness in American Nature Writing*. Salt Lake City: University of Utah Press, 1992.

Smith, Harold F. *American Travellers Abroad: A Bibliography of Accounts Published Before 1900*. Carbondale & Edwardsville: Library of Southern Illinois University, 1969.

Spurr, David. *The Rhetoric of Empire: Colonial Discourse in Journalism, Travel Writing, and Imperial Administration*. Durham, N.C.: Duke University Press, 1993.

Stafford, Barbara M. *Voyage into Substance: Art, Science, Nature, and the Illustrated Travel Account, 1760–1840*. Cambridge, Mass.: MIT Press, 1984.

Stowe, William. *Going Abroad: European Travel in Nineteenth-Century American Culture*. Princeton: Princeton University Press, 1994.

Swinglehurst, Edmund. *Cook's Tours: The Story of Popular Travel*. Poole, Dorset: Blandford, 1982.

Trease, Robert G. *The Grand Tour*. London: Heinemann, 1967.

U.S. Department of State. *The American Passport: Its History and a Digest of Laws, Rulings, and Regulations Governing Its Issuance by the Department of State*. Washington, D.C.: Government Printing Office, 1898.

Vaucaire, Michel. *Paul Du Chaillu: Gorilla Hunter*. New York: Harper, 1930.

White, Hayden. *Tropics of Discourse: Essays in Cultural Criticism*. Baltimore: Johns Hopkins University Press, 1978.

Zboray, Ronald J. *A Fictive People: Antebellum Economic Development and the American Reading Public*. New York: Oxford University Press, 1993.

Contributors

M. D. Allen..*University of Wisconsin–Fox Valley*
Xavier Baron...*University of Wisconsin–Milwaukee*
Linda S. Bergmann ....*Illinois Institute of Technology*
James E. Canacci..*Youngstown State University*
Roger Célestin ....*University of Connecticut*
Laurie Delaney..*University of Cincinnati*
Mary K. Edmonds...*Carrboro, North Carolina*
James L. Gray ....*Indiana University of Pennsylvania*
Kristine Harrington ....*Kent State University, Trumbull Campus*
Kevin J. Hayes..*University of Central Oklahoma*
Elizabeth Hewitt ....*Grinnell College*
Sherrie A. Inness ....*Miami University*
Lisa Logan..*Kent State University*
Anna E. Lomando ....*Pennsylvania State University, New Kensington*
Jeffrey Alan Melton...*Auburn University at Montgomery*
Linda Ledford-Miller...*University of Scranton*
Taimi Olsen..*Tusculum College*
Martha I. Pallante..*Youngstown State University*
Brendan A. Rapple ....*Boston College*
Barbara Ryan ....*Michigan Society of Fellows*
James J. Schramer...*Youngstown State University*
Alan Spearman...*University of North Carolina at Chapel Hill*
Eric Sterling ....*Auburn University at Montgomery*
Carole Sims Tabor..*Louisiana Tech University*
Stephanie A. Tingley..*Youngstown State University*
Sarah Wadsworth...*University of Minnesota, Twin Cities*
Craig White ....*University of Houston–Clear Lake*
James A. Wren..*University of Hawaii at Mānoa*
Sarah Bird Wright..*College of William and Mary*

Cumulative Index

Dictionary of Literary Biography, Volumes 1-189
Dictionary of Literary Biography Yearbook, 1980-1996
Dictionary of Literary Biography Documentary Series, Volumes 1-16

Cumulative Index

DLB before number: *Dictionary of Literary Biography*, Volumes 1-189
Y before number: *Dictionary of Literary Biography Yearbook*, 1980-1996
DS before number: *Dictionary of Literary Biography Documentary Series*, Volumes 1-16

B

C

E

F

G

S

W